ANGLO-AMERICAN CATALOGUING RULES

Second Edition
1998 Revision

Prepared under the direction of

THE JOINT STEERING COMMITTEE FOR REVISION OF AACR
a committee of:
The American Library Association
The Australian Committee on Cataloguing
The British Library
The Canadian Committee on Cataloguing
The Library Association
The Library of Congress

CANADIAN LIBRARY ASSOCIATION / *Ottawa*
LIBRARY ASSOCIATION PUBLISHING / *London*
AMERICAN LIBRARY ASSOCIATION / *Chicago*

Published 1998 by

AMERICAN LIBRARY ASSOCIATION
50 East Huron Street, Chicago, Illinois 60611
ISBN 0-8389-2197-3 (electronic, single user)
ISBN 0-8389-2198-1 (electronic, network)
ISBN 0-8389-3485-4 (paperbound)
ISBN 0-8389-3486-2 (cloth)

CANADIAN LIBRARY ASSOCIATION
200 Elgin Street, Ottawa, Ontario K2P 1L5
ISBN 0-88802-279-4 (electronic, single user)
ISBN 0-88802-285-9 (electronic, network)
ISBN 0-88802-282-4 (paperbound)
ISBN 0-88802-284-0 (cloth)

LIBRARY ASSOCIATION PUBLISHING
7 Ridgmount Street, London WC1E 7AE
ISBN 1-85604-229-4 (electronic)
ISBN 1-85604-154-9 (paperbound)
ISBN 1-85604-313-4 (cloth)

British Library Cataloguing in Publication Data

A catalogue record for this book is available from the British Library

Canadian Cataloguing in Publication Data

Main entry under title:

  Anglo-American cataloguing rules

2nd ed., 1998 revision.
Co-published by: Library Association, American Library Association.
Originally published (1967) in two versions under the following
    titles : Anglo-American cataloging rules. North American
    text; Anglo-American cataloging rules. British text.
Includes bibliographical references and index.
ISBN 0-88802-284-0 (bound) - ISBN 0-88802-282-4 (pbk.)

    1. Descriptive cataloging—Rules.   I. Gorman, Michael,
1941-   II. Winkler, Paul W., (Paul Walter)   III. Joint Steering
Committee for Revision of AACR.   IV. Canadian Library Association.
V. Library Association.   VI. American Library Association
Z694.15.A56A53 1998   025.3'2   C98-900686-7

Library of Congress Cataloging-in-Publication Data

Anglo-American cataloguing rules / prepared under the direction of the Joint
    Steering Committee for Revision of AACR, a committee of the American
    Library Association, the Australian Committee on Cataloguing, the British
    Library, the Canadian Committee on Cataloguing, the Library Association,
    the Library of Congress. — 2nd ed., 1998 revision.
        p. cm.
    Includes index.
    ISBN 0-8389-3486-2. — ISBN 0-8389-3485-4 (pbk.)
    1. Descriptive cataloging—Rules. I. Joint Steering Committee
for Revision of AACR. II. American Library Association.
Z694.15.A56A53 1998
025.3'2–dc21   98-8479

02   01   00   5   4

CONTENTS

PART I

Description

PART II

Headings, Uniform Titles, and References

Committees

The following lists, in alphabetical order by country, show committee membership and liaisons as of March 1998.

AUSTRALIA
AUSTRALIAN COMMITTEE ON CATALOGUING

Chair
Pam Dunlop (1995–)
Andrew Wells (1993–1994)
David Toll (1992)
Simon McMillan (1988–1991)
Anthony Ketley (1986–1987)
Jeffrey Scrivener (1984–1986)
Warwick Cathro (1982–1983)
Allan Horton (1981–1982)

Olivia Abbay (1984–1989)
Judith Baskin (1981)
Stan Bastow (1981–1985)
Louise Burmester (1992)
Warwick Cathro (1981–1983)
Diana Dack (1986–1994)
Pam Dunlop (1994–)
Warwick Dunstan (1988–1989)
Maggie Exon (1989–1991)
Jan Fullerton (1981–1987)
Pam Gatenby (1989–1990)
Gaye Gericke (1991)
Eugenie Greig (1981–1982)
Peter Haddad (1981–1982, 1985–1987)
Elaine Hall (1981–1989)
Twila Herr (1986, 1990–1992)

Helen Hoffmann (1981–1988, 1991–)
Ann Huthwaite (1992–)
Fontaine Ip (1988–1990)
Anthony Ketley (1983–1986)
Robert Langker (1983–1984)
Giles Martin (1990–)
Simon McMillan (1986–1988, 1993)
Susanne Moir (1995–)
Margareta Nicholas (1990–1995)
Jeanette Rosengren (1988–1990)
Jeffrey Scrivener (1982–1986)
Chris Taylor (1996–)
John Thompson (1988–1991)
Janet Thorp (1993–)
Julia Trainor (1993–)
Andrew Wells (1992–1994)

CANADA
CANADIAN COMMITTEE ON CATALOGUING
COMITÉ CANADIEN DE CATALOGAGE

Chair
Ralph W. Manning (1986–)
Jean Weihs (1981–1986)
Ronald Hagler (1979–1980)
Edwin Buchinski (1975–1978)
Jean Lunn (1974–1975)

Edwin Buchinski (1975–1980)
Jack Cain (1974–1978)
Clarisse Cardin (Secretary, 1975–1983)
Joseph Cox (1996–)

Thomas Delsey (1979–1983)
Pierre Deslauriers (1974–1981)
Charlotte Dionne (1988–1991)
Mary Dykstra (1986–1995)
Louise Filion (1994–)

Gaston Fournier (1991–)
Derek R. Francis (1981–1983)
Robert Giroux (1979–1986)
Ronald Hagler (1974–1980)
Lise Lavigne (1982–1994)
Jean Lunn (1974–1975)
Deb MacLean (1993–1997)
Ralph W. Manning (1984–)
Pierre Manseau (1986–1988)

Wendy Moriarity (1984–1986)
Christine Oliver (1997–)
André Paul (1981–1996)
Paule Rolland-Thomas (1974–1979)
Hlib Sirko (1974–1979)
Donna Slater (Secretary, 1984–1985)
Jane Thacker (Secretary, 1986–)
Jean Weihs (1979–1986)
Nancy Williamson (1986–1993)

Resource Groups

Association of Canadian Map Libraries and Archives (formerly Association of Canadian Map Libraries): Vivien Cartmell (1979–1984); Velma Parker (1984–)

Bureau of Canadian Archivists: Kent Haworth (1990–1996); Mireille Miniggio (1996–)

Canadian Association for Graduate Education in Library, Archival, and Information Studies (formerly Canadian Association of Library Schools): Nancy Williamson (1980–1986); Donald Cook (1987–1989); John Leide (1989–1995)

Canadian Association for Information Science: Donna Duncan (1980–1983); David LaFranchise (1985–1991); Pat Johnston (1991–1997); Mary Nash (1997–)

Canadian Association of Law Libraries: Shih-Sheng Hu (1979–1983); Dana Dvorak (1983–1987); Humayun Rashid (1987–1989); Lenore Rapkin (1989–)

Canadian Association of Music Libraries: Gerald Parker (1979–1982); Joan Colquhoun (1983–1987); Alison Hall (1987–1989); Vivien Taylor (1989–1993); Lisa Emberson (1993–1996); Brenda Muir (1996–)

Canadian Association of Research Libraries: Yvon Richer (1979–1989); Earle Ferguson (1989–1992); Mary Curran (1992–)

Canadian Council of Library Schools: Michèle Hudon (1996–)

Special Libraries Association, Eastern Canada Chapter: Anne M. Galler (1980–1983); John Leide (1984–)

Special Libraries Association, Toronto Chapter: Mary-Lois Williams (1979–1982); Pamela Stoksik (1983–1985); Linda Reid (1986–1988)

UNITED KINGDOM

LIBRARY ASSOCIATION/BRITISH LIBRARY COMMITTEE ON AACR2

Chair
Susan Brown (1989–)
Alan Jeffreys (1980–1988)
Geoffrey Hamilton (1974–1978)

Philip Beresford (1988–1989)
Susan Brown (1987–)
Rodney Brunt (1987–)
Joyce Butcher (1974–1986; 1990–1994)
Roger Butcher (1983–1986)
John Byford (1981–1989)
Richard Carpenter (Secretary, 1980–1981)
Catherine Charnley (1996–)
Richard Christophers (1974–1987; Secretary, 1974–1978)

Joel C. Downing (1974–1981)
Nick Eden (1996–)
James Elliot (1994–1996)
Phillip K. Escreet (1974–1978)
Lesley Firth (Secretary, 1997–)
Robert Fulford (1974–1978)
Jasia Glowczewska (Secretary, 1993–1997)
Isobel Gordon (Secretary, 1990)
Tony Hall (1980–1981)
Geoffrey Hamilton (1974–1978)

Michael Hoey (1988–1990)
Jennifer Hunt (Secretary, 1986–1989)
Eric Hunter (1975–1985)
Duncan Irvine (1986)
Alan Jeffreys (1974–1990)
Mary Jesper (1974–1978)
Peter R. Lewis (1974–1978)
Anthony Long (1987)
Wilma Minty (1992–)
Janet Mitchell (1986–1995)
Pat Oddy (Secretary, 1981–1986;
    1987–)

Lis Phelan (1980–1986)
Christopher Ravilious (1976–1978)
Heather Rosie (1997–)
Malcolm Shifrin (1974–1978)
Sally Strutt (1994–)
John Thomas (1982–1985)
Elizabeth Traynor (Secretary, 1989)
Robert Vickers (Secretary, 1991–1993)
Janice Wrench (1990–1994)

UNITED STATES (through 1978)

AMERICAN LIBRARY ASSOCIATION
RESOURCES AND TECHNICAL SERVICES DIVISION
CATALOG CODE REVISION COMMITTEE

Chair
John D. Byrum

Lizbeth Bishoff
Winifred Duncan
Neal L. Edgar
Barbara Gates (1977–1978)
Doralyn J. Hickey
Frances Hinton
Carol Ishimoto (1974–1976)

Paul Kebabian (1974–1976)
Åke Koel
Joan Marshall (1977–1978)
Marian Sanner (1974)
Helen Schmierer (1976–1978)
Edith Scott
Gordon Stevenson (1974–1976)

Resource person
C. Sumner Spalding (1975–1977)

Recording secretary
Marilyn Jones (1977–1978)
Ann Murphy (1974–1976)

SUBCOMMITTEE ON RULES
  FOR CATALOGING MACHINE-READABLE DATA FILES

Chair
Elizabeth Herman

Laurence W.S. Auld
Geraldine Dobbin (1974–1976)
Walter J. Fraser
Carolyn Kacena

Judith Rowe
Henriette Avram
Sharon Chapple Henry (1975–1978)

Consultants
AACR Revision Study Committee, Resources and Technical Services Division, ALA,
    Judith Cannan (1975–1978)
American Association of Law Librarians, Cecilia Kwan (1975–1978)
American Association of School Librarians, Robert Little
American Library History Round Table, ALA, Constance Rinehart

American Library Trustee Association, ALA, Lee Brawner (1974)
American National Standards Institute (1975–1976)
American Theological Library Association, Lydia Lo (1975–1978)
Art Libraries Society of North America, Nancy John
Association for Asian Studies (1975–1978)
Association for Educational Communications and Technology, Alma Tillin (1975–
    1976); William Quinly (1976–1978)
Association of American Library Schools, Constance Rinehart (1975–1978)
Association of College and Research Libraries, ALA, LeRoy D. Ortopan
Audiovisual Committee, ALA, Evelyn G. Clement (1975)
Catholic Library Association, Arnold M. Rzepecki (1975); Rev. Thomas Pater (1975–
    1978)
Children's Services Division, ALA, Annette Shockey (1974–1976)
Church and Synagogue Library Association (1975)
Committee on Computer Filing, Resources and Technical Services Division, ALA,
    Joseph Rosenthal (1975–1976)
Council on Library Resources (1975–1978)
Educational Media Council, Carolyn Whitenack (1975–1976)
Federal Librarians Round Table, ALA, Mary Sauer
Government Documents Round Table, ALA, Bernadine Hoduski
Health and Rehabilitative Library Services Division, ALA, Dallas R. Shawkey (1974);
    Marilyn Jones (1975–1978)
Information Science and Automation Division, ALA, Barbara Gates
Intellectual Freedom Round Table, Sanford Berman (1974); James R. Dwyer (1974–
    1978)
Joint Advisory Committee on Nonbook Materials, Margaret Chisholm (1975);
    Suzanne Massonneau (1975–1978)
Library Administration Division, ALA, Morris Schertz (1974–1976)
Library Research Round Table, ALA, Lawrence Leonard (1974); Helen Schmierer
    (1975–1978)
Medical Library Association, Emilie Wiggins (1975–1978)
Middle East Librarians Association, John A. Eilts (1975–1978)
Music Library Association, Katherine Skrobela (1975–1978)
National Federation of Abstracting and Indexing Services (1975–1978)
Reference and Adult Services Division, ALA, Concetta Sacco (1974–1976); David F.
    Kohl (1976–1978)
*Representation in Machine-Readable Form of Bibliographic Information Committee,
    ALA*, Ruth Tighe (1975); John Knapp (1975–1977)
Social Responsibilities Round Table, Sanford Berman (1974–1975); Joan Marshall
    (1975–1978)
Society of American Archivists (1975–1978)
Special Libraries Association (1975–1978)
Young Adult Services Division, ALA, Mary K. Chelton (1974)

DESCRIPTIVE CATALOGING COMMITTEE

Chair
Michael J. Fitzgerald (from 1976)
Carolyn J. McMillen (to 1976)

Allen Cohen (1977–)	Frances R.L. Needleman (1974–1976)
Arlene T. Dowell (1977–)	Leila Payne (1976–1978)
Oliver T. Field (1974–1978)	Carolyn A. Small (1975–)
Eugene R. Hanson (1973–1977)	Gordon Stevenson (to 1975)
Frances R. Ladd (1975–)	Donald E. Talkington (to 1975)
Shirley Lewis (1975–1977)	Alma Tillin (to 1975)

UNITED STATES (from 1979)
AMERICAN LIBRARY ASSOCIATION
RESOURCES AND TECHNICAL SERVICES DIVISION
CATALOGING AND CLASSIFICATION SECTION
COMMITTEE ON CATALOGING: DESCRIPTION AND ACCESS

Chair
Daniel W. Kinney (1997–)
Joan Swanekamp (1995–1997)
Frank E. Sadowski, Jr. (1993–1995)
Brian E.C. Schottlacndcr (1992–1993)
Edward Swanson (1990–1992)
Verna Urbanski (1988–1990)
Richard P. Smiraglia (1986–1988)
Dorothy McGarry (1985–1986)
Olivia M.A. Madison (1984–1985)
Patricia M. Thomas (1983–1984)
Nancy R. John (1980–1983)
Allen Cohen (1979–1980)
Frances Ladd (1979)

Members

John Attig (1986–1990)
Elizabeth Ruth Baughman (1984–1986)
Matthew Beacom (1996–)
Pamela P. Brown (1987–1991)
Jo Lynne Byrd (1995–1997)
Michael Carpenter (1988–1992)
Allen Cohen (1979–1981)
Eleanor R. Crary (1979–1980)
Nancy Davey (1991–1995)
Nancy E. Douglas (1985–1989)
Arlene T. Dowell (1979–1981)
John K. Duke (1989–1993)
Ann Fiegen (1993–1997)
Elizabeth Herman (1983–1987)
Doralyn J. Hickey (1979–1981)
Carol Hixson (1997–)
Christa F.B. Hoffmann (1979–1983)
Lynne C. Howarth (1993–1997)
Laurel Jizba (1989–1993)
Nancy R. John (1980–1984)
Bruce Chr. Johnson (1990–1994)
Sherry Kelley (1996–)
Daniel W. Kinney (1997–)
Frances Ladd (1979)
Jay H. Lambrecht (1986–1990)
Mary L. Larsgaard (1997–)
Lee W. Leighton (1990–1994)

Olivia M.A. Madison (1981–1985)
Marilyn Jones McClaskey (1979–1982)
Dorothy McGarry (1982–1986)
Ingrid Mifflin (1991–1995)
Monty L. Montee (1985–1989)
Patricia G. Oyler (1983–)
Janet G. Padway (1988–1990)
Carlen M. Ruschoff (1984–1988)
Frank E. Sadowski, Jr. (1992–1996)
Adam L. Schiff (1997–)
Kim M. Schmidt (1979–1980)
Brian E.C. Schottlaender (1989–1993)
Judith C. Singleton (1979–1981)
Richard P. Smiraglia (1984–1988)
Christopher L. Sugnet (1985–1989)
Janet Swan Hill (1980–1984)
Joan Swanekamp (1993–1997)
Edward Swanson (1979–1983,
    1990–1992)
Patricia M. Thomas (1980–1984)
Karen A. Trainer (1981–1985)
Mitch L. Turitz (1995–)
Verna Urbanski (1987–1991)
Arnold Wajenberg (1981–1985)
Mark R. Watson (1992–1996)
Martha Yee (1994–)
J. Bradford Young (1994–)

Interns

Jo Lynne Byrd (1993–1995)
Ann Fiegen (1992–1993)
Susan M. Hayes (1997–)
Carol Hixson (1995–1997)
Shirley J. Lincicum (1997–)
John A. Richardson (1995–1997)

Patrick J. Stevens (1993–1995)
Patricia S. Vanderberg (1988–1990)
Mark R. Watson (1991–1992)
Tamara Weintraub (1992–1993)
Philip Youngholm (1990–1992)

Ex Officio: ALA Representative to the Joint Steering Committee for Revision of AACR, Frances Hinton (1979–1983); Helen F. Schmierer (1983–1989); Janet Swan Hill (1989–1995); Brian E.C. Schottlaender (1995–). Association for Library Collections & Technical Services, William I. Bunnell (1979–1987); Karen Muller (1987–). Library of Congress, Ben R. Tucker (1979–1992); Sarah E. Thomas (1992–1994); Barbara B. Tillett (1994–). OCLC, Inc., Glenn E. Patton (1982–). Research Libraries Group, Inc., Charles Stewart (1979–1980); Ed Glazier (1981–).

REPRESENTATIVES TO THE COMMITTEE

From the American Library Association

Divisions
Association for Library Collections & Technical Services (formerly Resources and Technical Services Division)
ALCTS/LITA/RUSA Representation in Machine-Readable Form of Bibliographic Information Committee (MARBI), John Attig (1982–1986); Anne Highsmith (1986–1990); Sherman Clarke (1990–1994); Catherine Gerhart (1995–)
Acquisition of Library Materials Section, Beth Jacoby (1992–1993); Jean Hudgins (1994–1996)
Audiovisual Committee, Sheila S. Intner (1983–1985); Martha Yee (1985–1986); Bruce Chr. Johnson (1986–1990); Marilyn L. Kercher (1990–1991); Joan Swanekamp (1991–1993); Eric Childress (1993–1995); Mary Beth Fecko (1995–1996); Marlyn Hackett (1997–)
Cataloging and Classification Section, Committee on Cataloging: Asian and African Materials, Michael J. Fitzgerald (1984–1986); Dona S. Straley (1986–1988); Gertrude Koh (1988–1989); Dorothy Niekamp (1990–1991); Karl K. Kahler (1992–1994); James Maccaferri (1995–1996); David Reynolds (1996); James Gentner (1997); Clare Dunkle (1997–)
Cataloging and Classification Section, Committee on Cataloging: Children's Materials, Robert E. Boyer (1983–1984); Laura Colberg (1984–1985); Patricia M. Thomas (1985–1988); Doris C. Dale (1988–1991); Dorothy M. Shields (1992–1994); Jianrong Wang (1996–)
Collection Management and Development Section, Matthew W. Wise (1992–1996); Betsy Simpson (1996–)
Preservation and Reproduction Section, Cecilia S. Sercan (1995–)
Preservation of Library Materials Section, G. David Anderson (1984–1986); Paul J. Weiss (1986–1991); Willy Cromwell (1992–1994)
Reproduction of Library Materials Section, Charles Willard (1979–1983); Colleen Hyslop (1984–1986); Laurel Jizba (1986–1990); Crystal Graham (1990–1992); Cecilia S. Sercan (1992–1994)
Resources Section, Susan Vita (1979–1981); Miriam W. Palm (1981–1985); Ceres Birkhead (1985–1988); D. Whitney Coe (1988–1991)
Serials Section, Judith Kuhagen (1979–1982); Dea Szatkowski (1982–1983); Jim Cole (1983–1985); Crystal Graham (1985–1988); Patrick Callahan (1988–1990); Mitch L. Turitz (1990–1992); Jean P. Altschuler (1992–1995); Marguerite E. Horn (1995–1997); Carolynne Myall (1997–)
Technical Services Costs Committee, Michael Shelley (1985–1988); Peri Irish Switzer (1988–1991); Cliff Glaviano (1992–1993)
Technical Services Measurements Committee, Cliff Glaviano (1993–1995); Victoria Mills (1995–1996)
Association for Library Service to Children, Doris Clack (1984–1986)
Association of College and Research Libraries, LeRoy D. Ortopan (1979–1983); Jennifer Younger (1983–1984); Ellen Waite (1984–1989); Frank D'Andraia (1988–1990); Colby Mariva Riggs (1990–1992); Norma H. Martin (1993); Marie Morgan (1995–)
Association of Specialized and Cooperative Library Agencies, Elizabeth A. Breedlove (1979–1980)

Library and Information Technology Association, Karen Bendorf (1979–1982); Pamela S. Cenzer (1982–1983); Carol White (1983–1984); Jeff Rehbach (1984–1985); Peter R. Young (1985–1989); V. Louise Saylor (1989–1991); Judith Hopkins (1992–1994); Brad Eden (1995–   )

Public Library Association, Jerome Pennington (1979–1982); Gail Shurgot (1982–1983); Susan Nesbitt (1983–1985); Sheryl Nichin (1985–1988); Donna Cranmer (1988–1990); Judith H. Rossoff (1990–1993); Margaret Shen (1995–   )

Reference and User Services Association (formerly Reference and Adult Services Division), Sandy Whiteley (1979–1982); Joseph R. Matthews (1982–1984); Joan Kuklinski (1984–1988); Sally Wayman Kalin (1988–1989); Noelle Van Pulis (1990–1995)

Round Tables

American Library History Round Table, Francis L. Miksa, Jr. (1979–1983)

Federal Librarians Round Table, Sue Ellen Sloca (1979–1983); David Brunell (1984); Hollis Landrun (1985); Mary Stewart-Taylor (1986–   )

Government Documents Round Table, Bernadine Hoduski (1979–1983); Judy Meyers (1985–1986); David J. Hardgrove (1986–1988); Gary Cornwell (1988–1990); Mary A. Martin (1991); Rhonda Marker (1992–   )

Intellectual Freedom Round Table, Karen Tallman (1984); Beth Rile (1985–1988)

International Relations Round Table, Elizabeth A. Widenmann (1988–1992); Laurel Jizba (1993–   )

Junior Members Round Table, Joseph R. Edelen, Jr. (1979–1981); John B. Graves (1981–1982); Donna Cranmer (1982–1984); Antonia Snee (1984–1986); Josephine Crawford (1986–1988); David Fiste (1988–1989); Mark Watson (1989–1990)

Map and Geography Round Table, Robert Karrow (1979–1980, 1981–1983); Alice Hudson (1980–1981); Janet Swan Hill (1984–1985); Mary Anne Waltz (1985–1988); Ellen Caplan (1988–1989); Nancy J. Edstrom (1989–1991); Elizabeth Mangan (1991–   )

New Members Round Table, Mark R. Watson (1990–1991); Kathryn Sorury (1992–1993); Karen Cook (1993–1995); Jimmie Lundgren (1995–   )

Social Responsibilities Round Table, Joan K. Marshall (1979–1982); Patricia A. Young (1982–1983); Gary L. Strawn (1983–1990); Sherry Kelley (1990–1996); Larry Heiman (1997–   )

From Organizations outside the American Library Association

African Studies Association, Gail Junion (1981–1983)

American Association of Law Libraries, Phyllis Marion (1979–1985); Lee W. Leighton (1985–1989); Regina Wallen (1990–1993); Ann Sitkin (1993–   )

American Theological Library Association, Elvire Hilgert (1983–1984); Joyce L. Farris (1984–1992); Sally B. Berlowitz (1993–1996); Chris Schone (1997–   )

Art Libraries Society of North America, Nancy R. John (1979–1980); Bethany R. Mendenhall (1980–1982); Karen Muller (1982–1985); Sherman Clarke (1985–1991); Karen L. Meizner (1992–1994); Daniel Starr (1995–   )

Association for Asian Studies, Committee on East Asian Libraries, Thomas H. Lee (1981–1983)

Association for Recorded Sound Collections, Charles W. Simpson (1979–1987); Daniel W. Kinney (1987–1997)

Association of American Library Schools, Martha Mannheimer (1979–1983)

Association of Jewish Libraries, Ellen S. Kovacic (1985–1986); Mischa F. Oppenheim (1986–1988); Rosalie E. Katchen (1988–1990); Yael Herbsman (1991–1992); Rita Lifton (1992–1993); Ruth A. Rin (1993–1995); Rachel Simon (1995–   )

Association of Research Libraries, Carol Mandel (1979–1982); George Gibbs (1982–1983)

Catholic Library Association, Rev. Thomas Pater (1981–1984); Tina-Karen Forman (1984–1997); Gertrude Koh (1997–   )

Chinese American Librarians Association, Roy Ting-Kwo Chang (1979–1981); Sally C. Tseng (1981–1983)

Church and Synagogue Library Association, Ruth Sawyer (1979–1983)

Council of National Library and Information Associations, Donald Seibert (1979–1982); Margaret Maes Axtmann (1982–1983)

International Association for Social Science Information Services and Technology, Sue A. Dodd (1979–1988); Elizabeth Stephenson (1988–1989); Patricia S. Vanderberg (1990–   )

Medical Library Association, James E. Raper, Jr. (1979–1983); Sally Sinn (1984–1988); Laurie L. Thompson (1988–1991); Steve Squires (1991–   )

Middle East Librarians Association, Frances Morton (1979–1982)

Music Library Association, Katherine C. Skrobela (1979–1980); Richard P. Smiraglia (1980–1983); Joan Swanekamp (1983–1988); Jennifer B. Bowen (1988–1991); Philip Schreur (1992–1997); Matthew W. Wise (1997–   )

Online Audiovisual Catalogers, Nancy B. Olson (1981–1983)

Society of American Archivists, Miriam I. Crawford (1979–1983); John Lancaster (1983–1985); Lauren Brown (1985–1986); Saundra Taylor (1986–1988); Michael Fox (1988–1990); Jackie M. Dooley (1990–1992); Marion Matters (1993–1995); Michael Fox (1996–   )

Southwestern Library Association, Margaret F. Maxwell (1979–1983)

Special Libraries Association, Marguerite C. Soroka (1979–1981); Mary L. Larsgaard (1982–1983); Claire Tozier (1984–1985); Chris Grabenstatter (1985–1986); Dorothy McGarry (1986–1988); Ronda E. Breitbard (1988–1991); Dorothy L. Malcolm (1992); Dorothy McGarry (1992–1993); Adam L. Schiff (1993–1997); Cynthia M. Whitacre (1997–   )

Consultants

John Duke, Ann Fox, Judith Hopkins, Thomas Jedele, Julie Nilson

PREFACE TO THE 1998 REVISION

The publication of the 1998 Revision to the second edition of the *Anglo-American Cataloguing Rules* (AACR2) coincides with a major new development in the history of AACR2: this revision is published concurrently in print and in electronic form. The content of the two formats is identical except for those changes in formatting that are dictated by the requirements of the electronic medium. The 1998 Revision incorporates the group of revisions previously published as Amendments 1993 and additional revisions approved between 1992 and 1996. These previously unpublished revisions will appear in a subfile as the New Amendments List in the electronic format and in the preliminaries of the print version. In addition, the index has been completely reviewed to reflect all amendments and to correct errors in the previous version.

Acceptance of AACR2 continues to grow throughout the world. Since the last revision in 1988, additional translations have been licensed for Czech, Catalan, Greek, and Russian. The sharing of cataloguing among libraries has become an essential component of management planning, particularly in national libraries, and this has continued to encourage international cooperation and harmonization of cataloguing practices beyond national boundaries.

As noted in the Preface to the 1988 revision, cataloguing rules must respond to changing needs. In recognition of this fact, a formal agreement was established in 1989 between the American Library Association, the British Library, the Canadian Library Association, the Library Association (of the United Kingdom), and the Library of Congress in order to clarify the responsibilities and relationship of the various bodies charged with the production and publication of AACR2. In 1991, the National Library of Canada also became a party to the agreement. These six organizations became known as the Principals of AACR and form the Committee of Principals. The key functions of the Committee of Principals include reviewing developments and progress in the work of the Joint Steering Committee for Revision of AACR and reviewing the state and application of the Common Revision Fund of AACR2. The Fund continues to be maintained for purposes related to the support of the Joint Steering Committee, the Committee of Principals, and other development and research related to AACR2. Copyright and publication matters are dealt with by the three association members of the Committee of Principals.

The ongoing process of rule revision is the responsibility of the Joint Steering Committee for Revision of AACR (JSC), which was formally re-established by the Committee of Principals in 1989. According to that agreement, the JSC is responsible for:

- Reviewing the need for revisions and consolidations of AACR;
- Preparing the text of any such revisions and revised or consolidated editions and submitting them to the publishers;
- Advising the Committee of Principals on programmes and activities appropriate for the receipt of financial support from the AACR Fund.

In support of this work, JSC subsequently developed an internal statement of policy for rule revision which confirmed that rule revision proposals should be submitted through a JSC member body or through the Chair, who would submit appropriate proposals from outside the member bodies. An important element of the JSC policy for rule revision is the commitment to ongoing revision as a means of ensuring that the code continues to meet the needs of its users while also ensuring that careful consideration be given to the real value of and need for change. In weighing the merits of a proposed change, JSC takes into account the following points:

- The rules are intended primarily for catalogue users in English language communities;
- AACR2 is intended to cover all library materials following a consistent approach;
- Wherever possible, changes to AACR2 should be coordinated with relevant international standards, particularly the ISBDs and other standards applied in the communities using AACR, and with the principles of Universal Bibliographic Control;
- The potential impact on existing catalogues and files is assessed;
- Consideration is given to technological developments and their future capabilities;
- The possibility that some minor amplifications to the rules, such as those not seriously affecting uniform application of the code, may be better suited to interpretative manuals is taken into account.

As part of its ongoing mandate to respond to changing needs, JSC undertook, with the support of the Committee of Principals, the International Conference on the Principles and Future Development of AACR. This invitational conference was held in October 1997 in Toronto and generated a number of action items which will be dealt with by JSC and the Committee of Principals over the next months and years, always balancing the need for change with its impact on libraries and their catalogues.

Work of the JSC continues to be supported by each of the participating countries. The Australian Committee on Cataloguing, established in 1981, and the Canadian Committee on Cataloguing, established in 1974, are each made up of representatives from the national library and national library associations and are advised by specialized interest groups. The Library Association/British Library Committee on AACR2, reconstituted in 1980, represents the British Library and the Library Association. In the United States, the Committee on Cataloging: Description and Access, a committee of the Association for Library Collections & Technical Services, serves as a wide forum for consultation on matters related to AACR2. In addition to its ongoing commitment to AACR2, the Library of Congress has provided strong leadership as founding member and continuing secretariat for the Program for Cooperative Cataloging.

Since the last Revision of AACR2, JSC has carefully considered formal proposals from its constituent organizations at seven meetings held between April 1989 and June 1996. Meeting locations rotate among the members of the committee: Washington (1989), Perth (1990), Ottawa (1991), York (1992), Boulder (1994), Leeds (1995), Washington (1996).

The introductory pages to this publication list the many people who have contributed their time and energy to the continued maintenance of AACR2. We continue to acknowledge the many unnamed people who have made comments or provided information, and in particular we acknowledge the considerable contribution of the following institutions that have supported JSC's work in various ways, but particularly by donating the time of the members of JSC: Leeds Metropolitan University, Library of Congress, London Borough of Redbridge, National Library of Australia, National Library of Canada, Queensland University of Technology, State Library of New South Wales, The British Library, University of California at Los Angeles, University of Chicago, University of Colorado at Boulder, University of Newcastle upon Tyne.

RALPH W. MANNING, *Chair*
Joint Steering Committee for Revision of AACR

PREFACE TO THE 1988 REVISION

The ten-year period between the publication of the second edition of the *Anglo-American Cataloguing Rules* (AACR 2) and this revision of AACR 2 has been marked by the general adoption of these rules in most English-speaking countries. This process has been hastened by the ever-increasing commitment to networks and shared cataloguing. At the same time a growing acceptance has also been developing throughout the world. AACR 2 has been translated, or is in the process of translation, into Arabic, Bahasa Malaysia, Chinese, Danish, Finnish, French, Italian, Japanese, Norwegian, Portuguese, Spanish, Swedish, Turkish, and Urdu.

Cataloguing rules cannot be static; they must be allowed to respond to changing needs. Recognizing this fact, the five bodies responsible for the second edition entered into new agreements following the completion of that text. In 1977 the American Library Association, the British Library, the Canadian Library Association (acting on behalf of the Canadian Committee on Cataloguing/Comité canadien de catalogage), the Library Association, and the Library of Congress established a second Joint Steering Committee for Revision of AACR for a two-year term. This agreement has been renewed several times for varying periods and defined the Committee's membership as one representative for each of the five bodies and two editors. A committee to administer the Common Revision Fund was established in 1978. This fund is the repository for royalties from the sales of AACR 2, and monies from the fund support publishing and other rule-related activities, including the work of the Joint Steering Committee.

Because Australian cataloguers had for some time been contributing to code revision and to the review of draft documents sent from overseas, the Australian Committee on Cataloguing has been invited, since 1981, to send a representative to Joint Steering Committee meetings. In 1986, the Australian Committee on Cataloguing was made a full participant in the Committee.

TERMS OF REFERENCE

The terms of reference for the Joint Steering Committee as set down in the 1977 agreement are:

1) to advise the editor of the abridged edition of AACR 2 and to approve the text of the said abridged edition prior to its publication
2) to assess the use and sale of AACR 2 and the abridged edition and to advise the users of AACR 2 and the abridged edition on implementation or adoption of the rules; to advise as required on the granting of permissions to translate
3) to keep under review the need for amendment and revision of the second edition and abridgement, in the light of representations from users of the texts; and to prepare any necessary amendments and revisions for publication by the copyright owners on an agreed schedule for the issue of amendment revision bulletins
4) to act as a forum for discussion of proposals on rule interpretation so as to ensure consistent use of AACR 2 and to promulgate agreed rule interpretations
5) to define and propose appropriate activities associated with AACR 2 in accordance with the funding agreement made with the Council on Library Resources

6) to maintain liaison with IFLA and the UBC Office, in order to facilitate the interests of users of AACR 2 in any programmes of international standardization in the cataloguing field carried out by those bodies.

The Joint Steering Committee has devoted time to all but one of these tasks. It quickly became obvious that it would be both time-consuming and costly for the Committee to discuss the large number of rule interpretations published by national bibliographic agencies. Rule interpretations that contravened the basic tenets of AACR 2 were discussed only after a formal complaint had been submitted by a national committee. The Committee then used moral suasion to encourage amendment of the rule interpretation or, if the rule interpretation had merit, requested a proposal for rule revision.

Work associated with the first term of reference culminated in the publication in 1981 of *The Concise AACR2* by Michael Gorman.

In accomplishing tasks 2 and 5, Committee members have cooperated with the publishers and professional organizations, singly and as a group, to assist in the implementation and promotion of AACR 2 by initiating, coordinating, and participating in many training programmes and other activities.

The Joint Steering Committee has also maintained liaison with international groups such as committees of the International Federation of Library Associations and Institutions (IFLA), and the International Serials Data System; some Joint Steering Committee representatives have also been members of these committees. Frances Hinton, chair of the Joint Steering Committee from 1981 to 1983, played an active role on the IFLA ISBD Review Committee and was chairperson of the ISBD(M) Working Group.

However, most of the Joint Steering Committee's work has been devoted to refining the rules. This revision incorporates the decisions taken by the Joint Steering Committee in the past ten years. In addition, it corrects obvious errors, modifies wording for ease of understanding, changes rules that have proven inadequate, and adds rules and examples to deal with new cases. It is not a new edition; it has not changed basic concepts.

The use of the rules by many cataloguers in different libraries and in various countries and the acts of translation into other languages revealed ambiguous wording, omissions, and typographical errors. Errors and omissions have been corrected, some rules reworded or rearranged, other rules given appropriate references.

Technological change is reflected in rule revisions. For example, videodiscs are different in important ways from those available in 1978, and microcomputer files have become part of many library collections.

In order to keep cataloguers informed, three sets of rule revisions were published, in 1982, 1983, and 1985. These revisions are found in this revised second edition as well as the unpublished revisions authorized by the Joint Steering Committee since 1985.

STRUCTURE AND WORKING METHODS

The Joint Steering Committee has, for the most part, worked by consensus. A vote was necessary only in the case of a very few rules because one or more representatives were unable to support a particular proposal. In these few cases attempts were made, often successfully, to satisfy the concerns of the dissenting members.

Only proposals presented by members of the Joint Steering Committee were discussed. The decision to forward a proposal to the Joint Steering Committee was made by the national committees, the Library of Congress, or the editors after comments, criticisms, and suggestions received from their constituencies had been discussed at national meetings. From such discussions, those matters determined to be appropriate for the Joint Steering Committee's agenda were written as formal proposals and submitted to the Joint Steering Committee. In addition, proposals presented by other members of the Joint Steering Committee were considered and formal responses prepared. The national committees are structured distinctively to meet the needs of their constituencies.

The primary function of the Australian Committee on Cataloguing (ACOC), since its establishment in 1981, has been to prepare, review, and comment on Joint Steering Committee proposals for rule revision, and to brief the Australian representative to the Joint Steering Committee. ACOC is made up of representatives from the National Library of Australia, the Library Association of Australia, and the Australian Advisory Council on Bibliographical Services (AACOBS). The AACOBS Secretariat, headed by Marion Newman, provides the secretarial support to the Committee. With ACOC's broad representative base, and taking advice from interested individuals, organizations, and institutions as appropriate, the Committee has been able to represent to the Joint Steering Committee the views of the Australian cataloguing community and, in turn, through its participation in the Joint Steering Committee, keep that community and library management informed of AACR 2 developments.

The voting members of the Canadian Committee on Cataloguing/Comité canadien de catalogage (CCC) continue to be the representatives of the three national bodies that were its original core—l'Association pour l'avancement des sciences et des techniques de la documentation, the Canadian Library Association, and the National Library of Canada—with financial and secretarial support for the Committee provided by the National Library of Canada. In addition, eight organizations were invited to send nonvoting representatives to Committee meetings. Although CCC's terms of reference include the broad field of cataloguing, the discussions at its semiannual meetings were largely devoted to AACR 2 and National Library of Canada rule interpretations. Decisions on new proposals and on the Canadian response to proposals from other countries were usually determined by the consensus of the larger committee. Particular attention was paid to the remarks of the representatives of special interest groups when rules pertaining to their fields of interest were discussed. From time to time people with special expertise or experience were consulted.

In the United Kingdom, the Library Association/British Library Committee on AACR 2 was reconstituted in 1980 with four representatives from the Library Association and four from the British Library, with the chair elected from the Library Association representatives. Three meetings a year were held. Through most of this period, Pat Oddy of the British Library Bibliographic Services served ably as its secretary. Although the Committee received and welcomed suggestions for revision not only from librarians in the British Isles but also from those in the wider context of the countries of the Commonwealth (excluding Australasia) and throughout the English-speaking world outside the Americas, it was decided early that the profession would best be served by a period of relative stability following the publication of AACR 2. Revision was supported where necessary and in particular much time was spent, with the expert help of Ray Templeton and Alan Poulter, on chapter 9.

In the United States, the ALA/RTSD/CCS Committee on Cataloging: Description and Access (CC:DA) was constituted in 1979 as the successor committee to the ALA/RTSD Catalog Code Revision Committee and the ALA/RTSD/CCS Descriptive Cataloging Committee. Charged with the responsibility to develop official ALA positions on descriptive cataloguing proposals in consultation with other appropriate ALA units and organizations in the United States, CC:DA has met twice annually in open public meetings at all ALA Conferences and Midwinter Meetings. In 1983, ALA representation to CC:DA was restructured to include liaison persons from all ALA divisions and round tables, all RTSD sections, and appropriate RTSD and Cataloging and Classification Section committees. At the same time, eligibility for participation by organizations outside ALA was limited to national or international organizations that do not duplicate interests of ALA units and that contain a body charged to formulate positions on cataloguing policy. The CC:DA roster regularly has included some forty representatives and liaison persons in addition to its voting and *ex officio* members. Much of the work of the committee has been accomplished by task forces whose membership included outside consultants as well as CC:DA members, liaison persons, and representatives.

Formal proposals from these four committees, the Library of Congress, and the editors were considered by the Joint Steering Committee at its nine meetings held between August 1979 and October 1986: Tallahassee (1979), Vancouver (1980), San Francisco (1981), London (1982), Ottawa (1983), Glasgow (1984), Chicago (1985), Toronto (March 1986), London (October 1986). The decisions made at these meetings are to be found either in this publication or, in some instances, in the rule interpretations issued by national bibliographic agencies.

SOURCES

This revision of AACR 2 is, of course, based on the same sources as those listed in the 1978 Preface, printed below. The principal published sources for the revision of chapter 9 are *Study of Cataloguing Computer Software : Applying AACR2 to Microcomputer Programs* / Ray Templeton and Anita Witten. — [London] : British Library, c1984. — (Library and Information Research Report ; 28) and *Guidelines for Using AACR2 Chapter 9 for Cataloging Microcomputer Software* / Committee on Cataloging: Description and Access, Cataloging and Classification Section, American Library Association. — Chicago : ALA, 1984.

ACKNOWLEDGMENTS

The people listed on the preceding pages have contributed their time and energy to the work of rule revision, both in generating ideas and in reviewing the proposals of others. We recognize also the many unnamed people who made helpful comments or provided further information. An additional thank you is extended to Lisa Boise, for responding to Joint Steering Committee requests promptly and pleasantly. We owe a great debt to Ronald Hagler, who contributed a keen eye for errors and inconsistencies and, even more importantly, his great expertise and unflagging diligence. This publication owes many of its virtues and none of its faults to Ronald Hagler.

We are indebted to those people in the United Kingdom and in the United States who worked on special committees and task forces dealing with the cataloguing of computer files. Without their initial efforts the work of the Joint Steering Committee in this area would have been much more prolonged. We also acknowledge the leadership provided by music cataloguers in North America, whose initiatives led to the reorganization of the rules for music uniform titles.

Not least of the contributions made to this revision of the second edition of AACR is the financial one. Many organizations contributed indirectly by allowing their staff members to spend time and resources preparing documents that helped national committees and the Joint Steering Committee make decisions. We wish to mention particularly the following organizations which either underwrote national meetings or donated Joint Steering Committee representatives' time and secretarial costs: The British Library, Free Library of Philadelphia, Library of Congress, Liverpool Polytechnic, National Library of Australia, National Library of Canada, Seneca College of Applied Arts and Technology (Toronto), State Library of New South Wales, University of Chicago, University of Illinois at Urbana-Champaign, and University of Newcastle upon Tyne.

JEAN WEIHS, *Chair*
Joint Steering Committee for Revision of AACR

PREFACE TO THE ANGLO-AMERICAN CATALOGUING RULES, SECOND EDITION (1978)

The first edition of the *Anglo-American Cataloguing Rules*, in its separately published North American and British texts, was the product of the inspired editorship successively of Seymour Lubetzky and C. Sumner Spalding and the culmination of many years' activity by a large number of individuals, to whom credit and acknowledgment were given in that edition. This second edition does not supersede their work, but continues it: for, in spite of the changes in presentation and content which it introduces, these are still the *Anglo-American Cataloguing Rules*, having the same principles and underlying objectives as the first edition, and being firmly based on the achievement of those who created the work, first published in 1967.

The starting point for this new edition is, indeed, the very clear success of the 1967 texts in meeting the needs of large numbers—and many different kinds—of libraries during a period in which there have been considerable growth in libraries and extensions of catalogue processes, bibliographic services, and national library services; not only in the three "Anglo-American" countries for which AACR was established, but throughout the world. AACR has been adopted by major libraries and agencies in most English-speaking countries, and has had a considerable influence on the formation or revision of local and national cataloguing rules in a number of others. For ten years it has thus been subjected to the critical test of application over a very wide range of professional practice across the world.

During this time mechanization, the growth of centralized and cooperative bibliographic services and networks, the development and unification of services in the national libraries (especially, in the AACR context, those of the United Kingdom and Canada)—all these have had, as they continue to have, significant effects on the assembly, transmission, and catalogue exploitation of bibliographic information, both within libraries and between libraries. And, the introduction into most libraries of increasing numbers of the new media that have established themselves in the same period as having a parallel importance, for many library users, with the paper-based and printed documents traditionally the staple of the processing and cataloguing department, has created or intensified integrative problems on a scale unpredictable by those who wrought the 1967 texts.

A "memorandum of agreement" of 1966 between the American Library Association (ALA) and the [British] Library Association provided a means of continuing review by these two bodies of the 1967 texts after publication, so that appropriate action by amendment and addition might be taken to deal with any problems encountered by users on account either of errors and ambiguities or of changing circumstances. The forum for that review was the Descriptive Cataloging Committee (DCC) of the ALA Resources and Technical Services Division; and from 1969 to 1974 regular meetings of DCC were attended by representatives of the Cataloguing Rules Committee established by the Library Association, with formal representation also of the Library of Congress and the Canadian Library Association. At these meetings a number of amendments and changes of the 1967 texts were agreed and promulgated; and some of the problems arising from changing circumstances were addressed for the first time, particularly those of the treatment of nonbook materials. However, the memorandum did not stipulate agreement among all parties as a condition of amendment to either text and, while in one or two important respects the differences between the two texts were diminished, there were some not unimportant issues on which they seemed in some danger of moving further apart. Furthermore, some significant problems were identified on which, although all parties were agreed on the line of development needed, the procedural mechanisms provided by the memorandum were not wholly adequate for thorough examination and effective action.

At this stage, two new factors made it both propitious and desirable to find a new means of consolidating development since 1967 and of providing for the ascertainable requirements of bibliographic control in the 1980s and beyond. These were, first, the proposed conclusion by the Library of Congress of the policy of "superimposition" by which its adoption of AACR had been limited; and, second, the establishment by the newly formed British Library of its policies of working alongside the Library of Congress, the National Library of Canada, and other libraries and agencies, in the framework of national and international networks and standards for bibliographic records. Another contributory factor was the emergence, from the International Meeting of Cataloguing Experts held in Copenhagen in 1969, of a programme of International Standard Bibliographic Description (ISBD) under the aegis of the International Federation of Library Associations and Institutions (IFLA). This programme commenced with a standard for monographs, ISBD(M), which was incorporated into the two texts of AACR in 1974 by means of separately published revisions of chapter 6.

For these reasons, and on the initiatives of ALA and the British Library, there took place at ALA headquarters in Chicago, in March 1974, a tripartite meeting—consisting of one delegate each from the three "Anglo-American" countries, representing in each case both the library association and the national library—to draw up a new memorandum of agreement and to complete the planning of the project for a second edition of AACR.

OBJECTIVES AND POLICIES

The objectives established in the memorandum of the tripartite meeting may be briefly stated as follows:

1) to reconcile in a single text the North American and British texts of 1967
2) to incorporate in the single text all amendments and changes already agreed and implemented under the previous mechanisms
3) to consider for inclusion in AACR all proposals for amendment currently under discussion between the American Library Association, the Library Association, the Library of Congress, and the Canadian Library Association; any new proposals put forward by these bodies and the British Library; and any proposals of national committees of other countries in which AACR is in use
4) to provide for international interest in AACR by facilitating its use in countries other than the United States, Canada, and the United Kingdom. This final objective was later intensified, as a condition of funding by the Council on Library Resources, to one of making a contribution to the development of an international cataloguing code.

The tripartite meeting set up a Joint Steering Committee for Revision of AACR (JSCAACR), consisting of one voting and one nonvoting representative of each of the five participating organizations, and provided for two editors, one from either side of the Atlantic. JSCAACR's function has been to appoint the editors, to consider all proposals and determine questions of policy with the editors, to assess for approval the rules framed by the editors, and to present the final text for publication; and thus to be the ultimate authority for the content and presentation of this second edition.

An early result of JSCAACR's consideration of the objectives and its own terms of reference was its declaration of the guidelines by which policy questions and new proposals were to be determined. These guidelines were stated publicly at the commencement of the project; they have been sustained throughout the two and a half years of its completion, and they may be summarized as follows:

1) maintenance of general conformity with the Paris Principles of 1961, as manifested in the first edition
2) particular attention to developments in the machine processing of bibliographic records
3) continuance of conformity with the ISBD(M) as a basis for the bibliographic description of monographs, and commitment to the principle of standardization in the bibliographic description of all types of materials
4) determination of the treatment of nonbook materials primarily from a consideration of the published cataloguing rules of the Canadian Library Association, the Library Association, and the Association for Educational Communications and Technology; and of the ALA revision of chapter 12 of the 1967 text.[1]

With regard to the first of the guidelines, the second edition continues to reflect the tendency to closer conformity with the Paris Principles that was already embodied in amendments to the 1967 texts promulgated before work on the edition began, specifically the abandonment of entry under the name of a place of certain institutional bodies, as related to section 9.4 of the Paris Principles[2]; and some other shortfalls in conformity have been made good during the course of approving new proposals, notably by the substitution of uniform titles for form subheadings in relation to section 9.5.

With regard to the second guideline, the single most important contribution of this edition to meeting the needs of machine processing resides, in the submission of the authors, in the achievement of an integrated and standardized framework for the systematic description of all library materials, as presented by part I. This achievement, being also the first such comprehensive systematization to be related to the goals of international standardization, is also presented by the authors as the principal fulfilment of the undertaking (in objective 4 above) to make a contribution to the development of an international cataloguing code, and as a major development in its own right.

It is also the principal means by which the third and fourth guidelines have been sustained, and by which resolution has been achieved of the conflict that was soon

---

1. See "Sources" on page xxx for full citations.

2. See the Introduction to the 1967 edition of AACR (pp. 2–4 North American text; pp. 2–3 British text) for a summary statement on the initial relationship with the Paris Principles; and *Statement of Principles . . . Paris . . . 1961. Annotated Edition* (full citation at "Sources," below, p. xxx) for an extensive commentary with texts of the *Principles*.

apparent between them and the programme initiated by IFLA, under the general heading of Universal Bibliographical Control (UBC), for the development of separate ISBDs for such materials as serials, maps, and nonbook materials.

Seeking to establish means of uniform description for all materials, JSCAACR could not easily reconcile AACR users' needs with those of the UBC programme on two counts: (1) the timetables of AACR revision and UBC were not in phase with each other; and (2) although harmonized in general terms with ISBD(M), the available drafts from the new ISBD working groups contained indications that in their final forms they would be insufficiently uniform in their relations with ISBD(M) and with each other; and thus they might be neither anticipated nor utilized in AACR as an integrated code.

Mindful of its undertaking to the Council on Library Resources, JSCAACR took the initiative of proposing to the IFLA Committee on Cataloguing that a standardized general framework, drawn up by joint editor Michael Gorman after scrutiny of the four main sources for nonbook materials and of other sources, should be developed jointly by JSCAACR and IFLA as a constraint within which both AACR and the evolving special-material ISBDs should be held; so that the fullest uniformity might be achieved within AACR, within ISBDs, and between ISBDs and AACR. The first meeting between JSCAACR (represented by all but one of its voting members and by both editors) and the IFLA committee with the chairpersons of all the then established ISBD working groups was held in Paris in October 1975, and substantial agreement was reached on the implementation of a general framework, to be known as ISBD(G). Further agreement on some modifications was reached at subsequent meetings, and part I of this edition is based on the ISBD(G) framework determined by these agreements.

STRUCTURE AND WORKING METHODS

In each of the three participating countries the Joint Steering Committee's work has been supported and stimulated by a national committee, which initiated and/or screened very many of the proposals for revision and then reviewed and commented on the draft texts before their final form in this edition was settled.

In the United States the ALA/RTSD Catalog Code Revision Committee (CCRC) organized rule review and revision proposal teams to identify systematically the rules needing attention and to make their own proposals in respect of them, as well as to process those of other bodies. CCRC established working relations with other ALA/ RTSD groups, notably the Serials Section's AACR Revision Study Committee, the Filing Committee, and with the Interdivisional Committee on Representation in Machine-Readable Form of Bibliographic Information (MARBI); and the entire membership of the Descriptive Cataloging Committee also participated in its work. Thirty organizations outside ALA were invited either to designate representatives to CCRC or to receive and comment on the Committee's documents.

In the United Kingdom a joint Library Association/British Library Committee on Revision of AACR, having equal representation from both organizations, performed a similar task in respect of the British text. A close relationship was maintained with the Library Association Cataloguing and Indexing Group, under whose aegis consultations and meetings with representatives of numerous other interest groups and organizations were held; and a joint conference was convened with AACR-oriented library representatives of the Nordic countries of Europe. The formal input of comments and proposals from these and other countries outside the "Anglo-American" triangle was processed for JSCAACR by its Library of Congress representative; but the British committee was responsible for arranging and monitoring the review of final drafts by those other English-speaking countries who contributed to the input. This wider input and review were greatly assisted by the good offices of the Director of the IFLA International Office for UBC.

In Canada the Canadian Committee on Cataloguing/Comité canadien de catalogage (CCC) expressed the interests of the three national bodies that appoint its members: L'Association pour l'avancement des sciences et des techniques de la documentation, the Canadian Library Association, and the National Library of Canada. The committee called on the Canadian Association of Law Libraries, the Association of Canadian Map Libraries, and the Joint Advisory Committee for Nonbook Materials throughout the revision project for assistance in formulating its positions.

The input from these sources, from the Library of Congress's discussions among its own staff, and from the editors, was considered by JSCAACR at seven meetings between January 1975 and December 1976; five in the United States (New York, Washington (2), Chicago, and Princeton University), and one each in Canada (Toronto) and the United Kingdom (London). In January 1977 a draft of the emergent text of part I was distributed for review to the national committees and by them to a wide range of outside organizations. This draft was followed by drafts of part II in April 1977, in which month a special meeting of JSCAACR in Washington planned the concluding stages of drafting and copy preparation. The ninth and final meeting, to consider all proposals and comments of reviewers, to approve the whole text, and to authorize its presentation for publication, was held in Washington in August 1977.

ADOPTION STRATEGIES

In fulfilling their brief the Joint Steering Committee and the editors have striven to maintain as conservative an approach to revision as the demands of text reconciliation and closer uniformity, and the evidence of new needs from new circumstances, will allow. Most of what is here was already in the first edition, only made (if the attempt has been successful in this respect) more accessible to cataloguers and bibliographers in language and articulation, and more nearly related to what are seen as the normal sequences of cataloguing decision making in current practice, than before.

Some of the contents of the first edition (AACR 1) are not now included. They are those in which were provided options or alternatives inappropriate to the objectives of reconciliation and uniformity and those that treated of matters at a level of detail more appropriate to the interpretations and "in-house" rules of a single institution than to a code for all types and sizes of institutions. The absence of such details does not necessarily mean that observances of them by particular libraries should be abandoned.

Some of what is new does no more than extend the coverage of AACR to the newer categories of library materials with which cataloguers and bibliographers nowadays have to deal; and in this respect there should be little difficulty in adopting the new text.

There are also some areas in which—looking ahead from current developments and seeking resolution of problems that, for all its excellence, AACR 1 did not entirely resolve—AACR 2 has introduced some changes and new directions that will lead to differences in the bibliographic record and in the types and forms of heading at which it is displayed. The treatment of description, corporate headings, uniform titles, and fullness of names are instanced.

Such changes have not been introduced without awareness of the difficulties that they raise for libraries with large retrospective files. Indeed, these difficulties were acknowledged to be at the heart of the compromises and occasional inconsistencies in AACR 1 of which, from the sheer weight of evidence of the need for better resolution, JSCAACR has felt most strongly impelled to attempt amelioration for the sake of future practice. It has also been felt that, with the increased flexibility of modern systems for processing bibliographic data and of catalogue formats, the inertia of the retrospective file is much less than it has been in the past. Many of the larger research libraries have, or may expect soon to have, the capability of relatively inexpensive conversion of at least part of their catalogues to more flexible forms of storage; and, too, there appears generally a much wider acceptance in libraries of the propriety and utility of simply closing old catalogues when they become too large to respond easily to new requirements of their users and starting new ones alongside them.

JSCAACR therefore envisions libraries and bibliographic agencies adopting first those rules (principally in part I) the application of which has no significant effect on the arrangement and collocation of existing bibliographic records, even though some differences of style and content may occur between one record and another. The remaining provisions, where they differ from AACR 1 or from previous local practice, may then be most easily adopted at the time when newly designed cataloguing and bibliographic systems allow earlier records to be converted or reconciled or when a new sequence or catalogue is to come into being. In this connection there is a chronological checkpoint in the announced intention, earlier in 1978, of the Library of Congress, the National Library of Canada, the British Library, and the Australian National Library to adopt AACR 2 as of January 1981, so that cumulations of their published bibliographic records from that date will reflect the new rules.

SOURCES

The principal published sources for this edition include, in addition to the texts for the first edition itself, the amendments and changes to the North American text published in the Library of Congress *Cataloging Service* and to the British text published in the Library Association *Anglo-American Cataloguing Rules Amendment Bulletin*, 1969 through 1975; the two revised texts of chapter 6 published respectively by ALA and the Library Association in 1974; and the North American text revision of chapter 12 (ALA, 1975).

The other three primary sources for the development of rules for nonbook materials are *Non-book Materials Cataloguing Rules* / prepared by the Library Association Media Cataloguing Rules Committee. — London : National Council for Educational Technology, 1973. — (Working paper ; no. 11); *Nonbook Materials : the Organization of Integrated Collections* / by Jean Riddle Weihs, Shirley Lewis, Janet Macdonald. — 1st ed. — Ottawa : Canadian Library Association, 1973; and *Standards for Cataloging Nonprint Materials : an Interpretation and Practical Application* / by Alma Tillin and William J. Quinly. — 4th ed. — Washington : Association for Educational Communications and Technology, 1976.

Relevant sections of part I, as of the revised chapter 6 above, are based on *ISBD(M) : International Standard Bibliographic Description for Monographic Publications*. — 1st standard ed. — London : IFLA Committee on Cataloguing, 1974; and, as noted above, part I as a whole is closely related to *ISBD(G) : General International Standard Bibliographic Description : Annotated Text* / prepared by the Working Group on the General International Standard Bibliographic Description set up by the IFLA Committee on Cataloguing. – London : IFLA International Office for UBC, 1977.

In consideration of part II, a principal reference source has been *Statement of Principles Adopted at the International Conference on Cataloguing Principles, Paris, October 1961.* – Annotated ed. with commentary and examples / by Eva Verona, assisted by . . . [others]. – London : IFLA Committee on Cataloguing, 1971. JSCAACR and the editors also acknowledge their debt to Eva Verona's *Corporate Headings : Their Use in Library Catalogues and National Bibliographies : a Comparative and Critical Study.* – London : IFLA Committee on Cataloguing, 1975.

ACKNOWLEDGMENTS

In his prefatorial acknowledgment of all those who contributed to the first edition, the chairman of the then Catalog Code Revision Committee observed that "rules are not lightly made or changed." Working on this edition, though with more limited objectives and occupying fewer years of their lives, has proved no less arduous for the many individuals who have been engaged in it. The members of the ALA Catalog Code Revision Committee, the Library Association/British Library Committee on Revision of AACR, and the Canadian Committee on Cataloguing, and the senior staff of the Library of Congress deserve very special thanks for the formidable accomplishment of their contributions: and their names are on the following pages. Our thanks extend to the many organizations and committees in several countries whose members are not listed in the following pages, but who have devoted time and trouble to assist in this, a truly international enterprise; and, of course, to the members of the Joint Steering Committee for Revision of AACR themselves, with an admirable record of 100 percent attendance through all the long and often weary meetings at which this edition has taken shape.

Our debt to the editors, for the commitment and inspiration they brought to their task, is obvious; but to the acknowledgment they will surely receive from those who discover the merits of their work by applying it, an addition of particular gratitude from those for whom they toiled is commanded for their achievement in meeting the very onerous deadlines that the schedule of the project required of them. A similar encomium is deserved by Carol Kelm, then executive secretary of ALA/RTSD, who acted as secretary to the Joint Steering Committee and without whose organizational, documentational, and administrative talents the committee's work could scarcely have been accomplished in this time. Mention must also be made of the special documentational contributions of Helen Schmierer and Robert M. Hiatt, both being important factors in the completion on schedule of the review of draft texts.

Finally, grateful acknowledgment is made to the American Library Association, the British Library, the Library Association, the Library of Congress, and the National Library of Canada for the financial and other supportive resources with which they sustained the project at both national and international levels; and to the Council on Library Resources, without whose generous financial support of the Joint Steering Committee and the editors this edition could not have been undertaken.

PETER R. LEWIS, *Chair*
Joint Steering Committee for Revision of AACR

NEW AMENDMENTS LIST

Following is a list of revisions that were approved between 1992 and 1996 but have not been published separately. They are now incorporated, along with Amendments 1993, in the 1998 Revision in both the electronic and print formats.

rule 1.1C1. Add paragraph 4 under footnote 2:

Use *kit* for any item fitting the definition of this term in the Glossary, appendix D; note that this term may apply to certain categories of textual material.

rule 1.1G2 to read:

1.1G2. If, in an item lacking a collective title, no one work predominates, *either* describe the item as a unit (see 1.1G3) *or* make a separate description for each separately titled work, linking the separate descriptions with notes (see 1.7B21).

rule 2.5C1 to read:

2.5C1. Give *ill.* for an illustrated printed monograph. Tables containing only words and/or numbers are not illustrations. Disregard illustrated title pages and minor illustrations.

> 327 p. : ill.

rule 2.5C2 to read:

2.5C2. *Optionally*, if the illustrations are all of one or more of the following types, and are considered to be important, give the appropriate term(s) or abbreviation(s) in alphabetical order: coats of arms, facsimiles, forms, genealogical tables, maps, music, plans, portraits (use for both single and group portraits), samples. If none of these terms adequately describes the illustrations, use another term as appropriate.

> 333 p. : maps
>
> 256 p. : coats of arms, facsims., ports.
>
> 147 p. : computer drawings

If only some of the illustrations are of types considered to be important, give *ill.* followed by the appropriate term(s) or abbreviations(s) in alphabetical order.

> 230 p. : ill., maps, music, ports.
>
> 1 v. (loose-leaf) : ill., plans
>
> 199 p. : ill., cross sections, forms

rule 2.5C3. Add a new example:

> : ill. (chiefly col.), plans

rule 2.5C5 (formerly 2.5C6) to read:

2.5C5. If the publication consists wholly or predominantly of illustrations, give *all ill.* or *chiefly ill.*, as appropriate. *Optionally*, if those illustrations are all of one type, give *all* [*name of type*] or *chiefly* [*name of type*].

> : all ill.

> : chiefly maps

rule 4.0A1. 1st sentence to read:

4.0A1. The rules in this chapter cover the description of manuscript (including typescript or printout) materials of all kinds, including manuscript books, dissertations, letters, speeches, etc., legal papers (including printed forms completed in manuscript), and collections of such manuscripts.

rule 4.7B1 to read:

4.7B1. Nature, scope, or form. Make notes on the nature of a manuscript or a collection of manuscripts unless it is apparent from the rest of the description. Use one of the following terms, as appropriate:

> holograph(s) (for manuscripts handwritten by the person(s)
>   responsible for the work(s) contained therein)
> ms. (for all other handwritten manuscripts)
> mss. (for all other collections of handwritten manuscripts)
> printout(s)
> typescript(s)

> Holograph

> Ms.

> Typescripts

If the item is signed, add *signed.*

> Holograph, signed

If the item or collection being described is a copy or consists of copies, add *(carbon copy)*, *(photocopy)*, or *(transcript)*, or the plural of one of these. If a photocopy is negative, add *negative*. Add *handwritten*, *typewritten*, or *printout* to *transcript(s)*.

> Holograph (carbon copy)

> Ms. (photocopy, negative)

> Ms., signed (photocopy)

> Mss. (transcripts, handwritten)

> Typescript (photocopy)

If the items in a collection are not all of the same nature, word the qualification to indicate this.

Mss. (some photocopies)

Mss. (transcripts, handwritten, and photocopies)

Mss. (photocopies, some negative)

If the item is a copy, add the location of the original if this can be readily ascertained.

Ms. (photocopy) of original in the British Library Humanities and Social Sciences

Holograph, signed (photocopy), original in possession of W.S. Mcrwin

Indicate the scope or form of a manuscript item if it is not apparent from the rest of the description.

Poem

Journal and account book

Typescript of sound recording

Printout of catalog

[remainder of rule is unchanged]

rule 7.0B2 to read:

7.0B2. Prescribed sources of information. The prescribed source(s) of information for each area of the description of motion pictures and videorecordings is set out below. Enclose information taken from outside the prescribed source(s) in square brackets.

AREA	PRESCRIBED SOURCES OF INFORMATION
Title and statement of responsibility	Chief source of information
Edition	Chief source of information, accompanying material, container
Publication, distribution, etc.	Chief source of information, accompanying material, container
Physical description	Any source
Series	Chief source of information, accompanying material, container
Note	Any source
Standard number and terms of availability	Any source

rule 7.7B2 to read:

7.7B2. Language. Give the language(s) of the spoken, sung, or written content of a motion picture or videorecording unless this is apparent from the rest of the description. Indicate captioning or signing.

In French

French dialogue, English subtitles

Dubbed into English

Closed-captioned

rule 9.0B1 to read:

9.0B1. Chief source of information. The chief source of information for computer files is the title screen(s).

If there is no title screen, take the information from other formally presented internal evidence (e.g., main menus, program statements, first display of information, the header to the file including "Subject:" lines, information at the end of the file). In case of variation in fullness of information found in these sources, prefer the source with the most complete information.

If the computer file is unreadable without processing (e.g., compressed file, printer-formatted file), take the information from the file after it has been uncompressed, printed out, or otherwise processed for use.

If the information required is not available[1] from internal sources, take it from the following sources (in this order of preference):

> the physical carrier or its labels[2]
> information issued by the publisher, creator, etc., with the file (sometimes called "documentation")
> information printed on the container issued by the publisher, distributor, etc.

If the item being described consists of two or more separate physical parts, treat a container or its permanently affixed label that is the unifying element as the chief source of information if it furnishes a collective title and the formally presented information in, or the labels on, the parts themselves do not.

If the information required is not available from the chief source or the sources listed above, take it from the following sources (in this order of preference):

> other published descriptions of the file
> other sources

rule 9.1F1 to read:

9.1F1. Transcribe statements of responsibility relating to those persons or bodies credited with a major role in creating the content of the file as instructed in 1.1F.

> Database [GMD] / Paul Fellows

> The China study [GMD] / principal investigator, Angus Campbell

> Memory castle [GMD] / designed by Donna Stanger ; programmed by Lon Koenig

> Class records system [GMD] / by Quercus

> Moby Dick [GMD] / by Herman Melville ; compiled and produced by Princeton University Computer Center under the direction of Robert Knight

Give all other statements of responsibility in notes (see 9.7B6).

rule 9.3B2 to read:

9.3B2. Number of records, statements, etc. If a file designation is given and if the information is readily available, give the number or approximate number of files that make up the content (use *file* or *files* preceded by an arabic numeral) and/or these other details:

a) *Data.* Give the number or approximate number of records (use *records*) and/or bytes (give the term in either abbreviated or full form).

  Computer data (1 file : 350 records)

  Computer data (550 records)

  Computer data (1 file : 600 records, 240,000 bytes)

  Computer data (1 file : 2.5 gb)

  Computer data (1 file : 1.2 megabytes)

b) *Programs.* Give the number or approximate number of statements (use *statements*) and/or bytes (give the term in either abbreviated or full form).

  Computer program (1 file : 200 statements)

  Computer program (2150 statements)

c) Multipart files. Give the number or approximate number of records and/or bytes, or statements and/or bytes, in each part according to a) and b) above.

  Computer data (3 files : 100, 460, 550 records)

  Computer programs (2 files : 4300, 1250 bytes)

  Computer data (2 files : ca. 330 records each)

  Computer data (2 files : 800, 1250 records) and programs (3 files : 7260, 3490, 5076 bytes)

  Computer data (2 files : 3.5, 2 megabytes)

If such numbering cannot be given succinctly, omit the information from this area. If desired, give it in a note (see 9.7B8).

rule 9.5B1 to read:

9.5B1. Record the number of physical units of the carrier by giving the number of them in arabic numerals and one of the following terms as appropriate:[4]

> computer cartridge
> computer cassette
> computer disk
> computer optical disc
> computer reel

> 1 computer disk
>
> 2 computer cassettes
>
> 1 computer reel
>
> 1 computer optical disc

When new physical carriers are developed for which none of these terms is appropriate, give the specific name of the physical carrier as concisely as possible, preferably qualified by *computer*.

> 1 computer card

If the information is readily available and if desired, indicate the specific type of physical medium.

> 1 computer chip cartridge
>
> 1 computer tape cartridge
>
> 1 computer tape reel
>
> 1 computer optical card

Optionally, if general material designations are used (see 1.1C1), omit *computer* from the specific material designation.

Give a trade name or other similar specification in a note (see 9.7B1b).

rule 9.5B1. Add a footnote to read:

> 4. The following rules apply to the terms:
>   1) Use *computer disk* for magnetically encoded computer disks.
>   2) Use *computer optical disc* for optically encoded computer discs.

rule 9.5D1. Paragraph a) to read:

> a) *Discs/Disks*. Give the diameter of the disc or disk in inches, to the next ¼ inch up.
>
>> 1 computer disk : col. ; 5¼ in.
>>
>> 1 computer optical disc : col. ; 4¾ in.

rule 9.7B8. Examples at the 2nd paragraph to read:

> File size: 520, 300, 280, 400, 320, 400, 500 records
>
> File size: ca. 520, 300, 400, 320 statements
>
> File size: 75, 65, 63, 92, 81, 109 kilobytes

rule 21.1B4 to be deleted.

rule 22.5A1. 1st paragraph and examples to read:

22.5A1. Enter a name containing a surname or consisting only of a surname under that surname unless subsequent rules (e.g., 22.6, 22.10, 22.28) provide for entry under a different element.

> **Bernhardt, Sarah**

Fitzgerald, Ella

Byatt, A.S.

Ching, Francis K.W.

Mantovani

rule 22.5D1. Add as a first example under *ENGLISH*

À Beckett, Gilbert Abbott

rule 22.5D2. Delete the second example.

rule 22.28D2. Example to read:

Phra Thammathatsanāthǫn (Thǫngsuk)
   x Thammathatsanāthǫn (Thǫngsuk), *Phra*
   x Thǫngsuk Suthatsō
   x Suthatsō, Thǫngsuk
   x Thǫngsuk Čhantharakhačhǫn
   x Čhantharakhačhǫn, Thǫngsuk
   x Sutsasa, *Thēra*

rule 24.26A to read:

24.26A. Enter a delegation, commission, etc., representing a country in an international or intergovernmental body, conference, undertaking, etc., under the heading for the country represented, followed by the name of the delegation, etc. Give the subheading in the language (see 24.3A) of the country represented. Omit from the subheading the name or abbreviation of the name of the government in noun form unless such an omission would result in objectionable distortion. If the name of the delegation, etc., is uncertain, give *Delegation [Mission, etc.]* (or equivalent terms in the language of the country represented). If considered necessary to distinguish the delegation, etc., from others of the same name, add the name, in the form and language used for it as a heading, of the international or intergovernmental body, conference, undertaking, etc., to which the delegation, etc., is accredited. Make explanatory references as necessary from the heading for the international body, etc., followed by an appropriate subheading (see 26.3C1).

   Mexico. *Delegación (Inter-American Conference for the Maintenance of Peace (1936: Buenos Aires, Argentina))*

   Germany. *Reichskommission für die Weltausstellung in Chicago*

   United States. *Delegation (International Conference on Maritime Law (3rd : 1909 : Brussels, Belgium))*

   United States. *Mission (United Nations)*
   Explanatory reference:
   United Nations. Missions
     Delegations, missions, etc., from member nations to the United Nations and to its subordinate units are entered under the name of the nation followed by the name of the delegation, mission, etc.; e.g.,
   United States. *Mission (United Nations)*

United States. *Delegation (United Nations. General Assembly)*
Uruguay. *Delegación (United Nations)*

Make the same explanatory reference under **United Nations.** *Delegations, and under* **United Nations.** *General Assembly. Delegations, and under other appropriate headings*

If it is uncertain that a delegation represents the government of a country, enter it under its own name.

rule 26.2A2 to read:

26.2A2. Different forms of the name. Refer from a form of name used by a person, or found in reference sources, or resulting from a different romanization of the name, if it differs significantly from the form used in the heading for that person. Typical instances are:

[examples remain unchanged]

rule A.4A1. Footnote 2 to read:

If a romanized title (title proper, alternative title, parallel title, quoted title, etc.) begins with the Arabic article *al* in any of its various orthographic forms (e.g., *al, el, es*) or with the Hebrew article *ha (he)*, do not capitalize the article, whether written separately or hyphenated with the following word.

> ha-Milon he-hadash : Ivri-Angli, Angli-Ivri
> (Milon *is considered the first word and is therefore capitalized*)

rule A.10A to read:

A.10A. Capitalize the first word in each note or an abbreviation beginning a note. If a note consists of more than one sentence, capitalize the first word of each subsequent sentence. See A.4A-A.4D for the capitalization of titles. Capitalize other words as instructed in the rules for the language involved.

> Title from container.

> Facsim. reprint. Originally published: London: I. Walsh, ca. 1734

Glossary. Definition for Game to read:

Game. An item or set of materials designed for play according to prescribed or implicit rules and intended for recreation or instruction. *See also* Activity card, Kit, Toy.

Glossary. Definition for Model to read:

Model. A three-dimensional representation of a real thing. *See also* Toy.

Glossary. Delete the definition for "Production company (Motion pictures)" and add a definition for "Producer":

Producer. 1. A person or corporate body that has artistic and/or intellectual responsibility for the form and content of an item. 2. An individual or organization that has responsibility for the technical aspect(s) (e.g., mixing of sound), manufacture or production of an item.

Glossary. Definition for Realia to read:

Realia. An artefact or naturally occurring entity, as opposed to a replica. *See also* Object, Toy.

Glossary. Add the definition:

Toy. An object designed for imaginative play or one from which to derive amusement. *See also* Game, Model, Realia.

Appendix

The following open marks of omission in normal weight type should be corrected to closed marks of omission in normal weight type:

rule 1.0C1. General rule, 5th paragraph

rule 4.7B23. Example commencing "Tractatus begins"

rule 11.7B6. Example

rule 21.25A. 1st example, 1st mark of omission

The following open marks of omission in bold type should be deleted:

rule 21.4B1. 2nd example, 2nd mark of omission

The following closed marks of omission in normal weight type should be corrected to open marks of omission in bold type:

rule 21.6B1. 1st example and 4th example

The following open marks of omission in normal weight type should be corrected to open marks of omission in bold type:

rule 21.10A. 5th example commencing "The pilgrim's progress"
rule 22.8C1. 4th example commencing "**Eleanor,** *of Acquitaine*"

The following open marks of omission in normal weight type should be deleted:

rule 21.21A. 2nd example

GENERAL INTRODUCTION

0.1. These rules are designed for use in the construction of catalogues and other lists in general libraries of all sizes. They are not specifically intended for specialist and archival libraries, but such libraries are recommended to use the rules as the basis of their cataloguing and to augment their provisions as necessary. The rules cover the description of, and the provision of access points for, all library materials commonly collected at the present time. The integrated structure of the text makes the general rules usable as a basis for cataloguing uncommonly collected materials of all kinds and library materials yet unknown.

0.2. The second edition of the rules is based on a reconciliation of the British and North American texts of the 1967 edition. This extends to style, which is generally in accordance with the *Chicago Manual of Style*,[1] and to spellings, which are those of Webster's *New International Dictionary*.[2] Where Webster's gives as a permitted alternative a British spelling (e.g., *catalogue, centre*), it has been used in the rules; where the American usage is the only one specified (e.g., *capitalize*), it has been used in the rules. Agreement on terminology has similarly resulted sometimes in the use of an American term (e.g., *membership in*) and sometimes in a British term (e.g., *full stop*).

STRUCTURE OF THE RULES

0.3. The rules follow the sequence of cataloguers' operations in most present-day libraries and bibliographic agencies. Part I deals with the provision of information describing the item being catalogued and part II deals with the determination and establishment of headings (access points) under which the descriptive information is to be presented to catalogue users, and with the making of references to those headings. The introductions to parts I and II begin on page 7 and page 305 respectively.

0.4. In both parts the rules proceed from the general to the specific. In part I the specificity relates to the physical medium of the item being catalogued, to

---

1. *The Chicago Manual of Style : for Authors, Editors, and Copywriters.* — 13th ed., rev. and expanded. — Chicago ; London : University of Chicago Press, 1982.

2. *Webster's Third New International Dictionary of the English Language, Unabridged* / editor in chief, Philip Babcock Gove and the Merriam-Webster editorial staff. — Springfield, Mass. : Merriam-Webster ; Harlow, Essex : Distributed by Longman Group, c1986.

the level of detail required for each element of the description, and to the analysis of an item containing separate parts.

MAIN ENTRY AND ALTERNATIVE HEADINGS

0.5. In part II the rules are based on the proposition that one *main entry* is made for each item described, and that this is supplemented by *added entries*. The question of the use of *alternative heading entries* (i.e., sets of equal entries for each item described) was discussed but not embodied in the rules. It is recognized, however, that many libraries do not distinguish between the main entry and other entries. It is recommended that such libraries use chapter 21 as guidance in determining all the entries required in particular instances. It will be necessary, however, for all libraries to distinguish the main entry from the others when:

        a) making a single entry listing
or b) making a single citation for a work (as required for entries for related works and for some subject entries).

In addition, the concept of main entry is considered to be useful in assigning uniform titles and in promoting the standardization of bibliographic citation.

STRUCTURE OF ENTRIES

0.6. Distinguish a name heading and/or uniform title assigned to a description from the descriptive data:

either a) by giving them on separate lines above the description
  or b) by separating them from the description by a full stop and two spaces.

If an entry begins with a title proper (i.e., the first element of the description):

either a) repeat the title proper on a separate line above the description
  or b) give the description alone.

ALTERNATIVES AND OPTIONS

0.7. Some rules are designated as *alternative rules* or as *optional additions*, and some other rules or parts of rules are introduced by *optionally*. These provisions arise from the recognition that different solutions to a problem and differing levels of detail and specificity are appropriate in different contexts. Decide some alternatives and options as a matter of cataloguing policy for a particular catalogue or bibliographic agency and, therefore, exercise them either always or never. Exercise other alternatives and options case by case. All cataloguing agencies should distinguish between these two types of option and keep a record of their policy decisions and of the circumstances in which a particular option may be applied.

0.8. The word *prominently* (used in such phrases as *prominently named* and *stated prominently*) means that a statement to which it applies must be a formal statement found in one of the prescribed sources of information (see 1.0A) for areas 1 and 2 for the class of material to which the item being catalogued belongs.

0.9. These rules recognize the necessity for judgement and interpretation by the cataloguer. Such judgement and interpretation may be based on the requirements of a particular catalogue or upon the use of the items being catalogued. The need for judgement is indicated in these rules by words and phrases such as *if appropriate*, *important*, and *if necessary*. Such words and phrases indicate recognition of the fact that uniform legislation for all types and sizes of catalogue is neither possible nor desirable, and encourage the application of individual judgement based on specific local knowledge. This statement in no way contradicts the value of standardization. Apply such judgements consistently within a particular context and record the cataloguing agency's policy.

APPENDICES

0.10. Matters of general application (abbreviations, capitalization, and the treatment of numerals) are dealt with in appendices. The instructions given in those appendices are rules and must be applied consistently. A glossary is given as the final appendix.

STYLE

0.11. In matters of style not covered by the rules and appendices (e.g., matters of punctuation other than prescribed punctuation), follow the *Chicago Manual of Style.*

LANGUAGE PREFERENCES

0.12. The rules contain some instances in which a decision is made on the basis of language and in which English is preferred. Users of the rules who do not use English as their working language should replace the specified preference for English by a preference for their working language. Authorized translations will do the same.

0.13. The ALA/LC romanization tables[3] are used in examples in which romanization occurs. This usage is based on the recognition that these tables are used by the overwhelming majority of libraries in Australia, Canada, the United Kingdom, and the United States. Authorized translations will, in examples, substitute romanizations derived from the standard romanization tables prevailing in libraries in the countries or areas for which the translation is intended.

EXAMPLES

0.14. The examples used throughout these rules are illustrative and not prescriptive. That is, they illuminate the provisions of the rule to which they are attached, rather than extend those provisions. Do not take the examples or the form in which they are presented as instructions unless specifically told to do so by the accompanying text.

Examples often have explanatory notes in italics added to them. Do not confuse them with notes to be added to the description by the cataloguer (see 1.7). In part I of the rules, a note to be added to the description is indicated in the examples by *Note*. Do not add this word to the actual description.

---

3. *Cataloging Service,* bulletin 118 (summer 1976)- . — Washington : Cataloging Distribution Service, Library of Congress, 1976-

Two marks of omission are used in examples. One indicates that the mark is to form a part of the actual catalogue entry. Its appearance is shown in the next line:

by Thomas Smith ... [et al.]

The other indicates the incompleteness of the example itself. Where it appears, the required wording (governed by a rule other than the one at which it appears) is to take its place in the actual catalogue entry. Its appearance is shown in the next line:

London : Walt Disney Productions .... — (Disney storyteller)

PART I. DESCRIPTION

INTRODUCTION

0.21. This part of the rules contains instructions on the formulation of descriptions of library materials. Those descriptions need (in most instances) headings and/or uniform titles added to them before they are usable as catalogue entries. For instructions on the formulation of such access points, see part II.

0.22. The rules for description are based on the general framework for the description of library materials, the General International Standard Bibliographic Description (ISBD(G)[1]) agreed between the International Federation of Library Associations and Institutions (IFLA) and the Joint Steering Committee for Revision of AACR. They follow that framework exactly in the order of elements and their prescribed punctuation. It was agreed with IFLA that it is not necessary for codes of rules to follow the terminology of the ISBD(G) exactly.

IFLA has developed, and is developing, specialized ISBDs for specific types of material, also on the basis of the ISBD(G). Close correspondence will therefore exist between chapters in part I and the corresponding ISBD.

STRUCTURE OF PART I

0.23. The basic rules for the description of all library materials are to be found in chapter 1, which sets out all the rules that are of general applicability. Then follow rules for specific types of material (chapters 2–10) and rules of partial generality (chapters 11–13). There are no chapters numbered 14–20; part II begins with chapter 21, the paragraphs of the Introduction to part II being numbered 20.1, 20.2, etc.

Chapter 1 is a general chapter containing those rules that apply to all library materials. For example, rule 1.4C deals with the place of publication, distribution, etc., and subsequent chapters in part I refer the user to that rule for guidance on that topic. Where types of material demand specific treatment of a certain element, the general chapter contains only brief guidance and the user of the rules will find specific guidance in the appropriate specific chapter. For example, rule 1.5 contains an indication of the type of information found in the physical description area; and detailed guidance on the physical description of sound recordings will be found in rule 6.5, on the physical description of motion pictures

---

1. *ISBD(G) : General International Standard Bibliographic Description : Annotated Text* / prepared by the Working Group on the General International Standard Bibliographic Description set up by the IFLA Committee on Cataloguing. — London : IFLA International Office for UBC, 1977.

and videorecordings in rule 7.5, and so on. Use the chapters in part I alone or in combination as the specific problem demands. For example, a difficult problem in describing a serial sound recording might lead the user to consult chapters 1, 6, and 12. The majority of problems, however, can be solved, once the rules have been studied comprehensively, by a single reference to a single rule.

Within the chapters the rule numbering has a mnemonic structure. For example, rule 1.4C is concerned with the place of publication, etc., for all materials, rule 2.4C is concerned with the place of publication, etc., for printed monographs, rule 3.4C is concerned with the place of publication, etc., for cartographic materials, and so on. If a particular rule appearing in chapter 1 is not applicable to the material treated in a subsequent chapter, the rule is omitted from that chapter. For example, there is no rule numbered 5.7B17 because rule 1.7B17 is not applicable to music.

METHODS OF PROCEDURE

0.24. It is a cardinal principle of the use of part I that the description of a physical item should be based in the first instance on the chapter dealing with the class of materials to which that item belongs. For example, describe a printed monograph in microform as a microform (using the rules in chapter 11). There will be need in many instances to consult the chapter dealing with the original form of the item, especially when constructing notes. So, using the same example, consult the chapter dealing with printed books (chapter 2) to supplement chapter 11. In short, the starting point for description is the physical form of the item in hand, not the original or any previous form in which the work has been published.

In describing serials, consult chapter 12 in conjunction with the chapter dealing with the physical form in which the serial is published. For example, in describing a serial motion picture, use both chapters 12 and 7.

0.25. The ISBD(G) contains an area for details that are special to a particular class of material or type of publication. This third area is used in these rules for cartographic materials (chapter 3), music (chapter 5), computer files (chapter 9), serial publications (chapter 12), and, in some circumstances, microforms (chapter 11). Do not use this area for any other materials treated in these rules. Where it is applicable and appropriate, repeat this area. For example, in describing a serial cartographic item or a serial computer file, give details relating to the cartographic material or the computer file and those relating to its seriality (in that order).

OPTIONS AND OMISSIONS

0.26. Although the rules for description are based upon a standard (the ISBD(G)), it is recognized that certain materials do not require every element of that standard. For this reason there are differences between the treatment of some materials and some others. For example, the extent of item element is called "number of volumes and/or pagination" in the chapter on books, pamphlets, and printed sheets (chapter 2). Again, the place of publication, etc., and the name of publisher, etc., elements are not used for manuscripts, some art originals, and some three-dimensional objects and artefacts.

0.27. All notes described in the chapters of part I are optional (unless a note is specifically stated to be mandatory) in that their inclusion in the entry depends on the nature of the item described and the purpose of the entry concerned. In addition, the wording of notes in the examples is not prescriptive (i.e., if desired, choose another wording provided that it meets the general requirements of brevity and clarity).

0.28. Not all measurements prescribed in part I for library materials are metric. They are the normal measurements used at this time in libraries in Australia, Canada, the United Kingdom, and the United States. Where no predominant system of measurement exists, metric measurements have been used. Substitute metric measurements for nonmetric measurements when:

either a) in the course of time a metric measurement becomes the normal measurement for the materials in question

   or b) the rules are being used in a country where only metric measurements are used.

0.29. Rule 1.0D contains a specification of three levels of description. Consider each of these levels as a minimum. When appropriate, add further information to the required set of data. The three levels of description allow libraries flexibility in their cataloguing policy, because they prescribe an entry that is in conformity with bibliographic standards and yet allow some materials to be described in more detail than others. Use the three levels of description:

either a) by choosing a level of description for all items catalogued in the library

   or b) by drawing up guidelines for the use of all three levels in one catalogue depending on the type of item being described.

This standardization at three levels of description will help in achieving uniformity of cataloguing, and it is recommended that each machine-readable record carry an indication of the level at which the item has been described.

GENERAL RULES FOR DESCRIPTION

Contents

11

1.0. GENERAL RULES

1.0A. Sources of information

1.0A1. Each chapter in part I contains a specification of the chief source of information for each material or type of publication covered by that chapter. A source of information may be unitary in nature (e.g., a title page) or may be collective (e.g., the credits sequence of a motion picture). Prefer information found in that chief source to information found elsewhere. When the other sources of information are placed in a ranking order by specific chapters, follow that order. For each area of the description one or more sources of information are prescribed. Enclose in square brackets information taken from outside the prescribed source(s).

1.0A2. Items lacking a chief source of information. If no part of the item supplies data that can be used as the basis of the description, take the necessary information from any available source, whether this be a reference work or the content of the item itself. This technique may be necessary for printed works, the title pages of which are lost; collections of pamphlets or other minor material assembled by the library or by a previous owner and that are to be catalogued as a single item; nonprocessed sound recordings, etc. In all such cases give in a note the reason for and/or source of the supplied data.

1.0B. Organization of the description

1.0B1. The description is divided into the following areas:

> Title and statement of responsibility
> Edition
> Material (or type of publication) specific details
> Publication, distribution, etc.
> Physical description
> Series
> Note
> Standard number and terms of availability

Each of these areas is divided into a number of elements as set out in the rules in this and in following chapters.

1.0C. Punctuation

1.0C1. Precede each area, other than the first area, or each occurrence of a note or standard number, etc., area, by a full stop, space, dash, space (. —) unless the area begins a new paragraph.

Precede or enclose each occurrence of an element of an area with standard punctuation prescribed at the head of each section of this chapter.

Precede each mark of prescribed punctuation by a space and follow it by a space, except for the comma, full stop, hyphen (see 12.3A1), and opening and closing parentheses and square brackets. The comma, full stop, hyphen, and closing parenthesis and square bracket are not preceded by a space; the hyphen and the opening parenthesis and square bracket are not followed by a space.

Precede the first element of each area, other than the first element of the first area or the first element of an area beginning a new paragraph, by a full stop, space, dash, space. When that element is not present in a description, precede the first element that is present by a full stop, space, dash, space instead of the prescribed preceding punctuation for that element.

Indicate an interpolation (i.e., data taken from outside the prescribed source(s) of information) by enclosing it in square brackets. Indicate a conjectural interpolation by adding a question mark within the square brackets. Indicate the omission of part of an element by the mark of omission (...). Precede and follow the mark of omission by a space. Omit any area or element that does not apply in describing an individual item; also omit its prescribed preceding or enclosing punctuation. Do not indicate the omission of an area or element by the mark of omission.

When adjacent elements within one area are to be enclosed in square brackets, enclose them in one set of square brackets unless one of the elements is a general material designation, which is always enclosed in its own set of square brackets.

> Skaterdater [GMD] / [produced by] Marshal Backlar

> *but*   [London : Phipps, 1870]

When adjacent elements are in different areas, enclose each element in a set of square brackets.

> [2nd ed.]. — [London] : Thomsons, 1973

When an element ends with an abbreviation followed by a full stop or ends with the mark of omission and the punctuation following that element either is or begins with a full stop, omit the full stop that constitutes or begins the prescribed punctuation.

> 261 p. ; 24 cm. — (Canadian Ethnic Studies Association series ; v. 4)
> *not*   261 p. ; 24 cm.. — (Canadian Ethnic Studies Association series ; v. 4)

When punctuation occurring within or at the end of an element is retained, give it with normal spacing. Prescribed punctuation is always added, even though double punctuation may result.

> Quo vadis? : a narrative from the time of Nero

1.0D. Levels of detail in the description

The elements of description provided in the rules in this and in following chapters constitute a maximum set of information. This rule sets out three recommended levels of description each containing those elements that must be given as a minimum by libraries and other cataloguing agencies choosing that level of description. Base the choice of a level of description on the purpose of the catalogue or catalogues for which the entry is constructed. Include this minimum set of elements for all items catalogued at the chosen level when the elements are applicable to the item being described and when, in the case of optional additions, the library has chosen to include an optional element. If the rules in part I specify other pieces of information in place of any of the elements set out below, include those other pieces of information. Consult individual rules in this chapter and in those following for the content of elements to be included. See also 0.29.

1.0D1. First level of description. For the first level of description, include at least the elements set out in this schematic illustration:

> Title proper / first statement of responsibility, if different from main entry heading in form or number or if there is no main entry heading. — Edition statement. — Material (or type of publication) specific details. — First publisher, etc., date of publication, etc. — Extent of item. — Note(s). — Standard number

See 1.1B, 1.1F, 1.2B, 1.3, 1.4D, 1.4F, 1.5B, 1.7, and 1.8B.

1.0D2. Second level of description. For the second level of description, include at least the elements set out in this schematic illustration:

> Title proper [general material designation] = Parallel title : other title information / first statement of responsibility ; each subsequent statement of responsibility. — Edition statement / first statement of responsibility relating to the edition. — Material (or type of publication) specific details. — First place of publication, etc. : first publisher, etc., date of publication, etc. — Extent of item : other physical details ; dimensions. — (Title proper of series / statement of responsibility relating to series, ISSN of series ; numbering within the series. Title of subseries, ISSN of subseries ; numbering within subseries). — Note(s). — Standard number

1.0D3. Third level of description. For the third level of description, include all elements set out in the following rules that are applicable to the item being described.

1.0E. Language and script of the description

1.0E1. In the following areas, give information transcribed from the item itself in the language and script (wherever practicable) in which it appears there:

> Title and statement of responsibility
> Edition
> Publication, distribution, etc.
> Series

For details given in the material (or type of publication) specific details area, follow the instructions in the relevant rules of the following chapters.

Replace symbols or other matter that cannot be reproduced by the facilities available with a cataloguer's description in square brackets. Make an explanatory note if necessary. (See also 1.1B1, 1.1F9, and 1.2B2.)

In general, give interpolations into these areas in the language and script of the other data in the area. Exceptions to this are:

a) prescribed interpolations and abbreviations
b) general material designations (see 1.1C)
c) supplied forms of the place of publication (see 1.4C2, 1.4C3, and 1.4C6)
d) statements of function of the publisher, distributor, etc. (see 1.4E).

If the other data are romanized, give interpolations according to the same romanization.

Give all elements in the other areas (other than the key-title (see 1.8C) and titles and quotations in notes) in the language and script of the cataloguing agency.

1.0F. Inaccuracies

1.0F1. In an area where transcription from the item is required, transcribe an inaccuracy or a misspelled word as it appears in the item. Follow such an inaccuracy either by *[sic]* or by *i.e.* and the correction within square brackets. Supply a missing letter or letters in square brackets.

> The wolrd [sic] of television

> The Paul Anthony Buck [i.e. Brick] lectures

> What your child really wants to know about sex, and why / by Will[i]am A. Block

1.0G. Accents and other diacritical marks

1.0G1. Add accents and other diacritical marks that are not present in the data found in the source of information in accordance with the usage of the language used in the context.

1.0H. Items with several chief sources of information

1.0H1. Single part items. Describe an item in one physical part from the first occurring chief source of information or the one that is designated as first, unless one of the following applies.

a) In cataloguing an item comprising different works and with no chief source of information pertaining to the whole item, treat the sources of information for the different works as if they were a single source. Common examples include books containing a number of works with title pages for each (see 1.1G3) and sound discs with a different label on each side (see 6.0B1).
b) Prefer a chief source of information bearing a later date of publication, distribution, etc.
c) If the chief sources present the item in different aspects (e.g., as an individual item and as part of a multipart item), prefer the source that corresponds to the aspect in which the item is to be treated.
d) For items that contain written, spoken, or sung words for which there are chief sources of information in more than one language or script, prefer (in this order):
  i) the source in the language or script of the written, spoken, or sung words if there is only one such language or script or only one predominant language or script

ii) the source in the original language or script of the work if the words are in more than one language or script, unless translation is known to be the purpose of the publication, in which case use the source in the language of the translation

iii) the source in the language or script that occurs first in the following list: English, French, German, Spanish, Latin, any other language using the roman alphabet, Greek, Russian, any other language using the cyrillic alphabet, Hebrew, any other language using the Hebrew alphabet, any other language.

1.0H2. Multipart items. Describe an item in several physical parts from the chief source of information for the first part. If the first part is not available, use the first part that is. If there is no discernible first part, use the part that gives the most information. Failing this, use any part or a container that is a unifying element. Show variations in the chief sources of information of subsequent parts in notes, or, when so instructed, by incorporating the data with those derived from the first part.

1.1. TITLE AND STATEMENT OF RESPONSIBILITY AREA

Contents:
    1.1A. Preliminary rule
    1.1B. Title proper
    1.1C. General material designation
    1.1D. Parallel titles
    1.1E. Other title information
    1.1F. Statements of responsibility
    1.1G. Items without a collective title

1.1A. Preliminary rule

1.1A1. Punctuation
For instructions on the use of spaces before and after prescribed punctuation, see 1.0C.
Precede the title of a supplement or section (see 1.1B9) by a full stop.
Enclose the general material designation in square brackets.
Precede each parallel title by an equals sign.
Precede each unit of other title information by a colon.
Precede the first statement of responsibility by a diagonal slash.
Precede each subsequent statement of responsibility by a semicolon.
For the punctuation of this area for items without a collective title, see 1.1G3.
For the use of the equals sign to precede parallel statements, see the appropriate rules following.

1.1A2. Sources of information. Take information recorded in this area from the chief source of information for the material to which the item being described belongs. Enclose information supplied from any other source in square brackets.
Give the elements of data in the order of the sequence of the following rules, even if this means transposing data. Transcribe the data as found, however, if

case endings are affected, if the grammatical construction of the data would be disturbed, or if one element is inseparably linked to another.

1.1B. Title proper

1.1B1. Transcribe the title proper exactly as to wording, order, and spelling, but not necessarily as to punctuation and capitalization. Give accentuation and other diacritical marks that are present in the chief source of information (see also 1.0G). Capitalize according to appendix A.

> Speedball technique charts
>
> Les misérables
>   (*Diacritic supplied*)
>
> The materials of architecture
>
> Supplement to The conquest of Peru and Mexico
>
> The 1919/20 Breasted Expedition to the Near East
>
> λ-calculus and computer theory
>
> Fourteen hours
>
> IV informe de gobierno

An alternative title is part of the title proper (see Glossary, appendix D). Precede and follow the word *or* (or its equivalent in another language) introducing an alternative title by a comma. Capitalize the first word of the alternative title.

> Marcel Marceau, ou, L'art du mime

If the title proper as given in the chief source of information includes the punctuation marks . . . or [ ], replace them by − and ( ), respectively.

> If elected−
>   (*Source of information reads:* If elected . . .)

If the title proper as given in the chief source of information includes symbols that cannot be reproduced by the facilities available, replace them with a cataloguer's description in square brackets. Make an explanatory note if necessary.

> Tables of the error function and its derivative, [reproduction of equations for the functions]

If the title proper is not taken from the chief source of information, give the source of the title in a note (see 1.7B3).

1.1B2. If the title proper includes a statement of responsibility or the name of a publisher, distributor, etc., and the statement or name is an integral part of the title proper (i.e., connected by a case ending or other grammatical construction), transcribe it as part of the title proper.

> Marlowe's plays
>
> Eileen Ford's a more beautiful you in 21 days

Ernst Günther läser Balzac

La route Shell

1.1B3. If the title proper consists solely of the name of a person or body responsible for the item, transcribe such a name as the title proper.

Georges Brassens

Conference on Industrial Development in the Arab Countries

1.1B4. Abridge a long title proper only if this can be done without loss of essential information. Never omit any of the first five words of the title proper (excluding the alternative title). Indicate omissions by the mark of omission.

1.1B5. If a letter or word appears only once but the design of the chief source of information makes it clear that it is intended to be read more than once, repeat the letter or word without the use of square brackets.

Canadian bibliographies = Bibliographies canadiennes
(*Source of information reads:* Canadian BIBLIOGRAPHIES canadiennes)

If the first level of description is used (see 1.0D1), the transcription of such a title is:

Canadian bibliographies

1.1B6. If a title proper includes separate letters or initials without full stops between them, transcribe such letters without spaces between them.

ALA rules for filing catalog cards

If such letters or initials have full stops between them, transcribe them with full stops and omit any internal spaces.

T.U.E.I. occasional papers in industrial relations

The most of S.J. Perelman

1.1B7. Supply a title proper for an item lacking a chief source of information from the rest of the item, or a reference source, or elsewhere. If no title can be found in any source, devise a brief descriptive title. Enclose such a supplied or devised title in square brackets.

[Carte de la lune]

[Photograph of Theodore Roosevelt]

1.1B8. If the chief source of information bears titles in two or more languages or scripts, transcribe as the title proper the one in the language or script of the main written, spoken, or sung content of the item. If this criterion is not applicable, choose the title proper by reference to the order of titles on, or the layout of, the chief source of information. Record the other titles as parallel titles (see 1.1D).

1.1B9. If the title proper for an item that is supplementary to, or a section of, another item appears in two or more parts not grammatically linked, give the title of the main work first, followed by the title(s) of the supplementary item(s) or section(s) in order of their dependence. Separate the parts of the title proper by full stops.

> Journal of biosocial science. Supplement
> (*Title appears on item as:*
> 　JOURNAL OF BIOSOCIAL SCIENCE
> 　Supplement ...)

> Faust. Part one

1.1B10. If the chief source of information bears both a collective title and the titles of individual works, give the collective title as the title proper and give the titles of the individual works in a contents note (see 1.7B18).

> Three notable stories
> *Note:* Contents: Love and peril / the Marquis of Lorne − To be or not to be / Mrs. Alexander − The melancholy hussar / Thomas Hardy

> Six Renoir drawings
> *Note:* Contents: La danse à la campagne − Les deux baigneuses − Pierre Renoir − Enfants jouant à la balle − Baigneuse assise − Étude d'une enfant

1.1C. *Optional addition.* **General material designation**

1.1C1. Choose one of the lists of general material designations given below and use terms from the chosen list in all descriptions for which general material designations are desired.[1]

If general material designations are to be used in cataloguing, British agencies should use terms from list 1 and agencies in Australia, Canada, and the United States should use terms from list 2.[2]

---

1. In all subsequent examples, other than those illustrating general material designations directly, the designation is indicated by *I GMDI*. The use of *I GMDI* in examples does not imply that a designation is required.

2. The following rules apply to list 2:
　1)　Use *map* for cartographic charts, not *chart*.
　2)　For material treated in chapter 8, use *picture* for any item not subsumed under one of the other terms in list 2.
　3)　Use *technical drawing* for any item fitting the definition of this term in the Glossary, appendix D; for architectural renderings, however, use *art original*, *art reproduction*, or *picture*, not *technical drawing*.
　4)　Use *kit* for any item fitting the definition of this term in the Glossary, appendix D; note that this term may apply to certain categories of textual material.

LIST 1	LIST 2
braille	activity card
cartographic material	art original
computer file	art reproduction
graphic	braille
manuscript	chart
microform	computer file
motion picture	diorama
multimedia	filmstrip
music	flash card
object	game
sound recording	globe
text	kit
videorecording	manuscript
	map
	microform
	microscope slide
	model
	motion picture
	music
	picture
	realia
	slide
	sound recording
	technical drawing
	text
	toy
	transparency
	videorecording

For materials for the visually impaired, add *(large print)* or *(tactile)*, when appropriate, to any term in list 2. Add *(braille)*, when appropriate, to any term in list 2 other than *braille* or *text*.

> ... [map (tactile)]
>
> ... [music (braille)]
>
> ... [text (large print)]

1.1C2. If an item consists of material falling within one category in the list chosen, give the appropriate designation immediately following the title proper (or the last part of the title proper, see 1.1B9).

> How the poor view their health [computer file]
>
> British masters of the albumen print [microform]
>
> Divina commedia. Inferno [text]

In the case of an item having no collective title, give the appropriate designation immediately following the first title (inclusive of part titles (see 1.1B9) and al-

21

ternative titles (see 1.1B1), but exclusive of parallel titles (see 1.1D) and other title information (see 1.1E)).

> The art of the fugue [sound recording] = Die Kunst der Fuge = L'art de la fugue : BMV 1080 (Contrapunctus 1-9) / Johann Sebastian Bach. Suites for harpsichord = Cembalo = Clavecin / Georg Friedrich Haendel

1.1C3. If the item is a reproduction in one material of a work originally presented in another material (e.g., a text as microform; a map on a slide), give the general material designation appropriate to the material being described (e.g., in the case of a map on a slide, give the designation appropriate to the slide).

1.1C4. If an item contains parts belonging to materials falling into two or more categories in the list chosen and if none of these is the predominant constituent of the item, give *multimedia* or *kit* (see 1.1C1 and 1.10C1).

> Changing Africa [multimedia]

> *or*   Changing Africa [kit]

1.1D. Parallel titles

1.1D1. Transcribe parallel titles in the order indicated by their sequence on, or by the layout of, the chief source of information.

1.1D2. In preparing a second-level description (see 1.0D2), give the first parallel title. Give any subsequent parallel title that is in English.

> Wood Cree [GMD] = Les Cris des forêts

> Einführung in die Blutmorphologie [GMD] = Introduction to the morphology of blood

> Strassenkarte der Schweiz [GMD] = Carte routière de la Suisse = Road map of Switzerland

If, in preparing a second-level description, all of the following conditions apply:
- a) the title proper is in a nonroman script
- b) the first parallel title recorded in accordance with the instructions in the preceding paragraph is in a nonroman script
- c) no title is in English

give as the second parallel title the one that is (in order of preference) in French, German, Spanish, Latin, any other roman alphabet language.

In preparing a third-level description (see 1.0D3), transcribe all parallel titles appearing in the chief source of information according to the instructions in 1.1B.

> Wood Cree [GMD] = Les Cris des forêts

> Einführung in die Blutmorphologie [GMD] = Introduction to the morphology of blood = Введение в морфологию крови

> Strassenkarte der Schweiz [GMD] = Carte routière de la Suisse = Carta stradale della Svizzera = Road map of Switzerland

22

1.1D3. Transcribe an original title in a language different from that of the title proper appearing in the chief source of information as a parallel title if the item contains all or some of the text in the original language, or if the original title appears before the title proper in the chief source of information. Transcribe as other title information an original title in the same language as the title proper (see 1.1E). In all other cases give the original title in a note.

> Twenty love poems and a song of despair [GMD] = 20 poemas de amor y una canción desesperada
> (*Contains parallel Spanish text and English translation*)

1.1D4. Give parallel titles appearing outside the chief source of information in a note (see 1.7B5).

1.1E. Other title information

1.1E1. Transcribe all other title information appearing in the chief source of information according to the instructions in 1.1B.

> Edgar Wallace [GMD] : the man who made his name

> Winterthur [GMD] : an adventure in the past

> SPSS primer [GMD] : statistical package for the social sciences primer

1.1E2. Transcribe other title information in the order indicated by the sequence on, or the layout of, the chief source of information.

> Distribution of the principal kinds of soil [GMD] : orders, suborders, and great groups : National Soil Survey classification of 1967

1.1E3. Lengthy other title information. If the other title information is lengthy, either give it in a note (see 1.7B5) or abridge it.

Abridge other title information only if this can be done without loss of essential information. Never omit any of the first five words of the other title information. Indicate omissions by the mark of omission.

1.1E4. If the other title information includes a statement of responsibility or the name of a publisher, distributor, etc., and the statement or name is an integral part of the other title information, transcribe it as such.

> The devil's dictionary [GMD] : a selection of the bitter definitions of Ambrose Bierce

> Robert Owen's American legacy [GMD] : proceedings of the Robert Owen Bicentennial Conference, Thrall Opera House, New Harmony, Indiana, October 15 and 16, 1971

1.1E5. Transcribe other title information following the whole or part of the title proper or the parallel title to which it pertains.

23

> On tour [GMD] : 10 British jewellers in Germany and Australia
> = Auf Tournee : zehn britische Goldschmiede in Deutschland
> und Australien

> Recreation information : opportunities for people with
> intellectual disability.   News sheet [GMD]

If there are no parallel titles and if other title information appears in more than one language or script, give the other title information that is in the language or script of the title proper. If this criterion does not apply, give the other title information that appears first. *Optionally*, give the other title information in other languages. Precede each parallel statement by an equals sign.

> Variations on a Czech love song [GMD] : for piano solo and
> woodwind choir = pour piano soliste et ensemble de bois

1.1E6. If the title proper needs explanation, supply a brief addition as other title information, in the language of the title proper.

> Longfellow [GMD] : [selections]

> Conference on Industrial Development in the Arab Countries
> [GMD] : [proceedings]

1.1F. Statements of responsibility

1.1F1. Transcribe statements of responsibility appearing prominently in the item in the form in which they appear there. If a statement of responsibility is taken from a source other than the chief source of information, enclose it in square brackets.

> All that jazz [GMD] / Fats Waller

> Stereogram book of fossils [GMD] : photographs of invertebrate
> fossils in 3 dimensions / by Philip A. Sandberg

> Obiter dicta [GMD] / [A. Birrell]
>   (*Statement appears on spine and cover only*)

> Handley Cross [GMD] : a sporting tale / by the Author of
> Jorrocks' jaunts and jollities

> George Gissing and H.G. Wells [GMD] : their friendship and
> correspondence / edited, with an introduction, by Royal A.
> Gettmann

> Map catalogue [GMD] / Ordnance Survey

> Common service book of the Lutheran church [GMD] /
> authorized by the United Lutheran Church of America

1.1F2. If no statement of responsibility appears prominently in the item, neither construct one nor extract one from the content of the item. Give the relevant information in a note (see 1.7B6).

Do not include in the title and statement of responsibility area statements of responsibility that do not appear prominently in the item. If such a statement is necessary, give it in a note.

1.1F3. If a statement of responsibility precedes the title proper in the chief source of information, transpose it to its required position unless it is an integral part of the title proper (see 1.1A2 and 1.1B2).

1.1F4. Transcribe a single statement of responsibility as such whether the two or more persons or corporate bodies named in it perform the same function or different functions.

> Thinking and reasoning [GMD] : selected readings / edited by P.C. Wason and P.N. Johnson-Laird

> Puzzled people [GMD] : a study in popular attitudes to religion, ethics, progress, and politics in a London borough / prepared for the Ethical Union by Mass-Observation

1.1F5. If a single statement of responsibility names more than three persons or corporate bodies performing the same function, or with the same degree of responsibility, omit all but the first of each group of such persons or bodies. Indicate the omission by the mark of omission (...) and add *et al.* (or its equivalent in a nonroman script) in square brackets.

> America's radical right [GMD] / Raymond Wolfinger ... [et al.]

> Dickens 1970 [GMD] : centenary essays / by Walter Allen ... [et al.] ; edited by Michael Slater

> A short-title catalogue of books printed in England, Scotland & Ireland ... 1475-1640 [GMD] / compiled by A.W. Pollard & G.R. Redgrave with the help of G.F. Barwick ... [et al.]

> Proceedings of the Workshop on Solar Collectors for Heating and Cooling of Buildings, New York City, November 21-23, 1974 [GMD] / sponsored by the National Science Foundation, RANN— Research Applied to National Needs ; coordinated by University of Maryland ... [et al.]

1.1F6. If there is more than one statement of responsibility, transcribe them in the order indicated by their sequence on, or the layout of, the chief source of information. If the sequence and layout are ambiguous or insufficient to determine the order, transcribe the statements in the order that makes the most sense. If statements of responsibility appear in sources other than the chief source, transcribe them in the order that makes the most sense.

> Bits of paradise [GMD] : twenty-one uncollected stories / by F. Scott and Zelda Fitzgerald ; selected by Scottie Fitzgerald Smith and Matthew J. Bruccoli ; with a foreword by Scottie Fitzgerald Smith

> A saint in Philadelphia [GMD] : John Neumann / Raymond C. Kammerer and Carl R. Steinbecker ; made by Creative Sights & Sounds

> Exploration of the solar system [GMD] / prepared by members of the AIAA Technical Committees on Space Systems and Space Atmospheric Physics ; edited by Arthur Henderson, Jr., and Jerry Grey

1.1F7. Include titles and abbreviations of titles of nobility, address, honour, and distinction, initials of societies, qualifications, date(s) of founding, mottoes, etc., in statements of responsibility if:

a) such data are necessary grammatically

> ... / ... ; prólogo del Excmo. Sr. D. Manuel Fraga Iribarne

b) the omission would leave only a person's given name or surname

> ... / by Miss Jane

> ... / by Miss Read

> ... / by Dr. Johnson

c) the title is necessary to identify a person

> ... / by Mrs. Charles H. Gibson

d) the title is a title of nobility, or is a British term of honour (*Sir, Dame, Lord,* or *Lady*).

> ... / by Baroness Orczy

> ... / by Sir Richard Acland

Otherwise, omit all such data from statements of responsibility. Do not use the mark of omission.

> ... / by Harry Smith
> (*Source of information reads:* by Dr. Harry Smith)

> ... / sponsored by the Library Association
> (*Source of information reads:* sponsored by the Library Association (founded 1877))

> ... / by T.A. Rennard
> (*Source of information reads:* by the late T.A. Rennard)

1.1F8. Add a word or short phrase to the statement of responsibility if the relationship between the title of the item and the person(s) or body (bodies) named in the statement is not clear.

> Baijun ballads [GMD] / [collected by] Chet Williams

> Piers Plowman [GMD] / [edited by] Elizabeth Salter

but

> Bleak House [GMD] / Charles Dickens

Brief guide [GMD] / National Gallery of Art

Beggars banquet [GMD] / the Rolling Stones

1.1F9. Replace symbols or other matter that cannot be reproduced by the facilities available with the cataloguer's description in square brackcts. Make an explanatory note if necessary.

Over the border [GMD] : Acadia, the home of "Evangeline" / by [E.B.C.]
Note: Author's initials represented by musical notes on title page

1.1F10. If an item has parallel titles but a statement(s) of responsibility in only one language or script, transcribe the statement of responsibility after all the parallel titles or other title information.

Jeux de cartes pour enfants [GMD] = Children's playing cards / par Giovanni Belgrado et Bruno Munari

If an item has parallel titles and a statement or statements of responsibility in more than one language or script, transcribe each statement after the title proper, parallel title, or other title information to which it relates.

Familias norte-americanas [GMD] : los De Stefano / colaborador de educación, Beryl L. Bailey = American families : the De Stefanos / educational collaborator, Beryl L. Bailey

If it is not practicable to give the statements of responsibility after the titles to which they relate, transcribe the statement of responsibility in the language or script of the title proper and omit the others.

Concerto in c-Moll für Cembalo (Klavier) und Streicher [GMD] = Concerto in C minor for harpsichord (piano) and strings / Carl Philipp Emanuel Bach ; herausgegeben von György Balla
(*Statement about editor appears in German and English*)

1.1F11. If there are no parallel titles and a statement of responsibility appears in more than one language or script, transcribe the statement in the language or script of the title proper. If this criterion does not apply, transcribe the statement that appears first.

Tin statistics [GMD] / International Tin Council

Optionally, transcribe the parallel statements, each preceded by an equals sign.

Tin statistics [GMD] / International Tin Council = Conseil international de l'étain = Consejo Internacional del Estaño

1.1F12. Treat a noun phrase occurring in conjunction with a statement of responsibility as other title information if it is indicative of the nature of the work.

Characters from Dickens [GMD] : dramatised adaptations / by Barry Campbell

If the noun or noun phrase is indicative of the role of the person(s) or body (bodies) named in the statement of responsibility rather than of the nature of the work, treat it as part of the statement of responsibility.

> Roman Britain [GMD] / research and text by Colin Barham

In case of doubt, treat the noun or noun phrase as part of the statement of responsibility.

1.1F13. When a name associated with responsibility for the item is transcribed as part of the title proper (see 1.1B2) or other title information (see 1.1E4), do not make any further statement relating to that name unless such a statement is required for clarity, or unless a separate statement of responsibility including or consisting of that name appears in the chief source of information.

> Goethes Stücke [GMD]

but

> Feminism and Vivian Gornick [GMD] / Vivian Gornick
> (*Name of author appears separately in the chief source of information as well as in the title proper*)

> Malo's complete guide to canoeing and canoe-camping [GMD] / by John Malo

> The John Franklin Bardin omnibus [GMD] / John Franklin Bardin
> (*Name of author appears separately in the chief source of information as well as in the title proper*)

1.1F14. Transcribe a statement of responsibility even if no person or body is named in that statement.

> Korean phrases [GMD] / by a group of students with a Korean resource person

> Call of love [GMD] / translated from the Danish

> ... / with a spoken commentary by the artist

A statement of responsibility may include words or phrases that are neither names nor linking words.

> ... / written by Jobe Hill in 1812

1.1F15. Omit statements found in the chief source of information that neither constitute other title information nor form part of statements of responsibility.

1.1G. Items without a collective title

1.1G1. If, in an item lacking a collective title, one work is the predominant part, treat the title of that work as the title proper and name the other work(s) in a contents note (see 1.7B18).

1.1G2. If, in an item lacking a collective title, no one work predominates, *either* describe the item as a unit (see 1.1G3) *or* make a separate description for each separately titled work, linking the separate descriptions with notes (see 1.7B21).

1.1G3. If describing the item as a unit, transcribe the titles of the individually titled works in the order in which they appear in the chief source of information or, if there is no single chief source of information, in the order in which they appear in the item, treating multiple sources of information as if they were one source (see 1.0H).

Separate the titles of the works by semicolons if the works are all by the same person(s) or emanate from the same body (bodies), even if the titles are linked by a connecting word or phrase. Follow the title of each work by its parallel title(s) and other title information.

> Clock symphony [GMD] : no. 101 ; Surprise symphony : no. 94 / Haydn

> Lord Macaulay's essays [GMD] ; and, Lays of ancient Rome

If the individual works are by different persons or emanate from different bodies, or in case of doubt, follow the title of each work by its parallel title(s), other title information, and statement(s) of responsibility. Separate the groups of data with a full stop followed by two spaces.

> Saudades do Brasil [GMD] : suite de danses pour orchestre / Darius Milhaud. Symphonie concertante pour trompette et orchestre / Henry Barraud

> Le prince [GMD] / Machiavel. Suivi de L'anti-Machiavel de Frédéric II
> > (*Title page reads:* Machiavel. Le prince, suivi de L'anti-Machiavel de Frédéric II)

1.1G4. If, in an item lacking a collective title, more than one (but not all) of the separately titled works predominate, treat the predominating works as instructed in 1.1G3, and name the other work(s) in contents notes (see 1.7B18).

1.2. EDITION AREA

Contents:
- 1.2A. Preliminary rule
- 1.2B. Edition statement
- 1.2C. Statements of responsibility relating to the edition
- 1.2D. Statement relating to a named revision of an edition
- 1.2E. Statements of responsibility relating to a named revision of an edition

1.2A. Preliminary rule

1.2A1. Punctuation

For instructions on the use of spaces before and after prescribed punctuation, see 1.0C.

Precede this area by a full stop, space, dash, space.

Precede a statement relating to a named revision of an edition by a comma.

Precede the first statement of responsibility following an edition statement by a diagonal slash.

Precede each subsequent statement of responsibility by a semicolon.

For the use of the equals sign to precede parallel statements, see the appropriate rules following.

1.2A2. Sources of information. Give in this area information taken from the chief source of information or from any other source prescribed for this area in the following chapters. Enclose information supplied from any other source in square brackets.

1.2B. Edition statement

1.2B1. Transcribe the edition statement as found on the item. Use abbreviations as instructed in appendix B and numerals as instructed in appendix C.

> Ny udg.
> (*Source of information reads:* Ny udgave)

> 2nd ed.
> (*Source of information reads:* Second edition)

1.2B2. If the edition statement consists solely or chiefly of characters that are neither numeric nor alphabetic, give the statement in words in the language and script of the title proper and enclose them in square brackets.

> [Three asterisks] ed.

If the edition statement consists of a letter or letters and/or a number or numbers without accompanying words, add an appropriate word or abbreviation.

> 3e [éd.]

> [State] B

1.2B3. In case of doubt about whether a statement is an edition statement, take the presence of such words as *edition*, *issue*, or *version* (or their equivalents in other languages) as evidence that such a statement is an edition statement, and transcribe it as such.

> South-west gazette [GMD]. — Somerset ed.

> Subbuteo table soccer [GMD]. — World Cup ed.

1.2B4. *Optional addition.* If an item lacks an edition statement but is known to contain significant changes from other editions, supply a suitable brief statement in the language and script of the title proper and enclose it in square brackets.

> [New ed.]

> [3e éd.]

> [2nd ed., partly rev.]

1.2B5. If an edition statement appears in more than one language or script, transcribe the statement in the language or script of the title proper. If this criterion does not apply, transcribe the statement that appears first.

Optionally, transcribe the parallel statement(s), each preceded by an equals sign.

> Rev. 1980 = Révision 1980
>
> 2e éd. = 2^a ed. = 2. Aufl.
>
> 2de herziene en verb. uitg. = 2^e éd., rev. et corr.

1.2B6. If an item lacking a collective title contains one or more works with an associated edition statement(s), transcribe each edition statement following the title and statement(s) of responsibility to which it relates, separated from them by a full stop.

> Le western [GMD] / textes rassemblés et présentés par Henri
> Agel. Nouv. éd. Évolution et renouveau du western (1967-1968)
> / par Jean A. Gili

1.2C. Statements of responsibility relating to the edition

1.2C1. Transcribe a statement of responsibility relating to one or more editions, but not to all editions, of a given work following the edition statement if there is one. Follow the instructions in 1.1F for the transcription and punctuation of such statements.

> The nether world [GMD] : a novel / George Gissing. — [New
> ed., repr.] / edited, with an introduction, by John Goode
>
> Shachiapang [GMD] : a modern revolutionary Peking opera. —
> May 1970 script / revised collectively by the Peking Opera Troupe
> of Peking

1.2C2. In case of doubt about whether a statement of responsibility applies to all editions or only to some, or if there is no edition statement, give such a statement in the title and statement of responsibility area.

> The prelude, 1798-1799 [GMD] / by William Wordsworth ; edited
> by Stephen Parrish

When describing the first edition, give all statements of responsibility in the title and statement of responsibility area (see 1.1F).

1.2C3. If an item has parallel edition statements that have been recorded (see 1.2B5) and a statement of responsibility relating to the edition in only one language or script, give the statement of responsibility after all the parallel edition statements.

> 3rd ed. = 3. uppl. / B. Larsen

1.2C4. *Optional addition.* If an item has both an edition statement and a statement of responsibility relating to the edition in more than one language or script, give each statement of responsibility after the edition statement to which it relates.

> 2nd ed. / edited by Larry C. Lewis = 2ᵉ éd. / rédigé par Larry C. Lewis

1.2C5. If an item has an edition statement in only one language or script and a statement of responsibility relating to the edition in more than one language or script, give the statement of responsibility in the language or script of the title proper. If this criterion does not apply, give the statement that appears first.

> 2. opl. / reviderade og udvidet af David Hohnen

Optionally, transcribe the parallel statements of responsibility after the edition statement, each preceded by an equals sign.

> 2. opl. / reviderade og udvidet af David Hohnen = revised and enlarged by David Hohnen

1.2D. Statement relating to a named revision of an edition

1.2D1. If an item is a revision of an edition (a named reissue of a particular edition containing changes from that edition), transcribe the statement relating to that revision following the edition statement and its statements of responsibility.

> The pocket Oxford dictionary of current English [GMD] / compiled by F.G. Fowler & H.W. Fowler. — 4th ed. / revised by H.G. Le Mesurier and E. McIntosh, Reprinted with corrections

> The natural history of Selborne in the county of Southampton [GMD] / by Gilbert White. — World's classics ed., New ed., rev., reset, and illustrated

1.2D2. If the statement relating to the revision appears in more than one language or script, follow the instructions in 1.2B5.

> 2nd ed., 3rd corr. impression

> *or*   2nd ed., 3rd corr. impression = 2ᵉ éd., 3ᵉ réimpr. corr.

1.2D3. Do not record statements relating to a reissue of an edition that contains no changes unless the item is considered to be of particular importance to the cataloguing agency.

1.2E. Statements of responsibility relating to a named revision of an edition

1.2E1. Transcribe a statement of responsibility relating to one or more named revisions of an edition (but not to all such revisions) following the statement relating to the revision(s). Follow the instructions in 1.1F for the transcription and punctuation of such statements of responsibility.

The elements of style [GMD] / by William Strunk, Jr. — Rev. ed. / with revisions, an introduction, and a chapter on writing by E.B. White, 2nd ed. / with the assistance of Eleanor Gould Packard

1.2E2. If an item has parallel statements relating to the revision of an edition that have been recorded (see 1.2D2) and a statement of responsibility relating to that revision in only one language or script, give the statement of responsibility following all the parallel statements relating to the revision.

4th ed., Corr. = 4ª ed., Corr. / G.A. Phelan

1.2E3. *Optional addition.* If the statement of responsibility referred to in 1.2E1 appears in more than one language or script, give each statement as instructed in 1.2C4 and 1.2C5.

2nd ed., 3rd revision / by N. Schmidt = 2. uppl., 3. utg. / af N. Schmidt

1.3. MATERIAL (OR TYPE OF PUBLICATION) SPECIFIC DETAILS AREA

1.3A. Precede this area by a full stop, space, dash, space.

This area is used in the description of cartographic materials (chapter 3), music (chapter 5), computer files (chapter 9), serial publications (chapter 12), and, in some circumstances, microforms (chapter 11). See those chapters for the contents of this area and its internal prescribed punctuation.

1.4. PUBLICATION, DISTRIBUTION, ETC., AREA

Contents:
    1.4A. Preliminary rule
    1.4B. General rule
    1.4C. Place of publication, distribution, etc.
    1.4D. Name of publisher, distributor, etc.
    1.4E. Statement of function of publisher, distributor, etc.
    1.4F. Date of publication, distribution, etc.
    1.4G. Place of manufacture, name of manufacturer, date of manufacture

1.4A. Preliminary rule

1.4A1. Punctuation

For instructions on the use of spaces before and after prescribed punctuation, see 1.0C.

Precede this area by a full stop, space, dash, space.

Precede a second or subsequently named place of publication, distribution, etc., by a semicolon.

Precede the name of a publisher, distributor, etc., by a colon.

Enclose a supplied statement of function of a publisher, distributor, etc., in square brackets.

Precede the date of publication, distribution, etc., by a comma.

Enclose the details of manufacture (place, name, date) in parentheses.

Precede the name of a manufacturer by a colon.

Precede the date of manufacture by a comma.

For the use of the equals sign to precede parallel statements, see the appropriate rules following.

1.4A2. Sources of information. Give in this area information taken from the chief source of information or from any other source prescribed for this area in the following chapters. Enclose in square brackets information supplied from a source other than those prescribed.

1.4B. General rule

1.4B1. In this area, record information about the place, name, and date of all types of publishing, distributing, releasing, and issuing activities. For unpublished materials, see 1.4C8, 1.4D9, and 1.4F9–1.4F10.

1.4B2. Record information relating to the manufacture of the item in this area.

1.4B3. When more than one place, name, or date is recorded in this area, give them in the order that is appropriate to the item being described.

1.4B4. Give names of places, persons, or bodies as they appear, omitting accompanying prepositions unless case endings would be affected. Use abbreviations as instructed in appendix B.

> Berolini
>
> ... : Im Deutschen Verlag

but

> Paris
not À Paris

> ... : University of Leeds, Dept. of Spanish
not ... : University of Leeds, Department of Spanish

1.4B5. If the original publication details are covered by a label containing publication details relating to a reproduction, reissue, etc., give the publication details of the later publication in this area. Give the publication details of the original in a note (see 1.7B9) if they can be ascertained readily.

1.4B6. If an item is known to have fictitious publication, distribution, etc., details, give them in the conventional order. Supply the real publication, distribution, etc., details as a correction if they are known.

> Belfast [i.e. Dublin : s.n.], 1982

> Paris : Impr. Vincent, 1798 [i.e. Bruxelles : Moens, 1883]

1.4C. Place of publication, distribution, etc.

1.4C1. Transcribe a place of publication, etc., in the form and the grammatical case in which it appears.

Köln

Lugduni Batavorum

Den Haag

If the name of a place appears in more than one language or script, give the form in the language or script of the title proper. If this criterion does not apply, give the form that appears first.

1.4C2. Supply another form of the name of a place if such an addition is considered desirable as an aid to identifying the place, using the English form of name if there is one.

Lerpwl [Liverpool]

Christiania [Oslo]

1.4C3. If the name of the country, state, province, etc., appears in the source of information, transcribe it after the name of the place if it is considered necessary for identification, or if it is considered necessary to distinguish the place from others of the same name. Supply the name of the country, state, province, etc., if it does not appear in the source of information but is considered necessary for identification or distinction, using the English form of name if there is one. Use abbreviations (see B.14).

City and country, etc., appear in prescribed source of information
Tolworth, England

Carbondale, Ill.

City alone appears in prescribed source of information
Waco [Tex.]

London [Ont.]

Santiago [Chile]

Renens [Switzerland]

1.4C4. If a place name is found only in an abbreviated form in the item, transcribe it as found, and add the full form or complete the name.

Mpls [i.e. Minneapolis]

Rio [de Janeiro]

1.4C5. If two or more places in which a publisher, distributor, etc., has offices are named in the item, give the first named place. Give any subsequently named place that is given prominence by the layout or typography of the source of information. If the first named place and any place given prominence are not in the home country of the cataloguing agency, give also the first of any subsequently named places that is in the home country. Omit all other places.

Toronto
(*Source of information reads:* Toronto, Buffalo, London.
Cataloguing agency in Canada)

Montréal ; Toronto
(Toronto *given prominence by typography*)

London ; New York
(*Cataloguing agency in the United States*)

Toronto ; London
(*Source of information reads:* Toronto, Buffalo, London.
Cataloguing agency in the United Kingdom)

New York ; London ; Sydney
(London *given prominence by typography. Cataloguing agency in
Australia*)

For items with two or more places of publication, distribution, etc., relating
to two or more publishers, distributors, etc., see 1.4D5.

1.4C6. If the place of publication, distribution, etc., is uncertain, supply the probable place in the English form of name if there is one, followed by a question
mark.

[Munich?]

If no probable place can be given, supply if possible the name of the country,
state, province, etc. If, in such a case, the country, state, province, etc., is not
certain, follow it by a question mark.

[Canada]

[Spain?]

If no place or probable place can be given, give *s.l.* (sine loco), or its equivalent
in a nonroman script.

[S.l.]

1.4C7. *Optionally*, give the full address of a publisher, distributor, etc., after the
name of the place. Enclose the full address in parentheses. Do not give the full
address for major trade publishers.

London (108 Gloucester Ave., London, NW1 8HX)

1.4C8. Do not record a place of publication, distribution, etc., for unpublished
items (manuscripts, art originals, naturally occurring objects that have not been
packaged for commercial distribution, unedited or unpublished film or video
materials, stock shots, nonprocessed sound recordings, unpublished computer
files, etc.). Do not record a place of publication, distribution, etc., for unpublished
collections (including those containing published items but not published as collections). Do not give *s.l.* in either case.

1.4D. Name of publisher, distributor, etc.

1.4D1. Give the name of the publisher, distributor, etc., following the place(s) to
which it relates.

London : Macmillan

Toronto : University of Toronto Press

New York ; London : McGraw-Hill

Montréal ; London : Grolier

London : Sussex Tapes ; Wakefield : Educational Productions

New York ; London ; Sydney : Oxford University Press

1.4D2. Give the name of a publisher, distributor, etc., in the shortest form in which it can be understood and identified internationally.

> : Penguin
> (*Source of information reads:* Penguin Books)

> : W.H. Allen   *not*   : Allen
> (*Avoids confusion with other publishers called Allen*)

> : Da Capo
> (*Source of information reads:* Da Capo Press, Inc., a subsidiary of Plenum Publishing Corporation)

If the shortest form of the name of the publisher, distributor, etc., is in more than one language or script, give the form that is in the language or script of the title proper. If this criterion does not apply, give the shortest form in the language or script that appears first.

Optionally, give the shortest form in each language or script. Precede each parallel statement by an equals sign. If the shortest form is the same in all languages or scripts, give it only once.

> : Éditions du peuple = Commoner's Pub.

> *but* : Høst
> *not* : Høst & Søns Forlag = Høst & Son Publisher

1.4D3. In giving the name of a publisher, distributor, etc., retain:

a) words or phrases indicating the function (other than solely publishing) performed by the person or body

> : Printed for the CLA by the Morriss Print. Co.

> : Distributed by New York Graphic Society

> : In Kommission bei O. Harrassowitz

> : Allen & Unwin
> (*Source of information reads:* Published by Allen & Unwin)

b) parts of the name required to differentiate between publishers, distributors, etc., or to identify subsidiary companies.

> : Longmans, Green

> *but* : Longmans Educational   *not*   : Longmans

1.4D4. If the name of the publisher, distributor, etc., appears in a recognizable form in the title and statement of responsibility area, give it in the publication, distribution, etc., area in the shortest possible form. If, in such a case, the publisher, distributor, etc., is a person, give the initials and the surname of the person.

> The wonder of new life [GMD] / Cleveland Health Museum. — Cleveland, Ohio : The Museum

> Fichier de terminologie [GMD] / Office de la langue française, Centre de terminologie. — Québec : O.L.F.

> Even the waitresses were poets [GMD] / Daisy Warren. — Iowa City : D. Warren

1.4D5. If an item has two or more publishers, distributors, etc., describe it in terms of the first named and the corresponding place(s). In the following cases, add subsequently named publishers, distributors, etc., and their corresponding places (if they are different from the place(s) already named):

a) when the first and subsequently named entities are linked in a single statement

> London : Macmillan for the University of York

b) when the first named entity is a distributor, releasing agency, etc., and a publisher is named subsequently

c) when a subsequently named entity is clearly distinguished as the principal publisher, distributor, etc., by layout or typography

> Toronto : McClelland and Stewart : World Crafts Council
> (*Second publisher given prominence by typography*)

d) when the subsequently named publisher, distributor, etc., is in the home country of the cataloguing agency and the first named publisher, distributor, etc., is not.

> Paris : Gauthier-Villars ; Chicago : University of Chicago Press
> (*Cataloguing agency in the United States*)

> New York : Dutton ; Toronto : Clarke, Irwin
> (*Cataloguing agency in Canada*)

Follow this rule for multipart items (see 1.0H2) when the publisher, etc., or the name of the publisher, etc., changes in the course of publication.

1.4D6. *Optionally*, give the name and, when appropriate, the place of a distributor when the first named entity is a publisher.

> Stockholm : Grammofon AB BIS ; New York : Distributed by Qualiton Imports

1.4D7. If the name of the publisher, distributor, etc., is unknown, give *s.n.* (sine nomine) or its equivalent in a nonroman script.

> Paris : [s.n.]

1.4D8. In case of doubt about whether a named agency is a publisher or a manufacturer, treat it as a publisher.

1.4D9. Do not record the name of a publisher, distributor, etc., for unpublished items (e.g., manuscripts, art originals, naturally occurring objects that have not been packaged for commercial distribution, unedited or unpublished film or video materials, stock shots, nonprocessed sound recordings, unpublished computer files). Do not record the name of a publisher, distributor, etc., for unpublished collections (including those containing published items but not published as collections). Do not give *s.n.* in either case.

1.4E. *Optional addition.* **Statement of function of publisher, distributor, etc.**

1.4E1. Add to the name of a publisher, distributor, etc., a term that clarifies the function of the publisher, distributor, etc., unless:

- a) the phrase naming the publisher, distributor, etc., includes words that indicate the function performed by the person(s) or body (bodies) named

or b) the function of the publishing, distributing, etc., agency is clear from the context.

> Montréal : National Film Board of Canada ; London : Guild Sound and Vision [distributor]

> London : Macmillan : Educational Service [distributor]

but

> New York : Released by Beaux Arts

> Oliver Twist [GMD] / Charles Dickens. — London : Chapman and Hall

1.4F. Date of publication, distribution, etc.

1.4F1. For published items, give the date (i.e., year) of publication, distribution, etc., of the edition, revision, etc., named in the edition area. If there is no edition statement, give the date of the first publication of the edition to which the item belongs. Give dates in Western-style arabic numerals. If the date found in the item is not of the Gregorian or Julian calendar, give the date as found and follow it with the year(s) of the Gregorian or Julian calendar.

> , 1975

> , 4308 [1975]

> , [4308 i.e. 1975]

> , 5730 [1969 or 1970]

> , anno 18 [1939]   *not*   , anno XVIII

> , 1976   *not*   ١٩٧٦

For unpublished items, see 1.4F9. For unpublished collections, see 1.4F10.

1.4F2. Give the date as found in the item even if it is known to be incorrect. If a date is known to be incorrect, add the correct date.

> , 1697 [i.e. 1967]

If necessary, explain any discrepancy in a note.

> , 1963 [i.e. 1971]
> *Note:* Originally issued as a sound disc in 1963; issued as a cassette in 1971.

1.4F3. Give the date of a named revision of an edition as the date of publication only if the revision is specified in the edition area (see 1.2D). In this case, give only the date of the named revision.

1.4F4. If the publication date differs from the date of distribution, add the date of distribution if it is considered to be significant by the cataloguing agency. If the publisher and distributor are different, give the date(s) after the name(s) to which they apply.

> London : Macmillan, 1971, [distributed 1973]

> London : Educational Records, 1973 ; New York : Edcorp [distributor], 1975

> Toronto : Royal Ontario Museum, 1971 ; Beckenham [England] : Edward Patterson [distributor]
> (*Distribution date known to be different but not recorded*)

If the publication and distribution dates are the same, give the date after the last named publisher, distributor, etc.

> New York : American Broadcasting Co. [production company] : Released by Xerox Films, 1973

1.4F5. *Optional addition.* Give the latest date of copyright following the publication, distribution, etc., date if the copyright date is different.

> , 1967, c1965

> , [1981], p1975

1.4F6. If the dates of publication, distribution, etc., are unknown, give the copyright date or, in its absence, the date of manufacture (indicated as such) in its place.

> , c1967

> , 1967 printing

> , p1983

> , 1979 pressing

1.4F7. If no date of publication, distribution, etc., copyright date, or date of manufacture appears in an item, supply an approximate date of publication.

, [1971 or 1972]	*one year or the other*
, [1969?]	*probable date*
, [between 1906 and 1912]	*use only for dates fewer than 20 years apart*
, [ca. 1960]	*approximate date*
, [197-]	*decade certain*
, [197-?]	*probable decade*
, [18--]	*century certain*
, [18--?]	*probable century*

Optionally, give an approximate date of publication if it differs significantly from the date(s) specified in 1.4F6.

, [1982?], c1949

1.4F8. If two or more dates are found on the various parts of a multipart item (e.g., when an item is published in parts over a number of years), give the earlier and later or earliest and latest dates, separated by a hyphen.

, 1968-1973

In describing a multipart item that is not yet complete, give the earliest or earlier date only, and follow it with a hyphen and four spaces.

, 1968-

Optionally, when the item is complete, add the latest or later date.

, 1968-1980

1.4F9. Do not record a date for naturally occurring objects that have not been packaged for commercial distribution. For other unpublished items (e.g., manuscripts, art originals, unedited or unpublished film or video materials, stock shots, nonprocessed sound recordings, unpublished computer files), give the date of production (creation, inscription, manufacture, recording, etc.).

1.4F10. Give the date or inclusive dates of unpublished collections (including those containing published items but not published as collections).

1.4G. Place of manufacture, name of manufacturer, date of manufacture

1.4G1. If the name of the publisher is unknown and the place and name of the manufacturer are found in the item, give the place and name of the manufacturer.

[S.l. : s.n.], 1970 (London : High Fidelity Sound Studios)

1.4G2. In recording the place and name of the manufacturer, follow the instructions in 1.4B–1.4D.

1.4G3. If the date of manufacture is given in place of an unknown date of publication, distribution, etc. (see 1.4F6), do not repeat it here.

1.4G4. *Optional addition.* Give the place, name of manufacturer, and/or date of manufacture if they are found in the item and differ from the place, name of publisher, distributor, etc., and date of publication, distribution, etc., and are considered important by the cataloguing agency.

> London : Arts Council of Great Britain, 1976
> (Twickenham : CTD Printers, 1974)

> Harmondsworth : Penguin, 1949 (1963 printing)

1.5. PHYSICAL DESCRIPTION AREA

Contents:
    1.5A. Preliminary rule
    1.5B. Extent of item (including specific material designation)
    1.5C. Other physical details
    1.5D. Dimensions
    1.5E. Accompanying material

1.5A. Preliminary rule

1.5A1. Punctuation

For instructions on the use of spaces before and after prescribed punctuation, see 1.0C.

Precede this area by a full stop, space, dash, space *or* start a new paragraph.
Precede other physical details (i.e., other than extent or dimensions) by a colon.
Precede dimensions by a semicolon.
Precede each statement of accompanying material by a plus sign.
Enclose physical details of accompanying material in parentheses.

1.5A2. Sources of information. Take information for this area from any source. Take explicitly or implicitly stated information from the item itself. Enclose information in square brackets only when specifically instructed by the following chapters.

1.5A3. If an item is available in different formats (e.g., as text and microfilm; as sound disc and sound tape reel), give the physical description of the format in hand. *Optionally*, make a note describing other formats in which it is available (see 1.7B16).

1.5B. Extent of item (including specific material designation)

1.5B1. Record the extent of the item by giving the number of physical units in arabic numerals and the specific material designation as instructed in subrule .5B in the chapter dealing with the type of material to which the item belongs.

> 3 microscope slides

> 1 jigsaw puzzle

> 3 v.

> 1 hand puppet

If the units of the item are identical, add *identical* before the specific material designation.

>   25 identical maps

>   50 identical sets of 10 slides

1.5B2. Describe a single-part printed text item as instructed in 2.5B.

>   327 p.

>   310 leaves of braille

1.5B3. Specify the number of components as instructed in the following chapters.

>   1 microfiche (150 fr.)

>   3 v. (1397 p.)

1.5B4. If the item being described has a playing time, give that playing time as follows.

a) If the playing time is stated on the item, give the playing time as stated.

>   1 sound cassette (40 min.)

>   1 film loop (3 min., 23 sec.)

>   2 sound discs (1 hr., 30 min.)

b) If the playing time is not stated on the item but is readily ascertainable, give it.

>   1 videoreel (30 min.)

c) *Optionally*, if the playing time is neither stated on the item nor readily ascertainable, give an approximate time.

>   1 piano roll (ca. 7 min.)

>   2 film reels (ca. 90 min.)

d) *Optionally*, if the parts of a multipart item have a stated uniform playing time or an approximate uniform playing time, give the playing time of each part followed by *each*. Otherwise, give the total duration.

>   31 sound cassettes (60 min. each)

>   11 sound cassettes (ca. 30 min. each)

>   2 videoreels (50 min.)

1.5B5. In describing a multipart item that is not yet complete, give the specific material designation alone preceded by three spaces.

>   microscope slides

>   v.

Optionally, when the item is complete, add the number of physical units.

1.5C. Other physical details

1.5C1. Give physical data (other than extent or dimensions) about an item as instructed in the following chapters.

> 1 filmstrip (70 fr.) : b&w
>
> 321 p. : ill. (some col.)
>
> 5 microscope slides : stained
>
> 1 sound disc (20 min.) : analog, 33⅓ rpm, mono.
>
> 1 model (4 pieces) : polystyrene

1.5D. Dimensions

1.5D1. Give the dimensions of an item as instructed in the following chapters.

> 1 wall chart : col. ; 24 × 48 cm.
>
> 321 p. : ill. (some col.) ; 23 cm.
>
> 6 microfilm reels ; 35 mm.
>
> 1 sound disc (56 min.) : digital, stereo. ; 4¾ in.
>
> 2 sound discs (1 hr., 15 min.) : analog, 33⅓ rpm, stereo. ; 10-12 in.

1.5D2. *Optionally*, if the item is in a container, name the container and give its dimensions *either* after the dimensions of the item *or* as the only dimensions.

> 12 paperweights : glass ; 12 cm. each in diam. in box 40 × 50 × 8 cm.
>
> 1 stone : malachite ; in box 12 × 9 × 18 cm.

1.5E. Accompanying material

1.5E1. Give details of accompanying material (see Glossary, appendix D) in one of the following ways:

> a) make a separate entry
> *or* b) make a multilevel description (see 13.6)
> *or* c) make a note (see 1.7B11)

> Accompanied by: A demographic atlas of north-west Ireland. 39 p. : col. maps ; 36 cm. Previously published separately in 1956
>
> Teacher's guide / by Robert Garry Shirts. 24 p.
>
> Accompanied by filmstrip entitled: Mexico and Central America

> *or* d) give the number of physical units in arabic numerals and the name of the accompanying material (using, when appropriate, a specific material designation) at the end of the physical description.

> 387 p. : ill. ; 27 cm. + 1 set of teacher's notes

32 p. : col. ill. ; 28 cm. + 7 maps

200 p. : ill. ; 25 cm. + 2 computer disks

271 p. : ill. ; 21 cm. + 1 atlas

1 stereograph reel (12 pairs of fr.) : col. + 1 pamphlet

1 score (32 p.) ; 26 cm. + 3 sound cassettes

1 computer disk ; 5¼ in. + 1 demonstration disk + 1 set of user's notes

Optional addition. If method d) is used and if more detail is desired, give the physical description of the accompanying material as instructed in the following chapters.

1 stereograph reel (12 pairs of fr.) : col. + 1 v. (12 p. : ill. ; 18 cm.)

1 filmstrip (70 fr.) : col. ; 35 mm. + 1 v. (39 p. ; 22 cm.)

271 p. : ill. ; 21 cm. + 1 atlas (95 p. : 85 col. maps ; 32 cm.)

1.6. SERIES AREA

Contents:
1.6A. Preliminary rule
1.6B. Title proper of series
1.6C. Parallel titles of series
1.6D. Other title information of series
1.6E. Statements of responsibility relating to series
1.6F. ISSN of series
1.6G. Numbering within series
1.6H. Subseries
1.6J. More than one series statement

1.6A. Preliminary rule

1.6A1. Punctuation
For instructions on the use of spaces before and after prescribed punctuation, see 1.0C.
Precede this area by a full stop, space, dash, space.
Enclose each series statement (see 1.6J) in parentheses.
Precede each parallel title by an equals sign.
Precede other title information by a colon.
Precede the first statement of responsibility by a diagonal slash.
Precede each subsequent statement of responsibility by a semicolon.
Precede the ISSN of a series or subseries by a comma.
Precede the numbering within a series or subseries by a semicolon.
Precede the title of a subseries by a full stop.
For the use of the equals sign to precede parallel statements, see the appropriate rules following.

1.6A2. Sources of information. Take information recorded in this area from the chief source of information or from any other source prescribed for this area in the following chapters. Enclose any information supplied from other sources in square brackets, within the parentheses enclosing each series statement.

1.6B. Title proper of series

1.6B1. If an item is issued in a series, transcribe the title proper of the series as instructed in 1.1B (see also 12.1B).

> Virago modern classics

> Great newspapers reprinted

1.6B2. If different forms of the title of the series (other than parallel titles) appear, choose the title given in the first of the prescribed sources for the series area as the title proper of the series. Give the other form(s) in the note area if of value in identifying the item.

If the title of the series does not appear in the first of the prescribed sources of information and different forms appear elsewhere in the item, choose the title given in the other prescribed sources in the order of preference for the sources (e.g., if different forms appear in the second and third sources, choose the one appearing in the second source).

1.6C. Parallel titles of series

1.6C1. Follow the instructions in 1.1D (second level of description) when transcribing the parallel titles of a series.

> Jeux visuels = Visual games

1.6D. Other title information of series

1.6D1. Give other title information of a series only if it provides valuable information identifying the series. Follow the instructions in 1.1E when transcribing other title information of a series.

> English linguistics, 1500-1750 : a collection of facsimile reprints

> Words : their origin, use, and spelling

1.6E. Statements of responsibility relating to series

1.6E1. Transcribe statements of responsibility appearing in conjunction with the series title only if they are considered to be necessary for identification of the series. Follow the instructions in 1.1F when transcribing a statement of responsibility relating to a series.

> Map supplement / Association of American Geographers

> Technical memorandum / Beach Erosion Board

Research monographs / Institute of Economic Affairs

Sämtliche Werke / Thomas Mann

1.6F. ISSN of series

1.6F1. Give the International Standard Serial Number (ISSN) of a series if it appears in the item being described (see also 1.6H4). Give the ISSN in the standard manner (i.e., *ISSN* followed by a space and two groups of four digits separated by a hyphen).

Western Canada series report, ISSN 0317-3127

1.6G. Numbering within series

1.6G1. Give the numbering of the item within the series in the terms given in the item. Use abbreviations as instructed in appendix B and numerals as instructed in appendix C.

Historic instruments at the Victoria and Albert Museum ; 4

Beatrix Potter jigsaw puzzles ; no. 1

Environment science research ; v. 6

Russian titles for the specialist, ISSN 0305-3741 ; no. 78

1.6G2. If the parts of a multipart item are separately numbered within a series, give the first and the last numbers if the numbering is continuous. Otherwise, give all the numbers. For numbering of a periodical series, see 12.6B.

; v. 11-15

; v. 131, 145, 152

1.6G3. If the item has a designation other than a number, give the designation as found.

; v. A

; 1971

1.6H. Subseries

1.6H1. If an item is one of a subseries (see Glossary, appendix D) and both the series and the subseries are named in the item, give the details of the main series (see 1.6A–1.6G) first and follow them with the name of the subseries and the details of that subseries.

Biblioteca del lavoro. Serie professionale

Geological Survey professional paper ; 683-D. Contributions to palaeontology

1.6H2. If the subseries has an alphabetic or numeric designation and no title, give the designation. If such a subseries has a title as well as a designation, give the title after the designation.

> Music for today. Series 2 ; no. 8

> Viewmaster science series. 4, Physics

1.6H3. Give parallel titles, other title information, and statements of responsibility relating to subseries as instructed in 1.6C, 1.6D, and 1.6E.

> World films. France today = La France d'aujourd'hui

> Papers and documents of the I.C.I.   Series C, Bibliographies = Travaux et documents de l'I.C.I.   Série C, Bibliographies

1.6H4. Give the ISSN of a subseries if it appears in the item being described; in such a case, omit the ISSN of the main series.

> Janua linguarum. Series maior, ISSN 0075-3114
> *not*   Janua linguarum, ISSN 0446-4796. Series maior, ISSN 0075-3114

1.6H5. Give the numbering within a subseries as instructed in 1.6G.

> Sciences. Physics ; TSP 1

> Biblioteca de arte hispánico ; 8. Artes aplicadas ; 1

1.6J. More than one series statement

1.6J1. The information relating to one series, or series and subseries, constitutes one series statement. If an item belongs to two or more series and/or two or more series and subseries, give separate series statements and enclose each statement in parentheses. Follow the instructions in 1.6A–1.6H in recording each series statement.

> (Video marvels ; no. 33) (Educational progress series ; no. 3)

If parts of an item belong to different series and this relationship cannot be stated clearly in the series area, give details of the series in a note (see 1.7B12).

1.7. NOTE AREA

Contents:
    1.7A. Preliminary rule
    1.7B. Notes

1.7A. Preliminary rule

1.7A1. Punctuation
Precede each note by a full stop, space, dash, space *or* start a new paragraph for each.
Separate introductory wording from the main content of a note by a colon followed but not preceded by a space.

1.7A2. Sources of information. Take data recorded in notes from any suitable source. Use square brackets only for interpolations within quoted material. See also 1.0E.

1.7A3. Form of notes

Order of information. If data in a note correspond to data found in the title and statement of responsibility, edition, material (or type of publication) specific details, publication, etc., physical description, and series areas, give the elements of the data in the order in which they appear in those areas. In such a case, use prescribed punctuation, except substitute a full stop for a full stop, space, dash, space.

>Adaptation of: Germinie Lacerteux / Edmond et Jules de Goncourt

>Originally published: London : Gray, 1871

>Revision of: 3rd ed. London : Macmillan, 1953

When giving names or titles originally in nonroman scripts, use the original script whenever possible rather than a romanization (see 1.0E).

>Based on: Братья Карамазовы / Ф.М. Достоевский

Quotations. Give quotations from the item or from other sources in quotation marks. Follow the quotation by an indication of its source, unless that source is the chief source of information. Do not use prescribed punctuation within quotations.

>"Published for the Royal Institute of Public Administration"

>"A textbook for 6th form students"—Pref.

>"Generally considered to be by William Langland"—Oxford companion to English literature

References. Refer to passages in the item, or in other sources, if these either support the cataloguer's own assertions or save repetition in the catalogue entry of information readily available from other sources.

>Introd. (p. xxix) refutes attribution to John Bodenham

>Detailed description in: Supplement to Hain's Repertorium bibliographicum / W.A. Copinger

Formal notes. Use formal notes employing an invariable introductory word or phrase or a standard form of words when uniformity of presentation assists in the recognition of the type of information being presented or when their use provides economy of space without loss of clarity.

Informal notes. When making informal notes, use statements that present the information as briefly as clarity, understandability, and grammar permit.

1.7A4. Notes citing other editions and works

Other editions. In citing another edition of the same work, give enough information to identify the edition cited.

>Revision of: 2nd ed., 1973

Other works and other manifestations of the same work. In citing other works and other manifestations of the same work (other than different editions with the same title), always give the title and (when applicable) the statement(s) of responsibility. Give the citation in the form: main entry heading, title proper; *or* in the form: title proper / statement of responsibility. When necessary, add the edition and/or date of publication of the work cited.

>Continues: Poetry in London. 1931-1947

>Translation of: Le deuxième sexe

>Previously published as: Mike. 1909

>Adaptation of: Wells, H.G. Kipps

>*or* Adaptation of: Kipps / by H.G. Wells

Notes relating to items reproduced. In describing an item that is a reproduction of another (e.g., a text reproduced in microform; a manuscript reproduced in book form; a set of maps reproduced as slides), give the notes relating to the reproduction and then the notes relating to the original. Combine the notes relating to the original in one note, giving the details in the order of the areas to which they relate.

1.7A5. Notes contain useful descriptive information that cannot be fitted into other areas of the description. A general outline of notes is given in 1.7B. Specific applications of 1.7B are provided in other chapters in part I. When appropriate, combine two or more notes to make one note.

1.7B. Notes

Give notes in the order in which they are listed here. However, give a particular note first when it has been decided that note is of primary importance.

1.7B1. Nature, scope, or artistic form

>Comedy in two acts

>Documentary

1.7B2. Language of the item and/or translation or adaptation

>Commentary in English

>Spanish version of: Brushing away tooth decay

1.7B3. Source of title proper

>Title from container

>Title from descriptive insert

1.7B4. Variations in title

Cover title: Giovanni da Firenze

Original title: L'éducation sentimentale

1.7B5. Parallel titles and other title information

Title on container: The four seasons

Subtitle: An enquiry into the present state of medicine including several recommendations as to how it may be improved and a discussion of the merits of the proposals of other persons

1.7B6. Statements of responsibility

Attributed to Thomas Dekker

Based on the novel by Thomas Hardy

Inspired by themes from the music of George Butterworth

1.7B7. Edition and history

Formerly available as: CAS 675

Continues: Monthly Scottish news bulletin

Rev. ed. of: The portable Dorothy Parker

1.7B8. Material (or type of publication) specific details

Scale of original: ca. 1:6,000

Military grid

File size varies

Vol. numbering irregular

Numbering begins each year with no. 1

1.7B9. Publication, distribution, etc.

Distributed in the U.K. by: EAV Ltd.

Published in London or Manchester, 1807-1899

1.7B10. Physical description

Printed area measures 30 × 46 cm.

Consists of head and torso made of clear plastic, ⅛ life size

Magnetic sound track

1.7B11. Accompanying material and supplements

Set includes booklet: New mathematics guide. 16 p.

Every 3rd issue includes supplement: EEC facts and statistics

Slides with every 7th issue

1.7B12. Series

> Originally issued in the series: Our world of today

> Pts. 1 and 2 in series: African perspective. Pts. 3 and 4 in series: Third World series. Pt. 5 in both series

1.7B13. Dissertations. If the item being described is a dissertation or thesis presented as part of the requirements for an academic degree, give *Thesis* followed by a brief statement of the degree for which the author was a candidate (e.g., (*M.A.*) or (*Ph.D.*), or, for theses to which conventional abbreviations do not apply, (*doctoral*) or (*master's*)), the name of the institution or faculty to which the thesis was presented, and the year in which the degree was granted.

> Thesis (Ph.D.)—University of Toronto, 1974

> Thesis (M.A.)—University College, London, 1969

> Thesis (doctoral)—Freie Universität, Berlin, 1973

If the publication is a revision or abridgement of a thesis, state this.

> Abstract of thesis (Ph.D.)—University of Illinois at Urbana-Champaign, 1974

If the thesis is a text by someone else edited by the candidate, give the candidate's name in the note.

> Karl Schmidt's thesis (doctoral)—München, 1965

If the publication lacks a formal thesis statement, give a bibliographic history note.

> Originally presented as the author's thesis (doctoral—Heidelberg) under the title: . . .

1.7B14. Audience

> Intended audience: Elementary grades

> For children aged 7-9

> Intended audience: Clinical students and postgraduate house officers

1.7B15. Reference to published descriptions

> References: HR6471; GW9101; Goff D-403

1.7B16. Other formats. Give the details of other formats in which the content of the item has been issued.

> Issued also on cassette and cartridge tapes

> Issued also in 16 mm. format

For details of other formats available in the library, see 1.7B20.

1.7B17. Summary

Summary: Pictures the highlights of the play Julius Caesar using photographs of an actual production

1.7B18. Contents

Partial contents: Introduction / Howard H. Brinton — William I. Hull : a biographical sketch / Janet Whitney — George Fox as a man / Frank Aydelotte

Contents: v. 1. Plain tales from the hills — v. 2-3. Soldiers three and military tales — v. 4. In black and white — v. 5. The phantom 'rickshaw and other stories — v. 6. Under the deodars. The story of the Gadsbys. Wee Willie Winkie

1.7B19. Numbers borne by the item (other than those covered in 1.8)

Supt. of Docs. no.: I 19.16:818

Warner Bros.: K56151

1.7B20. Copy being described, library's holdings, and restrictions on use. Give important descriptive details of the particular copy being described.

Ms. notes by author on endpapers

Lacks last 15 min. of recording

Give details of the library's holdings of a multipart item if those holdings are incomplete.

Library set lacks slides 7-9

Library has v. 1, 3-5, and 7

Indicate any restrictions on the use of the item.

Accessible after 2010

For graduate students only

1.7B21. "With" notes. If the title and statement of responsibility area contains a title that applies to only a part of an item lacking a collective title and, therefore, more than one description is made (see 1.1G2), make a note beginning *With:* and listing the other separately titled works in the item in the order in which they appear.

With: Candles at night / Alexandra Napier

With: Sonata in G, op. 1, no. 5 / Carlo Francesco Chabran — Sonata no. 1 in B flat / Pietro Nardini

1.7B22. Combined notes relating to the original. In making a note relating to an original, combine the data into a single note (see 1.7A4, 1.11F, and 11.7B22).

Facsim. of: A classification and subject index for cataloguing and arranging the books and pamphlets of a library. Amherst, Mass. :

[s.n.], 1876 (Hartford, Conn. : Case, Lockwood & Brainard). 44 p.
; 25 cm.

1.8. STANDARD NUMBER AND TERMS OF AVAILABILITY AREA

Contents:

1.8A. Preliminary rule

1.8A1. Punctuation
For instructions on the use of spaces before and after prescribed punctuation,
see 1.0C.
Precede this area by a full stop, space, dash, space *or* start a new paragraph.
Precede each repetition of this area by a full stop, space, dash, space.
Precede a key-title by an equals sign.
Precede terms of availability by a colon.
Enclose a qualification to the standard number or terms of availability in
parentheses.

1.8A2. Sources of information. Take information included in this area from any
source. Do not enclose any information in brackets.

1.8B. Standard number

1.8B1. Give the International Standard Book Number (ISBN), or International
Standard Serial Number (ISSN), or any other internationally agreed standard
number for the item being described. Give such numbers with the agreed abbreviation and with the standard spacing or hyphenation.

> ISBN 0-552-67587-3

> ISSN 0002-9769

1.8B2. If an item bears two or more such numbers, give the one that applies to
the item being described.
Optionally, give more than one number and add a qualification as prescribed
in 1.8E. Give a number for a complete set before the number(s) for the part(s).
Give numbers for parts in the order of the parts. Give a number for accompanying
material last.

> ISBN 0-379-00550-6 (set). — ISBN 0-379-00551-4 (v. 1)

1.8B3. Give any number of an item other than an International Standard Number
in a note (see 1.7B19).

1.8B4. If a number is known to be incorrectly printed in the item, give the correct number if it can be readily ascertained and add *(corrected)* to it.

ISBN 0-340-16427-1 (corrected)

1.8C. Key-title

1.8C1. Give the key-title of a serial, if it is found on the item or is otherwise readily available, after the International Standard Serial Number (ISSN). Give the key-title even if it is identical with the title proper. If no ISSN is given, do not record the key-title.

ISSN 0340-0352 = IFLA journal

1.8D. *Optional addition.* Terms of availability

1.8D1. Give the terms on which the item is available. These terms consist of the price (given in numerals with standard symbols) if the item is for sale, or a brief statement of other terms if the item is not for sale.

£2.50

Free to students of the college

For hire

1.8E. Qualification

1.8E1. Give, after the standard number, a brief qualification when an item bears two or more standard numbers.

ISBN 0-435-91660-2 (cased). − ISBN 0-435-91661-0 (pbk.)

ISBN 0-387-08266-2 (U.S.). − ISBN 3-540-08266-2 (Germany)

ISBN 0-684-14258-9 (bound) : $12.50. − ISBN 0-684-14257-0 (pbk.) : $6.95

Optionally, when the terms of availability (see 1.8D) need qualification, give one briefly.

£1.00 (£0.50 to members)

$12.00 ($6.00 to students)

1.8E2. If there is no standard number, give the terms of availability before any qualification.

$10.00 (pbk.)

1.9. SUPPLEMENTARY ITEMS

Contents:
　　1.9A. Supplementary items described independently
　　1.9B. Supplementary items described dependently

1.9A. Supplementary items described independently

1.9A1. Describe supplementary (including accompanying and related) items that are to be catalogued separately (see 21.28) as separate items. For instructions on the recording of the title proper of supplementary items, the titles proper of which consist of two or more parts, see 1.1B9.

1.9B. Supplementary items described dependently

1.9B1. Choose one of the following methods of describing supplementary (including accompanying and related) items described dependently:

a) record the item as accompanying material as instructed in 1.5E1d

> 48 photos. : b&w ; 20 × 16 cm. + 1 v.

> 5 v. : ill., facsims., ports ; 32 cm. + 1 atlas (135 p. ; 32 cm.)

or b) record minor supplementary items in a note (see 1.7B11)

> Accompanied by supplement (37 p.) issued in 1971

or c) use the multilevel description (see 13.6).

> The Nonesuch Dickens / published under the editorial direction of Arthur Waugh ... [et al.]. — Bloomsbury [England] : Nonesuch, 1937-1938. — 23 v. : ill. ; 26 cm.
> The Nonesuch Dickens. Retrospectus and prospectus. — 1937. — 130 p. : ill., facsims. — Contains facsim. pages from previous eds. of The Pickwick papers.

.10. ITEMS MADE UP OF SEVERAL TYPES OF MATERIAL

1.10A. This rule applies to items that are made up of two or more components, two or more of which belong to distinct material types (e.g., a sound recording and a printed text).

1.10B. If an item has one predominant component, describe it in terms of that component and give details of the subsidiary component(s) as accompanying material following the physical description (see 1.5E) or in a note (see 1.7B11).

> 47 slides : col. ; 5 × 5 cm. + 1 sound cassette

> 3 v. : ill. ; 30 cm.
> *Note:* Sound disc (12 min. : analog, 45 rpm, mono. ; 7 in.) in pocket at end of v. 3

1.10C. If an item has no predominant component, apply the following in addition to other relevant rules in this chapter and in the appropriate following chapters.

1.10C1. General material designation. If a general material designation is used (see 1.1C):

a) for an item without a collective title, give the appropriate designation after each title as instructed in 1.1C2

Life in the time of Charles Dickens [filmstrip] / editor, Albert Ammerman. The time, the life, the works of Charles Dickens, and excerpts from Dickens on America [sound recording] / read by Ian Brett and Peter Howell

b) for an item with a collective title, follow the instructions in 1.1C4.

... [kit]

or ... [multimedia]

1.10C2. Physical description. Apply whichever of the following three methods is appropriate to the item being described:

a) Give the extent of each part or group of parts belonging to each distinct class of material as the first element of the physical description (do this if no further physical description of each item is desired). *Optionally*, if the parts are in a container, name the container and give its dimensions.

400 lesson cards, 40 answer key booklets, 1 student record, 1 teacher's handbook, 1 placement test ; in container 18 × 25 × 19 cm.

12 slides, 1 sound cassette, 1 booklet, 1 map ; in box 16 × 30 × 20 cm.

b) Give a separate physical description for each part or group of parts belonging to each distinct class of material (do this if a further physical description of each item is desired). Give each physical description on a separate line. *Optionally*, if the parts are in a container, name the container after the last physical description and give its dimensions.

Beyond the reading list [GMD] : guidelines for research in the humanities / C.P. Ravilious ; University of Sussex Library. — Brighton [England] : University of Sussex Library, Audio-Visual Materials Room [distributor], 1975
46 slides : col.
1 sound cassette (15 min.) : analog, mono.
Summary: The bibliographic control of the humanities, with special reference to literature. A typical research project is followed through. — Intended audience: Postgraduates and research students

Hot deserts [GMD] / Ruth Way. — London ; Toronto : Visual Publications, [1975?]
1 filmstrip (39 fr.) : col. ; 35 mm.
1 sound cassette (ca. 18 min.) : analog, mono.
4 study prints : col. ; 29 × 88 cm. folded to 29 × 44 cm.
1 v. (15 p.) ; 22 cm.
1 folded sheet (4 p.) ; 22 cm.
All in container 33 × 47 × 5 cm.
(The earth & man. The earth without man ; 4). — Pictures on filmstrip and study prints identical. — Cassette has automatic and manual advance signals

c) For items with a large number of heterogeneous materials, give a general term as the extent. Give the number of such pieces unless it cannot be ascertained. *Optionally*, if the pieces are in a container, name the container and give its dimensions.

> various pieces

> 27 various pieces

> 42 various pieces ; in box 20 × 12 × 6 cm.

1.10C3. Notes. Give notes on particular parts of the item together following the series area or following the physical description(s) if no series area is present.

> Tape cassette also issued as disc. — Slides photographed in
> Death Valley, Calif.

1.10D. Multilevel description

1.10D1. *Optionally*, in describing a single part of a multimedia item, follow the instructions in 13.6.

1.11. FACSIMILES, PHOTOCOPIES, AND OTHER REPRODUCTIONS

1.11A. In describing a facsimile, photocopy, or other reproduction of printed texts, maps, manuscripts, printed music, and graphic items, give the data relating to the facsimile, etc., in all areas except the note area.

Give data relating to the original in the note area (but give numeric and/or alphabetic, chronological, etc., designations of serials in the material (or type of publication) specific details area).

If a facsimile, etc., is in a form of material different from that of the original (e.g., a manuscript reproduced as a book), use the chapter on the form of the facsimile, etc., in determining the sources of information (e.g., for a manuscript reproduced as a book, use 2.0B). In addition to instructions given in the relevant chapters, follow the instructions in this rule.

1.11B. If the facsimile, etc., has a title different from the original, give the title of the facsimile, etc., as the title proper. Give the original title as other title information if it appears on the chief source of information of the facsimile, etc. (see 1.1D3). Otherwise, give the title of the original in the note area (see 1.11F).

1.11C. If the facsimile, etc., has the edition statement, publication details, or series data of the original as well as those of the facsimile, etc., give those of the facsimile, etc., in the edition, publication, distribution, etc., and series areas. Give the details of the original in the note area (see 1.11F).

1.11D. Give the physical description of the facsimile, etc., in the physical description area. Give the physical description of the original in the note area (see 1.11F).

1.11E. If the facsimile, etc., has a standard number, give it in the standard number and terms of availability area, together with the key-title and terms of availability of the facsimile, etc. Give the standard number and key-title of the original in the note area (see 1.11F).

1.11F. Give all the details of the original of a facsimile, etc., in a single note (see also 1.7A4). Give the details of the original in the order of the areas of the description.

> The baby's bouquet [GMD] : a fresh bunch of old rhymes and tunes / arranged and decorated by Walter Crane ; the tunes collected and arranged by L.C. — London : Pan, 1974
> 56 p. : col. ill. ; 16 × 17 cm. — (A Piccolo book)
> Facsim. of: 2nd ed., rev. London : Routledge, 1877
> ISBN 0-330-24089-7 : £0.60

> Alice's adventures under ground [GMD] / by Lewis Carroll ; with a new introduction by Martin Gardner. — New York : Dover, 1965
> xiii, 91, [17] p. : ill., facsims. ; 22 cm.
> Contents: Complete facsimile of the British Museum manuscript of Alice's adventures under ground — Front matter of the Macmillan 1886 edition — Back matter of the Macmillan 1886 edition

> Pre-Raphaelite drawings [GMD] / by Dante Gabriel Rossetti ; [selected and introduced by] Andrea Rose. — Chicago : University of Chicago Press, 1977
> 3 microfiches (251 fr.) : all ill. ; 10 × 15 cm. + 1 booklet
> Reproductions of 251 drawings from Birmingham City Museums

BOOKS, PAMPHLETS, AND PRINTED SHEETS

Contents

Early Printed Monographs

2.0. GENERAL RULES

2.0A. Scope

2.0A1. The rules in this chapter cover the description of separately published monographic printed items other than cartographic items (see chapter 3) and printed music (see chapter 5). These are referred to hereafter in this chapter as printed monographs and comprise books, pamphlets, and single sheets. For microform reproductions of printed texts, see chapter 11. For serial printed texts, see also chapter 12.

2.0B. Sources of information

2.0B1. Chief source of information. The chief source of information for printed monographs is the title page or, if there is no title page, the source from within the publication that is used as a substitute for it. For printed monographs published without a title page, or without a title page applying to the whole work (as in the case of some editions of the Bible and some bilingual dictionaries), use the part of the item supplying the most complete information, whether this be the cover (excluding a separate book jacket), caption, colophon, running title, or other part. Specify the part used as a title page substitute in a note (see 2.7B3). If no part of the item supplies data that can be used as the basis of the description, take the necessary information from any available source. If the information traditionally given on the title page is given on facing pages or on pages on successive leaves, with or without repetition, treat those pages as the title page.

Use the colophon as the chief source of information for an oriental nonroman script publication if the colophon contains full bibliographic information and the following conditions apply:

- a) the page standing in the position of a title page bears only the title proper
- *or* b) the title page bears only a calligraphic version of the title proper
- *or* c) the title page bears only a western-language version of the title and other bibliographic information.

2.0B2. Prescribed sources of information. The prescribed source(s) of information for each area of the description of printed monographs is set out below. Enclose information taken from outside the prescribed source(s) in square brackets.

AREA	PRESCRIBED SOURCES OF INFORMATION
Title and statement of responsibility	Title page[1]
Edition	Title page, other preliminaries, colophon
Publication, distribution, etc.	Title page, other preliminaries, colophon

---

1. Hereafter in this chapter, *title page* includes any substitute (including, for oriental publications, a colophon specified in 2.0B1 as a title page substitute).

Physical description	The whole publication
Series	Series title page, monograph title page, cover, rest of the publication
Note	Any source
Standard number and terms of availability	Any source

2.0C. Punctuation
For the punctuation of the description as a whole, see 1.0C.
For the prescribed punctuation of elements, see the following rules.

2.0D. Levels of detail in the description
See 1.0D.

2.0E. Language and script of the description
See 1.0E.

2.0F. Inaccuracies
See 1.0F.

2.0G. Accents and other diacritical marks
See 1.0G.

2.0H. Items with several title pages
See 1.0H.

2.1. TITLE AND STATEMENT OF RESPONSIBILITY AREA
Contents:

2.1A. Preliminary rule

2.1A1. Punctuation
For instructions on the use of spaces before and after prescribed punctuation, see 1.0C.
Precede the title of a supplement or section (see 1.1B9) by a full stop.
Enclose the general material designation in square brackets.
Precede each parallel title by an equals sign.
Precede each unit of other title information by a colon.
Precede the first statement of responsibility by a diagonal slash.

Precede each subsequent statement of responsibility by a semicolon.
For the punctuation of this area for items without a collective title, see 1.1G.

2.1B. Title proper

2.1B1. Transcribe the title proper as instructed in 1.1B.

> The articulate mammal

> Why a duck?

> Classification décimale de Dewey et index

> Memoirs of the life of the late John Mytton, Esq.

> The ballroom of romance and other stories

> The first Rex Stout omnibus

> The most of P.G. Wodehouse

> Marlowe's plays

> Linda Goodman's sun signs

> Larousse's French-English dictionary

> Harriet said—
>   (*Title page reads:* Harriet said ...)

> Under the hill, or, The story of Venus and Tannhäuser

> 4.50 from Paddington

> Advanced calculus. Student handbook
>   (*Title proper consists of title of main work and title of handbook.*
>   *See 1.1B9*)

> Instructor's guide and key for The American economy

> Bank officer's handbook of commercial banking law, fourth
> edition, by Frederick K. Bentel. 1975 supplement
>   (*Title proper consists of title, statement of responsibility, and edition*
>   *statement of main work and designation of supplement*)

Specify the part used as a title page substitute in a note (see 2.7B3).

2.1C. *Optional addition.* General material designation

2.1C1. Give immediately following the title proper the appropriate general material designation as instructed in 1.1C.

2.1C2. If an item contains parts belonging to materials falling into two or more categories, and if none of these is the predominant constituent of the item, give either *multimedia* or *kit* as the designation (see 1.1C1 and 1.10C1).

2.1D. Parallel titles

2.1D1. Transcribe parallel titles as instructed in 1.1D.

Tyres and wheels = Pneus et roues = Reifen und Räder

Thumbelina = Tommelise

2.1E. Other title information

2.1E1. Transcribe other title information as instructed in 1.1E.

A Laodicean : a story of to-day

The age of neo-classicism : the fourteenth exhibition of the Council of Europe

Private eyeballs : a golden treasury of bad taste

Letters to an intimate stranger : a year in the life of Jack Trevor Story

2.1F. Statements of responsibility

2.1F1. Transcribe statements of responsibility relating to persons or bodies as instructed in 1.1F.

Shut up in Paris / by Nathan Sheppard

Great Britain : handbook for travellers / by Karl Baedeker

Le père Goriot / Honoré de Balzac

Statistics of homelessness / Home Office

Tynan right & left : plays, films, people, places, and events / Kenneth Tynan

Vas-y, Charlie Brown / par Charles M. Schulz

Dan Russel the fox : an episode in the life of Miss Rowan / by E.Œ. Somerville and Martin Ross

The world of the lion / by Samuel Devend ... [et al.]

Eventyr og historier / H.C. Andersen

A modern herbal / by Mrs. M. Grieve ; edited and introduced by Mrs. C.F. Leyel
    (*Lengthy other title information given in note area*)

Eldorado : a story of the Scarlet Pimpernel / by the Baroness Orczy

Letters from AE / selected and edited by Alan Denson ; with a foreword by Monk Gibbon

A French and English dictionary / compiled from the best authorities of both languages by Professors De Lolme and Wallace, and Henry Bridgeman

The diary of a country parson, 1758-1802 / by James Woodforde ; passages selected and edited by John Beresford

Hadrian the Seventh / Fr. Rolfe (Frederick, Baron Corvo)

Underwater acoustics : a report / by the Natural Environment Research Council Working Group on Underwater Acoustics

Proceedings / International Symposium on the Cataloguing, Coding, and Statistics of Audio-Visual Materials ; organised by ISO/TC46 Documentation in collaboration with IFLA and IFTC, 7-9 January 1976 in Strasbourg

American Ballet Theatre : thirty-six years of scenic and costume design, 1940-1976 / presented by Ballet Theatre Foundation, Inc., and the International Exhibitions Foundation

Scientific policy, research, and development in Canada : a bibliography / prepared by the National Science Library = La politique des sciences, la recherche et le développement au Canada : bibliographie / établie par la Bibliothèque nationale des sciences

Ramsay Traquair and his successors : guide to the archive / Canadian Architecture Collection, Blackader-Lauterman Library of Architecture and Art, McGill University ; Irena Murray, general editor = Ramsay Traquair et ses successeurs : guide du fonds / Collection d'architecture canadienne, Blackader-Lauterman Library of Architecture and Art, McGill University ; Irena Murray, directrice

Teach yourself Irish / Myles Dillon, Donncha Ó Cróinín

Swedenborgs korrespondenslära / av Inge Jonsson ; with a summary in English

Book of bores / drawings by Michael Heath

Sanditon / Jane Austen and another lady

2.1F2. Add a word or short phrase to the statement of responsibility if the relationship between the title and the person(s) or body (bodies) named in the statement is not clear.

Morte Arthure / [edited by] John Finlayson

The great ideas of Plato / [selected by] Eugene Freeman and David Appel

Research in human geography / by Michael Chisholm ; [for the] Social Science Research Council

> Palava Parrot / [illustrations by] Tamasin Cole ; story by James Cressey

> Antologija hrvatske poezije dvadesetog stoljeća od Kranjčevića do danas / [sastavili] Slavko Mihalić, Josip Pupačić, Anton Šoljan

2.1G. Items without a collective title

2.1G1. If a printed monograph lacks a collective title, transcribe the titles of the individual parts as instructed in 1.1G.

> The listing attic ; The unstrung harp / by Edward Gorey

> Flash and filigree ; and, The magic Christian / by Terry Southern

> Henry Esmond : a novel / by Thackeray.   Bleak House : a novel / by Dickens

> Humanismens krise / af H.C. Branner.   Eneren og massen / af Martin A. Hansen

2.1G2. Make the relationship between statements of responsibility and the parts of an item lacking a collective title clear by additions as instructed in 2.1F2.

> Man Friday : a play ; Mind your head : a return trip with songs / Adrian Mitchell ; music [for Man Friday] by Mike Westbrook ; music [for Mind your head] by Andy Roberts

2.2. EDITION AREA

Contents:
- 2.2A. Preliminary rule
- 2.2B. Edition statement
- 2.2C. Statements of responsibility relating to the edition
- 2.2D. Statement relating to a named revision of an edition
- 2.2E. Statements of responsibility relating to a named revision of an edition

2.2A. Preliminary rule

2.2A1. Punctuation
For instructions on the use of spaces before and after prescribed punctuation, see 1.0C.
Precede this area by a full stop, space, dash, space.
Precede a statement relating to a named revision of an edition by a comma.
Precede the first statement of responsibility following an edition statement by a diagonal slash.
Precede each subsequent statement of responsibility by a semicolon.

2.2B. Edition statement

2.2B1. Transcribe a statement relating to an edition of a work that contains differences from other editions of that work, or to a named reissue of a work, as instructed in 1.2B.

> 2nd ed.
>
> New ed., rev. and enl.
>
> 1st American ed.
>
> 1st illustrated ed.
>
> Household ed.
>
> 6. Aufl.
>
> Draft
>
> Facsim. ed.
>
> New Wessex ed.
>
> [3rd ed.]
>
> [New ed.]
>
> 3ª ed.

2.2B2. In case of doubt about whether a statement is an edition statement, follow the instructions in 1.2B3.

2.2B3. *Optional addition.* If an item lacks an edition statement but is known to contain significant changes from other editions, supply a suitable brief statement in the language and script of the title proper and enclose it in square brackets.

> [New ed.]
>
> [5ᵉ éd.]

2.2B4. If an edition statement appears in more than one language or script, transcribe the statement that is in the language or script of the title proper. If this criterion does not apply, transcribe the statement that appears first. *Optionally*, transcribe the parallel statement(s), each preceded by an equals sign.

2.2B5. If an item lacking a collective title contains one or more works with an associated edition statement, transcribe such statements following the titles and statements of responsibility to which they relate, separated from them by a full stop.

2.2C. Statements of responsibility relating to the edition

2.2C1. Transcribe a statement of responsibility relating to one or more editions, but not to all editions, of a work as instructed in 1.2C and 2.1F.

> Economic history of England : a study in social development /
> by H.O. Meredith. — 5th ed. / by C. Ellis

The well-beloved : a sketch of a temperament / Thomas Hardy. — New Wessex ed. / introduction by J. Hillis Miller ; notes by Edward Mendelson

A French and English dictionary / compiled from the best authorities of both languages by Professors De Lolme and Wallace, and Henry Bridgeman. — [New ed.] / revised, corrected, and considerably enlarged by E. Roubaud

A short history of the Catholic Church / by Philip Hughes. — 8th ed. / with a final chapter (1966-1974) by E.E.Y. Hales

2.2D. Statement relating to a named revision of an edition

2.2D1. If an item is a named revision of an edition, transcribe the statement relating to that revision as instructed in 1.2D.

Selected poems / D.H. Lawrence. — [New ed.] / edited, with an introduction, by Keith Sagar, Repr. with minor revisions

Ireland / edited by L. Russel Muirhead. — 3rd ed., 2nd (corr.) impression

Do not record statements relating to an impression or printing that contains no changes unless the item is considered to be of particular importance to the cataloguing agency.

2.2E. Statements of responsibility relating to a named revision of an edition

2.2E1. Transcribe a statement of responsibility relating to one or more named revisions of an edition (but not to all such revisions) as instructed in 1.2E and 2.1F.

2.3. MATERIAL (OR TYPE OF PUBLICATION) SPECIFIC DETAILS AREA

2.3A. This area is not used for printed monographs.

2.4. PUBLICATION, DISTRIBUTION, ETC., AREA

Contents:
2.4A. Preliminary rule
2.4B. General rule
2.4C. Place of publication, distribution, etc.
2.4D. Name of publisher, distributor, etc.
2.4E. Statement of function of publisher, distributor, etc.
2.4F. Date of publication, distribution, etc.
2.4G. Place of printing, name of printer, date of printing

2.4A. Preliminary rule

2.4A1. Punctuation

For instructions on the use of spaces before and after prescribed punctuation, see 1.0C.

Precede this area by a full stop, space, dash, space.

Precede a second or subsequently named place of publication, distribution, etc., by a semicolon.

Precede the name of a publisher, distributor, etc., by a colon.

Enclose a supplied statement of function of a publisher, distributor, etc., in square brackets.

Precede the date of publication, distribution, etc., by a comma.

Enclose the details of printing (place, name, date) in parentheses.

Precede the name of a printer by a colon.

Precede the date of printing by a comma.

2.4B. General rule

2.4B1. Record information about the place, name, and date of all types of publishing, distributing, etc., activities as instructed in 1.4B.

2.4C. Place of publication, distribution, etc.

2.4C1. Give the place of publication, distribution, etc., as instructed in 1.4C.

2.4D. Name of publisher, distributor, etc.

2.4D1. Give the name of the publisher, etc., and *optionally* the name of the distributor, as instructed in 1.4D.

London : Macmillan

New York : Dell

London : H.M.S.O.

Tucson : University of Arizona Press

Taunton, Somerset : Barnicotts

London : The Society : Sold by Longman

London : Oxford University Press

London : John Lane, the Bodley Head

Geneva : WHO

[Hove, England] : Fox

Göttingen : Vandenhoeck & Ruprecht

London : Benn ; Chicago : Rand McNally
  (*Cataloguing agency in the United States*)

Freiburg : Baedeker ; London : Allen & Unwin
  (*Cataloguing agency in the United Kingdom*)

New York : Dutton ; Toronto : Clarke, Irwin
(*Cataloguing agency in Canada*)

London : T. Wall and Sons
(*Title page reads:* Published in celebration of life's minor pleasures
by T. Wall and Sons (Ice-Cream) Ltd.)

2.4E. *Optional addition.* **Statement of function of publisher, distributor, etc.**

2.4E1. Add to the name of a publisher, distributor, etc., a statement of function
as instructed in 1.4E.

New York : Dover ; London : Constable [distributor]

2.4F. Date of publication, distribution, etc.

2.4F1. Give the date of publication, distribution, etc., as instructed in 1.4F.

London : Gollancz, 1951

New York : Dover, 1970 ; London : Constable [distributor],
1972

New York : Dell, [1985], c1983

2.4G. Place of printing, name of printer, date of printing

2.4G1. If the name of the publisher is unknown and the place and name of the
printer are found in the item, give that place and name as instructed in 1.4G.

London : [s.n.], 1971 (London : HiTimes Press)

[S.l. : s.n.], 1971 (London : Wiggs)

2.4G2. *Optional addition.* Give the place, name of printer, and/or date of printing
if they are found in the item and differ from the place, name of publisher, etc.,
and date of publication, etc., and are considered important by the cataloguing
agency.

London : The Society, 1971 (London : Ploughshare Press)

London : J. Lane, 1902 (1907 printing)

2.5. PHYSICAL DESCRIPTION AREA

Contents:
2.5A. Preliminary rule
2.5B. Number of volumes and/or pagination
2.5C. Illustrative matter
2.5D. Dimensions
2.5E. Accompanying material

2.5A. Preliminary rule

2.5A1. Punctuation

For instructions on the use of spaces before and after prescribed punctuation, see 1.0C.

Precede this area by a full stop, space, dash, space *or* start a new paragraph.
Precede details of illustrations by a colon.
Precede dimensions by a semicolon.
Precede each statement of accompanying material by a plus sign.
Enclose physical details of accompanying material in parentheses.

2.5B. Number of volumes and/or pagination

Single volumes

2.5B1. Give the number of pages or leaves in a publication in accordance with the terminology suggested by the volume. That is, describe a volume with leaves printed on both sides in terms of pages; describe a volume with leaves printed on only one side in terms of leaves; and describe a volume that has more than one column to a page and is numbered in columns in terms of columns.

If a publication contains sequences of leaves and pages, or pages and numbered columns, or leaves and numbered columns, record each sequence.[2] Describe a volume printed without numbering in terms of leaves or pages, but not of both. For the treatment of plates, see 2.5B10. Describe a broadside as such. Describe a single sheet (folded or not) as *sheet*. Describe a case or portfolio as such.

2.5B2. Give the number of pages, leaves, or columns in terms of the numbered or lettered sequences in the volume. Give the last numbered page, leaf, or column in each sequence[2] and follow it with the appropriate term or abbreviation.

> 327 p.
>
> 321 leaves
>
> 381 columns
>
> xvii, 323 p.
>
> 27 p., 300 leaves
>
> 1 broadside
>
> 1 sheet
>
> 1 portfolio

Give pages, etc., that are lettered inclusively in the form *A–K p.*, *a–d leaves*, etc. Give pages, etc., that are numbered in words or characters other than arabic or roman in arabic figures.

> A-Z p.
>   (*Pages lettered:* A–Z)

---

2. A sequence of pages or leaves is: (1) a separately numbered group of pages, leaves, etc.; (2) an unnumbered group of pages, etc., that stands apart from other groups in the publication; or (3) a number of pages or leaves of plates distributed throughout the publication.

32 p.
(*Pages numbered in words*)

2.5B3. Disregard unnumbered sequences, unless such a sequence constitutes the whole (see 2.5B7) or a substantial part (see also 2.5B8) of the publication, or unless an unnumbered sequence includes pages, etc., that are referred to in a note. When recording the number of unnumbered pages, etc., either give the estimated number preceded by *ca.*, without square brackets, or enclose the exact number in square brackets.

8, vii, ca. 300, 73 p.

33, [31] leaves

[8], 155 p.
Note: Bibliography: 6th prelim. page

Disregard unnumbered sequences of inessential matter (advertising, blank pages, etc.).

2.5B4. If the number printed on the last page or leaf of a sequence does not represent the total number of pages or leaves in that sequence, let it stand uncorrected unless it gives a completely false impression of the extent of the item, as, for instance, when only alternate pages are numbered or when the number on the last page or leaf of the sequence is misprinted. Supply corrections in such cases in square brackets.

48 [i.e. 96] p.

329 [i.e. 392] p.

2.5B5. If the numbering within a sequence changes (e.g., from roman to arabic numerals), ignore the numbering of the first part of the sequence.

176 p.
(*Pages numbered:* i–xii, 13–176)

2.5B6. If the pages, etc., are numbered as part of a larger sequence (e.g., one volume of a multivolume publication) or if the item appears to be incomplete (see also 2.5B16), give the first and last numbers of the pages or leaves, preceded by the appropriate term or abbreviation.

leaves 81-149

p. 713-797

2.5B7. If the pages or leaves of a volume are unnumbered and the number of pages or leaves is readily ascertainable, give the number in square brackets. If the number is not readily ascertainable, estimate the number of pages or leaves and give that estimated number without square brackets and preceded by *ca.*

[93] p.

[55] leaves

ca. 600 p.

ca. 300 leaves

2.5B8. If the volume has complicated or irregular paging, give the pagination using one of the following methods:

a) Give the total number of pages or leaves (excluding those which are blank or contain advertising or other inessential matter) followed by *in various pagings* or *in various foliations*.

1000 p. in various pagings

256 leaves in various foliations

b) Give the number of pages or leaves in the main sequences of the pagination and add the total number, in square brackets, of the remaining variously paged sequences.

226, [44] p.

366, 98, [99] p.

c) Give *1 v. (various pagings)*, *1 case*, or *1 portfolio*, as appropriate.

2.5B9. For loose-leaf publications that are designed to receive additions, give the number of volumes followed by *(loose-leaf)*.

1 v. (loose-leaf)

3 v. (loose-leaf)

2.5B10. Leaves or pages of plates. Give the number of leaves or pages of plates (see Glossary, appendix D) at the end of the sequence(s) of pagination, whether the plates are found together or distributed throughout the publication, or even if there is only one plate. If the numbering of the leaves or pages of plates is complex or irregular, follow the instructions in 2.5B8.

246 p., 32 p. of plates

xvi, 249 p., [12] leaves of plates

x, 32, 73 p., [1] leaf of plates

xii, 24 p., 212, [43] leaves of plates

If the volume contains both leaves and pages of plates, give the number in terms of whichever is predominant.

323 p., [19] p. of plates
    (*Contains 16 pages and 3 leaves of plates*)

2.5B11. Describe folded leaves as such.

122 folded leaves

230 p., 25 leaves of plates (some folded)

25 folded leaves of plates

2.5B12. If numbered pages or leaves are printed on a double leaf (e.g., books in the traditional oriental format), give them as pages or leaves according to their numbering. If they are unnumbered, count each double leaf as two pages.

2.5B13. If the paging is duplicated, as is sometimes the case with books having parallel texts, give both pagings and make an explanatory note (see 2.7B10).

> xii, 35, 35 p.
> *Note:* Opposite pages bear duplicate numbering

2.5B14. If a volume has a pagination of its own and also bears the pagination of a larger work of which it is a part, give the paging of the individual volume in this area and give the continuous paging in a note (see 2.7B10).

> 328 p.
> *Note:* Pages also numbered 501-828

2.5B15. If the volume has groups of pages numbered in opposite directions, as is sometimes the case with books having texts in two languages, give the pagings of the various sections in order, starting from the title page selected for cataloguing.

> ix, 155, 127, x p.

2.5B16. If the last part of a publication is missing and the paging of a complete copy cannot be ascertained, give the number of the last numbered page followed by + *p*. Make a note of the imperfection (see 2.7B20).

> xxiv, 179 + p.
> *Note:* Library's copy imperfect: all after p. 179 wanting

Publications in more than one volume

2.5B17. Give the number of volumes of a printed monograph in more than one physical volume.

> 3 v.

2.5B18. If *volume* is not appropriate for a multipart item, use one of the following terms.

Parts. Use for bibliographic units intended to be bound several to a volume, especially if so designated by the publisher.

Pamphlets. Use for collections of pamphlets bound together or assembled in a portfolio for cataloguing as a collection.

Pieces. Use for items of varying character (e.g., pamphlets, broadsides, clippings, maps) published, or assembled for cataloguing, as a collection.

Case(s). Use for either boxes containing bound or unbound material or containers of fascicles.

Portfolio(s). Use for containers holding loose papers, illustrative materials, etc. A portfolio usually consists of two covers joined together at the back and tied at the front, top, and/or bottom.

2.5B19. If the number of bibliographic volumes differs from the number of physical volumes, give the number of bibliographic volumes followed by *in* and the number of physical volumes.

>8 v. in 5

2.5B20. If a set of volumes is continuously paged, give the pagination in parentheses after the number of volumes. Ignore separately paged sequences of preliminary matter in volumes other than the first.

>2 v. (xxxxi, 999 p.)

>3 v. (xx, 800 p.)
>(*Pages numbered:* xx, 1–201; xx, 202–513; xxi, 514–800)

2.5B21. *Optional addition.* If the volumes in a multivolume set are individually paged, give the pagination of each volume in parentheses after the number of volumes.

>2 v. (xvi, 329; xx, 412 p.)

2.5B22. If a publication was planned to be in more than one volume, but not all have been published and it appears that publication will not be continued, describe the incomplete set as appropriate (i.e., give paging for a single volume *or* number of volumes for multiple volumes). Make a note (see 2.7B10) to the effect that no more volumes have been published.

2.5B23. Braille or other tactile systems. If an item consists of leaves or pages of braille or another tactile system, add an appropriate term (e.g., *of braille, of Moon type, of jumbo braille, of press braille, of computer braille, of solid dot braille*) to the statement of the number of volumes, leaves, or pages.

>310 leaves of braille

>125 leaves of Moon type

>4 v. of jumbo braille

>320 leaves of computer braille

>300 p. of press braille

>40 leaves of solid dot braille

If an item consists of eye-readable print and braille or another tactile writing system, or of two or more tactile writing systems, use a concise description of the combination (e.g., *of print and braille, of braille and Nemeth code*).

>300 p. of print and braille

>205 leaves of braille and Nemeth code

If an item is a thermoform copy, add *(thermoform)*.

>64 leaves of braille (thermoform)

For braille cassette items, see 10.5B1.

2.5B24. Large print. If an item is in large print intended for use by the visually impaired, add, to the statement of the number of volumes, leaves, or pages, *(large print)*.

>   3 v. (large print)

>   342 p. (large print)

Optionally, if a general material designation (see 1.1C1) including *large print* is used, omit this addition.

2.5C. Illustrative matter

2.5C1. Give *ill.* for an illustrated printed monograph. Tables containing only words and/or numbers are not illustrations. Disregard illustrated title pages and minor illustrations.

>   327 p. : ill.

2.5C2. *Optionally*, if the illustrations are all of one or more of the following types, and are considered to be important, give the appropriate term(s) or abbreviation(s) in alphabetical order: coats of arms, facsimiles, forms, genealogical tables, maps, music, plans, portraits (use for both single and group portraits), samples. If none of these terms adequately describes the illustrations, use another term as appropriate.

>   333 p. : maps

>   256 p. : coats of arms, facsims., ports.

>   147 p. : computer drawings

If only some of the illustrations are of types considered to be important, give *ill.* followed by the appropriate term(s) or abbreviation(s) in alphabetical order.

>   230 p. : ill., maps, music, ports.

>   1 v. (loose-leaf) : ill., plans

>   199 p. : ill., cross sections, forms

2.5C3. Describe coloured illustrations (i.e., those in two or more colours) as such.

>   : col. ill.

>   : ill., col. maps, ports. (some col.)

>   : ill. (some col.), maps, plans

>   : ill. (chiefly col.), plans

2.5C4. Give the number of illustrations if their number can be ascertained readily (e.g., when the illustrations are listed and their numbers stated).

>   : 48 ill.

>   : ill., 12 maps

>   : ill., 3 forms, 1 map

2.5C5. If the publication consists wholly or predominantly of illustrations, give *all ill.* or *chiefly ill.*, as appropriate. *Optionally*, if those illustrations are all of one type, give *all [name of type]* or *chiefly [name of type]*.

> : all ill.

> : chiefly maps

2.5C6. Describe illustrative matter issued in a pocket inside the cover of an item in the physical description. Specify the number of such items and their location in a note (see 2.7B10 and 2.7B11).

> : ill., col. maps
> *Note:* Four maps on 2 folded leaves in pocket

2.5D. Dimensions

2.5D1. Give the height of the item in centimetres, to the next whole centimetre up (e.g., if an item measures 17.2 centimetres, give *18 cm.*). Measure the height of the binding if the volume is bound. Otherwise, measure the height of the item itself. If the item measures less than 10 centimetres, give the height in millimetres.

2.5D2. If the width of the volume is either less than half the height or greater than the height, give the height × width.

> ; 20 × 8 cm.

> ; 20 × 32 cm.

2.5D3. If the volumes in a multipart item differ in size, give the smallest or smaller and the largest or larger size, separated by a hyphen.

> ; 24-28 cm.

2.5D4. Give the height and the width of a single sheet. If such a sheet is designed to be folded when issued, add the dimensions of the sheet when folded.

> ; 48 × 30 cm. folded to 24 × 15 cm.

If the sheet is designed to be read in pages when folded, describe it as *1 folded sheet* and give the number of imposed pages and the height of the sheet when folded.

> 1 folded sheet (8 p.) ; 18 cm.

2.5D5. If the item consists of separate physical units of varying height bound together, give the height of the binding only.

2.5E. Accompanying material

2.5E1. Give the details of accompanying material as instructed in 1.5E.

> 271 p. : ill. ; 21 cm. + 1 answer book

> 271 p. : ill. ; 21 cm. + 1 v. (37 p., 19 leaves : col. maps ; 37 cm.)

271 p. : ill. ; 21 cm. + 1 sound disc (25 min. : analog, 33⅓ rpm, mono. ; 12 in.)

2.5E2. If the accompanying material is issued in a pocket inside the cover of the publication, give its location in a note (see 2.5C6, 2.7B10, and 2.7B11).

2.6. SERIES AREA

Contents:
    2.6A. Preliminary rule
    2.6B. Series statements

2.6A. Preliminary rule

2.6A1. Punctuation
For instructions on the use of spaces before and after prescribed punctuation, see 1.0C.
Precede this area by a full stop, space, dash, space.
Enclose each series statement (see 1.6J) in parentheses.
Precede each parallel title by an equals sign.
Precede other title information by a colon.
Precede the first statement of responsibility by a diagonal slash.
Precede each subsequent statement of responsibility by a semicolon.
Precede the ISSN of a series or subseries by a comma.
Precede the numbering within a series or subseries by a semicolon.
Precede the title of a subseries by a full stop.

2.6B. Series statements

2.6B1. Record each series statement as instructed in 1.6.

(Typophile chap books ; 7)

(Britain advances ; 10)

(The king penguin books)

(Special paper / Geological Society of America)

(Publicación / Universidad de Chile, Departamento de Geología ; no. 28)

(Occasional papers / University of Sussex Centre for Continuing Education, ISSN 0306-1108 ; no. 4)

(Department of State publication ; 8583. East Asian and Pacific series ; 199)

(Olympia Press traveller's companion series ; no. 105)

(Acta Universitatis Stockholmiensis. Stockholm studies in the history of literature ; 10)

(Acta Universitatis Stockholmiensis. Studia Hungarica Stockholmiensia ; 6)

(Treaty series ; no. 66 (1976)) (Cmnd. ; 6580)
  (*Numbering of first series transcribed from the item*)

(Graeco-Roman memoirs, ISSN 0306-9222 ; no. 62)

(Scríbhinni Gaeilge na mBráthar Mionúr ; imleabhar 11)

(Works / Charles Dickens ; v. 12)

2.7. NOTE AREA

Contents:
> 2.7A. Preliminary rule
> 2.7B. Notes

2.7A. Preliminary rule

2.7A1. Punctuation
Precede each note by a full stop, space, dash, space *or* start a new paragraph for each.

Separate introductory wording from the main content of a note by a colon followed but not preceded by a space.

2.7A2. In making notes, follow the instructions in 1.7A.

2.7B. Notes
Make notes as set out in the following subrules and in the order given there. However, give a particular note first when it has been decided that note is of primary importance.

2.7B1. Nature, scope, or artistic form. Make notes on these matters unless they are apparent from the rest of the description.

> "Collection of essays on economic subjects"
>
> Arabic reader
>
> Play in 3 acts
>
> Scenario of film

2.7B2. Language of item and/or translation or adaptation. Make notes on the language(s) of the item, or on the fact that it is a translation or adaptation, unless this is apparent from the rest of the description.

> Translation of: La muerte de Artemio Cruz
>
> Author's adaptation of his Russian text
>
> Latin text, parallel English translation
>
> Adaptation of: The taming of the shrew / William Shakespeare

2.7B3. Source of title proper. Make notes on the source of the title proper if the chief source of information is a title page substitute.

Caption title

Title from spine

2.7B4. Variations in title. Make notes on titles borne by the item other than the title proper. *Optionally*, give a romanization of the title proper.

Added t.p. in Russian

Previously published as: Enter Psmith

Cover title: The fair American

2.7B5. Parallel titles and other title information. Give the title in another language and other title information not recorded in the title and statement of responsibility area if they are considered to be important.

Subtitle: The medicinal, culinary, cosmetic and economic
properties, cultivation, and folklore of herbs, grasses, fungi, shrubs,
and trees, with all their modern scientific uses

Title on added t.p.: Les rats

2.7B6. Statements of responsibility. Make notes on variant names of persons or bodies named in statements of responsibility if these are considered to be important for identification. Give statements of responsibility not recorded in the title and statement of responsibility area. Make notes on persons or bodies connected with a work, or significant persons or bodies connected with previous editions and not already named in the description.

At head of title: *[Name not used in the main entry heading and with indeterminate responsibility for the work]*

"Also attributed to Jonathan Swift"—Introd.

"Begun by Jane Austen in 1817 ... completed, some 160 years later, by another lady"—Cover

2.7B7. Edition and history. Make notes relating to the edition being described or to the bibliographic history of the work.

"This issue is founded on the second edition, printed by Rudolf
Ackermann in the year 1837 (with considerable additions) from
The new sporting magazine"—T.p. verso

Previous ed.: Harmondsworth : Penguin, 1950

Sequel to: Mémoires d'un médecin

2.7B9. Publication, distribution, etc. Make notes on publication, distribution, etc., details that are not included in the publication, distribution, etc., area and are considered to be important.

Imprint under label reads: Humanitas-Verlag Zürich

"Privately printed"

Published simultaneously in Canada

2.7B10. Physical description. Make notes on important physical details that are not included in the physical description area. Make notes on braille or other tactile books.

> Captions on verso of plates
>
> Printed on vellum
>
> Limited ed. of 60 signed and numbered copies
>
> Alternate pages blank
>
> No more published
>
> Two charts on folded leaves in pocket
>
> Tables on 4 leaves in pocket
>
> Grade 3 braille
>
> Alternate leaves of print and braille
>
> Coloured map of Australia on endpapers

2.7B11. Accompanying material. Make notes on the location of accompanying material if appropriate. Give details of accompanying material neither mentioned in the physical description area nor given a separate description (see 1.5E).

> Slides in pocket
>
> "Tables I, II, and III omitted by error from report" published as supplement (5 p.) and inserted at end
>
> Accompanied by: A demographic atlas of north-west Ireland. 39 p. : col. maps ; 36 cm. Previously published separately in 1956

2.7B12. Series. Make notes on series data that cannot be given in the series area.

> Series title romanized: Min hady al-Islām
>
> Also issued without series statement
>
> Originally issued in series: Environmental science series
>   (*For another edition*)

2.7B13. Dissertations. If the item being described is a dissertation, make a note as instructed in 1.7B13.

2.7B14. Audience. Make a brief note of the intended audience for, or intellectual level of, an item if this information is stated in the item.

> For 9-12 year olds
>
> Undergraduate text
>
> Intended audience: Preschool children

2.7B16. Other formats. Give the details of other formats in which the content of the item has been issued.

> Issued also as computer file

2.7B17. Summary. Give a brief objective summary of the content of an item unless another part of the description provides enough information.

> Summary: Kate and Ben follow their rabbit into a haunted house and discover the source of the house's ghostly sound

2.7B18. Contents. List the contents of an item, either selectively or fully, if it is considered necessary to show the presence of material not implied by the rest of the description; to stress items of particular importance; or to list the contents of a collection or of a multipart item. When recording titles formally, take them from the source in the item being catalogued that provides the best identification.

> Bibliography: p. 859-910

> Includes bibliographies

> Includes index

> Statistical tables cover periods between 1849 and 1960

> Contents: Love and peril / the Marquis of Lorne — To be or not to be / Mrs. Alexander — The melancholy hussar / Thomas Hardy

> Partial contents: Recent economic growth in historical perspective / by K. Ohkawa and H. Rosovsky — The place of Japan ... in world trade / by P.H. Tresize

> Contents: How these records were discovered — A short sketch of the Talmuds — Constantine's letter

2.7B19. Numbers. Give important numbers borne by the item other than ISBNs (see 2.8B).

> Supt. of Docs. no: HE20.8216:11

2.7B20. Copy being described, library's holdings, and restrictions on use. Make these notes as instructed in 1.7B20.

> Library's copy lacks appendices, p. 245-260

> Library has v. 1, 3-5, and 7 only

> Library's copy signed and with marginalia by the author

2.7B21. "With" notes. If the title and statement of responsibility area contains a title that applies to only a part of an item lacking a collective title and, therefore, more than one entry is made, make a note beginning *With:* and listing the other separately titled works in the item in the order in which they appear there.

> With: The reformed school / John Dury. London : Printed for R. Wadnothe, [1650]

> With: Out of the depths / Mary Ryan. [New York? : s.n., 1945?] — Label your luggage / Robert Nash. [New York? : s.n., 1945?]

> With: Of the sister arts / H. Jacob. New York : [s.n.], 1970

2.8. STANDARD NUMBER AND TERMS OF AVAILABILITY AREA

Contents:
  2.8A. Preliminary rule
  2.8B. International Standard Book Number
  2.8C. Terms of availability
  2.8D. Qualification

2.8A. Preliminary rule

2.8A1. Punctuation

For instructions on the use of spaces before and after prescribed punctuation, see 1.0C.

Precede this area by a full stop, space, dash, space *or* start a new paragraph.

Precede each repetition of this area by a full stop, space, dash, space.

Precede terms of availability by a colon.

Enclose a qualification to the International Standard Book Number (ISBN) or terms of availability in parentheses.

2.8B. International Standard Book Number (ISBN)

2.8B1. Give ISBNs as instructed in 1.8B.

> ISBN 0-904576-17-5

> ISBN 0-8352-0875-3 (corrected)

2.8B2. Give any other number in a note (see 2.7B19).

2.8C. *Optional addition.* Terms of availability

2.8C1. Give the price or other terms on which the item is available. Give the price in symbols and numbers, and other terms as concisely as possible.

> ISBN 0-85435-332-1 : £0.60

> ISBN 0-902573-45-4 : Subscribers only

> ISBN 0-7043-3100-4 : $1.95

2.8D. Qualification

2.8D1. Add qualifications (including the type of binding) to the ISBN and/or terms of availability as instructed in 1.8E. Additionally, if volumes in a set have different ISBNs, follow each ISBN with the designation of the volume to which it applies.

> ISBN 0-901212-04-0 (v. 38)

ISBN 0-19-212192-8 (cased). — ISBN 0-19-281123-1 (pbk.)

ISBN 0-08-019857-0 (set). — ISBN 0-08-019856-2 (v. 1 : pbk.)

ISBN 0-900002-92-1 (limited ed.) : £35.00 (£30.00 to members of the association)

ISBN 0-7225-0344-X (pbk.) : £8.75

2.9. SUPPLEMENTARY ITEMS

2.9A. Describe supplementary items as instructed in 1.9.

2.10. ITEMS MADE UP OF SEVERAL TYPES OF MATERIAL

2.10A. Describe items made up of several types of material as instructed in 1.10.

2.11. FACSIMILES, PHOTOCOPIES, AND OTHER REPRODUCTIONS

2.11A. Describe facsimiles, photocopies, and other reproductions as instructed in 1.11.

Early Printed Monographs

2.12. SCOPE

2.12A. The following rules (2.13–2.18) are extra rules for the description of early books, pamphlets, and broadsides (for the most part, pre-nineteenth-century publications). In general, follow the instructions in chapter 1 and in 2.1–2.11 for describing those materials and use the additional and modifying rules given below only when the conditions they state apply to the early book, etc., or when, as in 2.16, they contain instructions different from the previous rules. Consult specialized reference materials for more detailed treatment of early printed books, etc.

2.13. CHIEF SOURCE OF INFORMATION

2.13A. If the early book, etc., has a title page, use it as the chief source of information. If it has no title page, use the following sources (in this order of preference):

> caption
> colophon
> cover
> running title
> incipit *or* explicit
> privilege *or* imprimatur
> other sources

If the item has no title page, make a note indicating the source used (see 2.18B).

2.14. TITLE AND STATEMENT OF RESPONSIBILITY AREA

2.14A. If the item has no title page and if no other source furnishes a title proper, transcribe as the title proper as many of the opening words of the text as are sufficient to identify the item uniquely.

2.14B. In abridging a long title proper (see 1.1B4), omit first any alternative title and the connecting word (e.g., *or*), then omit inessential words or groups of words. Indicate omissions by the mark of omission.

> *Title appears as*:
>   Revelation examined with candour. Or a fair enquiry into the sense and use of the several revelations expressly declared or sufficiently implied to be given to mankind from the Creation as they are found in the Bible

> *Title proper recorded as*:
>   Revelation examined with candour ...

2.14C. Omit mottoes, quotations, dedications, statements, etc., appearing on the title page that are separate from the title proper.

2.14D. Treat additions to the title, even if they are linked to it by a preposition, conjunction, prepositional phrase, etc., as other title information, not as part of the title proper.

> The English Parliament represented in a vision : with an after-thought upon the speech delivered to His Most Christian Majesty by the deputies of the states of Britany on the 29th day of February last ... : to which is added at large the memorable representation of the House of Commons to the Queen in the year 1711/12 ...

2.14E. Transcription of certain letters

2.14E1. Transcribe capitals that are to be converted to lowercase according to the usage of the text. If the usage of the text is in doubt or if it is inconsistent, transcribe

> I as i
> J as i
> U as u (but as v when it is the first letter of the word)
> V as u (but as v when it is the first letter of the word)
> VV as uu (but as vv when it is the first letter of the word)

Transcribe gothic capitals in the form of J and U as I and V.

2.14F. Abridge lengthy other title information and statements of responsibility by omitting inessential words or groups of words. Include as many words of a statement of responsibility as are necessary to identify the person(s) concerned.

2.15. EDITION AREA

2.15A. In general, give an edition statement as it is found in the item. Otherwise, give standard abbreviations and arabic numerals in place of words as instructed in 1.2B.

Nunc primum in lucem aedita

Editio secunda auctior et correctior

Cinquième édition   *or*   5e éd.

2.15B. If the edition statement is an integral part of the title proper, other title information, or statement of responsibility, or if it is grammatically linked to any of these, give it as such and do not make a further edition statement.

Chirurgia / nunc iterum non mediocri studio atque diligentia a pluribus mendis purgata

2.16. PUBLICATION, ETC., AREA

2.16A. A publisher statement may refer to one or more publishers, distributors, booksellers, or printers.

2.16B. Transcribe the place of publication, etc., as it is found in the item. It may include the name(s) of publishers, printers, etc. Supply the modern name of the place if it is considered necessary for identification.

Augustae Treverorum [Trier]

2.16C. If more than one place of publication, etc., is found in the item, transcribe the first, and *optionally*, the others in the order in which they appear. If second or subsequent places are omitted, add *[etc.]*.

London [etc.]

or   Londres ; et se trouve à Paris

2.16D. Give the rest of the details relating to the publisher, etc., as they are given in the item. Separate the parts of a complex publisher, etc., statement only if they are presented separately in the item. If the publisher, etc., statement includes the name of a printer, give it here. Omit words in the publisher, etc., statement that do not aid in the identification of the item and do not indicate the role of the publisher, etc. Indicate omissions by the mark of omission.

London : R. Barker

London : Printed for the author and sold by J. Roberts

London : Impressi per me Wilhelmum de Machlinia in opulentissima civitate Londonarium iuxta pontem qui vulgariter dicitur Flete Brigge

London : Imprinted ... by Robt. Barker ... and by the assigns of John Bill

> Enprynted at Westmyster in Caxtons hous : By me Wynken the Worde
>
> Birmingham : Printed by John Baskerville for R. and J. Dodsley
>
> ...
>
> Paris : Chez Testu, imprimeur-libraire
>
> Paris : Ex officina Ascensiana : Impendio Joannis Parvi

2.16E. If there is more than one statement relating to publishers, etc., give the first statement, and *optionally*, the other statements in the order in which they appear. If subsequent statements are omitted, add *[etc.]*.

> London : Printed for the author and sold by J. Parsons [etc.]

2.16F. Give the date of publication or printing, including the day and month, as found in the item and add any necessary correction. Add the day and/or month in modern terms. Change roman numerals indicating the year to arabic numerals unless they are misprinted, in which case give the roman numerals and add a correction. Add the date in the modern chronology if this is considered to be necessary.

> 1716
>
> iv Ian 1497
>
> xii Kal. Sept. [21 Aug.] 1473
>
> In vigilia S. Laurentii Martyris [9 Aug.] 1492
>
> iii Mar. 1483 [i.e. 1484]
>
> 1733
>   (*Date in book:* MDCCXXXIII)
>
> DMLII [i.e. 1552]

Optionally, formalize the date if the statement appearing in the item is very long.

> 18 May 1507
>   (*Date in book:* Anno gratiae millesimo quingentesimo septimo die vero decimoctavo Maij)

2.16G. If the item is undated and the date of publication is unknown, give an approximate date.

> [1492?]
>
> [not after Aug. 21, 1492]
>
> [between 1711 and 1719]

2.16H. If the printer is named separately in the item and the printer can clearly be distinguished from the publisher or bookseller, give the place of printing and the name of the printer as instructed in 1.4G.

2.17. PHYSICAL DESCRIPTION AREA

2.17A. Extent

2.17A1. In recording the pagination of single volume or multivolume (see 2.5B) early books, etc., give each sequence of leaves, pages, or columns in the terms and form presented in the item. If the volume is printed in pages but numbered as leaves, give the numbering as leaves. If required, give more precise information about pagination, blank leaves, or other aspects of collation, by *either* expanding the statement of extent (if this can be done succinctly) *or* making a note.

> xi, 31 p.
>
> XII, 120 leaves
>
> x, 32 p., 90 leaves
>
> xi, [79] leaves
>
> [160] p.
>
> 40 leaves, [8] p.

Describe broadsides as such and other single sheets as *sheets*.

> 1 broadside
>
> 1 sheet
>
> [2] sheets
>
> VIII sheets

2.17B. Illustrations

2.17B1. Describe an illustrated item as instructed in 2.5C. *Optionally*, add *woodcuts*, *metal cuts*, etc., as appropriate.

> : ill. (woodcuts)
>
> : 30 ill. (cuts)
>
> : ill. (woodcuts, some col.)
>
> : ill. (woodcuts), ports.
>
> : ports. (woodcuts)
>
> : ports. (engravings)

If the item is illustrated by hand or if the illustrations are hand coloured, make a note (see 2.18E).

2.17C. Dimensions

2.17C1. Give the dimensions of the item as instructed in 2.5D. Add the format to the dimensions of a volume in an abbreviated form (e.g., *fol.*, *4to*, *8vo*, *12mo*).

> ; 23 cm. (4to)

> ; 20 cm. (8vo)

> ; 33 cm. (fol.)

> ; 23 cm. (4to)

> 1 sheet ; 48 × 27 cm.

2.18. NOTE AREA

2.18A. Make notes as instructed in 2.7 and follow the instructions given below. Always make the notes below for incunabula.

If the formalized description of the areas preceding the note area does not identify the edition or issue being catalogued clearly, make notes to identify the item unambiguously. When appropriate, refer to a detailed description in a standard catalogue or bibliography (see 2.18C).

2.18B. Source of title proper

2.18B1. Give the source of the title proper if it is not the title page.

> Title from colophon

> Title from: Incipit leaf [2][a]

2.18C. Bibliographic references

2.18C1. For incunabula, and *optionally* for other early books, etc., cite briefly descriptions in standard lists in accordance with standard practice.

> Reference: HR 6471

> *or* Reference: Hain-Reichling 6471

> References: BMC (XV cent.) II, p. 346 (IB.5874); Schramm, v. 4, p. 10, 50, and ill.

2.18D. Signatures

2.18D1. If desired, make a note giving details of the signatures.

> Signatures: a-v^8, x^6

2.18E. Physical description

2.18E1. If desired, give the number of columns or lines and the type measurements. Give fuller details of the illustrations if considered necessary. Make a note on colour printing.

24 lines; type 24G

Woodcuts on leaves B2[b] and C5[b] signed: b

Woodcuts: ill., initials, publisher's and printer's devices

Title and headings printed in red

2.18F. Copy being described

2.18F1. Make notes on special features of the copy in hand. These include rubrication, illumination and other hand colouring, manuscript additions, binding (if noteworthy), provenance, and imperfections.

Leaves I5-6 incorrectly bound between h3 and h4

Imperfect: wanting leaves 12 and 13 (b6 and c1); also the blank last leaf (S8)

On vellum. Illustrations and part of borders hand coloured. With illuminated initials. Rubricated in red and blue

Contemporary doeskin over boards; clasp. Stamp: Château de La Roche Guyon, Bibliothèque

Blind stamped pigskin binding (1644) with initials C.S.A.C.

Inscription on inside of front cover: Theodorinis ab Engelsberg

Signed: Alex. Pope

CHAPTER 3

CARTOGRAPHIC MATERIALS

Contents

3.0. GENERAL RULES

3.0A. Scope

3.0A1. The rules in this chapter cover the description of cartographic materials of all kinds. Cartographic materials include all materials that represent the whole or part of the earth or any celestial body. These include two- and three-dimensional maps and plans (including maps of imaginary places); aeronautical, navigational, and celestial charts; atlases; globes; block diagrams; map sections; aerial photographs with a cartographic purpose; bird's-eye views (map views); etc. They do not cover in detail the description of early or manuscript cartographic materials, though the use of an additional term in the physical description (see 3.5B) and/or the use of the specific instructions in chapter 4 will furnish a sufficiently detailed description for the general library catalogue. For items falling within the scope of other chapters but presenting cartographic information (e.g., some wall charts, some playing cards), consult the rules in this chapter in conjunction with those of the chapter appropriate to the item.

3.0B. Sources of information

3.0B1. For sources of information for a printed atlas, see 2.0B.

3.0B2. Chief source of information. The chief source of information for other than a printed atlas (in order of preference) is:

  a) the cartographic item itself; when an item is in a number of physical parts, treat all the parts (including a title sheet) as the cartographic item itself
  b) container (e.g., portfolio, cover, envelope) or case, the cradle and stand of a globe, etc.

If information is not available from the chief source, take it from any accompanying printed material (e.g., pamphlets, brochures).

3.0B3. Prescribed sources of information. The prescribed source(s) of information for each area of the description of cartographic materials is set out below. Enclose information taken from outside the prescribed source(s) in square brackets.

AREA	PRESCRIBED SOURCES OF INFORMATION
Title and statement of responsibility	Chief source of information
Edition	Chief source of information, accompanying printed material
Mathematical data	Chief source of information, accompanying printed material
Publication, distribution, etc.	Chief source of information, accompanying printed material

Physical description	Any source
Series	Chief source of information, accompanying printed material
Note	Any source
Standard number and terms of availability	Any source

3.0C. Punctuation

For the punctuation of the description as a whole, see 1.0C.
For the prescribed punctuation of elements, see the following rules.

3.0D. Levels of detail in the description

Follow the instructions in 1.0D. Additionally, in a first-level description include the scale in the mathematical data area and, in a second-level description, include all the mathematical data specified in 3.3.

3.0E. Language and script of the description

See 1.0E.

3.0F. Inaccuracies

See 1.0F.

3.0G. Accents and other diacritical marks

See 1.0G.

3.0H. Items with several chief sources of information

See 1.0H.

3.0J. Description of whole or part

3.0J1. In describing a collection of maps, describe the collection as a whole *or* describe each map (giving the name of the collection as the series), according to the needs of the cataloguing agency. If the collection is catalogued as a whole and descriptions of the individual parts are considered desirable, see chapter 13. If in doubt whether to describe the collection as a whole or to describe each part separately, describe the collection as a whole.

Description of the collection as a whole

Ordnance Survey of Great Britain one inch to one mile map [GMD] : seventh series. — Scale 1:63,360. — Chessington : The Survey, 1952-1974. — 190 maps : col. ; 71 × 64 cm.

[Plans of the Rideau Canal from Kingston Bay to Ottawa] [GMD] / [signed by] John By ... [et al.]. — Scales vary. — 1827-1828. — 28 ms. maps : col. ; 74 × 234 cm. or smaller. — Provenance stamps: Board of Ordnance, Inspector General of Fortifications; sheets AA3-6, 9-11, 13-32

Description of one map—separate description

Banbury [GMD] / Ordnance Survey. — [Ed.] B. — Scale 1:63,360. — Southampton : The Survey, 1968. — 1 map : col. ; 71 × 64 cm. — (Ordnance Survey of Great Britain one inch to one mile map : seventh series ; sheet 145). — "Fully revised 1965-66"

Locks and dams at Merrick Mills, sect. no. 5 [GMD] / [signed by] John By. — Scale [1:1,050]. — 1827 Oct. 25. — 1 ms. map : col. ; 65 × 75 cm. — ([Plans of the Rideau Canal from Kingston Bay to Ottawa / signed by] John By ... [et al.] ; sheet AA29). — Provenance stamps: Board of Ordnance, Inspector General of Fortifications

Description of one map—multilevel description

Ordnance Survey of Great Britain one inch to one mile map [GMD] : seventh series. — Scale 1:63,360. — Chessington : The Survey, 1952-1974. — 190 maps : col. ; 71 × 64 cm.
   Sheet 145: Banbury. — [Ed.] B. — Southampton, 1968. — 1 map : col. ; 71 × 64 cm. — "Fully revised 1965-66"

[Plans of the Rideau Canal from Kingston Bay to Ottawa] [GMD] / [signed by] John By ... [et al.]. — Scales vary. — 1827-1828. — 28 ms. maps : col. ; 74 × 234 cm. or smaller
   Sheet AA29: Locks and dams at Merrick Mills, sect. no. 5. — Scale [1:1,050]. — 1827 Oct. 25. — 1 ms. map : col. ; 65 × 75 cm. — Provenance stamps: Board of Ordnance, Inspector General of Fortifications

3.1. TITLE AND STATEMENT OF RESPONSIBILITY AREA

Contents:
   3.1A. Preliminary rule
   3.1B. Title proper
   3.1C. General material designation
   3.1D. Parallel titles
   3.1E. Other title information
   3.1F. Statements of responsibility
   3.1G. Items without a collective title

3.1A. Preliminary rule

3.1A1. Punctuation

For instructions on the use of spaces before and after prescribed punctuation, see 1.0C.
   Precede the title of a supplement or section (see 1.1B9) by a full stop.
   Enclose the general material designation in square brackets.
   Precede each parallel title by an equals sign.
   Precede each unit of other title information by a colon.
   Precede the first statement of responsibility by a diagonal slash.

Precede each subsequent statement of responsibility by a semicolon.
For the punctuation of this area for items without a collective title, see 1.1G.

3.1B. Title proper

3.1B1. Transcribe the title proper as instructed in 1.1B.

> Historical north England

> A map of the county of Essex

> Road map of 50 miles around London

> England & Wales

> The Edinburgh world atlas, or, Advanced atlas of modern geography

> Bouguer gravity anomaly map of Tennessee

> Františkovy Lázně orientačni plán

> British maps of the American Revolution

> The Faber atlas

> Map of Middle Earth

> Geographia marketing and sales maps of Europe

If the title proper is not taken from the chief source of information, give the source of the title in a note (see 3.7B3).

3.1B2. If the title proper includes a statement of the scale, include that statement in the transcription.

> Topographic 1:500,000 low flying chart

> New half-inch cycling road maps of England and Wales

3.1B3. If the chief source of information bears more than one title, choose the title proper as instructed in 1.1B8. If both or all of the titles are in the same language and script, choose the title proper on the basis of the sequence or layout of the titles. If these are insufficient to enable the choice to be made or are ambiguous, choose the most comprehensive title.

3.1B4. If the item lacks a title, supply one as instructed in 1.1B7. Always include in the supplied title the name of the area covered.

> [Map of Ontario]

> [Lunar globe]

> [Gravity anomaly map of Canada]

> [Relief model of California showing vegetation]

> [Nautical chart of the coast of Maine from Cape Elizabeth to Monhegan Island]

3.1C. *Optional addition.* **General material designation**

3.1C1. Give immediately following the title proper the appropriate general material designation as instructed in 1.1C.

> Central Europe [GMD]
>
> Camden's Britannia, 1695 [GMD]
>
> Decca aeronautical plotting chart [GMD]

3.1C2. If an item contains parts belonging to materials falling into two or more categories, and if none of these is the predominant constituent of the item, give either *multimedia* or *kit* as the designation (see 1.1C1 and 1.10C1).

3.1D. Parallel titles

3.1D1. Transcribe parallel titles as instructed in 1.1D.

> Suomi [GMD] = Finland
>
> International map of natural gas fields in Europe [GMD] = Carte internationale des champs de gaz naturel en Europe
>
> Mobil street map of Durban [GMD] = Straatkaart van Durban

3.1E. Other title information

3.1E1. Transcribe other title information as instructed in 1.1E.

> Canada [GMD] : a pictorial & historical map
>
> Ethelreda's Isle [GMD] : a pictorial map of the Isle of Ely to commemorate the 1300th anniversary of the founding of Ely's conventual church
>
> Motor road map of south-east England [GMD] : showing trunk and other classified roads
>
> Kaunispää-Kopsusjärvi [GMD] : ulkoilukartta

3.1E2. If the title proper does not include an indication of the geographic area covered by the item and if the other title information does not include such an indication or if there is no other title information, supply, as other title information, a word or brief phrase indicating the area covered.

> Vegetation [GMD] : [in Botswana]

3.1F. Statements of responsibility

3.1F1. Transcribe statements of responsibility relating to persons or bodies as instructed in 1.1F.

> Football history map of England and Wales [GMD] : showing ... the colours and locations of all the clubs in the Football League ... / compiled by John Carvosso

The English pilot, the fifth book [GMD] / J. Seller & C. Price

A map book of West Germany [GMD] / A.J.B. Tussler, A.J.L. Alden

Road atlas Europe [GMD] / Bartholomew

World atlas [GMD] / compiled by Rand McNally International

The Wills south coast yachting guide [GMD] / edited by The daily express

Flugbild Schweiz [GMD] = Vue aérienne Suisse = Air view Switzerland / Swissair Photo + Vermessungen AG

Maps & plans of the operations, movements, battles & sieges of the British Army, during the campaigns in Spain, Portugal, and the south of France, from 1808 to 1814 [GMD] / compiled by Lieut. Godwin ; engraved by Jas. Wyld

Glacial map of Tasmania [GMD] / compiled by E. Derbyshire ... [et al.]

[Pocket terrestrial globe] [GMD] / J. Moxon

Mondmapo [GMD] / laŭ la decidoj de Internacia Komisiono por Ordigo de Geografiaj Nomoj ; redaktis, Tibor Sekelj

Wheaton's atlas of British and world history [GMD] / by T.A. Rennard ; editors, H.E.L. Mellersh and B.S. Trinder ; maps prepared by David A. Hoxley

3.1F2. Add a word or short phrase to the statement of responsibility if the relationship between the title and the person(s) or body (bodies) named in the statement is not clear.

Maps of the Mid-west [GMD] / [edited by] D.M. Bagley

3.1G. Items without a collective title

3.1G1. If a cartographic item lacks a collective title, *either* describe the item as a unit (see 3.1G2 and 3.1G3), *or* make a separate description for each separately titled part (see 3.1G4), *or* (in certain circumstances) supply a collective title (see 3.1G5).

3.1G2. In describing as a unit a cartographic item lacking a collective title, transcribe the titles of the individual parts as instructed in 1.1G3.

Grand Teton [GMD] ; Yellowstone National Park
  (*Both maps produced by the same body*)

Daily mail motor road map of London and twelve miles round [GMD]. Motor road map of south-east England
  (*Maps produced by different bodies*)

3.1G3. Make the relationship between statements of responsibility and the parts of an item lacking a collective title and described as a unit clear by additions as instructed in 3.1F2.

>France [GMD] ; Germany / drawn by L. Scott [France] & P. McComb [Germany]

3.1G4. *Optionally*, make a separate description for each separately titled part of an item lacking a collective title. For the statement of the extent in each of these descriptions, see 3.5B4. Link the separate descriptions with notes (see 3.7B21).

3.1G5. If a cartographic item lacking a collective title consists of a large number of physically separate parts, supply a collective title as instructed in 3.1B4.

>[Maps of Denmark]

>[Collection of tourist maps of Thailand published by various authorities]

>[Ontario county and district maps colour series]

3.2. EDITION AREA

Contents:
>3.2A. Preliminary rule
>3.2B. Edition statement
>3.2C. Statements of responsibility relating to the edition
>3.2D. Statement relating to a named revision of an edition
>3.2E. Statements of responsibility relating to a named revision of an edition

3.2A. Preliminary rule

3.2A1. Punctuation
For instructions on the use of spaces before and after prescribed punctuation, see 1.0C.

Precede this area by a full stop, space, dash, space.

Precede a statement relating to a named revision of an edition by a comma.

Precede the first statement of responsibility following an edition statement by a diagonal slash.

Precede each subsequent statement of responsibility by a semicolon.

3.2B. Edition statement

3.2B1. Transcribe a statement relating to an edition of a work that contains differences from other editions of that work, or to a named reissue of a work, as instructed in 1.2B.

>2nd ed.

>1974 new ed.

>Rev. et corr.

Facsim. ed.

2ᵉ éd.

3.2B2. In case of doubt about whether a statement is an edition statement, follow the instructions in 1.2B3.

3.2B3. *Optional addition.* If an item lacks an edition statement but is known to contain significant changes from other editions, supply a suitable brief statement in the language and script of the title proper and enclose it in square brackets.

[5th ed.]

[Nouv. éd.]

3.2B4. If an edition statement appears in more than one language or script, transcribe the statement that is in the language or script of the title proper. If this criterion does not apply, transcribe the statement that appears first.

Carte géologique internationale de l'Europe [GMD] = International geological map of Europe. — 3ᵉ éd.

Optionally, transcribe the parallel statement(s), each preceded by an equals sign.

3.2B5. If an item lacking a collective title and described as a unit contains one or more works with an associated edition statement, transcribe such statements following the titles and statements of responsibility to which they relate, separated from them by a full stop.

3.2C. Statements of responsibility relating to the edition

3.2C1. Transcribe a statement of responsibility relating to one or more editions, but not to all editions, of a cartographic item as instructed in 1.2C and 3.1F.

3rd ed. / with maps redrawn by N. Manley

3.2D. Statement relating to a named revision of an edition

3.2D1. If an item is a named revision of an edition, transcribe the statement relating to that revision as instructed in 1.2D.

9th ed., Repr. with summary of the 1961 census and suppl. of additional names and amendments

4th ed., Roads rev.

[Ed.] A, [Three bars, one star]
(*Appears on item as:* A ≡ ★)

Do not record statements relating to a reissue that contains no changes unless the item is considered to be of particular importance to the cataloguing agency.

3.2E. Statements of responsibility relating to a named revision of an edition

3.2E1. Transcribe a statement of responsibility relating to one or more named revisions of an edition (but not to all such revisions) as instructed in 1.2E and 3.1F.

3.3. MATHEMATICAL DATA AREA

Contents:
>3.3A. Preliminary rule
>3.3B. Statement of scale
>3.3C. Statement of projection
>3.3D. Statement of coordinates and equinox

3.3A. Preliminary rule

3.3A1. Punctuation

For instructions on the use of spaces before and after prescribed punctuation, see 1.0C.

Precede this area by a full stop, space, dash, space.

Precede the projection statement by a semicolon.

Enclose the statement of coordinates and equinox in one pair of parentheses.

If both coordinates and equinox are given, precede the statement of equinox by a semicolon.

Precede the statement of epoch by a comma.

3.3A2. Use English words and abbreviations in this area.

3.3B. Statement of scale

3.3B1. Give the scale of a cartographic item (except as noted below) as a representative fraction expressed as a ratio (1:   ). Precede the ratio by *Scale*. Give the scale even if it is already recorded as part of the title proper or other title information.

>Scale ca. 1:36,000,000
>   (*Scale as it appears on the item*)

>Bartholomew one inch map of the Lake District [GMD]. — Rev. — Scale 1:63,360

If a scale statement found in the chief source of information or accompanying material is not expressed as a representative fraction, give it as a representative fraction in square brackets.

>Scale [1:253,440]
>   (*Scale statement reads:* 1 inch to 4 miles)

If a representative fraction or other scale statement is found in a source other than the chief source of information or accompanying material (e.g., on a container or case not used as the chief source), give the scale as a representative fraction in square brackets.

>Scale [1:63,360]

If no scale statement is found in the chief source of information or accompanying material or on the item's container or case, compute a representative fraction from a bar graph or a grid or by comparison with a map of known scale, and give it in square brackets preceded by *ca.*

> Scale [ca. 1:63,360]

If no scale can be determined by any of the above means, give *Scale indeterminable.*

3.3B2. *Optional addition.* Give additional scale information that is found on the item (such as a statement of comparative measures or limitation of the scale to particular parts of the item). Use standard abbreviations and numerals in place of words. Precede such additional information by a full stop.

> Scale 1:250,000. 1 in. to 3.95 miles. 1 cm. to 2.5 km.

Quote the additional scale information if:

> a) the statement presents unusual information that cannot be verified by the cataloguer

or b) a direct quotation is more precise than a statement in conventional form

or c) the statement on the item is in error or contains errors.

> Scale 1:59,403,960. "Along meridians only, 1 inch = 936 statute miles"

> Scale [ca. 1:90,000] not "1 inch to the mile"

3.3B3. If the scale within one item varies and the outside values are known, give both scales connected by a hyphen.

> Scale 1:15,000-1:25,000

If the values are not known, give *Scale varies.*

3.3B4. If the description is of a multipart item with two scales, give both. Give the larger scale first.

> Scale 1:100,000 and 1:200,000

3.3B5. If the description is of a multipart item with three or more scales, give *Scales vary.*

3.3B6. In describing a cartographic item in which all the main maps are of one or two scales, give the scale or both scales (in the latter case give the larger scale first). If the main maps are of three or more scales, give *Scales vary.*

3.3B7. Give a statement of scale for celestial charts, maps of imaginary places, views (bird's-eye views or map views), and maps with nonlinear scales only if the information appears on the item. If the item is not drawn to scale, give *Not drawn to scale.*

> Scale 1′ per 2 cm.

3.3B8. In describing a relief model or other three-dimensional item, give the vertical scale (specified as such) after the horizontal scale if the vertical scale can be ascertained.

       Scale 1:744,080. 1 in. to ca. 28 miles. Vertical scale ca. 1:96,000

       Scale 1:250,000. Vertical exaggeration 1:5

3.3C. Statement of projection

3.3C1. Give the statement of projection if it is found on the item, its container or case, or accompanying printed material. Use abbreviations as instructed in appendix B and numerals as instructed in appendix C.

       ; conic equidistant proj.

3.3C2. *Optional addition.* Give phrases associated with the projection statement in the source of information that concern, for example, meridians, parallels, and/ or ellipsoid.

       ; transverse Mercator proj. Everest spheroid

       ; azimuthal equidistant proj. centered on Nicosia, N 35° 10′, E 33° 22′

3.3D. *Optional addition.* Statement of coordinates and equinox

3.3D1. For terrestrial maps, etc., give the coordinates in the following order:

           westernmost extent of area covered by item (longitude)
           easternmost extent of area covered by item (longitude)
           northernmost extent of area covered by item (latitude)
           southernmost extent of area covered by item (latitude)

Express the coordinates in degrees (°), minutes (′), and seconds (″) of the sexagesimal system (360° circle) taken from the Greenwich prime meridian. Precede each coordinate by W, E, N, or S, as appropriate. Separate the two sets of latitude and longitude by a diagonal slash neither preceded nor followed by a space. Separate each longitude or latitude from its counterpart by a dash.

       (E 79°–E 86°/N 20°–N 12°)

       (E 15° 00′ 00″–E 17° 30′ 45″/N 1° 30′ 12″–S 2° 30′ 35″)

       (W 74° 50′–W 74° 40′/N 45° 05′–N 45° 00′)

Optionally, give other meridians found on the item in the note area (see 3.7B8).

3.3D2. For celestial charts, give as coordinates the right ascension of the item, or the right ascensions of the western and eastern limits of its collective coverage, and the declination of the centre of the item, or the northern and southern limits of its collective coverage.

Designate the right ascension by *RA*, followed by the hours and, when necessary, minutes and seconds of the twenty-four-hour clock.

Designate the declination by *Decl.*, followed by the degrees (°) and, when necessary, minutes (') and seconds ('') of the sexagesimal system (360° circle), using a plus sign (+) for the northern celestial hemisphere and a minus sign (−) for the southern celestial hemisphere.

Separate right ascensions and declinations from each other by a diagonal slash, neither preceded nor followed by a space. When two right ascensions are found, give both separated by *to*. When two declinations are found, give both separated by *to*.

When coordinates are given, give also the statement of equinox. Express the equinox as a year preceded by a semicolon and *eq*. Give also a statement of the epoch when it is known to differ from the equinox. Separate it from the statement of the equinox by a comma, and precede it by *epoch*.

> (RA 16 hr. 30 min. to 19 hr. 30 min./Decl. − 16° to − 49° ; eq. 1950, epoch 1948.5)

> (RA 16 hr./Decl. − 23° ; eq. 1950)

> (RA 2 hr./Decl. + 30° ; eq. 1950)

> (RA 2 hr. 00 min. to 2 hr. 30 min./Decl. − 30° to − 45° ; eq. 1950)

For charts centered on a pole, give the declination limit.

> (Centered at South Pole/Decl. limit − 60°)

For atlases or collections of charts arranged in declination zones, give the declination limits of each zone, but omit the statement of right ascension. If the zones are numerous, give the declination limits of the first few zones followed by the mark of omission and the declination limit of the last zone.

> (Zones + 90° to + 81°, + 81° to + 63°, + 63° to + 45° ; eq. 1950)

> (Zones + 90° to + 81°, + 81° to + 63°, ... − 81° to − 90° ; eq. 1950)

3.4. PUBLICATION, DISTRIBUTION, ETC., AREA

Contents:

3.4A. Preliminary rule

3.4A1. Punctuation

For instructions on the use of spaces before and after prescribed punctuation, see 1.0C.

Precede this area by a full stop, space, dash, space.

Precede a second or subsequently named place of publication, distribution, etc., by a semicolon.

Precede the name of a publisher, distributor, etc., by a colon.

Enclose a supplied statement of function of a publisher, distributor, etc., in square brackets.

Precede the date of publication, distribution, etc., by a comma.

Enclose the details of printing, etc., (place, name, date) in parentheses.

Precede the name of a printer, etc., by a colon.

Precede the date of printing, etc., by a comma.

3.4B. General rule

3.4B1. Record information about the place, name, and date of all types of publishing, distributing, etc., activities as instructed in 1.4B.

3.4B2. Early cartographic items. Give the publication, etc., details of early cartographic items as instructed in 2.16.

3.4C. Place of publication, distribution, etc.

3.4C1. Give the place of publication, distribution, etc., of a published item as instructed in 1.4C.

3.4C2. Do not record a place of publication, distribution, etc., for an unpublished cartographic item. Do not record *s.l.* in such a case.

3.4D. Name of publisher, distributor, etc.

3.4D1. Give the name of the publisher, etc., and *optionally* the distributor, as instructed in 1.4D.

> Southampton : Ordnance Survey
>
> Point Reyes, Calif. : Drake Navigators Guild
>
> Paris : Institut géographique internationale
>
> [London] : Royal Geographical Society
>
> Montréal : Éditions FM
>
> [Chicago] : Chicago Area Transportation Study
>
> Amsterdam ; London : North-Holland Pub. Co.
>   (*Cataloguing agency in the United Kingdom*)
>
> London : Royal Geographical Society ; Lympne Castle, Kent : H. Margary
>   (*Second publisher given prominence by layout*)
>
> Southampton : Ordnance Survey for the Institute of Geological Sciences.
>
> Tananarive : Service géographique de Madagascar

3.4D2. Do not record the name of a publisher, distributor, etc., for an unpublished cartographic item. Do not record *s.n.* in such a case.

3.4E. *Optional addition.* **Statement of function of publisher, distributor, etc.**

3.4E1. Add to the name of a publisher, distributor, etc., a statement of function as instructed in 1.4E.

> København : Geodætisk Institut ; [London] : Stanford [distributor]

3.4F. Date of publication, distribution, etc.

3.4F1. Give the date of publication, distribution, etc., of a published cartographic item as instructed in 1.4F.

> Washington, D.C. : Secretaría General de la Organización de los Estados Americanos, 1969
>
> Sevenoaks, Kent : Geographers' Map Co., [1973]
>
> Zürich : Orell Füssli, c1973
>
> Helsinki : Maanmittaushallitus, 1965-1967

3.4F2. Give the date of a map manuscript as instructed in 4.4B1.

3.4G. Place of printing, etc., name of printer, etc., date of printing, etc.

3.4G1. If the name of the publisher is unknown and the place and name of the printer or manufacturer are found in the item, give that place and name as instructed in 1.4G.

> Paris : [s.n., ca. 1898] (Paris : LeBrun)

3.4G2. *Optional addition.* Give the place, name of printer, etc., and/or date of printing, etc., if they are found on the item or its container or case or accompanying printed material and differ from the place, name of publisher, etc., and date of publication, etc., and are considered important by the cataloguing agency.

> London : Laurie & Whittle, 1804 (1810 printing)

3.5. PHYSICAL DESCRIPTION AREA

Contents:
    3.5A. Preliminary rule
    3.5B. Extent of item (including specific material designation)
    3.5C. Other physical details
    3.5D. Dimensions
    3.5E. Accompanying material

3.5A. Preliminary rule

3.5A1. Punctuation

For instructions on the use of spaces before and after prescribed punctuation, see 1.0C.

Precede this area by a full stop, space, dash, space *or* start a new paragraph.

Precede other physical details by a colon.

Precede dimensions by a semicolon.

Precede each statement of accompanying material by a plus sign.

Enclose physical details of accompanying material in parentheses.

3.5B. Extent of item (including specific material designation)

3.5B1. Give the extent of a cartographic item. In the case of atlases and globes, give the number of physical units. In the case of other cartographic items, give the number of maps, etc. Use arabic numerals and one of the following terms. If the item is a manuscript, precede the term by *ms*.

> atlas
> diagram
> globe
> map
> map section
> profile
> relief model
> remote-sensing image
> view

> 1 globe
>
> 1 map
>
> 1 ms. map
>
> 3 diagrams
>
> 10 identical maps

If a cartographic item is not comprehended by one of the above terms, use an appropriate term taken from subrule .5B of one of the chapters of part I.

> 7 wall charts
>
> 52 playing cards

If the parts of an item are very numerous and the exact number cannot be readily ascertained, give an approximate number.

> ca. 800 maps

If a cartographic item contains, or consists of, tactile data, follow the instructions in 3.5B5.

3.5B2. If there is more than one map, etc., on one or more sheets, specify the number of maps, etc., and the number of sheets.

> 6 maps on 1 sheet

> 8 map sections on 3 sheets

If the maps, etc., are printed in two or more segments designed to fit together to form one or more maps, etc., give the number of complete maps, etc., and:

a) the number of segments if all the segments are on a single sheet

> 1 map section in 4 segments

> 2 views in 6 segments

b) the number of sheets if the segments are on separate sheets.

> 1 map on 4 sheets

Optionally, omit the specification of the number of sheets or segments from the specific material designation and, if desired, give such information in a note (see 3.7B10).

> 6 maps
> *Note:* Maps on one sheet

> 2 views
> *Note:* Each view in 6 segments

If an item consists of a number of sheets each of which is a complete map, etc., treat it as a collection and describe it as instructed in 3.5B1.

3.5B3. Add, to the statement of extent for an atlas, the pagination or number of volumes as instructed in 2.5B.

> 1 atlas (3 v.)

> 1 atlas (xvii, 37 p., 74 leaves of plates)

3.5B4. If the description is of a separately titled part of a cartographic item lacking a collective title (see 3.1G4) and the part is physically separate from the rest of the item, give the statement of extent as instructed in 3.5B1–3.5B3.

> 1 globe

If the description is of a separately titled part of a cartographic item lacking a collective title (see 3.1G4) and the part is not physically separate from the rest of the item, express the fractional extent in the form *on sheet 3 of 4 maps* (if the parts are numbered or lettered in a single sequence) or *on 1 side of 4 maps* (if there is no sequential numbering).

> on side 1 of 1 map

> on 1 side of 1 map

> 2 map sections in 6 segments

3.5B5. If a cartographic item contains visual data and tactile data (i.e., braille letters or other tactile systems intended for the visually impaired), add a concise term (e.g., *print and tactile*) to the extent of item (see 3.5B1–3.5B4).

109

>   1 map (print and tactile)
>
>   1 atlas (print and tactile)
>
>   1 map in 4 segments (print, braille, and tactile)
>
>   1 globe (print and tactile)

If a cartographic item contains only tactile data, add, to the statement of extent (see 3.5B1–3.5B4), *braille*, *press braille*, *solid dot braille*, *tactile*, etc., as appropriate.

>   1 map (braille)
>
>   1 map (tactile)
>
>   1 globe (tactile)
>
>   1 atlas (3 v., tactile)
>
>   1 atlas (100 p., braille and tactile)

Optionally, if general material designations are used (see 1.1C1) and the general material designation indicates the tactile nature of the item, omit the addition.

If the item is a thermoform copy, add *thermoform* to the parenthetic addition, preceded by a comma. If there is no parenthetic addition (see *option* above), add *thermoform* in parentheses.

>   1 map (braille, thermoform)
>
> *or* 1 map (thermoform)
>
>   1 map (print and braille, thermoform)

3.5C. Other physical details

3.5C1. Give the following details, as appropriate, in the order set out here:

>   number of maps in an atlas
>   colour
>   material
>   mounting

3.5C2. Give the number of maps in an atlas as instructed in 2.5C.

>   1 atlas (xvi, 97, 100 p.) : 35 col. maps
>
>   1 atlas (330 p.) : 100 col. maps (some folded)
>
>   1 atlas (207 p.) : ca. 190 maps

3.5C3. Colour. If the item is coloured or partly coloured, indicate this. Disregard coloured matter outside a map, etc., border.

>   1 map : col.
>
>   4 maps : 2 col.

1 globe : col.

1 ms. map : col.

10 maps : some col.

3.5C4. Material. Give the material of which the item is made if it is considered to be significant (e.g., if a map is printed on a substance other than paper).

1 map : col., plastic

1 map : col., silk

1 globe : col., wood

1 ms. map : col., vellum

3.5C5. Mounting. If a map, etc., is mounted, indicate this. Indicate the mounting of a globe.

1 map : col., mounted on linen

1 globe : col., wood, on brass stand

1 globe : plastic, on metal stand

3.5D. Dimensions

3.5D1. Maps, plans, etc. Give the height × width in centimetres, to the next whole centimetre up, of a two-dimensional cartographic item (e.g., if a measurement is 37.1 centimetres, record it as *38 cm.*). *Optionally*, for early and manuscript cartographic items, give the dimensions to the nearest millimetre. Give the measurements of the face of the map, etc., measured within the neat line. Give the diameter of a circular map, etc., and specify it as such. If a map, etc., is irregularly shaped, or if it has no neat line, or if it bleeds off the edge, give the greater or greatest dimensions of the map itself. If it is difficult to determine the points for measuring the height and the width of the map, etc. (e.g., when the shape is extremely irregular, or when it was printed without one or more of its borders), give the height × width of the sheet specified as such.

1 map : col. ; 25 × 35 cm.

1 wall chart ; 40 × 23 cm.

1 ms. map ; 123.5 × 152.4 cm.

1 map : col. ; 45 cm. in diam.

1 map : col. ; on sheet 45 × 33 cm.

If a map, etc., is on sheets of two sizes, give both sets of dimensions. If the sheets are of more than two sizes, give the greatest height of any of them followed by the greatest width of any of them and *or smaller.*

1 map on 2 sheets ; 25 × 35 cm. and 30 × 35 cm.

1 map on 4 sheets ; 30 × 40 cm. or smaller

If a map, etc., is on one or more sheets in two or more segments designed to fit together to form one map, etc., give the dimensions of the complete map, etc., followed by the dimensions of the sheet(s). If such a map, etc., is mounted, give the dimensions of the whole map, etc., alone.

> 1 map in 4 segments ; 10 × 60 cm. on sheet 25 × 35 cm.

> 1 map on 9 sheets ; 264 × 375 cm. on sheets 96 × 142 cm.

> 1 map ; 120 × 276 cm.
> (*Mounted map created from several segments*)

If it is difficult to determine the points for measuring the height and width of a complete map, etc., that is in segments, or if it is difficult to assemble the map, etc., for measuring, give only the height and width of the sheet(s) specified as such.

> 1 map on 3 sheets ; sheets 30 × 40 cm.

> 2 maps on 6 sheets ; sheets 60 × 60 cm. or smaller

If the size of either dimension of a map, etc., is less than half the same dimension of the sheet on which it is printed or if there is substantial additional information on the sheet (e.g., text), give the sheet size as well as the size of the map, etc.

> 1 map ; 20 × 31 cm. on sheet 42 × 50 cm.

If a map, etc., is printed with an outer cover within which it is intended to be folded or if the sheet itself contains a panel or section designed to appear on the outside when the sheet is folded, give the sheet size in folded form as well as the size of the map, etc.

> 1 map ; 80 × 57 cm. folded to 21 × 10 cm.

> 1 map : col. ; 9 × 20 cm. on sheet 40 × 60 cm. folded to 21 × 10 cm.

If a map, etc., is printed on both sides of a sheet at a consistent scale, give the dimensions of the map, etc., as a whole, and give the sheet size. If it is difficult to measure such a map, etc., give the sheet size alone.

> 1 map ; 45 × 80 cm. on sheet 50 × 44 cm.
> (*Printed on both sides of sheet with line for joining indicated*)

> 1 map ; on sheet 45 × 30 cm.
> (*Printed on both sides of sheet*)

If the maps, etc., in a collection are of two sizes, give both. If they are of more than two sizes, give the greatest height of any of them followed by the greatest width of any of them and *or smaller*.

> 60 maps ; 44 × 55 cm. and 48 × 75 cm.

> 60 maps ; 60 × 90 cm. or smaller

> 10 map sections in 25 segments : col. ; 100 × 90 cm. or smaller

3.5D2. Atlases. Give the dimensions of an atlas as instructed in 2.5D.

>   1 atlas (xii, 100, 32 p.) : 100 col. maps ; 29 cm.

3.5D3. Relief models. Give the height × width of a relief model in centimetres as instructed in 3.5D1. *Optionally*, add the depth.

>   1 relief model : col., plastic ; 45 × 35 × 2 cm.

3.5D4. Globes. Give the diameter of a globe, specified as such.

>   1 globe : col., wood, on metal stand ; 12 cm. in diam.

3.5D5. *Optional addition.* **Containers.** Add the description of a container and its dimensions to the dimensions of the item.

>   1 globe : col., plastic, on metal stand ; 20 cm. in diam. in box 40 × 12 × 12 cm.

>   1 map : col. ; 200 × 350 cm. folded to 20 × 15 cm. in plastic case 25 × 20 cm.

3.5E. Accompanying material

3.5E1. Give the details of accompanying material as instructed in 1.5E.

>   17 maps ; 90 × 96 cm. + 1 v. (xvii, 272 p. ; 25 cm.)

3.6. SERIES AREA

Contents:
>   3.6A. Preliminary rule
>   3.6B. Series statements

3.6A. Preliminary rule

3.6A1. Punctuation

For instructions on the use of spaces before and after prescribed punctuation, see 1.0C.

Precede this area by a full stop, space, dash, space.

Enclose each series statement (see 1.6J) in parentheses.

Precede each parallel title by an equals sign.

Precede other title information by a colon.

Precede the first statement of responsibility by a diagonal slash.

Precede each subsequent statement of responsibility by a semicolon.

Precede the ISSN of a series or subseries by a comma.

Precede the numbering within a series or subseries by a semicolon.

Precede the title of a subseries by a full stop.

3.6B. Series statements

3.6B1. Record each series statement as instructed in 1.6.

>   (Climatological studies ; no. 8)

(A1 street atlas series)

(Carte géographique de l'Angleterre ; no 16)

(Deutscher Planungsatlas ; Bd. 8)

(Bartholomew world travel series)

(Nouvelle collection / Maurice Le Lannou)

(Communications of the Dublin Institute for Advanced Studies. Series D, Geophysical bulletin ; no. 29)

(Series of atlases in facsimile / Theatrum Orbis Terrarum. 6th series ; v. 1)

(Saggi e memorie di storia dell'arte ; v. 7)

(Graeco-Roman memoirs, ISSN 0306-9992 ; no. 93)

([Geological Survey of Canada A series] ; 1245A)

(Military city map : series A902 1:25,000 = Carte militaire de la ville : série A902 1:25,000 / Mapping and Charting Establishment, Department of National Defence ; MCE 329)

3.7. NOTE AREA

Contents:
 3.7A. Preliminary rule
 3.7B. Notes

3.7A. Preliminary rule

3.7A1. Punctuation
Precede each note by a full stop, space, dash, space *or* start a new paragraph for each.

Separate introductory wording from the main content of a note by a colon followed but not preceded by a space.

3.7A2. In making notes, follow the instructions in 1.7A.

3.7B. Notes
Make notes as set out in the following subrules and in the order given there. However, give a particular note first when it has been decided that note is of primary importance.

3.7B1. Nature and scope of the item. Make notes on the nature or scope of a cartographic item unless it is apparent from the rest of the description. Also make a note on unusual or unexpected features of the item.

Shows all of western Europe and some of eastern Europe
 (*Item entitled:* Germany)

Maps dissected and pasted onto the sides of 42 wooden blocks to form an educational game

Shows the routes of Amundsen, Byrd, and Gould

Shows southernmost extent of the midnight sun

Shows the main battles of 1944-1945
(*Item entitled:* The Asian struggle)

Free ball globe in transparent plastic cradle with graduated horizon circle and "geometer"

Shows dioceses

"Contour interval 20 feet"

Relief shown by contours, hachures, and spot heights

Based on 1981 statistics

3.7B2. Language. Give the language(s) of captions, etc., and text unless this is apparent from the rest of the description.

In Esperanto

Includes text in Finnish, Swedish, English, and German

Place names in Italian

Legend in English and Afrikaans

Except for title and "La mer du Nord" the map is in English

3.7B3. Source of title proper. Make notes on the source of the title proper if it is other than the chief source of information.

Title from container

Title from separate wrapper

Title from: A list of maps of America / P.L. Phillips. p. 502

3.7B4. Variations in title. Make notes on titles borne by the item other than the title proper. *Optionally*, give a romanization of the title proper.

Panel title: Welcome to big Wyoming

Title in left margin: Ville de Aix-les-Bains, Savoie

Romanized title: Moskovskaia oblast'

3.7B5. Parallel titles and other title information. Give the title in another language and other title information not recorded in the title and statement of responsibility area if they are considered to be important.

Added title in Spanish

Subtitle on wrapper: Showing population changes 1951-60

3.7B6. Statements of responsibility. Make notes on variant names of persons or bodies named in statements of responsibility if these are considered to be important for identification. Give statements of responsibility not recorded in the title and statement of responsibility area. Make notes on persons or bodies connected with a work, or significant persons or bodies connected with previous editions and not already named in the description.

>Engraved by T.J. Newman

>"Ch. Smith sculp."—Cover

>"Plotted ... by G. Petrie and D.P. Nicol, University of Glasgow, 1965. Field reconnaissance, 1962, and geomorphological interpretation by R.J. Price as part of project no. 1469 of the Institute of Polar Studies, the Ohio State University"

>Attributed to Blaeu in: Atlantes Neerlandici / C. Koeman

3.7B7. Edition and history. Make notes relating to the edition being described or to the history of the cartographic item.

>First ed. published 1954

>Sheets of various eds.

>A later state of the map first published in 1715 and later in 1745. This state has the additions of "King's roads" and an advertisement for Overton's large map of the British Isles, dated 1746

>Facsim. of: "The 52 countries [i.e. counties] of England and Wales described in a pack of cards. Sold by Robert Morton ... [et al.] in 1676"

>Copied from:

>Based on:

>Red overprinting on the author's Greater Germany, administrative divisions 1 July 1944 (no. 3817-R&A, OSS)

>"Roads and railways fully revised, 1971"—Wrapper

>A later state of the map first published in 1772

>From: Atlas élémentaire de géographie physique et politique / E. Mentelle et P.G. Chanlaire. [1798]

>First ed. published as: Atlas of comparative geography for junior classes / edited by George Philip. 1903

3.7B8. Mathematical and other cartographic data. Make notes on the magnitude of celestial charts.

>Limiting magnitude 3.5

Give mathematical data not already included in the mathematical data area for remote-sensing images.

>f5.944, alt. 12,000 ft.

Give other mathematical and cartographic data additional to, or elaborating on, that given in the mathematical data area.

Scale of original: ca. 1:1,300

Oriented with north to right

Prime meridians: Ferro and Paris

Scale departure graph: "Statute miles Mercator projection"

Military grid

If the scales vary (see 3.3B5) and if one or more of the scales is readily discernible and can be expressed concisely, give the scale(s).

Scale of third and fourth maps: 1:540,000

Scales: 1:250,000, 1:200,000, 1:150,000

Predominant scale: 1:250,000

3.7B9. Publication, distribution, etc. Make notes on publication, distribution, etc., details that are not included in the publication, distribution, etc., area and are considered to be important.

All previous eds. published by:

Maps dated between 1780 and 1813

The imprint of Gerard Valck has been substituted for the erased imprint of Joan. Blaeu, who probably first published the map ca. 1672

Imprint of W. & S. Jones pasted onto the terrestrial and celestial globe gores

3.7B10. Physical description. Make notes on important physical details that are not included in the physical description area, especially if these affect the use of the item. If the item is a photoreproduction, give the method of reproduction if it is likely to affect the use of the item (e.g., when it is a blueline print).

Irregularly shaped

Hand coloured

Printed on both sides of sheet

Photocopy

Blueprint

Photocopy, negative

Watermark: C. & I. Honig

In wooden case bearing, on its inner faces, representations of the celestial hemispheres

Bound in vellum

Legends in braille

County boundaries tactile

Mounted map created from several segments

3.7B11. Accompanying material. Make notes on the location of accompanying material if appropriate. Give details of accompanying material neither mentioned in the physical description area nor given a separate description (see 1.5E).

> Accompanied by filmstrip entitled: Mexico and Central America

> Accompanied by the same maps in sheet form first published in: Géographie générale / M.J.C. Barbié Du Bocage. 1842

> Each sheet accompanied by a sheet of geological sections

3.7B12. Series. Make notes on series data that cannot be given in the series area.

> Some maps have series designation: Direct route map

3.7B13. Dissertations. If the item being described is a dissertation, make a note as instructed in 1.7B13.

3.7B14. Audience. Make a brief note of the intended audience for, or intellectual level of, an item if this information is stated in the item.

> Intended audience: Primary schools

3.7B16. Other formats. Give the details of other formats in which the content of the item has been issued.

> Also issued as a set of wall charts

> Also issued on microfiche

3.7B18. Contents. If a collection of maps is described as a unit (see 3.0J), make notes on the state of the collection at the time of description and indicate the composition of the complete collection if possible. Give variations between sheets in the collection. Complete this note when the collection is complete.

> Complete in 174 sheets. Set includes various editions of some sheets including some reissued by the U.S. Army Map Service. Some sheets, prepared under the direction of the Chief of Engineers, U.S. Army, have series designation "Provisional G.S. G.S. 4145"

List the contents of an item, either selectively or fully, including: insets; maps, etc., printed on the verso of a map, etc., sheet; illustrations, etc. Make notes on maps, insets, etc., on the recto before those on the verso of a sheet. Give the scale of insets, etc., if it is consistent. If the insets, etc., are numerous and/or minor, make a note in general terms.

> Includes index

> Includes "Glossary"

> Includes key to 140 place names

> With two additional unnumbered parts: The stars in six maps. 1830 — The terrestrial globe in six maps. 1831

> Includes an index and illustrations of the Wangapeka Track

Insets: Connaught Place — Chanakyapuri — Delhi & New Delhi City. Scale [ca. 1:23,000]

Insets: Political and economic alliances — Air distances from London — Membership of international organisations

On verso: New map of South Hadley, Mass. Scale [ca. 1:15,000]

On verso: Indiana — Iowa — Missouri. Scale 1:60,000

Insets: Harrow — Wembley — Ruislip. On verso: Map of N.W. London

Includes 7 insets

Contents: The world in 3000 B.C. — The world in 1500 B.C. — The world in 500 B.C. — The world in A.D. 1

Contents: Ancient Orient before the rise of the Greeks. Scale 1:4,752,000 — Palestine about 860 B.C. Scale 1:506,880

Contents: Colonial organization of the world 1937 — Achievement of independence 1958-1966

3.7B19. Numbers. Give important numbers borne by the item other than ISBNs or ISSNs (see 3.8B).

Publisher's no.: LB 3721-9

3.7B20. Copy being described, library's holdings, and restrictions on use. Make these notes as instructed in 1.7B20.

Library's copy annotated in red ink to show land owners

Originally published on 4 sheets

Library's copy imperfect: Upper left corner missing

Library's set lacks sheets 9-13 and sheet 27

3.7B21. "With" notes. If the title and statement of responsibility area contains a title that applies to only a part of an item lacking a collective title and, therefore, more than one entry is made, make a note beginning *With:* and listing the other separately titled works in the item in the order in which they appear there.

With a separate map on same sheet: Queen Maud Range

With (on verso): Motor road map of south-east England

Mounted on a wooden stand to form a pair with: Bale's new celestial globe. 1845

With: Atlas de France. Paris : Desnos, 1775

3.8. STANDARD NUMBER AND TERMS OF AVAILABILITY AREA

Contents:
3.8A. Preliminary rule
3.8B. Standard number
3.8C. Key-title
3.8D. Terms of availability
3.8E. Qualification

3.8A. Preliminary rule

3.8A1. Punctuation

For instructions on the use of spaces before and after prescribed punctuation, see 1.0C.

Precede this area by a full stop, space, dash, space *or* start a new paragraph.
Precede each repetition of this area by a full stop, space, dash, space.
Precede a key-title by an equals sign.
Precede terms of availability by a colon.
Enclose a qualification to the standard number or terms of availability in parentheses.

3.8B. Standard number

3.8B1. Give the International Standard Book Number (ISBN) or International Standard Serial Number (ISSN) assigned to an item as instructed in 1.8B.

ISBN 0-85152-392-7

ISSN 0085-4859

3.8B2. Give any other number in a note (see 3.7B19).

3.8C. Key-title

3.8C1. Give the key-title of a serial item as instructed in 1.8C.

3.8D. *Optional addition.* Terms of availability

3.8D1. Give the terms on which the item is available as instructed in 1.8D.

£4.40 (complete collection). − £0.55 (individual sheets)

3.8E. Qualification

3.8E1. Add qualifications to the standard number and/or terms of availability as instructed in 1.8E.

3.9. SUPPLEMENTARY ITEMS

3.9A. Describe supplementary items as instructed in 1.9.

3.10. ITEMS MADE UP OF SEVERAL TYPES OF MATERIAL

3.10A. Describe items made up of several types of material as instructed in 1.10.

3.11. FACSIMILES, PHOTOCOPIES, AND OTHER REPRODUCTIONS

3.11A. Describe facsimiles, photocopies, and other reproductions as instructed in 1.11.

CHAPTER 4

MANUSCRIPTS (INCLUDING MANUSCRIPT COLLECTIONS)

Contents

4.0. GENERAL RULES

4.0A. Scope

4.0A1. The rules in this chapter cover the description of manuscript (including typescript or printout) materials of all kinds, including manuscript books, dissertations, letters, speeches, etc., legal papers (including printed forms completed in manuscript), and collections of such manuscripts. For reproductions of manuscripts published in multiple copies, see chapter 2 or chapter 11, as appropriate. For manuscript cartographic items, see also chapter 3. For manuscript music, see also chapter 5.

4.0B. Sources of information

4.0B1. Chief source of information. The chief source of information for manuscripts is the manuscript itself. Within manuscripts, use (in this order of preference) information from the:

> title page
> colophon
> caption, heading, etc.
> content of the manuscript

However, prefer a source that is part of the original manuscript to sources that have been supplied later. If information is not available from the chief source, take it from the following sources (in this order of preference):

> another manuscript copy of the item
> a published edition of the item
> reference sources
> other sources

For collections of manuscripts, treat the whole collection as the chief source.

4.0B2. Prescribed sources of information. The prescribed source(s) of information for each area of the description of manuscripts is set out below. Enclose information taken from outside the prescribed source(s) in square brackets.

AREA	PRESCRIBED SOURCES OF INFORMATION
Title and statement of responsibility	Chief source of information, published copies of manuscript
Edition	Chief source of information, published copies of manuscript
Date	Chief source of information, published copies of manuscript
Physical description	Any source
Note	Any source

4.0C. Punctuation

For the punctuation of the description as a whole, see 1.0C.
For the prescribed punctuation of elements, see the following rules.

4.0D. Levels of detail in the description

See 1.0D.

4.0E. Language and script of the description

See 1.0E.

4.0F. Inaccuracies

See 1.0F.

4.0G. Accents and other diacritical marks

See 1.0G.

4.1. TITLE AND STATEMENT OF RESPONSIBILITY AREA

Contents:
4.1A. Preliminary rule
4.1B. Title proper
4.1C. General material designation
4.1D. Parallel titles
4.1E. Other title information
4.1F. Statements of responsibility
4.1G. Items without a collective title

4.1A. Preliminary rule

4.1A1. Punctuation

For instructions on the use of spaces before and after prescribed punctuation, see 1.0C.

Enclose the general material designation in square brackets.

Precede each parallel title by an equals sign.

Precede each unit of other title information by a colon.

Precede the first statement of responsibility by a diagonal slash.

Precede each subsequent statement of responsibility by a semicolon.

For the punctuation of this area for items without a collective title, see 1.1G.

4.1B. Title proper

4.1B1. Transcribe the title proper as instructed in 1.1B.

> Life of Romney

> A Declaration of the Representatives of the United States of America in Congress Assembled

> The waste land

> Death in Leamington Spa

If the title proper is not taken from the chief source of information, give the source of the title in a note (see 4.7B3).

4.1B2. If a manuscript or manuscript collection lacks a title, supply one as instructed below. Give the source of a supplied title (other than one composed by the cataloguer) in the note area (see 4.7B3).

Manuscript volumes and similar material. Supply a brief title indicating the nature of the material for literary manuscripts, diaries, journals, memorandum books, account books, etc. For manuscripts of subsequently published texts, give the title by which the work is known.

> [Diary]

> [Seventeen poems]

Ancient, medieval, and Renaissance manuscripts and oriental manuscripts lacking a title page.[1] Follow, when appropriate, the provisions for early printed monographs (see 2.14). If those rules do not apply, supply a title by which the work is known or a title indicating the nature of the material.

> [De re militari]

> [Treatise on arithmetic]

Single letters, postcards, telegrams, radiograms, etc. Supply a title consisting of *Letter* (or *Postcard*, *Telegram*, etc.), the date of writing (expressed as year, month, day), the place of writing, the name of the addressee, and place to which addressed. Enclose any details not taken from the letter, etc., its envelope, or enclosures, in square brackets.

> [Letter, ca. 1898 Jan. 1] Worcester Park, Surrey [to] George Gissing, Rome

---

1. This rule is intended for general guidance only.

[Postcard] 1898 March 1, Rome [to] H.G. Wells, Worcester Park, Surrey

[Telegram] 1889 Feb. 8, London [to] James McNeill Whistler, Chelsea, London

Speeches, sermons, etc. Supply a title consisting of an appropriate word (e.g., *Speech*, *Address*) followed by the place and/or the occasion of the delivery.

[Lecture, Royal College of Medicine, London]

[Address, before Goucher College, Baltimore, Md., in the First Methodist Episcopal Church]

Legal documents (wills, deeds, mortgages, leases, warrants, commissions, etc.). Supply a title consisting of a word or brief phrase characterizing the document, the date of signing (expressed as year, month, day), the name(s) of persons concerned other than those responsible for the document, and the occasion for the document if it can be expressed concisely. Enclose any details not taken from the document in square brackets.

[Will] 1943 Feb. 8

[Commission, ca. 1851 Apr. 9] appointing J.E. Bradshaw to command the Peshawar Battalion

[Lease, 1937 Oct. 17, of shop in Bridge St., Harrow, Middlesex]

Collections of manuscript materials formed by or around a person, family, corporate body, or subject. The materials may be in their original form or reproductions, and may include photographs and printed materials. Give the title by which the collection is known, or supply a title indicating the nature of the collection. Unless more specific terms are used, use *Letters* for letters by an individual, *Correspondence* for letters between persons or to a person or persons, *Papers* for miscellaneous personal or family material, and *Records* for materials relating to a corporate body.

[Letters]

[Records]

[Mercantile records]

[Indian papers]

[Literary remains]

Miscellaneous single manuscripts. For a manuscript not covered by the above sections, give the title by which it is known, or supply a title indicating the nature of the material.

[Chart for Tender is the night]

4.1C. *Optional addition.* **General material designation**

4.1C1. Give immediately following the title proper the appropriate general material designation as instructed in 1.1C.

> Gondal poems [GMD]

4.1D. Parallel titles

4.1D1. Transcribe parallel titles as instructed in 1.1D.

4.1E. Other title information

4.1E1. Transcribe other title information as instructed in 1.1E.

> The need of redirected rural schools [GMD] : address, before the Iowa State Teachers' Association, [Des Moines], Oct. 4, 1910

4.1E2. If a letter, etc., speech, sermon, etc., or legal document has a title lacking some information specified for supplied titles for those documents (see 4.1B2), add that information as other title information.

> Why no Baal? [GMD] : [sermon, Westminster Cathedral]

> In place of uncertainty [GMD] : a speech [to the Peace Pledge Union and Society of Friends, Friends Hall, London]

4.1F. Statements of responsibility

4.1F1. Transcribe statements of responsibility relating to persons or bodies appearing on the manuscript as instructed in 1.1F.

> Exil [GMD] / St.-J. Perse

> [Letter] 1899 Jan. 3, Dorking, Surrey [to] H.G. Wells, Worcester Park, Surrey [GMD] / George Gissing

> Three sonnets of Shakespeare [GMD] / written in the italic hand by Pamela Thomson

4.1F2. *Optional addition.* If the name appended to, or the signature on, a manuscript is incomplete, complete the name.

> [Letter] 1929 Feb. 8, New York to F. Scott Fitzgerald, Wilmington, Del. [GMD] / Zelda [Fitzgerald]

> [Letter] 1898 July 19, Dorking, Surrey [to] H.G. Wells, Worcester Park, Surrey [GMD] / G.G. [George Gissing]

4.1F3. If a manuscript lacks a signature or statement of responsibility, supply the name(s) of the person(s) responsible for it, if known.

> Speech, Trafalgar Square, London [GMD] / [William Morris]

> The waste land [GMD] / T.S. Eliot ; [with ms. amendments by Ezra Pound]

4.1G. Items without a collective title

4.1G1. If a single manuscript lacks a collective title, transcribe the titles of the individual parts as instructed in 1.1G.

> Gold shoes [GMD] ; The other world / J.M. Morgan

> Speculum regum [GMD] / Godefridus Viterbiensis. Tractatus de occultatione vitiorum sub specie virtutum

4.2. EDITION AREA

Contents:
    4.2A.   Preliminary rule
    4.2B.   Edition statement
    4.2C.   Statements of responsibility relating to the edition

4.2A. Preliminary rule

4.2A1. Scope. Use this area to give statements relating to versions of manuscript works existing in two or more versions or states in single or multiple copies. Examples are different manuscript drafts of a work and filmscripts existing in various versions.

4.2A2. Punctuation

For instructions on the use of spaces before or after prescribed punctuation, see 1.0C.

Precede this area by a full stop, space, dash, space.

Precede the first statement of responsibility following an edition statement by a diagonal slash.

Precede each subsequent statement of responsibility by a semicolon.

4.2B. Edition statement

4.2B1. Transcribe a statement relating to a version of a manuscript that is different from other versions, or that is a named revision, as instructed in 1.2B.

> Prelim. draft

> 3rd script

> 2nd draft continuity

> Estimating script

4.2B2. In case of doubt about whether a statement is an edition statement, do not treat it as such.

4.2B3. *Optional addition.* If an item lacks an edition statement but is known to contain significant changes from other versions, supply a suitable brief statement in the language and script of the title proper and enclose it in square brackets.

> [2nd draft]

> [3. Konzept]

[Continuity]

[Mar. 1970 draft]

[Rev. screenplay]

4.2C. Statements of responsibility relating to the edition

4.2C1. Transcribe a statement of responsibility relating to an edition as instructed in 1.2C and 4.1F.

Continuity / written by Waldemar Young

3rd draft / edited by Paul Watson

4.3. MATERIAL (OR TYPE OF PUBLICATION) SPECIFIC DETAILS AREA

4.3A. This area is not used for manuscripts.

4.4. DATE AREA

Contents:
4.4A. Preliminary rule
4.4B. Date of the manuscript

4.4A. Preliminary rule

4.4A1. Punctuation
Precede this area by a full stop, space, dash, space.

4.4B. Date of the manuscript

4.4B1. Give the date or inclusive dates of the manuscript or manuscript collection unless it is already included in the title (as with letters and legal documents). Give the year or years of the manuscript(s), and *optionally* the month and day (in the case of single manuscripts), in that order. For the dating of a collection, see 1.4F8.

Exil [GMD] / St.-J. Perse. — 1941

Correspondence [GMD] / William Allen. — 1821-1879

Records [GMD] / American Colonization Society. — 1816-1908

Alice's adventures under ground [GMD] : a Christmas gift to a dear child in memory of a summer day / [Lewis Carroll (Rev. C.L. Dodgson)]. — 1864

Sonnet, To Genevra [GMD] / [Lord Byron]. — 1813 Dec. 17

4.4B2. If the date of delivery of a speech, sermon, etc., differs from the date of the manuscript, give the date of delivery in a note unless this date is part of the title information.

[Speech] Glasgow Labour Club [GMD] / James Maxton. — 1928
Jan. 13
Note: Delivered Feb. 8, 1928

4.5. PHYSICAL DESCRIPTION AREA

Contents:
    4.5A. Preliminary rule
    4.5B. Extent of item
    4.5C. Other physical details
    4.5D. Dimensions

4.5A. Preliminary rule

4.5A1. Punctuation

For instructions on the use of spaces before and after prescribed punctuation, see 1.0C.

Precede this area by a full stop, space, dash, space *or* start a new paragraph.

Precede other physical details by a colon.

Precede dimensions by a semicolon.

4.5B. Extent of item

4.5B1. Single manuscripts. Give the number of leaves or pages as instructed in 2.5B.

23 leaves

iv, 103 leaves

[63] leaves

[4] p.

[4], 103 p.

leaves 51-71

If the manuscript has been bound, add *bound* at the end of the statement of extent.

[70] leaves, bound

4, [20], 30 p., bound

Add, to the pagination, etc., of ancient, medieval, and Renaissance manuscripts, the number of columns (if more than one) and the average number of lines to the page.

[208] leaves (41 lines)

[26] leaves (2 columns, 45-47 lines)

Optional addition. If a pagination is given, add the number of leaves.

[2] p. on 1 leaf

[5] p. on 3 leaves

4.5B2. Collections of manuscripts. If a collection occupies one linear foot or less of shelf space, give the extent in terms of the number or approximate number of items[2] (the number of bound and unbound items separately expressed), or the number of containers or volumes. *Optionally*, if the number of volumes or containers is given, add the number or approximate number of items.

> 123 items
>
> ca. 400 items
>
> 6 v.
>
> 3 v. (183 items)

If the collection occupies more than one linear foot of shelf space, give the extent in terms of the number of linear feet occupied. *Optionally*, add the number or approximate number of containers or volumes and/or items.

> 40 ft.
>
> 3 ft. (ca. 2250 items)
>
> 6 ft. (75 v.)
>
> 5 ft. (30 items bound, 37 items unbound)
>
> 2 ft. (ca. 70 items, 12 bound)
>
> 10 ft. (12 boxes)
>
> 15 ft. (12 boxes, ca. 1000 items)

4.5B3. If a manuscript consists of leaves or pages of braille or another tactile system, add *of braille*, etc., as appropriate (see also 2.5B23).

> 12 leaves of braille

Optionally, if general material designations are used (see 1.1C1) and the general material designation indicates the tactile nature of the item, omit the addition.

4.5C. Other physical details

4.5C1. Name the material on which the item being described is written if it is other than paper.

> [1] leaf : parchment
>
> [20] leaves : vellum

4.5C2. If a manuscript is illustrated or if a collection of manuscripts includes illustrated items, give an illustration statement as instructed in 2.5C.

> 30 p. : ill.
>
> [3], 20 leaves : vellum, ill., maps

---

2. *Item* here means a separate manuscript. For example, a letter with several leaves and an enclosure is counted as one item.

> 30 p. : col. ill.
>
> 6 v. : ill.
>
> 3 v. (183 items) : ill. (some col.)

If a manuscript or collection of manuscripts consists of illustrations, follow the instructions in 8.5C.

4.5D. Dimensions

4.5D1. Single manuscripts. Give the height of an unbound manuscript in centimetres to the next whole centimetre up. Add the width if it is less than half the height or greater than the height. If the manuscript is kept folded, add the dimensions when folded.

> 6 p. ; 24 cm.
>
> [7] p. ; 24 × 30 cm.
>
> 12 leaves : ill. ; 20 cm. folded to 10 × 12 cm.
>
> [1] leaf : parchment ; 35 × 66 cm. folded to 10 × 19 cm.

Give the dimensions of a bound volume as instructed in 2.5D.

> 131 leaves, bound ; 26 cm.

4.5D2. Collections of manuscripts. If the size of the items, containers, or volumes (depending on the terms of the first statement of extent) is uniform, give that size as instructed in 4.5D1, or, in the case of containers, give the height, width, and depth.

> 20 items ; 20 × 30 cm.
>
> 6 v. ; 30 cm.
>
> 12 boxes ; 27 × 40 × 50 cm.
>
> 6 v. ; 24-30 cm.

4.6. SERIES AREA

4.6A. This area is not used for manuscripts.

4.7. NOTE AREA

Contents:
4.7A. Preliminary rule
4.7B. Notes

4.7A. Preliminary rule

4.7A1. Punctuation
Precede each note by a full stop, space, dash, space *or* start a new paragraph for each.

Separate introductory wording from the main content of a note by a colon followed but not preceded by a space.

4.7A2. In making notes, follow the instructions in 1.7A.

4.7B. Notes

Make notes as set out in the following subrules and in the order given there. However, give a particular note first when it has been decided that note is of primary importance. For additional notes on ancient, medieval, and Renaissance manuscripts, see 4.7B23.

4.7B1. Nature, scope, or form. Make notes on the nature of a manuscript or a collection of manuscripts unless it is apparent from the rest of the description. Use one of the following terms, as appropriate:

> holograph(s) (for manuscripts handwritten by the per-
>   son(s) responsible for the work(s) contained therein)
> ms. (for all other handwritten manuscripts)
> mss. (for all other collections of handwritten manu-
>   scripts)
> printout(s)
> typescript(s)

> Holograph

> Ms.

> Typescripts

If the item is signed, add *signed*.

> Holograph, signed

If the item or collection being described is a copy or consists of copies, add *(carbon copy)*, *(photocopy)*, or *(transcript)*, or the plural of one of these. If a photocopy is negative, add *negative*. Add *handwritten*, *typewritten*, or *printout* to *transcript(s)*.

> Holograph (carbon copy)

> Ms. (photocopy, negative)

> Ms., signed (photocopy)

> Mss. (transcripts, handwritten)

> Typescript (photocopy)

If the items in a collection are not all of the same nature, word the qualification to indicate this.

> Mss. (some photocopies)

> Mss. (transcripts, handwritten, and photocopies)

> Mss. (photocopies, some negative)

If the item is a copy, add the location of the original if this can be readily ascertained.

> Ms. (photocopy) of original in the British Library Humanities and Social Sciences

> Holograph, signed (photocopy), original in possession of W.S. Merwin

Indicate the scope or form of a manuscript item if it is not apparent from the rest of the description.

> Poem

> Journal and account book

> Typescript of sound recording

> Printout of catalog

In describing a collection of manuscripts, name the types of papers, etc., constituting the collection and mention any other features that characterize it. If the collection is of personal papers, give enough data to identify the person, either as a brief initial statement or as part of the summary of the nature of the collection. If necessary, give the contents (see 4.7B18) as part of that summary.

> Paleontologist and educator. Correspondence, reports, notes, articles, maps, printed matter, and other papers, mainly relating to the Carnegie Institution, the National Academy of Sciences, the National Research Council, and national parks

> Papers covering (in the main) Allen's service as U.S. senator, 1837-1848, and as governor of Ohio, 1873-1874. Includes some of his speeches, drafts of his letters, and letters from various correspondents on political matters in Ohio

> Includes records of the Banking Board, 1911-1939, and those of the Bureau of Insurance, 1897-1943

> Writer. Personal papers, letters, etc., drafts of some poems, including the complete text of the verse drama "The pierrot of the minute"

4.7B2. Language. Make notes on the language(s) of the item, or on the fact that it is a translation or adaptation, unless this is apparent from the rest of the description.

> In Swedish

> Latin with English marginalia

> Some items in English, some in French

> English with typewritten French translation

4.7B3. Source of title proper. Make notes on the source of the title proper if it is other than the chief source of information.

Title from cover

Title from: Guide to manuscript collections in the William L. Clements Library / compiled by H.H. Peckham. 1942

4.7B4. Variations in title. Make notes on titles borne by the item other than the title proper. *Optionally*, give a romanization of the title proper.

Also known as: The Thynne papers

4.7B5. Parallel titles and other title information. Give the title in another language and other title information not recorded in the title and statement of responsibility area if they are considered to be important.

4.7B6. Statements of responsibility. Make notes on variant names of persons or bodies named in statements of responsibility if these are considered to be important for identification. Give statements of responsibility not recorded in the title and statement of responsibility area. Make notes on persons or bodies connected with a work or the manuscript and not already named in the description.

Original, signed by John Hancock

Marginalia by Robert Graves

Collection made by P.M. Townshend

Dictated to Clare Wheeler

4.7B7. Donor, source, etc., and previous owner(s). Make notes on the donor or source of a manuscript or manuscript collection, and on previous owners if readily ascertainable. Add the year or years of accession to the name of the donor or source, and add the years of ownership to the name of a previous owner.

Gift of Worthington C. Ford, 1907

Purchase, 1951-1968

Purchased from the Del Monte collection, 1901

Gift of Mr. Wright, 1938-1954

Previously owned by L. McGarry, 1951-1963

4.7B8. Place of writing. Give the name of the place in which a manuscript was written if it is found in the item and is not given elsewhere in the description. Give the source of the information.

At end: Long Beach Island

On t.p.: London-Zagreb-Trieste

4.7B9. Published versions. If the work contained in a manuscript or the content of a collection of manuscripts has been, or is being, published, give the publication details.

Published as: The life of George Romney. London : T. Payne, 1809

> Published in: Poetry : a magazine of verse. Vol. 59 (1942).
> p. 295-308

> Entire collection, with Jefferson papers from the Library of
> Congress and elsewhere, is being published in: The papers of
> Thomas Jefferson / edited by J.P. Boyd and Charles Cullen. 1950-

4.7B10. Physical description. Make notes on important physical details that are
not given elsewhere in the description.

> Paper watermarked: KS and a crown

> Two seals, pendant

> Ms. torn in half and rejoined

> Lacks top right corner

> Some papers stained by water

> Red ink on yellow paper

> In case 20 × 24 cm.

4.7B11. Accompanying material. Give details of materials accompanying a manuscript or manuscript collection, especially (for letters) envelopes, enclosures, and
endorsements; (for legal documents) accompanying papers and endorsements;
and (for collections) unpublished guides.

> Accompanied by autobiographical sketch (2 p., holograph)

> Accompanied by slip containing emendations

> In envelope, with enclosure (4 p. on 2 leaves, holograph, signed)

> Endorsement: Thomas Kitchen to Ellen Montgomery Jones

> Accompanied by photocopies of documents relating to the
> probate of the will

> Unpublished guide in the library

> Indexed in the library's catalogue

4.7B13. Dissertations. If the item being described is a dissertation, make a note
as instructed in 1.7B13.

> Presented as the author's thesis (Ph.D.)—University of Chicago

4.7B14. Access and literary rights. Give, as specifically as possible, all restrictions
on access to a manuscript or collection of manuscripts.

> Accessible after 2008

> Open to researchers under library restrictions

If the literary rights in a collection have been reserved for a specified period
or are dedicated to the public and a document stating this is available, give *Information on literary rights available.*

4.7B15. Reference to published descriptions. Make notes on the best or fullest published descriptions of a manuscript or a collection of manuscripts and on published indexes or calendars.

> Calendar: Spanish manuscripts concerning Peru, 1531-1651. Washington, D.C. : Library of Congress, 1932

> Described in: Virginia Woolf : a list of manuscripts. London : Spencer, 1986

4.7B17. Summary. Give a brief objective summary of the content of an item unless another part of the description provides enough information.

4.7B18. Contents. List the contents of an item, either selectively or fully, if it is considered necessary to show the presence of material not implied by the rest of the description; to stress items of particular importance; or to list the contents of a collection. When recording titles formally, take them from the head of the part to which they refer rather than from contents lists, etc.

> Includes petition to the King from the citizens of London, 1783, in scroll form

> Also contains two short prose pieces dated 1937

> Contains letters to Mrs. Wells and Gabrielle Gissing

4.7B23. Ancient, medieval, and Renaissance manuscripts. In addition to the notes specified above, give the following notes for ancient, medieval, and Renaissance manuscripts and collections of such manuscripts.

Style of writing. Give the script used in a manuscript or the predominant script in a collection.

> Textura script with marginal corrections in roman script

Illustrative matter. Give ornamentation, rubrication, illumination, etc., and important details of other illustrative matter.

> Rubricated

> Headings in red, with sepia drawings

> Col. drawing of Jacob's dream on leaf [23][a]

Collation. Give the number of gatherings with mention of blank, damaged, or missing leaves, and any earlier foliation.

> Signatures (with catchwords at the end of each): [4] leaves (on vellum), $[a]^{10}$, b^{10+2} (1st and last leaves on vellum), c-f^{10}, g^{10+2}, h-p^{10}, q^{10+2} (2nd and 11th leaves on vellum), r-t^{10}, v^8 (the last 2 leaves blank)

Other physical details. Give details of owner's annotations, the binding, and any other important physical details.

> Annotated by previous owner, signed M.B.

> Bound in calf, gold stamped, with Bellini arms on spine

137

Opening words. If the manuscript is given a supplied title, quote as many of the opening words of the main part of the text as will enable the item to be identified.

> Tractatus begins (on leaf [17]ᵃ): Est via que videtʳ homī rcta nouissima ...

4.8. STANDARD NUMBER AND TERMS OF AVAILABILITY AREA

4.8A. This area is not used for manuscripts.

MUSIC

Contents

5.0. GENERAL RULES

5.0A. Scope

5.0A1. The rules in this chapter cover the description of published music. They do not cover manuscript or other unpublished music in detail, though the use of an additional term in the physical description (see 5.5B) and the use of the specific provisions of chapter 4 will furnish a sufficiently detailed description for the general library catalogue. For the description of recorded music, see chapter 6. For microform reproductions of music, see chapter 11.

5.0B. Sources of information

5.0B1. Chief source of information. If the title page consists of a list of titles including the title of the item being catalogued, use as the chief source of information whichever of the "list" title page, the cover, or the caption furnishes the fullest information. In all other cases, use the title page or title page substitute (see 2.0B1) as the chief source of information.

If information is not available from the chief source, take it from the following sources (in this order of preference):

> caption
> cover
> colophon
> other preliminaries
> other sources

5.0B2. Prescribed sources of information. The prescribed source(s) of information for each area of the description of published music is set out below. Enclose information taken from outside the prescribed source(s) in square brackets.

AREA	PRESCRIBED SOURCES OF INFORMATION
Title and statement of responsibility	Chief source of information
Edition	Chief source of information, caption, cover, colophon, other preliminaries
Musical presentation	Chief source of information
Publication, distribution, etc.	Chief source of information, caption, cover, colophon, other preliminaries, first page of music
Physical description	Any source
Series	Series title page, caption, cover, title page, colophon, other preliminaries
Note	Any source
Standard number and terms of availability	Any source

5.0C. Punctuation

For the punctuation of the description as a whole, see 1.0C.
For the prescribed punctuation of elements, see the following rules.

5.0D. Levels of detail in the description
See 1.0D.

5.0E. Language and script of the description
See 1.0E.

5.0F. Inaccuracies
See 1.0F.

5.0G. Accents and other diacritical marks
See 1.0G.

5.0H. Items with several chief sources of information
See 1.0H.

5.1. TITLE AND STATEMENT OF RESPONSIBILITY AREA

Contents:
> 5.1A. Preliminary rule
> 5.1B. Title proper
> 5.1C. General material designation
> 5.1D. Parallel titles
> 5.1E. Other title information
> 5.1F. Statements of responsibility
> 5.1G. Items without a collective title

5.1A. Preliminary rule

5.1A1. Punctuation

For instructions on the use of spaces before and after prescribed punctuation, see 1.0C.

Precede the title of a supplement or section (see 1.1B9) by a full stop.

Enclose the general material designation in square brackets.

Precede each parallel title by an equals sign.

Precede each unit of other title information by a colon.

Precede the first statement of responsibility by a diagonal slash.

Precede each subsequent statement of responsibility by a semicolon.

For the punctuation of this area for items without a collective title, see 1.1G.

5.1B. Title proper

5.1B1. Transcribe the title proper as instructed in 1.1B. If a title consists of the name(s) of one or more type(s) of composition, or one or more type(s) of composition and one or more of the following:

> medium of performance
> key
> date of composition
> number

treat type of composition, medium of performance, etc., as the title proper.

> Rhapsody
>
> Songs & folk music
>
> Violin-Sonaten 1,2,3
>
> String quartet 5

Sonate en ré majeur, opus 3, pour violon

Scherzo for two pianos, four hands

Symphony no. 3, A major, opus 56

String quintet no. 1, A major, op. 18

Zwei Praeludien und Fugen für Orgel, op. posth. 7

Musik für Saiteninstrumente, Schlagzeug, und Celeste

Două piese pentru orchestră

Prelude and fugue in A minor

Sinfonia I (1970)

VIII. Symphonie c-Moll

In all other cases, if one or more statements of medium of performance, key, date of composition, and/or number are found in the source of information, treat those elements as other title information (see 5.1E).

Die Meistersinger von Nürnberg

Sinfonia mazedonia

Little suite

Easter fresco

Georgia moon

Gigi

3 D.H. Lawrence love poems

Hymne à la joie

Charles Aznavour présente ses plus grands succès

The vocal score and libretto of The merry widow

The Beatles song book

1952 electronic tape music

In case of doubt, treat statements of medium of performance, key, date of composition, and number as part of the title proper.

If the title proper is not taken from the chief source of information, give the source of the title in a note (see 5.7B3).

5.1B2. In a supplied title proper (see 1.1B7), give all of the elements prescribed for uniform titles for music in the order prescribed in 25.25–25.35.

[Trios, piano, strings, no. 2, op. 66, C minor]

5.1C. *Optional addition.* **General material designation**

5.1C1. Give immediately following the title proper the appropriate general material designation as instructed in 1.1C.

> Sonata for viola and piano, op. 147 [GMD]
>
> Fugue for 6 cellos on themes by Beethoven [GMD]
>
> Sechs Partiten für Flöte [GMD]
>
> Sunday morning coming down [GMD]

5.1C2. If an item contains parts belonging to materials falling into two or more categories, and if none of these is the predominant constituent of the item, give either *multimedia* or *kit* as the designation (see 1.1C1 and 1.10C1).

5.1D. Parallel titles

5.1D1. Transcribe parallel titles as instructed in 1.1D.

> Gold und Silber [GMD] = L'or et l'argent = Gold and silver
>
> Album for the young [GMD] = Album für die Jugend
>
> Concerto, D-Dur, für Horn und Orchester [GMD] = Concerto, D major, for horn and orchestra = Concerto, ré majeur, pour cor et orchestre

If the chief source includes statements of medium of performance, key, date of composition, and/or number that are treated as part of the title proper (see 5.1B1) in two or more languages or scripts, transcribe such information in the order in which it appears in the chief source of information. Precede each set of parallel statements by an equals sign.

> Konzert Nr. 1 für Klarinette und Orchester, Es-Dur [GMD] = E♭-major = mi♭-majeur
>
> Sonate à 3, en mi mineur, pour 2 violons ou hautbois (flûtes) et basse continue [GMD] = e-Moll, für 2 Violinen oder Oboen (Flöten) und Generalbass = in E minor, for 2 violins or oboes (flutes) and thorough-bass

5.1E. Other title information

5.1E1. Transcribe other title information as instructed in 1.1E.

> Angelo mio [GMD] : valse
>
> 6 succès d'Elvis Presley [GMD] : album : piano, chant et guitare
>
> Fugue on Hey diddle diddle [GMD] : for SATB unaccompanied
>
> Kleine Meditationen [GMD] : für Streichtrio und Harfe = Short meditations : for string trio and harp
>
> Officium pastorum [GMD] = The shepherds at the manger : an acting version of a 13th-century liturgical music drama : for six soloists (three sopranos and three basses, or two sopranos, one tenor, and three basses) and treble (or soprano) chorus with suggested accompaniment for chamber organ and chime bells

5.1F. Statements of responsibility

5.1F1. Transcribe statements of responsibility relating to persons or bodies as instructed in 1.1F.

> Traces [GMD] : pour violoncelle seul / Jacques Lenot

> Overture from La sultane suite [GMD] / by François Couperin

> La vie parisienne [GMD] : operetta in three acts / Jacques Offenbach ; music adapted and arranged by Ronald Hanmer ; new book and lyrics by Phil Park

> Door number three [GMD] / Steve Goodman, Jimmy Buffett

> The liber usualis [GMD] : with introduction and rubrics in English / edited by the Benedictines of Solesmes

> Song to the Virgin Mary [GMD] : for mixed chorus a capella or 6 solo voices / by Andrzej Panufnik ; words anonymous

> Three songs for America [GMD] : bass voice and instruments (woodwind quintet and string quintet) / David Amram ; piano reduction by the composer ; words by John F. Kennedy, Martin Luther King, and Robert F. Kennedy

5.1F2. Add a word or short phrase to the statement of responsibility if the relationship between the title and the person(s) or body (bodies) named in the statement is not clear.

> A Collection of ancient piobaireachd or Highland pipe music [GMD] / [collected] by Angus Mackay

> Der Prozess [GMD] / [Musik von] Gottfried von Einem ; [Text von] Boris Blacher und Heinz von Cramer

5.1G. Items without a collective title

5.1G1. If an item lacks a collective title, transcribe the titles of the individual parts as instructed in 1.1G.

> Four small dances [GMD] ; and, Six Hungarian folksongs / Béla Bártok ; arranged for junior string orchestra by Gábor Darvas

> Her silver will [GMD] ; Looking back at Sposalizio : medium voice / Gordon Binkerd ; poems by Emily Dickinson

> Neosa [GMD] : march / Phil B. Catelinet. The wonder of Christmas : suite / Leslie Condon. I come to thee : meditation / Stuart Johnson. Rejoicing every day / selection by Neville McFarlane

5.1G2. Make the relationship between statements of responsibility and the parts of an item lacking a collective title clear by additions as instructed in 5.1F2.

5.2. EDITION AREA

Contents:

5.2A. Preliminary rule

5.2A1. Punctuation

For instructions on the use of spaces before and after prescribed punctuation, see 1.0C.

Precede this area by a full stop, space, dash, space.

Precede a statement relating to a named revision of an edition by a comma.

Precede the first statement of responsibility following an edition statement by a diagonal slash.

Precede each subsequent statement of responsibility by a semicolon.

5.2A2. Manuscript music. For manuscript music existing in different versions, see 4.2.

5.2B. Edition statement

5.2B1. Transcribe a statement relating to an edition of a work that contains differences from other editions of that work, or to a named reissue of a work, as instructed in 1.2B.

> 2nd ed.

> 2ᵉ éd. du recueil noté

> 6. udg.

> Urtextausg.

5.2B2. In case of doubt about whether a statement is an edition statement, follow the instructions in 1.2B3.

5.2B3. *Optional addition.* If an item lacks an edition statement but is known to contain significant changes from other editions, supply a suitable brief statement in the language and script of the title proper and enclose it in square brackets.

> [3rd ed.]

> [Nouv. éd. augm. des Lectures chantées, parue en 1968]

5.2B4. If an edition statement appears in more than one language or script, transcribe the statement that is in the language or script of the title proper. If this criterion does not apply, transcribe the statement that appears first. *Optionally*, transcribe the parallel statement(s), each preceded by an equals sign.

5.2B5. If an item lacking a collective title contains one or more works with an associated edition statement, transcribe such statements following the titles and statements of responsibility to which they relate, separated from them by a full stop.

5.2C. Statements of responsibility relating to the edition

5.2C1. Transcribe a statement of responsibility relating to one or more editions, but not to all editions, of a work as instructed in 1.2C and 5.1F.

> Nolo mortem peccatoris [GMD] / Thomas Morley ; edited by Sylvia Townsend Warner. — Rev. ed. / by John Morehen

> Piano concerto, A major, K. 414 [GMD] / Wolfgang Amadeus Mozart. — Rev. ed. / foreword by Paul Badura-Skoda

5.2D. Statement relating to a named revision of an edition

5.2D1. If an item is a named revision of an edition, transcribe the statement relating to that revision as instructed in 1.2D.

Do not record statements relating to an impression or printing that contains no changes unless the item is considered to be of particular importance to the cataloguing agency.

5.2E. Statements of responsibility relating to a named revision of an edition

5.2E1. Transcribe a statement of responsibility relating to one or more named revisions of an edition (but not to all such revisions) as instructed in 1.2E and 5.1F.

5.3. *Optional area.* MUSICAL PRESENTATION STATEMENT AREA

Contents:
5.3A. Preliminary rule
5.3B. Musical presentation statement

5.3A. Preliminary rule

5.3A1. Punctuation

Precede this area by a full stop, space, dash, space.

5.3B. Musical presentation statement

5.3B1. Transcribe a statement found in the chief source of information indicating the physical presentation of the music.

> Orchester-Partitur

> Score and set of parts

> Miniature score

> Playing score

If the statement appears in two or more languages or scripts, transcribe the one that is in the language or script of the title proper. If this criterion does not apply, transcribe the one that appears first.

Optionally, transcribe the parallel statements, each preceded by an equals sign.

> Partitura = Partition

> Játszópartitúra = Playing score

In case of doubt about whether a statement is a musical presentation statement (as, for example, when it is associated with a statement of responsibility), do not treat it as one.

> . . . ; full score reconstructed by Julian Woodruff from the manuscript parts

5.3B2. If a musical presentation statement is an inseparable part of another area and is recorded as such, do not repeat it here.

5.4. PUBLICATION, DISTRIBUTION, ETC., AREA

Contents:
5.4A. Preliminary rule
5.4B. General rule
5.4C. Place of publication, distribution, etc.
5.4D. Name of publisher, distributor, etc.
5.4E. Statement of function of publisher, distributor, etc.
5.4F. Date of publication, distribution, etc.
5.4G. Place of printing, name of printer, date of printing

5.4A. Preliminary rule

5.4A1. Punctuation

For instructions on the use of spaces before and after prescribed punctuation, see 1.0C.

Precede this area by a full stop, space, dash, space.

Precede a second or subsequently named place of publication, distribution, etc., by a semicolon.

Precede the name of a publisher, distributor, etc., by a colon.

Enclose a supplied statement of function of a publisher, distributor, etc., in square brackets.

Precede the date of publication, distribution, etc., by a comma.

Enclose the details of printing (place, name, date) in parentheses.

Precede the name of a printer by a colon.

Precede the date of printing by a comma.

5.4B. General rule

5.4B1. Record information about the place, name, and date of all types of publishing, distributing, etc., activities as instructed in 1.4B.

5.4B2. Early printed music. Give the publication, etc., details of items published before 1821 as instructed in 2.16.

5.4C. Place of publication, distribution, etc.

5.4C1. Give the place of publication, distribution, etc., as instructed in 1.4C.

5.4C2. Do not record a place of publication, distribution, etc., for an unpublished item. Do not record *s.l.* in such a case.

5.4D. Name of publisher, distributor, etc.

5.4D1. Give the name of the publisher, etc., and *optionally* the distributor, as instructed in 1.4D.

> London : Faber Music
>
> Leipzig : Breitkopf & Härtel
>
> Mainz ; London : Schott

5.4D2. Do not record the name of a publisher, distributor, etc., for an unpublished item. Do not record *s.n.* in such a case.

5.4D3. Publisher's numbers and plate numbers. Give publisher's numbers and plate numbers in the note area (see 5.7B19).

5.4E. *Optional addition.* **Statement of function of publisher, distributor, etc.**

5.4E1. Add to the name of a publisher, distributor, etc., a statement of function as instructed in 1.4E.

> New York : Warner ; [London] : Blossom [distributor]

5.4F. Date of publication, distribution, etc.

5.4F1. Give the date of publication, distribution, etc., of a published music item as instructed in 1.4F. If the copyright date is found only on the first page of the music, do not enclose it in square brackets.

> New York ; London : Peters, 1975
>
> Leipzig : Peters, c1971

5.4F2. Give the date of a music manuscript as instructed in 4.4B1.

5.4G. Place of printing, name of printer, date of printing

5.4G1. If the name of the publisher is unknown and the place and name of the printer are found in the item, give that place and name as instructed in 1.4G.

> [London? : s.n.], 1871 (London : Lord's Press)

5.4G2. *Optional addition.* Give the place, name of printer, and/or date of printing if they are found in the item and differ from the place, name of publisher, etc., and date of publication, etc., and are considered important by the cataloguing agency.

> Madrid : Real Academia de Bellas Artes de San Fernando, [1890] (Madrid : Tip. de las Huérfanos)

5.5. PHYSICAL DESCRIPTION AREA

Contents:
5.5A. Preliminary rule
5.5B. Extent of item (including specific material designation)
5.5C. Illustrative matter
5.5D. Dimensions
5.5E. Accompanying material

5.5A. Preliminary rule

5.5A1. Punctuation

For instructions on the use of spaces before and after prescribed punctuation, see 1.0C.

Precede this area by a full stop, space, dash, space *or* start a new paragraph.

Precede details of illustrations by a colon.

Precede dimensions by a semicolon.

Precede each statement of accompanying material by a plus sign.

Enclose physical details of accompanying material in parentheses.

5.5B. Extent of item (including specific material designation)

5.5B1. Record the number of physical units of an item by giving the number of scores or parts in arabic numerals and one of the following terms as appropriate:

> score
> condensed score
> close score
> miniature score[1]
> piano [violin, etc.] conductor part
> vocal score
> piano score
> chorus score
> part

> 1 score

> 1 vocal score

> 4 parts

For special types of music, use an appropriate specific term (e.g., *choir book, table book*).

> 1 choir book

---

1. Use for scores reduced in size and not intended primarily for performance.

If none of the terms above is appropriate, use *v. of music, p. of music,* or *leaves of music.* If a general material designation (see 1.1C1) is used, *optionally* omit *of music.*

> xx p., 55 p. of music

If the item is a manuscript, precede the term by *ms.*

> 1 ms. score

5.5B2. Give the number of scores and/or parts issued by the publisher.

> 1 score and part
> *Note:* Part printed on p. 5 of the score

If the item consists of different types of score, or a score and parts separately, or different types of score and parts, give the details of each in the order of the list in 5.5B1, separated from each other by a space, plus sign, space.
Add the pagination or number of volumes as instructed in 2.5B.

> 1 score (vi, 27 p.)
>
> 1 score (2 v.)
>
> 2 scores (20 p. each)
>
> 1 miniature score (3 v.)
>
> 1 score (viii, 278 p.) + 24 parts
>
> 1 score (23 p.) + 1 piano conductor part (8 p.) + 16 parts
>
> 1 score (2 sheets)

5.5B3. If the item is in braille or another tactile format, add *(braille), (press braille), (tactile),* etc., to the appropriate term.

> 1 score (2 v., braille)
>
> 1 v. of music (press braille)
>
> 23 leaves of music (braille)

Optionally, if general material designations are used (see 1.1C1) and the general material designation indicates the tactile nature of the item, omit the addition.
If the item is a thermoform copy, add *thermoform* to the parenthetic addition, preceded by a comma.

> 1 score (30 p., braille, thermoform)
>
> *or* 1 score (30 p., thermoform)

If there is no parenthetic addition (see *option* above), add *thermoform* in parentheses.
If the item is in large print intended for use by the visually impaired, add *(large print)* to the appropriate term.

> 1 vocal score (xvii, 378 p., large print)

Optionally, if a general material designation (see 1.1C1) including *large print* is used, omit this addition.

5.5C. Illustrative matter

5.5C1. Give details of illustrative matter as instructed in 2.5C.

>   1 score (vi, 27 p.) : ill.
>
>   1 score (23 p.) : port.
>
>   1 score (23 p.) : ill. + 16 parts

5.5D. Dimensions

5.5D1. Give the dimensions of the item as instructed in 2.5D. If the item consists of score(s) and part(s), give the dimensions after all the details of the score(s) and part(s). If the dimensions of the score(s) and part(s) differ, give the dimensions of each after the details to which they apply.

>   1 miniature score (34 p.) : ill. ; 18 cm.
>
>   1 score (20 p.) + 1 part ; 28 cm.
>
>   4 parts ; 25-27 cm.
>
>   1 score (vi, 63 p.) ; 20 cm. + 16 parts ; 32 cm.

5.5E. Accompanying material

5.5E1. Give the details of accompanying material as instructed in 1.5E.

>   1 score (32 p.) + 5 parts ; 26 cm. + 1 sound tape reel
>
>   1 score (vii, 32 p.) ; 28 cm. + 1 sound tape reel (60 min. : analog, 7½ ips, mono. ; 7 in., ½ in. tape)
>
>   1 score (30 p.) + 4 parts ; 24 cm. + 1 booklet

5.6. SERIES AREA

Contents:
>   5.6A. Preliminary rule
>   5.6B. Series statements

5.6A. Preliminary rule

5.6A1. Punctuation

For instructions on the use of spaces before and after prescribed punctuation, see 1.0C.

Precede this area by a full stop, space, dash, space.

Enclose each series statement (see 1.6J) in parentheses.

Precede each parallel title by an equals sign.

Precede other title information by a colon.

Precede the first statement of responsibility by a diagonal slash.
Precede each subsequent statement of responsibility by a semicolon.
Precede the ISSN of a series or subseries by a comma.
Precede the numbering within a series or subseries by a semicolon.
Precede the title of a subseries by a full stop.

5.6B. Series statements

5.6B1. Record each series statement as instructed in 1.6.

> (Master choruses for Lent and Easter)

> (Early English church music ; no. 7)

> (Music for today. Series 2 ; no. 8)

> (The Salvation Army brass band journal. General series ; no. 1565-1568)

> (Ashdown vocal duets ; no. 384)

> (Yesterday's music, ISSN 4344-1277 ; no. 56)

5.7. NOTE AREA

Contents:
5.7A. Preliminary rule
5.7B. Notes

5.7A. Preliminary rule

5.7A1. Punctuation

Precede each note by a full stop, space, dash, space *or* start a new paragraph for each.

Separate introductory wording from the main content of a note by a colon followed but not preceded by a space.

5.7A2. In making notes, follow the instructions in 1.7A.

5.7B. Notes

Make notes as set out in the following subrules and in the order given there. However, give a particular note first when it has been decided that note is of primary importance.

5.7B1. Form of composition and medium of performance. If the musical form of a work is not apparent from the rest of the description, give the form in a word or brief phrase.

> Carol

> Opera in two acts

Name the medium of performance for which a musical work is intended unless it is named in the rest of the description in English or in foreign language terms that can be readily understood. Name voices before instruments. Name the voices and then the instruments in the order in which they are listed in the item being described. Name a voice or instrument in English unless there is no satisfactory English equivalent.

If the work is for solo instruments, name them all if no more than eleven would be named. If the work is for an orchestra, band, etc., do not list the instruments involved. In describing ensemble vocal music, add to the appropriate term a parenthetical statement of the component voice parts, using *S* (soprano), *Mz* (mezzo-soprano), *A* (alto), *T* (tenor), *Bar* (baritone), and *B* (bass). Repeat an abbreviation, if necessary, to indicate the number of parts.

> For organ
>
> For unacc. child's voice
>
> For voice and piano
>
> For voice, 2 violins, and violoncello
>
> Arr. for guitar
>
> Electronic music
>
> For alto saxophone and piano
>
> For soprano and electronic tape
>
> Reduction for clarinet and piano
>
> For piano, 4 hands
>
> For soprano and piano
>
> For voice and sitar
>
> For solo voices (SATB), chorus (SSATB), and orchestra
>
> For 2 treble recorders, 2 oboes, 2 violins, and basso continuo
>
> For superius, contratenor, tenor, and bassus

If the information relating to the medium of performance given in the rest of the description is ambiguous or insufficient, record supplementary information here.

> Part for piano only
>
> Score for violoncello and piano, part for clarinet
> (*Title page reads:* For violoncello or clarinet or viola, and piano)

5.7B2. Language. Give the language(s) of the textual content of the work unless this is apparent from the rest of the description. Indicate vocal texts published with part of the music.

> French and English words
>
> Latin words

Russian, German, and English words

Words in Hebrew (romanized)

Arbitrary syllables as text

Original text with English translation

Macaronic text (Latin and German)

French words, English translation on p. v-xxii

English words, includes principal melodics

5.7B3. Source of title proper. Make notes on the source of the title proper if it is other than the chief source of information.

Title from publisher's catalogue

5.7B4. Variations in title. Make notes on titles borne by the item other than the title proper. *Optionally*, give a romanization of the title proper.

Title on cover: Love songs of Lennon & McCartney

5.7B5. Parallel titles and other title information. Give the title in another language and other title information not recorded in the title and statement of responsibility area if they are considered to be important.

5.7B6. Statements of responsibility. Make notes on variant names of persons or bodies named in statements of responsibility if these are considered to be important for identification. Give statements of responsibility not recorded in the title and statement of responsibility area. Make notes on persons or bodies connected with a work, or significant persons or bodies connected with previous editions and not already named in the description.

Arr. by Charles Graveney

Previously attributed to Handel

"Based on themes in the poems of Thomas Hardy"—T.p. verso

Transcriptions of recordings made by Alan Lomax

Libretto by Arrigo Boito, based on Victor Hugo's Angelo

5.7B7. Edition and history. Make notes relating to the edition being described or to the bibliographic history of the work.

Reprinted from the 1712 ed.

Reprint in reduced format of the full score: Berlin : Harmonie, 1910

Rev. ed. of: Complete organ works. London : Schott, 1958

Facsim. reprint. Originally published: London : I. Walsh, [ca. 1734]

5.7B8. Notation. Give the notation used in an item if it is not the notation normally found in that type of item.

> Lute tablature and staff notation on opposite pages

> Plainsong notation

> Modern staff notation
> (*Use to describe a work that would normally be in plainsong notation*)

> Tonic sol-fa notation

> Graphic notation

> Melody in both staff and tonic sol-fa notation

5.7B9. Publication, distribution, etc. Make notes on publication, distribution, etc., details that are not included in the publication, distribution, etc., area and are considered to be important.

> Distributed by: London : Peters

5.7B10. Duration of performance and physical description. Give the duration of performance if it is stated in the item. Give the duration in English and in abbreviated form.

> Duration: 18 min.

> Duration: about 1 hr., 10 min.

Make notes on important physical details that are not included in the physical description area.

> Each copy signed by the composer and numbered

5.7B11. Accompanying material. Make notes on the location of accompanying material if appropriate. Give details of accompanying material neither mentioned in the physical description area nor given a separate description (see 1.5E).

> Three photos. of first performance in pocket inside each cover

5.7B12. Series. Make notes on series data that cannot be given in the series area.

> Also issued without series statement

5.7B13. Dissertations. If the item being described is a dissertation, make a note as instructed in 1.7B13.

> Thesis (M. Mus.)—University of Western Ontario, 1972

> Thesis (M.M.A.)—McGill University, 1971

5.7B14. Audience. Make a brief note of the intended audience for, or intellectual level of, an item if this information is stated in the item.

> For 7-9 year olds

> Intended audience: First-year undergraduate students

5.7B16. Other formats. Give the details of other formats in which the content of the item has been issued.

> Issued also on microfilm

5.7B18. Contents. List the separately titled works contained in an item. Add to the titles opus numbers (if they are necessary to identify the works named) and statements of responsibility not already included in the title and statement of responsibility area. If the works in a collection are all in the same musical form and that form is named in the title proper of the item, do not repeat the musical form in the titles in the contents note.

> Contents: Sailing homeward — People call me the Pied Piper — The piper's theme

> Contents: The matron cat's song / words by Ruth Pitter — My cat Jeffry / words by Christopher Smart — The song of the Jellicles / words by T.S. Eliot

> Contents: Komm Heiliger Geist, Herre Gott = Come, O Holy Ghost, God and Lord / by Lucas Osiander ; text by Lucas Osiander — Psalm 121 / by Heinrich Schütz ; freely translated by Cornelius Becker

> Contents: Sonata in D major, op. 6 — Three marches, op. 45 — Variations in C major, op. 23 — Variations in C major, op. 34

> Contents: v. 1. No. 1 (op. 1, no. 1b) E minor. No. 2 (op. 1, no. 2) G minor. No. 3 (op. 1, no. 5) G major. No. 4 (op. 1, no. 7) C major — v. 2. No. 5 (op. 1, no. 11) F major. No. 6 (op. 1, no. 9) B minor. No. 7 (op. 1, no. 4) A minor. No. 8, A minor

Make notes on additional or partial contents when appropriate.

> Includes a song by George Harrison

5.7B19. Publishers' numbers and plate numbers. Give publishers' numbers and/ or plate numbers that appear on the item. Precede the numbers by *Publisher's no.:* or *Pl. no.:*, as appropriate. If a number is preceded by an abbreviation, word, or phrase designating a publisher, give that abbreviation, word, or phrase as part of the number.

In describing an item in several volumes, give inclusive numbers if the numbering is consecutive; otherwise give individual numbers or, if there are more than three of these, the first number and the last number separated by a diagonal slash. Give letters preceding a number before the first number, letters following a number after the last number, but letters preceding and following numbers in conjunction with each number.

> Pl. no.: S. & B. 4081

> Publisher's no.: 6139

> Pl. no.: B. & H. 8797-8806

> Pl. no.: B. M. Co. 10162, 10261, 10311

Publisher's no.: 6201/9935
(*The complete set of numbers is* 6201, 6654, 7006, 7212, 7635, 7788, 8847, 9158, 9664, 9935)

Pl. no.: 9674-9676 H.L.

Pl. no.: R.10150E.-R.10155E.

In describing a reprint, give the plate or publisher's number(s) together with the statement that the item is a reprint (see 5.7B7).

Reissued from Brandus plates. Pl. no.: B. et Cie 4520

5.7B20. Copy being described, library's holdings, and restrictions on use. Make these notes as instructed in 1.7B20.

Library has 6 parts

Library's copy signed by the composer

Library has 3 copies of each score, 2 copies of each part

5.7B21. "With" notes. If the title and statement of responsibility area contains a title that applies to only a part of an item lacking a collective title and, therefore, more than one entry is made, make a note beginning *With:* and listing the other separately titled works in the item in the order in which they appear there.

With: Die Mittagshexe ; and, Das goldene Spinnrad / Antonín Dvořák

5.8. STANDARD NUMBER AND TERMS OF AVAILABILITY AREA

Contents:
5.8A. Preliminary rule
5.8B. Standard number
5.8C. Key-title
5.8D. Terms of availability
5.8E. Qualification

5.8A. Preliminary rule

5.8A1. Punctuation
For instructions on the use of spaces before and after prescribed punctuation, see 1.0C.
Precede this area by a full stop, space, dash, space *or* start a new paragraph.
Precede each repetition of this area by a full stop, space, dash, space.
Precede a key-title by an equals sign.
Precede terms of availability by a colon.
Enclose a qualification to the standard number or terms of availability in parentheses.

5.8B. Standard number

5.8B1. Give the International Standard Book Number (ISBN) or International Standard Serial Number (ISSN) assigned to an item as instructed in 1.8B.

ISBN 0-19-341508-9

5.8B2. Give any other number in a note (see 5.7B19).

5.8C. Key-title

5.8C1. Give the key-title of a serial item as instructed in 1.8C.

5.8D. *Optional addition.* **Terms of availability**

5.8D1. Give the terms on which the item is available as instructed in 1.8D.

ISBN 0-333-17848-3 : £4.50

Free to students and members of the association

5.8E. Qualification

5.8E1. Add qualifications to the standard number and/or terms of availability as instructed in 1.8E and 2.8D.

ISBN 0-573-08042-9 (pbk.)

5.9. SUPPLEMENTARY ITEMS

5.9A. Describe supplementary items as instructed in 1.9.

5.10. ITEMS MADE UP OF SEVERAL TYPES OF MATERIAL

5.10A. Describe items made up of several types of material as instructed in 1.10.

5.11. FACSIMILES, PHOTOCOPIES, AND OTHER REPRODUCTIONS

5.11A. Describe facsimiles, photocopies, and other reproductions as instructed in 1.11.

CHAPTER 6

SOUND RECORDINGS

Contents

6.0. GENERAL RULES

6.0A. Scope

6.0A1. The rules in this chapter cover the description of sound recordings in all media, i.e., discs, tapes (open reel-to-reel, cartridges, cassettes), piano rolls (and other rolls), and sound recordings on film (other than those intended to accompany visual images, for which see chapter 7). They do not cover specifically recordings in other forms (e.g., wires, cylinders) or in various experimental media, though the use of appropriate specifications in the physical description (see 6.5) and special notes will furnish a sufficiently detailed description for such items.

6.0B. Sources of information

6.0B1. Chief source of information. The chief source of information for each major type of sound recording is set out here.

TYPE	CHIEF SOURCE
Disc	Disc and label[1]
Tape (open reel-to-reel)	Reel and label
Tape cassette	Cassette and label
Tape cartridge	Cartridge and label
Roll	Label
Sound recording on film	Container and label

If there are two or more chief sources of information as defined above (e.g., two labels on a disc), treat these as a single chief source.

Treat accompanying textual material or a container as the chief source of information if it furnishes a collective title and the parts themselves and their labels do not. In this case, make a note (see 6.7B3) indicating the source of information.

If information is not available from the chief source, take it from the following sources (in this order of preference):

> accompanying textual material
> container (e.g., sleeve, box)
> other sources

Prefer textual data to sound data. For example, if a sound disc has a label and also information presented in sound form on the disc, prefer the label information.

6.0B2. Prescribed sources of information. The prescribed source(s) of information for each area of the description of sound recordings is set out below. Enclose information taken from outside the prescribed source(s) in square brackets.

AREA	PRESCRIBED SOURCES OF INFORMATION
Title and statement of responsibility	Chief source of information
Edition	Chief source of information, accompanying textual material, container

---

1. *Label* means any permanently affixed paper, plastic, etc., label as opposed to the container itself, which may have data embossed or printed on it.

Publication, distribution, etc.	Chief source of information, accompanying textual material, container
Physical description	Any source
Series	Chief source of information, accompanying textual material, container
Note	Any source
Standard number and terms of availability	Any source

6.0C. Punctuation

For the punctuation of the description as a whole, see 1.0C.
For the prescribed punctuation of elements, see the following rules.

6.0D. Levels of detail in the description

See 1.0D.

6.0E. Language and script of the description

See 1.0E.

6.0F. Inaccuracies

See 1.0F.

6.0G. Accents and other diacritical marks

See 1.0G.

6.0H. Items with several chief sources of information

See 1.0H.

6.1. TITLE AND STATEMENT OF RESPONSIBILITY AREA

Contents:
6.1A. Preliminary rule
6.1B. Title proper
6.1C. General material designation
6.1D. Parallel titles
6.1E. Other title information
6.1F. Statements of responsibility
6.1G. Items without a collective title

6.1A. Preliminary rule

6.1A1. Punctuation

For instructions on the use of spaces before and after prescribed punctuation, see 1.0C.
Precede the title of a supplement or section (see 1.1B9) by a full stop.
Enclose the general material designation in square brackets.
Precede each parallel title by an equals sign.

Precede each unit of other title information by a colon.
Precede the first statement of responsibility by a diagonal slash.
Precede each subsequent statement of responsibility by a semicolon.
For the punctuation of this area for items without a collective title, see 1.1G.

6.1B. Title proper

6.1B1. Transcribe the title proper as instructed in 1.1B. For data to be included in titles proper for musical items, see 5.1B.

> Music from Fiddler on the roof

> Greatest hits

> The little match girl and other tales

> Living and dying in 3/4 time

> Symphony no. 3, A major, op. 56

> The very best of Melanie

> Braverman's condensed cream of Beatles

> Antoine de Saint-Exupéry

> The Beatles

> Institute on International Standards as Related to Universal Bibliographic Control

> [Address to high school students, discussing good writing]

> [Recording of W.B. Yeats reading The lake isle of Innisfree]

> [Sonatas, piano, no. 17, op. 31, no. 2, D minor]

If the title proper is not taken from the chief source of information or if it is taken from a container that is a unifying element, give the source of the title in a note (see 6.7B3).

6.1C. *Optional addition.* General material designation

6.1C1. Give immediately following the title proper the appropriate general material designation as instructed in 1.1C.

> Faustus [GMD]

> Music for flute and tape [GMD]

> Elite Hotel [GMD]

> Woody Guthrie [GMD]

6.1C2. If an item contains parts belonging to materials falling into two or more categories, and if none of these is the predominant constituent of the item, give either *multimedia* or *kit* as the designation (see 1.1C1 and 1.10C1).

6.1D. Parallel titles

6.1D1. Transcribe parallel titles as instructed in 1.1D and 5.1D.

> Quattro concerti per l'organo ed altri stromenti [GMD] = Vier Orgelkonzerte = Four organ concertos = Quatre concertos pour orgue

> Русские народные песни [GMD] = Russian folk songs

6.1E. Other title information

6.1E1. Transcribe other title information as instructed in 1.1E.

> Hello Dolly! [GMD] : original motion picture soundtrack

> Valedictory [GMD] : for computer and soprano

6.1F. Statements of responsibility

6.1F1. Transcribe statements of responsibility relating to those persons or bodies credited with a major role in creating the intellectual content of the sound recording (e.g., as writers of spoken words, composers of performed music, collectors of field material, producers having artistic and/or intellectual responsibility) as instructed in 1.1F. If the participation of the person(s) or body (bodies) named in a statement found in the chief source of information goes beyond that of performance, execution, or interpretation of a work (as is commonly the case with "popular," rock, and jazz music), give such a statement as a statement of responsibility. If, however, the participation is confined to performance, execution, or interpretation (as is commonly the case with "serious" or classical music and recorded speech), give the statement in the note area (see 6.7B6).

> Prometheus bound [GMD] : a play for radio / Robert Lowell

> Famous overtures [GMD] / Offenbach

> Melville [GMD] / written and narrated by Thomas S. Klise

> Texas country [GMD] / Willie Nelson ... [et al.]

> Bury my heart at Wounded Knee [GMD] / by Dee Brown
> *Note:* "Dramatically presented by Harry Madden and Manu Tupon"—Accompanying leaflet

> Subterranean homesick blues [GMD] / Bob Dylan

> Piano rags [GMD] / Scott Joplin
> *Note:* Piano: Joshua Rifkin

> The Afro-American's quest for education [GMD] : a Black odyssey / produced by Pepsi-Cola Co. ; script writer, Norman McRae

> Natty dread [GMD] / Bob Marley and the Wailers

> Beach Boys greatest hits [GMD] / Beach Boys

Thriller [GMD] / produced by Quincy Jones ; co-produced by Michael Jackson

6.1F2. If the members of a group, ensemble, company, etc., are named in the chief source of information as well as the name of the group, etc., give them in the note area (see 6.7B6) if they are considered important. Otherwise omit them.

Quartet in F major [GMD] / Ravel
Note: Budapest String Quartet (J. Roisman and A. Schneider, violins; B. Kroyt, viola; M. Schneider, cello)

6.1F3. Add a word or short phrase to the statement of responsibility if the relationship between the title and the person(s) or body (bodies) named in the statement is not clear.

Born to run [GMD] / [written and performed by] Bruce Springsteen

6.1G. Items without a collective title

6.1G1. If a sound recording lacks a collective title, *either* describe the item as a unit (see 6.1G2 and 6.1G3) *or* make a separate description for each separately titled part (see 6.1G4).

6.1G2. In describing as a unit a sound recording lacking a collective title, transcribe the titles of the individual works as instructed in 1.1G3.

La mer [GMD] ; Khamma ; Rhapsody for clarinet and orchestra / Claude Debussy

How come? [GMD] ; Tell everyone ; Done this one before / Ronnie Lane ; accompanied by the band Slim Chance

Prelude, the afternoon of a faun [GMD] / Claude Debussy. Peer Gynt (Suite) no. 1-2 / Edvard Grieg. Till Eulenspiegels lustige Streiche / Richard Strauss

Dreamboat [GMD] / Linzer ; [performed by] Limmie & Family Cookin'. Made in heaven / Levine, Russell Brown ; [performed by] Limmie & Family Cookin'
Label side A: Dreamboat
(Linzer)
Limmie & Family Cookin'
Label side B: Made in heaven
(Levine-Russell Brown)
Limmie & Family Cookin'

6.1G3. Make the relationship between statements of responsibility and the parts of an item lacking a collective title and described as a unit clear by additions as instructed in 6.1F3.

6.1G4. *Optionally*, make a separate description for each separately titled work on a sound recording. For the statement of the extent in each of these descriptions, see 6.5B3. Link the separate descriptions with notes (see 6.7B21). For instructions on sources of information, see 6.0B.

6.2. EDITION AREA

Contents:
6.2A. Preliminary rule
6.2B. Edition statement
6.2C. Statements of responsibility relating to thc cdition
6.2D. Statement relating to a named revision of an edition
6.2E. Statements of responsibility relating to a named revision of an edition

6.2A. Preliminary rule

6.2A1. Punctuation

For instructions on the use of spaces before and after prescribed punctuation, see 1.0C.

Precede this area by a full stop, space, dash, space.

Precede a statement relating to a named revision of an edition by a comma.

Precede the first statement of responsibility following an edition statement by a diagonal slash.

Precede each subsequent statement of responsibility by a semicolon.

6.2B. Edition statement

6.2B1. Transcribe a statement relating to an edition of a sound recording that contains differences from other editions, or to a named reissue of a recording, as instructed in 1.2B.

6.2B2. In case of doubt about whether a statement is an edition statement, follow the instructions in 1.2B3.

> Viens vers le Père [GMD] / Office catéchistique provincial du Québec. — Éd. spéciale

6.2B3. *Optional addition.* If an item lacks an edition statement but is known to contain significant changes from other editions, supply a suitable brief statement in the language and script of the title proper and enclose it in square brackets.

6.2B4. If an edition statement appears in more than one language or script, transcribe the statement that is in the language or script of the title proper. If this criterion does not apply, transcribe the statement that appears first. *Optionally*, transcribe the parallel statement(s), each preceded by an equals sign.

6.2B5. If an item lacking a collective title and described as a unit contains one or more works with an associated edition statement, transcribe such statements following the titles and statements of responsibility to which they relate, separated from them by a full stop.

6.2C. Statements of responsibility relating to the edition

6.2C1. Transcribe a statement of responsibility relating to one or more editions, but not to all editions, of a sound recording as instructed in 1.2C and 6.1F.

6.2D. Statement relating to a named revision of an edition

6.2D1. If an item is a named revision of an edition, transcribe the statement relating to that revision as instructed in 1.2D.

Do not record statements relating to a reissue that contains no changes unless the item is considered to be of particular importance to the cataloguing agency.

6.2E. Statements of responsibility relating to a named revision of an edition

6.2E1. Transcribe a statement of responsibility relating to one or more named revisions of an edition (but not to all such revisions) as instructed in 1.2E and 6.1F.

6.3. MATERIAL (OR TYPE OF PUBLICATION) SPECIFIC DETAILS AREA

6.3A. This area is not used for sound recordings.

6.4. PUBLICATION, DISTRIBUTION, ETC., AREA

Contents:
- 6.4A.   Preliminary rule
- 6.4B.   General rule
- 6.4C.   Place of publication, distribution, etc.
- 6.4D.   Name of publisher, distributor, etc.
- 6.4E.   Statement of function of publisher, distributor, etc.
- 6.4F.   Date of publication, distribution, etc.
- 6.4G.   Place of manufacture, name of manufacturer, date of manufacture

6.4A. Preliminary rule

6.4A1. Punctuation

For instructions on the use of spaces before and after prescribed punctuation, see 1.0C.

Precede this area by a full stop, space, dash, space.

Precede a second or subsequently named place of publication, distribution, etc., by a semicolon.

Precede the name of a publisher, distributor, etc., by a colon.

Enclose a supplied statement of function of a publisher, distributor, etc., in square brackets.

Precede the date of publication, distribution, etc., by a comma.

Enclose the details of manufacture (place, name, date) in parentheses.

Precede the name of a manufacturer by a colon.

Precede the date of manufacture by a comma.

6.4B. General rule

6.4B1. Record information about the place, name, and date of all types of publishing, distributing, etc., activities as instructed in 1.4B.

6.4C. Place of publication, distribution, etc.

6.4C1. Give the place of publication, distribution, etc., of a published sound recording as instructed in 1.4C.

6.4C2. Do not record a place of publication, distribution, etc., for a nonprocessed sound recording.[2] Do not record *s.l.* in such a case.

6.4D. Name of publisher, distributor, etc.

6.4D1. Give the name of the publisher, etc., and *optionally* the distributor, as instructed in 1.4D.

> [London] : Warner
>
> New York : RCA Victor
>
> London : Gandalf Records : Distributed by Middle Earth Co.

6.4D2. If a sound recording bears both the name of the publishing company and the name of a subdivision of that company or a trade name or brand name used by that company, give the name of the subdivision or the trade name or brand name as the name of the publisher.

> [London] : Ace of Diamonds
>   (*Source of information reads:* Decca Record Company. Ace of Diamonds)

6.4D3. If, however, a trade name appears to be the name of a series rather than of a publishing subdivision, give it as a series title (see 6.6). In case of doubt, treat the name as a series title.

> London : Walt Disney Productions .... — (Disney storyteller)
>   (*Source of information reads:* Disney Storyteller. Walt Disney Productions)

6.4D4. Do not give the name of a publisher, distributor, etc., for a nonprocessed sound recording. Do not record *s.n.* in such a case.

6.4E. *Optional addition.* Statement of function of publisher, distributor, etc.

6.4E1. Add to the name of a publisher, distributor, etc., a statement of function as instructed in 1.4E.

> New York : Sunflower ; [London] : Virgin Records [distributor]

---

2. A *nonprocessed sound recording* is a noncommercial recording that generally exists in a unique copy.

6.4F. Date of publication, distribution, etc.

6.4F1. Give the date of publication, distribution, etc., of a published sound re-cording as instructed in 1.4F.

>   [Los Angeles] : CREDR Corp., c1976
>
>   Chicago : Mercury, 1973
>
>   New York : Polydor, p1979

6.4F2. If the date of recording appears on a published sound recording, give it in a note (see 6.7B7).

>   [New York] : Music Guild, 1971
>   *Note:* Recorded in 1961

6.4F3. Give the date of recording of a nonprocessed sound recording.

6.4G. Place of manufacture, name of manufacturer, date of manufacture

6.4G1. If the name of the publisher is unknown and the place and name of the manufacturer are found in the item, give that place and name as instructed in 1.4G.

>   [S.l. : s.n.], 1970 (London : High Fidelity Sound Studios)

6.4G2. *Optional addition.* Give the place, name of manufacturer, and/or date of manufacture if they are found in the item and differ from the place, name of publisher, etc., and date of publication, etc., and are considered important by the cataloguing agency.

6.5. PHYSICAL DESCRIPTION AREA

Contents:
>   6.5A. Preliminary rule
>   6.5B. Extent of item (including specific material designation)
>   6.5C. Other physical details
>   6.5D. Dimensions
>   6.5E. Accompanying material

6.5A. Preliminary rule

6.5A1. Punctuation
For instructions on the use of spaces before and after prescribed punctuation, see 1.0C.
Precede this area by a full stop, space, dash, space *or* start a new paragraph.
Precede other physical details by a colon.
Precede dimensions by a semicolon.
Precede each statement of accompanying material by a plus sign.
Enclose physical details of accompanying material in parentheses.

6.5B. Extent of item (including specific material designation)

6.5B1. Record the number of physical units of a sound recording by giving the number of parts in arabic numerals and one of the following terms as appropriate:

> sound cartridge
> sound cassette
> sound disc
> sound tape reel
> sound track film

> 1 sound cartridge

> 2 sound cassettes

Add *reel*, *cassette*, etc., as appropriate, to *sound track film*.

> 1 sound track film reel

Use [*name of instrument*] *roll*, as appropriate, for rolls.

> 2 piano rolls

If none of these terms is appropriate, give the specific name of the item as concisely as possible.

Optionally, if general material designations are used (see 1.1C1), omit *sound* from the specific material designation unless it is needed to make the designation understandable (as with *sound track film*).

6.5B2. Give the playing time of a sound recording as instructed in 1.5B4.

> 1 sound disc (50 min.)

> 1 sound tape reel (ca. 90 min.)

> 3 sound cassettes (40 min. each)

6.5B3. If the description is of a separately titled part of a sound recording lacking a collective title (see 6.1G4), express the fractional extent in the form *on side 3 of 2 sound discs*, *on reel 3 of 4 sound tape reels*, etc. (if the parts are numbered or lettered in a single sequence) or *on 1 side of 2 sound discs*, *on 1 reel of 3 sound tape reels*, etc. (if there is no sequential numbering). Add the duration of the part to such a statement.

> on 1 side of 1 sound disc (13 min.)

> on cassettes 3-4 of 4 sound cassettes (67 min.)

> on 1 side of 2 sound discs (ca. 25 min.)

6.5C. Other physical details

6.5C1. Give the following details, as appropriate, in the order set out here:

> type of recording
> playing speed
> groove characteristic (analog discs)

track configuration (sound track films)
number of tracks (tapes)
number of sound channels
recording and reproduction characteristics

6.5C2. Type of recording. Give, for a disc or tape, the type of recording (i.e., the way in which the sound is encoded on the item).

1 sound disc (45 min.) : analog

1 sound disc (56 min.) : digital

1 sound cassette (90 min.) : analog

1 sound cassette (60 min.) : digital

Give, for a sound track film, the type of recording (e.g., *optical*, *magnetic*).

1 sound track film reel (10 min.) : magnetic

6.5C3. Playing speed. Give the playing speed of an analog disc in revolutions per minute (*rpm*).

1 sound disc (45 min.) : analog, 33⅓ rpm

Give the playing speed of a digital disc in metres per second (*m. per sec.*). Give the playing speed of an analog tape in inches per second (*ips*).

1 sound tape reel (16 min.) : analog, 7½ ips

1 sound cassette (120 min.) : analog, 1⁵⁄₁₆ ips

Give the playing speed of a sound track film in frames per second (*fps*).

1 sound track film reel (10 min.) : magnetic, 24 fps

Do not give the playing speed if it is standard for the type of item (e.g., 1⅞ inches per second for an analog tape cassette; 1.4 metres per second for a digital disc).

6.5C4. Groove characteristic. Give the groove characteristic of an analog disc if it is not standard for the type of disc.

1 sound disc (7 min.) : analog, 78 rpm, microgroove

6.5C5. Track configuration. For sound track films, give the track configuration (e.g., *centre track*, *edge track*).

1 sound track film reel (10 min.) : magnetic, 25 fps, centre track

6.5C6. Number of tracks. For tape cartridges, cassettes, and reels, give the number of tracks, unless the number of tracks is standard for the item (e.g., the standard number of tracks for a cartridge is 8 and for an analog cassette 4).

6.5C7. Number of sound channels. Give the number of sound channels, if the information is readily available, using one or more of the following terms as appropriate:

mono.
stereo.
quad.

1 sound disc (56 min.) : digital, stereo.

1 sound tape reel (ca. 60 min.) : analog, 7½ ips, 2 track, mono.

2 sound discs (66 min.) : analog, 33⅓ rpm, mono., stereo.

6.5C8. *Optional addition.* **Recording and reproduction characteristics.** Give the recording and reproduction characteristics (e.g., *Dolby processed*, *NAB standard*).

1 sound cassette (60 min.) : analog, stereo., Dolby processed

6.5D. Dimensions

6.5D1. Give the dimensions of a sound recording as set out in the following rules.
If the sound recordings in a multipart item differ in size, give the smallest or smaller and the largest or larger size, separated by a hyphen.

6.5D2. Sound discs. Give the diameter of a disc in inches.

1 sound disc (20 min.) : analog, 33⅓ rpm, stereo. ; 12 in.

1 sound disc (56 min.) : digital, stereo. ; 4¾ in.

5 sound discs : analog, 33⅓ rpm, stereo. ; 10-12 in.

6.5D3. Sound track films. Give the gauge (width) of a film in millimetres.

1 sound track film reel (10 min.) : magnetic, 25 fps, centre track ; 16 mm.

6.5D4. Sound cartridges. Give the dimensions of a cartridge in inches if other than the standard dimensions (5¼ × 3⅞ in.). Give the width of the tape in fractions of an inch if other than the standard width (¼ in.).

6.5D5. Sound cassettes. Give the dimensions of a cassette if other than the standard dimensions (e.g., the standard dimensions of an analog cassette are 3⅞ × 2½ in.). Give the width of a tape if other than the standard width (e.g., the standard width of an analog tape is ⅛ in.).

1 sound cassette (85 min.) : analog, mono. ; 7¼ × 3½ in., ¼ in. tape

6.5D6. Sound tape reels. Give the diameter of a reel in inches. Give the width of a tape in fractions of an inch if other than the standard width (¼ in.).

1 sound tape reel (60 min.) : analog, 7½ ips, 2 tracks, mono. ; 7 in., ½ in. tape

> 3 sound tape reels (ca. 60 min. each) : analog, 7½ ips, 4 tracks, stereo. ; 5-7 in., ½ in. tape

6.5D7. Rolls. Do not give any dimensions.

6.5E. Accompanying material

6.5E1. Give the details of accompanying material as instructed in 1.5E.

> 1 sound disc (50 min.) : analog, 33⅓ rpm, stereo. ; 12 in. + 1 pamphlet (11 p. : col. ill. ; 32 cm.)

6.6. SERIES AREA

Contents:
    6.6A.　Preliminary rule
    6.6B.　Series statements

6.6A. Preliminary rule

6.6A1. Punctuation
For instructions on the use of spaces before and after prescribed punctuation, see 1.0C.
Precede this area by a full stop, space, dash, space.
Enclose each series statement (see 1.6J) in parentheses.
Precede each parallel title by an equals sign.
Precede other title information by a colon.
Precede the first statement of responsibility by a diagonal slash.
Precede each subsequent statement of responsibility by a semicolon.
Precede the ISSN of a series or subseries by a comma.
Precede the numbering within a series or subseries by a semicolon.
Precede the title of a subseries by a full stop.

6.6B. Series statements

6.6B1. Record each series statement as instructed in 1.6.

> (Historic instruments at the Victoria and Albert Museum ; 2)

> (Standard radio super sound effects. Trains)

> (Audio-cassette library for professional librarians ; L-510)

> ([Development digest. Premier series])

> (Disney storyteller)

> (Sounds of the eighties, ISSN 7981-5137 ; no. 54)

6.7. NOTE AREA

Contents:
    6.7A.　Preliminary rule
    6.7B.　Notes

6.7A. Preliminary rule

6.7A1. Punctuation

Precede each note by a full stop, space, dash, space *or* start a new paragraph for each.

Separate introductory wording from the main content of a note by a colon followed but not preceded by a space.

6.7A2. In making notes, follow the instructions in 1.7A.

6.7B. Notes

Make notes as set out in the following subrules and in the order given there. However, give a particular note first when it has been decided that note is of primary importance.

6.7B1. Nature or artistic form and medium of performance. Make notes on the form of a literary work or the type of musical or other work unless it is apparent from the rest of the description.

> Play for child actors

> Opera in two acts

> Field recording of birdsong

Name the medium of performance when necessary, as instructed in 5.7B1.

> Singer, bass, 2 electric guitars, drums

6.7B2. Language. Give the language(s) of the spoken or sung content of a recording unless this is apparent from the rest of the description.

> Sung in French

> In French, introduced in English

6.7B3. Source of title proper. Make notes on the source of the title proper if it is other than the chief source of information or if it is a container or accompanying textual material (see 6.0B1).

> Title from container

> Title from accompanying typewritten notes (4 p.)

6.7B4. Variations in title. Make notes on titles borne by the item other than the title proper. *Optionally*, give a romanization of the title proper.

> Title on container: The four seasons

6.7B5. Parallel titles and other title information. Give the title in another language and other title information not recorded in the title and statement of responsibility area if they are considered to be important.

> Subtitle: Songs of redemption

6.7B6. Statements of responsibility. Make notes on variant names of persons or bodies named in statements of responsibility if these are considered to be important for identification. Give the names of performers and the medium in which they perform if they have not been named in the statements of responsibility and if they are judged necessary. Make notes relating to any other persons or bodies connected with a work that are not named in the statements of responsibility.

> Based on music by Franz Schubert

> Genevieve Warner, Lois Hunt, Genevieve Rowe, sopranos; Elizabeth Brown, Virginia Paris, contraltos; Frank Rogier, baritone; Columbia Chamber Orchestra, Leon Engel, conductor

> Backing by Coral Reefer Band

> Recordings by Willie Nelson (side 1), Bob Wills and His Texas Playboys (side 2), Asleep at the Wheel (side 3), and Freddy Fender (side 4)

> Piano: Joshua Rifkin

Incorporate the names of performers into the contents note if appropriate (see 6.7B18).

6.7B7. Edition and history. Make notes relating to the edition being described, to the edition of the work performed, or to the history of the recording.

> Reissue of: Caedmon TC 1125 (1952)

> Ed. recorded: New York : Farrar, 1937

> Recorded in Vienna in 1961, previously released as Westminster WST 17035

> "The twenty-four songs on these two discs are drawn from sessions that took place between June and October 1967 in the basement of Big Pink, West Saugherties, New York"—Container notes

> An abridgement of: Bury my heart at Wounded Knee / by Dee Brown. Text originally published: New York : Holt, Rinehart & Winston, 1971

For a nonprocessed sound recording, give the available details of the event.

> Recording of speech given at the University of Kentucky Academic Library Institute, Lexington, Ky., May 24, 1984.

6.7B9. Publication, distribution, etc. Make notes on publication, distribution, etc., details that are not included in the publication, distribution, etc., area and are considered to be important.

> Distributed in the U.K. by: Hobbit & Son

6.7B10. Physical description. Make notes on important physical details that are not included in the physical description area, especially if these affect the use of the item. Do not give any physical details that are standard to the item being described (e.g., assume that all analog discs are electrically recorded, laterally cut, and designed for playing from the outside inward).

> *Discs*
>> In 2 containers
>>
>> Acoustic recording
>>
>> Impressed on rectangular surface 20 × 20 cm.
>>
>> Vertically cut from inside outward
>>
>> Compact disc
>>
>> Analog recording
>>> (*For a digital disc made from an analog original*)
>>
>> Digital recording
>>> (*For an analog disc made from a digital original*)
>
> *Rolls*
>> For 65-note player piano
>
> *Tape*
>> Paper tape
>>
>> Recording made with stacked heads
>>
>> Recorded on both sides
>>
>> Digital recording
>>> (*For an analog tape made from a digital original*)

Give the duration of each part contained in an item without a collective title and described as a unit (see 6.1G2 and 6.1G3; see also 6.7B18).

> Durations: 17 min. ; 23 min. ; 9 min.

6.7B11. Accompanying material. Make notes on the location of accompanying material if appropriate. Give details of accompanying material neither mentioned in the physical description area nor given a separate description (see 1.5E).

> Lyrics on sheets in container

6.7B12. Series. Make notes on series data that cannot be given in the series area.

> Originally issued in the series: Sound effects

6.7B13. Dissertations. If the item being described is a dissertation, make a note as instructed in 1.7B13.

6.7B14. Audience. Make a brief note of the intended audience for, or intellectual level of, a sound recording if this information is stated in the item, its container, or accompanying textual material.

> Intended audience: First year undergraduates
>
> Intended audience: G.C.E. "A" level students

6.7B16. Other formats. Give the details of other formats in which the content of the item has been issued.

> Issued also as cassette and as cartridge

6.7B17. Summary. Give a brief objective summary of the content of a sound recording (other than one that consists entirely or predominantly of music) unless another part of the description provides enough information.

> Summary: Episodes from the novel, read by Ed Begley

> Summary: A brief historical account up to the introduction of wave mechanics

6.7B18. Contents. List the titles of individual works contained on a sound recording. Add to each title statements of responsibility not included in the title and statement of responsibility area and the duration of the piece (see 1.5B4).

> Contents: The golden age of rock'n'roll — Born late 58 — Trudi's song — Pearl'n'Roy — Roll away the stone — Marionette — Alice — Crash Street kids — Through the looking glass

> Contents: The fourth millennium / Henry Brant (9 min.) — Music for brass quintet (14 min.)

> Contents: Louise. Depuis le jour / G. Charpentier (Mary Garden, soprano, with orchestra) — Tosca. Vissi d'arte / Puccini (Maria Jeritza, soprano, with piano)

Make notes on additional or partial contents when appropriate.

> With musical extracts from the works of the composer

6.7B19. Publishers' numbers. Give the publisher's stock number (usually an alphabetic and/or numeric symbol) as found on the item. Precede each number by the brand or trade name associated with it on the label or container (see 6.4D2) and a colon.

> Tamla Motown: STMA 8007

> Island: ILPS 9281

If the item has two or more numbers, give the principal number if one can be ascertained, otherwise give both or all. If one of the numbers applies to the set as a whole, give it first and designate it as such.

If the item consists of separately numbered units, give inclusive numbers if the numbering is consecutive; otherwise give individual numbers or, if there are more than three of these, the first number and the last number separated by a diagonal slash.

6.7B20. Copy being described, library's holdings, and restrictions on use. Make these notes as instructed in 1.7B20.

> Library's copy scratched but playable

6.7B21. "With" notes. If the title and statement of responsibility area contains a title that applies to only a part of an item lacking a collective title and, therefore, more than one entry is made, make a note beginning *With:* and listing the other separately titled works in the item in the order in which they appear there. If the individual works are not titled, supply titles as instructed in 6.1B1.

With: Peer Gynt (Suite) no. 1-2 / Edvard Grieg — Till Eulenspiegels lustige Streiche / Richard Strauss

6.8. STANDARD NUMBER AND TERMS OF AVAILABILITY AREA

Contents:
6.8A. Preliminary rule
6.8B. Standard number
6.8C. Key-title
6.8D. Terms of availability
6.8E. Qualification

6.8A. Preliminary rule

6.8A1. Punctuation
For instructions on the use of spaces before and after prescribed punctuation, see 1.0C.
Precede this area by a full stop, space, dash, space *or* start a new paragraph.
Precede each repetition of this area by a full stop, space, dash, space.
Precede a key-title by an equals sign.
Precede terms of availability by a colon.
Enclose a qualification to the standard number or terms of availability in parentheses.

6.8B. Standard number

6.8B1. Give the International Standard Book Number (ISBN) or International Standard Serial Number (ISSN) assigned to an item as instructed in 1.8B.

6.8B2. Give any other number in a note (see 6.7B19).

6.8C. Key-title

6.8C1. Give the key-title of a serial item as instructed in 1.8C.

6.8D. *Optional addition.* **Terms of availability**

6.8D1. Give the terms on which the item is available as instructed in 1.8D.

$14.00

Free to members of the Association

179

6.8E. Qualification

6.8E1. Add qualifications to the standard number and/or terms of availability as instructed in 1.8E.

6.9. SUPPLEMENTARY ITEMS

6.9A. Describe supplementary items as instructed in 1.9.

6.10. ITEMS MADE UP OF SEVERAL TYPES OF MATERIAL

6.10A. Describe items made up of several types of material as instructed in 1.10.

CHAPTER 7

MOTION PICTURES AND VIDEORECORDINGS

Contents

7.0. GENERAL RULES

7.0A. Scope

7.0A1. The rules in this chapter cover the description of motion pictures and videorecordings of all kinds, including complete films and programmes, compilations, trailers, newscasts and newsfilms, stock shots, and unedited material. For other visual material, see chapter 8. For sound track film not accompanied by visual material, see chapter 6.

7.0B. Sources of information

7.0B1. Chief source of information. The chief source of information for motion pictures and videorecordings is (in this order of preference):

a) the item itself (e.g., the title frames)
b) its container (and container label) if the container is an integral part of the piece (e.g., a cassette).

If the information is not available from the chief source, take it from the following sources (in this order of preference):

> accompanying textual material (e.g., scripts, shot lists, publicity material)
> container (if not an integral part of the piece)
> other sources

7.0B2. Prescribed sources of information. The prescribed source(s) of information for each area of the description of motion pictures and videorecordings is set out below. Enclose information taken from outside the prescribed source(s) in square brackets.

AREA	PRESCRIBED SOURCES OF INFORMATION
Title and statement of responsibility	Chief source of information
Edition	Chief source of information, accompanying material, container
Publication, distribution, etc.	Chief source of information, accompanying material, container
Physical description	Any source
Series	Chief source of information, accompanying material, container
Note	Any source
Standard number and terms of availability	Any source

7.0C. Punctuation
For the punctuation of the description as a whole, see 1.0C.
For the prescribed punctuation of elements, see the following rules.

7.0D. Levels of detail in the description
See 1.0D.

7.0E. Language and script of the description
See 1.0E.

7.0F. Inaccuracies
See 1.0F.

7.0G. Accents and other diacritical marks
See 1.0G.

7.0H. Items with several chief sources of information
See 1.0H.

7.1. TITLE AND STATEMENT OF RESPONSIBILITY AREA

Contents:
7.1A. Preliminary rule
7.1B. Title proper
7.1C. General material designation
7.1D. Parallel titles
7.1E. Other title information
7.1F. Statements of responsibility
7.1G. Items without a collective title

7.1A. Preliminary rule

7.1A1. Punctuation
For instructions on the use of spaces before and after prescribed punctuation, see 1.0C.
Precede the title of a supplement or section (see 1.1B9) by a full stop.
Enclose the general material designation in square brackets.
Precede each parallel title by an equals sign.
Precede each unit of other title information by a colon.
Precede the first statement of responsibility by a diagonal slash.
Precede each subsequent statement of responsibility by a semicolon.
For the punctuation of this area for items without a collective title, see 1.1G.

7.1B. Title proper

7.1B1. Transcribe the title proper as instructed in 1.1B.

> Jules et Jim
>
> How to steal a diamond in four uneasy lessons
>
> Pulse generator basics
>
> Lost by a hare on my terra pin pin
>
> Gullible's travails, or, How the meter met her match
>
> Little Roquefort in Good mousekeeping
>
> Walt Whitman's Civil War

If the title proper is not taken from the chief source of information, give the source of the title in a note (see 7.7B3).

7.1B2. If an item lacks a title, supply one as instructed in 1.1B7 and also follow these particular instructions.

Commercials. Supply for a short advertising film a title consisting of the name of the product, service, etc., advertised, and the word *advertisement*.

> [Manikin cigar advertisement]

> [Road safety campaign advertisement]

Unedited material and newsfilm. Include in a supplied title for unedited material, stock shots, and newsfilm all the major elements present in the picture in order of their occurrence (e.g., place, date of event, date of shooting (if different), personalities, and subjects).

> [Phantom jet landing at R.A.F. Leuchars, July 1971]

Optionally, give a description of the action and length of each shot in a note (see 7.7B18).

7.1C. *Optional addition.* **General material designation**

7.1C1. Give immediately following the title proper the appropriate general material designation as instructed in 1.1C.

> The Pickwick papers [GMD]

> The administration of justice [GMD]

7.1C2. If an item contains parts belonging to materials falling into two or more categories, and if none of these is the predominant constituent of the item, give either *multimedia* or *kit* as the designation (see 1.1C1 and 1.10C1).

Treat a sound track (recorded sound physically integrated or synchronized with the item and intended to be played with it) as an integral part of the motion picture or videorecording, and give the general material designation appropriate to the motion picture or videorecording alone. See also 7.5C3 and 7.7B10a.

7.1D. Parallel titles

7.1D1. Transcribe parallel titles as instructed in 1.1D.

> Clima de la calle [GMD] = Climate in the streets

7.1D2. Transcribe an original title in another language appearing in the chief source of information as a parallel title.

> Breathless [GMD] = À bout de souffle

7.1E. Other title information

7.1E1. Transcribe other title information as instructed in 1.1E.

> Jury and juror [GMD] : function and responsibility

> Le tambou [GMD] : drum of Haiti

7.1E2. If the item is a trailer containing extracts from a larger film, add *[trailer]* as other title information.

>   Annie Hall [GMD] : [trailer]

7.1F. Statements of responsibility

7.1F1. Transcribe statements of responsibility relating to those persons or bodies credited in the chief source of information with a major role in creating a film (e.g., as producer, director, animator) as instructed in 1.1F. Give all other statements of responsibility (including those relating to performance) in notes.

>   Flowering and fruiting of papaya [GMD] / produced by the Department of Botany, Iowa State University

>   Classroom control [GMD] / University of London Audio Visual Centre ; produced, directed, and edited by N.C. Collins

>   Food [GMD] : green grow the profits / ABC News ; producer and writer, James Benjamin ; director, Al Niggemeyer

>   Square pegs, round holes [GMD] / director, Dan Bessie ; writer, Phyllis Harvey ; animation, B. Davis ; editor, I. Dryer

7.1F2. Add a word or short phrase to the statement of responsibility if the relationship between the title and the person(s) or body (bodies) named in the statement is not clear.

>   Skaterdater [GMD] / [produced by] Marshal Backlar

7.1F3. If a statement of responsibility names both the agency responsible for the production of a motion picture or videorecording and the agency for which it is produced, give the statement as found.

>   New readers begin here [GMD] / University of Salford Audiovisual Media for University of Salford Library

7.1G. Items without a collective title

7.1G1. If a motion picture or videorecording lacks a collective title, *either* describe the item as a unit (see 7.1G2 and 7.1G3) *or* make a separate description for each separately titled part (see 7.1G4).

7.1G2. In describing as a unit a motion picture or videorecording lacking a collective title, transcribe the titles of the individual parts as instructed in 1.1G3.

>   Infancy [GMD] ; Childhood / [written by] J. Thornton Wilder

>   The Truman story [GMD]. They're in the army now

7.1G3. Make the relationship between statements of responsibility and the parts of an item lacking a collective title and described as a unit clear by additions as instructed in 7.1F2.

7.1G4. *Optionally*, make a separate description for each separately titled work on a motion picture or videorecording. For the statement of the extent in each of these descriptions, see 7.5B3. Link the separate descriptions with notes (see 7.7B21).

7.2. EDITION AREA

Contents:
7.2A. Preliminary rule
7.2B. Edition statement
7.2C. Statements of responsibility relating to the edition
7.2D. Statement relating to a named revision of an edition
7.2E. Statements of responsibility relating to a named revision of an edition

7.2A. Preliminary rule

7.2A1. Punctuation

For instructions on the use of spaces before and after prescribed punctuation, see 1.0C.

Precede this area by a full stop, space, dash, space.

Precede a statement relating to a named revision of an edition by a comma.

Precede the first statement of responsibility following an edition statement by a diagonal slash.

Precede each subsequent statement of responsibility by a semicolon.

7.2B. Edition statement

7.2B1. Transcribe a statement relating to an edition of a motion picture or videorecording that contains differences from other editions of that film, etc., or to a named reissue of a film, etc., as instructed in 1.2B.

> 2nd ed.

> Re-edited version

7.2B2. In case of doubt about whether a statement is an edition statement, follow the instructions in 1.2B3.

7.2B3. *Optional addition.* If a motion picture or videorecording lacks an edition statement but is known to contain significant changes from other editions, supply a suitable brief statement in the language and script of the title proper and enclose it in square brackets.

7.2B4. If an edition statement appears in more than one language or script, transcribe the statement that is in the language or script of the title proper. If this criterion does not apply, transcribe the statement that appears first. *Optionally*, transcribe the parallel statement(s), each preceded by an equals sign.

7.2B5. If an item lacking a collective title and described as a unit contains one or more works with an associated edition statement, transcribe such statements following the titles and statements of responsibility to which they relate, separated from them by a full stop.

7.2C. Statements of responsibility relating to the edition

7.2C1. Transcribe a statement of responsibility relating to one or more editions, but not to all editions, of a motion picture or videorecording as instructed in 1.2C and 7.1F.

7.2D. Statement relating to a named revision of an edition

7.2D1. If an item is a named revision of an edition, transcribe the statement relating to that revision as instructed in 1.2D.

Do not record statements relating to a reissue that contains no changes unless the item is considered to be of particular importance to the cataloguing agency.

7.2E. Statements of responsibility relating to a named revision of an edition

7.2E1. Transcribe a statement of responsibility relating to one or more named revisions of an edition (but not to all such revisions) as instructed in 1.2E and 7.1F.

7.3. MATERIAL (OR TYPE OF PUBLICATION) SPECIFIC DETAILS AREA

7.3A. This area is not used for motion pictures and videorecordings.

7.4. PUBLICATION, DISTRIBUTION, ETC., AREA

Contents:
- 7.4A. Preliminary rule
- 7.4B. General rule
- 7.4C. Place of publication, distribution, etc.
- 7.4D. Name of publisher, distributor, etc.
- 7.4E. Statement of function of publisher, distributor, etc.
- 7.4F. Date of publication, distribution, etc.
- 7.4G. Place of manufacture, name of manufacturer, date of manufacture

7.4A. Preliminary rule

7.4A1. Punctuation
For instructions on the use of spaces before and after prescribed punctuation, see 1.0C.

Precede this area by a full stop, space, dash, space.

Precede a second or subsequently named place of publication, distribution, etc., by a semicolon.

Precede the name of a publisher, distributor, etc., by a colon.

Enclose a supplied statement of function of a publisher, distributor, etc., in square brackets.

Precede the date of publication, distribution, etc., by a comma.

Enclose the details of manufacture (place, name, date) in parentheses.
Precede the name of a manufacturer by a colon.
Precede the date of manufacture by a comma.

7.4B. General rule

7.4B1. Record information about the place, name, and date of all types of publishing, distributing, etc., activities as instructed in 1.4B.

7.4C. Place of publication, distribution, etc.

7.4C1. Give the place of publication, distribution, etc., of a published item as instructed in 1.4C.

7.4C2. Do not record a place of publication, distribution, etc., for an unpublished item. Do not record *s.l.* in such a case.

7.4D. Name of publisher, distributor, etc.

7.4D1. Give the name of the publisher, etc., and *optionally* the name of the distributor, releasing agency, etc., as instructed in 1.4D.

> New York : National Society for the Prevention of Blindness

> Rochester, N.Y. : Modern Learning Aids

7.4D2. Do not record the name of a publisher, distributor, etc., for an unpublished item. Do not record *s.n.* in such a case.

7.4E. *Optional addition.* Statement of function of publisher, distributor, etc.

7.4E1. Add to the name of a publisher, distributor, releasing agency, etc., a statement of function as instructed in 1.4E.

> Manchester : University of Manchester, Dept. of Medical Biochemistry [distributor]

7.4F. Date of publication, distribution, etc.

7.4F1. Give the date of publication, distribution, release, etc., of a published item as instructed in 1.4F.

> Santa Ana, Calif. : Doubleday Multimedia, 1973

> Big Spring, Tex. : Creative Visuals, [197-?]

7.4F2. *Optionally*, give a date of original production differing from the date of publication, distribution, etc., of a published item in the note area (see 7.7B9).

> Santa Monica [Calif.] : Pyramid Films [distributor], 1971
> *Note:* Made in 1934

7.4F3. Give the date of creation of unedited or unpublished film or video material and of stock shots.

7.4G. Place of manufacture, name of manufacturer, date of manufacture

7.4G1. If the name of the publisher is unknown and the place and name of the manufacturer are found in the item, give that place and name as instructed in 1.4G.

7.4G2. *Optional addition.* Give the place, name of manufacturer, and/or date of manufacture if they are found in the item and differ from the place, name of publisher, etc., and date of publication, etc., and are considered important by the cataloguing agency.

7.5. PHYSICAL DESCRIPTION AREA

Contents:
    7.5A. Preliminary rule
    7.5B. Extent of item (including specific material designation)
    7.5C. Other physical details
    7.5D. Dimensions
    7.5E. Accompanying material

7.5A. Preliminary rule

7.5A1. Punctuation
For instructions on the use of spaces before and after prescribed punctuation, see 1.0C.
Precede this area by a full stop, space, dash, space *or* start a new paragraph.
Precede other physical details by a colon.
Precede dimensions by a semicolon.
Precede each statement of accompanying material by a plus sign.
Enclose physical details of accompanying material in parentheses.

7.5B. Extent of item (including specific material designation)

7.5B1. Record the number of physical units of a motion picture or videorecording by giving the number of parts in arabic numerals and one of the following terms as appropriate:

> film cartridge
> film cassette
> film loop
> film reel
> videocartridge
> videocassette
> videodisc
> videoreel

1 film cassette

3 film reels

1 videoreel

2 videodiscs

If none of these terms is appropriate, give the specific name of the item as concisely as possible.

Optionally, if general material designations are used (see 1.1C1), and the general material designation indicates that the item is a motion picture or video-recording, omit *film* or *video* from the specific material designation.

1 reel

1 disc

Give a trade name or other similar specification in a note (see 7.7B10).

7.5B2. Give the playing time of a motion picture or videorecording (other than a videodisc, see below) as instructed in 1.5B4.

1 film loop (4 min., 30 sec.)

2 film cassettes (25 min. each)

1 videoreel (ca. 75 min.)

Give the playing time of a videodisc as set out in the following subrules:

Videodiscs consisting of moving images. Give the playing time as instructed in 1.5B4.

1 videodisc (ca. 50 min.)

Videodiscs consisting of frames of still images. If the playing time is stated on the item, give it as stated.

1 videodisc (80 min.)

If the playing time is not stated on the item, do not give a playing time. *Optionally*, give the number of frames if that number is readily ascertainable.

1 videodisc (45,876 fr.)

Videodiscs consisting of both moving images and still images. If the playing time is stated on the item, give it as stated. *Optionally*, whether the playing time is stated on the item or not, give in a note the number of frames of still images and the duration of the moving images (see 7.7B10j).

7.5B3. If the description is of a separately titled part of a motion picture or videorecording lacking a collective title (see 7.1G4), express the fractional extent in the form *on reel 3 of 4 film reels* (if the parts are numbered or lettered in a single sequence) or *on 1 cassette of 3 videocassettes* (if there is no sequential numbering). Add the duration of the part to such a statement.

>   on reel 1 of 2 film reels (13 min.)

>   on 2 cassettes of 4 videocassettes (50 min.)

7.5C. Other physical details

7.5C1. Give the following details, as appropriate, in the order set out here:

>   aspect ratio and special projection characteristics (motion pictures)
>   sound characteristics
>   colour
>   projection speed (motion pictures)

7.5C2. Aspect ratio and special projection characteristics. If a film has special projection requirements, give them as succinctly as possible (e.g., *Cinerama*, *Panavision*, *multiprojector*; and whether anamorphic, techniscope, stereoscopic, or multiscreen).

>   14 film reels (157 min.) : Panavision

7.5C3. Sound characteristics. Give *sd.* (sound) or *si.* (silent) to indicate the presence or absence of a sound track. If a silent film is known to be photographed at the speed of sound film, give *si. at sd. speed*.

>   1 videoreel (15 min.) : sd.

7.5C4. Colour. Give *col.* or *b&w* to indicate whether an item is in colour or black and white. Give *b&w* for a sepia print (see also 7.7B10).

>   1 film reel (10 min.) : sd., col.

Give a succinct statement to indicate that an item is in a combination of colour and black and white.

>   1 film reel (30 min.) : sd., col. with b&w sequences

>   1 videocassette (24 min.) : sd., b&w with col. introductory sequence

7.5C5. Projection speed. Give the projection speed of a film in frames per second (*fps*), if this information is considered important.

>   1 film reel (1 min., 17 sec.) : si., col., 25 fps

Do not give the projection speed if it is standard for the item (24 fps for a sound film; 16 fps for a silent film).

7.5D. Dimensions

7.5D1. Give the dimensions of a motion picture or videorecording as set out in the following rules.
If the motion pictures or videorecordings in a multipart item differ in size, give the smallest or smaller and the largest or larger size, separated by a hyphen.

7.5D2. Give the gauge (width) of a motion picture in millimetres. If 8 mm., state whether single, standard, super, or Maurer.

> 1 film reel (12 min.) : sd., b&w ; 16mm.

> 1 film cassette (21 min.) : sd., col. ; standard 8 mm.

> 2 film reels (ca. 30 min. each) : b&w ; 16-35 mm.

7.5D3. Give the gauge (width) of a videotape in inches or millimetres.

> 1 videoreel (30 min.) : sd., b&w ; ½ in.

7.5D4. Give the diameter of a videodisc in inches.

> 1 videodisc (ca. 20 min.) : sd., b&w ; 8 in.

> 1 videodisc (38 min.) : sd., col. ; 12 in.

7.5E. Accompanying material

7.5E1. Give the details of accompanying material as instructed in 1.5E.

> 1 film cassette (21 min.) : sd., col. ; standard 8 mm. + 1 teacher's guide

or   1 film cassette (21 min.) : sd., col. ; standard 8 mm. + 1 v. (28 p. : ill. ; 22 cm.)

> 2 film cassettes (30 min. each) : sd., col. ; standard 8 mm. + 1 v. (35 p. ; 24 cm.)

7.6. SERIES AREA

Contents:
> 7.6A. Preliminary rule
> 7.6B. Series statements

7.6A. Preliminary rule

7.6A1. Punctuation
For instructions on the use of spaces before and after prescribed punctuation, see 1.0C.
Precede this area by a full stop, space, dash, space.
Enclose each series statement (see 1.6J) in parentheses.
Precede each parallel title by an equals sign.
Precede other title information by a colon.
Precede the first statement of responsibility by a diagonal slash.
Precede each subsequent statement of responsibility by a semicolon.
Precede the ISSN of a series or subseries by a comma.
Precede the numbering within a series or subseries by a semicolon.
Precede the title of a subseries by a full stop.

7.6B. Series statements

7.6B1. Record each series statement as instructed in 1.6.

> (Allstate simulation film library)

> (Ecology : communities in nature)

> (Automotive damage correction series. Set 5)

> (Mathematics for elementary school students. Whole numbers ; no. 10)

> (Fant anthology of literature in Ameslan)

> (Welding series. Gas metal arc (mig) welding)

> (Images of the seventies, ISSN 7745-2251 ; no. 22)

> (Visual media from the American Folklife Center ; no. 1)

7.7. NOTE AREA

Contents:
7.7A. Preliminary rule
7.7B. Notes

7.7A. Preliminary rule

7.7A1. Punctuation
Precede each note by a full stop, space, dash, space *or* start a new paragraph for each.
Separate introductory wording from the main content of a note by a colon followed but not preceded by a space.

7.7A2. In making notes, follow the instructions in 1.7A.

7.7B. Notes
Make notes as set out in the following subrules and in the order given there. However, give a particular note first when it has been decided that note is of primary importance.

7.7B1. Nature or form. Make notes on the nature or form of a motion picture or videorecording unless it is apparent from the rest of the description.

> Documentary

> TV play

7.7B2. Language. Give the language(s) of the spoken, sung, or written content of a motion picture or videorecording unless this is apparent from the rest of the description. Indicate captioning or signing.

> In French

> French dialogue, English subtitles

Dubbed into English

Closed-captioned

7.7B3. Source of title proper. Make notes on the source of the title proper if it is other than the chief source of information.

Title from script

7.7B4. Variations in title. Make notes on titles borne by the item other than the title proper. *Optionally*, give a romanization of the title proper.

Title on container: Papaya and guava

Title in English on title frame: 400 blows

Title on containers of parts 3, 5-6 varies slightly

7.7B5. Parallel titles and other title information. Give the title in another language and other title information not recorded in the title and statement of responsibility area if they are considered to be important.

Subtitle: Les fleurs anglaises

7.7B6. Statements of responsibility

Cast. List featured players, performers, narrators, and/or presenters.

Presenter: Jackie Glanville

Cast: Laurence Harvey, Mia Farrow, Lionel Stander, Harry Andrews

Cast: Gilles Behat (Charles IV), Jean Deschamps (Charles de Valois), Hélène Duc (Mahaut d'Artois)

Incorporate names of the cast into the contents note if appropriate (see 7.7B18).

Credits. List persons (other than the cast) who have contributed to the artistic and/or technical production of a motion picture or videorecording and who are not named in the statements of responsibility (see 7.1F). Do not include the names of assistants, associates, etc., or any other persons making only a minor contribution. Preface each name or group of names with a statement of function.

Credits: Screenplay, Harold Pinter; music, John Dankworth; camera, Gerry Fisher; editor, Reginald Beck

Credits: Script, John Taylor; calligraphy and design, Alan Haigh; commentator, Derek G. Holroyde

7.7B7. Edition and history. Make notes relating to the edition being described or to the history of the motion picture or videorecording.

Shorter version of the 1969 motion picture of the same name

Censored version. 3 min. sequence missing on reel 3. Censorship certificate C-132, May 4, 1946, of the U.S. Dept. of the Army

> Spanish version of the 1956 motion picture entitled: Jenny's birthday book. Based on: Jenny's birthday book / by Esther Averill

> Remake of the 1933 motion picture of the same name

> Based on the novel by Nicolas Mosley

7.7B9. Publication, distribution, etc., and date. Make notes on publication, distribution, etc., details that are not included in the publication, distribution, etc., area and are considered to be important.

> Distributed in the U.S. by: Stamford, Conn. : Educational Dimensions

Give a date of original production differing from the date of publication, distribution, etc.

> Made in 1927

Give the country of original release if it is not stated or implied elsewhere in the description.

> First released in Yugoslavia

7.7B10. Physical description. Make the following notes on the physical description when appropriate and if this level of detail is desired:

a) *Sound characteristics.* Give any special characteristics of the sound component of a motion picture or videorecording (e.g., optical or magnetic, whether the sound track is physically integrated with the film or the sound is separate on a synchronized recording).

> Magnetic sound track

> Dolby stereo., mono. compatible

b) *Length of film or tape.* Give the length in feet of a motion picture (from first frame to last) or videotape (from first programme signal to last).

> Film: 14,139 ft.

c) *Colour.* Give the process or colour recording system of a motion picture or videorecording, or any other details of the colour.

> Technicolor

> Colour recording system: SECAM

> Sepia print

d) *Form of print.* Give the form of print of a film (e.g., *negative, positive, reversal, reversal internegative, internegative, interpositive, colour separation, duplicate, fine grain duplicating positive, fine grain duplicating negative*). For master material held in checkerboard cutting form, state if A, B, C, etc., roll.

e) *Film base.* Give the film base (i.e., *nitrate, acetate,* or *polyester*).

f) *Videorecording system.* Give the system(s) used for a videorecording.

   Beta

   Laser optical CAV

   VHS Hi-fi

   LaserVision CAV

   For videotape, give the number of lines and fields, followed by the modulation frequency (e.g., *high band*, *low band*).

   Standard: 405 lines, 50 field, high band

g) *Generation of copy.* For videotapes, give the generation of the copy and either *master copy* or *show copy.*

   Second generation, show copy

h) *Special projection requirements.* Give special projection requirements not given in the physical description area (see 7.5C2).

   Three-dimensional film

j) *Videodiscs: duration and number of frames.* Give the duration of the moving images and the number of frames of still images for videodiscs that contain both.

   Eighty min. of moving images and 2400 fr. of still images

k) *Other.* Give any other physical details that are important to the use or storage of the motion picture or videorecording.

   One side CAV, one side CLV

7.7B11. Accompanying material. Make notes on the location of accompanying material if appropriate. Give details of accompanying material neither mentioned in the physical description area nor given a separate description (see 1.5E).

   Cast list and credits on box

   With shot list

   With instruction manual

7.7B12. Series. Make notes on series data that cannot be given in the series area.

   Originally issued in the series: Disney classics

7.7B13. Dissertations. If the item being described is a dissertation, make a note as instructed in 1.7B13.

7.7B14. Audience. Make a brief note of the intended audience for, or intellectual level of, an item if this information is stated in the item, its container, or accompanying textual material.

   Intended audience: Elementary grades

7.7B16. Other formats. Give the details of other formats in which the content of the item has been issued.

> Issued also as cassette (VHS or Sony U-Matic)

7.7B17. Summary. Give a brief objective summary of the content of an item unless another part of the description provides enough information.

> Summary: Presents several brief sketches showing communication problems in a family, in a business, and in school in order to analyze and correct failures in interpersonal relations

7.7B18. Contents. List the titles of individual works contained in, or the parts of, a motion picture or videorecording. Add to each title any statements of responsibility not included in the title and statement of responsibility area, and the duration if known.

> Contents: pt. 1. The cause of liberty (24 min.) — pt. 2. The impossible war (25 min.)

Make notes on additional or partial contents when appropriate.

> Also contains newsfilm on the Trooping of the Colour

Unedited material and newsfilm. Give a description, using standard abbreviations, of the action and length of each shot of unedited material, newsfilm, or stock shots.

> Shots: LS through heat haze of jet landing towards camera (20 ft.). CU front view of jet as it taxis towards camera (40 ft.). CU fuselage turning right to left through picture (30 ft.). CU braking parachute as it is discarded (52 ft.). CU nose and engines (57 ft.)

7.7B19. Numbers. Give important numbers borne by the item other than ISBNs or ISSNs (see 7.8B).

7.7B20. Copy being described, library's holdings, and restrictions on use. Make these notes as instructed in 1.7B20.

> Library's set lacks third reel

7.7B21. "With" notes. If the title and statement of responsibility area contains a title that applies to only a part of an item lacking a collective title and, therefore, more than one entry is made, make a note beginning *With:* and listing the other separately titled works in the item in the order in which they appear there.

> With: The Truman story

> With: Frilly follies — The shy mouse — The night hawk — No more cheese!

7.8. STANDARD NUMBER AND TERMS OF AVAILABILITY AREA

Contents:
7.8A. Preliminary rule
7.8B. Standard number

7.8C. Key-title
7.8D. Terms of availability
7.8E. Qualification

7.8A. Preliminary rule

7.8A1. Punctuation

For instructions on the use of spaces before and after prescribed punctuation, see 1.0C.

Precede this area by a full stop, space, dash, space *or* start a new paragraph.

Precede each repetition of this area by a full stop, space, dash, space.

Precede a key-title by an equals sign.

Precede terms of availability by a colon.

Enclose a qualification to the standard number or terms of availability in parentheses.

7.8B. Standard number

7.8B1. Give the International Standard Book Number (ISBN) or International Standard Serial Number (ISSN) assigned to an item as instructed in 1.8B.

7.8B2. Give any other number in a note (see 7.7B19).

7.8C. Key-title

7.8C1. Give the key-title of a serial item as instructed in 1.8C.

7.8D. *Optional addition.* **Terms of availability**

7.8D1. Give the terms on which the item is available as instructed in 1.8D.

For hire or sale (£15.00)

Free to universities and colleges

7.8E. Qualification

7.8E1. Add qualifications to the standard number and/or terms of availability as instructed in 1.8E.

7.9. SUPPLEMENTARY ITEMS

7.9A. Describe supplementary items as instructed in 1.9.

7.10. ITEMS MADE UP OF SEVERAL TYPES OF MATERIAL

7.10A. Describe items made up of several types of material as instructed in 1.10.

CHAPTER 8

GRAPHIC MATERIALS

Contents

8.0. GENERAL RULES

8.0A. Scope

8.0A1. The rules in this chapter cover the description of graphic materials of all kinds, whether opaque (e.g., two-dimensional art originals and reproductions, charts, photographs, technical drawings) or intended to be projected or viewed (e.g., filmstrips, radiographs, slides), and collections of such graphic materials. For unpublished graphic materials, see also the instructions in chapter 4. For visual material recorded on film and intended to be projected so as to create the illusion of movement, see chapter 7. For microforms, see chapter 11. For maps, etc., see chapter 3. For microscope slides, see chapter 10.

8.0B. Sources of information

8.0B1. Chief source of information. The chief source of information for graphic materials is the item itself including any labels, etc., that are permanently affixed to the item or a container that is an integral part of the item. If the item being described consists of two or more separate physical parts (e.g., a slide set), treat a container that is the unifying element as the chief source of information if it furnishes a collective title and the items themselves and their labels do not. In this case, make a note (see 8.7B3) indicating the source of information. If information is not available from the chief source, take it from the following sources (in this order of preference):

> container (e.g., box, frame)
> accompanying textual material (e.g., manuals, leaflets)
> other sources

In describing a collection of graphic materials as a unit, treat the whole collection as the chief source.

8.0B2. Prescribed sources of information. The prescribed source(s) of information for each area of the description of graphic materials is set out below. Enclose information taken from outside the prescribed source(s) in square brackets.

AREA	PRESCRIBED SOURCES OF INFORMATION
Title and statement of responsibility	Chief source of information
Edition	Chief source of information, container, accompanying material
Publication, distribution, etc.	Chief source of information, container, accompanying material
Physical description	Any source
Series	Chief source of information, container, accompanying material
Note	Any source
Standard number and terms of availability	Any source

8.0C. Punctuation

For the punctuation of the description as a whole, see 1.0C.
For the prescribed punctuation of elements, see the following rules.

8.0D. Levels of detail in the description
See 1.0D.

8.0E. Language and script of the description
See 1.0E.

8.0F. Inaccuracies
See 1.0F.

8.0G. Accents and other diacritical marks
See 1.0G.

8.0H. Items with several chief sources of information
See 1.0H.

8.1. TITLE AND STATEMENT OF RESPONSIBILITY AREA

Contents:
8.1A. Preliminary rule
8.1B. Title proper
8.1C. General material designation
8.1D. Parallel titles
8.1E. Other title information
8.1F.   Statements of responsibility
8.1G. Items without a collective title

8.1A. Preliminary rule

8.1A1. Punctuation
For instructions on the use of spaces before and after prescribed punctuation, see 1.0C.
Precede the title of a supplement or section (see 1.1B9) by a full stop.
Enclose the general material designation in square brackets.
Precede each parallel title by an equals sign.
Precede each unit of other title information by a colon.
Precede the first statement of responsibility by a diagonal slash.
Precede each subsequent statement of responsibility by a semicolon.
For the punctuation of this area for items without a collective title, see 1.1G.

8.1B. Title proper

8.1B1. Transcribe the title proper as instructed in 1.1B.

Searching British patent literature

Ancient Greek coins

Napoleon

19th century developments in art

Walt Disney's Disneyland

Advanced diagnostic ultrasound (two-dimensional ultrasonography)

If the title proper is taken from a container that is a unifying element, or if it is not taken from the chief source of information, give the source of the title in a note (see 8.7B3).

8.1B2. If a single graphic item lacks a title, supply one as instructed in 1.1B7.

[Birds of Jamaica]

[Photograph of Alice Liddell]

8.1B3. If a collection of graphic items lacks a title, supply a title by which the collection is known or a title indicating the nature of the collection.

[Dance posters]

8.1C. *Optional addition.* **General material designation**

8.1C1. Give immediately following the title proper the appropriate general material designation as instructed in 1.1C.

8.1C2. If a graphic item contains parts belonging to materials falling into two or more categories, and if none of these is the predominant constituent of the item, give either *multimedia* or *kit* as the designation (see 1.1C1 and 1.10C1).

8.1D. Parallel titles

8.1D1. Transcribe parallel titles as instructed in 1.1D.

French colonies in America [GMD] = Colonies françaises d'Amérique

8.1E. Other title information

8.1E1. Transcribe other title information as instructed in 1.1E.

Basic principles in chemistry—stoichiometry [GMD] : atomic weights, molecular weights, and the mole concept

Bulgaria [GMD] : my country

Personal communication [GMD] : gestures, expressions, and body English

8.1F. Statements of responsibility

8.1F1. Transcribe statements of responsibility relating to persons or bodies credited with a major role in creating or participating in the creation or production of a graphic item (e.g., directors, producers, artists, designers, developers, sponsors) as instructed in 1.1F. Give all other statements of responsibility in notes.

The beach [GMD] / Walt Smith

> Searching British patent literature [GMD] / British Library Science Reference and Information Service

> The histomap of religion [GMD] : the story of man's search for spiritual unity / John B. Sparks

> A picture study of the settlement of the West [GMD] / prepared by Historical Services and Consultants under the direction of John T. Saywell and John C. Ricker

> Two dancers on a stage [GMD] / Degas

> A girl with a broom [GMD] / Rembrandt ; National Gallery of Art

> Introduction to printmaking [GMD] / Crystal Productions ; writer, Corry Hubbard

> Soil, the growth medium [GMD] / Prentice-Hall Media ; produced by the Sun Group ; producer and director, Arthur Custer ; writer, Roger Scott

> Childcare shapes the future [GMD] : anti-racist strategies / developed by the Council on Interracial Books for Children, Inc., and the Multicultural Project for Communication and Education, Inc. ; produced by the Council on Interracial Books for Children, Inc.

8.1F2. Add a word or short phrase to the statement of responsibility if the relationship between the title and the person(s) or body (bodies) named in the statement is not clear.

8.1G. Items without a collective title

8.1G1. If a graphic item lacks a collective title, transcribe the titles of the individual parts as instructed in 1.1G.

> The great big enormous turnip [GMD] / Alexei Tolstoy ; with pictures by Helen Oxenbury. The three poor tailors / Victor G. Ambrus
> (*A filmstrip based on two children's books*)

8.1G2. Make the relationship between statements of responsibility and the parts of an item lacking a collective title clear by additions as instructed in 8.1F2.

8.2. EDITION AREA

Contents:

8.2A. Preliminary rule

8.2A1. Punctuation

For instructions on the use of spaces before and after prescribed punctuation, see 1.0C.

Precede this area by a full stop, space, dash, space.

Precede a statement relating to a named revision of an edition by a comma.

Precede the first statement of responsibility following an edition statement by a diagonal slash.

Precede each subsequent statement of responsibility by a semicolon.

8.2A2. Unpublished graphic items. For unpublished graphic items existing in different versions, see 4.2.

8.2B. Edition statement

8.2B1. Transcribe a statement relating to an edition of a graphic item that contains differences from other editions of that item, or to a named reissue of an item, as instructed in 1.2B.

> Britain's government at work [GMD] / by John A. Hawgood. — 3rd ed.

8.2B2. In case of doubt about whether a statement is an edition statement, follow the instructions in 1.2B3.

8.2B3. *Optional addition.* If a graphic item lacks an edition statement but is known to contain significant changes from other editions, supply a suitable brief statement in the language and script of the title proper and enclose it in square brackets.

> Wooded landscape with church, cow, and figure [GMD] / T. Gainsborough fecit aqua forte ; J. Wood perfecit. — [3rd state]

> The story of the Pied Piper [GMD] / Encyclopaedia Britannica Educational Corporation. — [New ed.]

8.2B4. If an edition statement appears in more than one language or script, transcribe the statement that is in the language or script of the title proper. If this criterion does not apply, transcribe the statement that appears first. *Optionally,* transcribe the parallel statement(s), each preceded by an equals sign.

8.2B5. If an item lacking a collective title contains one or more works with an associated edition statement, transcribe such statements following the titles and statements of responsibility to which they relate, separated from them by a full stop.

8.2C. Statements of responsibility relating to the edition

8.2C1. Transcribe a statement of responsibility relating to one or more editions, but not to all editions, of a graphic item as instructed in 1.2C and 8.1F.

Precambrian and older Palaeozoic eras [GMD] / by Knud Dreyer
Jorgenson. — [New issue] / re-edited in Great Britain by D.E.
Owen

8.2D. Statement relating to a named revision of an edition

8.2D1. If an item is a named revision of an edition, transcribe the statement
relating to that revision as instructed in 1.2D.

Do not record statements relating to a reissue that contains no changes unless
the item is considered to be of particular importance to the cataloguing agency.

8.2E. Statements of responsibility relating to a named revision of an edition

8.2E1. Transcribe a statement of responsibility relating to one or more named
revisions of an edition (but not to all such revisions) as instructed in 1.2E and
8.1F.

8.3. MATERIAL (OR TYPE OF PUBLICATION) SPECIFIC DETAILS AREA

8.3A. This area is not used for graphic materials.

8.4. PUBLICATION, DISTRIBUTION, ETC., AREA

Contents:
  8.4A. Preliminary rule
  8.4B. General rule
  8.4C. Place of publication, distribution, etc.
  8.4D. Name of publisher, distributor, etc.
  8.4E. Statement of function of publisher, distributor, etc.
  8.4F. Date of publication, distribution, etc.
  8.4G. Place of manufacture, name of manufacturer, date of
         manufacture

8.4A. Preliminary rule

8.4A1. Punctuation
For instructions on the use of spaces before and after prescribed punctuation,
see 1.0C.

Precede this area by a full stop, space, dash, space.

Precede a second or subsequently named place of publication, distribution,
etc., by a semicolon.

Precede the name of a publisher, distributor, etc., by a colon.

Enclose a supplied statement of function of a publisher, distributor, etc., in
square brackets.

Precede the date of publication, distribution, etc., by a comma.

Enclose the details of manufacture (place, name, date) in parentheses.

Precede the name of a manufacturer by a colon.

Precede the date of manufacture by a comma.

8.4B. General rule

8.4B1. Record information about the place, name, and date of all types of publishing, distributing, etc., activities as instructed in 1.4B.

8.4C. Place of publication, distribution, etc.

8.4C1. Give the place of publication, distribution, etc., of a published graphic item as instructed in 1.4C.

8.4C2. Do not record a place of publication, distribution, etc., for an unpublished graphic item, or for an unpublished collection of graphic items (including those containing published items but not published as collections). Do not record *s.l.* in either case.

8.4D. Name of publisher, distributor, etc.

8.4D1. Give the name of the publisher, etc., and *optionally* the distributor, of a published graphic item as instructed in 1.4D.

> Trowbridge, Wiltshire : Micro Colour (International)
>
> [Fullerton, Calif.] : Ruhle and Associates
>
> [Leeds] : University of Leeds, Dept. of Spanish

8.4D2. Do not record the name of a publisher, distributor, etc., for an unpublished graphic item, or for an unpublished collection of graphic items (including those containing published items but not published as collections). Do not record *s.n.* in either case.

8.4E. *Optional addition.* **Statement of function of publisher, distributor, etc.**

8.4E1. Add to the name of a publisher, distributor, etc., a statement of function as instructed in 1.4E.

> London : Rickett Encyclopedia of Slides [publisher] : Voluntary Committee on Overseas Aid & Development [distributor]

8.4F. Date of publication, distribution, etc.

8.4F1. Give the date of publication, distribution, etc., of a published graphic item as instructed in 1.4F.

> Melbourne : University of Melbourne ; London : EFVA [distributor], 1966
>
> Toronto : Royal Ontario Museum, [197-]
>
> New York : Personality Posters, c1966

8.4F2. Give the date of creation of an art original, unpublished photograph, or other unpublished graphic item.

Fair Rosamund [GMD] / E. Burne-Jones. — 1863
(*Dated gouache*)

Portrait of Charles Dickens [GMD]. — [1861?]
(*Undated photograph*)

8.4F3. Give the inclusive dates of a collection of graphic materials.

[Pen drawings of birds and flowers of Dorset] [GMD]. — [1910-1937]

8.4G. Place of manufacture, name of manufacturer, date of manufacture

8.4G1. If the name of the publisher is unknown and the place and name of the manufacturer are found in the item, give that place and name as instructed in 1.4G.

[S.l. : s.n., 1966?] (London : Curwen Press)

8.4G2. *Optional addition.* Give the place, name of manufacturer, and/or date of manufacture if they are found on the item and differ from the place, name of publisher, etc., and date of publication, etc., and are considered important by the cataloguing agency.

8.5. PHYSICAL DESCRIPTION AREA

Contents:
8.5A. Preliminary rule
8.5B. Extent of item (including specific material designation)
8.5C. Other physical details
8.5D. Dimensions
8.5E. Accompanying material

8.5A. Preliminary rule

8.5A1. Punctuation
For instructions on the use of spaces before and after prescribed punctuation, see 1.0C.
Precede this area by a full stop, space, dash, space *or* start a new paragraph.
Precede other physical details by a colon.
Precede dimensions by a semicolon.
Precede each statement of accompanying material by a plus sign.
Enclose physical details of accompanying material in parentheses.

8.5B. Extent of item (including specific material designation)

8.5B1. Record the number of physical units of a graphic item by giving the number of parts in arabic numerals and one of the following terms as appropriate:

activity card
art original
art print
art reproduction

chart
filmslip
filmstrip
flash card
flip chart
photograph
picture
postcard
poster
radiograph
slide
stereograph
study print
technical drawing
transparency
wall chart

1 wall chart

3 wall charts

100 slides

12 transparencies

Add *cartridge* or *reel* to *filmstrip* and *stereograph* when appropriate.

1 filmstrip cartridge

3 stereograph reels

Optionally, add a more specific term to one of those listed above.

50 identical sets of 10 slides

If none of the terms listed above is appropriate, give the specific name of the item as concisely as possible.

7 flannel board pieces

If the parts of the item are very numerous and the exact number cannot be readily ascertained, give an approximate number.

ca. 1,000 photographs

8.5B2. Add, to the designation for a filmslip or filmstrip, the number of frames or double frames.

1 filmstrip (36 fr.)

1 filmstrip (10 double fr.)

Add, to the designation for a stereograph, the number of pairs of frames.

1 stereograph reel (7 pairs of fr.)

If the frames are unnumbered and their number cannot be readily ascertained, give an approximate number.

1 filmstrip (ca. 100 fr.)

If the title frames are separately numbered, give the number of title frames after the number of other frames.

1 filmstrip (41 fr., 4 title fr.)

8.5B3. Add, to the designation for flip charts, the number or approximate number of sheets.

1 flip chart (8 sheets)

8.5B4. Add, to the designation for transparencies, the number or approximate number of overlays, if any. If the overlays are attached, indicate this.

1 transparency (5 overlays)

1 transparency (5 attached overlays)

8.5B5. If the parts of a multipart filmslip, filmstrip, stereograph, flip chart, or transparency have the same number of components (e.g., frames, sheets) or approximately the same number of components, use the form *3 filmstrips (50 fr. each)* or *3 transparencies (ca. 10 overlays each)*, etc. Otherwise, give the total number of components if they are consecutively numbered or omit the statement of the number of components.

4 filmstrips (50 double fr. each)

2 transparencies (20 overlays)

4 flip charts

8.5B6. If the item is in a raised image format, add *(tactile)* to the statement of extent (see 8.5B1–8.5B5).

1 chart (tactile)

Optionally, if general material designations are used (see 1.1C1) and the general material designation indicates the tactile nature of the item, omit the addition.

If the item is a thermoform copy, add *thermoform* to the parenthetic addition, preceded by a comma. If there is no parenthetic addition (see *option* above), add *thermoform* in parentheses.

1 chart (tactile, thermoform)

or 1 chart (thermoform)

8.5C. Other physical details

8.5C1. Medium-specific details. Give, for each of the media listed below, the details specified.

a) *Art originals.* Give the medium (e.g., *chalk*, *oil*, *pastel*) and the base (e.g., *board*, *canvas*, *fabric*).

1 art original : oil on canvas

b) *Art prints.* Give the process in general terms (e.g., *engraving, lithograph*) or specific terms (e.g., *copper engraving, chromolithograph*).

>   2 art prints : engraving
>
>   1 art print : sugar lift aquatint

c) *Art reproductions.* Give the method of reproduction (e.g., *photogravure, collotype*).

>   1 art reproduction : photogravure

d) *Charts and flip charts.* If the charts are double sided, indicate this.

>   1 flip chart (8 sheets) : double sided

e) *Filmstrips and filmslips.* Give *sd.* if the sound is integral. If the sound is not integral, describe the accompanying sound as accompanying material (see 8.5E).

>   1 filmstrip (41 fr., 4 title fr.) : sd.

f) *Flash cards.* Give *sd.* if the sound is integral. If the sound is not integral, describe the accompanying sound as accompanying material (see 8.5E).

>   200 flash cards : sd.

g) *Photographs.* If the photograph is a transparency not designed for projection or a negative print, indicate this. *Optionally*, give the process used.

>   3 photographs : negative
>
>   1 photograph : glass photonegative

h) *Slides.* Give *sd.* if the sound is integral. If the sound is not integral, describe the accompanying sound as accompanying material (see 8.5E).

>   12 slides : sd.

j) *Technical drawings.* Give the method of reproduction (e.g., *blueprint, photocopy*), if appropriate.

>   1 technical drawing : blueprint

8.5C2. Colour. Give an indication of colour (e.g., *col., b&w, sepia*) for all graphic media other than art originals, radiographs, and technical drawings.

>   1 art print : engraving, tinted
>
>   3 filmslips : col.
>
>   16 flash cards : col.
>
>   1 photograph : sepia
>
>   1 picture : col.
>
>   4 postcards : tinted
>
>   7 posters : blue and white

14 slides : b&w and col.

1 stereograph reel (7 pairs of fr.) : col.

1 study print : col.

3 transparencies (5 overlays each) : col.

8.5D. Dimensions

8.5D1. Give the height × width in centimetres, to the next whole centimetre up, for all graphic materials except filmstrips, filmslips, and stereographs. For these latter, see 8.5D2 and 8.5D3. For additional instructions on the dimensions of art works, slides, technical drawings, transparencies, and wall charts, see 8.5D4–8.5D6.

16 flash cards : col. ; 28 × 10 cm.

1 flip chart (8 sheets) : double sided, col. ; 23 × 18 cm.

24 photographs : b&w ; 13 × 8 cm.

1 picture : b&w ; 20 × 25 cm.

1 radiograph ; 38 × 38 cm.

1 study print : col. ; 34 × 47 cm.

1 technical drawing : blueprint ; 87 × 87 cm.

If the graphic materials in a multipart item differ in size, give the smallest or smaller and the largest or larger size, separated by a hyphen.

8.5D2. Filmstrips and filmslips. Give the gauge (width) of the film in millimetres.

1 filmstrip (50 fr.) : col. ; 35 mm.

8.5D3. Stereographs. Do not give the dimensions.

8.5D4. Art originals, art prints, art reproductions, and transparencies. Give the height × width of the item, excluding any frame or mount (see also 8.7B10).

1 art print : lithograph, col. ; 28 × 36 cm.

3 transparencies (15 overlays) : b&w ; 26 × 22 cm.

2 art originals : oil on canvas ; 28 × 40 cm.-30 × 45 cm.

8.5D5. Slides. Do not give the dimensions if they are 5 × 5 cm. (2 × 2 in.).

1 slide : col.

1 slide : b&w ; 7 × 7 cm.

8.5D6. Technical drawings and wall charts. Give the height × width when extended and (when appropriate) folded.

1 wall chart : col. ; 244 × 26 cm. folded to 30 × 26 cm.

3 technical drawings : blueprint ; 100 × 40 cm.-120 × 60 cm.

8.5E. Accompanying material

8.5E1. Give the details of accompanying material as instructed in 1.5E.

> 1 stereograph reel (12 pairs of fr.) : col. + 1 booklet

> 40 slides : col. + 1 sound disc (30 min. : analog, 33⅓ rpm, mono. ; 12 in.)

> 1 filmstrip (70 fr.) : sd., col. ; 35 mm. + 1 set of teacher's notes

Give details of integral sound systems as part of "other physical details" (see 8.5C1).

8.6. SERIES AREA

Contents:
  8.6A. Preliminary rule
  8.6B. Series statements

8.6A. Preliminary rule

8.6A1. Punctuation

For instructions on the use of spaces before and after prescribed punctuation, see 1.0C.
Precede this area by a full stop, space, dash, space.
Enclose each series statement (see 1.6J) in parentheses.
Precede each parallel title by an equals sign.
Precede other title information by a colon.
Precede the first statement of responsibility by a diagonal slash.
Precede each subsequent statement of responsibility by a semicolon.
Precede the ISSN of a series or subseries by a comma.
Precede the numbering within a series or subseries by a semicolon.
Precede the title of a subseries by a full stop.

8.6B. Series statements

8.6B1. Record each series statement as instructed in 1.6.

> (Listening, looking, and feeling)

> (At-a-flash time line cards ; set 1)

> (Ward's solo-learn system)

> (The sciences. Man and his environment ; TSB 3)

> (Viewmaster science series. 4, Physics)

> (How the health are you? ; no. 3)

> (Environmental studies, ISSN 8372-7639 ; v. 32)

8.7. NOTE AREA

Contents:
8.7A. Preliminary rule
8.7B. Notes

8.7A. Preliminary rule

8.7A1. Punctuation

Precede each note by a full stop, space, dash, space *or* start a new paragraph for each.

Separate introductory wording from the main content of a note by a colon followed but not preceded by a space.

8.7A2. In making notes, follow the instructions in 1.7A.

8.7B. Notes

Make notes as set out in the following subrules and in the order given there. However, give a particular note first when it has been decided that note is of primary importance.

8.7B1. Nature or artistic form. Make notes on the nature or artistic form of a graphic item unless it is apparent from the rest of the description.

> Cross-cultural survey

8.7B2. Language. Give the language(s) of the spoken or written content of a graphic item and its accompanying sound unless this is apparent from the rest of the description.

> Captions in Spanish

> Sound tape in Spanish and English

8.7B3. Source of title proper. Make notes on the source of the title proper if it is a container or if it is other than the chief source of information (see 8.0B1).

> Title from manufacturer's catalogue

8.7B4. Variations in title. Make notes on titles borne by the item other than the title proper. *Optionally*, give a romanization of the title proper.

> Also known as: The blue boy

> Title on container: Japan

8.7B5. Parallel titles and other title information. Give the title in another language and other title information not recorded in the title and statement of responsibility area if they are considered to be important.

> Subtitle: Cereals of the world

8.7B6. Statements of responsibility. Make notes on variant names of persons or bodies named in statements of responsibility if these are considered to be important for identification. Give statements of responsibility not recorded in the title and statement of responsibility area. Make notes on persons or bodies connected with a work, or significant persons or bodies connected with previous editions and not already named in the description.

> Narrator: Rod Serling

> Teacher's guide / by M. McComb

> Variously attributed to Mathew B. Brady, to Dan Adams, and to Anthony, Edwards & Co.

Donor, source, etc., and previous owner(s). Make notes on the donor or source of an original graphic item and on previous owners if they can be easily ascertained. Add the year or years of accession to the name of the donor or source, and the year or years of ownership to the name of a previous owner.

8.7B7. Edition and history. Make notes relating to the edition being described or to the history of the item.

> Originally released in 1965 with sound disc

> Spanish version of: Your mouth speaking

> Based on the fairy tale by H.C. Andersen

8.7B9. Publication, distribution, etc. Make notes on publication, distribution, etc., details that are not included in the publication, distribution, etc., area and are considered to be important.

> First released in 1969

8.7B10. Physical description. Make notes on important physical details that are not included in the physical description area, especially if these affect the use of the item.

> Scales vary

> Composite photo.

> Collage of wood, fabric, and paper

> Filmslip mounted in rigid format for use with Phono-viewer

> Images placed in frame both horizontally and vertically

> Text on verso

> Unmounted

> Size when framed: 40 × 35 cm.

8.7B11. Accompanying material. Make notes on the location of accompanying material if appropriate. Give details of accompanying material neither mentioned in the physical description area nor given a separate description (see 1.5E).

> With 2 exhibition catalogues: 19th century America : furniture and other decorative arts / by Marilynn Johnson, Marvin D.

216

Schwartz, and Suzanne Boorsch — 19th century America :
paintings and sculpture / by John K. Howat and others

8.7B12. Series. Make notes on series data that cannot be given in the series area.

Originally issued in the series:

Series title on container:
(*Container bears a variant form of the series title*)

8.7B13. Dissertations. If the item being described is a dissertation, make a note as instructed in 1.7B13.

8.7B14. Audience. Make a brief note of the intended audience for, or intellectual level of, a graphic item if this information is stated in the item, its container, or accompanying material.

Intended audience: Elementary grades

For remedial reading programmes

8.7B16. Other formats. Give the details of other formats in which the content of the item has been issued.

Issued also with sound

Issued also with double frames

8.7B17. Summary. Give a brief objective summary of the content of an item unless another part of the description provides enough information.

Aerial view of Champaign-Urbana, Ill.

Summary: Uses the children's tale of Goldilocks and the three bears in a programme of Spanish language instruction

Summary: A reading exercise which presents some little-known facts about gopher snakes, crocodiles, and sea turtles

8.7B18. Contents. List the titles of individually named parts of a graphic item. Add to each title any statements of responsibility not included in the title and statement of responsibility area, and the number of cards, frames, slides, etc., when appropriate.

Contents: Penny, nickel, dime, quarter — Nickel, dime, quarter, half-dollar — Dollar — Use of cent and dollar notation — Addition and subtraction — Making change — Story problems

Contents: Getting ahead of the game (81 fr.) — Decisions, decisions (55 fr.) — Your money (72 fr.) — How to be a loser (65 fr.) — The law and your pocketbook (70 fr.) — The all-American consumer (63 fr.)

Make notes on additional or partial contents when appropriate.

End frames reproduce 5 famous Spanish paintings

8.7B19. Numbers. Give important numbers borne by the item other than ISBNs or ISSNs (see 8.8B).

8.7B20. Copy being described, library's holdings, and restrictions on use. Make these notes as instructed in 1.7B20.

>   Print (no. 45) signed by artist

8.7B21. "With" notes. If the title and statement of responsibility area contains a title that applies to only a part of an item lacking a collective title and, therefore, more than one entry is made, make a note beginning *With:* and listing the other separately titled works in the item in the order in which they appear there.

>   With: The doom fulfilled — Ariadne

8.7B22. Note relating to the original. Make a note relating to the original of a reproduced art work as instructed in 1.7B22.

>   Reproduction of: Femme nue en plein air. 1876. 1 art original :
>   oil on canvas, col. ; 79 × 64 cm. In Louvre Museum, Paris.

8.8. STANDARD NUMBER AND TERMS OF AVAILABILITY AREA

Contents:
8.8A. Preliminary rule
8.8B. Standard number
8.8C. Key-title
8.8D. Terms of availability
8.8E. Qualification

8.8A. Preliminary rule

8.8A1. Punctuation

For instructions on the use of spaces before and after prescribed punctuation, see 1.0C.

Precede this area by a full stop, space, dash, space *or* start a new paragraph.

Precede each repetition of this area by a full stop, space, dash, space.

Precede a key-title by an equals sign.

Precede terms of availability by a colon.

Enclose a qualification to the standard number or terms of availability in parentheses.

8.8B. Standard number

8.8B1. Give the International Standard Book Number (ISBN) or International Standard Serial Number (ISSN) assigned to an item as instructed in 1.8B.

8.8B2. Give any other number in a note (see 8.7B19).

8.8C. Key-title

8.8C1. Give the key-title of a serial item as instructed in 1.8C.

8.8D. *Optional addition.* **Terms of availability**

8.8D1. Give the terms on which the item is available as instructed in 1.8D.

>Free loan to students

>For rent or sale ($10.00)

8.8E. Qualification

8.8E1. Add qualifications to the standard number and/or terms of availability as instructed in 1.8E.

8.9. SUPPLEMENTARY ITEMS

8.9A. Describe supplementary items as instructed in 1.9.

8.10. ITEMS MADE UP OF SEVERAL TYPES OF MATERIAL

8.10A. Describe items made up of several types of material as instructed in 1.10.

8.11. FACSIMILES, PHOTOCOPIES, AND OTHER REPRODUCTIONS

8.11A. Describe facsimiles, photocopies, and other reproductions as instructed in 1.11.

CHAPTER 9

COMPUTER FILES

Contents

9.0. GENERAL RULES

9.0A. Scope

9.0A1. The rules in this chapter cover the description of files that are encoded for manipulation by computer. These files comprise data and programs. Computer files may be stored on, or contained in, carriers available for direct access or by remote access.

The rules in this chapter do not cover electronic devices such as calculators, etc.; see chapter 10 for such materials. Programs residing in the permanent memory of a computer (ROM) or firmware are considered to be part of the device and should be described in conjunction with the device (e.g., the programming language of a particular computer, such as: Applesoft in ROM).

9.0B. Sources of information

9.0B1. Chief source of information. The chief source of information for computer files is the title screen(s).

If there is no title screen, take the information from other formally presented internal evidence (e.g., main menus, program statements, first display of information, the header to the file including "Subject:" lines, information at the end of the file). In case of variation in fullness of information found in these sources, prefer the source with the most complete information.

If the computer file is unreadable without processing (e.g., compressed file, printer-formatted file), take the information from the file after it has been uncompressed, printed out, or otherwise processed for use.

If the information required is not available[1] from internal sources, take it from the following sources (in this order of preference):

> the physical carrier or its labels[2]
> information issued by the publisher, creator, etc., with the file (sometimes called "documentation")
> information printed on the container issued by the publisher, distributor, etc.

If the item being described consists of two or more separate physical parts, treat a container or its permanently affixed label that is the unifying element as the chief source of information if it furnishes a collective title and the formally presented information in, or the labels on, the parts themselves do not.

If the information required is not available from the chief source or the sources listed above, take it from the following sources (in this order of preference):

> other published descriptions of the file
> other sources

9.0B2. Prescribed sources of information. The prescribed source(s) of information for each area of the description of computer files is set out below. Enclose information taken from outside the prescribed source(s) in square brackets.

AREA	PRESCRIBED SOURCES OF INFORMATION
Title and statement of responsibility	Chief source of information, the carrier or its labels, information issued by the publisher, creator, etc., container
Edition	Chief source of information, the carrier or its labels, information issued by the publisher, creator, etc., container

---

1. *Available*, in this context, includes the cataloguer's access to equipment to mount or read the file.

2. *Label* means any permanently affixed paper, plastic, etc., label that is added by the publisher, creator, etc., of the file, as opposed to those added locally, and as opposed to the container itself, which may have data embossed or printed on it.

File characteristics	Any source
Publication, distribution, etc.	Chief source of information, the carrier or its labels, information issued by the publisher, creator, etc., container
Physical description	Any source
Series	Chief source of information, the carrier or its labels, information issued by the publisher, creator, etc., container
Note	Any source
Standard number and terms of availability	Any source

9.0C. Punctuation
For the punctuation of the description as a whole, see 1.0C.
For the prescribed punctuation of elements, see the following rules.

9.0D. Levels of detail in the description
See 1.0D.

9.0E. Language and script of the description
See 1.0E.

9.0F. Inaccuracies
See 1.0F.

9.0G. Accents and other diacritical marks
See 1.0G.

9.0H. Items with several chief sources of information
See 1.0H.

9.1. TITLE AND STATEMENT OF RESPONSIBILITY AREA

Contents:
9.1A. Preliminary rule
9.1B. Title proper
9.1C. General material designation
9.1D. Parallel titles
9.1E. Other title information
9.1F. Statements of responsibility
9.1G. Items without a collective title

9.1A. Preliminary rule

9.1A1. Punctuation
For instructions on the use of spaces before and after prescribed punctuation, see 1.0C.

223

Precede the title of a supplement or section (see 1.1B9) by a full stop.
Enclose the general material designation in square brackets.
Precede each parallel title by an equals sign.
Precede each unit of other title information by a colon.
Precede the first statement of responsibility by a diagonal slash.
Precede each subsequent statement of responsibility by a semicolon.
For the punctuation of this area for items without a collective title, see 1.1G.

9.1B. Title proper

9.1B1. Transcribe the title proper as instructed in 1.1B.

> WordStar
>
> Practicalc II
>
> Demon attack
>
> The CPS 1974 American national election survey
>
> Krell's logo
>
> Visitrend + visiplot

9.1B2. Always give the source of the title proper in a note (see 9.7B3). If the title has been supplied (see 1.1B7), give the source of the supplied title in a note (see 9.7B3).

9.1B3. Do not record a file name or a data set name as the title proper unless it is the only name given in the chief source. If desired, give a file name or data set name not used as the title proper in a note (see 9.7B4).

9.1C. *Optional addition.* General material designation

9.1C1. Give immediately following the title proper the appropriate general material designation as instructed in 1.1C.

> Gertrude's puzzles [GMD]

9.1C2. If a computer file contains parts belonging to materials falling into two or more categories, and if none of these is the predominant constituent of the item, give either *multimedia* or *kit* as the designation (see 1.1C1 and 1.10C1).

9.1D. Parallel titles

9.1D1. Transcribe parallel titles as instructed in 1.1D.

> Citizen participation in non-work-time activities [GMD] =
> Participation des citoyens aux activités hors des heures de travail
>
> El asistente del instructor [GMD] = Teaching assistant

9.1E. Other title information

9.1E1. Transcribe other title information as instructed in 1.1E.

> Vufile [GMD] : an information retrieval system for use with files, lists, and data bases of all kinds

> A.C.E. [GMD] : Applesoft command editor

9.1F. Statements of responsibility

9.1F1. Transcribe statements of responsibility relating to those persons or bodies credited with a major role in creating the content of the file as instructed in 1.1F.

> Database [GMD] / Paul Fellows

> The China study [GMD] / principal investigator, Angus Campbell

> Memory castle [GMD] / designed by Donna Stanger ; programmed by Lon Koenig

> Class records system [GMD] / by Quercus

> Moby Dick [GMD] / by Herman Melville ; compiled and produced by Princeton University Computer Center under the direction of Robert Knight

Give all other statements of responsibility in notes (see 9.7B6).

9.1F2. Add a word or short phrase to the statement of responsibility if the relationship between the title and the person(s) or body (bodies) named in the statement is not clear.

> A reconstruction of Oliver Benson's Simple diplomatic game [GMD] / [developed by] Jeff Krend

> Redistricting program [GMD] / [prepared by] Stuart Nagel [for the] Inter-University Consortium for Political Research

9.1G. Items without a collective title

9.1G1. If a computer file lacks a collective title, *either* describe the item as a unit (see 9.1G2 and 9.1G3) *or* make a separate description for each separately titled part (see 9.1G4).

9.1G2. In describing as a unit a computer file lacking a collective title, transcribe the titles of the individual parts as instructed in 1.1G3.

> Personal bibliographic system [GMD] / by Victor Rosenberg. Data transfer system / written by Cyrus Galambor and Peter Rycus

> Let's go to a beer bust [GMD] / written by Sue Beall and Wayne Wyllie ; programmed by Kathy Kothmann. Time out / written by Ruth Cady ; programmed by Kathy Kothmann. Blood alcohol content / by Robert S. Gold

225

9.1G3. Make the relationship between statements of responsibility and the parts of an item lacking a collective title and described as a unit clear by additions as instructed in 9.1F2.

9.1G4. *Optionally*, make a separate description for each separately titled part of an item lacking a collective title. For the statement of the extent in each of these descriptions, see 9.5B2. Link the separate descriptions with notes (see 9.7B21). For instructions on sources of information, see 9.0B.

9.2. EDITION AREA

Contents:
- 9.2A. Preliminary rule
- 9.2B. Edition statement
- 9.2C. Statements of responsibility relating to the edition
- 9.2D. Statement relating to a named revision of an edition
- 9.2E. Statements of responsibility relating to a named revision of an edition

9.2A. Preliminary rule

9.2A1. Punctuation

For instructions on the use of spaces before and after prescribed punctuation, see 1.0C.

Precede this area by a full stop, space, dash, space.

Precede a statement relating to a named revision of an edition by a comma.

Precede the first statement of responsibility following an edition statement by a diagonal slash.

Precede each subsequent statement of responsibility by a semicolon.

9.2B. Edition statement

9.2B1. Transcribe a statement relating to an edition of a computer file that contains differences from other editions of that file, or to a named reissue of a file, as instructed in 1.2B.

> Rev. ed.
>
> NORC test ed.
>
> Level 3.4
>
> Rev. ed. 10/2/82
>
> 3rd update
>
> Version 5.20
>
> [Version] 1.1
>
> Prelim. release 0.5

Give the source of the edition statement in a note (see 9.7B7) if it is different from the source of the title proper.

226

9.2B2. In case of doubt about whether a statement is an edition statement, take the presence of words such as *edition, issue, version, release, level, update* (or their equivalents in other languages) as evidence that the statement is an edition statement, and transcribe it as such.

9.2B3. *Optional addition.* If a computer file lacks an edition statement but is known to contain significant changes from other editions (e.g., changes in the data involving content, standardized coding, etc.; changes in the programming including changes in the program statements, programming language, and programming routines and operations; the addition of sound or graphics; improvement of graphics), supply a suitable brief statement in the language and script of the title proper and enclose it in square brackets.

[Version 7]

9.2B4. Do not treat an issue of a file that incorporates minor changes as a new edition. Such minor changes include corrections of misspellings of data, changes in the arrangement of the contents, changes in the output format or the display medium, and changes in the physical characteristics (e.g., blocking factors, recording density). If desired, give the details of such changes in a note (see 9.7B7).

9.2B5. Transcribe an edition statement appearing in accompanying material only if it also refers to the file. In case of doubt, do not record such an edition statement.

9.2B6. If an edition statement appears in more than one language or script, transcribe the statement that is in the language or script of the title proper. If this criterion does not apply, transcribe the statement that appears first. *Optionally*, transcribe the parallel statement(s), each preceded by an equals sign.

9.2B7. If an item lacking a collective title and described as a unit contains one or more works with an associated edition statement, transcribe such statements following the titles and statements of responsibility to which they relate, separated from them by a full stop.

9.2C. Statements of responsibility relating to the edition

9.2C1. Transcribe a statement of responsibility relating to one or more editions, but not to all editions, of a file as instructed in 1.2C and 9.1F. If desired, transcribe other statements of responsibility relating to the edition in a note (see 9.7B7).

Rev. ed. / program has been converted from BASIC to
FORTRAN IV by Allen P. Smith

9.2D. Statement relating to a named revision of an edition

9.2D1. If an item is a named revision of an edition, transcribe the statement relating to that revision as instructed in 1.2D.

ICPSR ed., OSIRIS IV version

Do not record statements relating to a named revision of an edition when the changes are of a minor nature (see 9.2B4).

Do not record statements relating to a reissue that contains no changes unless the item is considered to be of particular importance to the cataloguing agency.

9.2E. Statements of responsibility relating to a named revision of an edition

9.2E1. Transcribe a statement of responsibility relating to one or more named revisions of an edition (but not to all such revisions) as instructed in 1.2E and 9.1F.

3rd ed., Version 1.2 / programmed by W.G. Toepfer

9.3. FILE CHARACTERISTICS AREA

Contents:
9.3A. Preliminary rule
9.3B. File characteristics

9.3A. Preliminary rule

9.3A1. Punctuation
For instructions on the use of spaces before and after prescribed punctuation, see 1.0C.
Precede this area by a full stop, space, dash, space.
Enclose each statement of the number of records, statements, etc., in parentheses.
Precede a statement of the number of records, statements, etc., by a colon when that number follows the number of files.

9.3B. File characteristics

9.3B1. Designation. When the information is readily available, indicate the type of file. Use one of the following terms:

computer data
computer program(s)
computer data and program(s)

Optionally, if general material designations are used (see 1.1C1), omit *computer* from the file designation.

9.3B2. Number of records, statements, etc. If a file designation is given and if the information is readily available, give the number or approximate number of files that make up the content (use *file* or *files* preceded by an arabic numeral) and/ or these other details:

a) *Data.* Give the number or approximate number of records (use *records*) and/or bytes (give the term in either abbreviated or full form).

Computer data (1 file : 350 records)

Computer data (550 records)

Computer data (1 file : 600 records, 240,000 bytes)

228

Computer data (1 file : 2.5 gb)

Computer data (1 file : 1.2 megabytes)

b) *Programs.* Give the number or approximate number of statements (use *statements*) and/or bytes (give the term in either abbreviated or full form).

Computer program (1 file : 200 statements)

Computer program (2150 statements)

c) *Multipart files.* Give the number or approximate number of records and/or bytes, or statements and/or bytes, in each part according to a) and b) above.

Computer data (3 files : 100, 460, 550 records)

Computer programs (2 files : 4300, 1250 bytes)

Computer data (2 files : ca. 330 records each)

Computer data (2 files : 800, 1250 records) and programs (3 files : 7260, 3490, 5076 bytes)

Computer data (2 files : 3.5, 2 megabytes)

If such numbering cannot be given succinctly, omit the information from this area. If desired, give it in a note (see 9.7B8).

9.4. PUBLICATION, DISTRIBUTION, ETC., AREA

Contents:
9.4A. Preliminary rule
9.4B. General rule
9.4C. Place of publication, distribution, etc.
9.4D. Name of publisher, distributor, etc.
9.4E. Statement of function of publisher, distributor, etc.
9.4F. Date of publication, distribution, etc.
9.4G. Place of manufacture, name of manufacturer, date of manufacture

9.4A. Preliminary rule

9.4A1. Punctuation

For instructions on the use of spaces before and after prescribed punctuation, see 1.0C.

Precede this area by a full stop, space, dash, space.

Precede a second or subsequently named place of publication, distribution, etc., by a semicolon.

Precede the name of a publisher, distributor, etc., by a colon.

Enclose a supplied statement of function of a publisher, distributor, etc., in square brackets.

Precede the date of publication, distribution, etc., by a comma.

Enclose the details of manufacture (place, name, date) in parentheses.

Precede the name of a manufacturer by a colon.

Precede the date of manufacture by a comma.

9.4B. General rule

9.4B1. Record information about the place, name, and date of all types of publishing, distributing, etc., activities as instructed in 1.4B.

9.4C. Place of publication, distribution, etc.

9.4C1. Give the place of publication, distribution, etc., of a published computer file as instructed in 1.4C.

9.4C2. Do not record a place of publication, distribution, etc., for an unpublished computer file. Do not record *s.l.* in such a case.

9.4D. Name of publisher, distributor, etc.

9.4D1. Give the name of the publisher, etc., and *optionally* the distributor, of a published computer file as instructed in 1.4D.

> London : Psion

> Newton Upper Falls, Mass. ; Ipswich : Practicorp
>   (*Cataloguing agency in the United Kingdom*)

> Prague : [s.n.]

> [S.l.] : Bruce & James Program Publishers ; [New York : Distributed by Simon & Schuster]

> Bellevue, Wash. : Temporal Acuity Products ; Owatonna, Minn. : Distributed exclusively by Musictronic

9.4D2. Do not record the name of a publisher, distributor, etc., for an unpublished computer file. Do not record *s.n.* in such a case.

9.4E. *Optional addition.* Statement of function of publisher, distributor, etc.

9.4E1. Add to the name of a publisher, distributor, etc., a statement of function as instructed in 1.4E.

> Chicago : National Opinion Research Center ; Storrs, Conn. : Roper Public Opinion Research Center [distributor]

9.4F. Date of publication, distribution, etc.

9.4F1. Give the date of publication, distribution, etc., of a published computer file as instructed in 1.4F.

> Ann Arbor : University of Michigan, Institute for Social Research, 1968

> Chicago : University of Chicago, 1961-1962

> Richmond, Va. : Rhiannon Software, c1985

> [United States : s.n., 198-]

9.4F2. Give the date of creation of an unpublished computer file.

9.4F3. Give any other useful dates (e.g., dates of collection of data) in a note (see 9.7B7 and 9.7B9).

9.4G. Place of manufacture, name of manufacturer, date of manufacture

9.4G1. If the name of the publisher is unknown and the place and name of the manufacturer are found in the item, give that place and name as instructed in 1.4G.

> [S.l. : s.n.], 1986 (Cleveland, Ohio : CD Wonderworks)

9.4G2. *Optional addition.* Give the place, name of manufacturer, and/or date of manufacture if they are found in the item and differ from the place, name of publisher, etc., and date of publication, etc., and are considered important by the cataloguing agency.

9.5. PHYSICAL DESCRIPTION AREA[3]

Contents:
    9.5A. Preliminary rule
    9.5B. Extent of item (including specific material designation)
    9.5C. Other physical details
    9.5D. Dimensions
    9.5E. Accompanying material

9.5A. Preliminary rule

9.5A1. Punctuation
For instructions on the use of spaces before and after prescribed punctuation, see 1.0C.
Precede this area by a full stop, space, dash, space *or* start a new paragraph.
Precede other physical details by a colon.
Precede dimensions by a semicolon.
Precede each statement of accompanying material by a plus sign.
Enclose physical details of accompanying material in parentheses.

9.5B. Extent of item (including specific material designation)

9.5B1. Record the number of physical units of the carrier by giving the number of them in arabic numerals and one of the following terms as appropriate:[4]

> computer cartridge
> computer cassette

---

3. Do not give a physical description for a computer file that is available only by remote access. See 9.7B1c and 9.7B10.

4. The following rules apply to the terms:
    1) Use *computer disk* for magnetically encoded computer disks.
    2) Use *computer optical disc* for optically encoded computer discs.

> computer disk
> computer optical disc
> computer reel

1 computer disk

2 computer cassettes

1 computer reel

1 computer optical disc

When new physical carriers are developed for which none of these terms is appropriate, give the specific name of the physical carrier as concisely as possible, preferably qualified by *computer*.

> 1 computer card

If the information is readily available and if desired, indicate the specific type of physical medium.

> 1 computer chip cartridge

> 1 computer tape cartridge

> 1 computer tape reel

> 1 computer optical card

Optionally, if general material designations are used (see 1.1C1), omit *computer* from the specific material designation.

Give a trade name or other similar specification in a note (see 9.7B1b).

9.5B2. If the description is of a separately titled part of an item lacking a collective title (see 9.1G4), express the fractional extent in the form *on reel 2, on 3 of 5 disks, on 1 disk*, etc.

9.5C. Other physical details

9.5C1. If the file is encoded to produce sound, give *sd*. If the file is encoded to display in two or more colours, give *col*.

> 1 computer chip cartridge : sd.

> 1 computer disk : col.

> 1 computer disk cartridge : sd., col.

Give details of the requirements for the production of sound or the display of colour in a note (see 9.7B1b).

9.5C2. *Optionally*, give the following physical characteristics, if readily available and if they are considered to be important:

> number of sides used
> recording density (e.g., number of bytes per inch (*bpi*),
>   single, double)
> sectoring

1 computer disk : sd., col., single sided, single density, soft sectored

2 computer tape reels : 6,250 bpi

9.5D. Dimensions

9.5D1. Give the dimensions of the physical carrier as instructed below.

a) *Discs/Disks*. Give the diameter of the disc or disk in inches, to the next ¼ inch up.

1 computer disk : col. ; 5¼ in.

1 computer optical disc : col. ; 4¾ in.

b) *Cartridges*. Give, in inches to the next ¼ inch up, the length of the side of the cartridge that is to be inserted into the machine.

1 computer chip cartridge ; 3½ in.

c) *Cassettes*. Give the length and height of the face of the cassette in inches, to the next ⅛ inch up.

1 computer cassette ; 3⅞ × 2½ in.

d) *Reels*. Do not give dimensions for reels.

e) *Other carriers*. Give the appropriate dimensions of other physical carriers in centimetres to the next whole centimetre up.

1 computer card ; 9 × 6 cm.

9.5D2. If the item consists of more than one physical carrier and they differ in size, give the smallest or smaller and the largest or larger size, separated by a hyphen.

3 computer disks ; 3½-5¼ in.

9.5E. Accompanying material

9.5E1. Give the details of accompanying material as instructed in 1.5E.

1 computer disk ; 5¼ in. + 1 user's guide

1 computer disk : col. ; 3½ in. + 1 v. (51 p. : ill. ; 20 cm.)

1 computer disk ; 5¼ in. + 1 user manual and addendum
(*Accompanying material has title:* User manual and addendum)

1 computer cassette : col. ; 3⅞ × 2½ in. + 1 sound cassette (20 min. : analog, stereo.)

1 computer disk ; 3½ in. + 1 demonstration disk + 1 codebook

2 computer disks ; 5¼ in.
Note: Second disk is back-up

1 computer cassette ; 3⅞ × 2½ in. + 7 maps

9.5E2. If no physical description is given (see footnote 3 at 9.5), give details of any accompanying material in a note (see 9.7B11).

9.6. SERIES AREA

Contents:
> 9.6A. Preliminary rule
> 9.6B. Series statements

9.6A. Preliminary rule

9.6A1. Punctuation
For instructions on the use of spaces before and after prescribed punctuation, see 1.0C.

Precede this area by a full stop, space, dash, space.

Enclose each series statement (see 1.6J) in parentheses.

Precede each parallel title by an equals sign.

Precede other title information by a colon.

Precede the first statement of responsibility by a diagonal slash.

Precede each subsequent statement of responsibility by a semicolon.

Precede the ISSN of a series or subseries by a comma.

Precede the numbering within a series or subseries by a semicolon.

Precede the title of a subseries by a full stop.

9.6B. Series statements

9.6B1. Record each series statement as instructed in 1.6.

> (Practicorp no-nonsense software)

> (American national election study series ; no. 13)

> (Series C. Machine-readable texts of Greek authors)

9.7. NOTE AREA

Contents:
> 9.7A. Preliminary rule
> 9.7B. Notes

9.7A. Preliminary rule

9.7A1. Punctuation
Precede each note by a full stop, space, dash, space *or* start a new paragraph for each.

Separate introductory wording from the main content of a note by a colon followed but not preceded by a space.

9.7A2. In making notes, follow the instructions in 1.7A.

9.7B. Notes

Make notes as set out in the following subrules and in the order given there. However, give a particular note first when it has been decided that note is of primary importance.

9.7B1. Nature and scope and system requirements

a) *Nature and scope.* Make notes on the nature or scope of the file unless it is apparent from the rest of the description.

> Game

> Word processor

> Combined time series analysis and graph plotting system

> Spread sheet, with word processing and graphic capabilities

b) *System requirements.* Make a note on the system requirements of the file if the information is readily available. Begin the note with *System require-ments:*. Give the following characteristics in the order in which they are listed below. Precede each characteristic, other than the first, by a semicolon.

> the make and model of the computer(s) on which the file is designed to run
> the amount of memory required
> the name of the operating system
> the software requirements (including the programming language)
> the kind and characteristics of any required or recom-mended peripherals

> System requirements: 48K RAM; Apple Disk II with controller; col. monitor
> (*File requires colour monitor for display*)

> System requirements: Apple family; 48K RAM; DOS 3.3

> System requirements: IBM PC; 64K; colour card; 2 disk drives

> System requirements: Commodore Super PET SP9000; 64K; Commodore BASIC, version 4.0; dual disk drive

> System requirements: Apple II, II+, or IIe; 48K; DOS 3.3; Applesoft in ROM

> System requirements: Apple II or higher; 48K; DOS 3.3; Applesoft BASIC; some programs require game paddles

> System requirements: IBM PC or 100% compatible; 128K; DOS 1.1 to DOS 2.1

> System requirements: RTI Series 500 CD-ROM DataDrive

> System requirements: IBM PC AT or XT; CD-ROM player and drive

c) *Mode of access.* If a file is available only by remote access, always specify the mode of access.

> Online access via AUSINET

> Mode of access: Electronic mail using ARPA

9.7B2. Language and script. Give the language(s) and/or script(s) of the spoken or written content of a file unless this is apparent from the rest of the description.

> In German

> Greek language transcribed in medieval manuscript tradition

Record the programming language as part of the system requirements note (see 9.7B1b).

9.7B3. Source of title proper. Always give the source of the title proper.

> Title from title screen

> Title from "catalogue record" provided by the producer

> Title from codebook

> Title supplied in correspondence by creator of the file

> Title supplied by cataloguer

9.7B4. Variations in title. Make notes on titles borne by the item other than the title proper. *Optionally*, give a romanization of the title proper.

> Title on manual: Compu-math decimals

> Also known as: MAXLIK

Optionally, transcribe a file name or data set name if it differs from the title proper. For a locally assigned file name or data set name, see 9.7B20.

> File name: CC.RIDER

9.7B5. Parallel titles and other title information. Give the title in another language and other title information not recorded in the title and statement of responsibility area if they are considered to be important.

9.7B6. Statements of responsibility. Make notes on variant names of persons or bodies named in statements of responsibility if they are considered to be important for identification. Give statements of responsibility not recorded in the title and statement of responsibility area. Make notes on persons or bodies connected with a work, or significant persons or bodies connected with previous editions and not already named in the description.

> Data collected in collaboration with Christiane Klapisch, École pratique des hautes études, Paris

> Additional contributors to program: Eric Rosenfeld, Debra Spencer

Simulation rev. and reprogrammed by John Smith for use in an online time-sharing environment

Systems designer, Henry Letow ; sound, LF Acoustics

User's guide by John Unger Zussman

9.7B7. Edition and history. Give the source of the edition statement if it is different from that of the title proper.

Ed. statement from container label

Make notes relating to the edition being described or to the history of the item.

Updated version of 1982 program

Program first issued in 1981

Give details of minor changes such as those listed in 9.2B4 if they are considered to be important.

Mnemonic tags substituted for numeric tags

Monochrome version recoded for colour

Cite other works upon which the item depends for its content.

Based on: Historiae / Thucydides ; edited by H.S. Jones and J.E. Powell. Oxford : Clarendon Press, 1967-1970

Give the following dates and details about them if they are considered to be important to the understanding of the content, use, or nature of the file:

the date(s) covered by the content of a file
the date(s) when data were collected
the date(s) of accompanying material not described separately if they differ from those of the file being described

New England sermons, 1790-1900

Data collected May-Aug. 1981

Manual dated 1983

Includes supplementary file dated 1981

9.7B8. File characteristics. Give important file characteristics that are not included in the file characteristics area.

Hierarchical file structure

Number of variables: 960

Number of routines: 102

File size varies

File size unknown

ASCII character set

Blocked BCDs, 40 records per block, 90 characters per record

If a file consists of numerous parts the numbering of which cannot be given succinctly in the file characteristics area, and if the information is considered to be important, give the number or approximate number of records, statements, etc., in each part.

File size: 520, 300, 280, 400, 320, 400, 500 records

File size: ca. 520, 300, 400, 320 statements

File size: 75, 65, 63, 92, 81, 109 kilobytes

9.7B9. Publication, distribution, etc. Make notes on publication, distribution, etc., details that are not included in the publication, distribution, etc., area and are considered to be important.

Solely distributed by the Laboratory

User's manual distributed by the American Political Science Association, Washington, D.C.

9.7B10. Physical description. Make notes on important physical details that are not included in the physical description area, especially if these affect the use of the item. If the file is available only by remote access, give physical details (e.g., colour, sound) if they are readily available and considered important.

Stereo. sd.

Displays in red, yellow, and blue

Not copy-protected

Second disk is back-up

9.7B11. Accompanying material. Make notes on the location of accompanying material if appropriate. Give details of accompanying material neither mentioned in the physical description area nor given a separate description (see 1.5E).

Accompanied by a series of 5 programs in PL/1, with assembler subroutines

Accompanied by documentation: 1980 census user's guide. Pts. 1-2. Washington, D.C. : Supt. of Docs., 1982

9.7B12. Series. Make notes on series data that cannot be given in the series area.

Originally issued in series: European Community study series

9.7B13. Dissertations. If the item being described is a dissertation, make a note as instructed in 1.7B13.

Thesis (M.A.)—University of Illinois at Urbana-Champaign, 1984

9.7B14. Audience. Make a brief note of the intended audience for, or intellectual level of, a file if this information is stated in or on the item, its container, or accompanying material.

> For ages 7-10

> Intended audience: High school students

> For use by qualified medical practitioners only

> Designed for those with a professional interest in analyzing spatial data (e.g., geographers, planners, meteorologists)

9.7B16. Other formats. Give the details of other formats in which the content of the file has been issued.

> Data issued also in printed form and in microform

> Issued also for IBM PC and PC-compatible hardware

9.7B17. Summary. Give a brief objective summary of the purpose and content of an item unless another part of the description provides enough information.

> Summary: Can be used to manipulate, weigh, and aggregate raw data in any manner desired. By assigning values to the coordinate locations of data points or data zones, the user may produce three types of map: contour, proximal, or conformant

> Summary: Responses of New York City adults to Harris study questionnaire used during Apr. and May 1969

> Summary: Eight versions of a video game for 1-2 players. To survive, players use laser cannons to destroy flying demons

> Summary: A simulation of Operation Barbarossa, the German invasion of Russia during World War II

9.7B18. Contents. List the parts of a file.

> Contents: 1. Idaho − 2. Montana − 3. Oregon − 4. Washington

> Contents: Moby Dick − Last of the Mohicans − Huckleberry Finn − Scarlet letter

Make notes on additional or partial contents when appropriate.

> Contains information on all 50 states

> Each record contains selected fields from the records with fewer than 2049 characters issued on LC MARC tape v. 6, no. 5

9.7B19. Numbers. Give important numbers borne by the item other than ISBNs or ISSNs (see 9.8B).

> APX-10050

9.7B20. Copy being described, library's holdings, and restrictions on use. Make these notes as instructed in 1.7B20. If desired, give a locally assigned file or data set name. If desired, give the date when the content of the file was copied from, or transferred to, another source.

> Local data set name: RBBIT.1
>
> Library's set lacks disk 7
>
> Copied June 1983
>
> File closed until Jan. 1990
>
> Restricted to scholarly use

9.7B21. "With" notes. If the title and statement of responsibility area contains a title that applies to only a part of an item lacking a collective title and, therefore, more than one entry is made, make a note beginning *With:* and listing the other separately titled works in the item in the order in which they appear there.

> With: Uncle Sam's jigsaw — U.S. Constitution tutor — Scramble

9.8. STANDARD NUMBER AND TERMS OF AVAILABILITY AREA

Contents:
9.8A. Preliminary rule
9.8B. Standard number
9.8C. Key-title
9.8D. Terms of availability
9.8E. Qualification

9.8A. Preliminary rule

9.8A1. Punctuation

For instructions on the use of spaces before and after prescribed punctuation, see 1.0C.

Precede this area by a full stop, space, dash, space *or* start a new paragraph.

Precede each repetition of this area by a full stop, space, dash, space.

Precede a key-title by an equals sign.

Precede terms of availability by a colon.

Enclose a qualification to the standard number or terms of availability in parentheses.

9.8B. Standard number

9.8B1. Give the International Standard Book Number (ISBN) or International Standard Serial Number (ISSN) assigned to a published file as instructed in 1.8B.

> ISBN 0-89138-111-2 (codebook)

9.8B2. Give any other number assigned to a file in a note (see 9.7B19).

9.8C. Key-title

9.8C1. Give the key-title of a serial file as instructed in 1.8C.

9.8D. *Optional addition.* **Terms of availability**

9.8D1. Give the terms on which the item is available as instructed in 1.8D.

$800.00

ISBN 0-87085-315-5 : $99.95

Free to universities and colleges, for hire to others

9.8E. Qualification

9.8E1. Add qualifications to the standard number and/or terms of availability as instructed in 1.8E.

ISBN 0-87490-399-8 : $49.00 ($19.00 for students)

9.9. SUPPLEMENTARY ITEMS

9.9A. Describe supplementary items as instructed in 1.9.

9.10. ITEMS MADE UP OF SEVERAL TYPES OF MATERIAL

9.10A. Describe items made up of several types of material as instructed in 1.10.

CHAPTER 10

THREE-DIMENSIONAL ARTEFACTS AND REALIA

Contents

10.0. GENERAL RULES

10.0A. Scope

10.0A1. The rules in this chapter cover the description of three-dimensional objects of all kinds (other than those covered in previous chapters), including models, dioramas, games (including puzzles and simulations), braille cassettes, sculptures and other three-dimensional art works, exhibits, machines, and clothing. They also cover the description of naturally occurring objects, including microscope specimens (or representations of them) and other specimens mounted for viewing. For the description of three-dimensional cartographic materials (e.g., relief models, globes), see chapter 3.

10.0B. Sources of information

10.0B1. Chief source of information. The chief source of information for the materials covered in this chapter is the object itself together with any accompanying textual material and container issued by the publisher or manufacturer of the item. Prefer information found on the object itself (including any permanently affixed labels) to information found in the accompanying textual material or on a container.

10.0B2. Prescribed sources of information. The prescribed source(s) of information for each area of the description of these materials is set out below. Enclose information taken from outside the prescribed source(s) in square brackets.

AREA	PRESCRIBED SOURCES OF INFORMATION
Title and statement of responsibility	Chief source of information
Edition	Chief source of information
Publication, distribution, etc.	Chief source of information
Physical description	Any source
Series	Chief source of information
Note	Any source
Standard number and terms of availability	Any source

10.0C. Punctuation

For the punctuation of the description as a whole, see 1.0C.
For the prescribed punctuation of elements, see the following rules.

10.0D. Levels of detail in the description

See 1.0D.

10.0E. Language and script of the description

See 1.0E.

10.0F. Inaccuracies

See 1.0F.

10.0G. Accents and other diacritical marks

See 1.0G.

10.0H. Items with several chief sources of information

10.0H1. Multipart items with a container that is a unifying element. Prefer information found on a container that is the unifying element of a multipart item to information found on the objects.

10.0H2. Multipart items without a container that is a unifying element. See 1.0H.

10.0H3. Single part items. See 1.0H.

10.1. TITLE AND STATEMENT OF RESPONSIBILITY AREA

Contents:

10.1A. Preliminary rule
10.1B. Title proper
10.1C. General material designation
10.1D. Parallel titles
10.1E. Other title information
10.1F. Statements of responsibility
10.1G. Items without a collective title

10.1A. Preliminary rule

10.1A1. Punctuation

For instructions on the use of spaces before and after prescribed punctuation, see 1.0C.

Enclose the general material designation in square brackets.

Precede each parallel title by an equals sign.

Precede each unit of other title information by a colon.

Precede the first statement of responsibility by a diagonal slash.

Precede each subsequent statement of responsibility by a semicolon.

For the punctuation of this area for items without a collective title, see 1.1G.

10.1B. Title proper

10.1B1. Transcribe the title proper as instructed in 1.1B.

Human development models

Solar system simulator

Muscular dynamism, or, Unique forms of continuity in space

1787

Adventure with sea-shells

[Woman's dress]

Tooth development

[United States silver dollar]

Pet rock

If the title proper is not taken from the chief source of information, give the source of the title in a note (see 10.7B3).

10.1C. *Optional addition.* **General material designation**

10.1C1. Give immediately following the title proper the appropriate general material designation as instructed in 1.1C.

10.1C2. If an item contains parts belonging to materials falling into two or more categories, and if none of these is the predominant constituent of the item, give either *multimedia* or *kit* as the designation (see 1.1C1 and 1.10C1).

10.1D. Parallel titles

10.1D1. Transcribe parallel titles as instructed in 1.1D.

>   Tarot cards [GMD] = L'ancien tarot

10.1E. Other title information

10.1E1. Transcribe other title information as instructed in 1.1E.

>   The language arts box [GMD] : 150 games, activities, manipulatives

10.1F. Statements of responsibility

10.1F1. Transcribe statements relating to persons or bodies responsible for the creation of the item, or for its display or selection, as instructed in 1.1F.

>   Hang-up [GMD] / developed by W.J. Gordon and T. Poze

>   Rosetta Stone unit [GMD] / consultant, Edward L.B. Terrace

>   A trip to the zoo [GMD] / created by the fourth grade class of Washington Elementary School, Berkeley, CA

10.1F2. Add a word or short phrase to the statement of responsibility if the relationship between the title and the person(s) or body (bodies) named in the statement is not clear.

10.1G. Items without a collective title

10.1G1. If an item lacks a collective title, transcribe the titles of the individual parts as instructed in 1.1G.

10.1G2. Make the relationship between statements of responsibility and the parts of an item lacking a collective title clear by additions as instructed in 10.1F2.

10.2. EDITION AREA

Contents:

10.2A. Preliminary rule

10.2A1. Punctuation

For instructions on the use of spaces before and after prescribed punctuation, see 1.0C.

Precede this area by a full stop, space, dash, space.

Precede a statement relating to a named revision of an edition by a comma.

Precede the first statement of responsibility following an edition statement by a diagonal slash.

Precede each subsequent statement of responsibility by a semicolon.

10.2B. Edition statement

10.2B1. Transcribe a statement relating to an edition of an artefact that contains differences from other editions of that artefact, or to a named reissue of an artefact, as instructed in 1.2B.

> The fable game [GMD] = Il gioco delle favole / Enzo Mari. — 2nd ed. / with cards re-drawn in colour

> Subbuteo table soccer [GMD]. — World Cup ed.

10.2B2. In case of doubt about whether a statement is an edition statement, follow the instructions in 1.2B3.

10.2B3. *Optional addition.* If an item lacks an edition statement but is known to contain significant changes from other editions, supply a suitable brief statement in the language and script of the title proper and enclose it in square brackets.

> [New ed.]

> [5e éd.]

10.2B4. If an edition statement appears in more than one language or script, transcribe the statement that is in the language or script of the title proper. If this criterion does not apply, transcribe the statement that appears first. *Optionally*, transcribe the parallel statement(s), each preceded by an equals sign.

10.2B5. If an item lacking a collective title contains one or more works with an associated edition statement, transcribe such statements following the titles and statements of responsibility to which they relate, separated from them by a full stop.

10.2C. Statements of responsibility relating to the edition

10.2C1. Transcribe a statement of responsibility relating to one or more editions, but not to all editions, of an artefact as instructed in 1.2C and 10.1F.

10.2D. Statement relating to a named revision of an edition

10.2D1. If an item is a named revision of an edition, transcribe the statement relating to that revision as instructed in 1.2D.

Do not record statements relating to a reissue that contains no changes unless the item is considered to be of particular importance to the cataloguing agency.

10.2E. Statements of responsibility relating to a named revision of an edition

10.2E1. Transcribe a statement of responsibility relating to one or more named revisions of an edition (but not to all such revisions) as instructed in 1.2E and 10.1F.

10.3. MATERIAL (OR TYPE OF PUBLICATION) SPECIFIC DETAILS AREA

10.3A. This area is not used for three-dimensional artefacts and realia.

10.4. PUBLICATION, DISTRIBUTION, ETC., AREA

Contents:

10.4A. Preliminary rule

10.4A1. Punctuation

For instructions on the use of spaces before and after prescribed punctuation, see 1.0C.

Precede this area by a full stop, space, dash, space.

Precede a second or subsequently named place of publication, distribution, etc., by a semicolon.

Precede the name of a publisher, distributor, etc., by a colon.

Enclose a supplied statement of function of a publisher, distributor, etc., in square brackets.

Precede the date of publication, distribution, etc., by a comma.

Enclose the details of manufacture (place, name, date) in parentheses.

Precede the name of a manufacturer by a colon.

Precede the date of manufacture by a comma.

10.4B. General rule

10.4B1. Record information about the place, name, and date of all types of publishing, distributing, etc., activities as instructed in 1.4B.

10.4C. Place of publication, distribution, etc.

10.4C1. Give the place of publication, distribution, etc., of a published artefact as instructed in 1.4C.

10.4C2. Do not record a place of publication, distribution, etc., for a naturally occurring object (other than one mounted for viewing or packaged for presentation) or for an artefact not intended primarily for communication. Do not record *s.l.* in such a case.

10.4D. Name of publisher, distributor, etc.

10.4D1. Give the name of the publisher, etc., and *optionally* the distributor, as instructed in 1.4D.

> Philadelphia : DCA Educational Products

> Circle Pines, Minn. : American Guidance Service

10.4D2. Do not record the name of a publisher, distributor, etc., for a naturally occurring object (other than one mounted for viewing or packaged for presentation) or for an artefact not intended primarily for communication. Do not record *s.n.* in such a case.

10.4E. *Optional addition.* **Statement of function of publisher, distributor, etc.**

10.4E1. Add to the name of a publisher, distributor, etc., a statement of function as instructed in 1.4E.

10.4F. Date of publication, distribution, etc.

10.4F1. Give the date of publication, distribution, etc., as instructed in 1.4F.

> Chicago : Science Research Associates, 1971

> Cambridge, Mass. : Synetics Education Systems, c1969

10.4F2. In the case of naturally occurring objects (other than those mounted for viewing or packaged for presentation), do not give a date. In the case of artefacts not intended primarily for communication, give the date of manufacture.

> [English Victorian costume] [GMD]. — [186-?]

> [United States silver dollar] [GMD]. — 1931

10.4G. Place of manufacture, name of manufacturer, date of manufacture

10.4G1. If the name of the publisher is unknown or if there is no publisher (see 10.4C2 and 10.4D2), and the place and the name of the manufacturer are known, give that place and name as instructed in 1.4G.

> [Wooden chair] [GMD]. — 1881 (Chiswick : Morris & Co.)

> [Millefiori paperweight] [GMD]. — [1890?] (Paris : Reynaud frères)

10.4G2. If the person or body responsible for the manufacture of the object has been named in a statement of responsibility (see 10.1F), do not repeat the place and name here.

> [Appliqué quilt, album style, Baltimore, Md.] [GMD] / Anna Putney Farrington. — 1857
> > (*Quilt is signed and dated*)

10.4G3. *Optional addition.* Give the place, name of manufacturer, and/or date of manufacture if they are found on the item or in accompanying textual material or on a container and differ from the place, name of publisher, etc., and date of publication, etc., and are considered important by the cataloguing agency.

> London : Her Majesty's Stationery Office, 1976 (London : UDO (Litho))

10.5. PHYSICAL DESCRIPTION AREA

Contents:
- 10.5A. Preliminary rule
- 10.5B. Extent of item (including specific material designation)
- 10.5C. Other physical details
- 10.5D. Dimensions
- 10.5E. Accompanying material

10.5A. Preliminary rule

10.5A1. Punctuation

For instructions on the use of spaces before and after prescribed punctuation, see 1.0C.

Precede this area by a full stop, space, dash, space *or* start a new paragraph.

Precede other physical details by a colon.

Precede dimensions by a semicolon.

Precede each statement of accompanying material by a plus sign.

Enclose physical details of accompanying material in parentheses.

10.5B. Extent of item (including specific material designation)

10.5B1. Record the number of physical units of a three-dimensional artefact or object by giving the number of parts in arabic numerals and one of the terms listed below, as appropriate.

> art original
> art reproduction
> braille cassette
> diorama
> exhibit
> game
> microscope slide
> mock-up
> model

1 game

2 dioramas

1 microscope slide

2 braille cassettes

6 microscope slides

If none of these terms is appropriate, give the specific name of the item or the names of the parts of the item as concisely as possible.

> 1 clockwork toy train
>
> 2 jigsaw puzzles
>
> 3 hand puppets
>
> 2 feather headbands, 1 pair beaded moccasins
>
> 3 quilts

Optionally, if general material designations are used (see 1.1C1) and the general material designation consists of one of the above listed terms, omit that term and give a description of the components alone (see 10.5B2).

> 1 board, 32 pieces, 2 poker dice

10.5B2. Add to the designation, when appropriate, the number and the name(s) of the component pieces.

> 1 jigsaw puzzle (1,000 pieces)
>
> 1 game (1 board, 50 cards, 5 role cards, 2 dice)

If the pieces cannot be named concisely or if their number cannot be readily ascertained, add *(various pieces)* and *optionally* give the details of the pieces in a note (see 10.7B10).

> 2 games (various pieces)
>
> 1 diorama (various pieces)
> *Note:* Contains 1 small stage, 5 foreground transparencies, 2 backgrounds, 5 story sheets, and 1 easel

10.5C. Other physical details

10.5C1. Material. When appropriate, give the material(s) of which the object is made. If the material(s) cannot be named concisely, either omit the statement or give it in a note. Give the material of which a microscope slide is made if it is other than glass.

> 2 models (various pieces) : polystyrene
>
> 1 diorama (various pieces) : plywood and papier mâché
>
> 1 statue : marble
>
> 2 paperweights : glass
>
> 1 quilt : cotton
>
> 1 jigsaw puzzle : wood
>
> 1 microscope slide : plastic

10.5C2. Colour. When appropriate, give *col.* for multicoloured objects, or name the colour(s) of the object if it is in one or two colours, or give *b&w* for black and white objects. If a microscope slide is stained, state this.

1 bowl : porcelain, blue and white

1 model : wood, blue

1 paperweight : glass, col.

1 model : balsa wood and paper, b&w

1 microscope slide : stained

10.5D. Dimensions

10.5D1. When appropriate, give the dimensions of the object. Give them in centimetres, to the next whole centimetre up. If necessary, add a word to indicate which dimension is being given. If multiple dimensions are given, give them as height × width × depth (for microscope slides, height × width).

1 sculpture : polished bronze ; 110 cm. high

6 microscope slides : stained ; 3 × 8 cm.

10.5D2. If the object is in a container, name the container and give its dimensions either after the dimensions of the object or as the only dimensions.

1 model (10 pieces) : col. ; 16 × 32 × 3 cm. in case 17 × 34 × 6 cm.

1 diorama (various pieces) : col. ; in box 30 × 25 × 13 cm.

1 jigsaw puzzle : wood, col. ; in box 25 × 32 × 5 cm.

10.5D3. If, in a multipart item, the objects and/or their containers differ in size, give the smallest or smaller and the largest or larger size, separated by a hyphen.

3 sculptures : marble ; 150-210 cm. high

2 jigsaw puzzles : cardboard, col. ; in boxes 20 × 30 × 5 cm.-26 × 35 × 6 cm.

10.5E. Accompanying material

10.5E1. Give the details of accompanying material as instructed in 1.5E.

5 models : col. ; in box 20 × 20 × 12 cm. + 1 teacher's guide (3 v. ; 30 cm.)

1 hand puppet : red and blue ; 20 cm. long + 1 sound disc (20 min. : analog, 33⅓ rpm, mono. ; 12 in.)

10.6. SERIES AREA

Contents:

10.6A. Preliminary rule

10.6A1. Punctuation

For instructions on the use of spaces before and after prescribed punctuation, see 1.0C.

Precede this area by a full stop, space, dash, space.

Enclose each series statement (see 1.6J) in parentheses.

Precede each parallel title by an equals sign.

Precede other title information by a colon.

Precede the first statement of responsibility by a diagonal slash.

Precede each subsequent statement of responsibility by a semicolon.

Precede the ISSN of a series or subseries by a comma.

Precede the numbering within a series or subseries by a semicolon.

Precede the title of a subseries by a full stop.

10.6B. Series statements

10.6B1. Record each series statement as instructed in 1.6.

(Dioramas of American history ; 7)

(Beatrix Potter jigsaw puzzles ; no. 3)

10.7. NOTE AREA

Contents:
10.7A. Preliminary rule
10.7B. Notes

10.7A. Preliminary rule

10.7A1. Punctuation

Precede each note by a full stop, space, dash, space *or* start a new paragraph for each.

Separate introductory wording from the main content of a note by a colon followed but not preceded by a space.

10.7A2. In making notes, follow the instructions in 1.7A.

10.7B. Notes

Make notes as set out in the following subrules and in the order given there. However, give a particular note first when it has been decided that note is of primary importance.

10.7B1. Nature of the item. Give the nature of the item unless it is apparent from the rest of the description.

Study of a figure in motion

Section of fetal pig mandible

10.7B3. Source of title proper. Make notes on the source of the title proper if it is other than the chief source of information.

> Title supplied by cataloguer

> Title taken from sales catalogue

10.7B4. Variations in title. Make notes on titles borne by the item other than the title proper. *Optionally*, give a romanization of the title proper.

> Title on container: DNA-RNA protein synthesis model kit

10.7B5. Parallel titles and other title information. Give the title in another language and other title information not recorded in the title and statement of responsibility area if they are considered to be important.

> Subtitle on container: Elementary dental model

10.7B6. Statements of responsibility. Make notes on variant names of persons or bodies named in statements of responsibility if these are considered to be important for identification. Give statements of responsibility not recorded in the title and statement of responsibility area. Make notes on persons or bodies connected with a work, or significant persons or bodies connected with previous editions and not already named in the description.

> "Developed by Frederick A. Rasmussen of E[ducational]
> R[esearch] C[ouncil of America]"

10.7B7. Edition and history. Make notes relating to the edition being described or to the history of the item. Cite other works upon which the item depends for its intellectual or artistic content.

> Recast in bronze from artist's plaster original of 1903

> Game based on: Lateral thinking / by M. Freedman

10.7B9. Publication, distribution, etc. Make notes on publication, distribution, etc., details that are not included in the publication, distribution, etc., area and are considered to be important.

10.7B10. Physical description. Make notes on important physical details that are not included in the physical description area, especially if these affect the use of the item. If the physical description includes *various pieces* and a description of the pieces is considered to be useful, give such a description.

> Four times actual size. — The parts of the ear are painted to
> show anatomical structure

> Includes headdress, beaded shirt, trousers, and moccasins

> Pattern: Pennsylvania wild goose

> Contains 1 small stage, 5 foreground transparencies, 2
> backgrounds, 5 story sheets, and 1 easel

10.7B11. Accompanying material. Make notes on the location of accompanying material if appropriate. Give details of accompanying material neither mentioned in the physical description area nor given a separate description (see 1.5E).

254

> Teacher's guide / by Robert Garry Shirts. 24 p.

> With instructor and student guides, 16 taped lectures, cassette recorder, and course guide (4 v.)

> Book (in container) entitled: The adventure book of shells / by Eva Knox Evans

10.7B12. Series. Make notes on series data that cannot be given in the series area.

10.7B13. Dissertations. If the item being described is a dissertation, make a note as instructed in 1.7B13.

> Thesis (M.I.D.)–Rhode Island School of Design, 1990

10.7B14. Audience. Make a brief note of the intended audience for, or intellectual level of, an item if this information is stated in the item.

> For medical students

> Intended audience: Junior high and up

10.7B17. Summary. Give a brief objective summary of the content of an item unless another part of the description provides enough information.

> Summary: Illustrations of animals and background scenery, with stands, which may be rearranged to create various scenes of animals at the zoo

> Summary: Puppets from a set designed to dramatize real-life situations

10.7B18. Contents. List the individually named parts of an object. Make notes on additional or partial contents when appropriate.

> Contents: Colony − Frontier − Reconstruction − Promotion − Intervention − Development

> Contents: Sperm cell in uterus − 2-week embryo − 7- to 8-week fetus − 13-week fetus − 18- to 20-week fetus

> Includes a simplified version of the game

10.7B19. Numbers. Give important numbers borne by the item other than ISBNs or ISSNs (see 10.8B).

10.7B20. Copy being described, library's holdings, and restrictions on use. Make these notes as instructed in 1.7B20.

> Set lacks 2 puppets

10.7B21. "With" notes. If the title and statement of responsibility area contains a title that applies to only a part of an item lacking a collective title and, therefore, more than one entry is made, make a note beginning *With:* and listing the other separately titled works in the item in the order in which they appear there.

> With: Backgammon − Checkers

10.8. STANDARD NUMBER AND TERMS OF AVAILABILITY AREA

Contents:
10.8A. Preliminary rule
10.8B. Standard number
10.8C. Key-title
10.8D. Terms of availability
10.8E. Qualification

10.8A. Preliminary rule

10.8A1. Punctuation

For instructions on the use of spaces before and after prescribed punctuation, see 1.0C.

Precede this area by a full stop, space, dash, space *or* start a new paragraph.

Precede each repetition of this area by a full stop, space, dash, space.

Precede a key-title by an equals sign.

Precede terms of availability by a colon.

Enclose a qualification to the standard number or terms of availability in parentheses.

10.8B. Standard number

10.8B1. Give the International Standard Book Number (ISBN) or International Standard Serial Number (ISSN) assigned to an item as instructed in 1.8B.

10.8B2. Give any other number in a note (see 10.7B19).

10.8C. Key-title

10.8C1. Give the key-title of a serial item as instructed in 1.8C.

10.8D. *Optional addition.* Terms of availability

10.8D1. Give the terms on which the item is available as instructed in 1.8D.

Free loan to medical students

$9.00 (medical students only)

10.8E. Qualification

10.8E1. Add qualifications to the standard number and/or terms of availability as instructed in 1.8E.

10.9. SUPPLEMENTARY ITEMS

10.9A. Describe supplementary items as instructed in 1.9.

10.10. ITEMS MADE UP OF SEVERAL TYPES OF MATERIAL

10.10A. Describe items made up of several types of material as instructed in 1.10.

CHAPTER 11

MICROFORMS

Contents

11.0. GENERAL RULES

11.0A. Scope

11.0A1. The rules in this chapter cover the description of all kinds of material in microform. Microforms include microfilms, microfiches, microopaques, and aperture cards. Microforms may be reproductions of existing textual or graphic materials or they may be original publications.

11.0B. Sources of information

11.0B1. Chief source of information. The chief source of information for microfilms is the title frame (i.e., a frame, usually at the beginning of the item, bearing the full title and, normally, publication details of the item). The chief source of information for aperture cards is, in the case of a set of cards, the title card, or, in the case of a single card, the card itself. The chief source of information for microfiches and microopaques is the title frame. If there is no such information or if the information is insufficient, treat the eye-readable data printed at the top of the fiche or opaque as the chief source of information. If, however, the title appears in a shortened form on the "header" and appears in a fuller form on the accompanying eye-readable materials or the container, treat the accompanying eye-readable materials or the container as the chief source of information and make a note (see 11.7B3) giving the source of the title proper. If information normally presented on the title frame or title card is presented on successive frames or cards, treat these frames or cards as the chief source of information.

If information is not available from the chief source, take it from the following sources (in this order of preference):

the rest of the item (including a container that is an integral part of the item)
container
accompanying eye-readable material
any other source

11.0B2. Prescribed sources of information. The prescribed source(s) of information for each area of the description of microforms is set out below. Enclose information taken from outside the prescribed source(s) in square brackets.

AREA	PRESCRIBED SOURCES OF INFORMATION
Title and statement of responsibility	Chief source of information
Edition	Chief source of information, rest of the item, container
Special data	Chief source of information, rest of the item, container
Publication, distribution, etc.	Chief source of information, rest of the item, container
Physical description	Any source
Series	Chief source of information, rest of the item, container
Note	Any source
Standard number and terms of availability	Any source

11.0C. Punctuation

For the punctuation of the description as a whole, see 1.0C.
For the prescribed punctuation of elements, see the following rules.

259

11.0D. Levels of detail in the description
See 1.0D.

11.0E. Language and script of the description
See 1.0E.

11.0F. Inaccuracies
See 1.0F.

11.0G. Accents and other diacritical marks
See 1.0G.

11.0H. Items with several chief sources of information
See 1.0H.

11.1. TITLE AND STATEMENT OF RESPONSIBILITY AREA

Contents:
    11.1A. Preliminary rule
    11.1B. Title proper
    11.1C. General material designation
    11.1D. Parallel titles
    11.1E. Other title information
    11.1F.   Statements of responsibility
    11.1G. Items without a collective title

11.1A. Preliminary rule

11.1A1. Punctuation
For instructions on the use of spaces before and after prescribed punctuation, see 1.0C.
Precede the title of a supplement or section (see 1.1B9) by a full stop.
Enclose the general material designation in square brackets.
Precede each parallel title by an equals sign.
Precede each unit of other title information by a colon.
Precede the first statement of responsibility by a diagonal slash.
Precede each subsequent statement of responsibility by a semicolon.
For the punctuation of this area for items without a collective title, see 1.1G.

11.1B. Title proper

11.1B1. Transcribe the title proper as instructed in 1.1B.

      Early narratives of the Northwest

      Grimm's fairy tales

      Library resources & technical services

      Records of the Socialist Labor Party of America

      Index to Sussex parish registers and bishops transcripts

> Beethoven's symphonies

> British masters of the albumen print

If the title proper is not taken from the chief source of information, or if the chief source of information is a container or eye-readable matter, give the source of the title in a note (see 11.7B3).

11.1C. *Optional addition.* **General material designation**

11.1C1. Give immediately following the title proper the appropriate general material designation as instructed in 1.1C.

> A history of Dalhousie University Main Library, 1867-1931 [GMD]

11.1C2. If an item contains parts belonging to materials falling into two or more categories, and if none of these is the predominant constituent of the item, give either *multimedia* or *kit* as the designation (see 1.1C1 and 1.10C1).

11.1D. Parallel titles

11.1D1. Transcribe parallel titles as instructed in 1.1D.

> Deutschland [GMD] = Allemagne = Germany

11.1E. Other title information

11.1E1. Transcribe other title information as instructed in 1.1E.

> The gentleman of Venice [GMD] : a tragi-comedie presented at the private house in Salisbury Court by Her Majesties servants

> A collection in the making [GMD] : works from the Phillipps Collection

11.1F. Statements of responsibility

11.1F1. Transcribe statements of responsibility relating to persons or bodies as instructed in 1.1F.

> The principles of psychology [GMD] / William James

> Books in English [GMD] / British Library Bibliographic Services

> Selections from the permanent collection [GMD] / Whitney Museum of American Art

11.1F2. Add a word or short phrase to the statement of responsibility if the relationship between the title and the person(s) or body (bodies) named in the statement is not clear.

11.1G. Items without a collective title

11.1G1. If a microform lacks a collective title, *either* describe the item as a unit (see 11.1G2 and 11.1G3) *or* make a separate description for each separately titled part (see 11.1G4).

11.1G2. In describing as a unit a microform lacking a collective title, transcribe the titles of the individual parts as instructed in 1.1G3.

> Don Juan [GMD] ; and, Childe Harold / Lord Byron

> Analysis of the results of the general population census 1964 [GMD] ; The supply of labour in Libya / Libya, Ministry of Economy and Commerce, Census and Statistical Department

> The Wilson papers [GMD]. The Cole-Hatt papers

11.1G3. Make the relationship between statements of responsibility and the parts of an item lacking a collective title and described as a unit clear by additions as instructed in 11.1F2.

11.1G4. *Optionally*, make a separate description for each separately titled work on a microform. For the description of the extent in each of these descriptions, see 11.5B3. Link the separate descriptions with notes (see 11.7B21).

11.2. EDITION AREA

Contents:
11.2A.   Preliminary rule
11.2B.   Edition statement
11.2C.   Statements of responsibility relating to the edition
11.2D.   Statement relating to a named revision of an edition
11.2E.   Statements of responsibility relating to a named revision of an edition

11.2A. Preliminary rule

11.2A1. Punctuation

For instructions on the use of spaces before and after prescribed punctuation, see 1.0C.

Precede this area by a full stop, space, dash, space.

Precede a statement relating to a named revision of an edition by a comma.

Precede the first statement of responsibility following an edition statement by a diagonal slash.

Precede each subsequent statement of responsibility by a semicolon.

11.2B. Edition statement

11.2B1. Transcribe a statement relating to an edition of a microform that contains differences from other editions of that microform, or to a named reissue of a microform, as instructed in 1.2B.

2nd ed.

New ed.

Memorial ed.

Micro ed.

11.2B2. In case of doubt about whether a statement is an edition statement, follow the instructions in 1.2B3.

11.2B3. *Optional addition.* If a microform lacks an edition statement but is known to contain significant changes from other editions, supply a suitable brief statement in the language and script of the title proper and enclose it in square brackets.

[New ed.]

[3rd ed.]

11.2B4. If an edition statement appears in more than one language or script, transcribe the statement that is in the language or script of the title proper. If this criterion does not apply, transcribe the statement that appears first. *Optionally*, transcribe the parallel statement(s), each preceded by an equals sign.

11.2B5. If an item lacking a collective title and described as a unit contains one or more works with an associated edition statement, transcribe such statements following the titles and statements of responsibility to which they relate, separated from them by a full stop.

Finnegans wake [GMD]. 2nd ed. ; Ulysses / James Joyce

11.2C. Statements of responsibility relating to the edition

11.2C1. Transcribe a statement of responsibility relating to one or more editions, but not to all editions, of a microform as instructed in 1.2C and 11.1F.

3rd ed. / with an introduction by Tom Barbellion

11.2D. Statement relating to a named revision of an edition

11.2D1. If the item is a named revision of an edition, transcribe the statement relating to that revision as instructed in 1.2D.

3rd ed., Corr.

Do not record statements relating to a reissue that contains no changes unless the item is considered to be of particular importance to the cataloguing agency.

11.2E. Statements of responsibility relating to a named revision of an edition

11.2E1. Transcribe a statement of responsibility relating to one or more named revisions of an edition (but not to all such revisions) as instructed in 1.2E and 11.1F.

11.3. SPECIAL DATA FOR CARTOGRAPHIC MATERIALS, MUSIC, AND SERIALS

11.3A. Cartographic materials

11.3A1. Give the mathematical data of a cartographic item in microform as instructed in 3.3.

11.3B. Music

11.3B1. Give the physical presentation of music in microform as instructed in 5.3.

11.3C. Serials

11.3C1. Give the numeric and/or alphabetic, chronological, or other designation of a serial microform or a serial reproduced in microform as instructed in 12.3.

> Library resources & technical services [GMD]. — Vol. 16, no. 1 (winter 1972)-

> The yellow book [GMD] : an illustrated quarterly. — Vol. 1 (Apr. 1894)-v. 13 (Apr. 1897)

11.4. PUBLICATION, DISTRIBUTION, ETC., AREA

Contents:
- 11.4A. Preliminary rule
- 11.4B. General rule
- 11.4C. Place of publication, distribution, etc.
- 11.4D. Name of publisher, distributor, etc.
- 11.4E. Statement of function of publisher, distributor, etc.
- 11.4F. Date of publication, distribution, etc.

11.4A. Preliminary rule

11.4A1. Punctuation
For instructions on the use of spaces before and after prescribed punctuation, see 1.0C.

Precede this area by a full stop, space, dash, space.

Precede a second or subsequently named place of publication, distribution, etc., by a semicolon.

Precede the name of a publisher, distributor, etc., by a colon.

Enclose a supplied statement of function of a publisher, distributor, etc., in square brackets.

Precede the date of publication, distribution, etc., by a comma.

11.4B. General rule

11.4B1. Record information about the place, name, and date of all types of publishing, distributing, etc., activities as instructed in 1.4B.

11.4C. Place of publication, distribution, etc.

11.4C1. Give the place of publication, distribution, etc., of a published microform as instructed in 1.4C.

11.4C2. Do not record a place of publication, distribution, etc., for an unpublished microform. Do not record *s.l.* in such a case.

11.4D. Name of publisher, distributor, etc.

11.4D1. Give the name of the publisher of a published microform, and *optionally* the distributor, as instructed in 1.4D.

> Los Angeles : University of Southern California
>
> London : Grossman
>
> New York : Readex Microprint
>
> Ann Arbor, Mich. : Xerox University Microfilms
>   (*Cataloguing agency in the United States*)
>
> Ann Arbor, Mich. ; Tylers Green, Buckinghamshire : Xerox
> University Microfilms
>   (*Cataloguing agency in the United Kingdom*)

11.4D2. Do not record the name of a publisher, distributor, etc., for an unpublished microform. Do not record *s.n.* in such a case.

11.4E. *Optional addition.* **Statement of function of publisher, distributor, etc.**

11.4E1. Add to the name of a publisher, distributor, etc., a statement of function as instructed in 1.4E.

> New York : Charles & Brown ; London : Salemis [distributor]

11.4F. Date of publication, distribution, etc.

11.4F1. Give the date of publication, distribution, etc., of a published microform as instructed in 1.4F.

> New York : Readex Microprint, 1953
>
> London : Challon, 1969
>
> Ann Arbor, Mich. : Xerox University Microfilms, 1973-
>
> Chicago : Library Resources, c1970

11.4F2. Give the date of creation of an unpublished microform, if readily available. Do not record a date if none is readily available.

> [Victorian literary letters from the Morgan-Krane Collection]
> [GMD]. — 1971
>   (*Title frame contains:* Filmed in 1971)

11.5. PHYSICAL DESCRIPTION AREA

Contents:
    11.5A.   Preliminary rule
    11.5B.   Extent of item (including specific material designation)
    11.5C.   Other physical details
    11.5D.   Dimensions
    11.5E.   Accompanying material

11.5A. Preliminary rule

11.5A1. Punctuation

For instructions on the use of spaces before and after prescribed punctuation, see 1.0C.

Precede this area by a full stop, space, dash, space *or* start a new paragraph.

Precede other physical details by a colon.

Precede dimensions by a semicolon.

Precede each statement of accompanying material by a plus sign.

Enclose physical details of accompanying material in parentheses.

11.5B. Extent of item (including specific material designation)

11.5B1. Record the number of physical units of a microform item by giving the number of them in arabic numerals and one of the following terms as appropriate:

> aperture card
> microfiche
> microfilm
> microopaque

Add *cartridge*, *cassette*, or *reel*, as appropriate, to *microfilm*. Add *cassette* if appropriate, to *microfiche*.

> 25 aperture cards

> 1 microfilm cassette

> 2 microfilm reels

> 3 microfiches

> 10 microopaques

Optionally, if general material designations are used (see 1.1C1), omit *micro* from the specific material designation.

11.5B2. Add the number of frames of a microfiche or microfiche set if that number can be readily ascertained.

> 2 microfiches (147 fr.)

> 1 microfiche (120 fr.)

> 3 microfiches (ca. 120 fr. each)

11.5B3. If the description is of a separately titled part of a microform lacking a collective title (see 11.1G4), express the fractional extent in the form *on reel 2 of 3 microfilm reels*, *on no. 4 of 5 microfiches*, etc. (if the parts are numbered or lettered in a single sequence) or *on 1 reel of 3 microfilm reels*, *on 1 of 5 microfiches*, etc. (if there is no sequential numbering).

> on no. 3 of 4 microfilm cassettes

> on 3 of 5 microopaques

11.5C. Other physical details

11.5C1. If a microform is negative, indicate this.

> 1 microfilm reel : negative

11.5C2. If a microform contains, or consists of, illustrations, indicate this as instructed in 2.5C.

> 1 microfilm cassette : ill.

> 1 microfiche : all ill.

> 1 microfiche : ill., music

> 1 microfiche : chiefly music

> 1 microfilm reel : negative, ill.

11.5C3. If a microform is wholly or partly coloured, indicate this by giving *col.* (for a coloured microform without illustrations), or *col. & ill.* (for a coloured microform with illustrations), or *col. ill.*, etc. (for a microform on which only the illustrations are coloured).

> 1 microfilm reel : col.

> 1 microfilm reel : col. & ill.

> 1 microfilm reel : col. ill., col. maps

11.5D. Dimensions

11.5D1. Give the dimensions of a microform as set out in the following rules. Give a fraction of a centimetre as the next whole centimetre up.

If the microforms in a multipart item differ in size, give the smallest or smaller and the largest or larger size, separated by a hyphen.

11.5D2. Aperture cards. Give the height × width of an aperture card mount in centimetres.

> 20 aperture cards ; 9 × 19 cm.

11.5D3. Microfiches. If the dimensions of a microfiche are other than 10.5 × 14.8 cm., give the height × width in centimetres.

      1 microfiche ; 12 × 17 cm.

      2 microfiches ; 11 × 15 cm.-12 × 17 cm.

11.5D4. Microfilms. Give the width of a microfilm in millimetres.

      1 microfilm reel ; 16 mm.

      1 microfilm cartridge ; 35 mm.

11.5D5. Microopaques. Give the height × width of a microopaque in centimetres.

      5 microopaques ; 8 × 13 cm.

11.5E. Accompanying material

11.5E1. Give the details of accompanying material as instructed in 1.5E.

      1 microfilm reel ; 16 mm. + 1 manual

      1 microfilm reel ; 16 mm. + 1 v. (30 p. : ill. ; 22 cm.)

11.6. SERIES AREA

Contents:
      11.6A. Preliminary rule
      11.6B. Series statements

11.6A. Preliminary rule

11.6A1. Punctuation

For instructions on the use of spaces before and after prescribed punctuation, see 1.0C.

Precede this area by a full stop, space, dash, space.

Enclose each series statement (see 1.6J) in parentheses.

Precede each parallel title by an equals sign.

Precede other title information by a colon.

Precede the first statement of responsibility by a diagonal slash.

Precede each subsequent statement of responsibility by a semicolon.

Precede the ISSN of a series or subseries by a comma.

Precede the numbering within a series or subseries by a semicolon.

Precede the title of a subseries by a full stop.

11.6B. Series statements

11.6B1. Record each series statement relating to a microform as instructed in 1.6. If the original was published in a series, record it in a note (see 11.7B12).

      (Bibliotheca Asiatica ; v. 9)

      (PCMI collection)

      (AIP-DRP ; 63-2)

(Three centuries of drama. English, 1642-1700)

(Wright American fiction ; reel A-4)

11.7. NOTE AREA

Contents:
11.7A. Preliminary rule
11.7B. Notes

11.7A. Preliminary rule

11.7A1. Punctuation

Precede each note by a full stop, space, dash, space *or* start a new paragraph for each.

Separate introductory wording from the main content of a note by a colon followed but not preceded by a space.

11.7A2. In making notes, follow the instructions in 1.7A.

11.7B. Notes

Make notes as set out in the following subrules and in the order given there. However, give a particular note first when it has been decided that note is of primary importance. If the item being described is a reproduction of an original in another form, make one note on the original, giving the details in the order of the areas to which they relate (see 11.7B22).

11.7B1. Nature, scope, or artistic or other form of an item. Make notes on these matters unless they are apparent from the rest of the description.

Collection of 18th cent. mss.

11.7B2. Language. Make notes on the language(s) of the item, unless this is apparent from the rest of the description.

Latin, with English translations

11.7B3. Source of title proper. Make notes on the source of the title proper if it is other than the chief source of information, or when the chief source of information is a container or eye-readable matter (see 11.0B1).

Title from container

11.7B4. Variations in title. Make notes on titles borne by the item other than the title proper. *Optionally*, give a romanization of the title proper.

Also known as: NICEM index to educational slides

11.7B5. Parallel titles and other title information. Give the title in another language and other title information not recorded in the title and statement of responsibility area if they are considered to be important.

Subtitle: An analysis of world trends

11.7B6. Statements of responsibility. Make notes on variant names of persons or bodies named in statements of responsibility if these are considered to be important for identification. Give statements of responsibility not recorded in the title and statement of responsibility area. Make notes on persons or bodies connected with a work, or significant persons or bodies connected with previous editions and not already named in the description.

"Edited ... by T.N. Jackson"—Pref.

11.7B7. Edition and history. Make notes on other microform editions of the item being described.

Previous microfiche ed.: 1971

11.7B9. Publication, distribution, etc. Make notes on publication, distribution, etc., details that are not included in the publication, distribution, etc., area and are considered to be important.

Distributed in the U.K. by: MicroFilm Imports

11.7B10. Physical description. Make the following physical description notes.

Reduction ratio. Give the reduction ratio if it is outside the $16\times$–$30\times$ range. Use one of the following terms:

> low reduction (for less than $16\times$)
> high reduction (for $31\times$–$60\times$)
> very high reduction (for $61\times$–$90\times$)
> ultra high reduction (for over $90\times$; for ultra high reduction give also the specific ratio (e.g., *Ultra high reduction, 150×*))
> reduction ratio varies

Reader. Give the name of the reader on which a cassette or cartridge microfilm is to be used if it affects the use of the item.

For Information Design reader

Film. Give details of the nature of the film.

Silver based film

Other physical details. Make notes on other important physical details that are not included in the physical description area.

Image printed on thin paper

11.7B11. Accompanying material. Make notes on the location of accompanying material if appropriate. Give details of accompanying material neither mentioned in the physical description area nor given a separate description (see 1.5E).

With brief notes (3 p.)

In container with facsim. reproductions of p. 1-8 of original

11.7B12. Series. Make notes on any microform series in which the microform has also been issued.

> Originally issued in the series: The Afro-American experience
> (*Microform previously issued as such in a series*)

11.7B13. Dissertations. If the item being described is a dissertation, make a note as instructed in 1.7B13.

> Thesis (M.A.)–University of New Brunswick, 1975

11.7B14. Audience. Make a brief note of the intended audience for, or intellectual level of, a microform if this information is stated on the item, its container, or accompanying eye-readable material.

> Intended audience: High school students

11.7B16. Other formats. Give the details of other formats in which the content of the item has also been issued. For a reproduction of previously existing material, see 11.7B22.

> Issued also on 16 mm. microfilm

11.7B17. Summary. Give a brief objective summary of the content of an item unless another part of the description provides enough information.

> Summary: Lists the serial holdings of 27 college libraries in Iowa
> as of 1981

11.7B18. Contents. List the contents of an item, either selectively or fully, if it is considered necessary to show the presence of material not implied by the rest of the description; to stress items of particular importance; or to list the contents of a collection. When recording titles formally, take them from the head of the part to which they refer rather than from contents lists, etc.

> Includes bibliography

> Contents: Surrey – Kent – Middlesex – Essex

> Annual reports for 1957-1971

11.7B19. Numbers. Give important numbers borne by the item other than ISBNs or ISSNs (see 11.8B).

11.7B20. Copy being described, library's holdings, and restrictions on use. Make these notes as instructed in 1.7B20.

> Available only to researchers with written permission from the
> copyright holder

> Also available as computer file

11.7B21. "With" notes. If the title and statement of responsibility area contains a title that applies to only a part of an item lacking a collective title and, therefore, more than one entry is made, make a note beginning *With:* and listing the other separately titled works in the item in the order in which they appear there.

With: General Sherman / M. Force — Life and campaigns of
Major-General J.E.B. Stuart / H. McClennan — General Butler in
New Orleans / J. Parton — Life and public services of Ambrose E.
Burnside / B. Poore — Life of General George G. Meade / R.
Bache

11.7B22. Note relating to the original. Make a note relating to an original as
instructed in 1.7A4 and 1.11F.

Reproduction of: Endymion / by the Author of Lothair.
London : Longmans, Green, 1880. 3 v. ; 20 cm.

Reproduction of: 2nd ed. London : Royal Geographic Society,
1924. 1 atlas (5 v.) : 450 maps ; 31 cm. (Atlases of the Western
world ; no. 17)

Reproduction of: Vol. 3, no. 58 (Apr. 21, 1841)-v. 4, no. 146
(Sept. 26, 1843). Manchester, Lancashire : Printed and published
by John Gadsby, 1841-1843. 93 no. : ill., map, music ; 38-50 cm.
Frequency varies. Continues: Anti-Corn Law circular. Continued
by: The league

Reproduction of: London : Printed for the editor, [1798-1807]. 1
score (3 v.) ; 32 cm.

11.8. STANDARD NUMBER AND TERMS OF AVAILABILITY AREA

Contents:
11.8A. Preliminary rule
11.8B. Standard number
11.8C. Key-title
11.8D. Terms of availability
11.8E. Qualification

11.8A. Preliminary rule

11.8A1. Punctuation
For instructions on the use of spaces before and after prescribed punctuation,
see 1.0C.
Precede this area by a full stop, space, dash, space *or* start a new paragraph.
Precede each repetition of this area by a full stop, space, dash, space.
Precede a key-title by an equals sign.
Precede terms of availability by a colon.
Enclose a qualification to the standard number or terms of availability in
parentheses.

11.8B. Standard number

11.8B1. Give the International Standard Book Number (ISBN) or International
Standard Serial Number (ISSN) assigned to an item as instructed in 1.8B.

11.8B2. Give any other number in a note (see 11.7B19).

11.8C. Key-title

11.8C1. Give the key-title of a serial item as instructed in 1.8C.

11.8D. *Optional addition.* **Terms of availability**

11.8D1. Give the terms on which the item is available as instructed in 1.8D.

11.8E. Qualification

11.8E1. Add qualifications to the standard number and/or terms of availability as instructed in 1.8E.

11.9. SUPPLEMENTARY ITEMS

11.9A. Describe supplementary items as instructed in 1.9.

11.10. ITEMS MADE UP OF SEVERAL TYPES OF MATERIAL

11.10A. Describe items made up of several types of material as instructed in 1.10.

CHAPTER 12

SERIALS

Contents

274

12.0. GENERAL RULES

12.0A. Scope

12.0A1. The rules in this chapter cover the description of serial publications of all kinds and in all media. Consult this chapter in conjunction with the chapter dealing with the physical form in which the serial is published. For example, in describing a serial motion picture, use both chapter 12 and chapter 7.

12.0B. Sources of information

12.0B1. Printed serials

Chief source of information. The chief source of information for printed serials is the title page[1] (whether published with the issues or published later) or the title page substitute of the first issue of the serial. Failing this, the chief source of information is the title page of the first available issue. The title page substitute for an item lacking a title page is (in this order of preference) the analytical title page, cover, caption, masthead, editorial pages, colophon, other pages. Specify the source used as the title page substitute in a note (see 12.7B3). If information traditionally given on the title page is given on facing pages, with or without repetition, treat the two pages as the title page.

Use the colophon as the chief source of information for an oriental nonroman script printed serial if the colophon contains full bibliographic information and the following conditions apply:

      a) the page standing in the position of a title page bears only the title proper

or b) the title page bears only a calligraphic version of the title proper

or c) the title page bears only a western-language version of the title and other bibliographic information.

Prescribed sources of information. The prescribed source(s) of information for each area of the description of printed serials is set out below. Enclose information taken from outside the prescribed source(s) in square brackets.

AREA	PRESCRIBED SOURCES OF INFORMATION
Title and statement of responsibility	Title page
Edition	Title page, other preliminaries, colophon
Numeric and/or alphabetic, chronological, or other designation	The whole publication
Publication, distribution, etc.	The whole publication
Physical description	The whole publication
Series	The whole publication
Note	Any source
Standard number and terms of availability	Any source

12.0B2. Nonprint serials. Follow the instructions given in subrule .0B in the relevant chapter in part I (e.g., for sources of information for a serial sound recording, see 6.0B).

12.0C. Punctuation

For the punctuation of the description as a whole, see 1.0C.

For the prescribed punctuation of elements, see the following rules.

---

1. Hereafter in this chapter *title page* includes any substitute (including, for oriental publications, a colophon specified in 12.0B1 as a title page substitute).

12.0D. Levels of detail in the description
See 1.0D.

12.0E. Language and script of the description
See 1.0E.

12.0F. Inaccuracies
See 1.0F.

12.0G. Accents and other diacritical marks
See 1.0G.

12.0H. Items with several chief sources of information
See 1.0H.

12.1. TITLE AND STATEMENT OF RESPONSIBILITY AREA

Contents:
12.1A. Preliminary rule
12.1B. Title proper
12.1C. General material designation
12.1D. Parallel titles
12.1E. Other title information
12.1F. Statements of responsibility

12.1A. Preliminary rule

12.1A1. Punctuation
For instructions on the use of spaces before and after prescribed punctuation, see 1.0C.
Precede the title of a supplement or section (see 1.1B9) by a full stop.
Enclose the general material designation in square brackets.
Precede each parallel title by an equals sign.
Precede each unit of other title information by a colon.
Precede the first statement of responsibility by a diagonal slash.
Precede each subsequent statement of responsibility by a semicolon.

12.1B. Title proper

12.1B1. Transcribe the title proper as instructed in 1.1B.

Gallia

Bulletin

Le monde

Boston evening transcript

Champaign-Urbana news-gazette

Transactions for the year

> Catalogue & index
>
> Q
>
> Willing's press guide
>
> IAVRI bulletin
>
> Bulletin of the Malaysia-Singapore Commercial Association (Inc.)
>
> 941.1
>
> The audio lawyer
>
> Thesis theological cassettes
>
> Supplement to The journal of physics and chemistry of solids

If the title proper is not taken from the chief source of information or if, in a printed serial, it is taken from a title page substitute (see 12.0B1), give the source in a note (see 12.7B3).

12.1B2. When the title appears in full and in the form of an acronym or initialism in the chief source of information, choose the full form as the title proper unless the acronym or initialism is the only form of title presented in other locations in the serial.

> Linguistics and language behavior abstracts
> (*Title appears in full and as* LLBA *in the chief source. Full title appears in other locations*)

12.1B3. In case of doubt about whether a corporate body's name or an abbreviation of that name is part of the title proper, treat the name as such only if it is consistently so presented in various locations in the serial (cover, caption, masthead, editorial pages, etc.) and/or, when cataloguing retrospectively, in indexes, abstracts, or other lists.

12.1B4. If a serial is a separately published section of, or supplement to, another serial and its title proper as presented in the chief source of information consists of

> a) the title common to all sections (or the title of the main serial)
>
> *and*   b) the title of the section or supplement

and if these two parts are grammatically independent of each other, give the common title followed by the section or supplement title preceded by a full stop. In such a case disregard the order in which the parts of the title proper are presented in the chief source of information.

> Acta Universitatis Carolinae. Philologica
>
> Key abstracts. Industrial power and control systems
>
> Journal of the American Leather Chemists' Association. Supplement
>
> Études et documents tchadiens. Série B

12.1B5. If the title of such a section or supplement (see 12.1B4) is preceded by an enumeration or alphabetic designation, give the common title, followed by the designation preceded by a full stop, and the section or supplement title preceded by a comma.

> Journal of polymer science. Part A, General papers

> Progress in nuclear energy. Series II, Reactors

For enumeration used as a chronological series designation, see 12.3G.

12.1B6. If the title of a section or supplement is presented in the chief source of information without the title that is common to all sections, give the title of the section or supplement as the title proper. In the case of a section, give the title that is common to all sections as the title proper of the series (see 12.6B). In the case of a supplement, give the title of the main serial in a note (see 12.7B7j).

> British journal of applied physics .... — (Journal of
> physics ; D)
> > (*Section title only presented in chief source of information. Common title given as series*)

12.1B7. If the title includes a date or numbering that varies from issue to issue, omit this date or numbering and replace it by the mark of omission, unless it occurs at the beginning of the title, in which case do not give the mark of omission.

> Report on the ... Conference on Development Objectives and
> Strategy

> Supply estimates for the year ending 31st March ...

> Annual report   *not*   ... Annual report

12.1B8. If the title proper of a serial changes, make a new description (see 21.2C).

12.1C. *Optional addition.* **General material designation**

12.1C1. Give immediately following the title proper the appropriate general material designation as instructed in 1.1C.

> Yoga for health [GMD]

> Pathé pictorial [GMD]

> Audio arts [GMD]

12.1D. Parallel titles

12.1D1. Transcribe parallel titles as instructed in 1.1D.

> Bank of Canada review [GMD] = Revue de la Banque du
> Canada

> Internationale volkskundliche Bibliographie [GMD] =
> International folklore bibliography = Bibliographie internationale
> des arts et traditions populaires

Bulletin of the Association of African Universities [GMD] =
Bulletin de l'Association des universités africaines

12.1D2. If, in the case of a serial with a title proper made up of a title common
to a number of sections and a section title, the common title has a parallel title
and the section title has a parallel title, give the common title and the section
title that make up the title proper followed by the parallel common title and the
parallel section title (see 12.1B4).

Trade of Canada. Exports by commodities [GMD] = Commerce
du Canada. Exportations par marchandises

12.1E. Other title information

12.1E1. Transcribe other title information as instructed in 1.1E.

Red herring [GMD] : lesbian newsletter

12 millions d'immigrés [GMD] : feuille de lutte des travailleurs
immigrés en Europe = 12 milhões de imigrados : folha de luta
dos operarios imigrados na Europa

The greenwood tree [GMD] : newsletter of the Somerset and
Dorset Family History Society

941.1 [GMD] : newsletter of AAL in Scotland

When an acronym or initialism of the title and its full form appear in the chief
source of information, treat the one not chosen as the title proper as other title
information.

Twin Cities [GMD] : TC

REED [GMD] : review of environmental educational
developments

Q [GMD] : question : the independent political review : arts,
business, science

GACIRE [GMD] : gaceta de cooperación informativa regional

12.1F. Statements of responsibility

12.1F1. Transcribe statements of responsibility relating to persons or bodies as
instructed in 1.1F.

Quarterly review [GMD] / Soil Association

Sussex essays in anthropology [GMD] / Anthropology Society of
Sussex

Serie de culturas mesoamericanas [GMD] / Universidad Nacional
Autónoma de México, Instituto de Investigaciones Históricas

Bieler Jahrbuch [GMD] = Annales biennoises / Herausgeber,
Bibliotheksverein Biel

Moot [GMD] / Eunice Wilson

Statistics of energy [GMD] / Organisation for Economic Co-operation and Development = Statistiques de l'énergie / Organisation de cooperation et de développement économiques

Application statistics [GMD] / [prepared by] the Research Division of the Council of Ontario Universities and the Ontario Universities' Application Centre

12.1F2. If a statement of responsibility is transcribed, in full or in abbreviated form, as part of the title proper or other title information, do not give a further statement of responsibility unless such a statement appears separately in the chief source of information.

British Library news [GMD]

ARC research review [GMD]

Ethnic minorities and employment [GMD] : quarterly journal of the Employment Section, Community Relations Commission

but

League review [GMD] / League of St. George

EmPHASis [GMD] / Public Health Advisory Service

The K-H newsletter service [GMD] / Stephen King-Hall

12.1F3. Do not record as statements of responsibility statements relating to persons that are editors of serials. If a statement relating to an editor is considered necessary by the cataloguing agency, give it in a note (see 12.7B6).

La cause du peuple [GMD]
Note: Founded, edited, and published by Jean-Paul Sartre

R.L.C.'s museum gazette [GMD]
Note: Compiled and edited by Richard L. Coulton with the assistance of voluntary aid

12.1F4. In the case of a serial with a title proper made up of a title common to a number of sections and a section or supplement title, give a statement of responsibility after the part of the title proper to which it refers. In case of doubt, give the statements of responsibility at the end of the title proper.

Länderkurzberichte. Thailand [GMD] / Statistisches Bundesamt

12.2. EDITION AREA

Contents:
12.2A. Preliminary rule
12.2B. Edition statement
12.2C. Statements of responsibility relating to the edition
12.2D. Statement relating to a named revision of an edition

12.2E. Statements of responsibility relating to a named revision of an
        edition

12.2A. Preliminary rule

12.2A1. Punctuation

For instructions on the use of spaces before and after prescribed punctuation,
see 1.0C.

Precede this area by a full stop, space, dash, space.

Precede a statement relating to a named revision of an edition by a comma.

Precede the first statement of responsibility following an edition statement by
a diagonal slash.

Precede each subsequent statement of responsibility by a semicolon.

12.2B. Edition statement

12.2B1. If an edition statement belongs to one of the following types, transcribe
it as instructed in 1.2B:

a) local edition statements

   Northern ed.

b) special interest edition statements

   Éd. pour le médecin

c) special format or physical presentation statements

   Airmail ed.

   Braille ed.

   Library ed.

   Microform ed.

d) language edition statements

   English ed.

   Éd. française

e) reprint or reissue statements indicating a reissue or revision of the serial as
   a whole.

   Reprint ed.

   2nd ed.

12.2B2. Give statements indicating volume numbering or designation, or chronological coverage (e.g., *1st ed.*, *1916 ed.*) in the numeric and/or alphabetic, chronological, or other designation area (see 12.3). Give statements indicating regular
revision (e.g., *Rev. ed. issued every 6 months*) in the note area.

12.2B3. If an edition statement appears in more than one language or script,
transcribe the statement that is in the language or script of the title proper. If

this criterion does not apply, transcribe the statement that appears first. *Optionally*, transcribe the parallel statement(s), each preceded by an equals sign.

> Canadian ed. = Éd. canadienne

12.2B4. For serials published in numerous editions, see 12.7B7h.

12.2C. Statements of responsibility relating to the edition

12.2C1. Transcribe a statement of responsibility relating to one or more editions, but not to all editions, of a serial as instructed in 1.2C and 12.1F.

12.2D. Statement relating to a named revision of an edition

12.2D1. If the item is a named revision of an edition, transcribe the statement relating to that revision as instructed in 1.2D.

> English ed., 2nd ed.

Do not record statements relating to a reissue that contains no changes unless the item is considered to be of particular importance to the cataloguing agency.

12.2E. Statements of responsibility relating to a named revision of an edition

12.2E1. Transcribe a statement of responsibility relating to one or more named revisions of an edition (but not to all such revisions) as instructed in 1.2E and 12.1F.

12.3. NUMERIC AND/OR ALPHABETIC, CHRONOLOGICAL, OR OTHER DESIGNATION AREA

Contents:

12.3A. Preliminary rule
12.3B. Numeric and/or alphabetic designation
12.3C. Chronological designation
12.3D. No designation on first issue
12.3E. Alternative numbering, etc., systems
12.3F. Completed serials
12.3G. Successive designations

12.3A. Preliminary rule

12.3A1. Punctuation

For instructions on the use of spaces before and after prescribed punctuation, see 1.0C.

Precede this area by a full stop, space, dash, space.

Follow a numeric and/or alphabetic designation and/or the date of the first issue of a serial by a hyphen.

Enclose a date following a numeric and/or alphabetic designation in parentheses.

Precede an alternative numbering, etc., system by an equals sign when more than one system of designation is used.

Precede a new sequence of numbering, etc., by a semicolon.

12.3B. Numeric and/or alphabetic designation

12.3B1. Give the numeric and/or alphabetic designation of the first issue of a serial as given in that issue. Use abbreviations as instructed in appendix B and numerals as instructed in appendix C. In describing a facsimile or other reprint, give the numeric and/or alphabetic designation of the original.

Follow the hyphen with four spaces (see also 12.3F).

> Population trends [GMD]. — 1-

> Papers on formal linguistics [GMD]. — No. 1-

> Policy publications review [GMD]. — Vol. 1, no. 1-

> Poetry North-east [GMD]. — Issue no. 1-

> Magic touch [GMD] : the new weekly encyclopedia of fashion and home crafts. — Pt. 1-

> OPCS monitor. Population estimates [GMD]. — PPL, 75/1-

12.3B2. If a numeric and/or alphabetic designation appears in more than one language or script, give the designation that is in the language or script of the title proper. If this criterion does not apply, give the designation that appears first.

12.3B3. If a new description is made for a serial (see 12.1B8) but the sequence of numbering, etc., is continued from the previous description, give the numbering, etc., of the first issue under the new title.

> Word processing report [GMD]. — International ed. — Vol. 1, no. 6-

12.3C. Chronological designation

12.3C1. If the first issue of a serial is identified by a chronological designation, give it in the terms used in the item. Use abbreviations as instructed in appendix B and numerals as instructed in appendix C.

> Annual report on consumer policy in OECD member countries [GMD] / Organisation for Economic Co-operation and Development. — 1975-

> Buck Jones annual [GMD]. — 1957-

> Prince Edward Island tourist exit survey [GMD]. — 1967-

> Commonwealth immigration [GMD] : a monthly summary of news items from national and local papers relating to immigrants in the United Kingdom. — Jan./Feb. 1964-

International commercial television rate and data book [GMD]. —
1961-2-

Länderberichte. Ecuador [GMD] / Statististiches Bundesamt. —
1965-

12.3C2. If the chronological designation includes dates not of the Gregorian or
Julian calendar, add the corresponding dates of the Gregorian or Julian calendar
in square brackets.

مجلة الاقتصاد والادارة [GMD] . — العدد 1 (رجب 1395 [يوليو 1975])-

12.3C3. If a chronological designation appears in more than one language or
script, give the designation that is in the language or script of the title proper. If
this criterion does not apply, give the designation that appears first.

May 1977-   *not*   May 1977 = Mai 1977-

12.3C4. If the first issue of a serial is identified by both numbering, etc., and a
chronological designation, give the numbering, etc., before the chronological
designation.

SPEL [GMD] : selected publications in European languages. —
No. 1 (Feb. 1973)-

New locations [GMD]. — No. 1 (Apr./May 1973)-

Renewable energy bulletin [GMD]. — Vol. 1, no. 1 (Jan./Mar.
1974)-

The musical mainstream [GMD] / Division for the Blind and
Physically Handicapped, Library of Congress. — Vol. 1, no. 1 (Jan.-
Feb. 1977)-

IEEE transactions on acoustics, speech, and signal processing
[GMD]. — Vol. ASSP-22, no. 1 (Feb. 1974)-

12.3D. No designation on first issue

12.3D1. If the first issue of a serial lacks a numeric, alphabetic, chronological, or
other designation, give *[No. 1]-* or its equivalent in the language of the title
proper. If, however, subsequent issues adopt a numbering, follow that.

[No. 1]-

[Pt. 1]-
    (*Subsequent issues numbered:* Part 2, Part 3, *etc.*)

12.3E. Alternative numbering, etc., systems

12.3E1. If a serial has more than one separate system of designation, give the
systems in the order in which they are presented in the chief source of information.

Vol. 3, no. 7-   = no. 31-

12.3F. Completed serials

12.3F1. In describing a completed serial, give the designation of the first issue followed by the designation of the last issue.

> News magazine [GMD] / Regina Chamber of Commerce. —
> Vol. 3, no. 6 (Aug./Sept. 1970)-v. 5, no. 3 (Mar. 1972)

12.3G. Successive designations

12.3G1. If a serial starts a new sequence of numbering without changing its title proper, give the designation of the first and last issues under the old system, followed by the designation of the first issue under the new system.

> Inside Interior [GMD] / Department of the Interior. — Vol. 1,
> no. 1 (Nov. 1943)-v. 10, no. 12 (June 1953) ; no. 1 (July 1974)-

Distinguish between a serial with a common title and a section title (see 12.1B4–12.1B6) and a serial with a new designation system indicated by *new series* or similar wording.

12.4. PUBLICATION, DISTRIBUTION, ETC., AREA

Contents:
    12.4A. Preliminary rule
    12.4B. General rule
    12.4C. Place of publication, distribution, etc.
    12.4D. Name of publisher, distributor, etc.
    12.4E. Statement of function of publisher, distributor, etc.
    12.4F. Date of publication, distribution, etc.
    12.4G. Place of manufacture, name of manufacturer, date of manufacture

12.4A. Preliminary rule

12.4A1. Punctuation
For instructions on the use of spaces before and after prescribed punctuation, see 1.0C.
Precede this area by a full stop, space, dash, space.
Precede a second or subsequently named place of publication, distribution, etc., by a semicolon.
Precede the name of a publisher, distributor, etc., by a colon.
Enclose a supplied statement of function of a publisher, distributor, etc., in square brackets.
Precede the date of publication, distribution, etc., by a comma.
Enclose the details of manufacture (place, name, date) in parentheses.
Precede the name of a manufacturer by a colon.
Precede the date of manufacture by a comma.

12.4B. General rule

12.4B1. Record information about the place, name, and date of all types of publishing, distributing, etc., activities as instructed in 1.4B.

12.4C. Place of publication, distribution, etc.

12.4C1. Give the place of publication, distribution, etc., as instructed in 1.4C.

12.4D. Name of publisher, distributor, etc.

12.4D1. Give the name of the publisher, etc., and *optionally* the distributor, as instructed in 1.4D.

> London : On Target Publications
>
> Edinburgh : Palingenesis Press
>
> London : [s.n.]
>
> Ottawa : The Association
>
> London : Iron and Steel Board : British Iron and Steel
> Federation

12.4E. *Optional addition.* **Statement of function of publisher, distributor, etc.**

12.4E1. Add to the name of a publisher, distributor, etc., a statement of function as instructed in 1.4E.

> New York : Wiley ; Oxford : Pergamon [distributor]

12.4F. Date of publication, distribution, etc.

12.4F1. Give the date of publication of the first issue as instructed in 1.4F. Follow the date with a hyphen and four spaces.

> Windsor, Berkshire : Wax & Wane, 1975-

Give the date of publication even if it coincides, wholly or in part, with the date given as the chronological coverage.

> Social history [GMD]. — 1 (Jan. 1976)-   . — London :
> Methuen, 1976-

12.4F2. In describing a completed serial, give the dates of publication of the first issue and the last issue, separated by a hyphen.

> Membership list [GMD] / Canadian Association of Geographers
> = Liste des membres / Association canadienne des geographes. —
> 1968-1969. — Montréal : The Association, 1968-1969

12.4G. Place of manufacture, name of manufacturer, date of manufacture

12.4G1. If the name of the publisher is unknown and the place and name of the manufacturer are found in the serial, give that place and name as instructed in 1.4G.

12.4G2. *Optional addition.* Give the place, name of manufacturer, and/or date of manufacture if they are found in the serial and differ from the place, name of publisher, etc., and date of publication, etc., and are considered important by the cataloguing agency.

12.5. PHYSICAL DESCRIPTION AREA

Contents:
12.5A. Preliminary rule
12.5B. Extent of item (including specific material designation)
12.5C. Other physical details
12.5D. Dimensions
12.5E. Accompanying material

12.5A. Preliminary rule

12.5A1. Punctuation
For instructions on the use of spaces before and after prescribed punctuation, see 1.0C.
Precede this area by a full stop, space, dash, space *or* start a new paragraph.
Precede other physical details by a colon.
Precede dimensions by a semicolon.
Precede each statement of accompanying material by a plus sign.
Enclose physical details of accompanying material in parentheses.

12.5B. Extent of item (including specific material designation)

12.5B1. For a serial that is still in progress, give the relevant specific material designation (taken from subrule .5B in the chapter dealing with the type of material to which the serial belongs, e.g., 11.5B for microform serials) preceded by three spaces. For printed serials, the specific material designation is *v.*, *no.*, or *pt.*

wall charts

filmstrips

v.

microfiches

12.5B2. For a completed serial, precede the appropriate specific material designation by the number of parts in arabic numerals (see also 2.5B19).

27 posters

16 microfilm reels

103 v.

12.5B3. If a serial consists of, or contains, braille or another tactile system, make additions to the statement of extent as indicated in subrule .5B in the chapter dealing with the type of material to which the serial belongs.

v. of braille

12 v. of music (braille)

12.5C. Other physical details

12.5C1. Give the other physical details appropriate to the item being described as instructed in subrule .5C in the chapter dealing with the type of material to which the serial belongs (e.g., 6.5C for serial sound recordings).

> v. : ill. (some col.)
>
> slides : sd., col.
>
> posters : b&w
>
> sound cassettes : mono.

12.5D. Dimensions

12.5D1. Give the dimensions of the serial as instructed in subrule .5D in the chapter dealing with the type of material to which the serial belongs (e.g., 2.5D for printed serials).

> v. : ill. ; 25 cm.
>
> filmstrips : col. ; 35 mm.
>
> film cassettes : sd., col. ; standard 8 mm.
>
> v. : ill. ; 27-32 cm.

12.5E. Accompanying material

12.5E1. Give, as instructed in 1.5E, the details of accompanying material that is intended to be issued regularly. If using 1.5E1d and if the serial is still in progress, give the name of the accompanying material preceded by three spaces.

> v. : ill. ; 21 cm. +　　　slides
>
> filmstrips : col. ; 35 mm. +　　　booklets
>
> 108 v. : ill. ; 25 cm. + 18 maps (col. ; 65 × 90 cm. or smaller)
> (*Completed serial*)

Make a note on the frequency of accompanying material (see 12.7B11). If accompanying material is issued irregularly or is issued only once, describe it in a note or ignore it.

12.6. SERIES AREA

Contents:
12.6A.　Preliminary rule
12.6B.　Series statements

12.6A. Preliminary rule

12.6A1. Punctuation

For instructions on the use of spaces before and after prescribed punctuation, see 1.0C.

Precede this area by a full stop, space, dash, space.
Enclose each series statement (see 1.6J) in parentheses.
Precede each parallel title by an equals sign.
Precede other title information by a colon.
Precede the first statement of responsibility by a diagonal slash.
Precede each subsequent statement of responsibility by a semicolon.
Precede the ISSN of a series or subseries by a comma.
Precede the numbering within a series or subseries by a semicolon.
Precede the title of a subseries by a full stop.

12.6B. Series statements

12.6B1. Record each series statement as instructed in 1.6. Do not give series numberings if each issue is separately numbered within the series.

>   (Acta Universitatis Stockholmiensis)

>   (H.C.)

>   (Quellenwerke der Schweiz = Statistiques de la Suisse)

>   (Public Health Service publication ; no. 1124)

>   (Bulletin of the Iowa Highway Research Board) (Iowa State University bulletin)

>   (West Virginia University bulletin. Engineering Experiment Station bulletin, ISSN 0083-8640)

12.7. NOTE AREA

Contents:
>   12.7A.   Preliminary rule
>   12.7B.   Notes

12.7A. Preliminary rule

12.7A1. Punctuation
Precede each note by a full stop, space, dash, space *or* start a new paragraph for each.

Separate introductory wording from the main content of a note by a colon followed but not preceded by a space.

12.7A2. In making notes, follow the instructions in 1.7A.

In referring to another serial, use the title or name-title under which that serial is entered in the catalogue (see chapter 21). If the serial is not in the catalogue *or* if main entry is not used (see 0.5), use the title proper and statement of responsibility of the serial.

12.7B. Notes
Make notes as set out in the following subrules and in the order given there. However, give a particular note first when it has been decided that note is of primary importance.

If the serial being described is a reproduction, give also details of the original (see 1.7A4, 1.11F, and, for microform or other photographic reproductions, 11.7B22).

12.7B1. Frequency. Make notes on the frequency of the serial unless it is apparent from the content of the title and statement of responsibility area or is unknown. Also make notes on changes in frequency. (The examples given here do not constitute an exhaustive list.)

> Annual
>
> Quarterly
>
> Monthly (except Aug.)
>
> Monthly (during school year)
>
> Several times a week
>
> Issued twice a month
>
> Six issues yearly
>
> Irregular
>
> Six issues yearly, 1950-1961; monthly, 1962-
>
> Frequency varies

12.7B2. Language. Make notes on the language(s) of the serial unless this is apparent from the rest of the description.

> Text in French and English
>
> Text in Swedish, English summaries
>
> Text in English and French, French text on inverted pages

12.7B3. Source of title proper. Make notes on the source of the title proper if it is other than the chief source of information or if it is the title page substitute of a printed serial.

12.7B4. Variations in title. Make notes on titles borne by the serial other than the title proper. *Optionally*, give a romanization of the title proper.

> Cover title: Proceedings of the ... Annual Glass Symposium
>
> Some issues also have title: Ergonomics in the work-place
>
> Title varies slightly
>
> Title on added t.p.: Bulletin / Société canadienne d'histoire orale & sonore
>
> Added t.p. in Uzbek

If individual issues of a serial (other than a monographic series) have special titles, give the individual titles if they are considered important.

> Each volume has a distinctive title: 1939, Government, the
> citizens' business; 1940, Explorations in citizenship; 1941, Self-
> government under war pressure

12.7B5. Parallel titles and other title information. Give the title in another language and other title information not recorded in the title and statement of responsibility area if they are considered to be important. Make notes on variations
in parallel titles and other title information.

> Titles also in the organization's other official languages

> Subtitle varies

12.7B6. Statements of responsibility. Make notes on statements of responsibility
that do not appear in the title and statement of responsibility area.

> Official journal of: Concrete Products Association, Oct. 1920-
> Apr. 1930

Give a fuller form of the name of a person or body that appears only in abbreviated form in the rest of the description if the fuller form is considered to
be necessary.

> Journal of the Professional Institute [GMD]
> *Note:* Full name of the institute: Professional Institute of the
> Public Service of Canada

> Occasional newsletter [GMD] / Alra
> *Note:* Issued by: Abortion Law Reform Association

Give the name of any editor considered to be an important means of identifying
the serial (e.g., if a particular person edited the serial for all or most of its existence; if the person's name is likely to be better known than the title of the
serial).

> Editor: Wyndham Lewis

> Editor: 1939-1945, H.L. Mencken

> Founded, edited, and published by Jean-Paul Sartre

12.7B7. Relationships with other serials. Make notes on the relationship between
the serial being described and any immediately preceding, immediately succeeding, or simultaneously published serial.

a) *Translation.* If a serial is a translation of a previously published serial (as
   opposed to a different language edition of a serial, for which see 12.2B1),
   give the name of the original.

> Translation of: Blé dans le monde

b) *Continuation.* If a serial continues a previously published serial, whether
   the numbering continues or is different, give the name of the preceding
   serial. (See also 21.2C and 21.3B.)

> Continues: Monthly Scottish news bulletin

c) *Continued by.* If a serial is continued by a subsequently published serial, whether the numbering continues or is different, give the name of the succeeding serial, and *optionally* the date of the change. (See also 21.2C, 21.3B.)

Continued by: Regina

Continued by a section in: Canadian Association of Geographers' newsletter

d) *Merger.* If a serial is the result of the merger of two or more other serials, give the names of the serials that were merged.

Merger of: British abstracts. B1, Chemical engineering, fuels metallurgy, applied electrochemistry, and industrial inorganic chemistry, and: British abstracts. B2, Industrial organic chemistry

If a serial is merged with one or more other serials to form a serial with a new title, give the title(s) of the serial(s) with which it has merged and the title of the new serial.

Merged with: Journal / British Ceramic Society, to become: Transactions and journal of the British Ceramic Society

e) *Split.* If a serial is the result of the split of a previous serial into two or more parts, give the name of the serial that has been split, and *optionally* the name(s) of the other serial(s) resulting from the split.

Continues in part: Proceedings / the Institution of Mechanical Engineers

If a serial splits into two or more parts, give the names of the serials resulting from the split.

Split into: Report on research and development / Department of Energy, and: Report on research and development / Department of Industry

Continued by: Journal of environmental science and health. Part A, Environmental science & engineering, and: Journal of environmental science and health. Part B, Pesticides, food contaminants, and agricultural wastes, and: Journal of environmental science and health. Part C, Environmental health sciences

If a serial has separated from another serial, give the name of the serial of which it was once a part.

Separated from: Farm journal and country gentleman

f) *Absorption.* If a serial absorbs another serial, give the name of the serial absorbed and *optionally* the date of absorption.

Absorbed: The morning post

Absorbed: The worker's friend, 1936

Absorbed: Metals technology; and, in part: Mining and metallurgy

If a serial is absorbed by another serial, give the name of the absorbing serial.

>   Absorbed by: Quarterly review of marketing

g) *Edition.* If a serial is a subsidiary edition differing from the main edition in partial content and/or in language, give the name of the main edition.

>   English ed. of: Bulletin critique du livre français

If the title of the main edition is not readily available, make a general note.

>   Translation of the German edition

h) *Numerous editions.* If a serial is published in numerous editions, give *Numerous editions.*

j) *Supplements.* If a serial is a supplement to another serial, give the name of the main serial.

>   Supplement to: Philosophical magazine

If a serial has supplement(s) that are described separately, make notes identifying the supplement(s).

>   Supplement: Journal of the Royal Numismatic Society

Make brief general notes on irregular, informal, numerous, or unimportant supplements that are not described separately.

>   Supplements accompany some numbers

>   Numerous supplements

12.7B8. Numbering and chronological designation. Make notes on complex or irregular numbering, etc., not already specified in the numeric and/or alphabetic, chronological, or other designation area. Make notes on peculiarities in the numbering, etc.

>   Issues for Aug. 1973-Dec. 1974 also called v. 1, no. 7-v. 2, no. 12

>   Vol. numbering irregular: Vols. 15-18 omitted, v. 20-21 repeated

>   Introductory no., called v. 1, no. 0, issued Nov. 30, 1935

>   Numbering begins each year with v. 1

>   Numbering irregular

If the period covered by a volume, issue, etc., of an annual or less frequent serial is other than a calendar year, give the period covered.

>   Report year ends June 30

>   Report year varies

>   Each issue covers: Apr. 1-Mar. 31

>   Each issue covers: Every two years since 1961-1962

If a serial suspends publication with the intention of resuming at a later date, give this fact. If publication is resumed, give the dates or designation of the period of suspension.

> Suspended with v. 11

12.7B9. Publication, distribution, etc. Make notes on any variations, peculiarities, irregularities, etc., in the publication, distribution, etc., details of the serial. If these have been numerous, give a general statement.

> No. 4 published in 1939, no. 5 in 1946

> Imprint varies

12.7B10. Physical description. Make notes on important physical details that are not included in the physical description area.

> Printed on hand-made paper

> Alternate leaves of print and braille

> In container (28 cm.) with abstracts of contents

Make notes on variations in the physical details of issues of a serial.

> Vols. 3-6: 30 cm.

> Some issues illustrated

12.7B11. Accompanying material. Make notes on the location of accompanying material if appropriate. Give details of accompanying material neither mentioned in the physical description area nor given a separate description (see 1.5E). Give the frequency of accompanying materials that are a regular feature of the serial.

> Slides in pocket

> Sound disc with last issue of each year

> Vol. 7, no. 6 contains wall chart (col. ; 26 × 40 cm.)

> Slides with every 7th issue

12.7B12. Series. Give details of the numbering within a series when the numbering varies from issue to issue.

> Each issue numbered 10, 20, 30, etc., in the series

> Each issue individually numbered in the series

12.7B14. Audience. Make a brief note of the intended audience for, or intellectual level of, a serial if this information is stated in the serial.

12.7B16. Other formats. Give the details of other formats in which the content of the serial is, or has been, issued.

> Issued also as computer file

> Vols. 1-4 issued also on microfiche

12.7B17. Indexes. Make notes on the presence of cumulative indexes. When possible, give the type of index, the volumes, etc., of the serial indexed, the dates of the serial indexed, and the location of the index in the set or the numbering of the index if it is issued separately. Make a note also on separately published indexes.

> Indexes: Vols. 1 (1927)-25 (1951) in v. 26, no. 1

> Indexes: Vols. 10-17 issued as v. 18, no. 3

> Index published separately every Dec.

> Indexes: Subject index, v. 1-11 in v. 13. Author-title index, v. 1-11 in v. 14

> Each third volume is an index to all preceding volumes

> Indexes covering every 5 v. (beginning with v. 71 and excluding financial volumes) issued with title: Consolidated index-digest of reports of the Interstate Commerce Commission involving motor carrier operating rights

12.7B18. Contents. Give details of inserts, other serials included in the serial, and important special items with specific titles, unless they are catalogued separately. Do not give contents notes for monographic series.

> Includes: Bibliography of Northwest materials

> Issues for 1922-1931 include: The woman voter : official organ of the League of Women Voters

12.7B19. Numbers. Give important numbers borne by the item other than ISSNs (see 12.8B).

12.7B20. Copy being described, library's holdings, and restrictions on use. Make these notes as instructed in 1.7B20.

> Library lacks: Vol. 12, v. 16

> Vol. 17 lacks 3 illustrations

12.7B21. "Issued with" notes. If the description is of a serial issued with one or more others, make a note beginning *Issued with:* and listing the other serial(s).

> Issued with: Journal of environmental science and health. Part B, Pesticides, food contaminants, and agricultural wastes, and: Journal of environmental science and health. Part C, Environmental health sciences

> Issued with: Who's where in Manitoba

12.7B23. Item described. If the description is not based on the first issue, identify the issue used as the basis for the description.

> Description based on: Vol. 3, no. 3 (May/June 1975)

12.8. STANDARD NUMBER AND TERMS OF AVAILABILITY AREA

Contents:
12.8A. Preliminary rule
12.8B. International Standard Serial Number (ISSN)
12.8C. Key-title
12.8D. Terms of availability
12.8E. Qualification

12.8A. Preliminary rule

12.8A1. Punctuation

For instructions on the use of spaces before and after prescribed punctuation, see 1.0C.

Precede this area by a full stop, space, dash, space *or* start a new paragraph.

Precede each repetition of this area by a full stop, space, dash, space.

Precede a key-title by an equals sign.

Precede terms of availability by a colon.

Enclose a qualification to the standard number or terms of availability in parentheses.

12.8B. International Standard Serial Number (ISSN)

12.8B1. Give ISSNs as instructed in 1.8B.

ISSN 0075-2363

ISSN 0027-7495 (corrected)

12.8B2. Give any other number in a note (see 12.7B19).

12.8C. Key-title

12.8C1. Give the key-title of the serial, if it is found on the serial or is otherwise readily available, after the International Standard Serial Number (ISSN). Give the key-title even if it is identical to the title proper. If no ISSN is given, do not record the key-title.

ISSN 0479-7469 = Volunteer (Washington)

ISSN 0268-9707 = British Library Bibliographic Services newsletter

ISSN 0319-3012 = Image. Niagara edition

12.8D. *Optional addition.* Terms of availability

12.8D1. Give the terms on which the serial is available as instructed in 1.8D.

£0.50 per issue

$6.45 per year

12.8E. Qualification

12.8E1. Add qualifications to the standard number and/or terms of availability as instructed in 1.8E.

> $30.00 per year ($25.00 to association members)

> £3.00 to individuals (£8.40 to libraries)

12.9. SUPPLEMENTS

12.9A. Describe supplements as instructed in 1.9.

12.10. SECTIONS OF SERIALS

12.10A. Do not use the "multilevel" structure (see chapter 13) for the description of sections of a serial. Describe such sections as separate serials (see 12.1B4–12.1B6).

ANALYSIS

Contents

13.1. SCOPE

13.1A. Analysis is the process of preparing a bibliographic record that describes a part or parts of an item for which a comprehensive entry might be made. The rules in this chapter offer various ways of achieving analysis. Some of these methods of analysis are related to provisions found in other chapters, but all the methods are collected here with general guidelines to assist in the selection of one of the means of analysis. Cataloguing agencies have their own policies affecting analysis; in particular, a policy predetermining the creation of separate bibliographic records may override any other consideration.

Although the rules in this chapter are stated as instructions, apply them according to the policy of the cataloguing agency.

13.2. ANALYTICAL ADDED ENTRIES

13.2A. If, in a comprehensive entry for a larger work, a part is named either in the title and statement of responsibility area or in the note area, make an added entry for that part. The heading for the added entry consists of the main entry heading (which may include or consist of a uniform title) or title proper of the part (see 21.30M). This method is appropriate when direct access to the part is wanted without creating an additional bibliographic record for the part.

13.3. ANALYSIS OF MONOGRAPHIC SERIES AND MULTIPART MONOGRAPHS

13.3A. If the item is a part of a monographic series or a multipart monograph and has a title not dependent on that of the comprehensive item, prepare an analytical entry consisting of a complete bibliographic description of the part. Give details of the comprehensive item in the series area (see 1.6).

> English history, 1914-1945 [GMD] / A.J.P. Taylor. — Oxford : Clarendon Press, 1965. — xxvii, 709 p., [1] folded leaf of plates : ill., maps ; 23 cm. — (The Oxford history of England ; v. 15). — Bibliography: p. 602-639

13.4. NOTE AREA

13.4A. In making a comprehensive entry for a larger work, list the parts in a contents note. This technique is the simplest means of analysis; the bibliographic description of the part is usually limited to a citation of title or name and title.

> The art of Van Gogh [GMD]
> *Note:* Contents: v. 1. Plates — v. 2. Text

> The English Bible [GMD] : essays / by various writers
> *Note:* Contents: The noblest monument of English prose / by John Livingston Lowes — The English Bible / by W. Macneile Dixon — The English Bible / by A. Clutton-Brock — On reading the Bible / by Arthur Quiller-Couch

13.5. "IN" ANALYTICS

13.5A. If more bibliographic description is needed for the part than can be obtained by displaying it in the note area, make an "In" analytic entry.

The descriptive part of an "In" analytic entry consists of a description of the part analyzed followed by a short citation of the whole item in which the part occurs.

Make a description of the part analyzed consisting of those of the following elements that apply to the part:

> title proper, other title information, statement(s) of responsibility
> edition
> numeric or other designation (in the case of a serial)
> publication, distribution, etc., details
> extent and specific material designation (when appropriate, in terms of its physical position within the whole item)
> other physical details

> dimensions
> notes

Begin the citation of the whole item with *In* (italicized, underlined, or otherwise emphasized). Follow *In* by:

> name and/or uniform title heading (see part II) of the
>   whole item, if appropriate
> title proper
> statement(s) of responsibility when necessary for
>   identification
> edition statement
> numeric or other designation (of a serial) or publication
>   details (of a monographic item)

Miss Mapp [GMD] / E.F. Benson. — 310 p. ; 23 cm.
In [Heading]. All about Lucia. — New York : Sun Dial Press, 1940

The moving toyshop [GMD] : a detective story / by Edmund Crispin. — p. 210-450 ; 30 cm.
In The Gollancz detective omnibus. — London : Gollancz, 1951

The loved one [GMD] / by Evelyn Waugh. — p. 78-159 ; 17 cm.
In Horizon. — Vol. 17, no. 98 (Feb. 1948)

Index numbers of road traffic and inland goods transport [GMD]. — Feb. 1960-
In Monthly digest of statistics / British Central Statistical Office. — No. 170 (Feb. 1960)-

A view of Hampstead from the footway next the Great Road, Pond Street [GMD] = Vue de Hampstead de la chaussée près du Grand Chemin, rue du Bassin. — 1 art reproduction : b&w ; 30 × 35 cm. — Reprint of engraving originally published: London : Robert Sayer, 1745
In Twelve views of Camden, 1733-1875. — London : London Borough of Camden, Libraries and Arts Dept., 1971

Bob Wills and his Texas Playboys [GMD]. — side 4 of 2 sound discs (ca. 17 min.) : analog, 33⅓ rpm, stereo. ; 12 in.
In Texas country. — Los Angeles : United Artists, p1976

Nonbook materials (NBM) [GMD] / Ronald Hagler. — on side B of tape 2 of 3 sound cassettes : analog, mono.
In [Heading]. Institute on International Standards as Related to Universal Bibliographic Control. — [Los Angeles] : Development Digest, c1976

13.5B. Parts of "In" analytics

13.5B1. In making an "In" analytic entry for a part of an item that is itself catalogued by means of an "In" analytic entry, make an "In" analytic note containing information about the whole item and about the part containing the part being analyzed. Give information about the smaller item first, and then information about the comprehensive item in the form of a series statement.

> The Tâo teh king, or, The Tâo and its characteristics [GMD]. — p. [45]-124 ; 23 cm.
> *In* The texts of Taoism / translated by James Legge. Part 1. — Oxford : Clarendon Press, 1891. — (The sacred books of the East. The sacred books of China ; v. 39)

13.6. MULTILEVEL DESCRIPTION

13.6A. Multilevel description is normally used by national bibliographies and those cataloguing agencies that prepare entries needing complete identification of both part and comprehensive whole in a single record that shows as its primary element the description of the whole. Use it as an alternative to "In" analytic entries.

Divide the descriptive information into two or more levels. Give at the first level only information relating to the item as a whole. Give at the second level information relating to a group of parts or to the individual part being described. If information at the second level relates to a group of parts, give information relating to the individual part at a third level. Make the levels distinct by layout and/or other means.

> The sacred books of the East [GMD] / translated by various oriental scholars and edited by F. Max Müller. — Oxford : Clarendon Press, 1879-1910. — 50 v. ; 23 cm.
> Vols. 39-40: The texts of Taoism / translated by James Legge. — 1891. — (The sacred books of China)
> Pt. 1: The Tâo teh king. The writings of Kwang-tsze, books I-XVII. — xxii, 396 p.

> American folklore [GMD] / co-ordinated for the Voice of America by Tristram Coffin. — Washington : United States Information Agency, 1967. — 28 sound tape reels : analog, 7½ ips, mono. ; 7 in. — (Forum series)
> 8: The American traditional ballad / G.M. Laws. — 1 sound tape reel (35 min.). — Includes illustrative excerpts

> Remembrance of things past [GMD] / Marcel Proust ; translated by C.K. Scott Moncrieff. — London : Chatto & Windus, 1957. — 12 v. ; 19 cm. — Translation of: À la recherche du temps perdu
> Vols. 1-2: Swann's way / illustrated by Philippe Jullian. — Translation of: Du côté de chez Swann. — This translation originally published in 1922
> Pt. 1: 1957 (1973 printing). — 303 p., 4 leaves of plates : ill. — ISBN 0-7011-1048-1

When all the parts are received, complete any element left open.

PART II. HEADINGS, UNIFORM TITLES, AND REFERENCES

INTRODUCTION

20.1. When a standard description for an item has been established according to the rules in part I, add headings and/or uniform titles to that description to create catalogue entries. The only exception is when an entry is made under title proper, in which case the entry may be made under the first words of the description. In this connection, see also 0.6.

The rules in part II deal with the choice of access points for main and added entries (chapter 21), with the form of name headings and uniform titles (chapters 22–25), and with references (chapter 26). In each chapter, general rules precede special rules. Where no specific rule exists for a specific problem, apply the more general rule(s).

The rules in part II apply to works and not to physical manifestations of those works, though the characteristics of an individual item are taken into account in some instances.

The rules in part II apply to all library materials, irrespective of the medium in which they are published or of whether they are serial or nonserial in nature.

20.2. Chapter 23 deals with geographic names. Though often used as part of corporate headings, these names pose a separate problem. Distinguish between the problem of establishing geographic names in a standard form and the related but separate problem of establishing corporate headings involving such names.

20.3. In chapters 22, 23, and 24, there are rules for additions to names used as headings (see 22.17–22.19, 23.4, and 24.4C). Always make such additions in cases of need to distinguish otherwise identical names in a catalogue, and in other cases called for by the rules. In addition, for the optional rules in chapter 22, *optionally* add these elements to all headings, in anticipation of future conflicts. In automated catalogues, such optional additions will always be recorded in the machine-readable record, but they need not necessarily form part of headings in printed entries derived from those records.

EXAMPLES

20.4. As with the examples in part I, those in part II are illustrative and not prescriptive. Moreover, they illustrate only the solutions to the problems dealt with in the rule to which they are appended. Other added entries (in chapter 21) or references (in chapters 22–25) may be necessary in the actual instances cited.

When an example prescribes main (or added) entry under title, interpret *title* as meaning title proper or uniform title as appropriate in the particular case. When a rule or example prescribes a name-title added entry, make an additional added entry under the title concerned, if appropriate.

The presentation of the examples (their layout and typography) is only intended to help in the use of the rules. Do not take it as implying a prescribed layout or typography for headings and uniform titles.

In chapters 22–25, *x* is used to indicate the necessity for a *see* reference and *xx* the necessity for a *see also* reference.

The elements of bibliographic description included in the examples in this part (principally in chapters 21 and 25) are set out according to the provisions of part I. These never constitute a complete description. The elements shown are only those that bear on the choice and/or form of the access point(s).

CHOICE OF ACCESS POINTS

Contents

Works of Mixed Responsibility

Works That Are Modifications of Other Works

Modifications of Texts

Art Works

Musical Works

Sound Recordings

Mixed Responsibility in New Works

Related Works

Added Entries

21.30C Writers
21.30D Editors and compilers
21.30E Corporate bodies
21.30F Other related persons or bodies
21.30G Related works
21.30H Other relationships
21.30J Titles
21.30K Special rules on added entries in certain cases
21.30K1   Translators
21.30K2   Illustrators
21.30L Series
21.30M Analytical entries

Special Rules

Certain Legal Publications

21.31 LAWS, ETC.

21.31A Scope
21.31B Laws of modern jurisdictions
21.31B1   Laws governing one jurisdiction
21.31B2   Laws governing more than one jurisdiction
21.31B3   Bills and drafts of legislation
21.31C Ancient laws, certain medieval laws, customary laws, etc.

21.32 ADMINISTRATIVE REGULATIONS, ETC.

21.32A Administrative regulations, etc., that are not laws
21.32B Administrative regulations, etc., that are laws
21.32C Collections of administrative regulations, etc.

21.33 CONSTITUTIONS, CHARTERS, AND OTHER FUNDAMENTAL LAWS
21.33C Drafts

21.34 COURT RULES

21.35 TREATIES, INTERGOVERNMENTAL AGREEMENTS, ETC.

21.35A International treaties, etc.
21.35A1   Treaties, etc., between two or three governments
21.35A2   Treaties, etc., between four or more governments
21.35B Agreements contracted by international intergovernmental bodies
21.35C Agreements contracted by the Holy See
21.35D Other agreements involving jurisdictions
21.35E Protocols, amendments, etc.
21.35F Collections

21.36 COURT DECISIONS, CASES, ETC.

21.36A Law reports
21.36A1   Reports of one court
21.36A2   Reports of more than one court
21.36B Citations, digests, etc.
21.36C Particular cases
21.36C1   Proceedings in the first instance. Criminal proceedings

---

21.0. INTRODUCTORY RULES

21.0A. Main and added entries

21.0A1. The rules in this chapter are rules for determining the choice of access points (headings) under which a bibliographic description (see part I) is entered in a catalogue. The rules give instructions on the choice of one of these access points as the main entry heading, the others being added entry headings. In general, each rule only gives instructions on those access points that are explicitly covered by the rule. Certain general points (e.g., series entries and title added entries) are dealt with in the rules on added entries (see 21.29–21.30).

21.0B. Sources for determining access points

21.0B1. Determine the access points for the item being catalogued from the chief source of information (see 1.0A) for the item or any part of the item that is being used as its substitute. Take other statements prominently stated in the item into account (see 0.8). Use information appearing only in the content of an item (e.g., the text of a book; the sound content of a sound recording) or appearing outside the item only when the statements appearing in the chief source of information are ambiguous or insufficient.

21.0C. Form of examples

21.0C1. The access points to be made are indicated without showing their forms. Determine the forms of these access points as instructed in chapters 22–25. When an example is followed by *Main* (or *Added*) *entry under title*, use the title proper or, when appropriate, the uniform title (see chapter 25).

Title added entries are indicated only when the rule involves consideration of the title as a possible main entry heading. See 21.30J for general rules on making title added entries.

21.0D. *Optional addition.* Designations of function

21.0D1. In the cases noted below, add an abbreviated designation of function to an added entry heading for a person.

FUNCTION PERFORMED	DESIGNATION
compiler	*comp.*
editor	*ed.*
illustrator	*ill.*
translator	*tr.*

Add other designations to headings as instructed in particular rules.

In specialist or archival cataloguing, when desirable for identification or file arrangement, add designations from standard lists appropriate to the material being catalogued.

21.1. GENERAL RULE

21.1A. Works of personal authorship

21.1A1. Definition. A personal author is the person chiefly responsible for the creation of the intellectual or artistic content of a work. For particular applications of this definition, see subsequent rules in this chapter. For persons who function solely as performers on sound recordings, see 21.23.

21.1A2. General rule. Enter a work by one or more persons under the heading for the personal author (see 21.4A), the principal personal author (see 21.6B), or the probable personal author (see 21.5B). In some cases of shared personal authorship (see 21.6) and mixed personal authorship (see 21.8–21.27), enter under the heading for the person named first. Make added entries as instructed in 21.29–21.30.

21.1B. Entry under corporate body

21.1B1. Definition. A corporate body is an organization or a group of persons that is identified by a particular name and that acts, or may act, as an entity. Consider a corporate body to have a name if the words referring to it are a specific appellation rather than a general description. Consider a body to have a name if, in a script and language using capital letters for proper names, the initial letters of the words referring to it are consistently capitalized, and/or if, in a language using articles, the words are always associated with a definite article. Typical examples of corporate bodies are associations, institutions, business firms, non-profit enterprises, governments, government agencies, projects and programmes, religious bodies, local church groups identified by the name of the church, and conferences.[1]

Some corporate bodies are subordinate to other bodies (e.g., the Peabody Museum of Natural History is subordinate to Yale University; the Annual General Meeting is subordinate to the Canadian Library Association).

Consider ad hoc events (such as athletic contests, exhibitions, expeditions, fairs, and festivals) and vessels (e.g., ships and spacecraft) to be corporate bodies.

21.1B2. General rule. Enter a work emanating[2] from one or more corporate bodies under the heading for the appropriate corporate body (see 21.4B, 21.5B) if it falls into one or more of the following categories:

a) those of an administrative nature dealing with the corporate body itself
   or   its internal policies, procedures, finances, and/or operations
   or   its officers, staff, and/or membership (e.g., directories)
   or   its resources (e.g., catalogues, inventories)
b) some legal, governmental, and religious works of the following types:[3]
   laws (see 21.31)
   decrees of the chief executive that have the force of law (see 21.31)
   administrative regulations (see 21.32)
   constitutions (see 21.33)
   court rules (see 21.34)
   treaties, etc. (see 21.35)
   court decisions (see 21.36)
   legislative hearings
   religious laws (e.g., canon law)
   liturgical works (see 21.39)
c) those that record the collective thought of the body (e.g., reports of commissions, committees, etc.; official statements of position on external policies)
d) those that report the collective activity of a conference (e.g., proceedings, collected papers), of an expedition (e.g., results of exploration, investigation), or of an event (e.g., an exhibition, fair, festival) falling within the definition of a corporate body (see 21.1B1), provided that the conference, expedition, or event is prominently named (see 0.8) in the item being catalogued
e) those that result from the collective activity of a performing group as a whole where the responsibility of the group goes beyond that of mere performance, execution, etc. Publications resulting from such activity include sound recordings, films, videorecordings, and written records of performances. (For corporate bodies that function solely as performers on sound recordings, see 21.23.)

---

1. Conferences are meetings of individuals or representatives of various bodies for the purpose of discussing and/or acting on topics of common interest, or meetings of representatives of a corporate body that constitute its legislative or governing body.

2. Consider a work to emanate from a corporate body if it is issued by that body *or* has been caused to be issued by that body *or* if it originated with that body.

3. Some legal and governmental works are entered under headings for bodies other than the body from which they emanate.

f) cartographic materials emanating from a corporate body other than a body that is merely responsible for their publication or distribution.

In case of doubt about whether a work falls into one or more of these categories, treat it as if it does not.

In some cases of shared responsibility (see 21.6) and mixed responsibility (see 21.8–21.27), enter such a work under the heading for the corporate body named first. Make added entries as instructed in 21.29–21.30.

21.1B3. If a work emanates from one or more corporate bodies and falls outside the categories given in 21.1B2, treat it as if no corporate body were involved. Make added entries under the headings for prominently named corporate bodies as instructed in 21.30E.

21.1C. Entry under title

21.1C1. Enter a work under its title proper or, when appropriate, uniform title (see chapter 25) if:

      a) the personal authorship is unknown (see 21.5) or diffuse (see 21.6C2), and the work does not emanate from a corporate body

or b) it is a collection of works by different persons or bodies (see 21.7)

or c) it emanates from a corporate body but does not fall into any of the categories given in 21.1B2 and is not of personal authorship

or d) it is accepted as sacred scripture by a religious group (see 21.37).

Make added entries as instructed in 21.29–21.30.

21.2. CHANGES IN TITLES PROPER

21.2A. Definition

21.2A1. In general, consider a title proper to have changed if any word other than an article, preposition, or conjunction is added, deleted, or changed, or if the order of the first five words (the first six words if the title begins with an article) is changed.

However, in general do not consider a title proper to have changed if:

a) the change is in the representation of a word or words (e.g., abbreviated word or symbol vs. spelled out form, singular vs. plural form, one spelling vs. another)

b) the addition, deletion, or change comes after the first five words (the first six words if the title begins with an article) and does not change the meaning of the title or indicate a different subject matter

c) the only change is the addition or deletion of the name of the issuing body (and any grammatical connection) at the end of the title

d) the only change is in the addition, deletion, or change of punctuation.

In case of doubt, consider the title proper to have changed.

As appropriate, give, in the note area (see 1.7B4), those changes not considered to constitute a change in the title proper. Make an added entry (see 21.30J) under any variant form considered necessary for access.

21.2B. Monographs

21.2B1. Monographs in one physical part. If the title proper of a monograph in one physical part changes between one edition and another, make a separate main entry for each edition. Follow the instructions in 25.1 in deciding whether to use uniform titles to assemble all the editions.

21.2B2. Monographs in more than one physical part. If the title proper of a monograph in more than one physical part changes between parts, give the title proper of the first part as the title of the whole monograph. If, however, another title proper appearing on later parts predominates, change the title proper of the whole monograph to the later title proper. If the title proper of a multipart monograph changes between editions, follow the instructions in 21.2B1.

21.2C. Serials

21.2C1. If the title proper of a serial changes, make a separate main entry for each title.

21.3. CHANGES OF PERSONS OR BODIES RESPONSIBLE FOR A WORK

21.3A. Monographs

21.3A1. If a monographic work is modified by a person or corporate body other than the person or body under which the work in its original edition was entered, enter it as instructed in 21.9–21.23.

21.3A2. If there is a change in responsibility between the parts of a multipart monograph, enter the monograph under the heading appropriate to the first part. If, however, a different person or corporate body responsible for later parts predominates, change the heading to that appropriate to the later parts and make an added entry under the heading for the earlier person or body. If more than three persons or corporate bodies are responsible for the completed work and no one is predominantly responsible, change to entry under title (see 21.6C2).

21.3B. Serials

21.3B1. Make a new entry for a serial when either of the following conditions arises, even if the title proper remains the same:

    a) if the heading for a corporate body under which a serial is entered changes

  or b) if the main entry for a serial is under a personal or corporate heading and the person or body named in that heading is no longer responsible for the serial.

21.4. WORKS FOR WHICH A SINGLE PERSON OR CORPORATE BODY IS RESPONSIBLE

21.4A. Works of single personal authorship

21.4A1. Enter a work, a collection of works, or selections from a work or works by one personal author (or any reprint, reissue, etc., of such a work) under the heading for that person whether named in the item being catalogued or not.

> The sun also rises / by Ernest Hemingway
> *Main entry under the heading for Hemingway*

> The doom fulfilled / Sir Edward Burne-Jones
> *Main entry under the heading for Burne-Jones*

> I.F. Stone's newsletter
> *Main entry under the heading for Stone*

> De bello Germanico ... / written in 1918 by the Author of
> Undertones of war
> *Main entry under the heading for the author of* Undertones of war,
>   *known to be Edmund Blunden*

> The poetic and dramatic works of Alfred, Lord Tennyson
> *Main entry under the heading for Tennyson*

> Virginia Woolf : selections from her essays
> *Main entry under the heading for Woolf*

> Symphony no. 4, E minor, for orchestra, op. 98 / by Johannes
> Brahms
> *Main entry under the heading for Brahms*

> The ecological crisis / Richard Felger
>   (*A filmstrip*)
> *Main entry under the heading for Felger*

> Diagnosis and management of abdominal emergencies / LeRoy
> H. Stahlgren
>   (*A set of slides*)
> *Main entry under the heading for Stahlgren*

> A short title catalogue of French books, 1601-1700, in the
> Library of the British Museum / by V.F. Goldsmith. — Folkestone
> : Dawsons
>   (*A catalogue not emanating from the library*)
> *Main entry under the heading for Goldsmith*

> Fifty years of modern art, 1916-1966 / Edward B. Henning. —
> [Cleveland] : Cleveland Museum of Art
>   (*A catalogue of a loan exhibition held at the museum*)
> *Main entry under the heading for Henning*

The Tate Gallery / John Rothenstein. — New York : Abrams
   (*A description of works from the gallery's collections*)
Main entry under the heading for Rothenstein

The indispensable Earl Hines
   (*A selection of recordings by the jazz pianist*)
Main entry under the heading for Hines

A tale of a tub : written for the universal improvement of
mankind
   (*Published anonymously; known to be by Jonathan Swift*)
Main entry under the heading for Swift

21.4B. Works emanating from a single corporate body

21.4B1. Enter a work, a collection of works, or selections from a work or works emanating from one corporate body (or any reprint, reissue, etc., of such a work) under the heading for the body if the work or collection falls into one or more of the categories given in 21.1B2.

Board of Directors meeting, 1972, ALA Annual Conference /
Association of State Library Agencies
   (*Minutes of an unnamed meeting of the parent body*)
Main entry under the heading for the association's board

M-Step today : interim report of project activities. — Baltimore
: Multi-State Teacher Education Project
Main entry under the heading for the project

The log of the Bon Homme Richard
Main entry under the heading for the ship

The book of discipline of the United Methodist Church, 1972
Main entry under the heading for the church

The book of common prayer and administration of the
sacraments and other rites and ceremonies of the church, according
to the use of the Church of England
Main entry under the heading for the church

Codex juris canonici / Pii X pontificis maximi iussu digestus
Benedicti papae XV auctoritate
Main entry under the heading for the Catholic Church

Directory / American Bar Association, Section of Patent,
Trademark, and Copyright Law
Main entry under the heading for the association's section

Constitution of the American Society of Zoologists
Main entry under the heading for the society

A room-to-room guide to the National Gallery / by Michael
Levey. — [London] : Publications Dept., the National Gallery
Main entry under the heading for the gallery

The art collection of the First National Bank of Chicago. —
Chicago : The Bank
      (*Catalogue of the collection*)
Main entry under the heading for the bank

Roman and pre-Roman glass in the Royal Ontario Museum : a
catalogue / John W. Hayes. — Toronto : The Museum
Main entry under the heading for the museum

Rembrandt in the National Gallery of Art. — Washington, D.C.
: The Gallery
      (*Catalogue of an exhibition of the gallery's holdings*)
Main entry under the heading for the gallery

Author-title catalog / Library, University of California, Berkeley.
— Boston : G.K. Hall
Main entry under the heading for the library

Oversight hearings on the Service Contract Act of 1965, as
amended : hearings before the Subcommittee on Labor-
Management Relations of the Committee on Education and Labor,
House of Representatives, Ninety-fourth Congress, second session
Main entry under the heading for the subcommittee

Courts organization : twelfth interim report of the Committee
on Court Practice and Procedure. — Dublin : Stationery Office
      (*Committee established to investigate the operations of the*
      courts and to recommend changes in practice, procedure, etc.)
Main entry under the heading for the committee

Firm action for a fair Britain : the Conservative manifesto, 1974.
— [Westminster : Conservative Central Office]
Main entry under the heading for the Conservative Party

Hydrogen sulfide health effects and recommended air quality
standard / prepared for the Illinois Institute of Environmental
Quality by the Environmental Health Resource Center
Main entry under the heading for the center

Northern communities consultation on local responsible
government : a consideration of the possible revision of the
Northern Affairs Act to allow thirty-six unincorporated
communities a larger role in local government responsibilities : a
report / prepared for the Honourable Minister of Northern
Affairs, Ron McBryde, by the Manitoba Human Relations Centre
      (*Recommendations with supporting data*)
Main entry under the heading for the centre

General safety standard for installations using non-medical X-ray
and sealed gamma-ray sources, energies up to 10 MeV : approved
May 24, 1974, American National Standards Institute ... /
American National Standards Subcommittee N43-5
Main entry under the heading for the institute's subcommittee

Capital and equality : report of a Labour Party study group
   (*The study group, which recommends policies to the party, is unnamed*)
Main entry under the heading for the party

Institute on International Standards as Related to Universal Bibliographic Control : [proceedings]
   (*A sound cassette*)
Main entry under the heading for the institute

Proceedings of the Symposium on Talc, Washington, D.C., May 8, 1973
Main entry under the heading for the symposium

Ceramics for high-performance applications : proceedings of the Second Army Materials Technology Conference, held at Hyannis, Massachusetts, November 13-16, 1973
Main entry under the heading for the conference

Canones et decreta sacrosancti oecvmenici et generalis Concilii Tridentini
Main entry under the heading for the council

High tide and green grass / the Rolling Stones
   (*Songs written and performed by the group*)
Main entry under the heading for the group

Paradise now / collective creation of the Living Theatre ; written down by Judith Malina and Julian Beck
   (*Written record of a play created by the group*)
Main entry under the heading for the group

Synchronicity concert / the Police ; executive producers, Miles Copland, Derek Power, Kim Turner ; directed by Godley and Creme
   (*Videorecording of a performance by the band the Police*)
Main entry under the heading for the band

Halley Bay, Coats Land, Falkland Island Dependencies, 1955-1959 / The Royal Society International Geophysical Year Antarctic Expedition
Main entry under the heading for the expedition

Offizielles Programm : 26.VII-20.VIII / Salzburger Festspiele, 1967
Main entry under the heading for the festival

Catalogo della 35ª esposizione biennale internazionale d'arte, Venezia
Main entry under the heading for the exhibition

Watford : 2½ inch map / Ordnance Survey
Main entry under the heading for the survey

South America / produced by the Cartographic Division,
National Geographic Society
   (*A map*)
Main entry under the heading for the society's division

21.4C. Works erroneously or fictitiously attributed to a person or corporate body

21.4C1. If responsibility for a work is known to be erroneously or fictitiously attributed to a person, enter under the actual personal author or under title if the actual personal author is not known. Make an added entry under the heading for the person to whom the authorship is attributed, unless he or she is not a real person.

The autobiography of Alice B. Toklas
   (*The life of Gertrude Stein written by herself as though it were
   an autobiography of her secretary, Alice B. Toklas*)
Main entry under the heading for Stein
Added entry under the heading for Toklas

The hums of Pooh / by Winnie the Pooh
   (*Written by A.A. Milne*)
Main entry under the heading for Milne

The adventure of the peerless peer / by John H. Watson ;
edited by Philip José Farmer
   (*Written by Farmer as if by the fictitious Dr. Watson*)
Main entry under the heading for Farmer

21.4C2. If responsibility for a work is known to be erroneously or fictitiously attributed to a corporate body, enter the work under the actual personal author, or under the actual corporate body responsible if the work falls into one of the categories given in 21.1B2, or under title if the actual author or responsible corporate body is unknown. Make an added entry under the heading for the corporate body to which responsibility is attributed, unless it is not a real body.

21.4D. Works by heads of state, other high government officials, popes, and other high ecclesiastical officials

21.4D1. Official communications. Enter a work that falls into one of the following categories under the corporate heading for the official (see 24.20 and 24.27B):

a) an official communication from a head of state, head of government, or head of an international body (e.g., a message to a legislature, a proclamation, an executive order other than one covered by 21.31)

b) an official communication from a pope, patriarch, bishop, etc. (e.g., an order, decree, pastoral letter, bull, encyclical, constitution, or an official message to a council, synod, etc.).

Make an added entry under the personal heading for the person.

A proclamation of Queen Anne for settling and ascertaining the
current rates for foreign coins in America
Main entry under the corporate heading for Anne as sovereign
Added entry under the personal heading for Anne

New York City at war : emergency services : report / by F.H. La Guardia, mayor
Main entry under the corporate heading for La Guardia as mayor
Added entry under the personal heading for La Guardia

Proclamations and executive orders by the President, under, and by virtue of, the Food Control Act of August 10, 1917 : November 25, 1918
    (*Communications of President Wilson*)
Main entry under the corporate heading for Wilson as president
Added entry under the personal heading for Wilson

Fulgens Corona : on the Marian Year and the dogma of the Immaculate Conception : encyclical letter of His Holiness, Pope Pius XII
Main entry under the corporate heading for Pius XII as Pope
Added entry under the personal heading for Pius XII

Carta pastoral sobre cursilhos de Cristandade / Antônio de Castro Mayer, bispo de Campos
Main entry under the corporate heading for Mayer as Bishop
Added entry under the personal heading for Mayer

Our vocation as children of Saint Francis : being the encyclical letter Divina Providentia of the Most Rev. Fr. General Pacific M. Perantoni, O.F.M.
Main entry under the corporate heading for Perantoni as Minister
    General of the order
Added entry under the personal heading for Perantoni

Enter a communication that merely accompanies and transmits a document under the heading for the document that it accompanies. Make an added entry under the corporate heading for the transmitting official.

Explosives Regulation Act : message from the President of the United States, transmitting to the Vice President a letter from the Secretary of the Interior, recommending an amendment to the Explosives Regulation Act
    (*Message of President Wilson*)
Main entry under the heading for the Interior Department
Added entry under the corporate heading for Wilson as president

Enter a collection of official communications of more than one holder of one of the offices listed in a) and b) above under the heading for the office. Make an added entry under the heading for a compiler named prominently in the item being catalogued.

Economic report of the President, transmitted to the Congress
    (*An annual*)
Main entry under the heading for the office of president of the
    United States

Tutte le encicliche dei sommi pontefici / raccolte e annotate da
Eucardio Momigliano
Main entry under the heading for the office of Pope
Added entry under the heading for Momigliano

21.4D2. Other works. Enter all other works of such a person under the personal
heading. Make an explanatory reference from the corporate heading to the personal heading (see 26.3C1).

Address of President Roosevelt to the Deep Waterway
Convention at Memphis, Tennessee, October 4, 1907
Main entry under the personal heading for Roosevelt

The second inaugural address of Abraham Lincoln
Main entry under the personal heading for Lincoln

Non-citizen Americans in the war emergency / by Fiorello H.
La Guardia, mayor
    (*A radio address*)
Main entry under the personal heading for La Guardia

Science and the existence of God ; and, Science and philosophy
: two addresses / Pope Pius XII
Main entry under the personal heading for Pius XII

21.4D3. Collections of official communications and other works. Enter a collection of official communications and other works by one person under the personal
heading. Make an added entry under the corporate heading.

The King to his people : being the speeches and messages of His
Majesty King George the Fifth delivered between July 1911 and
May 1935
Main entry under the personal heading for George V
Added entry under the corporate heading for George V as sovereign

Discorsi, messaggi, colloqui del Santo Padre Giovanni XXIII :
28 ottobre 1958-3 giugno 1963
Main entry under the personal heading for John XXIII
Added entry under the corporate heading for John XXIII as Pope

Enter a collection of official communications and other works by more than
one holder of an office as a collection (see 21.7). Make an added entry under
the heading for the office held.

Papal thought on the state : excerpts from encyclicals and other
writings of recent popes / edited by Gerard F. Yates
    (*Includes texts of public addresses*)
Main entry under title
Added entry under the heading for the office of Pope

A compilation of the messages and papers of the Presidents ... /
by James D. Richardson
Main entry under title
Added entry under the heading for the office of president of the
    United States

21.5. WORKS OF UNKNOWN OR UNCERTAIN AUTHORSHIP OR BY UNNAMED GROUPS

21.5A. If a work is of unknown or uncertain personal authorship or if it emanates from a body that lacks a name, enter it under title.

> The secret expedition : a farce (in two acts) as it has been
> represented upon the political theatre of Europe
> > (*Author unknown*)
> *Main entry under title*

> A memorial to Congress against an increase of duties on
> importations / by citizens of Boston and vicinity
> *Main entry under title*

> Orthogonal expansions and their continuous analogues :
> proceedings of a conference held at Southern Illinois University,
> Edwardsville, April 27-29, 1967 / edited by Deborah Tepper
> Haimo
> *Main entry under title*

If such a work has been attributed to one or more persons or corporate bodies, either in editions of the work or in reference sources, make added entries under the headings for these persons or corporate bodies.

> The law scrutiny, or, Attornies' guide
> > (*Variously attributed to Andrew Carmichael and William Norcott*)
> *Main entry under title*
> *Added entries under the headings for Carmichael and Norcott*

> La capucinière, ou, Le bijou enlevé à la course : poème
> > (*Possibly by Pierre-François Tissot; erroneously attributed to Pierre-*
> > *Jean-Baptiste Nougaret*)
> *Main entry under title*
> *Added entries under the headings for Tissot and Nougaret*

21.5B. If reference sources indicate that a person is the probable author of such a work, enter under the heading for that person. If a work falling into one or more of the categories given in 21.1B2 probably emanates from a particular corporate body, enter under the heading for that body. Make added entries under the headings for other persons or bodies to which the work has been attributed, and under title.

> A true character of Mr. Pope
> > (*Author uncertain; generally attributed to John Dennis*)
> *Main entry under the heading for Dennis*
> *Added entry under title*

> Portrait of Andrew Jackson
> > (*A daguerreotype once attributed to Mathew Brady but generally*
> > *thought to be by Edward Anthony*)
> *Main entry under the heading for Anthony*
> *Added entries under the heading for Brady and under title*

21.5C. If the name of a personal author is unknown and in the chief source of information of the item being catalogued the only indication of authorship is the appearance of a characterizing word or phrase or of a phrase naming another work by the person, enter under the word or phrase in the form given in 22.11D. Make an added entry under title.

> Memoir of Bowman Hendry ... / by a Physician
> > (*Name of author unknown*)
> *Main entry under the characterizing word*

> The unveiled heart : a simple story / by the Author of Early impressions
> > (*Name of author unknown*)
> *Main entry under the phrase*

If the only indication of authorship is a nonalphabetic and nonnumerical device, enter under title. Do not make an added entry under the device.

> Angry thoughts / by *!*!*
> > (*Name of author unknown*)
> *Main entry under title*

21.6. WORKS OF SHARED RESPONSIBILITY

21.6A. Scope

21.6A1. Apply this rule to:

a) works produced by the collaboration of two or more persons
b) works for which different persons have prepared separate contributions
c) works consisting of an exchange between two or more persons (e.g., correspondence, debates)
d) works falling into one or more of the categories given in 21.1B2 that emanate from two or more corporate bodies
e) works listed in a)–c) above that also contain contributions emanating from one or more corporate bodies
f) works resulting from a collaboration or exchange between a person and a corporate body.

Apply it also to cases of shared responsibility among adapters, arrangers, commentators, reporters, etc., when rules 21.8–21.27 prescribe main entry under the headings for such persons.

Do not apply this rule to works that are collections of previously existing works. For these, see 21.7.

For special types of collaboration, see the rules on mixed responsibility (21.8–21.27).

21.6B. Principal responsibility indicated

21.6B1. If, in a work of shared responsibility, principal responsibility is attributed (by the wording or the layout of the chief source of information of the item being catalogued) to one person or corporate body, enter under the heading for that person or body. If the name of another person or corporate body appears first in the chief source of information, make an added entry under the heading for that person or body. Make added entries under the headings for other persons or bodies involved if there are not more than two.

> The humanities and the library ... / by Lester Asheim and associates
> *Main entry under the heading for Asheim*

> Lady sings the blues / Billie Holiday with William Dufty
> *Main entry under the heading for Holiday*
> *Added entry under the heading for Dufty*

> Animal motivation : experimental studies on the albino rat / by C.J. Warden with the collaboration of T.N. Jenkins ... [et al.]
>> (*Three additional collaborators named on title page*)
> *Main entry under the heading for Warden*

> Faustus : a musical romance ... / composed by T. Cooke, Charles E. Horn, and Henry R. Bishop
>> (*Bishop's name is displayed more prominently than those of the others*)
> *Main entry under the heading for Bishop*
> *Added entries under the headings for Cooke and Horn*

> "Aaron, r.f." / by Henry Aaron as told to Furman Bisher
> *Main entry under the heading for Aaron*
> *Added entry under the heading for Bisher*

21.6B2. If principal responsibility is attributed to two or three persons or bodies, enter under the heading for the first named of these. Make added entries under the headings for the others. If a work is by two principal persons or corporate bodies and one collaborating person or body, make an added entry also for the third person or body.

> Calcium montmorillonite (fuller's earth) in the Lower Greensand of the Baulking area, Berkshire / E.G. Poole and B. Kelk with contributions from J.A. Bain ... [et al.]
>> (*Four additional contributors named on title page*)
> *Main entry under the heading for Poole*
> *Added entry under the heading for Kelk*

> The United Nations and economic and social co-operation / by Robert E. Asher, Walter M. Kotschnig, William Adams Brown, Jr., and associates
> *Main entry under the heading for Asher*
> *Added entries under the headings for Kotschnig and Brown*

> The geology of the southern part of the south Staffordshire coalfield ... / by Talbot H. Whitehead & T. Eastwood with contributions by T. Robertson
> *Main entry under the heading for Whitehead*
> *Added entries under the headings for Eastwood and Robertson*

21.6C. Principal responsibility not indicated

21.6C1. If responsibility is shared between two or three persons or bodies and principal responsibility is not attributed to any of them by wording or layout, enter under the heading for the one named first. Make added entries under the headings for the others.

> Health for effective living : a basic health education text for college students / Edward Johns, Wilfred C. Sutton, Lloyd E. Webster
> *Main entry under the heading for Johns*
> *Added entries under the headings for Sutton and Webster*

> Mrs. Wilson's diaries / Richard Ingrams and John Wells
> *Main entry under the heading for Ingrams*
> *Added entry under the heading for Wells*

> The basement tapes / Bob Dylan & the Band
> (*Songs written and performed by Dylan and the rock group the Band*)
> *Main entry under the heading for Dylan*
> *Added entry under the heading for the Band*

> Mail order and trade-paper advertising / by Homer J. Buckley, G.D. Crain, Jr., and Maxwell Droke
> (*Contains* Mail order advertising *by Homer J. Buckley,* Industrial and trade-paper advertising *by G.D. Crain, Jr.,* Advertising letters *by Maxwell Droke*)
> *Main entry under the heading for Buckley*
> *Added entries under the headings for Crain and Droke*

> The correspondence between Benjamin Harrison and James G. Blaine, 1882-1893
> *Main entry under the heading for Harrison*
> *Added entry under the heading for Blaine*

> Debate, subject, resolved that the United States continue the policy of prohibition as defined in the Eighteenth Amendment / Clarence Darrow, negative, versus John Haynes Holmes, affirmative
> *Main entry under the heading for Darrow*
> *Added entry under the heading for Holmes*

If the names of the persons or bodies appear in a different order in the chief sources of information of different editions of the work, enter each edition under the heading for the person or body named first in that edition.

> Decision systems for inventory management and production planning / Rein Peterson, Edward A. Silver
> *Main entry under the heading for Peterson*
> *Added entry under the heading for Silver*

Decision systems for inventory management and production
planning. — 2nd ed. / Edward A. Silver, Rein Peterson
Main entry under the heading for Silver
Added entry under the heading for Peterson

If the persons or bodies are not named in the item, enter under the one named
first in a previous edition or, if there is no previous edition, under the one whose
heading comes first in English alphabetic order.

21.6C2. If responsibility is shared among more than three persons or corporate
bodies and principal responsibility is not attributed to any one, two, or three,
enter under title. Make an added entry under the heading for the first person or
corporate body named prominently in the item being catalogued. If editors are
named prominently, make an added entry under the heading for each if there
are not more than three. If there are more than three named prominently, make
an added entry under the heading for the principal editor and/or for the one
named first.

Texas country / Willie Nelson ... [et al.]
(*A sound recording; three additional performers named on
labels*)
Main entry under title
Added entry under the heading for Nelson

Reforma agrária / Antônio de Castro Mayer ... [et al.]
(*Three additional authors named on title page*)
Main entry under title
Added entry under the heading for Mayer

Mélanges d'histoire du moyen âge / offerts à M. Ferdinand Lot
par ses amis et ses élèves
Main entry under title

A dictionary of music and musicians (A.D. 1450-1889) / by
eminent writers ... ; edited by Sir George Grove
Main entry under title
Added entry under the heading for Grove

A dictionary of American English on historical principles /
compiled at the University of Chicago under the editorship of Sir
William A. Craigie and James R. Hulbert
Main entry under title
Added entries under the headings for Craigie and Hulbert

Larousse de la musique / publié sous la direction de Norbert
Dufourcq avec la collaboration de Félix Raugel, Armand
Machabey
Main entry under title
*Added entries under the headings for Dufourcq, Raugel, and
Machabey*

327

21.6D. Shared pseudonyms

21.6D1. If two or more persons collaborate and use a single pseudonym, use the pseudonym as the heading for a work produced by their collaboration. Refer to the pseudonym from their names (see 26.2C1). If headings for one or more of the persons are also established in the catalogue, refer also from the pseudonym to those headings.

> Deadly weapon / Wade Miller
> (Wade Miller *is the joint pseudonym of Bill Miller and Bob Wade*)
> *Main entry under the pseudonym*
> *References to the pseudonym from the headings for Miller and Wade*

> The detective short story : a bibliography / by Ellery Queen
> (Ellery Queen *is the joint pseudonym of Frederic Dannay and Manfred B. Lee*)
> *Main entry under the pseudonym*
> *References to the pseudonym from the headings for Dannay and Lee*

> Philip : the story of a boy violinist / by T.W.O.
> (*Initials are the joint pseudonym of Mary C. Hungerford and Virginia C. Young*)
> *Main entry under the initials*
> *References to the pseudonym from the headings for Hungerford and Young*

> Rowntree's elect cocoa / Beggarstaff Brothers
> (*A poster*)
> (Beggarstaff Brothers *is the joint pseudonym of the artists James Pryde and Sir William Nicholson, who also did work under their own names*)
> *Main entry under the pseudonym*
> *References to the pseudonym from the headings for Pryde and Nicholson*
> *Reference to the headings for Pryde and Nicholson from the pseudonym*

21.7. COLLECTIONS OF WORKS BY DIFFERENT PERSONS OR BODIES

21.7A. Scope

21.7A1. Apply this rule to:

a) collections of independent works by different persons or bodies
b) collections consisting of extracts from independent works by different persons or bodies
c) works consisting partly of independent works and partly of contributions by different persons or bodies.

For collections of sound recordings, see 21.23C–21.23D.

21.7B. With collective title

21.7B1. Enter a work falling into one of the categories given in 21.7A under its title if it has a collective title. Make added entries under the headings for the compilers/editors if there are not more than three and if they are named prominently in the item being catalogued. If there are more than three compilers/editors named prominently, make an added entry under the heading for the principal compiler/editor and/or for the one named first.

> Working-class stories of the 1890s / edited, with an introduction, by P.J. Keating
> *Main entry under title*
> *Added entry under the heading for Keating*

> The Hamish Hamilton book of giants / edited by William Mayne
> *Main entry under title*
> *Added entry under the heading for Mayne*

> ، Economics of the environment : selected readings / edited by Robert Dorfman and Nancy S. Dorfman
> *Main entry under title*
> *Added entries under the headings for R. Dorfman and N. Dorfman*

> The Oxford dictionary of quotations
> ("*. . . under the general editorship of Miss Alice Mary Smyth, who worked, for purposes of selection, with a small committee formed of members of the Press itself"—P. xiii*)
> *Main entry under title*

> Journal of research of the U.S. Geological Survey
> (*Contains research papers written by staff members*)
> *Main entry under title*
> *Added entry under the heading for the survey*

> Motor bus laws and regulations : a complete code of all motor bus regulatory laws . . . / compiled and edited by John M. Meighan
> *Main entry under title*
> *Added entry under the heading for Meighan*

> Constitutions of nations / [compiled by] Amos J. Peaslee
> *Main entry under title*
> *Added entry under the heading for Peaslee*

> Treaty series : treaties and international agreements registered or filed and recorded with the Secretariat of the United Nations
> *Main entry under title*

> Conciliorum oecumenicorum decreta
> (*Contains decrees of councils from the 1st Council of Nicaea to the 1st Vatican Council*)
> *Main entry under title*

Codex canonum ecclesiae universae = The canons of the first
four general councils of the church, and those of the early local
Greek synods : in Greek, with Latin and revised English
translations ... / with notes selected by William Lambert
Main entry under title
Added entry under the heading for Lambert

The Ethiopic Didascalia, or, The Ethiopic version of the
Apostolical constitutions received in the Church of Abyssinia
Main entry under title

If such an item includes two or three works, make name-title added entries
for each of them.

Classic Irish drama / introduced by W.A. Armstrong
   (*Contains* The Countess Cathleen *by W.B. Yeats,* The playboy
   of the western world *by J.M. Synge,* Cock-a-doodle dandy *by
   Sean O'Casey*)
Main entry under title
*Added entries (name-title) under the headings for Yeats, Synge, and
   O'Casey*
Added entry under the heading for Armstrong

If there are more than three works but only two or three persons or bodies
responsible, make an added entry (or name-title added entry when appropriate)
under the heading for each person or body.

Regency poets : Byron, Shelley, Keats / compiled by C.R. Bull
Main entry under title
Added entries under the headings for Byron, Shelley, Keats, and Bull

A Cornish quintette : five original one-act plays from the
Cornwall Drama Festivals, 1970-2
   (*Contains* A skeleton in the cupboard *and* The happening at
   Botathen *by Donald R. Rawe,* Wheal Judas *and* The Christmas
   widow *by Burness Bunn,* Shadows of men *by Gwen Powell
   Jones*)
Main entry under title
Added entries under the headings for Rawe and Bunn
Added entry (name-title) under the heading for Jones

Traffic laws, city and state
   (*Contains ordinances of the city of Houston and laws of the
   state of Texas*)
Main entry under title
*Added entries under the headings for Houston and Texas with
   uniform titles for the ordinances and laws*

If more than three persons or bodies are named in the chief source of information, make an added entry under the first person or body named there.

330

21.7C. Without collective title

21.7C1. If a work falling into one of the categories given in 21.7A1 lacks a collective title, enter it under the heading appropriate to the first work named in the chief source of information of the item being catalogued. If the item lacks a collective chief source of information, enter it under the heading appropriate to the first work in the item. Make added entries for editors/compilers and for the other works as instructed in 21.7B1, insofar as it applies to works without a collective title.

> In praise of older women / Stephen Vizinczey. Feramontov / Desmond Cory. The graveyard shift / Harry Patterson
> *Main entry under the heading for Vizinczey*
> *Added entries (name-title) under the headings for Cory and Patterson*

> History of the elementary school contest in England / Francis Adams. Together with The struggle for national education / John Morley ; [both] edited, with an introduction, by Asa Briggs
> *Main entry under the heading for Adams*
> *Added entry (name-title) under the heading for Morley*
> *Added entry under the heading for Briggs*

Works of Mixed Responsibility

21.8. WORKS OF MIXED RESPONSIBILITY

21.8A. Scope

21.8A1. A work of mixed responsibility is one to which different persons or bodies make intellectual or artistic contributions by performing different kinds of activity (e.g., writing, adapting, illustrating, editing, arranging, translating).

The rules in this section are divided into the following two types of mixed responsibility:

a) previously existing works that have been modified (e.g., translations, musical arrangements, adaptations, see 21.9–21.23)
b) new works to which different persons or bodies have made different kinds of contributions (e.g., collaborative works by a writer and an artist, works reporting interviews, see 21.24–21.27).

Works That Are Modifications of Other Works

21.9. GENERAL RULE

21.9A. Enter a work that is a modification of another under the heading appropriate to the new work if the modification has substantially changed the nature and content of the original or if the medium of expression has been changed. If, however, the modification is an abridgement, rearrangement, etc., enter under the heading appropriate to the original. In some cases the wording of the chief source of information is taken into account; in other cases the nature of the work itself is the basis for the decision on entry.

For specific applications of this general rule, see 21.10–21.23.

Modifications of Texts

21.10. ADAPTATIONS OF TEXTS

21.10A. Enter a paraphrase, rewriting, adaptation for children, or version in a different literary form (e.g., novelization, dramatization) under the heading for the adapter. If the name of the adapter is unknown, enter under title. Make a name-title added entry for the original work. In case of doubt about whether a work is an adaptation, enter under the heading for the original work.

> The science of education : a paraphrase of Dr. Karl
> Rosenkranz's Paedagogik als System / by Anna C. Brackett
> *Main entry under the heading for Brackett*
> *Added entry (name-title) under the heading for Rosenkranz*

> Sinclair Lewis's Dodsworth / dramatized by Sidney Howard
> *Main entry under the heading for Howard*
> *Added entry (name-title) under the heading for Lewis*

> The green goddess / by Louise Jordan Miln . . . ; based on the
> play The green goddess by William Archer
> *Main entry under the heading for Miln*
> *Added entry (name-title) under the heading for Archer*

> Sam Weller, or, The Pickwickians : a farcical comedy . . . /
> arranged from Charles Dickens's work by W.T. Moncrieff
>   (*Dramatization of scenes from* The Pickwick papers)
> *Main entry under the heading for Moncrieff*
> *Added entry (name-title) under the heading for Dickens*

> Adventures of Tom Sawyer / by Mark Twain ; rewritten for
> young readers by Felix Sutton
> *Main entry under the heading for Sutton*
> *Added entry (name-title) under the heading for Twain*

> Harp and psaltery : a group of paraphrases of favorite Psalms /
> by Frank P. Fletcher
> *Main entry under the heading for Fletcher*
> *Added entry under the heading for the* Psalms

> The pilgrim's progress : for the young . . .
>   (*Adapted by an unknown person from John Bunyan's work*)
> *Main entry under title*
> *Added entry (name-title) under the heading for Bunyan*

Tristan / Gottfried von Strassburg ; translated ... With the surviving fragments of the Tristan of Thomas, newly translated ...
> (*Both works are versions of the* Tristan *story*)
> *Main entry under the heading for Gottfried*
> *Added entry* (*name-title*) *under the heading for Thomas*
> *Added entry under the heading for the* Tristan *story*

21.11. ILLUSTRATED TEXTS

21.11A. General rule

21.11A1. Enter a work that consists of a text for which an artist has provided illustrations under the heading appropriate to the text. Make an added entry under the heading for the illustrator if appropriate under the provisions of 21.30K2. For instructions on works of collaboration between a writer and an artist, see 21.24.

> The bedside manner, or, No more nightmares / by Robert Benchley ; with drawings by Gluyas Williams
> *Main entry under the heading for Benchley*

> British butterflies / by E.B. Ford ; with ... colour plates by Paxton Chadwick
> (*Illustrations occupy more than half the item*)
> *Main entry under the heading for Ford*
> *Added entry under the heading for Chadwick*

> Stories from the Arabian nights / retold by Laurence Housman ; with drawings by Edmund Dulac
> (*Dulac is a famous book illustrator*)
> *Main entry under the heading for Housman*
> *Added entry under the heading for Dulac*

21.11B. Illustrations published separately

21.11B1. If the illustrations for a text, or for several texts, by one artist are published separately, enter them under the heading for the artist. Make a name-title added entry for the work(s) illustrated if there are not more than three. If, however, the illustrations are for more than three works by one writer, make an added entry under the heading for the writer.

> The Doré illustrations for Dante's Divine comedy : 136 plates / by Gustave Doré
> *Main entry under the heading for Doré*
> *Added entry* (*name-title*) *under the heading for Dante*

21.12. REVISIONS OF TEXTS

21.12A. Original author considered responsible

21.12A1. Enter an edition of a work that has been revised, enlarged, updated, etc., under the heading for the original author if:

333

　　　　a) the original author is named in a statement of responsibility in the item being catalogued

or　b) the original author is named in the title proper and no other person is named in a statement of responsibility or other title information.

Make an added entry under the heading for the reviser, etc.

> Anatomy of the human body / by Henry Gray. — 25th ed. / edited by Charles Mayo Goss
> *Main entry under the heading for Gray*
> *Added entry under the heading for Goss*

> Guide to the study and use of reference books / by Alice Bertha Kroeger. — 3rd ed. / revised throughout and much enlarged by Isadore Gilbert Mudge
> *Main entry under the heading for Kroeger*
> *Added entry under the heading for Mudge*

> Leaves from our Tuscan kitchen ... / Janet Ross and Michael Waterfield
> 　　(*A revision by Waterfield of Ross' book of the same title*)
> *Main entry under the heading for Ross*
> *Added entry under the heading for Waterfield*

> A dictionary of modern English usage / by H.W. Fowler. — 2nd ed. / revised by Sir Ernest Gowers
> *Main entry under the heading for Fowler*
> *Added entry under the heading for Gowers*

> Hart's Rules for compositors and readers at the University Press, Oxford. — 39th ed., completely revised
> *Main entry under the heading for Hart*

> Boise's Manual of gem cutting. — 4th rev. ed.
> 　　(*Reviser, Gerhard Tucker, named only in the introduction*)
> *Main entry under the heading for Boise*
> *Added entry under the heading for Tucker*

Enter an abridgement of a work under the heading for the original author. Make an added entry under the heading for the abridger. For condensations that involve rewriting, see 21.10.

> John Evelyn's diary : a selection from the diary / edited by Philip Francis
> *Main entry under the heading for Evelyn*
> *Added entry under the heading for Francis*

> The people's Marx. — Abridged popular ed. of the three vols. of Capital / edited by Julian Borchardt ; translated by Stephen L. Trask
> *Main entry under the heading for Marx*
> *Added entry under the heading for Borchardt*

21.12B. Original author no longer considered responsible

21.12B1. Enter under the heading for the reviser, etc., or under title, as appropriate, if the wording of the chief source of information of the item being catalogued indicates that the person or body responsible for the original is no longer considered to be responsible for the work (e.g., when the original author is named only in the title proper and some other person or body is named as being primarily responsible in the statement of responsibility or in the statement of responsibility relating to the edition). Make a name-title added entry under the heading for the original author using, if it can be readily ascertained, the title of the last edition to have been entered under the heading for the person or body responsible for the original. Always make a title added entry if the title begins with the name of the original author and the main entry is under the name of the reviser, etc.

> Salmond on the law of torts. — 12th ed. / by R.V. Heuston
> *Main entry under the heading for Heuston*
> *Added entry (name-title) under the heading for Salmond*
> *Added entry under title*

> Roget's Thesaurus of English words and phrases. — New ed. / completely rev. and modernized by Robert A. Dutch
> *Main entry under the heading for Dutch*
> *Added entry (name-title) under the heading for Roget*
> *Added entry under title*

> Guide to reference books. — 7th ed. / by Constance M. Winchell
>   (*Based on Isadore Gilbert Mudge's sixth edition of the same work*)
> *Main entry under the heading for Winchell*
> *Added entry (name-title) under the heading for Mudge*

21.13. TEXTS PUBLISHED WITH COMMENTARY

21.13A. Scope

21.13A1. Apply this rule to works consisting of a text, or of texts, by the same person or body, and a commentary, interpretation, or exegesis by a different person or body.

21.13B. Commentary emphasized

21.13B1. If the chief source of information of the item being catalogued presents the item as a commentary, enter it as such (see 21.1–21.7). Make an added entry under the heading appropriate to the text.

> Commentary on the Rule of St. Augustine / by Robertus Richardinus
>   (*Includes the text of the* Regula)
> *Main entry under the heading for Richardinus*
> *Added entry (name-title) under the heading for St. Augustine*

Averrois Cordubensis Commentarium magnum in Aristotelis De
anima libros
(Includes a Latin text of De anima)
Main entry under the heading for Averroes
Added entry (name-title) under the heading for Aristotle

The Federal Expropriation Act : a commentary / by Eric C.E.
Todd
(Includes the text of the act)
Main entry under the heading for Todd
Added entry under the heading for the act

21.13C. Edition of the work emphasized

21.13C1. If the chief source of information presents the item as an edition of the
original work, enter it as such (see 21.1–21.7). Make an added entry under the
heading appropriate to the commentary.

Demosthenes : with an English commentary / by Robert
Whiston
Main entry under the heading for Demosthenes
Added entry under the heading for Whiston

The interpreter's Bible : the Holy Scriptures in the King James
and Revised Standard versions with general articles and
introduction, exegesis, exposition for each book of the Bible
Main entry under the heading for the Bible

The Employment Protection Act, 1975 : with annotations / by
Brian Bercusson
Main entry under the heading for the act
Added entry under the heading for Bercusson

Bundesbaugesetz : mit Kommentar / H. Knaup, H. Ingenstau
Main entry under the heading for the law
Added entries under the headings for Knaup and Ingenstau

21.13D. Chief source of information ambiguous

21.13D1. If the information given in the chief source of information is ambiguous,
enter the work as a commentary or edition in accordance with the aspect emphasized by (in this order of preference):

a) the prefatory material
b) the typographic presentation of the text and commentary
c) the relative extent of the text and the commentary.

In case of doubt, enter the work as an edition and make an added entry under
the heading appropriate to the commentary.

336

21.14. TRANSLATIONS

21.14A. Enter a translation under the heading appropriate to the original. Make an added entry under the heading for the translator if appropriate under the provisions of 21.30K1.

> The philosopher in the kitchen / Jean-Anthelme Brillat-Savarin ; translated by Anne Drayton
> > (*Only English translation*)
> *Main entry under the heading for Brillat-Savarin*

> A Christmas carol / Charles Dickens
> > (*A Tamil translation by V.A. Venkatachari; only Tamil translation*)
> *Main entry under the heading for Dickens*

> Fathers and sons / Ivan Turgenev ; translated by Rosemary Edmonds
> > (*One of several English translations*)
> *Main entry under the heading for Turgenev*
> *Added entry under the heading for Edmonds*

> The Mabinogion / translated by Gwyn Jones and Thomas Jones
> > (*An ancient collection*)
> *Main entry under the heading for the* Mabinogion
> *Added entries under the headings for G. Jones and T. Jones*

If the translation involves adaptation or is described as a "free" translation, treat it as an adaptation (see 21.10).

21.14B. Enter a collection of translations of works by different authors as a collection (see 21.7).

21.15. TEXTS PUBLISHED WITH BIOGRAPHICAL/CRITICAL MATERIAL

21.15A. If a work consisting of a work or works by a writer accompanied by (or interwoven with) biographical or critical material by another person is presented in the chief source of information of the item being catalogued as a biographical/critical work, enter it as such (see 21.1–21.7). Make an added entry under the heading appropriate to the work or works included.

> Life and letters of Mrs. Jason Lee ... / by Theressa Gay
> *Main entry under the heading for Gay*
> *Added entry under the heading for Lee*

21.15B. If the biographer/critic is represented as editor, compiler, etc., enter under the heading appropriate to the work or works included. Make an added entry under the heading for the biographer/critic.

> Life and letters of Catharine M. Sedgwick / edited by Mary E. Dewey
> *Main entry under the heading for Sedgwick*
> *Added entry under the heading for Dewey*

Art Works

21.16. ADAPTATIONS OF ART WORKS[4]

21.16A. Enter an adaptation from one medium of the graphic arts to another under the heading for the person responsible for the adaptation. If the name of the adapter is not known, enter under title. Make a name-title added entry for the original work.

> Children crying forfeits / engraved by C. Turner from an original painting by Joshua Reynolds
> *Main entry under the heading for Turner*
> *Added entry (name-title) under the heading for Reynolds*

> A summer night / by Albert Moore
> > (*An anonymous lithograph of Moore's painting*)
> *Main entry under title*
> *Added entry (name-title) under the heading for Moore*

21.16B. Enter a reproduction of an art work (e.g., a photograph, a photomechanical reproduction, or a reproduction of sculpture) under the heading for the original work. Make an added entry under the heading for the person or body responsible for the reproduction, unless the person or body is merely responsible for manufacture or publication.

> Child with a straw hat / Mary Cassatt
> > (*A photomechanical reproduction issued by the National Gallery of Art, Washington*)
> *Main entry under the heading for Cassatt*
> *Added entry under the heading for the gallery*

> Cat and butterfly : detail from a Japanese handscroll ... / by Katsushika Hokusai
> > (*A photomechanical reproduction*)
> *Main entry under the heading for Hokusai*

> Michelangelo's David
> > (*A plaster reproduction*)
> *Main entry under the heading for Michelangelo*

21.17. REPRODUCTIONS OF TWO OR MORE ART WORKS

21.17A. Without text

21.17A1. Enter a work consisting of reproductions of the works of an artist without accompanying text under the heading for the artist.

> The paintings of Alma-Tadema
> > (*Twelve coloured reproductions in a folder*)
> *Main entry under the heading for Alma-Tadema*

---

4. *Art works* include paintings, engravings, photographs, drawings, sculptures, etc., and any other creative work that can be represented pictorially (e.g., ceramic designs, tapestries, fabrics).

21.17B. With text

21.17B1. If a work consists of reproductions of the works of an artist and text about the artist and/or the works reproduced, enter under the heading appropriate to the text if the person who wrote it is represented as author in the chief source of information of the item being catalogued. Make an added entry under the heading for the artist. Otherwise, enter under the heading for the artist. In case of doubt, enter under the heading for the artist. If the work is entered under the heading for the artist, make an added entry under the heading for the person who wrote the text if his or her name appears in the chief source of information. For works emanating from a corporate body that are catalogues of the holdings of that body, see 21.1B2a.

> Mr. Lincoln's camera man, Mathew B. Brady / by Roy Meredith
> *Main entry under the heading for Meredith*
> *Added entry under the heading for Brady*

> Van Gogh / Palma Buccarelli
> *Main entry under the heading for Buccarelli*
> *Added entry under the heading for Van Gogh*

> Van Gogh / par A.-M. Rosset
> *Main entry under the heading for Rosset*
> *Added entry under the heading for Van Gogh*

> Renoir : paintings, drawings, lithographs, and etchings / selected and introduced by Nigel Lambourne
> *Main entry under the heading for Renoir*
> *Added entry under the heading for Lambourne*

> The landscapes of George Frederick Watts
>   (*Author of text, Walter Bayes, named in contents list*)
> *Main entry under the heading for Watts*

> Garden flowers : from plates by Jane Loudon / with an introduction and notes on the plates by Robert Gathorne-Hardy
> *Main entry under the heading for Loudon*
> *Added entry under the heading for Gathorne-Hardy*

Musical Works

21.18. GENERAL RULE

21.18A. Scope

21.18A1. Apply this rule to:

- a) arrangements, transcriptions, versions, settings, etc., in which music for one medium of performance has been rewritten for another
- b) simplified versions
- c) arrangements described as "freely transcribed," "based on . . . ," etc., and other arrangements incorporating new material
- d) arrangements in which the harmony or musical style of the original has been changed.

21.18B. Arrangements, transcriptions, etc.

21.18B1. Enter an arrangement, transcription, etc., of one or more works of one composer (or of parts of one composer's works) under the heading for that composer (see also 25.35C). If the original composer is unknown, enter under title. Make an added entry under the heading for the arranger or transcriber. *Optionally*, add *arr.* to the added entry heading.

> Divertimento, op. 12, no. 2 / L. van Beethoven ; transcribed for woodwind by George J. Trinkaus
> *Main entry under the heading for Beethoven*
> *Added entry under the heading for Trinkaus*

> Suite from The art of fugue / J.S. Bach ; arranged for chamber orchestra by Anthony Lewis
> *Main entry under the heading for Bach*
> *Added entry under the heading for Lewis*

> Michael, row the boat ashore : traditional / arranged by James Burt
>   (*An anonymous spiritual*)
> *Main entry under title*
> *Added entry under the heading for Burt*

21.18C. Adaptations

21.18C1. Enter any of the following types of adaptations of music under the heading for the adapter:

  a) a distinct alteration of another work (e.g., a free transcription)
  b) a paraphrase of various works or of the general style of another composer
  c) a work merely based on other music (e.g., variations on a theme).

If the name of the adapter is not known, enter under title.

If the work is related to one other work or to a part of a work with its own title or designation (e.g., a movement, an aria), make a name-title added entry for that work or part of a work. If the work is otherwise related to the music of another composer, make an added entry under the heading for that composer.

In case of doubt about whether a work is an arrangement, etc., or an adaptation, treat it as an arrangement, etc. (see 21.18B).

> Grande fantaisie de bravoure sur La clochette de Paganini : pour le piano-forte : œuvre 2 / par Fr. Liszt
> *Main entry under the heading for Liszt*
> *Added entry* (*name-title*) *under the heading for Paganini*

> Du alter Stefansturm : Viennese folk tune : free transcription for string orchestra / by J.M. Coopersmith
> *Main entry under the heading for Coopersmith*

Nouvelles soirées de Vienne : valses-caprices d'après J. Strauss / Ch. Tausig
Main entry under the heading for Tausig
Added entry under the heading for Strauss

Variationen über Là ci darem la mano : für das Pianoforte mit Begleitung des Orchesters / von Friedrich Chopin
(*Based on an aria from Mozart's* Don Giovanni)
Main entry under the heading for Chopin
Added entry (name-title) under the heading for Mozart

Rapsodie sur un thème de Paganini : pour piano et orchestre, op. 43 / S. Rachmaninoff
Main entry under the heading for Rachmaninoff
Added entry under the heading for Paganini

21.19. MUSICAL WORKS THAT INCLUDE WORDS

21.19A. General rule

21.19A1. Enter a musical work that includes words (e.g., a song, opera, musical comedy) under the heading for the composer. For librettos, see 21.28. Make added entries under the headings for the writers of the words if their work is fully represented in the item being catalogued (e.g., a full score, a vocal score). If the words are based on another text, make a name-title added entry under the heading for the original.

Dedication = Widmung : op. 25, no. 1 / Robert Schumann ; original poem by Friedrich Rückert
Main entry under the heading for Schumann
Added entry under the heading for Rückert

Rigoletto : opera in three acts / libretto by Francesco Maria Piave ; music by Giuseppe Verdi
(*A vocal score; libretto based on* Le roi s'amuse *by Victor Hugo*)
Main entry under the heading for Verdi
Added entry under the heading for Piave
Added entry (name-title) under the heading for Hugo

South Pacific : a musical play / music by Richard Rodgers ; lyrics by Oscar Hammerstein, 2nd ; book by Oscar Hammerstein, 2nd, and Joshua Logan
(*A vocal score; libretto based on* Tales of the South Pacific *by James A. Michener*)
Main entry under the heading for Rodgers
Added entries under the headings for Hammerstein and Logan
Added entry (name-title) under the heading for Michener

21.19B. Pasticcios, ballad operas, etc.

21.19B1. If the music of a pasticcio, ballad opera, etc., consists of previously existing ballads, songs, arias, etc., by various composers, enter the work under title. Make an added entry under the heading for the person who adapted or arranged the music and under the heading for the dramatist.

> The beggar's opera / written by Mr. Gay ; to which is prefix'd the musick to each song
>> (*The music for this work was adapted by John Christopher Pepusch*)
> *Main entry under title*
> *Added entries under the headings for Gay and Pepusch*

Enter a collection of musical excerpts from such a work under the title of the larger work. Enter a single song under the heading for its own composer, or under its title if the composer is unknown, and make a title added entry for the larger work.

> Songs in the opera call'd The beggar's wedding, as it is perform'd at the theatres
> *Main entry under the title of the opera*

21.19B2. If the music of a pasticcio, ballad opera, etc., was especially composed for it, enter the work as instructed in 21.6.

> The most favourite songs in the opera of Muzio Scaevola / composed by three famous masters
>> (*The composers are Amadei, Bononcini, and Handel*)
> *Main entry under the heading for Amadei*
> *Added entries under the headings for Bononcini and Handel*

21.19C. Writer's works set by several composers

21.19C1. Enter a collection of musical settings of songs, etc., by one writer made by two or more composers as a collection (see 21.7). Make an added entry under the heading for the writer.

> Songs from Shakespeare's tragedies : a collection of songs for concert or dramatic use / edited from contemporary sources by Frederick Sternfeld
> *Main entry under title*
> *Added entry under the headings for Shakespeare and Sternfeld*

> Et voici mes chansons / Minou Drouet ; mises en musique par Jean Françaix, Pierre Duclos, Paul Misraki, Bernard Boesch, Marc Lanjean
>> (*Drouet is the author of the words*)
> *Main entry under title*
> *Added entries under the headings for Drouet and Françaix*

21.20. MUSICAL SETTINGS FOR BALLETS, ETC.

21.20A. Enter a musical setting for a ballet, pantomime, etc., under the heading for the composer. Make added entries under the headings for choreographers and writers of scenarios, librettos, etc., whose names appear in the chief source of information of the item being catalogued.

> Robot : ballet / choreography by Stanislaw Povitch ; music by Walter L. Rosemont
> *Main entry under the heading for Rosemont*
> *Added entry under the heading for Povitch*

> Coppélia, ou, La fille aux yeux d'émail / ballet en 2 actes et 3 tableaux, de Ch. Nuitter et Saint-Léon ; musique de Léo Delibes
> *Main entry under the heading for Delibes*
> *Added entries under the headings for Nuitter and Saint-Léon*

> La fête chez Thérèse : ballet-pantomime / scénario de Catulle Mendès ; musique de Reynaldo Hahn
> *Main entry under the heading for Hahn*
> *Added entry under the heading for Mendès*

21.21. ADDED ACCOMPANIMENTS, ETC.

21.21A. Enter a musical work to which an instrumental accompaniment or additional parts have been added under the heading for the original work. Make an added entry under the heading for the composer of the accompaniment or the additional parts.

> Sechs Sonaten für Violine solo / von Joh. Seb. Bach ; herausgegeben von J. Hellmesberger ; Klavierbegleitung von Robert Schumann
> *Main entry under the heading for Bach*
> *Added entries under the headings for Hellmesberger and Schumann*

> O rosa bella
>> (*By John Dunstable, with optional contratenors and 3 additional voices by John Bedingham*)
> *Main entry under the heading for Dunstable*
> *Added entry under the heading for Bedingham*

21.22. LITURGICAL MUSIC

21.22A. Enter an edition of music that is officially prescribed as part of a liturgy as instructed in 21.39.

> The liber usualis : with introduction and rubrics in English / edited by the Benedictines of Solesmes
> *Main entry under the heading for the Catholic Church*

> The restored Holy Week liturgy : practical arrangement of the prescribed music for the average church choir / by Carlo Rossini
> *Main entry under the heading for the Catholic Church*

Sound Recordings

21.23. SOUND RECORDINGS

21.23A. One work

21.23A1. Enter a sound recording of one work (music, text, etc.) under the heading appropriate to that work. Make added entries under the headings for the principal performers[5] (e.g., singers, readers, orchestras) unless there are more than three. If there are more than three principal performers, make an added entry under the one named first.

> How many miles to Babylon? / author, Alison Uttley
>   (*Read by David Davis*)
> *Main entry under the heading for Uttley*
> *Added entry under the heading for Davis*

> The trout quintet : piano quintet in A major, op. 114 ... /
> Schubert
>   (*Performed by Smetana Quartet; Jan Panenka, piano; František
>   Pošta, double bass*)
> *Main entry under the heading for Schubert*
> *Added entries under the headings for the quartet, Panenka, and
>   Pošta*

> Bury my heart at Wounded Knee / by Dee Brown
>   (*An abridgement of Brown's book, dramatically presented by Henry
>   Madden and Manu Tupon*)
> *Main entry under the heading for Brown*
> *Added entries under the headings for Madden and Tupon*

21.23B. Two or more works by the same person(s) or body (bodies)

21.23B1. Enter a sound recording of two or more works all by the same person(s) or body (bodies) under the heading appropriate to those works. Make added entries under the headings for the principal performers unless there are more than three. If there are more than three principal performers, make an added entry under the one named first.

> Piano rags / Scott Joplin
>   (*Joshua Rifkin, piano*)
> *Main entry under the heading for Joplin*
> *Added entry under the heading for Rifkin*

> Any day now : songs of Bob Dylan
>   (*Sung by Joan Baez*)
> *Main entry under the heading for Dylan*
> *Added entry under the heading for Baez*

---

5. *Principal performers* are those given prominence (by wording or layout) in the chief source of information of the item being catalogued.

The best of Lennon and McCartney
(*Songs by Lennon and McCartney sung by Tommy James*)
Main entry under the heading for Lennon
Added entries under the headings for McCartney and James

The railway stories / W. Awdry
(*Read by Johnny Morris*)
Main entry under the heading for Awdry
Added entry under the heading for Morris

A tribute to Woody Guthrie
(*Songs and prose by Woody Guthrie, performed by Arlo Guthrie and others*)
Main entry under the heading for W. Guthrie
Added entry under the heading for A. Guthrie

21.23C. Works by different persons or bodies. Collective title

21.23C1. If a sound recording containing works by different persons or bodies has a collective title, enter it under the heading for the person or body represented as principal performer.

Pieces of the sky
(*Songs by various composers performed by Emmylou Harris*)
Main entry under the heading for Harris

All that jazz
(*Various pieces by several composers performed by Fats Waller*)
Main entry under the heading for Waller

Bonaparte's retreat
(*Folk tunes and songs by various composers performed by the band the Chieftains*)
Main entry under the heading for the band

Elisabeth Schumann
(*Vocal music by various composers sung by Schumann accompanied by various persons and bodies*)
Main entry under the heading for Schumann

Adrian Ruiz plays Niels Gade and Christian Sinding
(*Two works by Gade and six by Sinding performed by Ruiz*)
Main entry under the heading for Ruiz

If there are two or three persons or bodies represented as principal performers, enter under the heading for the first named and make added entries under the heading(s) for the other(s).

Great tenor arias
(*Arias by various composers sung by Carlo Bergonzi with the orchestra of the Accademia di Santa Cecilia, Rome*)
Main entry under the heading for Bergonzi
Added entry under the heading for the orchestra

Dancer with bruised knees / Kate & Anna McGarrigle
    (*Songs by the McGarrigle sisters and others performed by them*)
Main entry under the heading for K. McGarrigle
Added entry under the heading for A. McGarrigle

Irish rebel songs
    (*Sung by Mike Barrett and Joe Kiernan*)
Main entry under the heading for Barrett
Added entry under the heading for Kiernan

Orchestral suites of the British Isles
    (*Works by various composers performed by the Edmonton
    Symphony Orchestra; Uri Mayer, conductor*)
Main entry under the heading for the orchestra
Added entry under the heading for Mayer

If there are four or more persons or bodies represented as principal performers or if there is no principal performer, enter under title.

Music of nineteenth century England
    (*Several musical pieces performed by various persons and bodies*)
Main entry under title

Five centuries of music in Reims
    (*Pieces by various composers performed by various persons and
    bodies*)
Main entry under title

21.23D. Works by different persons or bodies. No collective title

21.23D1. If a sound recording containing works by different persons or bodies has no collective title and is to be catalogued as a unit (see 6.1G), follow one of the instructions below.

  a) If the item being catalogued contains works that are of a type in which the participation of the performer(s) goes beyond that of performance, execution, or interpretation (as is commonly the case in "popular," rock, and jazz music), enter under the heading for the person or body represented as principal performer.

I want to make you smile / Bill Medley ; [sung by] Kenny Rogers.   Coward of the county / R. Bowlings, B.E. Wheeler ; [sung by] Kenny Rogers
Main entry under the heading for Rogers

If there are two or three persons or bodies represented as principal performers, enter under the heading for the first named and make added entries under the heading(s) for the other(s).

All my love / Jolson, Akst, Chaplin ; Freddy Martin and his orchestra ; vocal refrain by Clyde Rogers and the Martin Men. When the white roses bloom in Red River Valley / Paul Herrick,

Ally Wrubel ; Freddy Martin and his orchestra ; vocal refrain by
Stuart Wade and the Martin Men
Main entry under the heading for Martin

If there are four or more persons or bodies represented as principal performers or if there is no principal performer, enter under the heading appropriate to the first work named.

Ko Ko Mo / Forest, Haven ; the Harmonaires with Bob Murray
Orchestra. Tweedle dee / Scott ; Joni Downs and the Starliners.
Ballad of Davy Crockett / Blackburn, Bruns ; Heck Johns and the
Pioneers. How important can it be? / Benjamin, Weiss ; Joan
Forrest with Jay Weston Orchestra
Main entry under the heading for Forest

b) If the works on the recording are of a type in which the participation of the
performer(s) does not go beyond that of performance, execution, and interpretation (as is commonly the case in classical and other "serious" music),
enter under the heading appropriate to the first work and make added entries for the other works as appropriate (see 21.7C). Make added entries
under the headings for the principal performers of each work as instructed
in 21.23A1.

Sinfonia in G minor, op. 6, no. 6 / Johann Christian Bach.
Symphony in G / Michael Haydn. Cassation in D, K. 62a /
Wolfgang Amadeus Mozart
   (*All performed by the Saint Paul Chamber Orchestra conducted by
   Dennis Russell Davies*)
Main entry under the heading for Bach
*Added entries (name-title) under the headings for Haydn and
   Mozart*
Added entries under the headings for Davies and the orchestra

Concerto grosso no. 1 for string orchestra with piano obbligato /
Bloch. Spirituals : for string choir and orchestra / Gould
   (*First work performed by Rafael Kubelik conducting the Chicago
   Symphony Orchestra. Second work performed by Antal Dorati
   conducting the Minneapolis Symphony Orchestra*)
Main entry under the heading for Bloch
Added entry (name-title) under the heading for Gould
*Added entries under the headings for Kubelik, Dorati, and the two
   orchestras*

The Pied Piper / Robert Browning. The hunting of the Snark /
Lewis Carroll
   (*Both works read by Boris Karloff*)
Main entry under the heading for Browning
Added entry (name-title) under the heading for Carroll
Added entry under the heading for Karloff

I look back ; Wistful ; Service of all the dead ; A child's grace ;
This glittering grief ; The ouselcock / Herbert Elwell. String

quartet no. 7 / John Verrall.   Spatials ; Sonata no. 2 ; Spektra / George Walker

> (*Elwell works performed by Maxine Makas, soprano; Anthony Makas, piano. Verrall work performed by the Berkshire Quartet. Walker works performed by the composer, piano*)

Main entry under the heading for Elwell
Added entry (*name-title*) *under the heading for Verrall*
Added entries under the headings for M. Makas, A. Makas, the quartet, and Walker

Mixed Responsibility in New Works

21.24. COLLABORATION BETWEEN ARTIST AND WRITER

21.24A. Enter a work that is, or appears to be, a work of collaboration between an artist and a writer under the heading for the one who is named first in the chief source of information of the item being catalogued unless the other's name is given greater prominence by the wording or the layout. Make an added entry under the heading for the other one. For instructions on illustrated texts, see 21.11A.

> A color guide to familiar garden and field birds, eggs, and nests / by Jiří Felix ; illustrated by Květoslav Hísek

> (*A collaborative work*)

Main entry under the heading for Felix
Added entry under the heading for Hísek

> A Carolina rice plantation of the fifties : 30 paintings in water-colour / by Alice R. Huger Smith ; narrative by Herbert Ravenel Sass ; with chapters from the unpublished memoirs of D.E. Huger Smith

Main entry under the heading for A. Smith
Added entries under the headings for Sass and D. Smith

> Say, is this the U.S.A.? / Erskine Caldwell and Margaret Bourke-White

> (*Text by Caldwell, photographs by Bourke-White*)

Main entry under the heading for Caldwell
Added entry under the heading for Bourke-White

> Goodbye baby & amen : a saraband for the sixties / David Bailey & Peter Evans

> (*Photographs by Bailey, text by Evans*)

Main entry under the heading for Bailey
Added entry under the heading for Evans

> Cartoons / by E.W. Kemble ; limericks by G. Mayo

Main entry under the heading for Kemble
Added entry under the heading for Mayo

Birds : a guide to the most familiar American birds / by
Herbert S. Zim and Ira N. Gabrielson ; illustrated by James
Gordon Irving
    (*A collaborative work*)
Main entry under the heading for Zim
Added entries under the headings for Gabrielson and Irving

21.25. REPORTS OF INTERVIEWS OR EXCHANGES

21.25A. If a report is essentially confined to the words of the person(s) interviewed or of the participants in an exchange (other than the reporter), enter
under the principal participant, participant named first in the chief source of
information of the item being catalogued, or title as instructed in 21.6. Make an
added entry under the heading for the reporter if he or she is named prominently
in the item.

Discussion at Workshop between the Rev. R.P. Blakeney ... and
the Rev. J.B. Naghten ... / reported verbatim by Thomas
Whitehead
Main entry under the heading for Blakeney
Added entries under the headings for Naghten and Whitehead

My wartime experiences in Singapore / Mamoru Shinozaki ;
interviewed by Lim Yoon Lin
Main entry under the heading for Shinozaki
Added entry under the heading for Lim

21.25B. If a report is to a considerable extent in the words of the reporter, enter
under the heading for the reporter. Make added entries under the headings for
the other person(s) involved if they are named in the chief source of information
and there are not more than three. If there are more than three such persons
named in the chief source of information, make an added entry under the one
named first.

Talks with Ralph Waldo Emerson / by Charles J. Woodbury
Main entry under the heading for Woodbury
Added entry under the heading for Emerson

Table-talk of G.B.S. : conversations on things in general
between George Bernard Shaw and his biographer / by Archibald
Henderson
Main entry under the heading for Henderson
Added entry under the heading for Shaw

Interviews impubliables / Gilbert Ganne
    (*Interviews with 23 persons; none named on the title page*)
Main entry under the heading for Ganne

21.26. SPIRIT COMMUNICATIONS

21.26A. Enter a communication presented as having been received from a spirit under the heading for the spirit (see 22.14). Make an added entry under the heading for the medium or other person recording the communication.

> Food for the million, or, Thoughts from beyond the borders of the material / by Theodore Parker ; through the hand of Sarah A. Ramsdell
> *Main entry under the heading for the spirit of Parker*
> *Added entry under the heading for Ramsdell*

21.27. ACADEMIC DISPUTATIONS

21.27A. Enter a work written for defence in an academic disputation (according to the custom prevailing in universities before the nineteenth century and continued in some cases thereafter) under the heading for the praeses (faculty moderator) unless the authorship of the respondent, defender, etc., can be established.[6] Make an added entry under the heading for whichever of the praeses, respondent, etc., is not chosen for the main entry. *Optionally*, add the appropriate designation (e.g., *praeses*, *respondent*, *defendant*) to the added entry headings. Do not make an added entry under the name of a person designated as an opponent.

> Principium Mosellae Ausonii, ad disputandum publice propositum / praeside Conrado Samuele Schurzfleischio ; respondente M. Godefrido Kupfender
> *Main entry under the heading for Schurzfleisch as praeses*
> *Added entry under the heading for Kupfender as respondent*

> Observationes circa vermes intestinales ... / praeside ... Ioanne Quistorp ; auctor Carolus Asmund Rudolphi
>   (*Rudolphi's authorship established*)
> *Main entry under the heading for Rudolphi*
> *Added entry under the heading for Quistorp as praeses*

If no one is named as praeses, enter under the heading for (in this order of preference) the proponent; the defendant or respondent.

---

6. Do not accept the designation *auctor* on the title page as proof of authorship without further evidence. For works dealing with this problem, see the following:

Eichler, Ferdinand. "Die Autorschaft der akademischen Disputationen," *Sammlung bibliothekswissenschaftlicher Arbeiten,* Heft 10 (1896), pp. 24–37; Heft 11 (1898), pp. 1-40.
Horn, Ewald. "Die Disputationen und Promotionen an den deutschen Universitäten, vornehmlich seit dem 16. Jahrhundert," *Centralblatt für Bibliothekswesen,* Beiheft XI (1893).
Kaufmann, Georg. "Zur Geschichte der academischen Grade und Disputationen," *ibid.,* XI. Jahrg. (Mai 1894), pp. [201]–225.
Wheatley, B.R. "On the Question of Authorship in Academical Dissertations," pp. 105–121 in Wheatley, H.B. *How to Catalogue a Library.* — (London : Stock, 1889).

Related Works

21.28. RELATED WORKS

21.28A. Scope

21.28A1. Apply this rule to a separately catalogued work (see also 1.1B9, 1.5E1a, and 1.9) that has a relationship to another work. Such works include:

> continuations and sequels
> supplements
> indexes
> concordances
> incidental music to dramatic works
> cadenzas
> scenarios, screenplays, etc.
> choreographies
> librettos and other texts set to music[7]
> subseries
> special numbers of serials
> collections of extracts from serials

Do not apply this rule to a work that has only a subject relationship to another work.

For particular types of relationship (e.g., adaptations, revisions, translations), see 21.8–21.27.

21.28B. General rule

21.28B1. Enter a related work under its own heading (personal author, corporate body, or title) according to the appropriate rule in this chapter. Make an added entry[8] (name-title or title, as appropriate) for the work to which it is related.

---

7. *Alternative rule.* Enter a libretto under the heading appropriate to the musical work. Make an added entry under the heading for the librettist. If the libretto is based on another text, make a name-title added entry under the heading for the original.

> Curlew River : a parable for church performance / by William Plomer ; set to music by Benjamin Britten
> > (*A libretto*)
> *Main entry under the heading for Britten*
> *Added entry under the heading for Plomer*

> Der Rosenkavalier : Komödie für Musik in 3 Aufzügen / von Hugo von Hofmannsthal ; Musik von Richard Strauss
> *Main entry under the heading for Strauss*
> *Added entry under the heading for Hofmannsthal*

If, however, a libretto is published without reference to its musical setting, enter it under the heading for the author of the libretto.

> Der Rosenkavalier : Komödie für Musik / von Hugo von Hofmannsthal
> > (*Published as a literary work*)
> *Main entry under the heading for Hofmannsthal*

Enter a collection of librettos for works by one composer under the heading for the composer.

8. Do not make an added entry for the related work in the case of a sequel by the same author.

An index to the Columbia edition of The works of John Milton /
by Frank Allen Patterson ; assisted by French Rowe Fogle
Main entry under the heading for Patterson
Added entry under the heading for Fogle
Added entry (name-title) under the heading for Milton

Teacher's manual / by W.D. Lewis ... to accompany Topical
studies in United States history by A.B. Blodgett
Main entry under the heading for Lewis
Added entry (name-title) under the heading for Blodgett

Supplement to The conquest of Peru and Mexico by the Moguls,
in the XIII century
*(By John Ranking, who is also the author of the work to which the
supplement is related)*
Main entry under the heading for Ranking
*Added entry (name-title) under the heading for Ranking as author of
the related work*

Supplement to Hain's Repertorium bibliographicum ... / by
W.A. Copinger
Main entry under the heading for Copinger
Added entry (name-title) under the heading for Hain

Ergänzungshefte zu den Blättern für Volksbibliotheken und
Lesehallen
Main entry under title
Added entry under the heading for the related work

Cumulative book index : a world list of books in the English
language ... supplementing The United States catalog
Main entry under title
Added entry under the heading for the related work

Histoire du peuple anglais au XIXe siècle. Épilogue (1895-1914)
/ Élie Halévy
Main entry under the heading for Halévy
Added entry (name-title) for the related work not required

A complete concordance to the Iliad of Homer / by Guy
Lushington Prendergast
Main entry under the heading for Prendergast
Added entry (name-title) under the heading for Homer

A complete concordance to the Holy Scriptures of the Old and
New Testament ... / by Alexander Cruden
Main entry under the heading for Cruden
Added entry under the heading for the Bible

Astronomie topographique : complément au Traité de
topographie générale : cours professé à l'École nationale du génie
rural / par A. Carrier
Main entry under the heading for Carrier
*Added entry (name-title) under the heading for Carrier as author of
the related work*

John Jasper's gatehouse : a sequel to the unfinished novel The mystery of Edwin Drood by Charles Dickens / by Edwin Harris
Main entry under the heading for Harris
Added entry (name-title) under the heading for Dickens

Over the garden wall : Mrs. H. and Mrs. C. gossip, as broadcast in Monday night at seven : a series of comedy episodes / by Guy Fane
Main entry under the heading for Fane
Added entry under the heading for Monday night at seven (*a radio programme*)

United nations : six radio dramatizations presented on The family hour
   (*Anonymous*)
Main entry under title
Added entry under the heading for The family hour (*a radio programme*)

Hiroshima mon amour : scénario et dialogues / Marguerite Duras
   (*A film scenario*)
Main entry under the heading for Duras
Added entry under the heading for the motion picture

Conrack
   (*Filmstrip based on* The water is wide *by Pat Conroy*)
Main entry under title
Added entry (name-title) under the heading for Conroy

Art in photography : with selected examples of European and American work / edited by Charles Holme
   (*Special number of the journal* The studio)
Main entry under title
Added entries under the headings for Holme and the journal

Studien zur Musikwissenschaft : Beihefte der Denkmäler der Tonkunst in Österreich
Main entry under title
Added entry under the heading for the Denkmäler

Eli Terry pillar & scroll shelf clocks / by Lockwood Barr
   (*Supplement to the* Bulletin of the National Association of Watch and Clock Collectors)
Main entry under the heading for Barr
Added entry under the heading for the journal

Youth and the new world : essays from The Atlantic monthly / edited by Ralph Boas
Main entry under title
Added entries under the headings for Boas and the journal

The Penguin book of Ximenes crosswords [from] The observer
Main entry under the heading for Ximenes
Added entry under the heading for the newspaper

Les CL Pseaumes de David escrites en diverses sortes de lettres / par Esther Anglois
(*A calligraphic work*)
Main entry under the heading for Anglois
Added entry under the heading for the Psalms

Rosamunde : Drama / von H. v. Chézy ; mit Musik von Franz Schubert
(*A musical score*)
Main entry under the heading for Schubert
Added entry (name-title) under the heading for Chézy

Cadenzas for the Flute concerto in G major (K.313) by Mozart / Georges Barrère
Main entry under the heading for Barrère
Added entry (name-title) under the heading for Mozart

Walt Disney's Alice in Wonderland
(*A sound recording of songs by Oliver Wallace from the motion picture* Alice in Wonderland)
Main entry under the heading for Wallace
Added entry under the heading for the motion picture

Curlew River : a parable for church performance / by William Plomer ; set to music by Benjamin Britten
(*A libretto*)
Main entry under the heading for Plomer
Added entry under the heading for Britten

Der Rosenkavalier : Komödie für Musik in 3 Aufzügen / von Hugo von Hofmannsthal ; Musik von Richard Strauss
(*A libretto*)
Main entry under the heading for Hofmannsthal
Added entry under the heading for Strauss

Added Entries

21.29. GENERAL RULE

21.29A. Make added entries to provide access to bibliographic descriptions in addition to the access provided by the main entry heading.

21.29B. Make added entries under headings for persons, corporate bodies, and titles as instructed in 21.30.

21.29C. In addition, make an added entry under the heading for a person or a corporate body or under a title if some catalogue users might suppose that the description of an item would be found under that heading or title rather than under the heading or title chosen for the main entry.

21.29D. If, in the context of a given catalogue, an added entry is required under a heading or title other than those prescribed in 21.30, make it.

21.29E. Construct a heading for an added entry according to the instructions in chapters 22–25. For instructions on the construction of name-title added entries, see 21.30G.

21.29F. If the reason for an added entry is not apparent from the description (e.g., if a person or body whose name is used as the basis for an added entry heading is not named in a statement of responsibility or in the publication details), provide a note giving, as appropriate, the name of the person or body (see 1.7B6) and/or the title (see 1.7B4).

21.29G. *Optionally*, use explanatory references in place of added entries in certain cases (see 26.5).

21.30. SPECIFIC RULES

21.30A. Two or more persons or bodies involved

21.30A1. If the following subrules refer to only one person or corporate body and two or three persons or bodies are involved in a particular instance, make added entries under the headings for each. If four or more persons or bodies are involved in a particular instance, make an added entry when appropriate under the heading for the one named first in the source from which the names are taken.

21.30B. Collaborators

21.30B1. If the main entry is under the heading for one of two or three collaborating persons or bodies, make added entries under the headings for the others.

If the main entry is under the heading for a corporate body or under a title, make added entries under the headings for collaborating persons if there are not more than three, or under the heading for the first named of four or more.

21.30C. Writers

21.30C1. Make an added entry under the heading for a prominently named writer of a work if the main entry is under the heading for another person or a corporate body or under title.

21.30D. Editors and compilers

21.30D1. Make an added entry under the heading for a prominently named editor or compiler of a monographic work. Make an added entry under the heading for an editor of a serial only in the rare instance when a serial is likely to be known by the editor's name.

21.30E. Corporate bodies

21.30E1. Make an added entry under the heading for a prominently named corporate body, unless it functions solely as distributor or manufacturer. Make an added entry under a prominently named publisher if the responsibility for the work extends beyond that of merely publishing the item being catalogued. In case of doubt, make an added entry.

21.30F. Other related persons or bodies

21.30F1. Make an added entry under the heading for a person or corporate body having a relationship to a work not treated in 21.1–21.28 if the heading provides an important access point (e.g., the addressee of a collection of letters; a person honoured by a Festschrift; a museum in which an exhibition is held).

21.30G. Related works

21.30G1. Make an added entry under the heading for a work to which the work being catalogued is closely related (see 21.8–21.28 for guidance in specific cases).

In such a case, the heading is that of the person or corporate body or the title under which the related work is, or would be, entered. If that heading is for a person or body, and the title of the related work differs from that of the work being catalogued, add the title of the related work to the heading to form a name-title added entry heading. When necessary, add the edition statement, date, etc., to the name-title or title added entry heading.

When appropriate, substitute a uniform title (see chapter 25) for a title proper in a name-title or title added entry heading for a related work.

21.30H. Other relationships

21.30H1. Make an added entry under the heading for any other name that would provide an important access point unless the relationship between the name and the work is purely that of a subject. For example, make added entries under the heading for the name of a collection from which reproductions of art works have been taken or under the heading for a collection of books upon which a bibliography is based.

When possible, formulate headings for such names by analogy with corporate name headings.

21.30J. Titles

21.30J1. Make an added entry under the title proper of every item entered under a personal heading, a corporate heading, or a uniform title unless:

    a) the title proper is essentially the same as the main entry heading or a reference to that heading

or b) the title proper has been composed by the cataloguer

or c) in a catalogue in which name-title and subject entries are interfiled, the title proper is identical to a subject heading assigned to the work or a direct reference to that subject heading *or* d) a conventionalized uniform title has been used as the uniform title for a musical work (see 25.25–25.35).

If considered necessary for access, make an added entry for any version of the title (e.g., cover title, caption title, running title) that, according to 21.2A, does not constitute a change in the title proper.

21.30K. Special rules on added entries in certain cases

21.30K1. Translators. Make an added entry under the heading for a translator if the main entry is under the heading for a corporate body or under title.

If the main entry is under the heading for a person, make an added entry under the heading for a translator if:

    a) the translation is in verse

or b) the translation is important in its own right

or c) the work has been translated into the same language more than once

or d) the wording of the chief source of information of the item being catalogued implies that the translator is the author

or e) the main entry heading may be difficult for catalogue users to find (e.g., as with many oriental and medieval works).

21.30K2. Illustrators. Make an added entry under the heading for an illustrator if:

    a) the illustrator's name is given equal or greater prominence in the chief source of information of the item being catalogued to that of the person or corporate body named in the main entry heading

or b) the illustrations occupy half or more of the item

or c) the illustrations are considered to be an important feature of the work.

21.30L. Series

21.30L1. Make an added entry under the heading for a series for each separately catalogued work in the series if it provides a useful collocation. *Optionally*, add the numeric or other designation of each work in the series.

Do not make added entries under the heading for a series if:

    a) the items in a series are related to each other only by common physical characteristics

or b) the numbering suggests that the parts have been numbered primarily for stock control or to benefit from lower postage rates.

In case of doubt, make a series added entry.

21.30M. Analytical entries

21.30M1. Make an analytical added entry under the heading for a work contained within the item being catalogued (see 21.7B–21.7C, 21.13B, and 21.15A for guidance in specific cases). Make additional analytical entries in accordance with the policy of the cataloguing agency. See also chapter 13.

In such a case, the heading is that of the person or corporate body or the title under which the work contained is, or would be, entered. If that heading is for a person or body, add the title of the work contained to form a name-title added entry heading. When necessary, add the edition statement, date, etc., to the name-title or title added entry heading.

When appropriate, substitute a uniform title (see chapter 25) for a title proper in a name-title or title analytical entry heading.

Special Rules

Certain Legal Publications

21.31. LAWS, ETC.

21.31A. Scope

21.31A1. Apply this rule to legislative enactments and decrees of a political jurisdiction and to decrees of a chief executive having the force of law (all hereinafter referred to as laws) other than:

a) administrative regulations that are not laws (see 21.32A)
b) constitutions and charters (see 21.33)
c) court rules (see 21.34)
d) treaties and similar formal agreements (see 21.35).

For annotated editions of laws and commentaries, see 21.13.

21.31B. Laws of modern jurisdictions

21.31B1. Laws governing one jurisdiction. Enter laws governing one jurisdiction under the heading for the jurisdiction governed by them. Add a uniform title as instructed in 25.15A. Make added entries under the headings for persons and corporate bodies (other than legislative bodies) responsible for compiling and issuing the laws.

> Canada Corporations Act : chap. 53, R.S.C. 1952, as amended.
> — 2nd ed. — Don Mills, Ont. : CCH Canadian
> *Main entry under the heading for Canada with uniform title for the*
> *law*
> *Added entry under the heading for CCH Canadian*

> Gesetz betreffend die Amortisation der Staatsschuld : auf
> Befehl e. h. Senats der Freien und Hansestadt Hamburg publicirt
> den 29. Mai 1865
> *Main entry under the heading for Hamburg with uniform title for the law*

> The school law of Illinois ... / prepared by T.A. Reynolds,
> assistant superintendent ; issued by John A. Wieland,
> superintendent of public instruction ; amended by the Fifty-ninth
> General Assembly
> *Main entry under the heading for Illinois with uniform title for the law*
> *Added entries under the headings for Reynolds and the Department*
> *of Public Instruction*

Building code of the city of Richmond, Virginia
Main entry under the heading for Richmond with uniform title for
the code

Byelaws for the regulation of motor hackney carriages and the
drivers thereof in the city of Glasgow
Main entry under the heading for Glasgow with uniform title for the
byelaws

The public health acts / annotated by William Golden Lumley
and Edmund Lumley
Main entry under the heading for the United Kingdom with uniform
title for the laws
Added entries under the headings for W.G. Lumley and E. Lumley

If the laws are enacted by a jurisdiction other than that governed by them,
make an added entry under the heading for the enacting jurisdiction. Add a
uniform title as instructed in 25.15A to the heading for the jurisdiction.

Code of the public local laws of Worcester County : article 24 of
the Code of public local laws of Maryland : comprising all the
local laws of the state of Maryland in force in Worcester County to
and inclusive of the Acts of the General Assembly of 1961 / edited
by Carl N. Everstine
Main entry under the heading for Worcester County with uniform
title for the laws
Added entry under the heading for Maryland with uniform title for
the laws
Added entry under the heading for Everstine

If the laws are decrees of a head of state, chief executive, or ruling executive
body (e.g., a junta), make an added entry under the corporate heading for the
official (see 24.20) or ruling executive body.

Notverordnungen des Reichspräsidenten
Main entry under the heading for Germany with uniform title for the
decrees
Added entry under the corporate heading for the Reichspräsident

Decretos-leyes de carácter electoral / dictados por la Junta
Militar de Gobierno
    (*Decrees of the ruling executive body of Bolivia*)
Main entry under the heading for Bolivia with uniform title for the
decree laws
Added entry under the heading for the junta

21.31B2. Laws governing more than one jurisdiction. Enter a compilation of laws
governing more than one jurisdiction as a collection (see 21.7).
    Make added entries under the headings for the jurisdictions governed if there
are two or three. If there are four or more jurisdictions and they are named in

the chief source of information of the item being catalogued, make an added entry under the heading for the one named first. If all the laws are enacted by a single jurisdiction, make an added entry under the heading for the enacting jurisdiction. Add a uniform title as instructed in 25.15A to each added entry heading.

> Motor bus laws and regulations : a complete code of all motor
> bus regulatory laws ... / compiled and edited by John M. Meighan
> *Main entry under title*
> *Added entry under the heading for Meighan*

21.31B3. Bills and drafts of legislation. Enter legislative bills under the heading for the appropriate legislative body (see 24.21). Enter other drafts of legislation as instructed in 21.1–21.7.

> A bill to designate a building site for the National Conservatory
> of Music of America, and for other purposes : 70th Congress, 1st
> session, S.2170
> *Main entry under the heading for the Senate of the United States*

> Draft of an act relating to the sale of goods / by Samuel
> Williston
> *Main entry under the heading for Williston*

> Draft of proposed tenement house law / Commission of
> Immigration and Housing of California
> *Main entry under the heading for the commission*

21.31C. Ancient laws, certain medieval laws, customary laws, etc.

21.31C1. Enter the laws of ancient jurisdictions; laws of non-western jurisdictions before the adoption of legislative institutions based on western models; and customary laws, tribal laws, etc., under (in this order of preference):

a) a uniform title consisting of the title by which the law or early compilation of laws is known (see 25.15B)
b) the title proper of the item being catalogued.

If there are one, two, or three compilers or enactors of such laws that are named prominently in the item being catalogued or are associated with the work in reference sources, make added entries under the heading(s) for the compiler(s), etc. If there are four or more such persons, make an added entry under the heading for the first.

> Lex Salica : the ten texts with the glosses and the Lex Emendata
> *Main entry under the uniform title for the* Lex Salica

> Edictum Diocletiani de pretiis rerum venalium
> *Main entry under the uniform title for the* Edictum

> The oldest code of laws in the world : the code of laws
> promulgated by Hammurabi, King of Babylon
> *Main entry under the uniform title for the laws*

Die Gesetze des Merowingerreiches, 481-714 / herausgegeben
von Karl August Eckhardt
Main entry under the title proper
Added entry under the heading for Eckhardt

Fontes iuris romani antejustiniani / in usum scholarum ediderunt
S. Riccobono ... [et al.]
(Four additional editors named on title page)
Main entry under the title proper
Added entry under the heading for Riccobono

21.32. ADMINISTRATIVE REGULATIONS, ETC.

21.32A. Administrative regulations, etc., that are not laws

21.32A1. If administrative regulations, rules, etc., are from jurisdictions in which
such regulations, etc., are promulgated by government agencies or agents under
authority granted by one or more laws (as is the case in the United States), enter
them under the heading for the agency or agent. If the regulations, etc., are issued
by an agency other than the promulgating agency, make an added entry under
the heading for the issuing agency. If the regulations, etc., derive from a particular
law, make an added entry under the heading and uniform title (see 25.15A) for
that law.

Rules and regulations for recreational areas : [Recreational
Area Licensing Act rules and regulations] / Department of Public
Health, Bureau of Environmental Health, Division of Swimming
Pools and Recreation
(Promulgated by the Department of Public Health, State of Illinois)
Main entry under the heading for the department
Added entry under the heading for the division
Added entry under the heading for Illinois with uniform title for the law

21.32A2. If a law or laws and the regulations, etc., derived from it are published
together, enter the item under the heading appropriate to whichever is mentioned
first in the chief source of information of the item being catalogued. Make an
added entry under the heading for the other. However, if only the law(s) or only
the regulations, etc., are named in the title proper, enter under the heading appropriate to the one mentioned and make an added entry under the heading for
the other. If the evidence of the chief source of information is ambiguous or
insufficient, enter under the heading for the law(s) and make an added entry
under the heading for the regulations, etc.

Regulations and principal statutes applicable to contractors and
subcontractors on public building and public work and on building
and work financed in whole or in part by loans or grants from the
United States / United States Department of Labor
(Includes several statutes, in whole and in part)
Main entry under the heading for the department
*Added entry under the heading for the United States with uniform
title for the laws*

Gewerbesteuer-Veranlagung 1966 : Gewerbesteuergesetz und
Gewerbesteuer-Durchführungsverordnung mit Gewerbesteuer-
Richtlinien ...
*(Regulations and guidelines included were promulgated by the
Bundesministerium der Finanzen of the Federal Republic of
Germany)*
*Main entry under the heading for the Federal Republic of Germany
with uniform title for the law*
Added entry under the heading for the ministry

21.32B. Administrative regulations, etc., that are laws

21.32B1. If administrative regulations, rules, etc., are from jurisdictions in which
such regulations, etc., are laws (as is the case in the United Kingdom and Canada),
enter them as instructed in 21.31. Make added entries under the headings for the
government agencies or agents promulgating and/or issuing them. If the regulations, etc., derive from a particular law, make an added entry under the heading
and uniform (see 25.15A) title for that law.

The Building Societies (Fee) Regulations, 1976
*(Promulgated by the Chief Registrar of Friendly Societies under
authority granted by* the Building Societies (Fee) Act)
*Main entry under the heading for the United Kingdom with uniform
title for the regulations*
Added entry under the heading for the chief registrar
*Added entry under the heading for the United Kingdom with
uniform title for the law*

Regulations under the Destructive Insect and Pest Act as they
apply to the importation of plants and plant products /
Department of Agriculture
(Promulgated by the Governor in Council)
*Main entry under the heading for Canada with uniform title for the
regulations*
Added entries under the headings for the governor and the department
Added entry under the heading for Canada with uniform title for the law

21.32C. Collections of administrative regulations, etc.

21.32C1. Enter a collection of regulations that are not laws as a collection (see
21.7). Enter a collection of regulations that are laws according to the instructions
in 21.32B.

21.33. CONSTITUTIONS, CHARTERS, AND OTHER FUNDAMENTAL LAWS

21.33A. Enter the constitution, charter, or other fundamental law of a jurisdiction
or international intergovernmental body[9] under the heading for that jurisdiction

---

9. *International intergovernmental body* means an international body created by intergovernmental action.

or body. Enter any amendments to such a document under the same heading. If the document is issued by a jurisdiction other than the one governed by it, make an added entry under the heading for the issuing jurisdiction. If the document is a law, add the appropriate uniform title as instructed in 25.15A to the added entry heading.

> The Constitution of the United States
> *Main entry under the heading for the United States*

> An Act for the Union of Canada, Nova Scotia, and New Brunswick, and the Government Thercof . . . at a Parliament begun and holden at Westminster the first day of February . . . 1866
> *Main entry under the heading for Canada*
> *Added entry under the heading for the United Kingdom with uniform title for the law*

> Kongeriget Norges grundlov
> *Main entry under the heading for Norway*

> Charter of the United Nations
> *Main entry under the heading for the United Nations*

> The Constitution of the state of Michigan
> *Main entry under the heading for Michigan*

> Constitución política del estado libre y soberano de Chihuahua
> *Main entry under the heading for Chihuahua*

> Constitution of the state of Connecticut, and historical antecedents
> *Main entry under the heading for Connecticut*

> Charter of the city of Detroit : revised to April 3, 1933 / adopted by the people of the city of Detroit
> *Main entry under the heading for Detroit*

> Charter of the city of Nashville, Tennessee : chapter no. 246, Private acts of the General Assembly of the state of Tennessee for the year 1947, as amended through the legislative session of 1949
> *Main entry under the heading for Nashville*
> *Added entry under the heading for Tennessee with uniform title for the law*

> The charter granted by His Majesty King Charles II to the Governour & Company of the English colony of Connecticut
> *Main entry under the heading for Connecticut*
> *Added entry under the corporate heading for Charles II as sovereign*

21.33B. Enter the constitution, charter, or other fundamental document of a body emanating from a jurisdiction but applying to a body other than a jurisdiction as instructed in the rule applying to the type of document (e.g., if the document is a law, see 21.31). Enter any amendments to such a document under the same heading. Make an added entry under the heading for the body governed by the constitution, etc., if the main entry is not under that heading.

> Charter of the Franklin Bank of Baltimore
>> (*An act of the Maryland legislature*)
> *Main entry under the heading for Maryland with uniform title for*
>> *the law*
> *Added entry under the heading for the bank*

For constitutions, etc., that neither apply to, nor emanate from, a jurisdiction or an intergovernmental body, see 21.1B and 21.4B.

21.33C. Drafts

21.33C1. If a draft of a constitution, charter, etc., is a legislative bill, enter it under the heading for the appropriate legislative body (see 24.21). Enter other drafts of such documents as instructed in 21.1–21.7.

21.34. COURT RULES

21.34A. Enter court rules governing a single court (regardless of their official nature, e.g., laws, administrative regulations) under the heading for that court. If the rules are laws, make an added entry under the heading for the jurisdiction enacting the law and add a uniform title as instructed in 25.15A. Make an added entry under the heading for the agency or agent promulgating the court rules.

> Rules of practice and procedure of United States Tax Court
> *Main entry under the heading for the court*

> The rules of the Supreme Court, 1965 ... / Lord Chancellor's Office
>> (*An administrative regulation promulgated by the Lord*
>> *Chancellor's Office*)
> *Main entry under the heading for the court*
> *Added entry under the heading for the office*
> *Added entry under the heading for the United Kingdom with*
>> *uniform title for the regulation*

21.34B. Enter a collection of rules governing more than one court of a single jurisdiction but enacted as laws of that jurisdiction as instructed in 21.31. Enter all other such collections of court rules under the heading for the agency or agent promulgating them.

If the rules govern two or three courts, make added entries under the headings for the courts governed. If the rules govern four or more courts, make an added entry under the heading for the one named first in the chief source of information of the item being catalogued.

> Code de procédure civile de la province de Québec : 13-14
> Elizabeth II chap. 80
> *Main entry under the heading for Québec with uniform title for the*
>> *law*

21.34C. Enter a collection of court rules that are the laws of more than one jurisdiction, or that are promulgated by more than one agency or agent, as a collection (see 21.7). Make an added entry under the heading for any corporate body involved in the compilation and named prominently in the item being catalogued unless it functions solely as a publisher.

> West's California rules of court, 1975, state and federal : with amendments received for January 1, 1975. — St. Paul, Minn. : West Pub. Co.
>> (*The rules apply to numerous state and federal courts in California; the state rules are promulgated by the California Judicial Council, which is named prominently*)
> *Main entry under title*
> *Added entries under the headings for the Judicial Council and for the publisher, which initiated the compilation*

21.35. TREATIES, INTERGOVERNMENTAL AGREEMENTS, ETC.

21.35A. International treaties, etc.

21.35A1. Treaties, etc., between two or three governments. Enter a treaty, or any other formal agreement, between two or three national governments[10] under (in this order of preference):

a) the heading for the government on one side if it is the only one on that side and there are two governments on the other
b) the heading for the government whose catalogue entry heading (see 24.3E) is first in English alphabetic order.

Make added entries under the headings for the other government(s). Add uniform titles as instructed in 25.16B1 to the main and added entry headings.

> Convention monétaire belgo-luxembourgeoise-néerlandaise
>> (*A convention between the government of the Netherlands, on the one side, and the governments of Belgium and Luxembourg on the other side*)
> *Main entry under the heading for the Netherlands with uniform title for the treaty*
> *Added entries under the headings for Belgium and Luxembourg, each with uniform title for the treaty*

> Special Economic Assistance : agreement between the United States of America and Burma, effected by exchange of notes
> *Main entry under the heading for Burma with uniform title for the treaty*
> *Added entry under the heading for the United States with uniform title for the treaty*

> Traité de paix entre le Japon et la Russie
> *Main entry under the heading for Japan with uniform title for the treaty*
> *Added entry under the heading for Russia with uniform title for the treaty*

---

10. *National governments* includes bodies exercising treaty powers such as Native American nations and African tribal governments.

> Convention between the governments of the United Kingdom,
> Belgium, and France regarding the supervision and preventive
> control of the African migratory locust
> *Main entry under the heading for Belgium with uniform title for the*
>   *treaty*
> *Added entries under the headings for France and the United*
>   *Kingdom, each with uniform title for the treaty*

21.35A2. Treaties, etc., between four or more governments. Enter a treaty, or
any other formal agreement, between four or more national governments under
title (either the title proper or a uniform title, see 25.16B2). Make an added entry
under the heading for the home government (i.e., the government of the cataloguing agency) if it is a signatory. Make an added entry under the heading for
any other government publishing the item being catalogued if that government
is a signatory. Make an added entry under the heading for the government named
first in the chief source of information if it is neither the home government nor
the publishing government. If the treaty, etc., is the product of an international
conference, make an added entry under the heading for the conference. Add
uniform titles as instructed in 25.16B1 to the added entry headings for parties
to the agreement.

> The definitive treaty of peace and friendship between His
> Britannick Majesty, the most Christian King, and the King of Spain
> : concluded at Paris, the 10th day of February, 1763 : to which the
> King of Portugal acceded on the same day
>   (*The signatories are Great Britain, France, Spain, and Portugal*)
> *Main entry under the uniform title for the treaty*
> *Added entry under the heading for Great Britain with uniform title*
>   *for the treaty*

> Universal Copyright Convention : with protocols 1, 2, and 3 :
> Geneva, September 6, 1952. − London : H.M.S.O., 1952
>   (*Drawn up by the Intergovernmental Conference on Copyright; the*
>   *United States and Canada are signatories*)
> *Main entry under the uniform title for the treaty*
> *Added entry under the heading for the United Kingdom (as*
>   *publisher) with uniform title for the treaty*
> *Added entry under the heading for Canada with uniform title for the*
>   *treaty*
>   (*Cataloguing agency in Canada*)
> *Added entry under the heading for the United States with uniform*
>   *title for the treaty*
>   (*Cataloguing agency in the United States*)
> *Added entry under the heading for the conference*

21.35B. Agreements contracted by international intergovernmental bodies

21.35B1. Enter as instructed in 21.35A an agreement between an international
intergovernmental body and one or more:

  a) other international intergovernmental bodies

or b) national governments
or c) jurisdictions other than national governments
or d) other corporate bodies.

In the case of c) and d) do not add uniform titles to either main or added entry headings.

> Guarantee agreement, Second Agricultural Project, between Republic of Iceland and International Bank for Reconstruction and Development
> *Main entry under the heading for Iceland with uniform title for the treaty*
> *Added entry under the heading for the bank with uniform title for the treaty*

> Agreement between the United Nations and the Food and Agriculture Organisation of the United Nations and the United Kingdom as administering power of the territories of Cyrenaica and Tripolitania regarding technical assistance for Cyrenaica and Tripolitania
> *Main entry under the heading for the Food and Agriculture Organisation with uniform title for the treaty*
> *Added entries under the headings for the United Kingdom and the United Nations, each with uniform title for the treaty*

> Project agreement (First Urban Sewerage Project) between International Bank for Reconstruction and Development and District de Tunis
> *Main entry under the heading for the bank*
> *Added entry under the heading for the district*

> Loan agreement, Paper and Pulp Project, between International Bank for Reconstruction and Development and Corporación de Fomento de la Producción and Compañía Manufacturera de Papeles y Cartones
> *Main entry under the heading for the bank*
> *Added entries under the headings for the corporation and the company*

Enter an agreement contracted by the member governments of an international intergovernmental body acting as individual entities rather than collectively as instructed in 21.35A.

> Agreement creating an association between the member states of the European Free Trade Association and the Republic of Finland
> .... – London : H.M.S.O., 1961
> > (*The signatories are the seven members of EFTA acting individually and Finland*)
> *Main entry under the uniform title for the treaty*
> *Added entries under the headings for the United Kingdom (as publisher) and Finland, each with uniform title for the treaty*

21.35C. Agreements contracted by the Holy See

21.35C1. Enter a concordat, *modus vivendi*, convention, or other formal agreement between the Holy See and a national government or other political jurisdiction under the party whose catalogue entry heading (see 24.3E) is first in English alphabetic order. Make an added entry under the heading for the other party. Add uniform titles as instructed in 25.16B1 to the main and added entry headings.

> Das Konkordat zwischen dem Heiligen Stuhle und dem
> Freistaate Baden
> *Main entry under the heading for Baden with uniform title for the*
> *treaty*
> *Added entry under the heading for the Catholic Church with*
> *uniform title for the treaty*

> Concordato celebrado entre su santidad Pío IX y el gobierno de
> Ecuador
> *Main entry under the heading for the Catholic Church with uniform*
> *title for the treaty*
> *Added entry under the heading for Ecuador with uniform title for*
> *the treaty*

21.35D. Other agreements involving jurisdictions

21.35D1. Enter an agreement between two or more jurisdictions below the national level, or between a national government and one or more jurisdictions within its country, as instructed in 21.6C.

> Memorandum of agreement between the government of the
> province of Ontario and the government of Canada pursuant to
> section 4(3) of the Anti-Inflation Act
> *Main entry under the heading for Ontario*
> *Added entry under the heading for Canada*

> Joint agreement between the state of Maine and the province of
> New Brunswick
> *Main entry under the heading for Maine*
> *Added entry under the heading for New Brunswick*

21.35D2. Enter an agreement involving jurisdictions below the national level and international intergovernmental bodies as instructed in 21.35B.

21.35D3. Enter an agreement between a national government and one or more jurisdictions below the national level outside its country as instructed in 21.35A, but do not add uniform titles to either main or added entry headings.

> Protocole relatif aux échanges entre le Québec et la France en
> matière d'éducation physique, de sport et d'éducation populaire :
> pris en application de l'entente franco-québécoise du 27 février

1965 sur un programme d'échange et de coopération dans le
domaine de l'éducation
Main entry under the heading for France
Added entry under the heading for Québec

21.35D4. Enter an agreement between a government at any level and a non-governmental corporate body as instructed in 21.6C. For agreements involving international intergovernmental bodies, see 21.35B.

Master agreement (PIPSC) : agreement between the Treasury
Board and the Professional Institute of the Public Service of
Canada
Main entry under the heading for the board
Added entry under the heading for the institute

Concession agreement between the Government of the Republic
of Liberia and Liberia Iron and Steel Corporation
Main entry under the heading for the government
Added entry under the heading for the corporation

21.35E. Protocols, amendments, etc.

21.35E1. Enter a separately published protocol, amendment, extension, or other agreement ancillary to a treaty, etc., under the heading for the basic agreement. Add uniform titles as instructed in 25.16B3.

21.35E2. Treat a general revision of a treaty, etc., as an independent work. Make an added entry under the heading for the revised treaty, etc., if the headings differ. Add uniform titles as appropriate.

21.35F. Collections

21.35F1. If a collection of treaties, etc., consists of those contracted between two parties, enter it under the heading for the one party in the same way as a single agreement between those parties (see 21.35A1, 21.35B–21.35E). Add uniform titles to the headings for the parties as instructed in 25.16A1. If such a collection has become known by a collective name, enter it under the uniform title for the name (see 25.16A1). Make an added entry under the heading for a compiler named prominently in the item being catalogued.

21.35F2. If a collection of treaties, etc., consists of those contracted between one party and two or more other parties, enter it under the heading for the one party. Make added entries under the headings for the other parties if there are two of them. Add uniform titles as instructed in 25.16A1 to the main and added entry headings for the parties. If such a collection has become known by a collective name, enter it under the uniform title for the name (see 25.16A1). Make an added entry under the heading for a compiler named prominently in the item being catalogued.

Treaties and other international agreements of the United States
of America, 1776-1949 / compiled under the direction of Charles I.
Bevans
*Main entry under the heading for the United States with uniform title
for the treaties*
Added entry under the heading for Bevans

21.35F3. Enter any other collection of treaties, etc., as a collection (see 21.7).

21.36. COURT DECISIONS, CASES, ETC.

21.36A. Law reports

21.36A1. Reports of one court. Enter law reports of one court that are not ascribed to a reporter or reporters by name under:

    a) the heading for the court if the reports are issued by or under the au-
thority of the court
or b) title if they are not.

Make an added entry under the heading for an editor or compiler named prominently in the item being catalogued. Make an added entry under the heading for
the publisher if its responsibility extends beyond that of publication. Make an
added entry under the heading for the court if it is not chosen as the main entry
heading.

Canada Federal Court reports / editor, Florence Rosenfeld
    (*Issued by the court*)
Main entry under the heading for the court
Added entry under the heading for Rosenfeld

Reports of cases argued and determined in the Court of Appeals
of Arizona . . . . – St. Paul : West Pub. Co.
    (*Publisher acts in an editorial capacity*)
Main entry under title
Added entries under the headings for the court and the publisher

Enter reports of one court that are ascribed to a reporter or to reporters by
name under the heading for the court or under the heading for the reporter or
first named reporter according to whichever is used as the basis for accepted legal
citation practice in the country where the court is located. If that practice cannot
be determined readily, enter under:

    a) the heading for the court if the reports are issued by or under the au-
thority of the court
or b) the heading for the reporter or first named reporter if they are not.

Make an added entry under the heading for the court or the reporter, whichever
is not chosen as the main entry heading. Make an added entry under the heading
for an editor, compiler, or additional reporter named prominently in the item
being catalogued. Make an added entry under the heading for the publisher if
its responsibility extends beyond that of publication.

370

Reports of cases determined in the Supreme Court of the state of California, October 23, 1969, to January 30, 1970 / Robert E. Formichi, reporter of decisions. — San Francisco : Bancroft-Whitney
(*Cited as* California reports)
Main entry under the heading for the court
Added entry under the heading for Formichi

Common bench reports : cases argued and determined in the Court of Common Pleas / [reported] by James Manning, T.C. Granger, and John Scott. — London : Benning
(*Cited as* Manning, Granger & Scott)
Main entry under the heading for Manning
Added entries under the headings for Granger, Scott, and the court

21.36A2. Reports of more than one court. Enter reports of more than one court under the heading for the reporter if responsible for the reports of all the cases reported. If there is more than one reporter, apply the instructions in 21.6. If the reporter(s) is not responsible for all the reports, or if no reporter is named in the chief source of information of the item being catalogued, enter under title. Make an added entry under the heading for the reporter named first in the chief source of information. Make added entries under the headings for the courts if there are two or three. If there are four or more, make an added entry under the heading for the court named first in the chief source of information. Make an added entry under the heading for an editor or compiler or a corporate body involved in the publication named prominently in the item being catalogued unless, in the latter case, it functions solely as the publisher.

Reports of cases argued and determined in the Courts of Common Pleas, and Exchequer Chamber, and in the House of Lords ... / by John Bernard Bosanquet and Christopher Puller
Main entry under the heading for Bosanquet
Added entries under the headings for Puller and the courts
    (*including the House of Lords*)

Australian law reports : being reports of judgments of the High Court of Australia and the Judicial Committee of the Privy Council and of state supreme courts exercising federal jurisdiction, other federal courts and tribunals, together with selected cases from the Supreme Court of the Northern Territory and reports of the Supreme Court of the Australian Capital Territory (authorized by the judges) / editor, Robert Hayes
(*The report for each case signed by its reporter*)
Main entry under title
Added entries under the headings for Hayes and the High Court

21.36B. Citations, digests, etc.

21.36B1. Enter citations to, and digests and indexes of, court reports under the heading for the person responsible for them if that person is named prominently in the item being catalogued. Otherwise, enter under title. Make an added entry

371

under the heading for a prominently named corporate body involved in the publication unless it functions solely as the publisher.

> Connecticut digest, 1785 to date ... / by Richard H. Phillips
> *Main entry under the heading for Phillips*

> Michie's digest of Virginia and West Virginia reports ... / under the editorial supervision of A. Hewson Michie
> *Main entry under the heading for Michie*

> Atlantic reporter digest, 1764 to date ... covering Atlantic reporter and corresponding cases in the reports of the Atlantic States ... . — St. Paul, Minn. : West Pub. Co., 1939-
>   (*Publisher acts in an editorial capacity*)
> *Main entry under title*
> *Added entry under the heading for the publisher*

21.36C. Particular cases

21.36C1. Proceedings in the first instance. Criminal proceedings. Enter the official proceedings and records of criminal trials, impeachments, courts-martial, etc., under the heading for the person or body prosecuted. If more than one person or body is prosecuted, apply the instructions in 21.6C. *Optionally*, add the appropriate legal designation (e.g., *defendant*, *libellee*) to the heading for a person or body prosecuted. Make an added entry under the heading for the court or other adjudicating body. Make an added entry under the heading for a reporter named prominently in the item being catalogued. Do not make an added entry under the heading for the jurisdiction bringing the prosecution.

> Report of the trial of Leavitt Alley, indicted for the murder of Abijah Ellis, in the Supreme Judicial Court of Massachusetts / reported by Franklin Fiske Heard
> *Main entry under the heading for Alley as defendant*
> *Added entries under the headings for the court and Heard*

> Report of the trial of Brig. General William Hull, commanding the North-western Army of the United States, by a court martial held at Albany on Monday, 3rd January, 1814, and succeeding days / taken by Lieut. Col. Forbes
> *Main entry under the heading for Hull as defendant*
> *Added entries under the headings for the court-martial and for Forbes*

> Report of the case of the steamship Meteor, libelled for alleged violation of the Neutrality Act ... / edited by F.V. Balch
> *Main entry under the heading for the ship as libellee*
> *Added entries under the headings for the various courts whose actions are reported and for Balch*

21.36C2. Proceedings in the first instance. Other proceedings. Enter the official proceedings and records of civil and other noncriminal proceedings in the first instance (including election cases) under the heading for the person or body bringing the action. If more than one person or body brings the action, apply the instructions in 21.6C. Make added entries under the headings for the persons or bodies on the opposing side if there are one, two, or three. If there are four or more persons or bodies on the opposing side, make an added entry under the heading for the one named first in the item being catalogued. *Optionally*, add the appropriate legal designation (e.g., *plaintiff, complainant, contestant, defendant, respondent, contestee*) to the heading for a party to the action. Make an added entry under the heading for the court or other adjudicating body. Make an added entry under the heading for a prominently named reporter.

> The case of William Brooks versus Ezekiel Byam and others, in equity, in the Circuit Court of the United States, for the First Circuit—District of Massachusetts
> *Main entry under the heading for Brooks as complainant*
> *Added entry under the heading for Byam as respondent*
> *Added entry under the heading for the court*

> Contested election case of John A. Smith, contestant, v. Edwin Y. Webb, contestee, from the Ninth Congressional District of North Carolina, before Committee on Elections No. 2
> *Main entry under the heading for Smith as contestant*
> *Added entry under the heading for Webb as contestee*
> *Added entry under the heading for the committee*

> The Goodwin Film and Camera Company, complainant, vs. Eastman Kodak Company, defendant
> > (*Case heard before the United States Circuit Court, Western District of New York*)
> *Main entry under the heading for the Goodwin Film and Camera Company as complainant*
> *Added entry under the heading for the Eastman Kodak Company as defendant*
> *Added entry under the heading for the court*

21.36C3. Appeal proceedings. Enter the official proceedings and records of appeal proceedings in the same way as the proceedings in the first instance. *Optionally*, add the legal designation appropriate to the appeal to that appropriate in the first instance (e.g., *defendant-appellee, defendant-appellant*).

> The Goodwin Film and Camera Company, complainant-appellee, vs. Eastman Kodak Company, defendant-appellant : transcript of record
> > (*Appeal heard before the United States Circuit Court of Appeals for the Second Circuit*)
> *Main entry under the heading for the Goodwin Film and Camera Company as complainant-appellee*
> *Added entry under the heading for the Eastman Kodak Company as defendant-appellant*
> *Added entry under the heading for the court*

21.36C4. Indictments. Enter an indictment as instructed in 21.36C1.

> Copy of an indictment (No. 1) in the Circuit Court of the United
> States in and for the Pennsylvania District of the Middle Circuit
> > (*Indictment of William Duane*)
> *Main entry under the heading for Duane as defendant*
> *Added entry under the heading for the court*

21.36C5. Charges to juries. Enter a charge to a jury under the heading for the court. Make an added entry under the heading for the judge delivering the charge. Make added entries under the headings for the first named party on each side, except for the jurisdiction in cases prosecuted by the jurisdiction. *Optionally*, add legal designations (see 21.36C1–21.36C3) to the added entry headings.

> The charge of Judge Patterson [i.e. Paterson] to the jury in the
> case of Vanhorne's lessee against Dorrance : tried at a Circuit
> Court for the United States, held at Philadelphia, April term, 1795
> > (*The lessee is not named*)
> *Main entry under the heading for the court*
> *Added entry under the heading for Dorrance as defendant*
> *Added entries under the headings for Paterson and Van Horne*

21.36C6. Judicial decisions. Enter a judgement or other decision of a court in a case under the heading for the court. Make an added entry under the heading for the first named party on each side, except for the jurisdiction in cases prosecuted by the jurisdiction. *Optionally*, add legal designations (see 21.36C1–21.36C3) to the added entry headings.

> Freedom of the press : opinion of the Supreme Court of the
> United States in the case of Alice Lee Grosjean, supervisor of
> public accounts for the state of Louisiana, appellant, v. American
> Press Company, Inc., et al.
> *Main entry under the heading for the court*
> *Added entries under the headings for the American Press Company*
> > *as plaintiff-appellee and Grosjean as defendant-appellant*

21.36C7. Judicial opinions. Enter an opinion of a judge under the heading for the judge. Make an added entry under the heading for the first named party on each side, except for the jurisdiction in cases prosecuted by the jurisdiction. *Optionally*, add legal designations (see 21.36C1–21.36C3) to the added entry headings.

> Dissenting opinion of Hon. Milton Sutliff, one of the judges : ex
> parte Simeon Bushnell : ex parte Charles Langston : on habeas
> corpus
> > (*At head of title:* Supreme Court of Ohio)
> *Main entry under the heading for Sutliff*
> *Added entry under the heading for Bushnell as defendant*

21.36C8. Records of one party. Enter a brief, plea, or other formal record of one party to a case under the heading for that party. If that party is not the one under which the proceedings of the trial would be entered (see 21.36C1–21.36C3), make an added entry under the heading for the other party (parties). *Optionally*, add legal designations (see 21.36C1–21.36C3) to the headings for the parties to the action. Make an added entry under the heading for the lawyer concerned.

> George B. Morewood, John R. Morewood, Frederic R. Routh, respondents, appellants versus Lorenzo N. Encquist, libellant, appellee : brief for appellants on admiralty jurisdiction / Robert Dodge, attorney for appellants
>   (*At head of title:* Supreme Court of the United States, no. 132)
> *Main entry under the heading for G. Morewood as respondent-appellant*
> *Added entries under the headings for J. Morewood as respondent-appellant, Routh as respondent-appellant, and Enequist as libellant-appellee*
> *Added entry under the heading for Dodge*

Enter a courtroom argument presented by a lawyer under the heading for the lawyer. Make an added entry under the heading for the party represented. If that party is not the one under which the proceedings of the trial would be entered (see 21.36C1–21.36C3), make an added entry under the heading for the other party (parties). *Optionally*, add legal designations (see 21.36C1–21.36C3) to the headings for the parties to the action.

> Argument of Franklin B. Gowen, Esq., of counsel for the Commonwealth in the case of the Commonwealth vs. Thomas Munley, indicted in the Court of Oyer and Terminer of Schuykill County, Pa., for the murder of Thomas Sanger ... / stenographically reported by R.A. West
> *Main entry under the heading for Gowen*
> *Added entry under the heading for Munley as defendant*

21.36C9. Collections. Enter a collection of the official proceedings or records of trials as a collection (see 21.7). Make added entries under the headings for the persons or bodies who are parties to all the trials if there are not more than three persons or bodies involved. *Optionally*, add legal designations (see 21.36C1–21.36C3) to the headings for the parties.

Certain Religious Publications

21.37. SACRED SCRIPTURES

21.37A. Enter a work that is accepted as sacred scripture by a religious group, or part of such a work, under title. When appropriate, use a uniform title as instructed in 25.17–25.18. Make an added entry under the heading for one, two, or three persons associated with the work and/or the item being catalogued. If there are four or more such persons, do not make added entries.

> The Book of Mormon : an account written by the hand of Mormon upon plates taken from the plates of Nephi / translated by Joseph Smith, Jun.

Main entry under the uniform title for the work
Added entry under the heading for Smith

The Koran / translated from the Arabic by J.M. Rodwell
Main entry under the uniform title for the work
Added entry under the heading for Rodwell

The book of Isaiah
Main entry under the uniform title for the work
Added entry under the heading for Isaiah

21.37B. Treat a harmony of different scriptural passages as an edition of the passages harmonized. Make an added entry under the heading for the harmonizer. For harmonies accompanied by commentary, see 21.13.

The life of Our Lord / compiled from the Gospels of the four Evangelists and presented in the very words of the Scriptures as one continuous narrative by Reginald G. Ponsonby
Main entry under the uniform title for the Gospels
Added entry under the heading for Ponsonby

21.38. THEOLOGICAL CREEDS, CONFESSIONS OF FAITH, ETC.

21.38A. Enter a theological creed, confession of faith, etc., accepted by more than one denominational body under title. When appropriate, use a uniform title as instructed in 25.19B. Make an added entry under the heading for one, two, or three persons or corporate bodies associated with the work and/or item being catalogued. If there are four or more such persons or bodies, do not make added entries.

The Assembly's Shorter catechism as used in the Presbyterian Church in the United States
    (*The catechism of the Westminster Assembly of Divines*)
Main entry under the uniform title for the Shorter catechism
Added entries under the headings for the church and the Westminster
    Assembly of Divines

The Augsburg Confession / translated ... by Richard Taverner ... edited for the use of the Joint Committee of the General Council, the General Synod, and the United Synod of the South ... by Henry E. Jacobs
Main entry under the uniform title for the Augsburg Confession
Added entries under the headings for Taverner, the Joint Committee,
    and Jacobs

21.39. LITURGICAL WORKS

21.39A. General rule

21.39A1. Enter a liturgical work[11] under the heading for the church or denominational body to which it pertains. When appropriate, add a uniform title as

---

11. *Liturgical work* includes officially sanctioned or traditionally accepted texts of religious observance, books of obligatory prayers to be offered at stated times, calendars and manuals of performance of religious observances, and prayer books known as "books of hours."

instructed in 25.19–25.23 to the main entry heading. If the work is special to the use of a particular body within the church (e.g., a diocese, cathedral, monastery, religious order), make an added entry under the heading for that body.

> The book of common worship as authorised by the Synod 1962
> (*Liturgical work of the Church of South India*)
> *Main entry under the heading for the church with uniform title for the work*

> Horae diurnae Breviarii Romani ex decreto sacrosancti Concilii Tridentini restituti
> *Main entry under the heading for the Catholic Church with uniform title for the work*

> Missale ad vsum sacri et canonici Ordinis Praemonstratensis
> *Main entry under the heading for the Catholic Church with uniform title for the work*
> *Added entry under the heading for the order*

> Common service book of the Lutheran church / authorized by the United Lutheran Church in America
> *Main entry under the heading for the United Lutheran Church with uniform title for the work*

> The coronation service of Her Majesty Queen Elizabeth II
> *Main entry under the heading for the Church of England with uniform title for the work*

21.39A2. Enter an item consisting of readings from sacred scriptures intended for use in a religious service as instructed in 21.39A1. However, enter a single passage from a sacred scripture used in religious services as instructed in 21.37.

> Epistles and Gospels for Sundays and holy days / prepared, with the addition of brief exegetical notes, by the Catholic Biblical Association of America
> *Main entry under the heading for the Catholic Church with uniform title for the work*

> Proper lessons for the Sundays and holy days throughout the year
> (*Published with* The book of common prayer ... according to the use of the Protestant Episcopal Church in the United States of America)
> *Main entry under the heading for the church with uniform title for the work*

> Miserere mei, Deus : Psalm LI : the morning prayer (Day 10) of the Church of England
> *Main entry under the uniform title for* Psalm LI
> *Added entry under the heading for the church*

21.39A3. Enter the following types of works as instructed in the general rules (21.1–21.7):

a) books intended for private devotions (*but* enter prayer books known as "books of hours" as liturgical works)
b) hymnals for congregations and choirs
c) proposals for orders of worship not officially approved
d) unofficial manuals
e) programmes of religious services
f) lectionaries without scriptural texts.

21.39B. Liturgical works of the Orthodox Eastern Church

21.39B1. Enter a liturgical work in the original language of the liturgy published for the use of a national Orthodox Church or another autocephalous body within the Orthodox Eastern Church as instructed in 21.39A1.

> Trebnik. — Sofiia̯ : Sv. Sinod na Bŭlgarskata tsŭrkva
>   (*Romanized title and publication details*)
> *Main entry under the heading for the Bulgarian church with uniform
>   title for the work*

Enter any other Orthodox liturgical work under the heading for the church as a whole. When appropriate, add a uniform title as instructed in 25.19–25.23 to the main entry heading.

> The ferial Menaion, or, The book of services for the twelve great
> festivals and the New-Year's Day / translated from a Slavonian
> edition
> *Main entry under the heading for the Orthodox Eastern Church with
>   uniform title for the work*

21.39C. Jewish liturgical works

21.39C1. Enter a Jewish liturgical work under its title. When appropriate, use a uniform title as instructed in 25.21–25.22. If the work is special to the use of a particular body (association, congregation, synagogue, etc.), make an added entry under the heading for that body.

> The Jewish marriage service . . .
> *Main entry under title*

> Services of the heart : weekday, Sabbath, and festival services
> and prayers for home and synagogue / Union of Liberal and
> Progressive Synagogues
> *Main entry under title*
> *Added entry under the heading for the union*

HEADINGS FOR PERSONS

Contents

Choice of Name

Entry Element

Additions to Names

General

Additions to Distinguish Identical Names

Special Rules for Names in Certain Languages

Choice of Name

22.1. GENERAL RULE

22.1A. In general, choose, as the basis of the heading for a person, the name by which he or she is commonly known. This may be the person's real name, pseudonym, title of nobility, nickname, initials, or other appellation. Treat a roman numeral associated with a given name (as, for example, in the case of some popes, royalty, and ecclesiastics) as part of the name. For the treatment of the names of authors using one or more pseudonyms or a real name and one or more pseudonyms, see 22.2B. For the form of name used in headings, see 22.4–22.16.

      Caedmon

      William Shakespeare

      D.W. Griffith
not David Wark Griffith

      Jimmy Carter
not James Earl Carter

      Capability Brown
not Lancelot Brown

      Anatole France
not Jacques-Anatole Thibault

      Ouida
not Marie Louise de la Ramée

      H.D.
not Hilda Doolittle

      Giorgione
not Giorgio Barbarelli

      Fra Angelico
not Giovanni da Fiesole
      Guido da Siena

      Maria Helena
not Maria Helena Vaquinhas de Carvalho

      Duke of Wellington
not Arthur Wellesley

      John Julius Norwich
not Viscount Norwich

      Sister Mary Hilary

      Sister Mary Joseph Cahill

      Queen Elizabeth II

      Pope John Paul II

      Patriarch Maximos V

      Duke Robert III

22.1B. Determine the name by which a person is commonly known from the chief sources of information (see 1.0A) of works by that person issued in his or her language. If the person works in a nonverbal context (e.g., a painter, a sculptor) or is not known primarily as an author, determine the name by which he or she is commonly known from reference sources[1] issued in his or her language or country of residence or activity.

---

1. *Reference sources*, as used in this chapter, includes books and articles written about a person.

22.1C. Include any titles of nobility or terms of honour (see also 22.12) or words or phrases (see also 22.8 and 22.15) that commonly appear in association with the name either wholly or in part. For the treatment of other terms appearing in association with the name, see 22.19B.

> Sir Richard Acland
>
> Duke of Wellington
>
> Viscountess Astor
>
> Fra Bartolommeo
>
> Andrea del Castagno
>
> Sister Mary Joseph

22.1D. Diacritical marks and hyphens

22.1D1. Accents, etc. Include accents and other diacritical marks appearing in a name. Supply them if it is certain that they are integral to a name but have been omitted in the source(s) from which the name is taken.

> Jacques Lefèvre d'Étaples
>
> Éliphas Lévi
> (*Sometimes appears without diacritical marks*)

22.1D2. Hyphens. Retain hyphens between given names if they are used by the bearer of the name.

> Gian-Carlo Menotti
>
> Jean-Léon Jaurès

Include hyphens in romanized names if they are prescribed by the romanization system adopted by the cataloguing agency.

> Ch'oe Sin-dŏk
>
> Jung-lu
>
> Li Fei-kan

Omit a hyphen that joins one of a person's forenames to the surname.

> Lucien Graux
> (*Name appears as:* Lucien-Graux)

22.2. CHOICE AMONG DIFFERENT NAMES

22.2A. Predominant name

22.2A1. If a person (other than one using a pseudonym or pseudonyms, see 22.2B) is known by more than one name, choose the name by which the person is clearly most commonly known, if there is one. Otherwise, choose one name or form of name according to the following order of preference:

a) the name that appears most frequently in the person's works
b) the name that appears most frequently in reference sources
c) the latest name.

22.2B. Pseudonyms

22.2B1. One pseudonym. If all the works by one person appear under one pseudonym, choose the pseudonym. If the real name is known, make a reference from the real name to the pseudonym.

> Yukio Mishima
> *not*   Kimitake Hiraoka

> George Orwell
> *not*   Eric Arthur Blair

> Martin Ross
> *not*   Violet Frances Martin

> Nevil Shute
> *not*   Nevil Shute Norway

> Woody Allen
> *not*   Allen Stewart Konigsberg

For the treatment of a pseudonym used jointly by two or more persons, see 21.6D.

22.2B2. Separate bibliographic identities. If a person has established two or more bibliographic identities, as indicated by the fact that works of one type appear under one pseudonym and works of other types appear under other pseudonyms or the person's real name, choose, as the basis for the heading for each group of works, the name by which works in that group are identified. Make references to connect the names (see 26.2C and 26.2D). In case of doubt, do not consider a person to have separate bibliographic identities (for contemporary authors see also 22.2B3).

> J.I.M. Stewart
>   (*Real name used in "serious" novels and critical works*)
> Michael Innes
>   (*Pseudonym used in detective novels*)

> C. Day-Lewis
>   (*Real name used in poetic and critical works*)
> Nicholas Blake
>   (*Pseudonym used in detective novels*)

> Charles L. Dodgson
>   (*Real name used in works on mathematics and logic*)
> Lewis Carroll
>   (*Pseudonym used in literary works*)

22.2B3. Contemporary authors. If a contemporary author uses more than one pseudonym or his or her real name and one or more pseudonyms, use, as the basis for the heading for each work, the name appearing in it. Make references to connect the names (see 26.2C and 26.2D).

> Ed McBain
> Evan Hunter
> (*Pseudonyms used by the same person*)

> Philippa Carr
> Victoria Holt
> Kathleen Kellow
> Jean Plaidy
> Ellalice Tate
> (*Pseudonyms used by the same person*)

> Howard Fast
> (*Real name used in some works*)
> E.V. Cunningham
> (*Pseudonym used in some works*)

> Molly Keane
> (*Real name used in some works*)
> M.J. Farrell
> (*Pseudonym used in some works*)

> Denys Watkins-Pitchford
> (*Real name used in some works*)
> BB
> (*Pseudonym used in some works*)

> Kingsley Amis
> (*Real name used in most works*)
> Robert Markham
> (*Pseudonym used in one work*)

If, in the works of contemporary authors, different names appear in different editions of the same work or two or more names appear in one edition, choose, for all editions, the name most frequently used in editions of the work. If that cannot be determined readily, choose the name appearing in the latest available edition of the work. Make name-title references from the other name or names (see 26.2B1).

> The rising tide / M.J. Farrell
> (*Two editions known. The later published under the name* Molly Keane)
> *Use* Molly Keane *as the basis for the heading*
> *Make a name-title reference using* M.J. Farrell *as the basis for the reference*

> Cut thin to win / Erle Stanley Gardner as A.A. Fair
> (*Two editions known. One published under the name* A.A. Fair, *the later as above*)
> *Use* Erle Stanley Gardner *as the basis for the heading*
> *Make a name-title reference using* A.A. Fair *as the basis for the reference*

22.2B4. If a person using more than one pseudonym or his or her real name and one or more pseudonyms

neither   has established separate bibliographic identities (see 22.2B2)
    nor   is a contemporary author (see 22.2B3)

choose, as the basis for the heading, the name by which that person has come to be identified in later editions of his or her works, in critical works, or in other reference sources[2] (in that order of preference). Make references from other names.

> Shimei Futabatei
> *not*   Tatsunosuke Hasegawa

> R.S. Surtees
> *not*   Author of Mr. Sponge's sporting tour

22.2C. Change of name

22.2C1. If a person (other than one using a pseudonym or pseudonyms) has changed his or her name, choose the latest name or form of name unless there is reason to believe that an earlier name will persist as the name by which the person is better known. Follow the same rule for a person who has acquired and become known by a title of nobility (see also 22.6).

> Dorothy Belle Hughes
> *not*   Dorothy Belle Flanagan
>   (*Name used in works before author's marriage*)

> Sister Mary Just
> *not*   Florence Didiez David
>   (*Name used in works before author entered a religious order*)

> Éloi-Gérard Talbot
> *not*   Frère Éloi-Gérard
>   (*Name without surname originally used in works*)

> Akiko Yosano
> *not*   Akiko Hō
>   (*Name used in works before author's marriage*)

> Jacqueline Onassis
> *not*   Jacqueline Bouvier
> Jacqueline Kennedy
>   (*Names used before marriage and during first marriage*)

> Ford Madox Ford
> *not*   Ford Madox Hueffer
>   (*Name changed from* Hueffer *to* Ford)

> Muhammad Ali
> *not*   Cassius Clay
>   (*Name changed from* Cassius Clay *to* Muhammad Ali)

---

2. Disregard reference sources that always enter persons under their real names.

> Earl of Longford
> *not* Francis Aungier Pakenham
> > (*Known successively by personal name, title as baron, and title as earl; best known by latest title*)
>
> Benjamin Disraeli
> *not* Earl of Beaconsfield
> > (*Title acquired late in life; better known by earlier name*)

22.3. CHOICE AMONG DIFFERENT FORMS OF THE SAME NAME

22.3A. Fullness

22.3A1. If the forms of a name vary in fullness, choose the form most commonly found. As required, make references from the other form(s).

> J. Barbey d'Aurevilly
> > (*Most common form:* J. Barbey d'Aurevilly)
> > (*Occasional forms:* Jules Barbey d'Aurevilly; Jules-Amédée Barbey d'Aurevilly)
> > (*Rare form:* J.-A. Barbey d'Aurevilly)
>
> Morris West
> > (*Most common form:* Morris West)
> > (*Occasional form:* Morris L. West)
>
> Juan Valera
> > (*Most common form:* Juan Valera)
> > (*Occasional form:* Juan Valera y Alcala Galiano)

If no one form predominates, choose the latest form. In case of doubt about which is the latest form, choose the fuller or fullest form.

22.3B. Language

22.3B1. Persons using more than one language. If the name of a person who has used more than one language appears in different language forms in his or her works, choose the form corresponding to the language of most of the works.

> George Mikes
> *not* György Mikes
>
> Philippe Garigue
> *not* Philip Garigue

If, however, one of the languages is Latin or Greek, apply 22.3B2.

In case of doubt, choose the form most commonly found in reference sources of the person's country of residence or activity. For persons identified by a well-established English form of name, see 22.3B3. If the name chosen is written in a nonroman script, see 22.3C.

22.3B2. Names in vernacular and Greek or Latin forms. If a name occurs in reference sources and/or in the person's works in a Greek or Latin form as well as in a form in the person's vernacular, choose the form most commonly found in reference sources.

> Sixt Birck
> *not*　Xystus Betulius

> Hugo Grotius
> *not*　Hugo de Groot

> Philipp Melanchthon
> *not*　Philipp Schwarzerd

> Friedrich Wilhelm Ritschl
> *not*　Fridericus Ritschelius

In case of doubt, choose the Latin or Greek form for persons who were active before, or mostly before, A.D. 1400. For persons active after that date, choose the vernacular form.

> Guilelmus Arvernus
> *not*　Guillaume d'Auvergne
> 　　(*Died 1249*)

> Giovanni da Imola
> *not*　Joannes de Imola
> 　　(*Died 1436*)

22.3B3. Names written in the roman alphabet and established in an English form. Choose the English form of name for a person entered under given name, etc. (see 22.8) or for a Roman of classical times (see 22.9A) whose name has become well established in an English form in English-language reference sources.

> Saint Francis of Assisi
> *not*　San Francesco d'Assisi

> Pope John XXIII
> *not*　Joannes Papa XXIII

> Horace
> *not*　Quintus Horatius Flaccus

> Pliny the Elder
> *not*　C. Plinius Secundus

> Charles V
> *not*　Karl V
> 　　　Carlos I

> King Philip II
> *not*　Rey Felipe II

> John Sobieski
> *not*　Jan III Sobieski

In case of doubt, use the vernacular or Latin form.

> Sainte Thérèse de Lisieux
> *not*　Saint Theresa of Lisieux

22.3B4. Other names. In all cases of names found in different language forms and not covered by 22.3B1–22.3B3, choose the form most frequently found in reference sources of the person's country of residence or activity.

> Hildegard Knef
>
> *not* Hildegarde Neff

22.3C. Names written in a nonroman script[3]

22.3C1. Persons entered under given name, etc. Choose the form of name that has become well-established in English-language reference sources for a person entered under given name, etc. (see 22.8) whose name is in a language written in a nonroman script. If variant English-language forms are found, choose the form that occurs most frequently. As required, make references from other forms.

> Alexander the Great
>
> *not* Alexandros ho Megas
>
> Avicenna
>
> *not* al-Ḥusayn ibn 'Abd Allāh ibn Sīnā
>
> Empress Catherine II
>
> *not* Imperatritsa Ekaterina II
>
> Confucius
>
> *not* K'ung-tzu
>
> Homer
>
> *not* Homeros
> Homerus
>
> Isaiah the Prophet
>
> *not* Yesha'yahu
>
> Maimonides
>
> *not* Moses ben Maimon
> Mosheh ben Maimon
>
> Theodore Metochites
>
> *not* Theodōros Metochitēs
>
> Omar Khayyam
>
> *not* 'Umar Khayyām
>
> King Paul I
>
> *not* Vasileus Paulos I

If no English romanization is found, or if no one romanization predominates, romanize the name according to the table for the language adopted by the cataloguing agency.

---

3. Systematic romanizations used in the examples in this chapter follow the tables (published by the Library of Congress in *Cataloging Service,* bulletin 118–   ) adopted jointly by the American Library Association, the Canadian Library Association, and the Library of Congress.

22.3C2. Persons entered under surname.[4] If the name of a person entered under surname (see 22.5) is written in a nonroman script, romanize the name according to the table for the language adopted by the cataloguing agency. Add vowels to names that are not vocalized. As required, make references from other romanized forms.

>　　　Lin Yü-t'ang
> *not*　Lin Yutang

>　　　Jamāl 'Abd al-Nāṣir
> *not*　Gamal Abdel Nasser

>　　　P.S. Irāmaccantiraṉ
> *not*　P.S. Ramachandran

>　　　Yi Sŭng-man
> *not*　Syngman Rhee

>　　　A.N. Skri͡abin
> *not*　A.N. Scriabin

>　　　Evgeniĭ Evtushenko
> *not*　Yevgeny Yevtushenko

>　　　Mosheh Dayan
> *not*　Moshe Dayan

---

4. *Alternative rule.* This alternative rule may be applied selectively language by language.
Persons entered under surname. Choose the romanized form of name that has become well-established in English-language reference sources for a person entered under surname (see 22.5) whose name is in a language written in a nonroman script. For a person who uses Hebrew or Yiddish and whose name is not found to be well-established in English-language reference sources, choose the romanized form appearing in his or her works.

If variant romanized forms are found in English-language reference sources, choose the form that occurs most frequently.

As required, make references from other romanized forms.

>　　　Lin Yutang
> *not*　Lin Yü-t'ang

>　　　Gamal Abdel Nasser
> *not*　Jamāl 'Abd al-Nāṣir

>　　　P.S. Ramachandran
> *not*　P.S. Irāmaccantiraṉ

>　　　Syngman Rhee
> *not*　Yi Sŭng-man

>　　　A.N. Scriabin
> *not*　A.N. Skri͡abin

>　　　Yevgeny Yevtushenko
> *not*　Evgeniĭ Evtushenko

>　　　Moshe Dayan
> *not*　Mosheh Dayan

>　　　Shlomit Cohen
> *not*　Shelomit Kohen

> Shelomit Kohen
> *not* Shlomit Cohen

If the name of a person is found only in a romanized form in his or her works, use it as found.

> Ghaoutsi Bouali
> *not* Ghawthī 'Abū 'Alī

If such a person's name is found in more than one romanized form in his or her works, choose the form that occurs most frequently.

If a name is written in more than one nonroman script, romanize it according to the table for the original language of most of the works. As required, make references from other romanized forms.

> 'Alī Muḥammad Irtiẓā
> *not* 'Alī Muḥammad Irtiḍā
> > (*Wrote primarily in Persian but also in Arabic*)

> Raghunātha Sūri
> *not* Irakunātasūri
> > (*Wrote primarily in Sanskrit but also in Tamil*)

In case of doubt as to which of two or more languages written in the Arabic script should be used for the romanization, base the choice on the nationality of the person or the language of the area of residence or activity. If these criteria do not apply, choose (in this order of preference): Urdu, Arabic, Persian, any other language.

22.3D. Spelling

22.3D1. If variant spellings of a person's name are found and these variations are not the result of different romanizations, choose the form resulting from an official change in orthography, or, if this does not apply, choose the predominant spelling. In case of doubt, choose the spelling found in the first item catalogued. For spelling differences resulting from different romanizations, see 22.3C.

Entry Element

22.4. GENERAL RULE

22.4A. If a person's name (chosen according to 22.1–22.3) consists of several parts, select as the entry element that part of the name under which the person would normally be listed in authoritative alphabetic lists[5] in his or her language or country of residence or activity. In applying this general rule, follow the instructions in 22.5–22.9. If, however, a person's preference is known to be different from the normal usage, follow that preference in selecting the entry element.

---

5. *Authoritative alphabetic lists* means publications of the "who's who" type, not telephone directories or similar compilations.

22.4B. Order of elements

22.4B1. If the entry element is the first element of the name, enter the name in direct order.

> **Ram Gopal**

22.4B2. If the first element is a surname, follow it by a comma.

> **Chiang, Kai-shek**
> (*Name:* Chiang Kai-shek)
> (*Surname:* Chiang)
>
> **Molnár, Ferenc**
> (*Name:* Molnár Ferenc)
> (*Surname:* Molnár)
>
> **Trịnh, Vân Thanh**
> (*Name:* Trịnh Vân Thanh)
> (*Surname:* Trịnh)

22.4B3. If the entry element is not the first element of the name, transpose the elements of the name preceding the entry element. Follow the entry element by a comma.

> **Cassatt, Mary**
> (*Name:* Mary Cassatt)

22.4B4. If the entry element is the proper name in a title of nobility (see 22.6), follow it by the personal name in direct order and then by the part of the title denoting rank. Precede the personal name and the part of the title denoting rank by commas.

> **Leighton, Frederick Leighton,** *Baron*
>
> **Caradon, Hugh Foot,** *Baron*

22.5. ENTRY UNDER SURNAME

22.5A. General rule

22.5A1. Enter a name containing a surname or consisting only of a surname under that surname unless subsequent rules (e.g., 22.6, 22.10, 22.28) provide for entry under a different element.

> **Bernhardt, Sarah**
>
> **Fitzgerald, Ella**
>
> **Byatt, A.S.**
>
> **Ching, Francis K.W.**
>
> **Mantovani**

If the surname is represented by an initial, but at least one element of the name is given in full, enter under the initial that represents the surname.

G., Michael

22.5B. Element other than the first treated as a surname[6]

22.5B1. If the name does not contain a surname but contains an element that identifies the individual and functions as a surname, enter under this element followed by a comma and the rest of the name.

Hus, Jan

Maḥfūẓ, Ḥusayn ʻAlī

al-Bāshā, ʻAbd al-Raḥmān

Ali, Muhammad
   (*The American boxer*)

X, Malcolm

Kurd ʻAlī, Muḥammad

22.5C. Compound surnames

22.5C1. Preliminary rule. The following rules deal with the entry of surnames consisting of two or more proper names (referred to as "compound surnames") and names that may or may not contain compound surnames. Apply the rules in the order given. Refer from elements of compound surnames not chosen as the entry element.

22.5C2. Preferred or established form known. Enter a name containing a compound surname under the element by which the person bearing the name prefers to be entered.[7] If this is unknown, enter the name under the element under which it is listed in reference sources[8] in the person's language or country of residence or activity.

Fénelon, François de Salignac de La Mothe-

---

6. For Islamic names, see 22.22, 22.26C1a, and 22.27.

7. Take regular or occasional initializing of an element preceding a surname as an indication that that element is not used as part of the surname.

> **Chavarri, Eduardo López**
> (*Name sometimes appears as:* Eduardo L. Chavarri)
>
> **Szentpál, Mária Sz.**
> (*Name appears as:* Sz. Szentpál Mária)
> (*Husband's surname:* Szilági)
>
> **Campbell, Julia Morilla de**
> (*Name sometimes appears as:* Julia M. de Campbell)

8. Disregard reference sources that list compound surnames in a uniform style regardless of preference or customary usage.

> **Lloyd George, David**
> (*Paternal surname:* George)

> **Machado de Assis, Joaquim Maria**
> (*Paternal surname:* de Assis)

22.5C3. Hyphenated surnames. If the elements of a compound surname are regularly or occasionally hyphenated, enter under the first element (see also 22.5E1).

> **Day-Lewis, C.**

> **Enäjärvi-Haavio, Elsa**

> **Chaput-Rolland, Solange**

> **Henry-Bordeaux, Paule**

> **Lykke-Seest, Hans**

> **Landová-Štychová, Luisa**

22.5C4. Other compound surnames, except those of married women whose surname consists of surname before marriage and husband's surname. Enter under the first element of the compound surname unless the person's language is Portuguese. If the person's language is Portuguese, enter under the last element.

> **Janković Mirijevski, Teodor**

> **Friis Møller, Kai**

> **Huber Noodt, Ulrich**

> **Johnson Smith, Geoffrey**

> **Hungry Wolf, Adolf**

> **Castres Saint Martin, Gaston**

> **Strauss und Torney, Lulu von**

> **Halasy Nagy, József**

> **Kőrösi Csoma, Sándor**

> **Imbriani Poerio, Matteo Renato**

> **Smitt Ingebretsen, Herman**

> **Budai Deleanu, Ion**

> **Cotarelo y Mori, Emilio**

> *but*   **Silva, Ovidio Saraiva de Carvalho e**

22.5C5. Other compound surnames. Married women whose surname consists of surname before marriage and husband's surname. Enter under the first element of the compound surname (regardless of its nature) if the person's language is Czech, French, Hungarian, Italian, or Spanish. In all other cases, enter under the husband's surname. For hyphenated names, see 22.5C3.

Semetkayné Schwanda, Magda
(*Language of person: Hungarian*)

Bonacci Brunamonti, Alinda
(*Language of person: Italian*)

Molina y Vedia de Bastianini, Delfina
(*Language of person: Spanish*)

but

Figueiredo, Adelpha Silva Rodrigues de
(*Language of person: Portuguese*)

Stowe, Harriet Beecher
(*Language of person: English*)

Wang Ma, Hsi-ch'un
(*Language of person: Chinese*)

22.5C6. Nature of surname uncertain. If a name has the appearance of a compound surname but its nature is not certain, treat it as a compound surname unless the language of the person is English, Danish, Faroese, Norwegian, or Swedish.

If the person's language is English, enter under the last part of the name and do not refer from the preceding part unless the name has been treated as a compound surname in reference sources.

Adams, John Crawford

Robertson, E. Arnot

If the person's language is Danish, Faroese, Norwegian, or Swedish, enter under the last part of the name and refer from the preceding part.

Mahrt, Haakon Bugge
x Bugge Mahrt, Haakon

Olsen, Ib Spang
x Spang Olsen, Ib

22.5C7. Place names added to surnames. Treat a place name added to a person's surname and connected to it by a hyphen as part of the surname (see 22.5C3).

Müller-Breslau, Heinrich

22.5C8. Words indicating relationship following surnames. Treat *Filho*, *Junior*, *Neto*, *Netto*, or *Sobrinho* following a Portuguese surname as part of the surname.

Castro Sobrinho, Antonio Ribeiro de

Marques Junior, Henrique

Omit similar terms (e.g., *Jr.*, *Sr.*, *fils*, *père*) occurring in languages other than Portuguese. If such a term is required to distinguish between two or more identical names, add it as instructed in 22.19B.

395

22.5D. Surnames with separately written prefixes

22.5D1. Articles and prepositions. If a surname includes an article or preposition or combination of the two, enter under the element most commonly used as entry element in alphabetically arranged directories, etc., in the person's language or country of residence or activity. The rules listed under languages and language groups below summarize entry element practice.

If such a name is listed in a nonstandard fashion in reference sources in the person's language or country of residence, enter under the entry element used in those sources.

If a person has used two or more languages, enter the name according to the language of most of that person's works. In case of doubt, follow the rules for English if English is one of the languages. Otherwise, if the person is known to have changed his or her country of residence, follow the rules for the language of the adopted country. As a last resort, follow the rules for the language of the name.

Languages and language groups:

AFRIKAANS. Enter under the prefix.

De Villiers, Anna Johanna Dorothea

Du Toit, Stephanus Johannes

Van der Post, Christiaan Willem Hendrik

Von Wielligh, Gideon Retief

CZECH AND SLOVAK. If the surname consists of a place name in the genitive case preceded by *z*, enter under the part following the prefix. Refer from the place name in the nominative case. Omit the *z* from the reference.

Žerotína, Karel z
    x Žerotín, Karel

DANISH. See Scandinavian languages.

DUTCH. If the surname is Dutch, enter under the part following the prefix unless the prefix is *ver*. In that case, enter under the prefix.

Aa, Pieter van der

Beeck, Leo op de

Braak, Menno ter

Brink, Jan ten

Driessche, Albert van

Hertog, Ary den

Hoff, Jacobus Henricus van 't

Wijngaert, Frank van den

Winter, Karel de

Ver Boven, Daisy

If the surname is not Dutch, enter the name of a Netherlander under the part following the prefix and the name of a Belgian according to the rules for the language of the name.

> **Faille, Jacob Baart de la**
> (*Netherlander*)

> **Long, Isaäc le**
> (*Netherlander*)

> **Du Jardin, Thomas**
> (*Belgian; French name*)

ENGLISH. Enter under the prefix.

> **À Beckett, Gilbert Abbott**

> **D'Anvers, Knightley**

> **De Morgan, Augustus**

> **De la Mare, Walter**

> **Du Maurier, Daphne**

> **Le Gallienne, Richard**

> **Van Buren, Martin**

> **Von Braun, Wernher**

FLEMISH. See Dutch.

FRENCH. If the prefix consists of an article or of a contraction of an article and a preposition, enter under the prefix.

> **Le Rouge, Gustave**

> **La Bruyère, René**

> **Du Méril, Édélestand Pontas**

> **Des Granges, Charles-Marc**

Otherwise, enter under the part of the name following the preposition.

> **Aubigné, Théodore Agrippa d'**

> **Musset, Alfred de**

> **La Fontaine, Jean de**

GERMAN. If the name is German and the prefix consists of an article or of a contraction of an article and a preposition, enter under the prefix.

> **Am Thym, August**

> **Aus'm Weerth, Ernst**

> **Vom Ende, Erich**

> **Zum Busch, Josef Paul**
>
> **Zur Linde, Otto**

Follow the same rule for Dutch names with a prefix consisting of an article or of a contraction of an article and a preposition.

> **De Boor, Hans Otto**
>   (*Name of Dutch origin*)
>
> **Ten Bruggencate, Paul**
>   (*Name of Dutch origin*)

Enter other German and Dutch names under the part of the name following the prefix.

> **Goethe, Johann Wolfgang von**
>
> **Mühll, Peter von der**
>
> **Urff, Georg Ludwig von und zu**

Enter names that are neither German nor Dutch according to the rules for the language of the name.

> **Du Bois-Reymond, Emil**
>
> **Le Fort, Gertrud**

ITALIAN. Enter modern names under the prefix.

> **A Prato, Giovanni**
>
> **D'Arienzo, Nicola**
>
> **Da Ponte, Lorenzo**
>
> **De Amicis, Pietro Maria**
>
> **Del Lungo, Isidoro**
>
> **Della Volpaia, Eufrosino**
>
> **Di Costanzo, Angelo**
>
> **Li Greci, Gioacchino**
>
> **Lo Savio, Niccolò**

For medieval and early modern names, consult reference sources about whether a prefix is part of a name. If a preposition is sometimes omitted from the name, enter under the part following the preposition. *De, de', degli, dei,* and *de li* occurring in names of the period are rarely part of the surname.

> **Alberti, Antonio degli**
>
> **Anghiera, Pietro Martire d'**
>
> **Medici, Lorenzo de'**

Do not treat the preposition in an Italian title of nobility used as an entry element (see 22.6A) as a prefix.

NORWEGIAN. See Scandinavian languages.

PORTUGUESE. Enter under the part of the name following the prefix.

Fonseca, Martinho Augusto da

Santos, João Adolpho dos

ROMANIAN. Enter under the prefix unless it is *de*. In that case, enter under the part of the name following the prefix.

A Mariei, Vasile

Pușcariu, Emil de

SCANDINAVIAN LANGUAGES. Enter under the part of the name following the prefix if the prefix is of Scandinavian, German, or Dutch origin (except for the Dutch *de*). If the prefix is the Dutch *de* or is of another origin, enter under the prefix.

Hallström, Gunnar Johannes af

Linné, Carl von

De Geer, Gerard

De la Gardie, Magnus Gabriel

La Cour, Jens Lassen

SLOVAK. See Czech and Slovak.

SPANISH. If the prefix consists of an article only, enter under it.

Las Heras, Manuel Antonio

Enter all other names under the part following the prefix.

Figueroa, Francisco de

Casas, Bartolomé de las

Río, Antonio del

SWEDISH. See Scandinavian languages.

22.5D2. Other prefixes. If the prefix is neither an article, nor a preposition, nor a combination of the two, enter under the prefix.

'Abd al-Ḥamīd, Aḥmad

Abū Zahrah, Muḥammad

Āl Yāsīn, Muḥammad Ḥasan

Ap Rhys Price, Henry Edward

Ben Maÿr, Berl

Ó Faoláin, Seán

Mac Muireadach, Niall Mór

22.5E. Prefixes hyphenated or combined with surnames

22.5E1. If the prefix is regularly or occasionally hyphenated or combined with the surname, enter the name under the prefix. As required, refer from the part of the name following the prefix.

> **FitzGerald, David**
>
> **MacDonald, William**
>
> **Tēr-Pōghosian, Petros**
>
> **Debure, Guillaume**
>   *x* Bure, Guillaume de
>
> **Fon-Lampe, A.A.**
>   *x* Lampe, A.A. Fon-

22.5F. Members of royal houses entered under surname, etc.

22.5F1. Enter the name of a member of a royal house no longer reigning or of a royal house that has lost or renounced its throne, and who is no longer identified as royalty, under surname or the part of the name by which he or she is identified in his or her works or in reference sources (e.g., name of the house or dynasty, territorial title) if there is no surname. Add titles that the person still uses as instructed in 22.12. Refer from the given name followed by the title as instructed in 22.16A1–22.16A4.

> **Bernadotte, Folke**
>   *x* Bernadotte af Wisborg, Folke, *greve*
>   *x* Folke, *Count Bernadotte of Wisborg*
>   *x* Wisborg, Folke Bernadotte, *greve af*
>
> **Habsburg, Otto**
>   *x* Otto, *Archduke of Austria*
>
> **Hohenzollern, Franz Joseph,** *Fürst von*
>   *x* Franz Joseph, *Prince of Hohenzollern*
>
> **Paris, Henri,** *comte de*
>   *x* Henri, *Count of Paris*
>
> **Wied, Maximilian,** *Prinz von*
>   *x* Maximilian, *Prince of Wied*

22.6. ENTRY UNDER TITLE OF NOBILITY

22.6A. General rule

22.6A1. Enter under the proper name in a title of nobility (including courtesy titles) if the person is commonly known by that title. Apply this rule to those persons who:

a) use their titles rather than their surnames in their works

or   b) are listed under their titles in reference sources.[9]

Follow the proper name in the title by the personal name (excluding unused forenames) in direct order and the term of rank[10] in the vernacular. Omit the surname and term of rank if the person does not use a term of rank or a substitute for it. Refer from the surname (see 26.2A3) unless the proper name in the title is the same as the surname.

> **Byron, George Gordon Byron,** *Baron*

> **Macaulay, Thomas Babington Macaulay,** *Baron*

> **Nairne, Carolina Nairne,** *Baroness*

> **Abrantès, Laure Junot,** *duchesse d'*
> *x* Junot, Laure, *duchesse d'Abrantès*

> **Bolingbroke, Henry St. John,** *Viscount*
> *x* St. John, Henry, *Viscount Bolingbroke*

> **Cavour, Camillo Benso,** *conte di*
> *x* Benso, Camillo, *conte di Cavour*

> **Willoughby de Broke, Richard Greville Verney,** *Baron*
> *x* Broke, Richard Greville Verney, *Baron Willoughby de*
> *x* Verney, Richard Greville, *Baron Willoughby de Broke*

> **Winchilsea, Anne Finch,** *Countess of*
> *x* Finch, Anne, *Countess of Winchilsea*

> **Monluc, Blaise de**
> (*Name appears as:* Blaise de Monluc)
> *x* Lasseran Massencome, Blaise de, *seigneur de Monluc*
> *x* Massencome, Blaise de Lasseran, *seigneur de Monluc*

> **Norwich, John Julius**
> (*Name appears as:* John Julius Norwich)
> *x* Cooper, John Julius, *Viscount Norwich*

22.6B. Special rules

22.6B1. Some titles in the United Kingdom peerage include a territorial designation that may or may not be an integral part of the title. If the territorial designation is an integral part of the title, include it.

> **Russell of Liverpool, Edward Frederick Langley Russell,** *Baron*

If it is not an integral part of the title, or if there is doubt that it is, omit it.

---

9. Disregard reference sources that list members of the nobility either all under title or all under surname.

10. The terms of rank in the United Kingdom peerage are *duke, duchess, marquess (marquis), marchioness, earl, countess, viscount, viscountess, baron,* and *baroness.* The heir of a British peer above the rank of baron usually takes the next to highest title of the peer during the peer's lifetime.

> **Bracken, Brendan Bracken,** *Viscount*
> *not*   Bracken of Christchurch, Brendan Bracken, *Viscount*

22.6B2. Apply 22.6A1 to judges of the Scottish Court of Session bearing a law title beginning with *Lord.*

> **Kames, Henry Home,** *Lord*
>   *x* Home, Henry, *Lord Kames*

22.6B3. If a person acquires a title of nobility, disclaims such a title, or acquires a new title of nobility, follow the instructions in 22.2C in choosing the name to be used as the basis for the heading.

> **Caradon, Hugh Foot,** *Baron*
>   (*Previously* Sir Hugh Foot)

> **George-Brown, George Brown,** *Baron*
>   (*Previously* George Brown)

> **Grigg, John**
>   (*Previously* Baron Altrincham; *peerage disclaimed*)

> **Hailsham of St. Marylebone, Quintin Hogg,** *Baron*
>   (*Originally* Quintin Hogg; *became* Viscount Hailsham, *1950; peerage disclaimed, 1963; became* Baron Hailsham of St. Marylebone, *1970*)

22.7. ENTRY UNDER ROMANIAN PATRONYMIC

22.7A. If a name of a person whose language is Romanian contains a patronymic with the suffix *ade*, enter under that patronymic.

> **Heliade Rădulescu, Ion**

22.8. ENTRY UNDER GIVEN NAME, ETC.[11]

22.8A. General rule

22.8A1. Enter a name that does not include a surname and that is borne by a person who is not identified by a title of nobility under the part of the name under which the person is listed in reference sources. In case of doubt, enter under the last element, following the instructions in 22.5B. Include in the name any words or phrases denoting place of origin, domicile, occupation, or other characteristics that are commonly associated with the name in works by the person or in reference sources. Precede such words or phrases by a comma. Refer, as appropriate, from the associated words or phrases, from variant forms of the name, and from other names by which the person is known.

> **John,** *the Baptist*

---

11. For Islamic names, see 22.22, 22.26C1, and 22.27.

Paulus, *Diaconus*
  x Paulus, *Casinensis*
  x Casinensis, Paulus
  x Paulus, *Levita*
  x Levita, Paulus
  x Paulus, *Warnefridus*
  x Warnefridus, Paulus
  x Paul, *the Deacon*
  x Paolo, *Diacono*

Iolo, *Goch*

Joannes, *Braidensis*
  x Braidensis, Joannes
  x Joannes, *de Brera*
  x Brera, Joannes de

Leonardo, *da Vinci*
  x Vinci, Leonardo da

Alexander, *of Aphrodisias*
  x Aphrodisias, Alexander of
  x Alexander, *Aphrodisiensis*
  x Alexander, *von Aphrodisias*
  x Alexandre, *d'Aphrodise*

Judah, *ha-Levi*
  x Halevi, Judah

Judas Iscariot
  x Iscariot, Judas

22.8A2. If a person with such a name is listed in reference sources by a part of the name other than the first, follow the instructions in 22.5B.

Planudes, Maximus

Helena, Maria

22.8B. Names including a patronymic

22.8B1. If a name consists of one or more given names and a patronymic, enter it under the first given name, followed by the rest of the name in direct order. If the patronymic precedes the given name(s), transpose the elements to bring the first given name into first position. Refer from the patronymic. For Icelandic names, see 22.9B.

'Abé Gubãnã
  (*Given name:* 'Abé)
  (*Patronymic:* Gubãnã)
  x Gubãnã, 'Abé

Solomon Gebre Christos
  (*Given name:* Solomon)
  (*Patronymic:* Gebre Christos)
  x Gebre Christos, Solomon

Kidāna Māryām Gétāhun
  (*Given names:* Kidāna Māryām)
  (*Patronymic:* Gétāhun)
  x Gétāhun, Kidāna Māryām

Gabra 'Iyasus H̲āyla Māryām
  (*Given names:* Gabra 'Iyasus)
  (*Patronymic:* H̲āyla Māryām)
  x H̲āyla Māryām, Gabra 'Iyasus

Isaac ben Aaron
  (*Given name:* Isaac)
  (*Patronymic:* ben Aaron)
  x Aaron, Isaac ben

Shirėndėv, B.
  (*Name appears as:* B. Shirėndėv)
  (*Initial of patronymic:* B.)
  (*Given name:* Shirėndėv)
  x B. Shirėndėv

Moses ben Jacob, *of Coucy*
  (*Given name:* Moses)
  (*Patronymic:* ben Jacob)
  (*Words denoting place:* of Coucy)
  x Jacob, Moses ben, *of Coucy*
  x Jacob, *of Coucy*, Moses ben
      (*To be made only when warranted in a particular
      catalogue*)

22.8C. Names of royal persons

22.8C1. If the name by which a royal person is known includes the name of a royal house, dynasty, territorial designation, etc., or a surname, enter the name in direct order. Add titles as instructed in 22.16A.

  John II Comnenus . . .

  Louis Bonaparte . . .

  Chandragupta Maurya . . .

  Eleanor, *of Aquitaine* . . .[12]

  Daulat Rao Sindhia . . .

  Ming T'ai-tsu . . .

  Shuja-ud-daulah . . .

---

12. For additions to the names of consorts of royal persons, see 22.16A3.

22.9. ENTRY OF OTHER NAMES

22.9A. Roman names

22.9A1. Enter a Roman active before, or mostly before, A.D. 476 under the part of the name most commonly used as entry element in reference sources.

> **Caesar, Gaius Julius**
>
> **Messalina, Valeria**
>
> **Messala Corvinus, Marcus Valerius**
>
> **Antoninus Pius**

In case of doubt, enter the name in direct order.

> **Martianus Capella**

22.9B. Icelandic names

22.9B1. Enter an Icelandic name under the first given name, followed by the other given names (if present), by the patronymic, and by the family name, in direct order. If a phrase naming a place follows the given name(s), patronymic, or family name, treat it as an integral part of the name. Refer from the patronymic and from the family name.

> **Svava Jakobsdóttir**
> (*Given name:* Svava)
> (*Patronymic:* Jakobsdóttir)
> *x* Jakobsdóttir, Svava
>
> **Halldór Laxness**
> (*Given name:* Halldór)
> (*Family name:* Laxness)
> *x* Laxness, Halldór
>
> **Bjarni Benediktsson frá Hofteigi**
> (*Given name:* Bjarni)
> (*Patronymic:* Benediktsson)
> (*Words denoting place:* frá Hofteigi)
> *x* Benediktsson frá Hofteigi, Bjarni
> *x* Benediktsson, Bjarni
> > (*To be made only when warranted in a particular catalogue*)
>
> **Jóhannes úr Kötlum**
> (*Given name:* Jóhannes)
> (*Words denoting place:* úr Kötlum)

22.10. ENTRY UNDER INITIALS, LETTERS, OR NUMERALS

22.10A. Enter a name consisting of initials, or separate letters, or numerals, or consisting primarily of initials, under those initials, letters, or numerals in direct

order. Include typographic devices when they appear as part of multi-letter abbreviations of a name, but omit them when they follow single-letter initials. Include any words or phrases associated with the initials, letters, or numerals. In
the case of initials or letters, make a name-title reference from an inverted form
beginning with the last letter for each item catalogued. Make a reference from
any phrase associated with the initials as required. In the case of numerals, make
a name-title reference from the numbers as words for each item catalogued.

> **H.D.**
>   *x* D., H.
>   By Avon River
>   *x* D., H.
>   Flowering of the rod
>   [*etc.*]
>
> **J.W.**
>   (*Name appears as:* J*** W*********)
>   *x* W., J.
>   Narrative of a commuted pensioner
>
> **A. de O.**
>   *x* O., A. de
>   Indiscretions of Dr. Carstairs
>
> **E. B——s**
>   *x* B——s, E.
>   Lettre sur la Grèce
>
> **B.,** *abbé de*
>   (*Name appears as:* abbé de B ...)
>
> **D.S.,** *Master*
>   *x* S., D., *Master*
>   *x* Master D.S.
>
> **i.e.,** *Master*
>   *x* e., i., *Master*
>   *x* Master i.e.
>
> **110908**
>   *x* One Hundred and Ten Thousand, Nine Hundred and Eight
>   Per ardua ad astra
>   *x* One, One, Zero, Nine, Zero, Eight
>   Per ardua ad astra

22.11. ENTRY UNDER PHRASE

22.11A. Enter in direct order a name that consists of a phrase or appellation that
does not contain a forename.

> **Dr. X**
>
> **Father Time**
>
> **Pan Painter**

Also enter in direct order a phrase that consists of a forename or forenames preceded by words other than a term of address or a title of position or office. Make a reference from the forename(s) followed by the initial word(s).

> **Poor Richard**
>   *x* Richard, *Poor*

> **Buckskin Bill**
>   *x* Bill, *Buckskin*

> **Calamity Jane**
>   *x* Janc, *Calamity*

> **Boy George**
>   *x* George, *Boy*

If, however, such a name has the appearance of a forename, forenames, or initials, and a surname, enter under the pseudosurname. Refer from the name in direct order.

> **Other, A.N.**
>   *x* A.N. Other

If such a name does not convey the idea of a person, add in parentheses a suitable designation in English.

> **River** (*Writer*)

> **Taj Mahal** (*Musician*)

22.11B. If a phrase consists of a forename preceded by a term of address (e.g., a word indicating relationship) or a title of position or office (e.g., a professional appellation), enter under the forename. Treat other word(s) as additions to the forename(s) (see 22.8A1). Refer from the name in direct order.

> **Fannie,** *Cousin*
>   *x* Cousin Fannie

> **Jemima,** *Aunt*
>   *x* Aunt Jemima

> **Marcelle,** *Tante*
>   *x* Tante Marcelle

> **Pierre,** *Chef*
>   *x* Chef Pierre

22.11C. If a phrase by which a person is commonly identified contains the name of another person, enter it in direct order. Make references to link the phrase and the heading for the other person if works by the person identified by the phrase have been ascribed to the other person (see 26.2C2 and 26.2D1).

> **Pseudo-Brutus**
>   *see also* **Brutus, Marcus Junius**

> **Brutus, Marcus Junius**
>   For the Greek letters erroneously attributed to this person, *see*
>   **Pseudo-Brutus**

22.11D. Enter a characterizing word or phrase, or a phrase naming another work by a person, in direct order. Omit an initial article. Consider such a word or phrase to be the heading for a person if that person is commonly identified by it in the chief sources of information of his or her works and in reference sources. Refer, when appropriate, from the title of the other work in the form [*Title*], *Author of*.

> **Physician**
> Memoir of Bowman Hendry ... / by a Physician

> **Author of Early impressions**
> The unveiled heart : a simple story / by the Author of Early impressions
> *x* Early impressions, Author of

If a person is commonly identified by a real name or another name (see 22.2A), and a word or phrase characterizing that person or including the title of another work has appeared in the chief source of information of any of his or her works, refer from the word or phrase. Also refer, when appropriate, from the title of the other work in the form [*Title*], *Author of*.

> **Bagnold, Enid**
> Serena Blandish, or, The difficulty of getting married / by a Lady of Quality
> *x* Lady of Quality

> **Sassoon, Siegfried**
> Memoirs of an infantry officer / by the Author of Memoirs of a fox-hunting man
> *x* Author of Memoirs of a fox-hunting man
> *x* Memoirs of a fox-hunting man, Author of

Additions to Names

General

22.12. TITLES OF NOBILITY AND TERMS OF HONOUR

22.12A. Titles of nobility

22.12A1. Add, to the name of a nobleman or noblewoman not entered under title (see 22.6), the title of nobility in the vernacular if the title or part of the title or a substitute for the title[13] commonly appears with the name in works by the person or in reference sources.[14] In case of doubt, add the title.

---

13. United Kingdom peers (other than dukes and duchesses) usually use the terms of address *Lord* or *Lady* in place of their titles. For example, George Gordon, Baron Byron, is almost invariably referred to as *Lord Byron*.

14. Disregard, in this context, reference sources dealing with the nobility.

Bismarck, Otto, *Fürst von*

Nagy, Pál, *felsőbüki*

Sévigné, Marie Rabutin-Chantal, *marquise de*

Johan, *de Middelste, Graaf van Nassau-Siegen*

but

Buchan, John
(*Title* Baron Tweedsmuir *not used in the majority of his works*)

Campbell, Patrick
(*Title* Baron Glenavy *not used in his works*)

Visconti, Luchino
(*Title* conte di Modrone *not used in his works*)

22.12B. British terms of honour

22.12B1. Add a British term of honour (*Sir*, *Dame*, *Lord*, or *Lady*) if the term commonly appears with the name in works by the person or in reference sources.[15] In case of doubt, add the term of honour.

Add the term at the end of the name if the person is entered under given name or if the person is the wife of a baronet or knight (unless she is also the daughter of a duke, duchess, marquess, marchioness, earl, or countess, see below).

Gregory, Augusta, *Lady*
(*Wife of a knight*)

Add the term before the forename(s) if the person is a baronet or knight, a dame of the Order of the British Empire (D.B.E.) or of the Royal Victorian Order (D.R.V.O.), a younger son of a duke, duchess, marquess, or marchioness, or a daughter of a duke, duchess, marquess, marchioness, earl, or countess.

Hess, *Dame* **Myra**
(*D.B.E.*)

West, *Dame* **Rebecca**
(*D.B.E.*)

Landseer, *Sir* **Edwin**
(*Knight*)

Beecham, *Sir* **Thomas**
(*Baronet*)

Gordon, *Lord* **George**
(*Younger son of a duke*)

---

15. Disregard, in this context, reference sources dealing with the nobility and gentry.

> **Greaves,** *Lady* **Rosamund**
> (*Daughter of a countess*)

> **Stanhope,** *Lady* **Hester**
> (*Daughter of an earl*)

but

> **Wodehouse, P.G.**
> (*Knight; term of honour* Sir *not used in his works*)

> **Christie, Agatha**
> (*D.B.E.; term of honour* Dame *not used in her works*)

> **Fraser, Antonia**
> (*Daughter of an earl; term of honour* Lady *not used in her works*)

22.13. SAINTS

22.13A. Add *Saint* after the name of a Christian saint, unless the person was a pope, emperor, empress, king, or queen, in which case follow 22.16A–22.16B.

> **Alban,** *Saint*

> **Teresa,** *of Avila, Saint*

> **Francis,** *of Assisi, Saint*

> **John,** *Climacus, Saint*

> **Francis Xavier,** *Saint*

> **More,** *Sir* **Thomas,** *Saint*

> **Seton, Elizabeth Ann,** *Saint*

> **Arundel, Philip Howard,** *Earl of, Saint*

> **Chantal, Jeanne-Françoise de,** *Saint*
> (*Not identified by title* baronne)

22.13B. Add any other suitable word or phrase necessary to distinguish between two saints.

> **Augustine,** *Saint, Archbishop of Canterbury*

> **Augustine,** *Saint, Bishop of Hippo*

22.14. SPIRITS

22.14A. Add *(Spirit)* to a heading established for a spirit communication (see 21.26).

> **Parker, Theodore** *(Spirit)*

> **Beethoven, Ludwig van** *(Spirit)*

> **Espirito Universal** *(Spirit)*

22.15. ADDITIONS TO NAMES ENTERED UNDER SURNAME

22.15A. If the name by which a person is known consists only of a surname, add the word or phrase associated with the name in works by the person or in reference sources. As required, refer from the name in direct order.

> **Deidier,** *abbé*

> **Moses,** *Grandma*
>   *x* Grandma Moses

> **Read,** *Miss*
>   *x* Miss Read

> **Seuss,** *Dr.*
>   *x* Dr. Seuss

If no such word or phrase exists, make additions to surnames alone only when they are needed to distinguish two or more persons with the same name (see 22.19B).

22.15B. Terms of address of married women

22.15B1. Add the term of address of a married woman if she is identified only by her husband's name.

> **Ward,** *Mrs.* **Humphry**

22.15B2. Include the enclitic *né* attached to the names of some Hungarian married women.

> **Magyary, Zoltánné**

> **Beniczkyné Bajza, Lenke**

22.15C. Do not add other titles or terms associated with names entered under surname unless they are required to distinguish between two or more persons with the same name and neither dates nor fuller forms of name are available (see 22.19B).

22.16. ADDITIONS TO NAMES ENTERED UNDER GIVEN NAME, ETC.

22.16A. Royalty

22.16A1. Add, to the name of the person with the highest royal status within a state or people,[16] a phrase consisting of a person's title (in English if there is a satisfactory English equivalent) and the name of the state or people in English.

---

16. Persons with such highest status are kings and queens, persons of imperial rank (emperors and empresses), and persons with other titles which denote such a status within a state or people (grand-dukes, grand-duchesses, princes, princesses, etc.). Rank is the only determining factor in applying these rules, not the degree of authority or power wielded by the person.

> **Clovis,** *King of the Franks*
>
> **Anne,** *Queen of Great Britain*
>
> **Elizabeth I,** *Queen of England*
>
> **Ferdinand I,** *Holy Roman Emperor*
>
> **Feisal II,** *King of Iraq*
>
> **Maximilian,** *Emperor of Mexico*
>
> **Victor Emmanuel II,** *King of Italy*
>
> **Gustaf I Vasa,** *King of Sweden*
>
> **John II Comnenus,** *Emperor of the East*
>
> **Robert III,** *Duke of Burgundy*
>
> **Ming T'ai-tsu,** *Emperor of China*
>
> **Shuja-ud-daulah,** *Nawab Wazir of Oudh*

22.16A2. Do not add other epithets associated with the name of such a person. Refer from the name with the epithet(s).

> **Catherine II,** *Empress of Russia*
>   x Catherine, *the Great*
>
> **Constantine I,** *Emperor of Rome*
>   x Constantine, *Saint*
>
> **Edward,** *King of the English*
>   x Edward, *the Confessor, Saint*
>
> **Charles IV,** *King of France*
>   x Charles, *the Fair*
>
> **Suleiman I,** *Sultan of the Turks*
>   x Suleiman, *the Magnificent*
>
> **Frederick I,** *Holy Roman Emperor*
>   x Frederick, *Barbarossa*

22.16A3. Consorts of royal persons. Add, to the name of a consort of a person with the highest royal status within a state or people, his or her title (in English if there is a satisfactory English equivalent) followed by *consort of* [the name of the royal person as prescribed in 22.16A1].

> **Philip,** *Prince, consort of Elizabeth II, Queen of the United Kingdom*
>
> **Anne,** *Queen, consort of Louis XIII, King of France*
>
> **Albert,** *Prince Consort, consort of Victoria, Queen of the United Kingdom*
>   (*His title was* Prince Consort)

412

> **Eleanor,** *of Aquitaine, Queen, consort of Henry II, King of England*
> *x* Eleanor, *Queen, consort of Henry II, King of England*

22.16A4. Children and grandchildren of royal persons. Add, to the name of a child or grandchild of a person with the highest royal status within a state or people, the title (in English if there is a satisfactory English equivalent) borne by him or her.

> **Carlos,** *Prince of Asturias*

> **Eulalia,** *Infanta of Spain*

If such a child or grandchild is known only as *Prince* or *Princess* (or a similar title in English or another language) without a territorial designation, add that title (in English if there is a satisfactory equivalent) followed by:

    a) another title associated with the name

or b) *daughter of . . ., son of . . ., granddaughter of . . ., or grandson of . . .* [the name and title of the parent or grandparent as prescribed in 22.16A1].

> **Mary,** *Princess Royal, Countess of Harewood*

> **Arthur,** *Prince, son of Victoria, Queen of the United Kingdom*

> **Alexis Petrovich,** *Prince, son of Peter I, Emperor of Russia*

> **Alexandra,** *Princess, granddaughter of George V, King of the United Kingdom*

> **Anne,** *Princess Royal, daughter of Elizabeth II, Queen of the United Kingdom*

22.16B. Popes

22.16B1. Add *Pope* to a name identifying a pope.

> **Pius XII,** *Pope*

> **Gregory I,** *Pope*
> *not* Gregory, *Saint, Pope Gregory I*
> Gregory, *the Great, Pope*

Add *Antipope* to a name identifying an antipope.

> **Clement VII,** *Antipope*

22.16C. Bishops, etc.

22.16C1. If a bishop, cardinal, archbishop, metropolitan, abbot, abbess, or other high ecclesiastical official is identified by a given name, add the title (in English if there is a satisfactory English equivalent). If the person has borne more than one such title, give the one of highest rank.

Use *Archbishop* for all archbishops other than cardinals. Use *Bishop* for all bishops other than cardinals. Use *Chorepiscopus* for persons so designated. Use *Cardinal* for cardinal-bishops, cardinal-priests, and cardinal-deacons. Add to the title of a diocesan bishop or archbishop or of a patriarch the name of the latest see, in English if there is an English form.

> **Bessarion,** *Cardinal*
>
> **Dositheos,** *Patriarch of Jerusalem*
>
> **Joannes,** *Bishop of Ephesus*
>
> **Platon,** *Metropolitan of Moscow*
>
> **John,** *Abbot of Ford*
>
> **Arnaldus,** *Abbot of Bonneval*
>
> **Ruricius I,** *Bishop of Limoges*
>
> **Maximos V,** *Ecumenical Patriarch of Constantinople*

If the name is of an ecclesiastical prince of the Holy Roman Empire, add *Prince-Bishop*, *Prince-Archbishop*, *Archbishop and Elector*, etc., as appropriate, and the name of the see. Add *Cardinal* also if appropriate.

> **Neithard,** *Prince-Bishop of Bamberg*
>
> **Albert,** *of Brandenburg, Archbishop and Elector of Mainz,*
>   *Cardinal*

22.16D. Other persons of religious vocation

22.16D1. Add the title, term of address, etc., in the vernacular to all other names of persons of religious vocation entered under given name, etc. If there is more than one such term, use the one that is most often associated with the name or is considered to be more important. Use spellings found in English-language dictionaries. For Thai names in religion, see also 22.28D.

> **Māhavijitāvī,** *Thera*
>
> **Angelico,** *fra*
>
> **Nyana,** *Ledi Sayadaw*
>
> **Claude,** *d'Abbeville, père*
>
> **Tathagata,** *Bhikshu*
>
> **Mary Loyola,** *Mother*
>
> **Vivekananda,** *Swami*
>
> **Dhammatinna,** *Ashin*

If such a title, etc., has become an integral part of the name, treat it as such.

> **Kakushin-ni**
> *not* Kakushin, *Ni*

Poďŏk Hwasang
not Poďŏk, *Hwasang*

Add also the initials of a Christian religious order if they are regularly used by the person.

Anselm, *Brother, F.S.C.*

Anselm, *Brother, O.F.M.Cap.*

Cuthbert, *Father, O.S.F.C.*

Mary Jeremy, *Sister, O.P.*

Additions to Distinguish Identical Names

22.17. DATES

22.17A. Add a person's dates (birth, death, etc.) in the form given below as the last element of a heading if the heading is otherwise identical to another.

Give dates in terms of the Christian era. Add *B.C.* when appropriate. Give dates from 1582 on in terms of the Gregorian calendar.[17]

---

17. The Gregorian calendar was adopted in France, Italy, Portugal, and Spain in 1582; by the Catholic states of Germany in 1583; by the United Kingdom in 1752; by Sweden in 1753; by Prussia in 1774; and by the Russian Republic in 1918. Convert dates from 1582 on from the Julian calendar to the Gregorian as set out in the following tables.

Table I. The following days in December under the Julian calendar fall in January of the next year under the Gregorian calendar:

YEAR (JULIAN)	DAYS (JULIAN)
1582–1699	Dec. 22–31
1700–1799	Dec. 21–31
1800–1899	Dec. 20–31
1900–1999	Dec. 19–31

Table II. The following days in the "old style" calendar used in the British Isles fall in the next later year under the Gregorian calendar:

BRITISH ISLES (EXCEPT SCOTLAND) AND COLONIES

YEAR (OLD STYLE)	DAYS (OLD STYLE)
1582–1699	Jan. 1–31
	Feb. 1–28 [29]
	Mar. 1–24
	Dec. 22–31
1700–1750	Jan. 1–31
	Feb. 1–28 [29]
	Mar. 1–24
	Dec. 21–31
1751	Dec. 21–31

SCOTLAND

YEAR (OLD STYLE)	DAYS (OLD STYLE)
1582–1599	Jan. 1–31
	Feb. 1–28 [29]
	Mar. 1–24
	Dec. 22–31
1600–1699	Dec. 22–31
1700–1751	Dec. 21–31

Optionally, add date(s) to any personal name, even if there is no need to distinguish between headings.

Smith, John, 1924-	*Living person*
Smith, John, 1900 Jan. 10- **Smith, John,** 1900 Mar. 2-	*Same name, same year*
Smith, John, 1837-1896	*Both years known*
Smith, John, 1836 *or* 7-1896	*Year of birth uncertain; known to be one of two years*
Smith, John, 1837?-1896	*Probable year of birth*
Smith, John, *ca.* 1837-1896	*Year of birth uncertain by several years*
Smith, John, 1837-*ca.* 1896	*Approximate year of death*
Smith, John, *ca.* 1837-*ca.* 1896	*Both years approximate*
Smith, John, *b.* 1825	*Year of death unknown*
Smith, John, *d.* 1859	*Year of birth unknown*
Johnson, Carl F., *fl.* 1893-1940 **Joannes,** *Diaconus, fl.* 1226-1240	*Years of birth and death unknown. Some years of activity known. Do not use* fl. *dates within the twentieth century.*
Joannes, *Diaconus,* 12th cent.	*Years of birth and death unknown, years of activity unknown, century known. Do not use for the twentieth century.*
Joannes, *Actuarius,* 13th/14th cent.	*Years of birth and death unknown. Years of activity unknown, but active in both centuries. Do not use for the twentieth century.*
Lin, Li, *chin shih* 1152	*Date at which a Chinese literary degree was conferred*

22.18. FULLER FORMS

22.18A. If a fuller form of a person's name is known and if the heading as prescribed by the preceding rules does not include all of that fuller form, add the fuller form to distinguish between headings that are otherwise identical. Add all the fuller form of the inverted part of the heading and/or the fuller form of the entry element, as appropriate. Enclose the addition in parentheses.

The most common instances of such additions occur when the heading as prescribed by the preceding rules contains initials and the spelled out form is known. Less common instances occur when known forenames, surnames, or initials are not part of the heading as prescribed.

Refer from the fuller form of the name when appropriate.

> **Smith, Russell E. (Russell Edgar)**
> *x* Smith, Russell Edgar

Smith, Russell E. (Russell Eugene)
  x Smith, Russell Eugene

Johnson, A.H. (Allison Heartz)
  x Johnson, Allison Heartz

Johnson, A.H. (Arthus Henry)
  x Johnson, Arthus Henry

Murray, Gilbert (Gilbert George Aimé)
  x Murray, Gilbert George Aimé

Murray, Gilbert (Gilbert John)
  x Murray, Gilbert John

Allen, Richard (Alexander Richard)
  x Allen, Alexander Richard

Allen, Richard (Richard Hugh Sedley)
  x Allen, Richard Hugh Sedley

Johnson, Barbara (Barbara A.)

Johnson, Barbara (Barbara E.)

Miller, *Mrs.* **J. (Anna)**
  x Miller, Anna

Miller, *Mrs.* **J. (Dorothea)**
  x Miller, Dorothea

Optionally, make the additions specified above even if they are not needed to distinguish between headings. However, when following this option, do not add:

> unused forenames to headings that contain forenames
> initials of names that are not part of the heading
> unused parts of surnames to headings that contain surnames.

Lawrence, D.H. (David Herbert)
  x Lawrence, David Herbert

H.D. (Hilda Doolittle)
  x Doolittle, Hilda

Rodríguez H., Guadalupe (Rodríguez Hernández)
  x Rodríguez Hernández, Guadalupe

González R., Pedro F. (Pedro Felipe González Rodríguez)
  x González Rodríguez, Pedro Felipe

Wanner, Joh. (Johann)

Beeton, *Mrs.* **(Isabella Mary)**
  x Beeton, Isabella Mary

but
         Welch, Denton
not Welch, Denton (Maurice Denton)

         Dickens, Charles
not Dickens, Charles (Charles John Huffam)

         Morgan, Percival
not Morgan, Percival (C. Percival)

         Wilson, Angus
not Wilson, Angus (Angus Frank Johnstone-Wilson)

22.19. DISTINGUISHING TERMS

22.19A. Names in which the entry element is a given name, etc.

22.19A1. If neither a fuller form of name nor dates are available to distinguish between identical headings of which the entry element is a given name, etc., devise a suitable brief term and add it in parentheses.

> **Johannes** *(Notary)*

> **Thomas** *(Anglo-Norman poet)*

22.19B. Names in which the entry element is a surname

22.19B1. If neither a fuller form of name nor dates are available to distinguish between identical headings of which the entry element is a surname, add a qualifier (e.g., term of address, title of position or office, initials of an academic degree, initials denoting membership in an organization) that appears with the name in works by the person or in reference sources.

> **Brown, George,** *Captain*

> **Brown, George,** *F.I.P.S.*

> **Brown, George,** *Rev.*

> **Valmer,** *capitaine*

> **Saur, Karl-Otto**

> **Saur, Karl-Otto,** *Jr.*

Do not use such a term if dates are available for one person and it seems likely that dates will eventually be available for the other(s).

> **Mudge, Lewis Seymour,** 1868-1945

> **Mudge, Lewis Seymour**
>   *(Name appears as:* Lewis Seymour Mudge, Jr.)

22.20. UNDIFFERENTIATED NAMES

22.20A. If no suitable addition (fuller form of name, dates, or distinguishing term) is available, use the same heading for all persons with the same name.

Müller, Heinrich
    80 Fotos und eine kurze Einführung in die Lage, Geschichte, und Sehenswürdigkeiten der Stadt Giessen

Müller, Heinrich
    Der Diebstahl im Urheberrecht

Müller, Heinrich
    Die Fussballregeln und ihre richtige Auslegung

Müller, Heinrich
    Historische Waffen

Müller, Heinrich
    Die Repser Burg

Special Rules for Names in Certain Languages

22.21. INTRODUCTORY RULE

22.21A. The preceding rules in this chapter give general guidance for personal names not written in the roman alphabet and for names in a non-European language written in the roman alphabet. For more detailed treatment of names in certain of these languages, follow the special rules given below. For more detailed treatment of names in other languages, see the IFLA International Office for UBC's survey of personal names.[18]

22.22. NAMES IN THE ARABIC ALPHABET[19]

22.22A. Scope

22.22A1. Apply this rule only to names (regardless of their origin) originally written in the Arabic alphabet that do not contain a surname or a name per-

---

18. *Names of Persons : National Usages for Entries in Catalogues* / compiled by the IFLA International Office for UBC. — 3rd ed. — London : The Office, 1977.

19. Major reference sources for names written in the Arabic alphabet and their treatment (note that romanization practices in these sources differ):

Babinger, Franz. *Die Geschichtsschreiber der Osmanen und ihre Werke* / mit einem Anhang, Osmanische Zeitrechnungen von Joachim Mayr. — Leipzig : Harrassowitz, 1927.
Brockelmann, Carl. *Geschichte der arabischen Literatur.* — 2. den Supplementbänden angepasste Aufl. — Leiden : Brill, 1943–1949. — 1.–3. Supplementband: Leiden : Brill, 1937–1942.
Caetani, Leone. *Onomasticon Arabicum* / compilato per cura di Leone Caetani e Giuseppe Gabrieli. — Roma : Casa editrice italiana, 1915.
The Encyclopaedia of Islām . . . / prepared by a number of leading orientalists ; edited by M. Th. Houtsma ... [et al.]. — Leyden : Brill, 1913–1934. — Supplement: Leiden : Brill, 1938.
The Encyclopaedia of Islam / prepared by a number of leading orientalists. — New ed. / edited by an editorial committee consisting of H.A.R. Gibb ... [et al.]. — Leiden : Brill, 1960–
İslâm ansiklopedisi : İslâm âlemi coğrafya, etnoğrafya ve biyografya lûgati / Beynelmilel Akademiler Birliğinin yardımı ve tanınmış müsteşriklerin iştiraki ile neşredenler M. Th. Houtsma ... [et al.]. — İstanbul : Maarif Matbaası, 1940–
Philologiae Turcicae Fundamenta . . . / una cum praestantibus Turcologis ediderunt Jean Deny ... [et al.]. — Aquis Mattiacis : Steiner, 1959–
Sezgin, Fuat. *Geschichte des arabischen Schrifttums.* — Leiden : Brill, 1967–
Storey, Charles Ambrose. *Persian Literature : A Bio-bibliographical Survey.* — London : Luzac, 1927–

forming the function of a surname. In case of doubt, assume that a name of a person active in the twentieth century includes a surname (see 22.5) and that other names do not.

22.22B. Entry element

22.22B1. Enter a name made up of a number of elements under the element or combination of elements by which the person is best known. Determine this from reference sources. When there is insufficient evidence available, enter under the first element. Refer from any part of the name not used as entry element if there is reason to believe that the person's name may be sought under that part. Refer as necessary from variant romanizations (see 22.3C).

22.22C. Essential elements

22.22C1. If the entry element is not the given name (ism) or a patronymic derived from the name of the father (a name usually following the given name and compounded with *ibn*), include these names unless they are not customarily used in the name by which the person is known. Include an additional name, descriptive epithet, or term of honour that is treated as part of the name if it aids in identifying the individual. Generally omit other elements of the name, particularly patronymics derived from anyone other than the father.

22.22D. Order of elements

22.22D1. When the elements of the name have been determined, place the best-known element or combination of elements first. Give the other elements in the following order: khiṭāb, kunyah, ism, patronymic, any other name. Insert a comma after the entry element unless it is the first part of the name.

KHIṬĀB (honorific compound of which the last part is typically *al-Dīn*)

> **Rashīd al-Dīn Ṭabīb**

> **Ṣadr al-Dīn al-Qūnawī, Muḥammad ibn Isḥāq**
> *x* Muḥammad ibn Isḥāq al-Qūnawī, Ṣadr al-Dīn
> *x* al-Qūnawī, Ṣadr al-Dīn Muḥammad ibn Isḥāq

KUNYAH (typically a compound with *Abū* as the first word)

> **Abū al-Barakāt Hibat Allāh ibn 'Alī**
> *x* Hibat Allāh ibn 'Alī, Abū al-Barakāt

> **Abū Ḥayyān al-Tawḥīdī, 'Alī ibn Muḥammad**
> *x* al-Tawḥīdī, Abū Ḥayyān 'Alī ibn Muḥammad
> *x* 'Alī ibn Muḥammad, Abū Ḥayyān al-Tawḥīdī

> **Abū Hurayrah**

ISM (given name)

> **'Alī ibn Abī Ṭālib,** *Caliph*

Bashshār ibn Burd

Mālik ibn Anas

Nashwān ibn Saʻīd al-Ḥimyāri
  x al-Ḥimyāri, Nashwān ibn Saʻīd

Ṭāhā Ḥusayn
  x Ḥusayn, Ṭāhā

Muḥammad Ismāʻīl Pānipātī
  x Pānīpatī, Muḥammad Ismāʻīl

Ghulām Ḥasan Khūyihāmī
  x Khūyihāmī, Ghulām Ḥasan

Nādirah Khātūn
  x Khātūn, Nādirah

PATRONYMIC (typically a compound with *Ibn* as the first word)

Ibn Hishām, ʻAbd al-Mālik
  x ʻAbd al-Mālik ibn Hishām

Ibn Ḥazm, ʻAlī ibn Aḥmad
  x ʻAlī ibn Aḥmad ibn Ḥazm

Ibn Sanāʼ al-Mulk, Hibat Allāh ibn Jaʻfar
  x Hibat Allāh ibn Jaʻfar ibn Sanāʼ al-Mulk

Ibn al-Muʻtazz, ʻAbd Allāh
  x ʻAbd Allāh ibn al-Muʻtazz

Ibn al-Muqaffaʻ, ʻAbd Allāh
  x ʻAbd Allāh ibn al-Muqaffaʻ

OTHER NAMES

Laqab (descriptive epithet)

al-Jāḥiẓ, ʻAmr ibn Baḥr
  x ʻAmr ibn Baḥr al-Jāḥiẓ

Abū Shāmah, ʻAbd al-Raḥmān ibn Ismāʻīl
  x ʻAbd al-Raḥmān ibn Ismāʻīl Abū Shāmah

al-Kātib al-Iṣfahānī, ʻImād al-Dīn Muḥammad ibn Muḥammad
  x Muḥammad ibn Muḥammad al-Kātib al-Iṣfahānī, ʻImād al-Dīn
  x al-Iṣfahānī, ʻImād al-Dīn Muḥammad ibn Muḥammad al-Kātib

al-Qāḍī al-Fāḍil, ʻAbd al-Raḥīm ibn ʻAlī
  x ʻAbd al-Raḥīm, ibn ʻAlī al-Qāḍī al-Fāḍil

Mirzā Khān Anṣārī
  x Anṣārī, Mirzā Khān

Nisbah (proper adjective ending in *ī*, indicating origin, residence, or other circumstances)

> **al-Bukhārī, Muḥammad ibn Ismāʻīl**
> *x* Muḥammad ibn Ismāʻīl al-Bukhārī

> **Māzandarānī, ʻAbd Allāh ibn Muḥammad**
> *x* ʻAbd Allāh ibn Muḥammad Māzandarānī

> **ʻAbbāsī, ʻAlī Aḥmad**
> *x* ʻAlī Aḥmad ʻAbbāsī

> **Hilālī, Muḥammad Khān Mīr**
> *x* Muḥammad Khān Mīr Hilālī

Takhalluṣ (pen name)

> **Qāʼānī, Ḥabib Allāh Shīrāzī**
> *x* Ḥabib Allāh Shīrāzī Qāʼānī

> **ʻIbrat, Ẓafar Ḥasan**
> *x* Ẓafar Ḥasan ʻIbrat

22.23. BURMESE AND KAREN NAMES

22.23A. Enter a Burmese or Karen name that includes a Western given name preceding the vernacular name(s) under the vernacular name(s). Transpose the Western name to the end.

> **Hla Gyaw, James**
> (*Name:* James Hla Gyaw)

22.23B. Add the term of address that usually accompanies a Burmese or Karen name. Add also any other distinguishing terms generally associated with the name. If the name of the same person is found with different terms of address, use the term of highest honour. Distinguish terms of address from the same words used as names.

> **Ba U,** *U*

> **Chit Maung,** *Saw*

> **Mya Sein,** *Daw*

> **Saw,** *U*

> **U Shan Maung,** *Maung*

> **Kaing, Katie,** *Naw*

> **Hla,** *Ludu U*

> **Ba Yin,** *Hanthawaddy U*

22.24. CHINESE NAMES CONTAINING A NON-CHINESE GIVEN NAME

22.24A. If a name of Chinese origin contains a non-Chinese given name and the name is found in the order [*non-Chinese given name*] [*surname*] [*Chinese given names*], enter the name as [*surname*], [*non-Chinese given name*] [*Chinese given names*]. Enter all other names as instructed in 22.5.

> **Loh, Philip Fook Seng**
> (*Name appears as:* Philip Loh Fook Seng)

22.25. INDIC NAMES

22.25A. Early names

22.25A1. Enter an Indic name borne by a person who flourished before the middle of the nineteenth century under the first element of the personal name, ignoring honorifics and religious terms of address that may precede it (e.g., *Shri (Sri)*, *Swami*, *Acharya*, *Muni*, *Bhikkhu*). For such terms as integral parts of names, see below. Do not include the enclitic *-ji* (or *-jee*) sometimes added to the personal element of the name.

> **Kālidāsa**
>
> **Pāṇini**
>
> **Īśvara Kaula**
>
> **Narmadashankar Lalshankar**

Enter the name of an ancient or medieval Sanskrit author or an author (usually Jain) of a Prakrit text under the Sanskrit form of the name. Refer from any significantly different form.

> **Āryabhaṭa**
> *x* Ārya Bhaṭa
>
> **Aśvaghosa**
> *x* Assaghoṣa
> *x* Ashwa Ghoshu
> *x* Açvaghosha
>
> **Bhaṭṭojī Dīkṣita**
>
> **Karṇapūra**

Include a title (e.g., *Shri (Sri)*, *Swami*, *Sastri*, *Acharya*, *Bhatta*, *Saraswati*, *Muni*, *Gani*) as an integral part of the name if it usually appears with the name in reference sources.

> **Narain Swami**
>
> **Śaṅkarācārya**
>
> **Śrīharṣa**
>
> **Śrīdharasvāmin**
> *but* **Rāmānuja**
> (*Sometimes appears as:* Rāmānujācārya)

Enter the name of a Buddhist author of a Pali text under the Pali form of the name. Refer from any significantly different form.

> **Dhammakitti**
> *x* Dharmakīrti
>
> **Ñāṇamoli,** *Bhikkhu*

22.25B. Modern names

22.25B1. With the exceptions specified in 22.25B2–22.25B3, enter an Indic name of a person flourishing after the middle of the nineteenth century under the surname or the name that the person is known to have used as a surname. If there is no surname, enter under the last name.

> **Dutt, Romesh Chunder**
>
> **Krishna Menon, V.K.**
>
> **Singh, Indrajit**
> (*For Sikh names ending in* Singh, *see 22.25B3*)
>
> **Das Gupta, Hemendra Nath**
>
> **Shastri,**[20] **Lal Bahadur**

22.25B2. Kannada, Malayalam, Tamil, and Telugu names. If a name in one of these languages does not contain a surname or a name known to have been used by the person who bears the name as a surname, enter under the given name. Given names in these languages are normally preceded by a place name and occasionally by the father's given name and may be followed by a caste name.

> **Kiruṣṇa Ayyaṅkār, Tiṭṭai**
> (*Given name:* Kiruṣṇa)
> (*Caste name:* Ayyaṅkār)
> (*Place name:* Tiṭṭai)
>
> **Sankaran Nair,** *Sir* **C.**
> (*Given name:* Sankaran)
> (*Caste name:* Nair)
> (*House name:* C. (Chettur))
>
> **Jōsaph, O.P.**
> (*Given name:* Jōsaph)
> (*Initials of place name and of father's given name:* O.P. (Oorakath Paul))
>
> **Radhakrishnan, S.**
> (*Given name:* Radhakrishnan)
> (*Initial of place name:* S. (Sarvepalli))

---

20. *Sastri (Shastri)* is sometimes used as a surname, sometimes as a religious title, sometimes as an appendage to a personal name, and sometimes as a reinforcement to another surname.

22.25B3. Sikh names. Enter the Sikh name of a person who does not use *Singh* or *Kaur* as a surname under the first of his or her names (the given name).

> **Amrit Kaur**
>
> **Mehtab Singh**

22.25B4. Religious names. Enter a modern person of religious vocation (whether Hindu, Buddhist, or Jain) under the religious name. Add the religious title.

> **Chinmayananda,** *Swami*
>
> **Ramana,** *Maharshi*
>
> **Punyavijaya,** *Muni*
>
> **Sangharakshita,** *Bhikshu*

22.26. INDONESIAN NAMES

22.26A. Scope

22.26A1. Apply this rule to names of Arabic, Chinese, Dutch, Indic, Javanese, Malayan, Sumatran, or other origin.

22.26B. Entry element

22.26B1. With the exceptions specified in 22.26C–22.26F, enter an Indonesian name consisting of more than one element under the last element of the name. Refer from the name in direct order unless the first element is a European name.

> **Hatta, Mohammad**
>   (*Compound given name*)
>   *x* Mohammad Hatta
>
> **Djajadiningrat, Idrus Nasir**
>   (*Given name plus surname*)
>   *x* Idrus Nasir Djajadiningrat
>
> **Purbatjaraka, Purnadi**
>   (*Given name plus father's name*)
>   *x* Purnadi Purbatjaraka
>
> **Nasution, Amir Hamzah**
>   (*Given name plus clan name*)
>   *x* Amir Hamzah Nasution
>
> **Ginarsa, Ktut**
>   (*Balinese name containing an element indicating seniority of children*)
>   *x* Ktut Ginarsa
>
> **Djelantik, I Gusti Ketut**
>   (*Balinese name*)
>   *x* I Gusti Ketut Djelantik
>   *x* Gusti Ketut Djelantik, I
>   *x* Ketut Djelantik, I Gusti

425

> **Sani, Sitti Nuraini**
> (*Married woman's name; last element may be the husband's or the father's name*)
> *x* Sitti Nuraini Sani

22.26C. Names entered under the first element

22.26C1. Enter the following categories of names under the first element of the name. Refer from the last element. If that element is an initial, refer also from the next to the last element.

a) A name consisting of a given name followed by an element denoting filial relationship (e.g., *bin*, *binti*, *ibni*) plus the father's name.

> **Abdullah bin Nuh**
> *x* Nuh, Abdullah bin

> **S. bin Umar**
> *x* Umar, S. bin

b) A name that may be written as one word or as separate words and that begins with one of the following elements: *Adi, Budi (Boedi), Joko (Djoko), Karta, Kusuma (Koesoema), Mangku (Mangkoe), Noto, Prawira, Pura (Poera), Sastra, Sri, Surya (Soerya, Surja, Suria)*, and *Tri*. (If the name of a particular person sometimes appears as one word and sometimes as separate words, use the one-word form.)

> **Adi Waskito**
> *x* Waskito, Adi

> **Adisendjaja**

> **Sri Muljono**
> *x* Muljono, Sri

c) A name containing an initial or abbreviation as the last element.

> **Djakaria N.E.**
> *x* E., Djakaria N.

22.26D. Names consisting of given name(s) plus *adat* title

22.26D1. Enter a name that includes one or more of the terms *gelar* (sometimes abbreviated as *gl.* or *glr.*), *Daeng*, *Datuk*, or *Sutan* under the element introduced by such words. Refer from the name in direct order.

> **Palindih, Rustam Sutan**
> *x* Rustam Sutan Palindih

> **Batuah, Ahmad gelar Datuk**
> *x* Ahmad gelar Datuk Batuah

> **Radjo Endah, Sjamsuddin Sutan**
> *x* Sjamsuddin Sutan Radjo Endah
> *x* Endah, Sjamsuddin Sutan Radjo

22.26E. Names containing place names

22.26E1. Enter a name consisting of personal names followed by a place name under the element preceding the place name. Treat the place name as an integral part of the name.

> **Abdullah Udjong Buloh**
>
> **Daud Beureuh, Muhammad**

22.26F. Names of Chinese origin

22.26F1. Enter a name of Chinese origin that follows the normal Chinese order (surname first) under the first element of the name. Refer from the last element of the name.

> **Lim, Yauw Tjin**
> (*Name appears as:* Lim Yauw Tjin)
> *x* Tjin, Lim Yauw
>
> **Oei, Tjong Bo**
> (*Name appears as:* Oei Tjong Bo)
> *x* Bo, Oei Tjong

22.26G. Titles[21]

22.26G1. Add titles and honorific words to an Indonesian name as instructed in 22.12A. Refer from the direct form of title plus name.

> **Purbatjaraka,** *Raden Mas Ngabei*
> *x* Raden Mas Ngabei Purbatjaraka

Refer from the direct form of title plus name even when the title is not used in the heading.

---

21. The following list of Indonesian titles and honorific words is incomplete as only some of the more commonly used titles are listed. A few variant spellings are also noted.

adipati	ide (ida)	raden pandji (*or* panji)
anak agung (*or* agoeng) gde	ide aju (ide ayu, ide ajoe)	raden roro
anak agung (*or* agoeng) istri	ide bagus (ide bagoes)	radja (raja)
andi	imam	ratu (ratoe, ratoh)
aria (arja, arya, arjo, aryo, ardjueh, arjueh)	marah	sidi
datuk (datoek, dato, datok)	mas	siti
desak	ngabei (ngabehi, ngabeui)	sultan (soeltan)
dewa gde (*or* gede)	nganten	susuhunan (soesoehoenan)
gusti (goesti)	pangeran	sutan (soetan)
gusti aju (gusti ayu, goesti ajoe)	pedanda	tengku (tungku, teuku, teungku)
gusti gde (goesti gede)	raden	tjokorde (cokorde)
hadji (haji)	raden adjeng (*or* ajeng)	tjokorde (*or* cokorde) gde
	raden aju (*or* ayu)	tjokorde (*or* cokorde) istri
	raden aria (*or* arya)	tubagus (*or* toebagoes)
	raden mas	tumenggung (toemenggoeng)
	raden nganten	tunku (toenkoe)

(continued)

Amrullah, Abdul Malik Karim
x Hadji Abdul Malik Karim Amrullah
x Abdul Malik Karim Amrullah

Distinguish titles used as such from the same words adopted by a person as elements of his or her name. When in doubt, treat the words as a title.

Rusli, Marah
(*Title* Marah *used as a personal name*)
x Marah Rusli

Djuanda, H.
(*Name and title* hadji Djuanda *appears as:* Dr. H. Djuanda)
x Djuanda, Hadji
x Hadji Djuanda

22.27. MALAY NAMES

22.27A. Scope

22.27A1. Apply this rule to Malay names, including names of Arabic origin beginning with the element *al-*, borne by persons living in Malaysia, Singapore, or Brunei. Apply this rule also to names from other ethnic groups native to Malaysia such as Ibans, Kedazans, etc. Enter a name from an ethnic group of non-Malay origin (e.g., Indian, Chinese) borne by a person living in one of these countries according to the rules for the language of the name.

22.27B. General rule

22.27B1. Enter a Malay name under the first element of the name and refer from the last element unless it is known that the bearer of the name treats another element of the name as a surname. In that case, enter under the surname and refer from the first element.

A. Samad Said
x Said, A. Samad

Rejab F.I.
x I., Rejab F.

Gelar, meaning "titled," often precedes an Indonesian title. Do not use the following terms of address in headings:

> bung (boeng)—brother, when used as a term of respect
> empu (mpu)—mister
> engku (ungku)—mister
> entjik (encik che, entje, inche, tje)—mister or mistress
> ibu (boe, bu, iboe)—mother, when used as a term of respect
> njonja (yonya)—mistress
> nona—miss
> pak (pa')—father, when used as a term of respect
> tuan (toean)—mister
> wan—mister

Shahnon Ahmad
  x Ahmad, Shahnon

Luat anak Jabu
  x Jabu, Luat anak

A.L. Bunggan
  x Bunggan, A.L.

William Duncan
  (*Full name:* William Duncan anak Ngadan)
  x Duncan, William
  x Ngadan, William Duncan anak

but
Merican, Faridah
  (*Surname:* Merican)
  x Faridah Merican

Nichol, Linda
  (*Surname:* Nichol)
  x Linda Nichol

22.27C. Filial indicators

22.27C1. Omit words or abbreviations denoting filial relationship[22] unless consistently used by the person.

Adibah Amin
  (*Sometimes appears as:* Khalidah Adibah binti Haji Amin)

but
Abdullah Sanusi bin Ahmad

Siti Norma bte. Ahmad

22.27C2. If the filial relationship is shown beyond one generation, include only the first unless more are required to distinguish between names that are otherwise identical.

Ali bin Ahmad
  (*Name appears as:* Ali bin Ahmad bin Hussein)
  x Ahmad, Ali bin
  x Ali bin Ahmad bin Hussein
  x Hussein, Ali bin Ahmad bin

---

22. Words denoting filial relationship are:

  anak (a., ak, *or* ak.)—child of
  bin (b.)—son of
  binte (bte.)—daughter of
  binti (bt.)—daughter of
  ibni—son of (royalty)

22.27D. Titles[23]

22.27D1. Add after the name titles of honour, rank, or position that are commonly associated with the name. Refer from the direct form of title plus name.

> **Abdul Majid bin Zainuddin,** *Haji*
> *x* Haji Abdul Majid bin Zainuddin
> *x* Zainuddin, Haji Abdul Majid bin

> **Hamzah Sendut,** *Tan Sri Datuk*
> *x* Tan Sri Datuk Hamzah Sendut
> *x* Sendut, Tan Sri Datuk Hamzah

> **Iskandar bin Raja Muhammad Zahid,** *Raja*
> *x* Raja Iskandar bin Raja Muhammad Zahid
> *x* Zahid, Raja Iskandar bin Raja Muhammad

22.28. THAI NAMES

22.28A. General rule

22.28A1. Enter a Thai name under the first element. Refer from the last element, which is normally a surname.[24] Omit a term of address (e.g., *Khun*, *Nāi*, *Nāng*, *Nāngsāo*) unless it is a title of nobility. In case of doubt, include it.

> **Dhanit Yupho**
> *x* Yupho, Dhanit

> **Prayut Sitthiphan**
> *x* Sitthiphan, Prayut

> **S. Bannakit**
> *x* Bannakit, S.

> **Maenmas Chavalit**
> *x* Chavalit, Maenmas

---

23. Iban titles are:

TITLES OF HONOUR	TITLES OF OFFICE
Tuai Serang	Penghulu Dalam
Tuai Kayau	Pengarah
Kepala Manok Sabong	Penghulu
Manok Sabong	Mandal
Kepala Pugu Menoa	Tuai rumah
Tuai Menoa	
Orang Kaya	
Orang Kaya Panglima	RELIGIOUS TITLES
Orang Kaya Pemanca	Kepala Lemambang
Orang Kaya Temenggong	Saut Lemambang
Patinggi	Lemambang
Temenggong	Manang Bali
Radin	Manang Mansau
Pateh	Manang Mengeris

24. Surnames became a legal requirement for most persons in 1915.

22.28B. Royalty

22.28B1. Make additions to the name of a king or queen of Thailand (and of a consort of a king or queen) as instructed in 22.16A.

> **Bhumibol Adulyadej,** *King of Thailand*
>
> **Chulalongkorn,** *King of Siam*
>
> **Saowaphā,** *Queen, consort of Chulalongkorn, King of Siam*
>
> **Thapthim,** *Čhaočhǫmmāndā, consort of Chulalongkorn, King of Siam*

22.28B2. Enter the name of a person of royal descent under the first element of the name, or latest name, that he or she uses. Add *Prince* or *Princess* for those of the ranks *Čhaofā* and *Phraʻong Čhao*. Use *M.C.*, *M.R.*, and *M.L.* for *Mǫm Čhao, Mǫm Rātchawong*, and *Mǫm Lūang*, respectively. If the person also bears a *krom* rank, do not add it. Refer from any earlier names, together with associated ranks and titles, borne by the person.

> **Damrongrāchānuphāp,** *Prince*
> *x* Ditsawǫnkumān, *Prince*

> **Seni Pramoj,** *M.R.*
> *x* Pramoj, Seni, *M.R.*
> *x* Prāmōt, Sēnī, *M.R.*

22.28C. Nobility (*Khunnāng*)

22.28C1. Enter a name containing a title of nobility under that title in the vernacular (*rātchathinanām*). If a person has more than one title, enter under the latest. Add the given name, when ascertainable, in parentheses. Add the vernacular rank (*yot bandāsak*) associated with the title. Refer from the given name, from the surname, and from any earlier titles borne by the person.

> **Prachākitkǫračhak (Chæm),** *Phrayā*
> *x* Chæm Bunnāk
> *x* Bunnāk, Chæm

> **Prachākitkǫračhak (Chup),** *Phrayā*
> *x* Chup ʻŌsathānon
> *x* ʻŌsathānon, Chup

> **Thammasakmontrī (Sanan),** *Čhaophrayā*
> *x* Sanan Thēphatsadin Na ʻAyutthayā

22.28C2. Enter the name of the wife of a man bearing a title of nobility under her own name, followed by the husband's title and the wife's conferred rank, if any.

> **Sangīam Phrasadetsurēntharāthibǫdī,** *Thānphūying*

22.28D. Buddhist monastics, ecclesiastics, and patriarchs

22.28D1. Monastics. Enter the name of a Buddhist monastic under the Pali name in religion unless the monastic is better known under the given name. Add *Phik-*

khu to a Pali name in religion. If the monastic is better known under the given name, enter under the given name and add the rank (*samanasak*) *Phra Mahā* or *Phra Khrū*. In the latter case, refer from the Pali name in religion if known.

> **Thammasārō,** *Phikkhu*

> **Khĩeo,** *Phra Mahā*
> *x* Thammathinnō, *Phikkhu*

22.28D2. Ecclesiastics. Enter the name of a Buddhist ecclesiastic under the latest title. Add the given name in parentheses. Add also any word indicating rank. Refer from the distinctive word in the title, from the given name, and from the surname.

> **Phra Thammathatsanāthǫn (Thǫngsuk)**
> *x* Thammathatsanāthǫn (Thǫngsuk), *Phra*
> *x* Thǫngsuk Suthatsō
> *x* Suthatsō, Thǫngsuk
> *x* Thǫngsuk Čhantharakhačhǫn
> *x* Čhantharakhačhǫn, Thǫngsuk
> *x* Sutsasa, *Thēra*

22.28D3. Supreme patriarchs. Enter the name of a supreme patriarch who is a commoner under the given name. Add *Supreme Patriarch* to the name. Refer from the surname and from any earlier names or titles by which the person is identified.

> **Plot,** *Supreme Patriarch*
> *x* Phra Wannarat (Plot), *Somdet*
> *x* Phra Phrommunī (Plot)
> *x* Phra 'Ariyawongsākhatayān (Plot), *Somdet*
> *x* Plot Kittisōphon
> *x* Kittisōphon, Plot
> *x* Kittisōphanō, *Mahāthēra*
> *x* Wannarat (Plot), *Somdet Phra*
> *x* Phrommunī (Plot), *Phra*
> *x* 'Ariyawongsākhatayān (Plot), *Somdet Phra*

Enter the name of a supreme patriarch of royal descent under the conferred name. Add the secular and ecclesiastical titles in that order. Refer from any earlier names or titles by which the person is identified.

> **Wachirayānawong,** *Prince, Supreme Patriarch*
> *x* Chū'n Nopphawong, *M.R.*
> *x* Nopphawong, Chū'n, *M.R.*
> *x* Phra Sukhunkhanāphǫn (Chū'n, *M.R.*)
> *x* Phra Yānwarāphǫn (Chū'n, *M.R.*)
> *x* Sukhunkhanāphǫn (Chū'n, *M.R.*), *Phra*
> *x* Yānwarāphǫn (Chū'n, *M.R.*), *Phra*

CHAPTER 23

GEOGRAPHIC NAMES

Contents

23.1. INTRODUCTORY NOTE

23.1A. The names of geographic entities (referred to throughout this chapter as "places") are used to distinguish between corporate bodies with the same name (see 24.4C); as additions to other corporate names (e.g., conference names, see 24.7B4); and, commonly, as the names of governments (see 24.3E) and communities that are not governments.

23.2. GENERAL RULES

23.2A. English form

23.2A1. Use the English form of the name of a place if there is one in general use. Determine this from gazetteers and other reference sources published in English-speaking countries. In case of doubt, use the vernacular form (see 23.2B).

>   **Austria**
> *not*   Österreich

>   **Copenhagen**
> *not*   København

>   **Florence**
> *not*   Firenze

>   **Ghent**
> *not*   Gent
>   Gand

>   **Sweden**
> *not*   Sverige

If the English form of the name of a place is the English name of the government that has jurisdiction over the place, use that form.

>   **Union of Soviet Socialist Republics**
> *not*   Soi͡uz Sovet͡skikh Sot͡sialisticheskikh Respublik
>   Russia

23.2B. Vernacular form

23.2B1. Use the form in the official language of the country if there is no English form in general use.

>   **Buenos Aires**

>   **Gorlovka**

>   **Tallinn**

>   **Livorno**
> *not*   Leghorn
>   (*English form no longer in general use*)

If the country has more than one official language, use the form most commonly found in English-language sources.

>   **Louvain**
> *not*   Leuven

>   **Helsinki**
> *not*   Helsingfors

434

23.3. CHANGES OF NAME

23.3A. If the name of a place changes, use as many of the names as are required by:

> 1) the rules on government names (24.3E) (e.g., use *Nyasaland* or *Malawi*, as appropriate)
>
> *or* 2) the rules on additions to corporate names (24.4C4) and conference names (24.7B4) (e.g., use *Léopoldville* or *Kinshasa*, as appropriate)
>
> *or* 3) other relevant rules in chapter 24.

23.4. ADDITIONS

23.4A. Punctuation

23.4A1. Make all additions to place names used as entry elements (see 24.3E) in parentheses.

> **Budapest** *(Hungary)*

If the place name is being used as an addition, precede the name of a larger place by a comma.

> **Magyar Nemzeti Galéria** *(Budapest, Hungary)*[1]

23.4B. General rule

23.4B1. Add to the name of a place (other than a country or a state, etc., listed in 23.4C1 or 23.4D1) the name of a larger place as instructed in 23.4C–23.4F. For additional instructions on distinguishing between place names used as the headings for governments, see 24.6. For instructions on abbreviating some place names used as additions, see B.14.

23.4C. Places in Australia, Canada, Malaysia, United States, U.S.S.R., or Yugoslavia

23.4C1. States, etc. Do not make any addition to the name of a state, province, territory, etc., of Australia, Canada, Malaysia, the United States, the U.S.S.R., or Yugoslavia.

> **Northern Territory**
>
> **Prince Edward Island**
>
> **District of Columbia**

23.4C2. Other places. If the place is in a state, province, territory, etc., of one of the countries listed above, add the name of the state, etc., in which it is located.

> **Darwin** *(N.T.)*

---

1. This example and the one above are included solely to show the punctuation patterns. For the construction of the heading, see the later rules in this chapter and those in chapter 24.

> **Jasper** *(Alta.)*
>
> **George Town** *(Penang)*
>
> **Cook County** *(Ill.)*
>
> **Alexandria** *(Va.)*
>
> **Washington** *(D.C.)*
>
> **Kiev** *(Ukraine)*
>
> **Split** *(Croatia)*

23.4D. Places in the British Isles

23.4D1. Do not make any addition to the names of the following parts of the British Isles: England, the Republic of Ireland, Northern Ireland, Scotland, Wales, the Isle of Man, the Channel Islands.

23.4D2. If a place is located in England, the Republic of Ireland, Northern Ireland, Scotland, Wales, the Isle of Man, or the Channel Islands, add *England*, *Ireland*, *Northern Ireland*, *Scotland*, *Wales*, *Isle of Man*, or *Channel Islands*, as appropriate.

> **Dorset** *(England)*
>
> **Pinner** *(England)*
>
> **Clare** *(Ireland)*
>
> **Waterville** *(Ireland)*
>
> **Bangor** *(Northern Ireland)*
>
> **Strathclyde** *(Scotland)*
>
> **Melrose** *(Scotland)*
>
> **Powys** *(Wales)*
>
> **Bangor** *(Wales)*
>
> **Ramsey** *(Isle of Man)*
>
> **Jersey** *(Channel Islands)*

23.4E. Other places

23.4E1. Add to the name of a place not covered by 23.4C–23.4D the name of the country in which the place is located.

> **Formosa** *(Argentina)*
>
> **Luanda** *(Angola)*
>
> **Lucca** *(Italy)*
>
> **Madras** *(India)*

Monrovia *(Liberia)*

Næsby *(Denmark)*

Paris *(France)*

Toledo *(Spain)*

23.4F. Further additions

23.4F1. Distinguishing between otherwise identical place names. If the addition of a larger place as instructed in 23.4C–23.4E is insufficient to distinguish between two or more places with the same name, include a word or phrase commonly used to distinguish them.

> **Villaviciosa de Asturias** *(Spain)*
>
> **Villaviciosa de Córdoba** *(Spain)*

If there is no such word or phrase, give the name of an appropriate smaller place before the name of the larger place.

> **Friedberg** *(Bavaria, Germany)*
>
> **Friedberg** *(Hesse, Germany)*
>
> **Tarbert** *(Strathclyde, Scotland)*
>
> **Tarbert** *(Western Isles, Scotland)*
>
> **Basildon** *(Essex, England)*
>
> **Basildon** *(Berkshire, England)*
>
> **Saint Anthony** *(Hennepin County, Minn.)*
>
> **Saint Anthony** *(Stearns County, Minn.)*

23.4F2. Identifying places. If considered necessary to identify the place (as in the case of a community within a city), give the name of an appropriate smaller place before the name of the larger place specified as an addition by the preceding rules.

> **Hyde Park** *(Chicago, Ill.)*
>
> **Chelsea** *(London, England)*
>
> **Everton** *(Liverpool, England)*
>
> **St. Peter Port** *(Guernsey, Channel Islands)*
>
> **Hataitai** *(Wellington, N.Z.)*
>
> **Palermo** *(Sicily, Italy)*
>
> **Swansea** *(Toronto, Ont.)*
>
> **11^e Arrondissement** *(Paris, France)*
>
> **Minato-ku** *(Tokyo, Japan)*

23.5. PLACE NAMES INCLUDING OR REQUIRING A TERM INDICATING A TYPE OF JURISDICTION

23.5A. If the first part of a place name is a term indicating a type of jurisdiction and the place is commonly listed under another element of its name in lists published in the language of the country in which it is located, omit the term indicating the type of jurisdiction.

> **Kerry** *(Ireland)*
> *not*   County Kerry *(Ireland)*

> **Ostholstein** *(Germany)*
> *not*   Kreis Ostholstein *(Germany)*

In all other cases, include the term indicating the type of jurisdiction.

> **Città di Castello** *(Italy)*

> **Ciudad Juárez** *(Mexico)*

> **District of Columbia**

> **Distrito Federal** *(Brazil)*

> **Mexico City** *(Mexico)*

23.5B. If a place name does not include a term indicating a type of jurisdiction and such a term is required to distinguish that place from another of the same name, follow the instructions in 24.6.

HEADINGS FOR CORPORATE BODIES

Contents

Additions, Omissions, and Modifications

Subordinate and Related Bodies

Special Rules

Government Bodies and Officials

Special Rules

440

Religious Bodies and Officials

24.1. GENERAL RULE

24.1A. Enter a corporate body[1] directly under the name by which it is commonly identified, except when the rules that follow provide for entering it under the name of a higher or related body (see 24.13) or under the name of a government (see 24.18).

Determine the name by which a corporate body is commonly identified from items issued by that body in its language (see also 24.3A), or, when this condition does not apply, from reference sources.[2]

If the name of a corporate body consists of or contains initials, omit or include full stops and other marks of punctuation according to the predominant usage of the body. In case of doubt, omit the full stops, etc. Do not leave a space between

---

1. For definition, see 21.1B1.

2. *Reference sources*, as used in this chapter, includes books and articles written about a corporate body.

a full stop, etc., and an initial following it. Do not leave spaces between the letters of an initialism written without full stops, etc.

Make references from other forms of the name of a corporate body as instructed in 26.3.

3 October-Vereeniging

Aeródromo de Puerto Juárez

Aslib

Breitkopf & Härtel

British Museum

Carnegie Library of Pittsburgh

Challenger Expedition . . .[3]

Chartered Insurance Institute

Colin Buchanan and Partners

École centrale lyonnaise

G. Mendel Memorial Symposium, 1865-1965 . . .

Help the Aged (Canada)

Lambeth Conference . . .

Light Fantastic Players

M. Robert Gomberg Memorial Committee

MEDCOM

Museum of American Folk Art

Paddington Chamber of Commerce

Radio Society of Great Britain

Real Academia de Bellas Artes de San Jorge

Royal Aeronautical Society

St. Annen-Museum

Symposium on Cognition . . .

United States Catholic Conference

University of Oxford

W.H. Ross Foundation for the Study of Prevention of Blindness

World Methodist Conference . . .

Yale University

---

3. For additions to the name of a conference, congress, expedition, etc., see 24.7B.

24.1B. Romanization[4]

24.1B1. If the name of the body is in a language written in a nonroman script, romanize the name according to the table for that language adopted by the cataloguing agency. Refer from other romanizations as necessary.

> **Chung-kuo wen tzu kai ko wei yüan hui[5]**
> *x* Zhongguo wenzi gaige weiyuanhui
>
> **Institut mezhdunarodnykh otnoshenii**
>
> **Keihanshin Kyūkō Dentetsu Rōdō Kumiai**

24.1C. Changes of name

24.1C1. If the name of a corporate body has changed (including change from one language to another), establish a new heading under the new name for items appearing under that name. Refer from the old heading to the new and from the new heading to the old (see 26.3C).

> **Pennsylvania State University**
> The name of the Farmers' High School was changed in 1862 to Agricultural College of Pennsylvania; in 1874 to Pennsylvania State College; in 1953 to Pennsylvania State University.
> Works by this body are entered under the name used at the time of publication.
> *Make the same explanatory reference under the other names*
>
> **National Association for the Study and Prevention of Tuberculosis**
> For works by this body, *see also* the later heading:
> **National Tuberculosis Association**
>
> **National Tuberculosis Association**
> For works by this body, *see also* the earlier heading:
> **National Association for the Study and Prevention of Tuberculosis**

24.2. VARIANT NAMES. GENERAL RULES

24.2A. Apply this rule if a body uses variant names in items issued by it. Apply the special rules in 24.3 as well when they are appropriate.

---

4. *Alternative rule.* **Romanization.** If the name of the body is in a language written in a nonroman script and a romanized form appears in items issued by the body, use that romanized form. Refer as necessary from other romanizations. If more than one romanized form is found, use the form resulting from romanization according to the table adopted by the cataloguing agency for the language.

> **Zhongguo wenzi gaige weiyuanhui**
> *x* Chung-kuo wen tzu kai ko wei yüan hui

5. Systematic romanizations used in the examples in this chapter follow the tables (published by the Library of Congress in *Cataloging Service,* bulletin 118–   ) adopted jointly by the American Library Association, the Canadian Library Association, and the Library of Congress.

24.2B. If variant forms[6] of the name are found in items issued by the body, use the name as it appears in the chief sources of information (see 1.0A) as opposed to forms found elsewhere in the items.

24.2C. If variant spellings of the name appear in items issued by the body, use the form resulting from an official change in orthography or, if this does not apply, use the predominant spelling. In case of doubt, use the spelling found in the first item catalogued.

24.2D. If variant names appear in the chief source of information, use the name that is presented formally. If no name is presented formally, or if all names are presented formally, use the predominant form of name.

If there is no predominant form, use a brief form (including an initialism or an acronym) that would differentiate the body from others with the same or similar brief names.

> **AFL–CIO**
> *not* American Federation of Labor and Congress of Industrial
>   Organizations
>
> **American Philosophical Society**
> *not* American Philosophical Society Held at Philadelphia for
>   Promoting Useful Knowledge
>
> **Euratom**
> *not* European Atomic Energy Community
>
> **Kung ch'ing t'uan**
> *not* Chung-kuo kung ch'an chu i ch'ing nien t'uan
>
> **Maryknoll Sisters**
> *not* Congregation of the Maryknoll Sisters
>
> **Rateksa**
> *not* Radiobranchens tekniske og kommercielle sammenslutning
>
> **Unesco**
> *not* United Nations Educational, Scientific, and Cultural
>   Organization

If the variant forms do not include a brief form that would differentiate two or more bodies with the same or similar brief names, use the form found in reference sources or the official form, in that order of preference.

> **Metropolitan Applied Research Center**
> (*Official name. Brief form sometimes used by the center,* MARC
> Corporation, *is the same as the name of another body located in
> New York*)

---

6. *Variant forms* do not include names that the body has abandoned in the past or adopted in the future. For these, see 24.1C.

24.3. VARIANT NAMES. SPECIAL RULES

24.3A. Language[7]

24.3A1. If the name appears in different languages, use the form in the official language of the body.

> **Société historique franco-américaine**
> *not* Franco-American Historical Society

If there is more than one official language and one of these is English, use the English form.

> **Canadian Committee on Cataloguing**
> *not* Comité canadien de catalogage

If English is not one of the official languages or if the official language is not known, use the form in the language used predominantly in items issued by the body.

> **Schweizerische Landesbibliothek**
> *not* Biblioteca nazionale svizzera
> Bibliothèque nationale suisse
> *(German is the language used predominantly by the body in its publications)*

In case of doubt, use the English, French, German, Spanish, or Russian form, in this order of preference. If there is no form in any of these languages, use the form in the language that comes first in English alphabetic order. Refer from form(s) in other languages.

24.3B. Language. International bodies

24.3B1. If the name of an international body appears in English on items issued by it, use the English form. In other cases, follow the instructions in 24.3A.

> **Arab League**
> *not* Union des états arabes
> Jāmi'at al-Duwal al-'Arabīyah

> **European Economic Community**
> *not* Communauté économique européenne
> Europese Economische Gemeenschap
> [*etc.*]

---

7. *Alternative rule.* **Language.** Use a form of name in a language suitable to the users of the catalogue if the body's name is in a language that is not familiar to those users.

> **Japan Productivity Center**
> *if not* **Nihon Seisansei Hombu**

> **Union of Chambers of Commerce, Industry, and Commodity Exchanges of Turkey**
> *if not* **Türkiye Ticaret Odaları, Sanayi Odaları ve Ticaret Borsaları Birliği**

International Federation of Library Associations and Institutions
not   Fédération internationale des associations de bibliothécaires et
       des bibliothèques
      Internationaler Verband der Bibliothekarischen Vereine und
       Institutionen
      Mezhdunarodnai͡a federat͡sii͡a bibliotechnykh assot͡siat͡sĭ i
       uchrezhdeniĭ
      [*etc.*]

Nordic Association for American Studies
not   Nordisk selskap for Amerikastudier
      Nordiska sällskapet för Amerikastudier
      [*etc.*]

Nordisk husholdningshøjskole
      (*Name appears in Danish, Finnish, Icelandic, Norwegian, and
       Swedish*)
not   Nordisk husholdshøgskole
      Nordiska hushållshögskolan
      Norrænn búsýsluháskóli
      Pohjoismainen kotitalouskorkeakoulu

24.3C. Conventional name

24.3C1. General rule. If a body is frequently identified by a conventional form of name in reference sources in its own language, use this conventional name.

Westminster Abbey
not   Collegiate Church of St. Peter in Westminster

Kunstakademiet
not   Kongelige Akademi for de skønne kunster
      Kongelige Danske kunstakademi

24.3C2. Ancient and international bodies.[8] If the name of a body of ancient origin or of one that is international in character has become firmly established in an English form in English language usage, use this English form.

Benedictines

Casablanca Conference . . .

Cluniacs

Coptic Church

Council of Nicaea . . .

Franciscans

---

8. Apply this rule, for example, to religious bodies, fraternal and knightly orders, church councils, and diplomatic conferences. If it is necessary to establish a heading for a diplomatic conference that has no formal name and has not yet acquired a conventional name, use the name found most commonly in periodical articles and newspaper accounts in English. If another name becomes established later, change the heading to that name.

Freemasons

Knights of Malta

Nestorian Church

Paris Peace Conference . . .

Poor Clares

Royal and Select Masters

Royal Arch Masons

Vatican Council . . .

24.3C3. Autocephalous patriarchates, archdioceses, etc. Enter an ancient autocephalous patriarchate, archdiocese, etc., of the Eastern Church under the place by which it is identified. Add a word or phrase designating the type of ecclesiastical jurisdiction.

Antioch (*Jacobite patriarchate*)

Antioch (*Orthodox patriarchate*)

Constantinople (*Ecumenical patriarchate*)

Cyprus (*Archdiocese*)

24.3D. Religious orders and societies

24.3D1. Use the best-known form of name, in English, if possible, for a religious order or society. In case of doubt, follow this order of preference:

a) the conventional name by which its members are known in English
b) the English form of name used by units of the order or society located in English-speaking countries
c) the name of the order or society in the language of the country of its origin.

    Franciscans
not Ordo Fratrum Minorum
    Order of St. Francis
    Minorites
    [*etc.*]

    Jesuits
not Societas Jesu
    Compañía de Jesús
    Society of Jesus
    [*etc.*]

    Poor Clares
not Order of St. Clare
    Clarisses
    Second Order of St. Francis
    Franciscans. *Second Order*
    Minoresses
    [*etc.*]

Brothers of Our Lady of the Fields

Community of the Resurrection

Dominican Nuns of the Second Order of Perpetual Adoration
not   Dominicans. *Second Order of Perpetual Adoration*

Dominican Sisters of the Perpetual Rosary

Sisters of Divine Providence
not   Sœurs de la divine providence

Society of Christ the King

Third Order Regular of St. Francis
not   Franciscans. *Third Order Regular*

Third Order Secular of St. Francis
not   Franciscans. *Third Order Secular*

Divine Consciousness Light Society
not   Hare Krishna Society

Zgromadzenie Służebnic Najświętszej Maryi Panny

24.3E. Governments

24.3E1. Use the conventional name of a government,[9] unless the official name is in common use. The conventional name of a government is the geographic name (see chapter 23) of the area (e.g., country, province, state, county, municipality) over which the government exercises jurisdiction. See also 24.6.

France
not   République française

Yugoslavia
not   Socijalistička Federativna Republika Jugoslavija
[*etc.*]

Massachusetts
not   Commonwealth of Massachusetts

Nottinghamshire (*England*)
not   County of Nottingham

Arlington (*Mass.*)
not   Town of Arlington

If the official name of the government is in common use, use it.

Greater Anchorage Borough (*Alaska*)

---

9. *Government* is used here to mean the totality of corporate bodies (executive, legislative, and judicial) exercising the powers of a jurisdiction. Treat as a government agency a corporate body known as *government*, or its equivalent in other languages, or a term with similar meaning, that is an executive element of a particular jurisdiction (see 24.18).

24.3F. Conferences, congresses, meetings, etc.

24.3F1. If, among the variant forms of a conference name appearing in the chief source of information, there is a form that includes the name or abbreviation of the name of a body associated with the meeting to which the meeting is not subordinate, use this form.

> **FAO Hybrid Maize Meeting . . .**

If, however, the name is of a body to which the meeting is subordinate (e.g., the annual meeting of an association), see 24.13A, type 6.

24.3F2. If a conference has both a specific name of its own and a more general name as one of a series of conferences, use the specific name.

> **Symposium on Protein Metabolism . . .**
>
> *not* Nutrition Symposium . . .
>
> **Symposium on Endocrines and Nutrition . . .**
>
> *not* Nutrition Symposium . . .

24.3G. Local churches, etc.

24.3G1. If variant forms of the name of a local church, cathedral, monastery, convent, abbey, temple, mosque, synagogue, etc., appear in the chief source of information of items issued by the body, use the predominant form. If there is no predominant form, follow this order of preference:

a) a name containing the name of the person(s), object(s), place(s), or event(s) to which the local church, etc., is dedicated or after which it is named

> **All Saints Church . . .**
>
> **Chapelle Saint-Louis . . .**
>
> **Church of the Holy Sepulchre . . .**
>
> **Duomo di Santa Maria Matricolare . . .**
>
> **Jāmiʻ ʻAmr ibn al-ʻĀṣ . . .**
>
> **Hōryūji . . .**
>
> **St. Clement's Church . . .**
>
> **St. Paul's Cathedral . . .**
>
> **Temple Emanu-El . . .**
>
> **Visitation Monastery . . .**

b) a name beginning with a word or phrase descriptive of a type of local church, etc.

> **Abtei Reichenau**
>
> **Great Synagogue . . .**
>
> **Jüdische Reformgemeinde in Berlin**

> **Monasterio de Clarisas . . .**
>
> **Parish Church of Limpsfield**
>
> **Unitarian Universalist Church . . .**

c) a name beginning with the name of the place in which the local church, etc., is situated.

> **Anerley Society of the New Church**
>
> **Beechen Grove Baptist Church . . .**
>
> **English River Congregation of the Church of the Brethren**
>
> **Kölner Dom**
>
> **Tenafly Presbyterian Church**
>
> **Westover Church . . .**
>
> **Winchester Cathedral**

For additions to the name of a local church, etc., see 24.10.

Additions, Omissions, and Modifications

24.4. ADDITIONS

24.4A. General rule

24.4A1. Make additions to the name of a corporate body as instructed in 24.4B–24.4C.

For additions to special types of corporate bodies (e.g., governments, conferences), see 24.6–24.11. Enclose in parentheses all additions required by rules in this chapter.

24.4B. Names not conveying the idea of a corporate body

24.4B1. If the name alone does not convey the idea of a corporate body, add a general designation in English.

> **Apollo 11** (*Spacecraft*)
>
> **Bounty** (*Ship*)
>
> **Elks** (*Fraternal order*)
>
> **Friedrich Witte** (*Firm*)

24.4C. Two or more bodies with the same or similar names

24.4C1. General rule. If two or more bodies have the same name, or names so similar that they may be confused, add a word or phrase to each name as instructed in 24.4C2–24.4C7. Add such a word or phrase to any other name if the addition assists in the understanding of the nature or purpose of the body.

Do not include the additions to names of places prescribed in 24.6 when the names of these places are used to indicate the location of corporate bodies.

24.4C2. Names of countries, states, provinces, etc. If a body has a character that is national, state, provincial, etc., add the name of the country, state, province, etc., in which it is located.

> **Republican Party** (*Ill.*)
>
> **Republican Party** (*Mo.*)
>
> **Sociedad Nacional de Minería** (*Chile*)
>
> **Sociedad Nacional de Minería** (*Peru*)
>
> **Governor's Highway Safety Program** (*N.C.*)
>
> **Governor's Highway Safety Program** (*Vt.*)
>
> **National Measurement Laboratory** (*U.S.*)
>
> **Midlands Museum** (*Zimbabwe*)

If such an addition does not provide sufficient identification or is inappropriate (as in the case of national, state, provincial, etc., universities of the same name serving the same country, state, province, etc.), follow the instructions in 24.4C3–24.4C7.

24.4C3. Local place names. In the case of any other body, add the name of the local place, whether it is a jurisdiction or not, that is most commonly associated with the name of the body, unless the name of an institution, the date(s) of the body, or other designation (see 24.4C5–24.4C7) provides better identification.

> **Salem College** (*Salem, W. Va.*)
>
> **Salem College** (*Winston-Salem, N.C.*)
>
> **Washington County Historical Society** (*Washington County, Ark.*)
>
> **Washington County Historical Society** (*Washington County, Md.*)
>
> **École française de papeterie** (*Grenoble, France*)
> (*School is located in St. Martin d'Hères, an incorporated suburb of Grenoble, but more closely associated with Grenoble*)
>
> **St. Barnabas Church of England School** (*Bradwell, England*)
>
> **St. Peter's Church** (*Hook Norton, England*)
>
> **St. Peter's Church** (*Sudbury, England*)
>
> **Red Lion Hotel** (*Newport, Wales*)
>
> **Red Lion Hotel** (*Newport, Isle of Wight, England*)
>
> **Red Lion Hotel** (*Newport, Shropshire, England*)

If further distinction is necessary, give the name of a particular area within the local place before the name of the local place.

> **St. John's Church** (*Georgetown, Washington, D.C.*)
>
> **St. John's Church** (*Lafayette Square, Washington, D.C.*)

24.4C4. Change of name of jurisdiction or locality. If the name of the local jurisdiction or geographic locality changes during the lifetime of the body, add the latest name in use in the lifetime of the body.

        St. Paul Lutheran Church (*Skokie, Ill.*)

not   St. Paul Lutheran Church (*Niles Center, Ill.*)
        (*Church founded in 1881. Place name changed in 1940*)

but   **Historisk samfund** (*Christiania, Norway*)
        (*Ceased to exist before Christiania became Oslo*)

24.4C5. Institutions. Add the name of an institution instead of the local place name if the institution's name is commonly associated with the name of the body. Give the name of the institution in the form and language used for it as a heading.

        Newman Club (*Brooklyn College*)

not   Newman Club (*Brooklyn, New York, N.Y.*)

        Newman Club (*University of Maryland*)

not   Newman Club (*College Park, Md.*)

        Center for Radiation Research (*National Measurement Laboratory* (*U.S.*))

        Institut geologiĭ (*Akademiia nauk SSSR. Komi filial*)

        Institut geologiĭ (*Akademiia nauk SSSR. Karel'skiĭ filial*)

24.4C6. Year(s). If the name has been used by two or more bodies that cannot be distinguished by place, add the year of founding or the inclusive years of existence.

        Scientific Society of San Antonio (*1892-1894*)

        Scientific Society of San Antonio (*1904-   *)

24.4C7. Other additions. If none of the place name, name of institution, or date(s) is sufficient or appropriate for distinguishing between two or more bodies, add an appropriate general designation in English.

        Church of God (*Adventist*)

        Church of God (*Apostolic*)

24.5. OMISSIONS

24.5A. Initial articles

24.5A1. Omit an initial article unless the heading is to file under the article (e.g., a corporate name that begins with an article that is the first part of the name of a person or place).

        Français de Grande-Bretagne (*Association*)

not   Les Français de Grande-Bretagne (*Association*)

        Library Association

not   The Library Association

Blaue Adler (*Association*)
not   Der Blaue Adler (*Association*)

Norske Nobelinstitutt
not   Det Norske Nobelinstitutt
but

Le Corbusier Sketchbook Publication Committee

Los Angeles Symphony (*Orchestra*)

24.5B. Citations of honours

24.5B1. Omit a phrase citing an honour or order awarded to the body.

Moskovskaia gosudarstvennaia konservatoriia imeni P.I. Chaĭkovskogo
not   Moskovskaia gosudarstvennaia ordena Lenina konservatoriia imeni P.I. Chaĭkovskogo

Moskovskiĭ khudozhestvennyĭ akademicheskiĭ teatr
not   Moskovskiĭ khudozhestvennyĭ ordena Lenina i Trudovogo krasnogo znameni akademicheskiĭ teatr

24.5C. Terms indicating incorporation and certain other terms

24.5C1. Omit an adjectival term or abbreviation indicating incorporation (e.g., *Incorporated, E.V., Ltd.*) or state ownership of a corporate body, and a word or phrase, abbreviated or in full, designating the type of incorporated entity (e.g., *Aktiebolaget, Gesellschaft mit beschränkter Haftung, Kabushiki Kaisha, Società per azione*), unless it is an integral part of the name or is needed to make it clear that the name is that of a corporate body.

    American Ethnological Society
      (*Without* Inc.)

    Automobiltechnische Gesellschaft
      (*Without* E.V.)

    Daiwa Ginkō
      (*Without* Kabushiki Kaisha)

    Thüringisches Kunstfaserwerk "Wilhelm Pieck"
      (*Without* VEB)

    Compañía Internacional Editora
      (*Without* S.a.)
but

Films Incorporated

Nihon Genshiryoku Hatsuden Kabushiki Kaisha

Peter Davies Limited

Vickers (Aviation) Limited

24.5C2. If such a term is needed to make it clear that the name is that of a corporate body and it occurs at the beginning of the name, transpose it to the end.

> **Elektrometall, Aktiebolaget**
> *not*   Aktiebolaget Elektrometall

> **Hochbauprojektierung Karl-Marx-Stadt, VEB**
> *not*   VEB Hochbauprojektierung Karl-Marx-Stadt

24.5C3. Omit an initial word or phrase in an oriental language indicating the private character of a corporate body (e.g., *Shiritsu*, *Ssu li*), unless the word or phrase is an integral part of the name.

> **Tan-chiang Ying yü chuan kʻo hsüeh hsiao**
> *not*   Ssu li Tan-chiang Ying yü chuan kʻo hsüeh hsiao

> *but*   **Shiritsu Daigaku Toshokan Kyōkai**

24.5C4. Omit abbreviations (e.g., *U.S.S.*, *H.M.S.*) occurring before the name of a ship.

> **Ark Royal** (*Ship*)
> *not*   H.M.S. Ark Royal

24.6. GOVERNMENTS. ADDITIONS

24.6A. Scope

24.6A1. Apply this rule to the names of governments that are not differentiated by the application of 23.4. Make the further additions prescribed here following a space, colon, space, and within the same parentheses that enclose the additions prescribed by 23.4.

24.6B. Add the type of jurisdiction in English if other than a city or a town. If there is no English equivalent for the vernacular term, or in case of doubt, use the vernacular term.

> **Cork** (*Ireland*)
>
> **Cork** (*Ireland : County*)
>
> **Darmstadt** (*Germany*)
>
> **Darmstadt** (*Germany : Landkreis*)
>
> **Darmstadt** (*Germany : Regierungsbezirk*)
>
> **Guadalajara** (*Mexico*)
>
> **Guadalajara** (*Spain*)
>
> **Guadalajara** (*Spain : Province*)
>
> **Lublin** (*Poland*)
>
> **Lublin** (*Poland : Voivodeship*)

New York (*N.Y.*)

New York (*State*)

Québec (*Province*)

Québec (*Québec*)

Québec (*Québec : County*)

Reşiţa (*Romania*)

Reşiţa (*Romania : Raion*)

24.6C. If the type of jurisdiction does not provide a satisfactory distinction, add an appropriate word or phrase.

Germany (*Democratic Republic*)

Germany (*Federal Republic*)

Berlin (*Germany : East*)

Berlin (*Germany : West*)

24.6D. If two or more governments lay claim to jurisdiction over the same area (e.g., as with occupying powers and insurgent governments), add a suitable designation to one or each of the governments, followed by the inclusive years of its existence.

France

France (*Territory under German occupation, 1940-1944*)

Algeria

Algeria (*Provisional government, 1958-1962*)

24.7. CONFERENCES, CONGRESSES, MEETINGS, ETC.

24.7A. Omissions

24.7A1. Omit from the name of a conference, etc., indications of its number, frequency, or year(s) of convocation.

Conference on Co-ordination of Galactic Research . . .
not   Second Conference on Co-ordination of Galactic Research . . .

Louisiana Cancer Conference . . .
not   Biennial Louisiana Cancer Conference . . .

Analogies Symposium . . .
not   1986 Analogies Symposium . . .

24.7B. Additions

24.7B1. General rule. Add to the name of a conference, etc. (including that of a conference entered subordinately, see 24.13), the number of the conference, etc. (if appropriate), the year(s), and the place(s) in which it was held. Separate these elements by a space, colon, space.

24.7B2. Number. If a conference, etc., is stated or inferred to be one of a series of numbered meetings of the same name, add the ordinal numeral in its English form (see C.8A).

> **Conference of British Teachers of Marketing at Advanced Level**
> (*3rd : . . .*)

If the numbering is irregular, do not add it. *Optionally*, provide an explanation of the irregularities in a note or an explanatory reference.

24.7B3. Date. If the heading is for a single meeting, add the year or years in which the conference, etc., was held.

> **Conference on Library Surveys** (*1965 : . . .*)

> **Conference on Technical Information Center Administration** (*3rd : 1966 : . . .*)

> **Study Institute on Special Education** (*1969-1970 : . . .*)

Add specific dates if necessary to distinguish between two or more meetings held in the same year.

> **Conférence agricole interalliée** (*1st : 1919 Feb. 11-15 : . . .*)

> **Conférence agricole interalliée** (*2nd : 1919 Mar. 17-19 : . . .*)

24.7B4. Location. Add the name of the local place or other location (institution, etc.) in which the conference, etc., was held. Give a local place name in the form prescribed in chapter 23. Give any other location in the nominative case in the language and form in which it is found in the item being catalogued.

> **Symposium on Glaucoma** (*1966 : New Orleans, La.*)

> **Konferentsiia po pochvovedeniiu i fiziologii kul'turnykh rastenii**
> (*1937 : Saratovskiĭ universitet*)

> **Workshop Conference on the Role of the Director of Medical Education in the Hospital** (*1959 : Chicago, Ill.*)

> **Regional Conference on Mental Measurements of the Blind** (*1st : 1951 : Perkins Institution*)

> **Louisiana Cancer Conference** (*2nd : 1958 : New Orleans, La.*)

> **International Conference on Atmospheric Emissions from Sulphate Pulping** (*1966 : Sanibel Island, Fla.*)

> **International Conference on the Biology of Whales** (*1971 : Shenandoah National Park*)

> **Conference "Systematics of the Old World Monkeys"** (*1969 : Burg Wartenstein*)

> **Conference on Cancer Public Education** (*1973 : Dulles Airport*)

If the heading is for a series of conferences, etc., do not add the location unless all were held in the same place.

> **Hybrid Corn Industry Research Conference**

If the location is part of the name of the conference, etc., do not repeat it.

> **Arden House Conference on Medicine and Anthropology** (*1961*)

> **Paris Symposium on Radio Astronomy** (*1958*)

If the sessions of a conference, etc., were held in two locations, add both names.

> **World Peace Congress** (*1st : 1949 : Paris, France, and Prague, Czechoslovakia*)

> **Institute on Diagnostic Problems in Mental Retardation** (*1957 : Long Beach State College and San Francisco State College*)

If the sessions of a conference, etc., were held in three or more locations, add the first named place followed by *etc.*

> **International Conference on Alternatives to War** (*1982 : San Francisco, Calif., etc.*)

24.8. EXHIBITIONS, FAIRS, FESTIVALS, ETC.

24.8A. Omissions

24.8A1. As instructed in 24.7A1, omit from the name of an exhibition, fair, festival, etc., word(s) that denote its number.

24.8B. Additions

24.8B1. As instructed in 24.7B, add to the name of an exhibition, fair, festival, etc., its number, date, and location. Do not add the date and/or location if they are integral parts of the name.

> **Biennale di Venezia** (*36th : 1972*)

> **World's Columbian Exposition** (*1893 : Chicago, Ill.*)

> **Expo 67** (*Montréal, Québec*)

24.9. CHAPTERS, BRANCHES, ETC.

24.9A. If a chapter, branch, etc., entered subordinately (see 24.13), carries out the activities of a corporate body in a particular locality or within a particular institution, add the name of the locality or institution, unless it is part of the name of the chapter, branch, etc.

> **Freemasons.** *Concordia Lodge, No. 13 (Baltimore, Md.)*

> **Freemasons.** *United Grand Lodge (England)*

> **Knights Templar** (*Masonic order*). *Grand Commandery (Me.)*

> **Scottish Rite** (*Masonic order*). *Oriental Consistory* (*Chicago, Ill.*)
>
> **Psi Upsilon** (*Fraternity*). *Gamma Chapter* (*Amherst College*)
>
> **Society of St. Vincent de Paul.** *Conference*[10] (*Cathedral of St. John the Baptist : Savannah, Ga.*)

but

> **American Heart Association.** *Illinois Affiliate*
>
> **American Red Cross.** *Champaign County Chapter*

24.10. LOCAL CHURCHES, ETC.

24.10A. If the name of a local church, etc., does not convey the idea of a church, etc., add a general designation in English.

> **Monte Cassino** (*Monastery*)

24.10B. Add to the name of a local church, etc., the name of the place or local ecclesiastical jurisdiction (e.g., parish, Pfarrei) in which it is located (see 24.4C3–24.4C4), unless the location is clear from the name itself.

> **All Saints Church** (*Birchington, England*)
>
> **St. Mary** (*Church : Aylesbury Vale, England*)
>
> **Visitation Monastery** (*Waldron, England*)
>
> **Westover Church** (*Charles City County, Va.*)
>
> **St. James' Church** (*Bronx, New York, N.Y.*)
>
> **Twin City Bible Church** (*Urbana, Ill.*)
>
> **Finnish Lutheran Church of Canberra**

If there are two or more local churches, etc., with the same name in the same locality, add a further suitable designation.

> **St. James' Church** (*Manhattan, New York, N.Y. : Catholic*)
>
> **St. James' Church** (*Manhattan, New York, N.Y. : Episcopal*)

24.11. RADIO AND TELEVISION STATIONS

24.11A. If the name of a radio or television station consists solely or principally of its call letters or if its name does not convey the idea of a radio or television station, add *Radio station* or *Television station* and the name of the place in which the station is located.

> **HVJ** (*Radio station : Vatican City*)
>
> **WCIA** (*Television station : Champaign, Ill.*)

---

10. *Conference* is used by this body as the generic word for its local units.

24.11B. Add to the name of any other radio or television station the place in which it is located unless the name of the place is an integral part of the name of the station.

>**Radio Maroc** (*Rabat, Morocco*)

>*but* **Radio London**

Subordinate and Related Bodies

24.12. GENERAL RULE

24.12A. Enter a subordinate body (other than a government agency entered under jurisdiction, see 24.18) or a related body directly under its own name (see 24.1–24.3) unless its name belongs to one or more of the types listed in 24.13. Refer to the name of a subordinate body entered directly from its name in the form of a subheading of the higher body (see 26.3A7).

>**Ansco**
>>*x* General Aniline and Film Corporation. *Ansco*

>**Association of College and Research Libraries**
>>*x* American Library Association. *Association of College and Research Libraries*

>**BBC Symphony Orchestra**
>>*x* British Broadcasting Corporation. *Symphony Orchestra*

>**Bodleian Library**
>>*x* University of Oxford. *Bodleian Library*

>**Congregation of the Most Holy Name of Jesus**
>>*x* Dominican Sisters. *Congregation of the Most Holy Name of Jesus*

>**Crane Theological School**
>>*x* Tufts University. *Crane Theological School*

>**Faculdade de Teologia de Lisboa**
>>*x* Universidade Católica Portuguesa. *Faculdade de Teologia de Lisboa*

>**Friends of IBBY**
>>*x* International Board on Books for Young People. *Friends*

>**Harvard Law School**
>>*x* Harvard University. *Law School*

24.13. SUBORDINATE AND RELATED BODIES ENTERED SUBORDINATELY

24.13A. Enter a subordinate or related body as a subheading of the name of the body to which it is subordinate or related if its name belongs to one or more of the following types.[11] Make it a direct or indirect subheading as instructed in 24.14. Omit from the subheading the name or abbreviation of the name of the higher or related body in noun form unless the omission would result in a heading that does not make sense.

TYPE 1. A name containing a term that by definition implies that the body is part of another (e.g., *Department, Division, Section, Branch*).

> **British Broadcasting Corporation.** *Engineering Division*
>
> **International Federation of Library Associations and Institutions.** *Section on Cataloguing*
>
> **Stanford University.** *Department of Civil Engineering*

TYPE 2. A name containing a word that normally implies administrative subordination (e.g., *Committee, Commission*) provided that the name of the higher body is required for the identification of the subordinate body.

> **Association of State Universities and Land-Grant Colleges.** *Committee on Traffic Safety Research and Education*
>
> **International Council on Social Welfare.** *Canadian Committee*
>
> **Timber Trade Federation of the United Kingdom.** *Statistical Co-ordinating Committee*
>
> **National Association of Insurance Commissioners.** *Securities Valuation Office*
>
> **University of Wales.** *University Commission*
> (*Name:* University Commission)

but **National Commission on United Methodist Higher Education**

TYPE 3. A name that is general in nature or that does no more than indicate a geographic, chronological, or numbered or lettered subdivision of a parent body.

> **American Dental Association.** *Research Institute*
> (*Name:* Research Institute)
>
> **Bell Telephone Laboratories.** *Technical Information Library*
> (*Name:* Technical Information Library)
>
> **Sondley Reference Library.** *Friends of the Library*
> (*Name:* Friends of the Library)
>
> **American Institute of Architects.** *Utah Society*
> (*Name:* Utah Society)
>
> **Canadian Jewish Congress.** *Central Region*
> (*Name:* Central Region)

---

11. Distinguish cases in which the subordinate body's name includes the names of higher bodies from cases in which the names of higher bodies appear only in association with the subordinate body's name.

California Home Economics Association. *Orange District*
(*Name:* Orange District)

International Labour Organisation. *European Regional Conference*
(*2nd : 1968 : Geneva, Switzerland*)
(*Name:* Second European Regional Conference)

Dartmouth College. *Class of 1980*
(*Name:* Class of 1980)

Knights of Labor. *District Assembly 99*
(*Name:* District Assembly 99)

U.S. Customs Service. *Region IX*
(*Name:* Region IX)

In case of doubt, enter the body directly.

Human Resources Centre (*London, England*)
x Tavistock Institute of Human Relations. *Human Resources Centre*

Research and Training Institute
x Human Resources Center (*Albertson, N.Y.*). *Research and Training Institute*

TYPE 4. A name that does not convey the idea of a corporate body.

British Library. *Collection Development*
(*Name:* Collection Development)

Bell Canada. *Corporate Public Relations*
(*Name:* Corporate Public Relations)

TYPE 5. A name of a university faculty, school, college, institute, laboratory, etc., that simply indicates a particular field of study.

Princeton University. *Bureau of Urban Research*

Syracuse University. *College of Medicine*

University College London. *Communication Research Centre*

University of London. *School of Pharmacy*

TYPE 6. A name that includes the entire name of the higher or related body.

American Legion. *Auxiliary*
(*Name:* American Legion Auxiliary)

Auburn University. *Agricultural Experiment Station*
(*Name:* Agricultural Experiment Station of Auburn University)

Friends of the Earth. *Camden Friends of the Earth*
(*Name:* Camden Friends of the Earth)

> **Labour Party** (*Great Britain*). *Conference (72nd : 1972 :
> Blackpool, England*)
> (*Name:* 72nd Annual Conference of the Labour Party)
> (*Activity of the Labour Party limited to Great Britain*)

> **United Methodist Church** (*U.S.*). *General Conference*
> (*Name:* General Conference of the United Methodist Church)

> **University of Southampton.** *Mathematical Society*
> (*Name:* Mathematical Society of the University of Southampton)

> **University of Vermont.** *Choral Union*
> (*Name:* University of Vermont Choral Union)

> **Yale University.** *Library*
> (*Name:* Yale University Library)

but   **BBC Symphony Orchestra**
not   British Broadcasting Corporation. *Symphony Orchestra*

24.14. DIRECT OR INDIRECT SUBHEADING

24.14A. Enter a body belonging to one or more of the types listed in 24.13 as a subheading of the lowest element in the hierarchy that is entered under its own name. Omit intervening elements in the hierarchy unless the name of the subordinate or related body has been, or is likely to be, used by another body entered under the name of the same higher or related body. In that case, interpose the name of the lowest element in the hierarchy that will distinguish between the bodies.

> **Public Library Association.** *Audiovisual Committee*
> *Hierarchy:* American Library Association
> Public Library Association
> Audiovisual Committee

> **American Library Association.** *Cataloging and Classification
> Section. Policy and Research Committee*
> *Hierarchy:* American Library Association
> Resources and Technical Services Division
> Cataloging and Classification Section
> Policy and Research Committee

> **American Library Association.** *Resources and Technical Services
> Division. Board of Directors*
> *Hierarchy:* American Library Association
> Resources and Technical Services Division
> Board of Directors

Refer from the name in the form of a subheading of the name of its immediately superior body when the heading does not include the name of that superior body (see 26.3A7).

American Library Association. *Committee on Outreach Programs for Young Adults (Ad Hoc)*
    Hierarchy: American Library Association
              Young Adult Services Division
              Committee on Outreach Programs for Young
                  Adults (Ad Hoc)
  x American Library Association. *Young Adult Services Division. Committee on Outreach Programs for Young Adults (Ad Hoc)*

American Library Association. *Cataloging and Classification Section*
    Hierarchy: American Library Association
              Resources and Technical Services Division
              Cataloging and Classification Section
  x American Library Association. *Resources and Technical Services Division. Cataloging and Classification Section*

Special Rules

24.15. JOINT COMMITTEES, COMMISSIONS, ETC.

24.15A. Enter a body made up of representatives of two or more other bodies directly under its own name.

Joint Committee on Individual Efficiency in Industry
    (*A joint committee of the Department of Scientific and Industrial Research and the Medical Research Council*)

Canadian Committee on MARC
    (*A joint committee of the Association pour l'avancement des sciences et des techniques de la documentation, the Canadian Library Association, and the National Library of Canada*)

Omit the names of the parent bodies when these occur within or at the end of the name and if the name of the joint unit is distinctive without them.

Joint Committee on Bathing Places
    (*Name:* Joint Committee on Bathing Places of the Conference of State Sanitary Engineers and the Engineering Section of the American Public Health Association)

but **Joint Commission of the Council for Education in World Citizenship and the London International Assembly**

24.15B. If the parent bodies are entered as subheadings of a common higher body, enter the joint unit as a subordinate body as instructed in 24.12–24.14.

American Library Association. *Joint Committee to Compile a List of International Subscription Agents*
    (*A joint committee of the Acquisitions and Serials sections of the American Library Association's Resources and Technical Services Division*)

24.16. CONVENTIONALIZED SUBHEADINGS FOR STATE AND LOCAL ELEMENTS OF UNITED STATES POLITICAL PARTIES

24.16A. Enter a state or local unit of a political party in the United States under the name of the party followed by the state or local name in parentheses and then the name of the unit. Omit from the name of the unit any indication of the name of the party or the state or locality.

> **Republican Party** (*Mo.*). *State Committee*
> (*Name:* Missouri Republican State Committee)

> **Republican Party** (*Ohio*). *State Executive Committee*
> (*Name:* Ohio State Republican Executive Committee)

> **Democratic Party** (*Tex.*). *State Convention* (*1857 : Waco, Tex.*)
> (*Name:* State Convention of the Democratic Party of the State of Texas)

Government Bodies and Officials

24.17. GENERAL RULE

24.17A. Enter a body created or controlled by a government directly under its own name (see 24.1–24.3) unless it belongs to one or more of the types listed in 24.18. However, if a body is subordinate to a higher body that is entered under its own name, formulate the heading for the subordinate body according to 24.12–24.14. Refer to the name of a government agency entered directly from its name in the form of a subheading of the name of the government (see 26.3A7).

> **American Battle Monuments Commission**
> *x* United States. *American Battle Monuments Commission*

> **Arts Council of Great Britain**
> *x* United Kingdom. *Arts Council*

> **Boundary Commission for England**
> *x* United Kingdom. *Boundary Commission for England*

> **Canada Institute for Scientific and Technical Information**
> *x* Canada. *Institute for Scientific and Technical Information*

> **Canadian National Railways**
> *x* Canada. *Canadian National Railways*

> **Consejo Superior de Investigaciones Científicas**
> *x* Spain. *Consejo Superior de Investigaciones Científicas*

> **Council on International Economic Policy**
> *x* United States. *Council on International Economic Policy*

> **Dundee Harbour Trust**
> *x* United Kingdom. *Dundee Harbour Trust*

> **University of British Columbia**
> *x* British Columbia. *University*

24.18. GOVERNMENT AGENCIES ENTERED SUBORDINATELY

24.18A. Enter a government agency subordinately to the name of the government if it belongs to one or more of the following types. Make it a direct or indirect subheading of the heading for the government as instructed in 24.19. Omit from the subheading the name or abbreviation of the name of the government in noun form unless such an omission would result in a heading that does not make sense.

> **Canada.** *Agriculture Canada*
>
> *not*　Canada. *Agriculture*

TYPE 1. An agency with a name containing a term that by definition implies that the body is part of another (e.g., *Department, Division, Section, Branch*, and their equivalents in other languages).

> **Vermont.** *Department of Water Resources*
>
> **Ottawa** (*Ont.*). *Department of Community Development*
>
> **United States.** *Division of Wildlife Services*

TYPE 2. An agency with a name containing a word that normally implies administrative subordination in the terminology of the government concerned (e.g., *Committee, Commission*), provided that the name of the government is required for the identification of the agency.

> **Australia.** *Bureau of Agricultural Economics*
>
> **Canada.** *Royal Commission on Banking and Finance*
>
> **United Kingdom.** *Royal Commission on the Press*
>
> **United Kingdom.** *Central Office of Information*
>
> **United States.** *Commission on Civil Rights*
>
> **United States.** *Committee on Retirement Policy for Federal Personnel*
>
> *but*　**Royal Commission on Higher Education in New Brunswick**

TYPE 3. An agency with a name that is general in nature or that does no more than indicate a geographic, chronological, or numbered or lettered subdivision of the government or of one of its agencies entered subordinately.

> **United States.** *National Labor Relations Board. Library*
> (*Name:* Library)
>
> **Niger.** *Commissariat général au développement. Centre de documentation*
> (*Name:* Centre de documentation)
>
> **Malaysia.** *Royal Customs and Excise Department. Sabah Region*
> (*Name:* Sabah Region)
>
> **United States.** *General Services Administration. Region 5*
> (*Name:* Region 5)

> **United States.** *Public Health Service. Region XI*
> (*Name:* Region XI)

In case of doubt, enter the body directly.

> **Governor's Internship Program**
> *not*   Minnesota. *Governor's Internship Program*

> **National Portrait Gallery** (*U.K.*)
> *not*   United Kingdom. *National Portrait Gallery*

> **Musée des beaux-arts** (*Béziers, France*)
> *not*   Béziers (*France*). *Musée des beaux-arts*

TYPE 4. An agency with a name that does not convey the idea of a corporate body and does not contain the name of the government.

> **Illinois.** *Bureau of Employment Security. Research and Analysis*
> (*Name:* Research and Analysis)

> **Lower Saxony** (*Germany*). *Landesvermessung*
> (*Name:* Landesvermessung)

> **United States.** *Naval Oceanography and Meteorology*
> (*Name:* Naval Oceanography and Meteorology)

> **Canada.** *Ocean and Aquatic Sciences*
> (*Name:* Ocean and Aquatic Sciences)

TYPE 5. An agency that is a ministry or similar major executive agency (i.e., one that has no other agency above it) as defined by official publications of the government in question.

> **United Kingdom.** *Home Office*

> **United Kingdom.** *Ministry of Defence*

> **Italy.** *Ministero del bilancio e della programmazione economica*

> **United States.** *National Aeronautics and Space Administration*

TYPE 6. A legislative body (see also 24.21).

> **Chicago** (*Ill.*). *City Council*

> **France.** *Assemblée nationale*

> **United Kingdom.** *Parliament*

> **United States.** *Congress*

TYPE 7. A court (see also 24.23).

> **Ontario.** *High Court of Justice*

> **United States.** *Supreme Court*

TYPE 8. A principal service of the armed forces of a government (see also 24.24).

> **Canada.** *Canadian Armed Forces*
>
> **Germany.** *Heer*
>
> **New York** (*State*). *Militia*
>
> **United Kingdom.** *Army*

TYPE 9. A head of state or head of government (see also 24.20).

> **United Kingdom.** *Sovereign*
>
> **Montréal** (*Québec*). *Mayor*
>
> **United States.** *President*
>
> **Virginia.** *Governor*

TYPE 10. An embassy, consulate, etc. (see also 24.25).

> **Canada.** *Embassy* (*U.S.*)
>
> **United Kingdom.** *Consulate* (*New York, N.Y.*)

TYPE 11. A delegation to an international or intergovernmental body (see also 24.26).

> **United Kingdom.** *Delegation* (*United Nations*)

24.19. DIRECT OR INDIRECT SUBHEADING

24.19A. Enter an agency belonging to one or more of the types listed in 24.18 as a direct subheading of the heading for the government unless the name of the agency has been, or is likely to be, used by another agency entered under the name of the same government. In that case, interpose the name of the lowest element in the hierarchy that will distinguish between the agencies.

> **United States.** *Office of Human Development Services*
> *Hierarchy:* United States
> Department of Health, Education, and Welfare
> Office of Human Development Services
>
> **Québec** (*Province*). *Service de l'exploration géologique*
> *Hierarchy:* Québec
> Ministère des richesses naturelles
> Direction générale des mines
> Direction de la géologie
> Service de l'exploration géologique
>
> **United States.** *Aviation Forecast Branch*
> *Hierarchy:* United States
> Department of Transportation
> Federal Aviation Administration
> Office of Aviation Policy
> Aviation Forecast Branch

> **United Kingdom.** *Nationality and Treaty Department*
> *Hierarchy:* United Kingdom
> Foreign and Commonwealth Office
> Nationality and Treaty Department

> **France.** *Commission centrale des marchés*
> *Hierarchy:* France
> Ministère de l'économie et des finances
> Commission centrale des marchés

but

> **United Kingdom.** *Department of Employment. Solicitors Office*
> *Hierarchy:* United Kingdom
> Department of Employment
> Solicitors Office
> (*Other ministries and departments have had subordinate units called* Solicitors Office)

> **France.** *Direction générale des impôts. Service de l'administration générale*
> *Hierarchy:* France
> Ministère de l'économie et des finances
> Direction générale des impôts
> Service de l'administration générale
> (*Other units within the same ministry are called* Service de l'administration générale)

Refer from the name in the form of a subheading of the name of its immediately superior body when the heading does not include the name of that superior body (see 26.3A7).

> **California.** *Employment Data and Research Division*
> *Hierarchy:* California
> Health and Welfare Agency
> Employment Development Department
> Employment Data and Research Division
> *x* California. *Employment Development Department. Employment Data and Research Division*

> **France.** *Ministère du travail, de l'emploi et de la population. Division de la statistique et des études*
> *Hierarchy:* France
> Ministère du travail, de l'emploi et de la population
> Service des études et prévisions
> Division de la statistique et des études
> *x* France. *Ministère du travail, de l'emploi et de la population. Service des études et prévisions. Division de la statistique et des études*

Special Rules

24.20. GOVERNMENT OFFICIALS

24.20A. Scope

24.20A1. Apply this rule only to officials of countries and other states that have existed in postmedieval times and to officials of international intergovernmental organizations.

24.20B. Heads of state, etc.

24.20B1. Enter a sovereign, president, other head of state, or governor acting in an official capacity (see 21.4D1) under the heading for the jurisdiction, followed by the title of the official in English (unless there is no equivalent English term). Add the inclusive years of the reign or incumbency and the name of the person in a brief form and in the language of the heading for that person.

> **United States.** *President (1953-1961 : Eisenhower)*
>
> **Illinois.** *Governor (1973-1977 : Walker)*
>
> **Iran.** *Shah (1941-1979 : Mohammed Reza Pahlavi)*
>
> **Papal States.** *Sovereign (1846-1870 : Pius IX)*

If the title varies with the gender of the incumbent, use a general term (e.g., *Sovereign* rather than *King* or *Queen*).

> **United Kingdom.** *Sovereign (1837-1901 : Victoria)*
>
> **Russia.** *Sovereign (1894-1917 : Nicholas II)*
>
> **Spain.** *Sovereign (1886-1931 : Alfonso XIII)*

If there are two or more nonconsecutive periods of incumbency, use separate headings.

> **United States.** *President (1885-1889 : Cleveland)*
>
> **United States.** *President (1893-1897 : Cleveland)*

If the heading applies to more than one incumbent (see 21.4D1), do not add the dates and names.

> **United States.** *President*

24.20B2. If a heading is established for an incumbent head of state, etc., as a person in addition to the heading as a head of state, etc., make an explanatory reference under the heading for the head of state, etc. (see 26.3C1).

24.20C. Heads of governments and of international intergovernmental bodies

24.20C1. Enter a head of government acting in an official capacity (see 21.4D1) who is not also a head of state under the heading for the jurisdiction, followed by the title of the official in the vernacular. Do not add dates or names.

> **United Kingdom.** *Prime Minister*
>
> **Philadelphia** (*Pa.*). *Mayor*
>
> **France.** *Premier ministre*
>
> **Italy.** *Presidente del Consiglio dei ministri*

24.20C2. Enter a head of an international intergovernmental organization acting in an official capacity under the heading for the organization, followed by the title of the official in the language of the heading for the organization.

> **United Nations.** *Secretary-General*

24.20D. Governors of dependent or occupied territories

24.20D1. Enter a governor of a dependent territory (e.g., a colony, protectorate) or of an occupied territory (see 24.6D) acting in an official capacity under the heading for the colony, territory, etc., followed by the title of the governor in the language of the governing power.

> **Hong Kong.** *Governor*
>
> **Jersey** (*Channel Islands*) (*Territory under German occupation, 1940-1945*). *Militärischer Befehlshaber*
>
> **Netherlands** (*Territory under German occupation, 1940-1945*). *Reichskommissar für die Besetzten Niederländischen Gebiete*
>
> **Germany** (*Territory under Allied occupation, 1945-1955 : U.S. Zone*). *Military Governor*

24.20E. Other officials

24.20E1. Enter any other official under the heading for the ministry or agency that the official represents.

> **United States.** *General Accounting Office*
> *not* United States. *Comptroller General*

24.20E2. Enter an official who is not part of a ministry, etc., or who is part of a ministry, etc., that is identified only by the title of the official, under the heading for the jurisdiction, followed by the title of the official.

> **United Kingdom.** *Lord Privy Seal*

24.21. LEGISLATIVE BODIES

24.21A. Enter a legislature under the name of the jurisdiction for which it legislates.

> **Iceland.** *Alþingi*

If a legislature has more than one chamber, enter each as a subheading of the heading for the legislature. Refer from the name of the chamber as a direct subheading of the jurisdiction.

> **United Kingdom.** *Parliament. House of Commons*
> *x* United Kingdom. *House of Commons*

> **United Kingdom.** *Parliament. House of Lords*
> *x* United Kingdom. *House of Lords*

24.21B. Enter a committee or other subordinate unit (other than a legislative subcommittee of the United States Congress, see 24.21C) as a subheading of the legislature or of a particular chamber, as appropriate.

> **United States.** *Congress. Joint Committee on the Library*

> **United States.** *Congress. House of Representatives. Select Committee on Government Organization*

24.21C. Enter a legislative subcommittee of the United States Congress as a subheading of the committee to which it is subordinate.

> **United States.** *Congress. Senate. Committee on Foreign Relations. Subcommittee on Canadian Affairs*
> *not* United States. *Congress. Senate. Subcommittee on Canadian Affairs*

24.21D. If successive legislatures are numbered consecutively, add the ordinal numeral and the year or years to the heading for the particular legislature or one of its chambers.

> **United States.** *Congress (87th : 1961-1962)*

> **United States.** *Congress (87th : 1961-1962). House of Representatives*

If, in such a case, numbered sessions are involved, add the session and its number and the year or years of the session to the number of the legislature.

> **United States.** *Congress (87th, 2nd session : 1962). House of Representatives*

24.22. CONSTITUTIONAL CONVENTIONS

24.22A. Enter a constitutional convention under the heading for the government that convened it, followed by the name of the convention. Add the year or years in which it was held.

> **Germany.** *Nationalversammlung (1919-1920)*

> **Portugal.** *Assembléia Nacional Constituinte (1911)*

24.22B. If there is variation in the forms of name of constitutional conventions convened by a jurisdiction using English as an official language, use *Constitutional Convention* as the subheading for each of the conventions.

> **New Hampshire.** *Constitutional Convention (1781)*
> *not* New Hampshire. *Convention for Framing a New Constitution or Form of Government (1781)*

> **New Hampshire.** *Constitutional Convention (1889)*

> **New Hampshire.** *Constitutional Convention (1912)*
> *not*   New Hampshire. *Convention to Revise the Constitution (1912)*

If English is not an official language of the jurisdiction, follow the instructions in 24.2 and 24.3.

24.23. COURTS

24.23A. Civil and criminal courts

24.23A1. Enter a civil or criminal court under the heading for the jurisdiction whose authority it exercises, followed by the name of the court.

> **Vermont.** *Court of Chancery*

Omit the name (or abbreviation of the name) of the place in which the court sits or the area which it serves unless the omission would result in objectionable distortion. If the name of the place or the area served is required to distinguish a court from others of the same name, add it in a conventionalized form.

> **France.** *Cour d'appel (Caen)*
> (*Name:* Cour d'appel de Caen)

> **United Kingdom.** *Crown Court (Manchester)*
> (*Name:* Manchester Crown Court)

> **United States.** *Court of Appeals (2nd Circuit)*
> (*Name:* United States Court of Appeals for the Second Circuit)

> **United States.** *Court of Appeals (District of Columbia Circuit)*
> (*Name:* United States Court of Appeals for the District of Columbia Circuit)

> **United States.** *District Court (Delaware)*
> (*Name:* United States District Court for the District of Delaware)

> **United States.** *District Court (North Carolina : Eastern District)*
> (*Name:* United States District Court for the Eastern District of North Carolina)

> **United States.** *District Court (Illinois : Northern District : Eastern Division)*
> (*Name:* United States District Court for the Eastern Division of the Northern District of Illinois)

> **California.** *Municipal Court (Los Angeles Judicial District)*
> (*Name:* Municipal Court, Los Angeles Judicial District)

> **California.** *Superior Court (San Bernardino County)*
> (*Name:* Superior Court of the State of California in and for San Bernardino County)

24.23B. Ad hoc military courts

24.23B1. Enter an ad hoc military court (e.g., court-martial, court of inquiry) under the heading for the particular military service (see 24.24), followed by the name of the court. Add the surname of the defendant and the year of the trial.

> **United States.** *Army. Court of Inquiry (Hall : 1863)*

> **Virginia.** *Militia. Court-martial (Yancey : 1806)*

24.24. ARMED FORCES

24.24A. Armed forces at the national level

24.24A1. Enter a principal service of the armed forces of a national government under the heading for the government, followed by the name of the service. Omit the name (or abbreviation of the name) of the government in noun form unless the omission would result in objectionable distortion.

> **Canada.** *Canadian Armed Forces*

> **United Kingdom.** *Royal Navy*

> **United States.** *Marine Corps*[12]

> **United Kingdom.** *Royal Marines*[13]

Enter a component branch, command district, or military unit, large or small, as a direct subheading of the heading for the principal service of which it is a part.

> **United Kingdom.** *Army. Royal Gloucestershire Hussars*

> **United Kingdom.** *Royal Air Force. Central Interpretation Unit*

> **United Kingdom.** *Royal Navy. Sea Cadet Corps*

> **United States.** *Army. General Staff*

> **United States.** *Army. Corps of Engineers*

> **United States.** *Army. District of Mindanao*

If the component branch, etc., is identified by a number, follow the style of numbering found in the name (spelled out, roman numerals, or arabic numerals) and place the numbering after the name.

> **United Kingdom.** *Army. Infantry Regiment, 57th*

> **United States.** *Army. Infantry Division, 27th*

> **United States.** *Navy. Fleet, 6th*

> **United States.** *Army. Army, First*

---

12. Treat the U.S. Marine Corps as a principal service.
13. Treat the Royal Marines as a principal service.

> **United States.** *Army. Corps, IV*
>
> **United States.** *Army. Engineer Combat Battalion, 2nd*
>
> **United States.** *Army. Volunteer Cavalry, 1st*
>
> **United States.** *Navy. Torpedo Squadron 8*
>
> **Confederate States of America.** *Army. Tennessee Regiment, 1st*
>
> **France.** *Armée. Régiment de dragons, 15ᵉ*
>
> **Germany.** *Heer. Panzerdivision, 11.*
>
> **Germany.** *Luftwaffe. Jagdgeschwader 26*
>
> **Germany.** *Luftwaffe. Luftgaukommando VII*
>
> **Union of Soviet Socialist Republics.** *Armii͡a. Vozdushnai͡a armii͡a, 16.*

If the name of such a component branch, etc., begins with the name, or an indication of the name, of the principal service, enter it as a direct subheading of the heading for the government.

> **United States.** *Army Map Service*
>
> **United States.** *Naval Air Transport Service*

If the name of such a component branch, etc., contains, but does not begin with, the name or an indication of the name of the principal service, enter it as a direct subheading of the heading for the service and omit the name or indication of the name unless objectionable distortion would result.

> **Canada.** *Canadian Army. Royal Canadian Army Medical Corps*

24.24B. Armed forces below the national level

24.24B1. Enter an armed force of a government below the national level under the heading for the government, followed by the name of the force.

> **New York** (*State*). *Militia*
>
> **New York** (*State*). *National Guard*

24.24B2. Enter a component branch of an armed force of a government below the national level as a subheading of the heading for the force as instructed in 24.24A.

> **New York** (*State*). *Militia. Regiment of Artillery, 9th*
> (*Name:* 9th Regiment of Artillery, N.Y.S.M.)
>
> **New York** (*State*). *National Guard. Coast Defense Command, 9th*

24.24B3. Enter a component branch, etc., of a force below the national level that has been absorbed into the national military forces as a component branch of the national force (see 24.24A).

United States. *Army. New York Volunteers, 83rd*

United States. *Army. Regiment Infantry, New York Volunteers, 9th*

24.25. EMBASSIES, CONSULATES, ETC.

24.25A. Enter an embassy, consulate, legation, or other continuing office representing one country in another under the heading for the country represented, followed by the name of the embassy, etc. Give the subheading in the language (see 24.3A) of the country represented, and omit from it the name of the country.

If the heading is for an embassy or legation, add the name of the country to which it is accredited.

> **Germany.** *Gesandschaft (Switzerland)*

> **United Kingdom.** *Embassy (U.S.)*

> **United States.** *Legation (Bulgaria)*

> **Yugoslavia.** *Poslanstvo (U.S.)*

> **Canada.** *Embassy (Belgium)*

If the heading is for a consulate or other local office, add the name of the city in which it is located.

> **France.** *Consulat (Buenos Aires, Argentina)*

> **United Kingdom.** *Consulate (Cairo, Egypt)*

24.26. DELEGATIONS TO INTERNATIONAL AND INTERGOVERNMENTAL BODIES

24.26A. Enter a delegation, commission, etc., representing a country in an international or intergovernmental body, conference, undertaking, etc., under the heading for the country represented, followed by the name of the delegation, etc. Give the subheading in the language (see 24.3A) of the country represented. Omit from the subheading the name or abbreviation of the name of the government in noun form unless such an omission would result in objectionable distortion. If the name of the delegation, etc., is uncertain, give *Delegation* [*Mission*, etc.] (or equivalent terms in the language of the country represented). If considered necessary to distinguish the delegation, etc., from others of the same name, add the name, in the form and language used for it as a heading, of the international or intergovernmental body, conference, undertaking, etc., to which the delegation, etc., is accredited. Make explanatory references as necessary from the heading for the international body, etc., followed by an appropriate subheading (see 26.3C1).

> **Mexico.** *Delegación (Inter-American Conference for the Maintenance of Peace (1936 : Buenos Aires, Argentina))*

> **Germany.** *Reichskommission für die Weltausstellung in Chicago*

> **United States.** *Delegation (International Conference on Maritime Law (3rd : 1909 : Brussels, Belgium))*

United States. *Mission* (*United Nations*)
   Explanatory reference:
United Nations. *Missions*
   Delegations, missions, etc., from member nations to the
United Nations and to its subordinate units are entered under
the name of the nation followed by the name of the delegation,
mission, etc.; e.g.,
United States. *Mission* (*United Nations*)
United States. *Delegation* (*United Nations. General Assembly*)
Uruguay. *Delegación* (*United Nations*)

   Make the same explanatory reference under United Nations.
   Delegations, and under United Nations. *General Assembly.*
   Delegations, and under other appropriate headings

If it is uncertain that a delegation represents the government of a country,
enter it under its own name.

Religious Bodies and Officials

24.27. RELIGIOUS BODIES AND OFFICIALS

24.27A. Councils, etc., of a single religious body

24.27A1. Enter a council, etc., of the clergy and/or membership (international,
national, regional, provincial, state, or local) of a single religious body under the
heading for the religious body, followed by the name of the council, etc. When
appropriate, make additions to the heading as instructed in 24.7B.

   Catholic Church. *Antilles Episcopal Conference*

   Society of Friends. *Philadelphia Yearly Meeting*[14]

   United Methodist Church (*U.S.*). *Northern Illinois Conference*

24.27A2. If the name of a council, etc., of the Catholic Church is given in more
than one language, use (in this order of preference) the English, Latin, French,
German, or Spanish name, and make appropriate references.

   Catholic Church. *Canadian Conference of Catholic Bishops*

   Catholic Church. *Plenary Council of Baltimore* (*2nd : 1866*)

   Catholic Church. *Concilium Plenarium Americae Latinae* (*1899 :
   Rome, Italy*)

24.27A3. If a council, etc., is subordinate to a particular district of the religious
body, enter it under the heading for that district (see 24.27C2–24.27C3), followed
by the name of the council, etc. If the name appears in more than one language,
use the name in the vernacular of the district.

---

14. *Yearly Meeting* is used by the Society of Friends to denote a particular level in its structure.

> **Catholic Church.** *Province of Baltimore. Provincial Council (10th : 1869)*

> **Catholic Church.** *Province of Mexico City. Concilio Provincial (3rd : 1585)*

24.27B. Religious officials

24.27B1. Enter a religious official (e.g., bishop, abbot, rabbi, moderator, mullah, patriarch) acting in an official capacity (see 21.4D1) under the heading for the religious jurisdiction (e.g., diocese, order, rabbinate, synod, denomination, see 24.27C2–24.27C3), followed by the title of the official in English (unless there is no equivalent English term). Add the inclusive years of incumbency and the name of the person in a brief form and in the language of the heading for that person.

> **Catholic Church.** *Diocese of Campos. Bishop (1949-1981 : Mayer)*

> **Franciscans.** *Minister General (1947-1951 : Perantoni)*

> **Catholic Church.** *Diocese of Winchester. Bishop (1367-1404 : William, of Wykeham)*

If the heading applies to more than one incumbent (see 21.4D1), do not add the dates and names.

> **Church of England.** *Diocese of Winchester. Bishop*

If a heading is established for the incumbent as a person in addition to the heading as a religious official, make an explanatory reference under the heading for the official (see 26.3C1).

24.27B2. Popes. Enter a pope acting in an official capacity (see 21.4D1) under *Catholic Church*, followed by *Pope*. Add the year or inclusive years of the reign, and the pontifical name in its catalogue entry form.

> **Catholic Church.** *Pope (1878-1903 : Leo XIII)*

> **Catholic Church.** *Pope (1978 : John Paul I)*

If the heading applies to more than one pope (see 21.4D1), do not add the dates and names.

> **Catholic Church.** *Pope*

If a heading is established for a pope as a person in addition to the heading as a religious official, make an explanatory reference under the heading for the official (see 26.3C1).

24.27C. Subordinate bodies

24.27C1. General rule. Except as provided in 24.27C2–24.27C4, enter subordinate religious bodies according to the instructions in 24.12–24.13. For religious orders and societies, see 24.3D.

24.27C2. Provinces, dioceses, synods, etc. Enter a province, diocese, synod, or other subordinate unit of a religious body having jurisdiction over a geographic area under the heading for the religious body, followed by the name of the province, etc.

> **Church of England.** *Diocese of Ely*
>
> **Evangelical and Reformed Church.** *Reading Synod*
>
> **Evangelische Kirche der Altpreussischen Union.** *Kirchenprovinz Sachsen*
>
> **Church of England.** *Archdeaconry of Surrey*
>
> **Nederlandse Hervormde Kerk.** *Classis Rotterdam*
>
> **Protestant Episcopal Church in the U.S.A.** *Diocese of Southern Virginia*
>
> **Russkaia pravoslavnaia tserkov'.** *Moskovskaia patriarkhiia*
>
> **Svenska kyrkan.** *Ärkestiftet Uppsala*
>
> **Church of England.** *Woking Deanery*

24.27C3. Catholic dioceses, etc. Use an English form of name for a patriarchate, diocese, province, etc., of the Catholic Church.

> **Catholic Church.** *Archdiocese of Santiago de Cuba*
>
> **Catholic Church.** *Diocese of Uppsala*
>
> **Catholic Church.** *Diocese of Ely*
>
> **Catholic Church.** *Diocese of Hexham and Newcastle*
>
> **Catholic Church.** *Patriarchate of Alexandria of the Copts*
>
> **Catholic Church.** *Province of Québec*
>
> **Catholic Church.** *Ukrainian Catholic Archeparchy of Philadelphia*
>
> **Catholic Church.** *Vicariate Apostolic of Zamora*

Do not apply this rule to an ecclesiastical principality (often called *Bistum*) of the Holy Roman Empire bearing the same name as a Catholic diocese and ruled by the same bishop.

> **Catholic Church.** *Diocese of Fulda*
>
> *but* **Fulda** (*Ecclesiastical principality*)

24.27C4. Central administrative organs of the Catholic Church (Roman Curia). Enter a congregation, tribunal, or other central administrative organ (i.e., one that is part of the Roman Curia) of the Catholic Church under *Catholic Church*, followed by the Latin form of the name of the congregation, etc. Omit any form of the word *sacer* when it is the first word of the name and make an explanatory reference (see 26.3C1) from the form of the name beginning with it.

> **Catholic Church.** *Congregatio Sacrorum Rituum*
>
> **Catholic Church.** *Congregatio de Propaganda Fide*
>
> **Catholic Church.** *Rota Romana*

24.27D. Papal diplomatic missions, etc.

24.27D1. Enter a diplomatic mission from the pope to a secular power under *Catholic Church*, followed by *Apostolic Nunciature* or *Apostolic Internunciature*, as appropriate. Add the heading for the government to which the mission is accredited.

> **Catholic Church.** *Apostolic Internunciature* (*India*)
>
> **Catholic Church.** *Apostolic Nunciature* (*Flanders*)

Enter a nondiplomatic apostolic delegation under *Catholic Church* followed by *Apostolic Delegation*. Add the name of the country or other jurisdiction in which the delegation functions.

> **Catholic Church.** *Apostolic Delegation* (*France*)

Enter an emissary of the pope acting in an official capacity (other than a nuncio, internuncio, or apostolic delegate) under *Catholic Church*, followed by the title of the emissary (in English if there is an equivalent term; otherwise in Latin). Add the name of the country or region in which the emissary functions.

> **Catholic Church.** *Legate* (*Colombia*)

If the country or region cannot be ascertained, add the name of the emissary in brief form.

> **Catholic Church.** *Commissary Apostolic* (*Robertus Castellensis*)

UNIFORM TITLES

Contents

25.12   UNIFORM TITLES FOR CYCLES AND FOR STORIES WITH MANY VERSIONS

Special Rules for Certain Types of Work

25.13   MANUSCRIPTS AND MANUSCRIPT GROUPS

25.14   INCUNABULA

Laws, Treaties, Etc.

25.15   LAWS, ETC.
   25.15A   Modern laws, etc.
   25.15A1   Collections
   25.15A2   Single laws, etc.
   25.15B   Ancient laws, certain medieval laws, customary laws, etc.

25.16   TREATIES, ETC.
   25.16A   Collections of treaties, etc.
   25.16B   One treaty, etc.
   25.16B1   Two or three parties
   25.16B2   Four or more parties
   25.16B3   Protocols, etc.

Sacred Scriptures

25.17   GENERAL RULE

25.18   PARTS OF SACRED SCRIPTURES AND ADDITIONS
   25.18A   Bible
   25.18A1   General rule
   25.18A2   Testaments
   25.18A3   Books
   25.18A4   Groups of books
   25.18A5   Apocrypha
   25.18A6   References
   25.18A7   Single selections
   25.18A8   Two selections
   25.18A9   Other selections
   25.18A10   Language
   25.18A11   Version
   25.18A12   Alternatives to version
   25.18A13   Year
   25.18A14   Apocryphal books
   25.18B   Talmud
   25.18C   Mishnah and Tosefta
   25.18D   References for the Talmud, Mishnah, and Tosefta
   25.18E   Midrashim
   25.18F   Buddhist scriptures
   25.18G   Vedas
   25.18H   Aranyakas, Brahmanas, Upanishads
   25.18J   Jaina Āgama

25.1. USE OF UNIFORM TITLES

25.1A. Uniform titles can be used for different purposes. They provide the means:

> for bringing together all catalogue entries for a work[1]
> when various manifestations (e.g., editions, transla-
> tions) of it have appeared under various titles;
> for identifying a work when the title by which it is
> known differs from the title proper of the item being
> catalogued;
> for differentiating between two or more works pub-
> lished under identical titles proper;
> for organizing the file.

The need to use uniform titles varies from one catalogue to another and varies within one catalogue. Base the decision whether to use a uniform title in a particular instance on one or more of the following, as appropriate:

1) how well the work is known
2) how many manifestations of the work are involved
3) whether another work with the same title proper has been identified (see 25.5B)
4) whether the main entry is under title (see 21.1C)
5) whether the work was originally in another language
6) the extent to which the catalogue is used for research purposes.

Although the rules in this chapter are stated as instructions, apply them according to the policy of the cataloguing agency.

25.2. GENERAL RULE

25.2A. Formulate a uniform title for a work as instructed in the rules that follow. Enclose the uniform title in square brackets. If the work is entered under title, give the uniform title as the heading within square brackets. *Optionally*, give a uniform title used as a main entry heading without square brackets.[2]

> **Dickens, Charles**
> [Martin Chuzzlewit]
> The life and adventures of Martin Chuzzlewit

> **Dickens, Charles**
> Martin Chuzzlewit

> **Dickens, Charles**
> [Martin Chuzzlewit]
> Martin Chuzzlewit's life and adventures

> **Blind date**
> Chance meeting
> (*Motion picture issued in the United Kingdom as:* Blind date.
> *Later issued in the United States as:* Chance meeting)

---

1. Unless otherwise indicated, *work* as used in this chapter includes collections and compilations catalogued as a unit.

2. In examples in this chapter uniform titles for works entered under title are shown as **bold** headings without square brackets.

25.2B. Do not use a uniform title for a manifestation of a work in the same language that is a revision or updating of the original work. Relate editions not connected by uniform titles by giving the title of the earlier edition in a note in the entry for the later edition (see 1.7B7, 2.7B7, etc.) and by making an added entry as appropriate (see 21.30G).

> **Scott, Franklin D.**
> The United States and Scandinavia ... 1950

> **Scott, Franklin D.**
> Scandinavia ... 1975
> (*Revised and enlarged edition of:* The United States and Scandinavia)

but **Hassenstein, Bernhard**
> [Biologische Kybernetik. English]
> Information and control in the living organism
> (*Verso of title page reads:* English edition revised from the third German edition)

25.2C. Initial articles

25.2C1. Omit an initial article unless the uniform title is to file under that article (e.g., a title that begins with the name of a person or place).

25.2D. Romanization

25.2D1. If the title selected as the uniform title is in a language written in a nonroman script, romanize it according to the table for that language adopted by the cataloguing agency.

25.2E. Added entries and references

25.2E1. Works entered under title. If a work is entered under a uniform title, make an added entry under the title proper of the item being catalogued unless the title proper is essentially the same as the main entry heading (see 21.30J). Refer from any other variants of the title, including variant romanizations found in the item (see 26.4).

> **Astronomy encyclopaedia**
> The international encyclopedia of astronomy
> (*Issued in the United Kingdom as:* The astronomy encyclopaedia. *Later issued in the United States as:* The international encyclopedia of astronomy)
> *Added entry under:* The international encyclopedia of astronomy

but **Christian educator** (*Nairobi, Kenya*)
> The Christian educator
> (*Several serials have the title:* The Christian educator)
> *No added entry under title proper*

25.2E2. Works entered under a personal or corporate heading. If a work is entered under a personal or corporate heading and a uniform title is used, make name-title reference(s) from the heading and the variant(s) of the title. Make an added entry under the title proper of the item being catalogued (see 21.30J).

Individual Titles

25.3. WORKS CREATED AFTER 1500

25.3A. Use the title or form of title in the original language by which a work created after 1500 has become known through use in manifestations of the work or in reference sources.

> **Dickens, Charles**
> [Pickwick papers]
> The posthumous papers of the Pickwick Club

> **Whitaker's almanack**
> An almanack for the year of Our Lord . . .

> **Hemingway, Ernest**
> [Sun also rises]
> Fiesta

> **Shakespeare, William**
> [Hamlet]
> The tragicall historie of Hamlet, Prince of Denmarke

> **Emerson, Ralph Waldo**
> [American scholar]
> An oration delivered before the Phi Beta Kappa Society, at Cambridge, August 31, 1837

> **Mozart, Wolfgang Amadeus**
> [Don Giovanni]
> Il dissoluto punito, ossia, Il don Giovanni

> **Swift, Jonathan**
> [Gulliver's travels]
> Travels into several remote nations of the world / by Lemuel Gulliver

> **Trial of treasure**
> A new and mery interlude called the Triall of treasure

25.3B. If no title in the original language is established as being the one by which the work is best known, or in case of doubt, use the title proper of the original edition. Omit from such titles:

1) introductory phrases (e.g., *Here beginneth the tale of*)
2) statements of responsibility that are part of the title proper (see 1.1B2), if such an omission is permissible grammatically and if the statement is not essential to the meaning of the title.

> **Gaunt, William**
> [Pre-Raphaelite tragedy]
> The Pre-Raphaelite dream

> **Criminal**
> The concrete jungle
> > (*Motion picture issued in the United Kingdom as:* The criminal. *Later issued in the United States as:* The concrete jungle)

> **Wodehouse, P.G.**
> [Ring for Jeeves]
> The return of Jeeves

> **Norway**
> [Grundlov]
> Kongeriget Norges grundlov

> **Treatyse of a galaunt**
> Here begynneth a Treatyse of a galaūt . . .

25.3C. Simultaneous publication under different titles

25.3C1. If a work is published simultaneously in the same language under different titles, use the title of the edition published in the home country of the cataloguing agency.

> *Cataloguing agency in the United States:*
> **Joesten, Joachim**
> Rats in the larder : the story of Nazi influence in Denmark
> > (*Published in New York, 1939*)

> **Joesten, Joachim**
> [Rats in the larder]
> Denmark's day of doom
> > (*Published in London, 1939*)

If the work is not published in the home country, use the title of the edition received first.

25.3C2. If a work entered under the heading for a corporate body is published simultaneously in different languages and under different titles, none of which is known to be the original language or title, use as the uniform title the title in the language in which the name of the corporate body is entered in the catalogue.

If there is no title in the language of the corporate heading, or if this criterion does not apply, follow the instructions in 25.3C3.

25.3C3. If any other work is published simultaneously in different languages and under different titles, none of which is known to be the original language or title, use as uniform title (in this order of preference) the title in English, French, German, Spanish, Russian. If there is no title in any of these languages, use the title of the edition received first.

25.4. WORKS CREATED BEFORE 1501

25.4A. General rule

25.4A1. Use the title, or form of title, in the original language by which a work created before 1501 (other than one covered by 25.4B–25.4C and 25.14) is identified in modern sources. If the evidence of modern reference sources is inconclusive, use (in this order of preference) the title most frequently found in:

a) modern editions
b) early editions
c) manuscript copies.

> **Avicenna**
> [Dānishnāmah-i ʻAlāʼi]

> **Beowulf**

> **Caesar, Julius**
> [De bello Gallico]

> **Chanson de Roland**

> **Chaucer, Geoffrey**
> [Pardoner's tale]

> **Nibelungenlied**

> **Edictum Theodorici**

25.4B. Classical and Byzantine Greek works

25.4B1. Use a well-established English title for a work originally written in classical Greek, or a work of a Greek church father or other Byzantine writer before 1453. If there is no such English title, use the Latin title. If there is neither a well-established English title nor a Latin title, use the Greek title.

> *English*

> **Aristophanes**
> [Birds]
> *not*   Aves
>   Ornithes

> **Comnena, Anna**
> [Alexiad]
> *not*   Alexias

Eusebius, *of Caesarea, Bishop*
[Ecclesiastical history]
not   Historia ecclesiastica
Ekklēsiastikē historia

Homer
[Iliad]
not   Ilias

Homer
[Odyssey]
not   Odyssea
Odysseia

Plato
[Republic]
not   Respublica
Politeia

Battle of the frogs and mice
not   Batrachomyomachia

Latin

Apollonius, *Rhodius*
[Argonautica]
not   Argonautika

Aristotle
[Meteorologica]
not   Meteōrologika

Origen
[Contra Celsum]
not   Kata Kelsou

Planudes, Maximus
[De processione Spiritus Sancti]
not   Peri tēs ekporeuseōs tou Hagiou Pneumatos

Plato
[Theaetetus]
not   Theaitētos

Greek

Manasses, Constantine
[Synopsis historikē]

Menander, *of Athens*
[Geōrgos]

Menander, *of Athens*
[Perikeiromenē]

Prodromus, Theodore
[Katamyomachia]

25.4C. Anonymous works written neither in Greek nor in roman script

25.4C1. If the original language of an anonymous work created before 1501 is written neither in Greek nor in roman script, use an established title in English if there is one.

> **Arabian nights**
>
> **Book of the dead**
>
> *but* **Slovo o polku Igoreve**
> (*Published in English under several titles including* Igor's tale *and* The campaign of Igor *and* The tale of the campaign of Igor)

25.5. ADDITIONS

25.5A. Scope

25.5A1. Make additions to uniform titles as instructed in this rule. For special additions, and for modifications of these rules, relating to special types of work, see 25.13–25.35.

25.5B. Conflict resolution

25.5B1. Add in parentheses an appropriate explanatory word, brief phrase, or other designation to distinguish a uniform title used as a heading from an identical or similar heading for a person or corporate body, or from an identical or similar uniform title used as a heading or reference.

> **Adoration of the shepherds** (*Chester plays*)
>
> **Adoration of the shepherds** (*Coventry plays*)
>
> **Arrow** (*Castlegar, B.C.*)
>
> **Arrow** (*Saskatoon, Sask.*)
>
> **Blue book contractors register** (*New York-New Jersey-Connecticut edition*)
>
> **Blue book contractors register** (*Southern California edition*)
>
> **Bulletin** (*Balai Pengolohan Galian (Indonesia)*)
>
> **Bulletin** (*California. Department of Water Resources*)
>
> **Charlemagne,** *Emperor*
>
> **Charlemagne** (*Play*)
>
> **Genesis** (*Anglo-Saxon poem*)
>
> **Genesis** (*Book of the Bible*)
> (*Use only as a reference*)
>
> **Genesis** (*Middle High German poem*)
>
> **Genesis** (*Old Saxon poem*)

Guillaume, 13th cent.

Guillaume (*Chanson de geste*)

King Kong (*1933*)

King Kong (*1976*)

San Francisco journal (*1944*)

San Francisco journal (*1980*)

Science bulletin (*Chicago, Ill.*)

Science bulletin (*Akron, Ohio : 1921*)

Science bulletin (*Akron, Ohio : 1980*)

Seven sages of Rome (*Northern version*)

Seven sages of Rome (*Southern version*)

Add in parentheses an appropriate designation to distinguish between identical uniform titles for works entered under the same personal or corporate heading.

> **Canada.** *Department of Public Works*
> [Annual report (1965)]
> Annual report . . .

> **Canada.** *Department of Public Works*
> [Annual report (1977)]
> Annual report . . .
>   (*Published 1972-1975 under title:* Report)

> **France**
> [Constitution (1946)]

> **France**
> [Constitution (1958)]

25.5C. Language

25.5C1. If the linguistic content of the item being catalogued is different from that of the original (e.g., a translation, a dubbed motion picture), add the name of the language of the item to the uniform title. Precede the language by a full stop.

> **Goncourt, Edmond de**
> [Frères Zemganno. English]
> The Zemganno brothers
>   (*An English translation of a French novel*)

> **Teorema.** *English*
> Theorem
>   (*An Italian motion picture dubbed into English*)

Do not add the name of the language to a uniform title for a motion picture with subtitles.

> **Jules et Jim**
> Jules and Jim
> (*A French motion picture with English subtitles*)

If the language of the item is an early form of a modern language, add the name of the modern language followed by the name of the early form in parentheses (e.g., *French (Old French)*, *French (Anglo-Norman)*, *English (Middle English)*).

> **Boethius**
> [De consolatione philosophiae. English (Middle English)]
> Chaucer's Boece

If an item is in two languages, name both. If one of the languages is the original language, name it second. Otherwise, name the languages in the following order: English, French, German, Spanish, Russian, other languages in alphabetic order of their names in English. If an item is in three or more languages, use *Polyglot* unless the original work is in three or more languages (e.g., a multilateral treaty), in which case give all the languages in the order specified above.

> **Caesar, Julius**
> [De bello Gallico. French & Latin]
> Les commentaires

> **United States**
> [Declaration of Independence. Polyglot]
> The Declaration of Independence of the United States, in ten languages

25.5D. *Optionally*, if general material designations are used (see 1.1C), add the designation.

> **Brunhoff, Jean de**
> [Babar en famille. English. Sound recording]
> Babar and his children

25.6. PARTS OF A WORK[3]

25.6A. One part

25.6A1. If a separately catalogued part of a work has a title of its own, use the title of the part by itself as the uniform title. Make a *see* reference from the heading for the whole work and the title of the part as a subheading of the title of the whole work (see 26.4B2). Include in the title in the reference the numeric designation of the part if there is one. Give the numeric designation in arabic numerals, but omit terms such as *volume*, *part*, *tome*, etc. Substitute an explanatory reference for the *see* reference if appropriate (see 26.4D2).

---

3. Apply 25.17–25.18 to parts of the Bible and certain other sacred scriptures; apply 25.23 to parts of liturgical works; apply 25.32 to parts of musical works.

Tolkien, J.R.R.
   [Two towers]
   x Tolkien, J.R.R. Lord of the rings. 2, Two towers

Proust, Marcel
   [Du côté de chez Swann]
   x Proust, Marcel. À la recherche du temps perdu. 1, Du côté de
      chez Swann

Raven, Simon
   [Come like shadows . . .][4]
   Explanatory reference:
   Raven, Simon
      Alms for oblivion
      For separately published novels in this series, *see*
   Raven, Simon
      Come like shadows
      Fielding Gray
      Friends in low places
      [*etc.*]

Sindbad the sailor
   Explanatory reference:
   Arabian nights
      For separately published stories from this collection, *see*
   Ali Baba
   Sindbad the sailor
   [*etc.*]

25.6A2. If a separately catalogued part of a work is identified only by a general term (with or without a number) such as

   Preface
   Detail (*for a graphic item*)
   Epilogue
   Book 1
   Part 2
   Number 1
   Band 3

use the designation of the part as a subheading of the title of the whole work. Give numeric designations in arabic numerals.

Goethe, Johann Wolfgang von
   [Faust. 1. Theil. English & German]

---

4. The marks of omission in uniform titles in examples here and subsequently indicate that one or more further elements may be required to complete the uniform title.

25.6B. More than one part

25.6B1. If the item being catalogued consists of consecutive parts of a work and the parts are numbered, use the designation of the parts in the singular as a subheading of the title of the whole work followed by the inclusive numbers of the parts. Treat them as a single part in applying 25.6B2–25.6B3.

> **Homer**
> [Iliad. Book 1-6]
> The first six books of Homer's Iliad

25.6B2. If the item consists of two unnumbered or nonconsecutively numbered parts of a work, use the uniform title (see 25.6A) of the first part as the uniform title for the item. Make a name-title added entry for the other part.

> **Dante Alighieri**
> [Purgatorio. English]
> The vision of Purgatory and Paradise
> *Added entry under:* **Dante Alighieri.** Paradiso. English

> **Homer**
> [Iliad. Book 1. English]
> Iliad, books I and VI
> *Added entry under:* **Homer.** Iliad. Book 6. English

> **Homer**
> [Odyssey. Book 6-14. English]
> The Odyssey, books VI-XIV, XVII-XXIV
> *Added entry under:* **Homer.** Odyssey. Book 17-24. English

25.6B3. If the item consists of three or more unnumbered or nonconsecutively numbered parts of, or of extracts from, a work, use the uniform title for the whole work followed by *Selections*.

> **Gibbon, Edward**
> [History of the decline and fall of the Roman Empire.
> Selections]

If the item is a translation, add *Selections* following the name of the language.

> **Dickens, Charles**
> [Sketches by Boz. German. Selections]
> Londoner Skizzen von Boz

25.7. TWO WORKS ISSUED TOGETHER

25.7A. If an item consisting of two works is entered under a personal or corporate heading, use the uniform title of the work that occurs first in the item. Make a name-title added entry using the uniform title of the second work.

> **Dickens, Charles**
> [Hard times]
> Dickens' new stories
>   (*Contains Hard times. Pictures from Italy*)
> *Added entry under:* **Dickens, Charles.** Pictures from Italy

Gibbons, Orlando
[O Lord, how do my woes increase]
Two anthems for four and five voices : from Leighton's teares or lamentations
> (*Contains O Lord, how do my woes increase. O Lord, I lift my heart to thee*)

Added entry under: **Gibbons, Orlando.** O Lord, I lift my heart to thee

Collective Titles

25.8. COMPLETE WORKS

25.8A. Use the collective title *Works* for an item that consists of, or purports to be, the complete works of a person, including those that are complete at the time of publication.

> **Maugham, W. Somerset**
> [Works]
> Complete works

> **Mirabeau, Honoré-Gabriel de Riqueti,** *comte de*
> [Works]
> Œuvres de Mirabeau

25.9. SELECTIONS

25.9A. Use the collective title *Selections* for items consisting of three or more works in various forms, or in one form if the person created works in one form only, and for items consisting of extracts, etc., from the works of one person. For musical works, see also 25.34B–25.34C.

> **Maugham, W. Somerset**
> [Selections]
> The Somerset Maugham pocket book
> > (*Contains Cakes and ale. The circle. Short stories. Travel sketches. Essays*)

> **Maugham, W. Somerset**
> [Selections]
> Wit and wisdom of Somerset Maugham

> **Morris, William**
> [Selections]
> Selected writings and designs

25.10. WORKS IN A SINGLE FORM

25.10A. Use one of the following collective titles for an item (other than music, see 25.34C) that consists of, or purports to be, the complete works of a person in one particular form.

> Correspondence
> Essays
> Novels
> Plays
> Poems
> Prose works
> Short stories
> Speeches

> **Maugham, W. Somerset**
> [Plays]
> Collected plays

> **Maugham, W. Somerset**
> [Short stories]
> Complete short stories

If none of these is appropriate, use an appropriate specific collective title (e.g., *Posters, Fragments*).

If the item consists of three or more but not all of the works of one person in a particular form, or of extracts, etc., from the works of one person in a particular form, add *Selections* to the collective title.

> **Maugham, W. Somerset**
> [Novels. Selections]
> Selected novels

> **Maugham, W. Somerset**
> [Plays. Selections]
> Six comedies

> **Maugham, W. Somerset**
> [Short stories. Selections]
> Best short stories of W. Somerset Maugham

25.11. TRANSLATIONS, ETC.

25.11A. If the linguistic content of a collection or selection of the works of one person is different from that of the originals, add the name of the language to the collective title as instructed in 25.5C. If *Selections* is added to a collective title, add the name of the language before that term.

> **Maugham, W. Somerset**
> [Works. Spanish]
> Obras completas

> **Archilochus**
> [Fragments. English]
> Archilochos / introduced, translated, and illustrated by
> Michael Ayrton

> **Maugham, W. Somerset**
> [Short stories. Spanish. Selections]
> En los mares del sur

25.12. UNIFORM TITLES FOR CYCLES AND FOR STORIES WITH MANY VERSIONS

25.12A. Use as the uniform title for a cycle (a collection of independent early poems, romances, etc., in the same language centered on a certain person, event, object, etc.) the generally accepted title for the cycle.

> **Guillaume d'Orange** (*Chansons de geste*)
>> Guillaume d'Orange : chansons de geste des XIᵉ et XIIᵉ
> siècles
>> (*Contains Li coronemens Looys. Li charrois de Nymes. La
>> prise d'Orenge. Li covenans Vivien. La bataille d'Aleschans*)

If the cycle is only identified by a descriptive phrase (e.g., "the Arthurian romances," "the Grail legends," "the St. Francis legends") or has no established title, enter it as instructed in 21.7.

> La légende arthurienne ... les plus anciens textes
> *Main entry under title proper*

25.12B. If an added entry is required for a basic story found in many versions, use the title that is established in English-language reference sources. Add the name of the language of the item being catalogued.

> Le roman de Renart
>> (*First of the Reynard stories*)
> *Added entry under:* **Reynard the Fox.** *French*

> The history of Reynard the Fox
>> (*Translation of a Dutch version*)
> *Added entry under:* **Reynard the Fox.** *English*

> Amis and Amiloun
>> (*Thirteenth century English version of a 12th century chanson de
>> geste*)
> *Added entry under:* **Amis et Amiles.** *English*

Special Rules for Certain Types of Work

25.13. MANUSCRIPTS AND MANUSCRIPT GROUPS

25.13A. Scope

25.13A1. Use this rule:

a) to formulate a uniform title for a work contained in a manuscript or manuscripts (including manuscript groups) when the preceding rules in this chapter do not provide a uniform title

b) to formulate a heading for a manuscript or manuscripts (including manuscript groups) when the item being catalogued merits an added entry for the manuscript(s).

25.13B. General rule

25.13B1. Use as the uniform title for a work contained in manuscript(s), or for a manuscript itself, or for a manuscript group (in this order of preference):

a) a title that has been assigned to the work subsequent to its creation or compilation

> **Domesday book**
>
> **Godwulf manuscript**

b) the name of the manuscript(s) if the work is identified only by that name

> **Book of Lismore**
>
> **Dead Sea scrolls**
>
> **Tell-el Amarna tablets**

c) the heading (see chapter 24) of the repository followed by *Manuscript* and the repository's designation for the manuscript(s). If the manuscript is a single item within a collection, add the foliation if known.

> **British Library. Manuscript. Arundel 384**
>
> **British Library. Manuscript. Additional 15233, fol. 11-27**

If the uniform title is chosen by the application of a) or b) above and the item has a repository designation, refer from that designation.

> **Codex Brucianus**
> *x* Bodleian Library. Manuscript. Bruce 96

25.14. INCUNABULA

25.14A. Use as the uniform title for an incunabulum the title found in standard reference sources for incunabula.

> **Victor, Sextus Aurelius**
> [De viris illustribus]
> Liber virorum illustrium . . .
>
> **Victor, Sextus Aurelius**
> [De viris illustribus]
> De rebus praeclare gestis virorum illustrium . . .

Laws, Treaties, Etc.

25.15. LAWS, ETC.

25.15A. Modern laws, etc.

25.15A1. Collections. Use *Laws, etc.* for a complete or partial collection of legislative enactments of a jurisdiction other than a compilation on a particular subject.

United Kingdom
[Laws, etc.]
Halsbury's statutes of England

United States
[Laws, etc.]
United States code

Ontario
[Laws, etc.]
Statutes of the province of Ontario passed in the session held
at Toronto in the twenty-third and twenty-fourth years of the
reign of Her Majesty Queen Elizabeth II

Boston (*Mass.*)
[Laws, etc.]
The revised ordinances of 1961 of the city of Boston

If a compilation of laws on a particular subject has a citation title, use that.
Otherwise, follow the instructions in 25.3.

California
[Agricultural code]
West's California agricultural code

United Kingdom
[Licensing acts]
Paterson's licensing acts

25.15A2. Single laws, etc. Use as the uniform title for a single legislative enactment (in this order of preference):

a) the official short title or citation title
b) an unofficial short title or citation title used in legal literature
c) the official title of the enactment
d) any other official designation (e.g., the number or date).

United Kingdom
[Field Monuments Act 1972]

New Zealand
[Copyright Act 1962]
   (*Citation title includes date of enactment*)

Canada
[Canada Corporations Act]

France
[Code pénal]

Argentina
[Ley no. 20.744]

If there are several different laws, etc., with the same title entered under the
heading for the same jurisdiction, add the year of promulgation.

United Kingdom
[Education Act (1944)]

25.15B. Ancient laws, certain medieval laws, customary laws, etc.

25.15B1. Follow the instructions in 25.3 or 25.4 for the uniform title for a collection of ancient, medieval, or customary laws identified by a name or for a single ancient, medieval, or customary law.

> **Lex Salica**
> Lex Salica : the ten texts

25.16. TREATIES, ETC.

25.16A. Collections of treaties, etc.

25.16A1. Use, as the uniform title for a collection of treaties and/or other agreements between two parties, *Treaties, etc.* followed by the name of the other party.

> **France**
> [Treaties, etc. United Kingdom]

Use *Treaties, etc.* alone for a collection of treaties between one party and two or more other parties.

> **United States**
> [Treaties, etc.]

If a collection of treaties, etc., is identified by a collective name, use that name followed in parentheses by the year, earlier year, or earliest year of signing for an item containing all the treaties, etc. For a single treaty, etc., in the collection, see 25.16B. Make *see also* references from the title of the collection to the headings and/or titles of the single treaties.

> **Treaty of Utrecht** (*1713*)
> *see also*
>
> **France**
> Treaties, etc. Prussia . . .
>
> **Spain**
> Treaties, etc. Great Britain . . .
> [*etc.*]

25.16B. One treaty, etc.

25.16B1. Two or three parties. Use a uniform title beginning *Treaties, etc.* for a treaty or other agreement between two or three of the following:

a) national governments
b) international intergovernmental bodies
c) the Holy See
d) jurisdictions now below the national level but retaining treaty-making powers.

If there is only one party on the other side, add the name of the other party. Add the date, earlier date, or earliest date of signing in the form: year, abbreviated name of the month (see B.15), number of the day.

Denmark
[Treaties, etc. United Kingdom, 1966 Mar. 3]
Agreement between the government of the United Kingdom of Great Britain and Northern Ireland and the kingdom of Denmark relating to the delimitation of the continental shelf between the two countries, London, 3 March 1966

Netherlands
[Treaties, etc. 1943 Oct. 21]
Convention monétaire belgo-luxembourgeoise-néerlandaise . . . 21 oct. 1943
> (*A treaty between the Netherlands on the one side and Belgium and Luxembourg on the other*)

France
[Treaties, etc. 1920 Aug. 10]
Tripartite agreement between the British Empire, France, and Italy . . . signed at Sèvres, August 10, 1920

Iceland
[Treaties, etc. International Bank for Reconstruction and Development, 1953 Sept. 4]
Guarantee agreement . . . between Republic of Iceland and International Bank for Reconstruction and Development, dated September 4, 1953

Baden (*Germany*)
[Treaties, etc. Catholic Church, 1932 Oct. 12]
Das Konkordat zwischen dem Heiligen Stuhle und dem Freistaate Baden, vom 12. Oktober 1932

25.16B2. Four or more parties. Use as the uniform title for a treaty, etc., between four or more parties the name by which the treaty is known. Use an English name if there is one. Add, in parentheses, the year, earlier year, or earliest year of signing. When making added entries for individual signatories to such an agreement (see 21.35A2), formulate the uniform title as instructed in 25.16B1.

> **Convention Regarding the Status of Aliens** (*1928*)
> Convención sobre condiciones de los extranjeros : celebrada entre los Estados Unidos Mexicanos y varias naciones : firmada en la ciudad de La Habana el 20 de febrero de 1928

> **Treaty of Paris** (*1763*)

> **Universal Copyright Convention** (*1952*)

25.16B3. Protocols, etc. Use as the uniform title for a separately catalogued protocol, amendment, extension, or other agreement ancillary to a treaty, etc., the uniform title for the original agreement followed by *Protocols, etc.* and the date of signing or, if more than one protocol, etc., is involved, the inclusive dates.

Poland
[Treaties, etc. United Kingdom, 1948 Mar. 2. Protocols, etc., 1951 Mar. 6]

Convention for the Protection of Human Rights and Fundamental Freedoms (*1950*). *Protocols, etc., 1963 Sept. 16*

Sacred Scriptures

25.17. GENERAL RULE

25.17A. Use as the uniform title for a sacred scripture (see 21.37) the title by which it is most commonly identified in English-language reference sources dealing with the religious group(s) to which the scripture belongs. If no such source is available, use general reference sources.

> **Avesta . . .**
>
> **Bible . . .**
>
> **Koran . . .**
>
> **Talmud . . .**
>
> **Tripiṭaka . . .**

For component parts of individual scriptures, see 25.18.

25.18. PARTS OF SACRED SCRIPTURES AND ADDITIONS

25.18A. Bible

25.18A1. General rule. Enter a Testament as a subheading of *Bible*. Enter a book of the Catholic or Protestant canon as a subheading of the appropriate Testament.

25.18A2. Testaments. Enter the Old Testament as **Bible.** *O.T.* and the New Testament as **Bible.** *N.T.*

25.18A3. Books. Use the brief citation form of the Authorized Version.

> **Bible.** *O.T. Ezra . . .*
>
> **Bible.** *N.T. Revelation . . .*

If the book is one of a numbered sequence of the same name, give its number after the name as an ordinal numeral in its English form (see C.8A).

> **Bible.** *N.T. Corinthians, 1st . . .*

If the item is part of a book (other than a single selection known by its title, see 25.18A7), give chapter (in roman numerals) and verse (in arabic numerals). Use inclusive numbering if appropriate.

> **Bible.** *O.T. Ecclesiastes III, 1-8 . . .*
>
> **Bible.** *O.T. Genesis XII, 1-XXV, 11 . . .*

25.18A4. Groups of books. Enter an item consisting of one of the following groups of books under the name given here as a subheading of the appropriate testament. For other groups of books, follow the instructions in 25.18A8–25.18A9.

Bible. *N.T. Catholic Epistles* ...
(*General Epistles of James, Peter, John, Jude*)

Bible. *N.T. Corinthians* ...
(*1–2 Corinthians*)

Bible. *N.T. Epistles* ...
(*All or miscellaneous Epistles*)

Bible. *N.T. Epistles of John* ...
(*1–3 John*)

Bible. *N.T. Epistles of Paul* ...

Bible. *N.T. Gospels* ...
(*Matthew, Mark, Luke, John*)

Bible. *N.T. Pastoral Epistles* ...
(*1–2 Timothy, Titus*)

Bible. *N.T. Peter* ...
(*1–2 Peter*)

Bible. *N.T. Thessalonians* ...
(*1–2 Thessalonians*)

Bible. *N.T. Timothy* ...
(*1–2 Timothy*)

Bible. *O.T. Chronicles* ...
(*1–2 Chronicles*)

Bible. *O.T. Five Scrolls* ...
(*Song of Solomon, Ruth, Lamentations, Ecclesiastes, Esther*)

Bible. *O.T. Former Prophets* ...
(*Joshua, Judges, 1–2 Samuel, 1–2 Kings*)

Bible. *O.T. Hagiographa* ...
(*Ruth, Chronicles, Ezra, Nehemiah, Esther, Job, Psalms, Proverbs, Ecclesiastes, Song of Solomon, Lamentations, Daniel*)

Bible. *O.T. Heptateuch* ...
(*Genesis, Exodus, Leviticus, Numbers, Deuteronomy, Joshua, Judges*)

Bible. *O.T. Hexateuch* ...
(*Genesis, Exodus, Leviticus, Numbers, Deuteronomy, Joshua*)

Bible. *O.T. Historical Books* ...
(*Joshua, Judges, Ruth, 1–2 Samuel, 1–2 Kings, Chronicles, Ezra, Nehemiah, Esther*)

Bible. *O.T. Kings* ...
(*1–2 Kings*)

> **Bible.** *O.T. Minor Prophets* . . .
> (*Hosea, Joel, Amos, Obadiah, Jonah, Micah, Nahum, Habakkuk, Zephaniah, Haggai, Zechariah, Malachi*)
>
> **Bible.** *O.T. Pentateuch* . . .
> (*Genesis, Exodus, Leviticus, Numbers, Deuteronomy*)
>
> **Bible.** *O.T. Prophets* . . .
> (*Isaiah, Jeremiah, Lamentations, Ezekiel, Daniel, Hosea, Joel, Amos, Obadiah, Jonah, Micah, Nahum, Habakkuk, Zephaniah, Haggai, Zechariah, Malachi*)
>
> **Bible.** *O.T. Prophets (Nevi'im)* . . .
> (*Joshua, Judges, 1–2 Samuel, 1–2 Kings, Isaiah, Jeremiah, Ezekiel, Minor Prophets*)
>
> **Bible.** *O.T. Samuel* . . .
> (*1–2 Samuel*)

25.18A5. Apocrypha. Enter the collection known as the Apocrypha (1–2 Esdras, Tobit, Judith, Rest of Esther, Wisdom of Solomon, Ecclesiasticus, Baruch, History of Susanna, Song of the Three Children, Bel and the Dragon, Prayer of Manasses, 1–2 Maccabees) under **Bible.** *O.T. Apocrypha.*[5] Enter an individual book as a further subheading. For apocryphal books, see 25.18A14.

> **Bible.** *O.T. Apocrypha* . . .
>
> **Bible.** *O.T. Apocrypha. Song of the Three Children* . . .
>
> **Bible.** *O.T. Apocrypha. Esdras, 1st* . . .

25.18A6. References. Refer, when appropriate, from the titles of individual books, from variant titles of individual books, and from the names of groups of books. Refer also from these as direct subheadings of *Bible*, and in the case of variant titles as subheadings of the appropriate testament.

> **Bible.** *O.T. Song of Solomon*
> *x* Song of Solomon (*Book of the Bible*)
> *x* Bible. *Song of Solomon*
>
> **Bible.** *N.T. Corinthians*
> *x* Corinthians (*Books of the Bible*)
> *x* Bible. *Corinthians*
>
> **Bible.** *O.T. Pentateuch*
> *x* Pentateuch
> *x* Torah (*Pentateuch*)
> *x* Ḥumash
> *x* Bible. *Pentateuch*
> *x* Bible. *Torah*
> *x* Bible. *Ḥumash*
> *x* Bible. *O.T. Torah*
> *x* Bible. *O.T. Ḥumash*

---

5. Do not treat an edition of the Bible lacking these books as being incomplete.

Make explanatory references when necessary.

> **Bible.** *O.T. Kings*
> Under this heading are found the books commonly called 1
> and 2 Kings but called 3 and 4 Kings in the Vulgate and versions
> based on it. For the books called 1 and 2 Kings in these versions,
> *see* Bible. *O.T. Samuel*
> *Make similar explanatory references under* **Bible.** *O.T. Kings, 1st,*
> *and* **Bible.** *O.T. Kings, 2nd*

25.18A7. Single selections. If a single selection is commonly identified by its own title (rather than its designation as part of the Bible), use that directly as the uniform title, and refer from the form of the title resulting from the application of 25.18A3.

> **Lord's prayer**
> *x* Bible. *N.T. Matthew VI, 9-13*
> *x* Bible. *N.T. Luke XI, 2-4*

> **Ten commandments**
> *x* Bible. *O.T. Exodus XX, 2-17*
> *x* Bible. *O.T. Deuteronomy V, 6-21*

> **Miserere**
> *x* Bible. *O.T. Psalms L (Vulgate)*
> *x* Bible. *O.T. Psalms LI*

Enter any other single selection as instructed in 25.18A3.

> **Bible.** *O.T. Psalms XXIII* ...

25.18A8. Two selections. If an item consists of two or more selections (including whole books) that are encompassed precisely by two uniform titles, enter under the uniform title for the first. Make an added entry under the uniform title for the second.

> **Bible.** *N.T. Gospels* ...
> Il Vangelo e gli Atti degli apostoli
> *Added entry under:* **Bible.** *N.T. Acts* ...

25.18A9. Other selections. Enter other selections (including miscellaneous extracts) under the most specific Bible heading. Add *Selections* after the language (see 25.18A10) and version (see 25.18A11–25.18A12) and before the year (see 25.18A13). If the selections were translated for the item in hand, do not give the translator's name as the version (see 25.18A11).

> **Bible.** *[language]. [version]. Selections. [year]*
> Memorable passages from the Bible (Authorized Version)

> **Bible.** *N.T. [language]. [version]. Selections. [year]*
> The records and letters of the Apostolic age
> (*Contains Acts. Epistles. Revelation*)

> **Bible.** *N.T. Gospels. [language]. Selections. [year]*
> The message of Jesus Christ : the tradition of the early
> Christian communities / restored and translated into German by
> Martin Dibelius ; translated into English by Frederick C. Grant

25.18A10. Language. Add the name of the language of the item after the designation for the Bible or part of the Bible.

> **Bible.** *English* . . .

> **Bible.** *N.T. English* . . .

> **Bible.** *N.T. Revelation. English* . . .

If the Old Testament is in Hebrew and the New Testament is in Greek, add *Hebrew-Greek*. Make a *see also* reference from **Bible.** *O.T. Hebrew* . . . and **Bible.** *N.T. Greek* . . .

In all other cases in which the item is in two languages, add (in this order of preference) the name of:

a) the early language if one is an early language and the other modern
b) the less widely known language if both are modern

If neither a) nor b) applies, add (in this order of preference) the name of:

c) the language given primary emphasis in the item
d) the language named first in the chief source of information
e) the language of the chief source of information chosen according to 1.0H
f) the language of the Biblical text that appears first.

Make an added entry under the designation followed by the name of the other language.

> **Bible.** *Latin* . . .
> La sainte Bible : texte latin et traduction française
> *Added entry under:* **Bible.** *French* . . .

> **Bible.** *Kikuyu* . . .
> The Bible in English and Kikuyu
> *Added entry under:* **Bible.** *English* . . .

If the item is in three or more languages, add *Polyglot*.

> **Bible.** *N.T. Epistles of John. Polyglot* . . .

25.18A11. Version. Give a brief form of the name of the version[6] following the name of the language. If the item is in three or more languages, do not add the name of the version.

> **Bible.** *Latin. Vulgate* . . .

> **Bible.** *N.T. Corinthians. English. Authorized* . . .

---

6. Here, *version* is used in its narrow sense of a translation. The version from which another version is made is ignored so far as entries and references are concerned.

If the version is identified by the name of the translator, use a short form of the translator's name. If there are two translators, hyphenate their names. If there are more than two, give the name of the first followed by *et al.*

> **Bible.** *English. Lamsa* ...

> **Bible.** *O.T. Anglo-Saxon. Ælfric* ...

> **Bible.** *English. Smith-Goodspeed* ...

Use *Douai* for Rheims-Douai-Challoner versions of the whole Bible. Use *Confraternity* for Confraternity-Douai-Challoner versions of the whole Bible.

> **Bible.** *English. Douai* ...
> The Holy Bible / translated from the Latin Vulgate ... being the edition published ... at Rheims, A.D. 1582 and at Douay, 1609 ; as revised and corrected in 1750, according to the Clementine edition of the Scriptures, by Richard Challoner

> **Bible.** *English. Confraternity* ...
> The Holy Bible. — Confraternity text (Genesis to Ruth, Psalms, New Testament) Douay-Challoner text (remaining books of the Old Testament)

If two versions are issued together, give the name of the one named first in the chief source of information, or, if neither is named there, the one appearing first in the item. Make an added entry under the Bible heading naming the other version.

> **Bible.** *English. Authorized* ...
> Johnson's worker's Bible : self-pronouncing edition of the Holy Scriptures arranged especially for workers, ministers, students ... showing a new and simple combination of the Authorized and Revised versions of the Old and New Testaments
> *Added entry under:* **Bible.** *English. Revised* ...

25.18A12. Alternatives to version. If the item is in the original language, if the version is unknown, if the text has been altered, if the version cannot be identified by name or translator, or if more than two versions are involved, give (in this order of preference):

a) the name of the manuscript or its repository designation (see 25.13) if the item is a manuscript, or a reproduction, transcription, edition, or translation of a manuscript

> **Bible.** *Greek. Codex Sinaiticus*
> Bibliorum Codex Sinaiticus Petropolitanus

b) the name of the person who has altered the text[7] if the altered text has no name of its own

---

7. Do not treat a harmony of different passages of the Bible as an altered text.

Bible. *English. Smith* . . .
  The Holy Scriptures : containing the Old and New Testaments
  : an inspired version of the Authorized Version / by Joseph
  Smith, Junior

c) a special name or phrase used in the chief source of information to identify
  the text.

Bible. *English. Anchor Bible* . . .
  The Anchor Bible

Bible. *English. Numerical Bible* . . .
  The Numerical Bible : being a revised translation of the Holy
  Scriptures with expository notes

If none of the above applies, do not add this element.

25.18A13. Year. Add the year of publication of the item to the uniform title.

Bible. *English. Revised Standard. 1959*

Bible. *French. Le Maistre. 1848*

Bible. *English. Revised Standard. 1961?*
  The Holy Bible : containing the Old and New Testaments. —
  Revised Standard Version . . . . — New York : Nelson, [1961?]

If the item was published over more than one year, add the earlier or earliest
year.

Bible. *Spanish. Torres Amat. 1871*
  La Sagrada Biblia / traducida . . . por Félix Torres Amat . . .
  1871-1873

If the item is a facsimile reproduction, give the year of publication of the original. Make an added entry under a heading containing the date of the facsimile.

Bible. *German. Luther. 1534*
  Biblia : das ist die gantze Heilige Schrifft / deudsch. Mart.
  Luth. — Leipzig : A. Foerster, 1934-1935
    (*Facsimile of a 1534 edition*)
  Added entry under: **Bible.** *German. Luther. 1934*

25.18A14. Apocryphal books. Use the title commonly found in English-language
sources as the uniform title of an apocryphal book (i.e., one included neither in
the Catholic canon nor in the Protestant Apocrypha). Make explanatory references from **Bible.** *Apocryphal books;* **Bible.** *N.T. Apocryphal books;* and **Bible.**
O.T. Apocryphal books.
  Enter a collection of apocryphal books as instructed in 21.7.

Book of Jubilees

Epistola Apostolorum

Gospel According to the Hebrews

508

Bible. *N.T. Apocryphal books*
  For individual apocryphal books of the New Testament, *see* the title of the book, e.g., **Shepherd of Hermas.**
  For collections of such books, *see* the title of the collection, e.g., Apocryphal New Testament.

Bible. *O.T. Apocryphal books*
  For individual apocryphal books of the Old Testament, *see* the title of the book, e.g., **Assumption of Moses.**
  For collections of such books, *see* the title of the collection, e.g., Forgotten books of Eden.
  For the Apocrypha of the Protestant Bible and its component books, *see* **Bible.** *O.T. Apocrypha.*

25.18B. Talmud

25.18B1. Enter a particular order (*seder*) or a tractate or treatise (*masekhet*) of the Talmud as a subheading of *Talmud* or *Talmud Yerushalmi*, as appropriate. Use the form of name of these parts found in the *Encyclopaedia Judaica*.

Talmud. *Ḥagigah* . . .
  Translation of the treatise Chagigah from the Babylonian Talmud

If the item is a translation only, make additions as instructed in 25.5C.

Talmud Yerushalmi. *French*
  Le Talmud de Jérusalem / traduit pour la première fois en français

However, if the item consists of the original text and a translation, do not add the name of the language to the uniform title. Make an added entry under a heading containing the name of the language of the translation.

Talmud
  New edition of the Babylonian Talmud : English translation, original text
  Added entry under: **Talmud.** *English*

If the item consists of selections, add *Selections* to the uniform title.

Talmud. *English. Selections*
  The Babylonian Talmud in selection / edited and translated from the original Hebrew and Aramaic by Leo Auerbach

25.18B2. Use the subheading *Minor tractates* for separately published editions of those tractates. If the item consists of a single tractate, add the title of the tractate as a further subheading.

Talmud. *Minor tractates*
  Seven minor tractates
  Added entry under: **Talmud.** *Minor tractates. English*

Talmud. *Minor tractates. Semaḥot. German*
  Der talmudische Tractat Ebel rabbathi, oder, S'machoth

25.18C. Mishnah and Tosefta

25.18C1. Enter a particular order or tractate of the Mishnah or Tosefta as a subheading of *Mishnah* or *Tosefta*. Use the form of name found in the *Encyclopaedia Judaica*. Add the name of the language of a translation and/or *Selections* as instructed in 25.18B1.

> **Mishnah**
> Die Mischna / Text, Übersetzung, und ausfürliche Erklärung
> ... herausgegeben von G. Beer
> *Added entry under:* **Mishnah.** *German*

> **Mishnah.** *Avot. English*
> Pirke Aboth = Sayings of the Fathers / edited, with
> translations and commentaries, by Isaac Unterman
> (*Text in English only*)

> **Tosefta.** *Beẓah*
> Der Tosefta-Traktat Jom Tob / Einleitung, Text, Übersetzung,
> und Erklärung ... von Michael Kern
> *Added entry under:* **Tosefta.** *Beẓah. German*

25.18D. References for the Talmud, Mishnah, and Tosefta

25.18D1. Refer from the titles of orders and tractates of the Talmud, Mishnah, and Tosefta to the uniform titles of those orders and tractates.

> **Bava kamma**
> *see*
> **Mishnah.** *Bava kamma*
> **Talmud.** *Bava kamma*
> **Talmud Yerushalmi.** *Bava kamma*
> **Tosefta.** *Bava kamma*

Make an explanatory reference from the uniform title of an order to the uniform titles of its tractates.

> **Talmud.** *Nezikin*
> For separately published tractates belonging to this order, *see*
> **Talmud.** *[name of tractate]*, *e.g.,* **Talmud.** *Bava kamma*

25.18E. Midrashim

25.18E1. Enter an anonymous midrash under its title. Use the form found in the *Encyclopaedia Judaica*.

> **Mekhilta**

> **Tanna de-Vei Eliyahu**

Add the name of the language of a translation and/or *Selections* as instructed in 25.18B1.

25.18E2. Use *Midrash ha-gadol*, *Midrash rabbah*, or *Sifrei* as the uniform titles for those midrashim. Enter any other collection of midrashim as instructed in 21.7.

25.18E3. Enter a separately published component of the *Midrash ha-gadol*, *Midrash rabbah*, or *Sifrei* under the uniform title for the midrashim. Add the English name of the book of the Bible with which it deals.

> **Midrash ha-gadol.** *Numbers*
>
> **Midrash rabbah.** *Ruth*
>
> **Sifrei.** *Deuteronomy*

25.18F. Buddhist scriptures

25.18F1. Enter a component division of the Pali canon (*Abhidhammapiṭaka*, *Suttapiṭaka*, *Vinayapiṭaka*) as a subheading of *Tipiṭaka*.

> **Tipiṭaka.** *Abhidhammapiṭaka*

Enter a separately published part of one of these component divisions as a subheading of the appropriate Piṭaka or of the appropriate division.

> **Tipiṭaka.** *Abhidhammapiṭaka. Dhātukathā*
>
> **Tipiṭaka.** *Suttapiṭaka. Khuddakanikāya. Jātaka*
>
> **Tipiṭaka.** *Vinayapiṭaka. Khandhaka. Mahāvagga*

25.18F2. Enter a component division of the Sanskrit canon (*Abhidharmapiṭaka*, *Sūtrapiṭaka*, *Vinayapiṭaka*) as a subheading of *Tripiṭaka*.

> **Tripiṭaka.** *Abhidharmapiṭaka*

Enter a separately published part of one of these component divisions as a subheading of the appropriate Piṭaka or of the appropriate division.

> **Tripiṭaka.** *Sūtrapiṭaka. Saddharmapundarikasutra*
>
> **Tripiṭaka.** *Vinayapiṭaka. Prātimokṣa*

25.18F3. Refer from the titles of individually published divisions and treatises to the appropriate uniform title.

> **Jātaka**
> *see* **Tipiṭaka.** *Suttapiṭaka. Khuddakanikāya. Jātaka*
>
> **Abhidharmapiṭaka**
> *see* **Tripiṭaka.** *Abhidharmapiṭaka*

25.18F4. Make other additions as instructed in 25.5 and 25.6B3.

25.18G. Vedas

25.18G1. Enter one of the four standard collections of Vedas (*Atharvaveda*, *Ṛgveda*, *Sāmaveda*, *Yajurveda*) as a subheading of *Vedas*. If the item is a particular version of one of these collections, add the name of the version in parentheses. Make other additions as instructed in 25.5 and 25.6B3.

> **Vedas.** *English. Selections*
>
> **Vedas.** *Atharvaveda*
>
> **Vedas.** *Ṛgveda. English. Selections*

Vedas. *Sāmaveda*

Vedas. *Yajurveda (Vājasaneyīsaṃhitā). English. Selections*

25.18H. Aranyakas, Brahmanas, Upanishads

25.18H1. Enter a component of the Aranyakas, Brahmanas, or Upanishads as a subheading of the title of the appropriate larger collection. Make other additions as instructed in 25.5 and 25.6B3.

> **Aranyakas.** *Aitareyāraṇyaka*
>
> **Brahmanas.** *Adbhutabrāhmaṇa*
>
> **Upanishads.** *English*
>
> **Upanishads.** *Chāndogyopaniṣad*

25.18J. Jaina Āgama

25.18J1. Enter one of the six component collections of the Jain canon (*Aṅga, Upāṅga, Prakīrnaka, Cheda, Mūla,* and *Cūlikā*) as a subheading of *Jaina Āgama.*

> **Jaina Āgama.** *Aṅga*

Enter a separately titled part of a component collection as a subheading of the title for the collection.

> **Jaina Āgama.** *Aṅga. Ācārāṅga*

Make other additions as instructed in 25.5 and 25.6B3.

25.18K. Avesta

25.18K1. Enter a main component part or a group of parts of the Avesta as a subheading of *Avesta.* Use the title by which it is identified in English-language sources. Make other additions as instructed in 25.5 and 25.6B3.

> **Avesta.** *Yasna*
>
> **Avesta.** *Khordah Avesta*

Enter an individually titled part of one of the main components as a subheading of the title for the main component.

> **Avesta.** *Yasna. Gathas*

25.18L. References for Vedas, Aranyakas, Brahmanas, Upanishads, Jaina Āgama, and Avesta

25.18L1. Refer from the titles of parts that are entered as subheadings of the larger work.

> **Atharvaveda**
>   *see* **Vedas.** *Atharvaveda*
>
> **Chāndogyopaniṣad**
>   *see* **Upanishads.** *Chāndogyopaniṣad*
>
> **Aṅga**
>   *see* **Jaina Āgama.** *Aṅga*

Ācāraṅga
　　see **Jaina Āgama.** *Aṅga. Ācāraṅga*

Gathas
　　see **Avesta.** *Yasna. Gathas*

25.18M. Koran

25.18M1. Enter a chapter (*sūrah*), one of the thirty parts (*juz'*), or a named grouping of selections of the Koran as a subheading of *Koran*. Precede the title of a chapter by *Sūrat*. Precede the title of a part by *Juz'*. Refer from *sūrah* or *juz'* number(s) using *Sūrah* or *Juz'* followed by the appropriate roman numeral(s). Refer from the titles of established groupings of selections. Make additions as instructed in 25.5 and 25.6B3.

> **Koran.** *Sūrat al-Baqarah*
> *x* Koran. *Sūrah II*
>
> **Koran.** *Juz' 'Amma*
> *x* Koran. *Juz' XXX*
>
> **Koran.** *Mu'awwidhatān*
> *x* Mu'awwidhatān

25.18M2. Enter a verse of a chapter as a subheading of *Koran* and add the arabic numeral of the verse to the title of the *sūrah*. Refer from the title of the verse and from the title of the verse as a subheading of *Koran*.

> **Koran.** *Sūrat al-Baqarah, 177*
> *x* Āyat al-Birr
> *x* Koran. *Āyat al-Birr*

Liturgical Works, Theological Creeds, Confessions of Faith, Etc.

25.19. GENERAL RULE[8]

25.19A. If the name of a body under which a liturgical work is entered is given in English, use as uniform title a well-established English title if there is one.

---

8. Consult the following works in cataloguing liturgical works of the Latin and Eastern rites of the Christian church:

Attwater, Donald. *A Catholic Dictionary.* — 3rd ed. — New York : Macmillan, 1958.
Cabrol, Fernand. *Dictionnaire d'archéologie chrétienne et de liturgie.* — Paris : Letouzey et Ané, 1907–1953.
International Federation of Library Associations and Institutions. Working Group on Uniform Headings of Liturgical Works. *List of Uniform Titles for Liturgical Works of the Latin Rites of the Catholic Church.* — 2nd ed., rev. — London : IFLA International Office for UBC, 1981.
Kapsner, Oliver L. *A Manual of Cataloging Practice for Catholic Author and Title Entries : Being Supplementary Aids to the A.L.A. and Vatican Library Cataloging Rules.* — Washington : Catholic University of America Press, 1953.
New Catholic Encyclopedia / prepared by an editorial staff at the Catholic University of America. — New York : McGraw-Hill, 1967–1979.

Church of England
[Book of common prayer]

Catholic Church
[Missal]
(*Full title in Latin:* Missale Romanum)

If there is no such title, or if the name of the body is given in a language other than English, use a brief title in the language of the liturgy.

Catholic Church
[Caeremoniale Romanum]

Catholic Church
[Ordo divini officii]
(*Full title:* Ordo divini officii recitandi sacrique peragendi)

Russkaia̅ pravoslavnaia̅ ts̅erkov'
[Sluzhebnik]

Svenska kyrkan
[Handbok]

25.19B. Use as the uniform title for a theological creed, confession of faith, etc., accepted by one or more denominational bodies a well-established English title if there is one. Otherwise, use a title in the original language.

Augsburg Confession

Westminster Confession of Faith

Nicene Creed

25.20. CATHOLIC LITURGICAL WORKS

25.20A. Early works

25.20A1. If a Catholic liturgical work compiled before the Council of Trent (1545–1563) has a close counterpart in a Tridentine work, use the Tridentine title.

Catholic Church
[Missal . . .]
Missale ad vsum insignis Ecclesie Sarum . . . 1527

If such a work has no close counterpart among Tridentine liturgical works, or in case of doubt, use the title by which the work is identified in reference sources.

Catholic Church
[Ordo Romanus primus . . .]
Ordo Romanus primus
(*An early work. Not the same as the later* Ordo divini officii)

25.20B. Recent works

25.20B1. Uniform titles of Tridentine texts are not applicable to those post-Vatican II texts that vary in language and content. Where such variations exist, use the individual title of each manifestation as the uniform title. Add a term to distinguish between different texts that have the same title.

> **Catholic Church**
> [Liturgy of the hours (U.S.)]

> **Catholic Church**
> [Liturgy of the hours (England)]

25.21. JEWISH LITURGICAL WORKS

25.21A. Use as the uniform title for a Jewish liturgical work its name as found in the *Encyclopaedia Judaica*.

> **Haggadah . . .**

> **Kinot . . .**

25.22. VARIANT AND SPECIAL TEXTS

25.22A. If the item being catalogued contains an authorized or traditional variant or special text of a liturgical work, add in parentheses (in this order of preference):

1) the name of a special rite (e.g., a Latin rite other than the Roman rite for Catholic works; a rite other than the unmodified Ashkenazic rite for Jewish works)

> **Catholic Church**
> [Vesperal (Ambrosian)]
> Liber vesperalis juxta ritum sanctae Ecclesiae Mediolanensis

> **Haggadah** (*Sephardic*)
> Haggadah de Péssah : transcrite en caractères latins, prononciation rite Sépharade

2) the name of the place (e.g., country, diocese) or institution (e.g., monastery) in which the variant is authorized or traditional; if necessary, add both elements, with the institution preceding the place

> **Catholic Church**
> [Ordo divini officii (Diocese of Trier)]
> Directorium Diocesis Treverensis, seu, Ordo divini officii recitandi missaeque celebrandae

> **Catholic Church**
> [Officia propria (Ireland)]
> Officia propria sanctorum insulae Hiberniae

> **Catholic Church**
> [Missal (St. Augustine's Abbey, Canterbury, England)]
> The missal of St. Augustine's Abbey, Canterbury

> **Kinot** (*Russia*)
> Seder kinot

3) the name of the religious order for which the variant is authorized or traditional.

Catholic Church
[Breviary (Benedictine)]
Brevarium monasticum

Catholic Church
[Missal (Dominican)]
Missale Dominicanum

If a single term is insufficient to identify the variant text, add a second term (e.g., the name of the editor).

Haggadah *(Reform, Guggenheim)*
Offenbacher Haggadah
(*Edited by Guggenheim*)

Haggadah *(Reform, Seligmann)*
Hagada : Liturgie für die häusliche Feier der Sederabende / in deutscher Sprache neu bearbeitet von C. Seligmann

25.22B. If the uniform title is for a particular manuscript, or a reproduction of a particular manuscript, add in parentheses *Ms.* followed by (in this order of preference):

1) a brief form of the name of a particular owner if that is how the manuscript is identified

Catholic Church
[Psalter (Ms. Queen Mary)]

2) any other name by which the manuscript is identified

Catholic Church
[Book of hours (Ms. Rohan)]

3) a brief form of the name of the repository followed by the repository's designation.

Catholic Church
[Sacramentary (Ms. Biblioteca Vaticana. Ottoboni 356)]

25.23. PARTS OF LITURGICAL WORKS

25.23A. If the item contains a specific liturgical observance, group of observances, or group of other texts extracted from a larger liturgical work, use as uniform title a well-established English title (if there is one) for the observance, group of observances, or other texts. Otherwise, use a brief title in the language of the liturgy. Refer from the title as a subheading of the title of the larger work.

Catholic Church
[Holy Week rite]
x Catholic Church. Missal. Holy Week rite

Albanian Orthodox Church in America
[Liturgy of St. John Chrysostom]
x Albanian Orthodox Church in America. Euchologion.
Liturgy of St. John Chrysostom

25.23B. Use *Office* or *Mass*, respectively, followed by a brief identification of the day or occasion, as the uniform title for an Office or for a proper of the Mass for a particular day. If the day is a saint's day, add only the saint's name in direct order and in the language of the heading for the saint. Make an explanatory reference from the Office or Mass as a subheading of the larger work.

> **Catholic Church**
> [Office, Assumption of the Blessed Virgin Mary]
> *Explanatory reference:*
>> **Catholic Church**
>> Breviary. Office
>> For the office of the Breviary for a particular day or
> occasion, *see*
>> **Catholic Church**
>> Office, [*name of day or occasion*], e.g.,
>> **Catholic Church**
>> Office, Assumption of the Blessed Virgin Mary

> **Catholic Church**
> [Mass, Sainte Thérèse]
> *Explanatory reference:*
>> **Catholic Church**
>> Missal. Mass
>> For the Mass for a particular day or occasion, *see*
>> **Catholic Church**
>> Mass, [*name of day or occasion*], e.g.,
>> **Catholic Church**
>> Mass, Sainte Thérèse

25.23C. Use *Mass*, followed by its number in the *Gradual*, as the uniform title for a numbered plainsong setting of the Ordinary of the Mass. Make an explanatory reference from the Ordinary as a subheading of *Gradual*.

> **Catholic Church**
> [Mass XVI]
> *Explanatory reference:*
>> **Catholic Church**
>> Gradual. Ordinary
>> For a single numbered Ordinary, *see*
>> **Catholic Church**
>> Mass [*number of the Ordinary*], e.g.,
>> **Catholic Church**
>> Mass XVI

Official Papal Communications, Etc.

25.24. OFFICIAL COMMUNICATIONS OF THE POPE AND THE ROMAN CURIA

25.24A. Use as the uniform title for an individual work entered under the official heading for a pope (see 21.4D1) the short title (generally the first word or words

517

of the text) by which it is generally known and cited in the original language (usually Latin).

> **Catholic Church.** *Pope* (*1963-1978 : Paul VI*)
> [Populorum progressio]

25.24B. If a communication of one of the tribunals, congregations, or offices of the Roman Curia is similarly known by a short title, use it as the uniform title.

> **Catholic Church.** *Congregatio Sancti Officii*
> [Lamentabili]

Musical Works

25.25. GENERAL RULE

25.25A. Formulate a uniform title for a musical work as instructed in 25.26–25.31. Formulate a uniform title for one or more parts of a musical work as instructed in 25.32. When two musical works, or one musical work and one part of another musical work, or one part of one musical work and one part of another musical work, by one composer are published together, follow the instructions in 25.33. Formulate a collective uniform title for music as instructed in 25.34. As appropriate, make additions to a uniform title to designate a particular manifestation as instructed in 25.35. Use general rules 25.1–25.7 insofar as they are applicable and are not contradicted by rules 25.26–25.35.

Individual Titles

25.26. GENERAL RULE

25.26A. Formulate the initial title element of the uniform title for a musical work as instructed in 25.27–25.29. Make additions to the initial title element as instructed in 25.30–25.32 and 25.35. If no additions are required, use the initial title element as the uniform title for the work.

25.27. SELECTION OF TITLE

25.27A. General rule

25.27A1. Use as the basis for the uniform title for a musical work the composer's original title in the language in which it was presented. Formulate the initial title element by applying 25.28–25.29 to the title selected.

> **Wagner, Richard**
> [Meistersinger von Nürnberg . . .]
> The mastersingers of Nuremberg

> **Berlioz, Hector**
> [Damnation de Faust . . .]
> Fausts Verdammung

Hardy, Françoise
[Tous les garçons et les filles . . .]
Todos los chicos y chicas

Grieg, Edvard
[Haugtussa . . .]
The mountain maid

Rimsky-Korsakov, Nikolay
[Zolotoĭ petushok . . .]
The golden cockerel

Bach, Johann Sebastian
[Präludium und Fuge . . .]
Präludium und Fuge, D-Dur für Orgel . . .

Frackenpohl, Arthur
[Rondo with fugato . . .]
Rondo with fugato . . .

Ravel, Maurice
[Introduction et allegro . . .]
Introduction et allegro . . .

If another title in the same language has become better known, if the title is very long, or if the title includes the name of a type of composition,[9] follow the instructions in 25.27B–25.27D.

25.27B. Better known title in the same language

25.27B1. If another title in the same language has become better known, use it (see also 25.1–25.4).

Mozart, Wolfgang Amadeus
[Don Giovanni . . .]
Il dissoluto punito, ossia, Il don Giovanni

Verdi, Giuseppe
[Nabucco . . .]
Nabucodonosor

25.27C. Long titles

25.27C1. If the title is very long, use (in this order of preference):

a) a brief title by which the work is commonly identified in reference sources

Schütz, Heinrich
[Historia der Auferstehung Jesu Christi . . .]
Historia der frölichen und siegreichen Auferstehung unsers
einigen Erlösers und Seligmachers Jesu Christi

---

9. The name of a type of composition, as distinguished from a distinctive title, is considered to be the name of a form, the name of a genre, or a generic term used frequently by different composers (e.g., *capriccio, concerto, intermezzo, Magnificat, mass, movement, muziek, nocturne, requiem, Stück, symphony, suite, Te Deum, trio sonata*). Other titles (including those that consist of such terms plus an additional word or words, e.g., *chamber concerto, Konzertstück, little suite*) are considered to be distinctive.

b) a brief title formulated by the cataloguer.

> **Schütz, Heinrich**
> [St. John Passion . . .]
> Historia des Leidens und Sterbens unsers Herrn und
> Heylandes Jesu Christi, nach dem Evangelisten St. Johannem

25.27D. Titles including the name of a type of composition

25.27D1. If all of a composer's works with titles (selected according to 25.27A–25.27C) that include the name of a type of composition are also cited as a numbered sequence of compositions of that type, use the name of the type of composition as basis for the uniform title (see 25.29).

> **Beethoven, Ludwig van**
> [Symphonies . . .]
> Sinfonia eroica
>   (*Also called:* Third symphony)

25.28. ISOLATION OF INITIAL TITLE ELEMENT

25.28A. When determining an initial title element, omit from the title selected according to 25.27:

1) a statement of medium of performance (even if such a statement is part of a compound word, provided that the resulting word(s) is the name of a type of composition)
2) key
3) serial, opus, and thematic index numbers
4) number(s) (unless they are an integral part of the title)
5) date of composition
6) adjectives and epithets not part of the original title of the work
7) an initial article (see 25.2C).

In the following examples the initial title element as defined above is underlined.

String <u>quartet</u>

<u>Streichquartett</u>

<u>Symphonie</u> no. 40

<u>Clavierübung</u>

<u>Kammersymphonie</u>

<u>Symphonie</u> fantastique

<u>Carnaval</u> op. 9

<u>Concerto</u> in A minor, op. 54

12 <u>sonatas</u>

<u>Nocturne</u> in F sharp minor, op. 15, no. 2

6 <u>Stücke</u> für Orchester

Fünf <u>Orchesterstücke</u>

Four orchestral <u>pieces</u>

Five <u>little pieces</u> for piano

Drei <u>Gesänge</u>

Vier <u>Orchesterlieder</u>, op. 22

Les <u>deux journées</u>

The <u>Ten commandments</u>

The <u>seventh trumpet</u>

Troisième <u>nocturne</u>

Mozart's favorite <u>minuet</u>

The celebrated <u>Sophie waltz</u>

<u>Grandes études</u>
  (*So named by the composer*)

Die <u>Zauberflöte</u>

<u>War requiem</u>

25.29. FORMULATION OF INITIAL TITLE ELEMENT

25.29A. Initial title elements consisting solely of the name of one type of composition

25.29A1. If the initial title element resulting from the application of 25.27 and 25.28 consists solely of the name of one type of composition, use the accepted English form of name if there are cognate forms in English, French, German, and Italian, or if the same name is used in all these languages. Give the name in the plural (this may be a non-English plural form, e.g., *divertimenti*) unless the composer wrote only one work of the type.

> **Boccherini, Luigi**
> [Quintets . . .]
> Quintetto VI in sol maggiore

> **Brahms, Johannes**
> [Ballades . . .]
> Vier Balladen

> **Geminiani, Francesco**
> [Sonatas . . .]
> Sonate a violino, violone, e cembalo

> **Geminiani, Francesco**
> [Concerti grossi . . .]
> Six concerti grossi for 2 violins, viola, and violoncello soli with strings and harpsichord

> **Mozart, Wolfgang Amadeus**
> [Divertimenti . . .]
> Divertimento Nr. 1

Do not use the English form of name for works intended for concert performance called *étude*, *fantasia*, or *sinfonia concertante* or their cognates.

> **Chopin, Frédéric**
> [Études . . .]
> Studies

25.29B. Duets

25.29B1. Use *Duets* for works variously titled *duos*, *duets*, etc.

> **Pleyel, Ignaz Joseph**
> [Duets . . .]
> Trois duos

25.29C. Trio sonatas

25.29C1. Use *Trio sonatas* for works of the seventeenth and eighteenth centuries variously titled *sonatas*, *trios*, *sonate a tre*, etc. These works are generally written for two treble instruments and continuo (usually violoncello and keyboard).

Corelli, Arcangelo
[Trio sonatas . . .]
Twelve sonatas for two violins and a violoncello, with a
thorough bass for harpsichord or organ

Corelli, Arcangelo
[Trio sonatas . . .]
Zwölf Triosonaten für zwei Violinen und Basso continuo

25.30. ADDITIONS TO INITIAL TITLE ELEMENTS CONSISTING OF THE NAME(S) OF ONE OR MORE TYPE(S) OF COMPOSITION

25.30A. General rule

25.30A1. If the initial title element consists solely of the name of a type, or of
two or more types, of composition, make additions to it as instructed in 25.30B–
25.30E. Make the additions in the order specified. Precede each element by a
comma. For all other title elements, see 25.31.

25.30B. Medium of performance

25.30B1. General rule. Add a statement of the medium of performance[10] if the
initial title element consists solely of the name of a type, or of two or more types,
of composition.

> [Sonatas, piano . . .]

> [Trios, sopranos, alto, piano . . .]

> [Introduction et allegro, harp, woodwinds, strings . . .]

Do not add a statement of the medium of performance if:

a) the medium is implied by the title

Chorale prelude
(*Implied medium: organ*)

Mass
(*Implied medium: voices, with or without accompaniment*)

Overture
(*Implied medium: orchestra*)

Songs, Lieder, etc.
(*Implied medium: solo voice(s) with accompaniment for keyboard
stringed instrument or, if in a "popular" idiom, solo voice(s) with
instrumental and/or vocal accompaniment*)

Symphony
(*Implied medium: orchestra*)

---

10. A statement of the medium of performance is a concise statement of the instrumental and/or
vocal medium of performance for which a musical work was originally intended.

If, however, the medium is other than that implied by the title, add the statement, e.g.,

> [Symphonies, organ . . .]

or b) the work consists of a set of compositions for different media, or is one of a series of works with the same title but for different media

> **Fesch, Willem de**
> [Sonatas . . .]
> 12 sonatas : six for a violin, with a thorough bass, several of them are proper for a German flute, and six for two violoncellos

> **Monteverdi, Claudio**
> [Madrigals, book 1 . . .]
> *(For 5 voices)*

> **Monteverdi, Claudio**
> [Madrigals, book 7 . . .]
> *(For 1–6 voices and instruments)*

> **Persichetti, Vincent**
> [Serenades, no. 14 . . .]
> *(For solo oboe)*

> **Persichetti, Vincent**
> [Serenades, no. 15 . . .]
> *(For harpsichord)*

or c) the medium was not designated by the composer
or d) the complexities of stating the medium are such that an arrangement by other identifying elements (e.g., thematic index number or opus number, see 25.30C) would be more useful.

> **Mozart, Wolfgang Amadeus**
> [Divertimenti, K. 251 . . .]

Record the medium of performance specifically, but do not use more than three elements except as instructed in 25.30B3. Give the elements in the following order:

> voices
> keyboard instrument if there is more than one non-
>   keyboard instrument
> the other instruments in score order
> continuo

> [Duets, voices, piano . . .]

> [Trio, piano, clarinet, violoncello . . .]

> [Sonatas, violin, piano . . .]

> [Trio sonatas, flute, bassoon, continuo . . .]

If there is more than one part for a particular instrument or voice, add the appropriate arabic numeral in parentheses after the name of that instrument or voice unless the number is otherwise implicit in the uniform title.

[Scherzos, flutes (2), clarinets (2) . . .]

[Galliards, viols (5) . . .]

but

[Quartets, violin, violas, violoncello . . .]

[Quartets, flutes, clarinets . . .]

25.30B2. Instrumental music intended for one performer to a part. For instrumental music intended for one performer to a part, record the medium of performance in one of, or a combination of, the following ways (in this order of preference):

a) by certain standard chamber music combinations (see 25.30B3)
b) by individual instruments (see 25.30B4)
c) by groups of instruments (see 25.30B5).

25.30B3. Standard combinations of instruments. For the following standard chamber music combinations, use the terms given in the column on the right:

COMBINATION	USE IN UNIFORM TITLE
string trio (violin, viola, violoncello)	[Trios, strings . . .]
string quartet (2 violins, viola, violoncello)	[Quartets, strings . . .]
woodwind quartet (flute, oboe, clarinet, bassoon)	[Quartets, woodwinds . . .]
wind quintet (flute, oboe, clarinet, horn, bassoon)	[Quintets, winds . . .]
piano trio (piano, violin, violoncello)	[Trios, piano, strings . . .]
piano quartet (piano, violin, viola, violoncello)	[Quartets, piano, strings . . .]
piano quintet (piano, 2 violins, viola, violoncello)	[Quintets, piano, strings . . .]

If the initial title element does not include *trio(s)*, *quartet(s)*, or *quintet(s)*, use the name of the standard combination as given in the left column above.

[Serenades, piano quartet . . .]

In uniform titles beginning *Trio*, *Quartet*, or *Quintet*, when the work is for a combination other than one listed above, record the full statement of medium even if more than three different instruments must be recorded. For the order of instruments, see 25.30B1.

[Quartets, violin, viola, violoncello, double bass . . .]

[Quartets, flute, oboe, saxophone, bassoon . . .]

[Quintets, piano, violin, viola, violoncello, double bass . . .]

[Quintets, flute, clarinets, bassoon, horn . . .]

25.30B4. Individual instruments. In naming an individual type of instrument, use an English term whenever possible. Use the following list of terms as a guide. When alternatives are given, choose a term and use it consistently.

> cello *or* violoncello
> cor anglais *or* English horn
> double bass (*not* bass viol *or* contrabass)
> double bassoon *or* contrabassoon
> harpsichord (*not* cembalo *or* virginal)
> horn (*not* French horn)
> kettle drums *or* timpani
> viol (*for sizes of viola da gamba other than bass*)
> viola da gamba (*not* bass viol *or* gamba)
> viols (*for viols of different sizes*)

For keyboard instruments use:

> piano (*for one instrument, 2 hands*)
> piano, 4 hands
> pianos (2) (*for two instruments, 4 hands*)
> pianos (2), 8 hands
> organs (2)

Omit the following elements:

a) the designation of the key in which an instrument is pitched

> clarinet (*not* clarinet in A)

b) the terms *alto*, *tenor*, *bass*, etc.

> recorder (*not* alto recorder)
> saxophone (*not* alto saxophone)

c) the names of alternative instruments.

Use *continuo* for a thorough bass part, with or without figures, realized or unrealized, whether it is named as *basso continuo*, *figured bass*, *thorough bass*, or *continuo*.

Marcello, Benedetto
[Sonatas, recorder, continuo . . .]
XII suonate a flauto solo, con il suo basso continuo per violoncello o cembalo

If the composition is intended for a keyboard instrument, but no particular instrument is named and the work can be played on any keyboard instrument, use *keyboard instrument*.

Gibbons, Orlando
[Fantazias, keyboard instrument . . .]
Fantazia of foure parts

Albrechtsberger, Johann Georg
  [Fugues, keyboard instrument . . .]
  Douze fugues pour le clavecin ou l'orgue

25.30B5. Groups of instruments. Use one of the following terms for a group of instruments:

> woodwinds
> brasses
> winds (*for woodwinds and brasses*)
> percussion
> plucked instruments
> keyboard instruments
> strings
> instrumental [string, wind, etc.] ensemble
>   (*for four or more diverse instruments*)

[Sextets, strings . . .]

[Divertimenti, piano, woodwinds . . .]

[Fanfares, brasses, percussion . . .]

[Concertos, instrumental ensemble . . .]

For standard chamber music combinations, see 25.30B3.

25.30B6. Instrumental music for orchestra, string orchestra, band. For instrumental music intended for orchestra, string orchestra, or band, use one of the following terms:

> orchestra (*for full or reduced orchestra*)
> string orchestra
> band

Ferguson, Howard
  [Partitas, orchestra . . .]

Hindemith, Paul
  [Symphonies, band . . .]

Bartók, Béla
  [Concertos, orchestra . . .]

Disregard continuo when it is part of an orchestra or string orchestra.

25.30B7. Solo instrument(s) and accompanying ensemble. For a work for one solo instrument and accompanying ensemble, use the name of the solo instrument followed by the name of the accompanying ensemble.

[Rhapsodies, violin, orchestra . . .]

[Concertos, piano, orchestra . . .]

[Concertos, harpsichord, instrumental ensemble . . .]

For a work for two or more solo instruments and accompanying ensemble, name the medium for the solo instruments as instructed in 25.30B1–25.30B6 followed by the name of the accompanying ensemble.

[Concertos, piano trio, orchestra . . .]

[Concertos, woodwind quartet, string orchestra . . .]

[Divertimenti, clarinets (2), string orchestra . . .]

[Sinfonie concertanti, violin, viola, orchestra . . .]

25.30B8. Solo voices. Use one of the following terms as appropriate to name a type of solo voice:

> soprano
> mezzo-soprano
> alto
> tenor
> baritone
> bass

[Cantatas, sopranos (2), alto, orchestra . . .]

[Romances, soprano, piano . . .]

Use other terms (e.g., *high voice*, *countertenor*) as appropriate.

Use one of the following terms for two or more solo voices of different ranges whenever it is necessary to reduce the number of elements in the medium statement to three or fewer:

> mixed solo voices
> men's solo voices
> women's solo voices

Use other terms (e.g., *children's solo voices*) as appropriate.

For compositions that include solo voices with chorus, give only the appropriate terms for the chorus (see 25.30B9) and the accompaniment, if any.

25.30B9. Choruses. Use one of the following terms as appropriate to name a choral ensemble:

> mixed voices
> men's voices
> women's voices
> unison voices

Use other terms (e.g., *children's voices*) as appropriate.

25.30B10. Accompaniment for songs, Lieder, etc. If a work (other than one in a "popular" idiom) requires an initial title element such as *Songs*, *Lieder*, etc., and is to be accompanied by anything other than a keyboard stringed instrument alone (see 25.30B1), add the name(s) of the accompanying instrument(s) and *acc.* If such a work is not accompanied add *unacc.*

[Chansons, guitar acc. . . .]

[Lieder, unacc. . . .]

[Songs, percussion acc. . . .]

25.30B11. Indeterminate medium of performance. Do not add a statement of medium of performance in the case of:

a) a work (especially one of the Renaissance period) intended for performance by voices and/or instruments
b) an instrumental chamber work for which the precise medium is not clearly defined.

> **Youll, Henry**
> [Canzonets]
> Canzonets to three voices

If, however, two or more such works with the same title are entered under the same heading, record the number of parts or voices. Use *voices* to designate both vocal and instrumental parts.

> **Morley, Thomas**
> [Canzonets, voices (4)]
> Canzonets, or, Little short songs to foure voyces

> **Morley, Thomas**
> [Canzonets, voices (5-6)]
> Canzonets, or, Little short aers to five and sixe voices

> **Maschera, Florentio**
> [Canzoni, voices (4) . . .]
> Libro primo de canzoni da sonare a quatro voci

> **Weelkes, Thomas**
> [Madrigals, voices (5-6)]
> Madrigals of 5 and 6 parts, apt for the viols and voices

25.30C. Numeric identifying elements

25.30C1. General rule. If the initial title element consists solely of the name(s) of type(s) of composition, add as many of the following identifying elements as can readily be ascertained. Add following the statement of medium of performance and in the order given:

a) serial number
b) opus number or thematic index number.

Precede each element by a comma.

25.30C2. Serial numbers. If works with the same title and the same medium of performance are consecutively numbered in music reference sources, add the number.

> [Quartets, strings, no. 2 . . .]

> [Symphonies, no. 5 . . .]

25.30C3. Opus numbers. Include the opus number, if any, and the number within the opus, if any.

> [Sonatas, piano, no. 1, op. 2, no. 1 . . .]

> [Sonatas, piano, no. 2, op. 2, no. 2 . . .]

If there is a conflict in opus numbering among works of the same title and medium, or if the overall opus numbering of a composer's works is confused and conflicting, add to the opus number the name of the publisher originally using the number chosen. Add the publisher's name in parentheses.

> **Cambini, Giovanni Giuseppe**
> [Duets, flute, violin, op. 20 (Bland) . . .]

> **Cambini, Giovanni Giuseppe**
> [Duets, flute, violin, op. 20 (LeDuc) . . .]

25.30C4. Thematic index numbers. In the case of certain composers, use the number assigned to a work in a recognized thematic index. Add the number in the absence of, or in preference to, a serial number and/or opus number. Precede the number by the initial letter(s) of the bibliographer's name (e.g., K. 453[11]) or a generally accepted abbreviation (e.g., BWV 232[12]).

25.30D. Key

25.30D1. Pre-twentieth-century works. For pre-twentieth-century works, give the key. If the mode is major or minor, add the appropriate word.

> **Mendelssohn-Bartholdy, Felix**
> [Trios, piano, strings, no. 2, op. 66, C minor]
> Trio, op. 66, piano, violin & violoncello

> **Haydn, Joseph**
> [Symphonies, H. I, no. 24, D major]
> Symphony in D major

25.30D2. Post-nineteenth-century works. For post-nineteenth-century works, give the key if it is stated prominently in the item being catalogued. If the mode is clearly major or minor, add the appropriate word.

> **Reizenstein, Franz**
> [Scherzo, piano, op. 20, A major]
> Scherzo in A for pianoforte

> **Reizenstein, Franz**
> [Trios, flute, clarinet, bassoon]
> Trio for flute, clarinet, and bassoon
> (*Key not stated prominently*)

> **Hindemith, Paul**
> [Symphonies, band, B♭]
> Symphony in B flat for concert band

---

11. Köchel, Ludwig. *Chronologisch-thematisches Verzeichnis sämtlicher Tonwerke Wolfgang Amadé Mozarts*

12. Schmieder, Wolfgang. *Thematisch-systematisches Verzeichnis der musikalischen Werke von Johann Sebastian Bach*

25.30E. Other identifying elements

25.30E1. If the medium of performance, numeric identifying elements, and key are not sufficient, or are not available, to distinguish between two or more works, add in parentheses (in this order of preference):

a) the year of completion of composition
b) the year of original publication
c) any other identifying element(s) (e.g., place of composition, name of first publisher).

> **Caix d'Hervelois, Louis de**
> [Pièces, flute, continuo (1726)]

> **Caix d'Hervelois, Louis de**
> [Pièces, flute, continuo (1731)]

25.31. ADDITIONS TO OTHER INITIAL TITLE ELEMENTS

25.31A. General rule

25.31A1. If the initial title element does not consist solely of the name of a type of composition, or the names of two or more types, make additions as necessary as instructed in 25.31B–21.31C.

25.31B. Conflict resolution

25.31B1. If there is a conflict between uniform titles entered under the same heading, add a statement of medium of performance (see 25.30B) preceded by a comma, or a descriptive word or phrase enclosed in parentheses. Use *either* the medium of performance *or* a descriptive phrase as an addition to each title.

> **Debussy, Claude**
> [Images, orchestra]

> **Debussy, Claude**
> [Images, piano]
> *not*   Images (Piano work)

> **Granados, Enrique**
> [Goyescas (Opera)]

> **Granados, Enrique**
> [Goyescas (Piano work)]
> *not*   Goyescas, piano

If these additions do not resolve the conflict, add one or more of the elements provided in 25.30C–25.30E.

> **Bach, Johann Sebastian**
> [Was Gott tut, das ist wohlgetan (Cantata), BWV 98 . . .]

> **Bach, Johann Sebastian**
> [Was Gott tut, das ist wohlgetan (Cantata), BWV 99 . . .]

Bach, Johann Sebastian
[Was Gott tut, das ist wohlgetan (Chorale prelude) . . .]

25.31C. Alterations of musico-dramatic works

25.31C1. If the text, plot, setting, or other verbal element of a musical work is adapted or if a new text is supplied, and the title has changed, use the uniform title of the original work followed in parentheses by the title of the adaptation.

Strauss, Johann
[Fledermaus . . .]

Strauss, Johann
[Fledermaus (Champagne sec) . . .]

Strauss, Johann
[Fledermaus (Gay Rosalinda) . . .]

Strauss, Johann
[Fledermaus (Rosalinda) . . .]

Mozart, Wolfgang Amadeus
[Così fan tutte (Dame Kobold) . . .]
Die Dame Kobold (Così fan tutte) / bearbeitet von Carl Scheidemantel
 (Scheidemantel substituted an entirely new libretto based on the play by Calderón de la Barca)

25.32. PARTS OF A WORK

25.32A. One part

25.32A1. Use as the uniform title for a separately published part of a musical work the uniform title for the whole work followed by the title or verbal designation and/or the number of the part as instructed below. If the part has a distinctive title, make a name-title reference from the heading for the composer and the title of the part.

a) If each of the parts is identified only by a number, use the number of the part being catalogued.

Brahms, Johannes
[Ungarische Tänze. Nr. 5]

b) If each of the parts is identified only by a title or other verbal designation, use the title or other verbal designation of the part being catalogued.

Verdi, Giuseppe
[Aïda. Celeste Aïda]
x Verdi, Giuseppe. Celeste Aïda

Beethoven, Ludwig van
[Symphonies, no. 1, op. 21, C major. Andante cantabile con moto]

531

c) If each of the parts is identified both by a number and by a title or other verbal designation, use the title or other verbal designation of the part being catalogued.

> **Mozart, Wolfgang Amadeus**
> [Così fan tutte. Come scoglio]
> > (*Each aria has a number (e.g.,* No. 14 *for* Come scoglio) *as well as a title*)
> *x* Mozart, Wolfgang Amadeus. Come scoglio

If each of the parts is identified both by a number and by the same title or other verbal designation, use the number of the part being catalogued.

> **Vivaldi, Antonio**
> [Estro armonico. N. 8]
> > (*Each part has the title* Concerto *as well as a number*)

d) If each of the parts is identified by a number, and some of the parts are also identified by a title or other verbal designation, use the number of the part being catalogued followed by the title or other designation if there is one.

> **Schumann, Robert**
> [Album für die Jugend. Nr. 30]

> **Schumann, Robert**
> [Album für die Jugend. Nr. 2, Soldatenmarsch]
> *x* Schumann, Robert. Soldatenmarsch

e) If the part being catalogued is part of a larger part that has a distinctive title, include the title of the larger part in the uniform title. Omit the designation of the larger part if it is not distinctive. However, if an indistinctive designation of the larger part is required to identify the smaller part, include the designation of the larger part.

> **Praetorius, Hieronymus**
> [Opus musicum. Cantiones sacrae. O vos omnes]
> *x* Praetorius, Hieronymus. O vos omnes

> **Handel, George Frideric**
> [Messiah. Pifa]
> *not*   Messiah. Part 1. Pifa

> **Verdi, Giuseppe**
> [Traviata. Atto 3°. Preludio]

25.32A2. If a part of a musical work is designated by the same general term as other parts and lacks a number, add enough of the identifying terms as instructed in 25.30–25.31 as are necessary to distinguish the part.

> **Cima, Giovanni Paolo**
> [Concerti ecclesiastici. Sonata, brasses, violin, continuo]

> **Cima, Giovanni Paolo**
> [Concerti ecclesiastici. Sonata, cornett, violin, continuo]

If such additions are not appropriate, determine the number of the part in the set and add it, enclosed in parentheses.

Milán, Luis
[Maestro. Pavana (No. 23)]

Milán, Luis
[Maestro. Pavana (No. 24)]

Milán, Luis
[Maestro. Fantasia del primero tono (No. 1)]

Milán, Luis
[Maestro. Fantasia del primero tono (No. 4)]

25.32B. More than one part

25.32B1. Follow the instructions in 25.6B.

Brahms, Johannes
[Ungarische Tänze. Nr. 5-6]

Rossini, Gioacchino
[Barbiere di Siviglia. Largo al factotum]
Largo al factotum ; and, Una voce poco fa : from The barber of Seville
Added entry under: **Rossini, Gioacchino.** Barbiere di Siviglia. Voce poco fa

Schubert, Franz
[Impromptus, piano, D. 899. No. 2]
Deux impromptus, op. 90, nos 2 et 4
Added entry under: **Schubert, Franz.** Impromptus, piano, D. 899. No. 4

Bach, Johann Sebastian
[Musikalisches Opfer. Selections]

Wagner, Richard
[Ring des Nibelungen. Rheingold. Selections]

25.32B2. If a composer assembles a group of excerpts from a larger work and calls the group *suite*, substitute that word for *Selections*.

Grieg, Edvard
[Peer Gynt. Suite, no. 2]

25.32C. Additions

25.32C1. Add to the uniform title for a single part, or for several parts, of a musical work any appropriate elements provided for in 25.35, when appropriate.

Wagner, Richard
[Ring des Nibelungen. Walküre. Libretto. English & German]

Bach, Johann Sebastian
[Weihnachts-Oratorium. 1.-2. Theil. Vocal score. English & German]

Handel, George Frideric
[Messiah. He shall feed His flock; arr.]

25.33. TWO WORKS ISSUED TOGETHER

25.33A. Follow the instructions in 25.7.

Schubert, Franz
[Symphonies, D. 589, C major]
Symphony no. 6 in C major ; Symphony no. 3 in D major
Added entry under: **Schubert, Franz.** Symphonies, D. 200, D
major

Collective Titles

25.34. COLLECTIVE TITLES

25.34A. Complete works

25.34A1. Follow the instructions in 25.8.

Purcell, Henry
[Works]
The works of Henry Purcell

25.34B. Selections

25.34B1. Use the collective title *Selections* for a collection containing various types of composition for various instrumental and vocal media by a single composer.

Poulenc, Francis
[Selections]
Les biches ; Bucolique ; Hommage à Marguerite Long ;
Pastourelle ; L'éventail de Jeanne ; Matelote provençale ; La
guirlande de Campra

25.34C. Works of various types in one broad or specific medium, and works of one type for one specific medium or various media

25.34C1. For a collection containing works of various types in one broad medium, use the designation of that medium.

[Chamber music]

[Choral music][13]

[Instrumental music]

---

13. Use *Choral music* also for collections of various types of works originally for one choral medium, with or without accompaniment.

[Keyboard music]

[Vocal music][14]

For a collection containing works of various types in one specific medium, use a collective title generally descriptive of that medium.

[Brass music]

[Orchestra music]

[Piano music]

[Piano music, 4 hands]

[Piano music, pianos (2)]

[String quartet music]

[Violin, piano music]

25.34C2. For a collection containing works of one type, use the name of that type. Add a statement of medium unless the medium is obvious or unless the works are for various media.

[Concertos]

[Operas]

[Polonaises, piano]

[Quartets, strings]

[Sonatas]

[Sonatas, violin, piano]

[Songs]

25.34C3. If a title formulated according to 25.34C1 or 25.34C2 is for a collection that is incomplete, add *Selections*.

[Instrumental music. Selections]

[Organ music. Selections]

[Nocturnes, piano. Selections]

[Sonatas, violin, piano. Selections]

If the selections constitute a consecutively numbered group, use the inclusive numbering instead of *Selections*.

Beethoven, Ludwig van
[Sonatas, piano, no. 21–23]
Sonata no. 21 in C major, op. 53 : Waldstein ; Sonata no. 22 in F major, op. 54 ; Sonata no. 23 in F minor, op. 57 : Appassionata

---

14. Use *Vocal music* also for collections of various types of works originally for one solo voice or one combination of solo voices, with or without accompaniment.

> **Beethoven, Ludwig van**
> [Symphonies, no. 1-3]
> First, second, and third symphonies

Additions

25.35. ADDITIONS FOR MUSICAL WORKS

25.35A. General rule

25.35A1. As appropriate, make other additions to uniform titles for musical works as instructed in 25.35B–25.35F. Make additions in the order given. If *Selections* is added to a uniform title (see 25.32B1 and 25.34C3), add it as the last element or as the next to last element when *arr.* is used (see 25.35C). Precede each addition by a full stop except where other punctuation is prescribed.

25.35B. Sketches

25.35B1. If a work consists of a composer's sketches for a musical composition(s), add *Sketches* in parentheses to the uniform title for the completed composition(s).

> **Beethoven, Ludwig van**
> [Quartets, strings, no. 1–6, op. 18 (Sketches)]

25.35C. Arrangements

25.35C1. If a work that belongs, broadly speaking, to the category of "serious," "classical," or "art" music is determined to be an arrangement, etc., and is entered under the heading for the original composer (see 21.18B), use the uniform title for the original work and add *arr.*, preceded by a semicolon. Apply this instruction also to a transcription by the original composer.

> **Berlioz, Hector**
> [Corsaire; arr.]
> The corsaire : overture for concert band / transcribed by
> Gunther Schuller
>   (*Originally for orchestra*)

> **Respighi, Ottorino**
> [Uccelli; arr.]
> The birds / Respighi
>   (*Arranged for Japanese instruments by H. Okano*)

> **Schubert, Franz**
> [Octet, woodwinds, horn, strings, D. 803, F major; arr.]
> Grosses Octett, op. 166
>   (*Arranged for piano, 4 hands*)

> **Wang, Wei**
> [Pa-wang hsieh chia; arr.]
>   (*An 8th century composition arranged and rewritten in modern notation by Li T'ing-sung*)

Ravel, Maurice
[Pavane pour une infante défunte; arr.]
Pavane pour une infante défunte : pour petit orchestre
(*Transcription by the composer*)

Satie, Erik
[Piano music. Selections; arr.]
Pièces pour guitare
(*Transcriptions of piano works for guitar*)

25.35C2. If a work that belongs, broadly speaking, to the category of music in the "popular" idiom (e.g., rock, jazz) is determined to be an arrangement, etc., and is entered under the heading for the original composer (see 21.18B), use the uniform title of the original work. Add *arr.* only if the work being catalogued is:

a) an instrumental work arranged for vocal or choral performance

or b) a vocal work arranged for instrumental performance.

MacDermot, Galt
[Hair. Selections; arr.]
Hair '72 : the American tribal love-rock musical / [lyrics] by James Rado, Gerome Ragni ; [music by] Galt MacDermot ; concert band arranged by Len Goldstyne
(*Vocal music arranged for band*)

but

Carmichael, Hoagy
[Songs. Selections]
Hoagy Carmichael : a choral portrait : for S.A.B. voices and piano with optional guitar, bass, drums, and vibraphone / music by Hoagy Carmichael ; arranged by Robert Sterling
(*Songs arranged for accompanied choral performance*)

25.35D. Vocal and chorus scores

25.35D1. If the item being catalogued is a vocal score or a chorus score, add *Vocal score(s)* or *Chorus score(s)* to the uniform title.

Handel, George Frideric
[Messiah. Vocal score . . .]

Sullivan, *Sir* **Arthur**
[Mikado. Chorus score . . .]

Wagner, Richard
[Operas. Vocal scores . . .]

25.35E. Librettos and song texts

25.35E1. If a libretto or song text is entered under the heading for the composer (see 21.28A), add *Libretto* to the uniform title if the item contains only the text of an opera, operetta, oratorio, or the like, or *Text* to the uniform title for the text of a song. For collections by a single composer, add *Librettos* if the collection contains only texts of operas, operettas, oratorios, or the like; otherwise add *Texts*.

> **Verdi, Giuseppe**
> [Forza del destino. Libretto . . .]

> **John, Elton**
> [Crocodile rock. Text . . .]
> The words of Elton's smash hit Crocodile rock / Bernie
> Taupin

> **Mozart, Wolfgang Amadeus**
> [Operas. Librettos . . .]

25.35F. Language

25.35F1. If the text of a vocal work is a translation, or if the texts of all the works in a collection are translations, add the name(s) of the language(s) as instructed in 25.5C.

> **Bizet, Georges**
> [Carmen. German]
> Carmen : Oper in 4 Akten

> **Gounod, Charles**
> [Faust. Hungarian. Selections]

> **Boito, Arrigo**
> [Mefistofele. Vocal score. English & Italian]

> **Handel, George Frideric**
> [Messiah. Vocal score. Dutch & English]

> **Lennon, John**
> [Let it be. French & English]
> Let it be : en anglais et français / Lennon & McCartney

> **Schubert, Franz**
> [Songs. English & German]

CHAPTER 26

REFERENCES

Contents

26.1. GENERAL RULE

26.1A. Make references as instructed in the previous rules in part II. In addition, follow the more general instructions in this chapter.

In making references, ensure that:

a) there is an entry in the catalogue under the name heading or uniform title to which the reference is made and/or from which a *see also* reference is made[1]
b) there is a record of every reference under the name heading or uniform title to which it refers in order to make possible the correction or deletion of the reference.

In case of doubt as to whether to make a reference, make it.
Omit an initial article from a title appearing in a reference.

26.1B. *See* references

26.1B1. Make a *see* reference from a form of the name of a person or a corporate body or title of a work that might reasonably be sought to the form that has been chosen as a name or uniform title heading, or as a title entry.

26.1C. *See also* references

26.1C1. Make a *see also* reference from one name or title heading to another related name heading, uniform title, or title.

26.1D. Name-title references

26.1D1. Make a *see* or *see also* reference from a title (or uniform title) that has been entered under a personal or corporate heading in the form of a name-title reference beginning with the personal or corporate heading followed by the title concerned.

---

1. *Optionally*, make *see also* references from headings under which there are, as yet, no entries if considered justifiable administratively.

26.1E. Explanatory references

26.1E1. If a *see* or *see also* reference does not give adequate guidance to the user of the catalogue, make an explanatory reference giving more explicit guidance.

26.1F. Form of references

26.1F1. In making a reference, give the name of a person, place, or corporate body from which reference is made in the same structure as it would have as a heading.

> **Guillaume d'Auvergne,** *Bishop of Paris*
> *see* **Guilelmus Arvernus,** *Bishop of Paris*

> **Gand** (*Belgium*)
> *see* **Ghent** (*Belgium*)

In making a reference to two or more different headings or titles from the same form, make one reference, listing all headings to which reference is being made.

> **Mahfouz, Naguib**
> *see*
> **Maḥfūẓ, Najīb,** 1882-1957
> **Maḥfūẓ, Najīb,** 1912-

> **A.B.M.**
> *see*
> **Associação Brasileira de Metais**
> **Associação Brasileira de Municípios**
> **Associação dos Bibliotecários Municipais de São Paulo**

> **Bava kamma**
> *see*
> **Mishnah.** *Bava kamma*
> **Talmud.** *Bava kamma*
> **Talmud Yerushalmi.** *Bava kamma*
> **Tosefta.** *Bava kamma*

> **Pennsylvania.** *Department of Public Welfare*
> *see also*
> **Pennsylvania.** *Department of Public Assistance*
> **Pennsylvania.** *Department of Welfare*

26.1G. The layout, arrangement, and wording of the examples in this chapter are not prescriptive (i.e., they represent one of several possible methods of making references).

26.1H. Do not make a reference if the reference is so similar to a heading (name and/or title) or to another reference as to be unnecessary.

26.1J. Use, as appropriate, additions to names as set out in rules 22.16–22.19, 23.4, 24.4, 24.6, and 25.5 to distinguish between names or titles from which references are made and other name headings or uniform titles or references.

26.2. NAMES OF PERSONS

26.2A. *See* references

26.2A1. Different names. Refer from a name used by a person, or found in reference sources, that is different from the name used in the heading for that person. (For persons entered under two or more different headings, see also 26.2C1 and 26.2D1.) Typical instances are:

> *Pseudonym to real name*
> **Saint-Aubin, Horace de**
>   *see* **Balzac, Honoré de**

> *Real name to pseudonym*
> **Robertson, Ethel Florence Lindesay**
>   *see* **Richardson, Henry Handel**

> **Dupin, Amandine-Lucile-Aurore,** *baronne Dudevant*
>   *see* **Sand, George**

> **Dudevant, Amandine-Lucile-Aurore Dupin,** *baronne*
>   *see* **Sand, George**

> **Munro, Hector Hugh**
>   *see* **Saki**

> **Russell, George William**
>   *see* **A.E.**

> *Phrase*
> **Bachelor knight**
>   *see* **Simms, W. Gilmore**

> **Author of Memoirs of a fox-hunting man**
>   *see* **Sassoon, Siegfried**

> **Memoirs of a fox-hunting man, Author of**
>   *see* **Sassoon, Siegfried**

> *Secular name*
> **Gysi, Lydia**
>   *see* **Maria,** *Mother*

> **Roncalli, Angelo Giuseppe**
>   *see* **John XXIII,** *Pope*

> *Name in religion*
> **Louis,** *Father,* 1894-1983
>   *see* **Biersack, Louis**

> **Louis,** *Father,* 1915-1969
>   *see* **Merton, Thomas**

> *Earlier name*
> **Kouyoumdjian, Dikran**
>   *see* **Arlen, Michael**

Thibault, Jacques-Anatole
see **France, Anatole**

Foot, *Sir* **Hugh**
see **Caradon, Hugh Foot,** *Baron*

Barrett, Elizabeth
see **Browning, Elizabeth Barrett**

Richthofen, Frieda von
see **Lawrence, Frieda**

Weekley, Frieda
see **Lawrence, Frieda**

Edward VIII, *King of the United Kingdom*
see **Windsor, Edward,** *Duke of*

Morris, James
see **Morris, Jan**

Later name

Nicholls, Charlotte
see **Brontë, Charlotte**

Beaconsfield, Benjamin Disraeli, *Earl of*
see **Disraeli, Benjamin**

26.2A2. Different forms of the name. Refer from a form of name used by a person, or found in reference sources, or resulting from a different romanization of the name, if it differs significantly from the form used in the heading for that person. Typical instances are:

Difference in fullness of name

Valera y Alcalá Galiano, Juan
see **Valera, Juan**

Schiller, Johann Christoph Friedrich von
see **Schiller, Friedrich von**

Davies, William Henry
see **Davies, W.H.**

Powell, Enoch
see **Powell, J. Enoch**

Embleton, G.A.
see **Embleton, Gerry**

Full name to initials used as heading

Worsley, Edward
see **E.W.**

Different language form

Domingo, *de Guzmán, Saint*
see **Dominic,** *Saint*

Jeanne, *d'Arc, Saint*
  see **Joan,** *of Arc, Saint*

Terentius Afer, Publius
  see **Terence**

Mikes, György
  see **Mikes, George**

Ó Maolruanaidh, Liam
  see **Rooney, William**

Meister des Amsterdamer Kabinetts
  see **Master of the Amsterdam Cabinet**

Different spelling
  Ralegh, *Sir* **Walter**
    see **Raleigh,** *Sir* **Walter**

  Luly, Jean
    see **Lœillet, Jean Baptiste**

Different romanization
  Cao, Xuequin
    see **Ts'ao, Hsüeh-ch'in**

  Dostoevsky, Anna
    see **Dostoevskaīa, A.G.**

  Garkavi, Avraam IAkovlevich
    see **Harkavi, Avraham Eliyahu**

26.2A3. Different entry elements. Refer from different elements of the heading for a person under which that name might reasonably be sought. Typical instances are:

Different elements of a compound name
  Lewis, C. Day-
    see **Day-Lewis, C.**

  Smith, Cecil Woodham-
    see **Woodham-Smith, Cecil**

  Saint-Hilaire, Étienne Geoffroy
    see **Geoffroy Saint-Hilaire, Étienne**

  Mori, Emilio Cotarelo y
    see **Cotarelo y Mori, Emilio**

Part of surname following a prefix
  Polnay, Peter de
    see **De Polnay, Peter**

  Balzo, Raimundo del
    see **Del Balzo, Raimundo**

Grunebaum, G.E. von
  see **Von Grunebaum, G.E.**

Annunzio, Gabriele d'
  see **D'Annunzio, Gabriele**

Sablière, Marguerite Hessein de La
  see **La Sablière, Marguerite Hessein de**

Prefix to surname used as entry element (see also 26.2D2)
  Von Hofmannsthal, Hugo
    see **Hofmannsthal, Hugo von**

  Van de Wetering, Janwillem
    see **Wetering, Janwillem van de**

Part of surname following a prefix combined with surname
  Bure, Guillaume de
    see **Debure, Guillaume**

First given name of person without surname when it is not the entry element
  Maria Helena
    see **Helena, Maria**

  'Ali ibn Muḥammad, Abū Ḥayyān al-Tawḥīdī
    see **Abu Ḥayyān al-Tawḥīdī, 'Ali ibn Muḥammad**

  'Abd al-Raḥmān al-Bāshā
    see **al-Bāshā, 'Abd al-Raḥmān**

Epithet or byname
  Aquinas, Thomas, *Saint*
    see **Thomas,** *Aquinas, Saint*

  Khayyām, Omar
    see **Omar Khayyām**

  Udine, Giovanni da
    see **Giovanni,** *da Udine*

Last element when it is not the entry element
  Barry, Jeanne Bécu, *comtesse Du*
    see **Du Barry, Jeanne Bécu,** *comtesse*

  Capella, Martianus
    see **Martianus Capella**

  al-Ḥimyarī, Nashwān ibn Sa'īd
    see **Nashwān ibn Sa'īd al-Ḥimyarī**

  Maung, Chit, *Saw*
    see **Chit Maung,** *Saw*

Person as saint
  Edward, *the Confessor, Saint*
    see **Edward,** *King of the English*

Constantine, *Saint*
  see **Constantine I,** *Emperor of Rome*

Family name of saint
Yepes y Alvarez, Juan de
  see **John of the Cross,** *Saint*

Soubirous, Marie-Bernarde
  see **Bernadette,** *Saint*

Family, dynastic, etc., name of ruler
Bonaparte, Napoléon
  see **Napoleon I,** *Emperor of the French*

Bernadotte, Jean-Baptiste-Jules
  see **Charles XIV John,** *King of Sweden and Norway*

Inverted form of initials entered in direct order (see also 26.2B2)
C., M.
  see **M.C.**

E., A.L.O.
  see **A.L.O.E.**

Direct form of inverted phrase heading
Miss Read
  see **Read,** *Miss*

Dr. Seuss
  see **Seuss,** *Dr.*

Inverted form of direct phrase heading
George, *Boy*
  see **Boy George**

X, *Dr.*
  see **Dr. X**

Honorary titles and terms of address when sometimes used as names
U Kyin U
  see **Kyin U,** *U*

26.2B. Name-title references

26.2B1. If the works of a person are entered under two or more different headings, make a name-title reference when the name appearing in a particular edition of a work is not the name used as the heading for that work.

Ashe, Gordon
  Croaker
    see **Creasey, John**
      (*Title page reads:* The croaker / John Creasey as Gordon Ashe)

Halliday, Michael
Edge of terror
see **York, Jeremy**
(*Title page reads:* The edge of terror / by Michael Halliday. *A later edition published under the name* Jeremy York)

26.2B2. Make a name-title reference from the inverted form of initials entered in direct order for each work entered under those initials.

D., H.
Helidora and other poems
see **H.D.**

D., H.
Hymen
see **H.D.**

D., H.
Sea garden
see **H.D.**

26.2B3. When two or more persons have used the same pseudonym and one or more is entered under another name, make a name-title reference from the pseudonym for each work of a person that is so entered.

Theophilus
Burmese loneliness
see **Enriquez, Colin Metcalf**

Theophilus
Defence of the dialogue entitled A display of God's special grace
see **Dickinson, Jonathan**

26.2B4. If a pseudonym consists of initials, a sequence of letters, or numerals, make a name-title reference from the real name for each item entered under the pseudonym.

Garcin, Étienne
Nouveau dictionnaire provençal-français
see **M.G.**
(*Initials stand for* Monsieur Garcin)

In addition, if the initials, etc., stand for a phrase other than a name, make a name-title reference from the phrase in direct order for each item entered under the pseudonym.

Lawrence, Curly
Betty the mongoliper
see **L.B.S.C.**

London, Brighton & South Coast
Betty the mongoliper
see **L.B.S.C.**

26.2C. *See also* references

26.2C1. If the works of one person are entered under two different headings, make a *see also* reference from each heading to the other (see also 26.2D1).

> **Innes, Michael**
>   *see also* **Stewart, J.I.M.**
>
> **Stewart, J.I.M.**
>   *see also* **Innes, Michael**

If the works of one person are entered under three or more different headings, make an explanatory reference as instructed in 26.2D.

26.2C2. If there are entries in the catalogue under the name of a known person and under the appellation of an unknown person including the name, or part of the name, of that known person, make a *see also* reference from the appellation to the name. Make an explanatory reference from the name to the appellation as instructed in 26.2D1.

> **Pseudo-Brutus**
>   *see also* **Brutus, Marcus Junius**

26.2D. Explanatory references

26.2D1. Make an explanatory reference when more guidance than a *see* or *see also* reference is required.

> **Gustaf Adolf,** *King of Sweden*
>   Kings of Sweden with this name are entered in a single
> sequence of all the kings of Sweden with the first name Gustaf,
> e.g.,
> **Gustaf I Vasa,** *King of Sweden*
> **Gustaf II Adolf,** *King of Sweden*
> **Gustaf III,** *King of Sweden*
> *Make a similar reference under* **Gustaf Vasa,** *King of Sweden*
>
> **Paine, Lauran**
>   For works of this author written under pseudonyms, *see*
> **Andrews, A.A.**
> **Benton, Will**
> **Bosworth, Frank**
> **Bradford, Will**
> **Bradley, Concho**
> *[etc., as required]*
>
> **Bradford, Will**
>   For works of this author written under other names, *see*
> **Andrews, A.A.**
> **Benton, Will**
> **Bosworth, Frank**
> **Bradley, Concho**
> **Paine, Lauran**
> *[etc., as required]*
> *Make similar references under the other pseudonyms*

Brutus, Marcus Junius
>For the Greek letters erroneously attributed to this person, *see*
Pseudo-Brutus

26.2D2. *Optionally*, make explanatory references under the various separately written prefixes of surnames to explain how names with such prefixes are entered in the catalogue.

De la
>Some names beginning with this prefix are also entered under
>**La** (e.g., La Bretèque, Pierre de) and others under the name
>following the prefix (e.g., Torre, Marie de la).
>*Make a similar reference under* **La**

26.3. GEOGRAPHIC NAMES AND NAMES OF CORPORATE BODIES

26.3A. *See* **references**

26.3A1. Different names. Refer from the name of a place found in reference sources that is significantly different from the form used as the entry element in a heading.

>**Aix-la-Chapelle** (*Germany*)
>   *see* **Aachen** (*Germany*)

>**Hellas**
>   *see* **Greece**

Refer from a name used by a body, or found in reference sources, that is significantly different from that used in the heading for that body.

>**Common Market**
>   *see* **European Economic Community**

>**Order of Preachers**
>   *see* **Dominicans**

>**Quakers**
>   *see* **Society of Friends**

Make an explanatory reference for a place or a body that has changed its name as instructed in 26.3C1.

26.3A2. General and specific names of conferences. Refer from a general name for a conference to the specific name used as the heading.

>**Nutrition Symposium** (*1953 : University of Toronto*)
>   *see* **Symposium on Protein Metabolism** (*1953 : University of Toronto*)

>**Nutrition Symposium** (*1956 : University of Michigan*)
>   *see* **Symposium on Endocrines and Nutrition** (*1956 : University of Michigan*)

26.3A3. Different forms of the name. Refer from a form of name used by a body, or from a form of name of a place or body found in reference sources or resulting from a different romanization, if that form differs significantly from the form used in the heading for that body or place. Typical instances are:

> *Different language forms*
>
> **Croix-Rouge suisse**
>   *see* **Schweizerisches Rotes Kreuz**
>
> **Nations Unies**
>   *see* **United Nations**
>
> **Uffizi Gallery**
>   *see* **Galleria degli Uffizi**
>
> **Danmark**
>   *see* **Denmark**
>
> **Deutschland** (*Bundesrepublik*)
>   *see* **Germany** (*Federal Republic*)
>
> *Initials and acronyms*
>
> **E.E.C.**
>   *see* **European Economic Community**
>
> **IDOT**
>   *see* **Illinois.** *Department of Transportation*
>
> **I.D.O.T.**
>   *see* **Illinois.** *Department of Transportation*
>
> *Full names*
>
> **Hertfordshire Technical Library and Information Service**
>   *see* **Hertis**
>
> **International Business Machines Corporation**
>   *see* **IBM**
>
> **European Atomic Energy Community**
>   *see* **Euratom**
>
> *Different spelling*
>
> **Organization for Economic Cooperation and Development**
>   *see* **Organisation for Economic Co-operation and Development**
>
> **Rumania**
>   *see* **Romania**
>
> *Different romanization*
>
> **Yaroslavsky tekhnologichesky institut**
>   *see* **ĨAroslavskiĭ tekhnologicheskiĭ institut**
>
> **Beijing** (*China*)
>   *see* **Peking** (*China*)

Other variants (*including shorter, fuller, and inverted forms*)

American Red Cross
see **American National Red Cross**

William Hayes Fogg Art Museum
see **Fogg Art Museum**

United States. *State Department*
see **United States.** *Department of State*

United Kingdom. *Army. Middlesex Regiment*
see **United Kingdom.** *Army. Infantry Regiment, 57th*

Religious Society of Friends
see **Society of Friends**

Friends, Society of
see **Society of Friends**

Luther College
see **Dr. Martin Luther College**

Martin Luther College
see **Dr. Martin Luther College**

St. Dominic, Order of
see **Dominicans**

William and Mary, College of
see **College of William and Mary**

Victoria University of Manchester
see **University of Manchester**

Roman Catholic Church
see **Catholic Church**

Jackson (D.G.) Advertising Service
see **D.G. Jackson Advertising Service**

Jackson Advertising Service
see **D.G. Jackson Advertising Service**

26.3A4. Initials. If a heading consists of an initialism or acronym and, in the catalogue, initials with full stops are filed differently from those without full stops, refer from one form to the other, depending on which has been used in the heading.

U.N.E.S.C.O.
see **Unesco**

NAAB
see **N.A.A.B.**

In the context of such a catalogue, *optionally* refer from initials without full stops, as well as with full stops (see 26.3A3), to a full name used as a heading (see also 26.3C2).

NATO
   see **North Atlantic Treaty Organization**

N.A.T.O.
   see **North Atlantic Treaty Organization**

USA
   see **United States**

U.S.A.
   see **United States**

26.3A5. Numbers. If, in the catalogue, numbers expressed as words are filed differently from numbers expressed as numerals, follow the instructions below if a heading begins with a number or contains a number in such a position that it affects the filing of the heading.

   a) If the number is expressed as a numeral, refer from the form of the heading with the number expressed as a word.

   Drie October-Vereeniging
      see **3 October-Vereeniging**

   Twentieth Century Heating & Ventilating Co.
      see **XXth Century Heating & Ventilating Co.**

   b) If the number is expressed as a word and if desirable, refer from the form of the heading with the number expressed as an arabic numeral.

   4 Corners Geological Society
      see **Four Corners Geological Society**

26.3A6. Abbreviations. If, in the catalogue, abbreviated words are filed differently from words written in full and if the heading begins with an abbreviated word or contains an abbreviated word in such a position that it affects the filing of the heading, refer from the form of the heading with the abbreviated word written in full in the language of the heading.

   Sankt Annen-Museum
      see **St. Annen-Museum**

   Société Saint-Jean-Baptiste de Montréal
      see **Société St-Jean-Baptiste de Montréal**

26.3A7. Different forms of heading. Refer from different forms of heading under which a corporate body might reasonably be sought. Typical instances are:

   Subordinate heading and its variants to a name entered directly
   American Library Association. *American Association of School Librarians*
      see **American Association of School Librarians**

   University of Oxford. *Bodleian Library*
      see **Bodleian Library**

London School of Economics and Political Science. *British Library of Political and Economic Science*
see **British Library of Political and Economic Science**

London School of Economics and Political Science. *Library*
see **British Library of Political and Economic Science**

University of London. *London School of Economics and Political Science*
see **London School of Economics and Political Science**

United Kingdom. *British Rail*
see **British Rail**

United States. *Tennessee Valley Authority*
see **Tennessee Valley Authority**

Name and its variants in the form of subheadings under the immediately superior body when the name has been entered under a body higher than the immediately superior body

American Library Association. *Resources and Technical Services Division. Cataloging and Classification Section*
see **American Library Association.** *Cataloging and Classification Section*

General Motors Corporation. *Fisher Body Division. Production Engineering Department. Engineering Pictorial Section*
see **General Motors Corporation.** *Fisher Body Division. Engineering Pictorial Section*

For bodies entered subordinately, the name and its variants in the form of independent headings whenever the name does not suggest subordinate entry

American Legion Auxiliary
see **American Legion.** *Auxiliary*

26.3B. *See also* references

26.3B1. Make *see also* references between independently entered corporate headings for bodies that are related:

British Ornithologists' Club
see also **British Ornithologists' Union**

British Ornithologists' Union
see also **British Ornithologists' Club**

British Iron and Steel Research Association
see also **Iron and Steel Institute**

Iron and Steel Institute
see also **British Iron and Steel Research Association**

26.3C. Explanatory references

26.3C1. General rule. Make an explanatory reference when more detailed guidance than a *see* or *see also* reference is required. Typical instances are:

a)   Scope of heading
    Freemasons
      Under subdivisions of this heading will be found publications of the lodges, grand lodges, etc., of the basic orders of Freemasonry (also called "craft" Masonry) in which are conferred the first three Masonic degrees.
      For publications of Masonic bodies conferring degrees beyond the first three, *see*
    Knights Templar (*Masonic order*)
    Royal and Select Masters
    Royal Arch Masons
    Scottish Rite (*Masonic order*)
      For publications of other Masonic bodies, *see* their names, e.g.,
    Order of the Secret Monitor

    Iran. *Shah* (*1941-1979 : Mohammed Reza Pahlavi*)
      Here are entered works of the Shah acting in his official capacity.
      For other works, *see*
    Mohammed Reza Pahlavi, *Shah of Iran*

    Pelham Books, Ltd.
      For works issued by Pelham Books, Ltd., under the designation John Dickson, Ph.D., *see*
    Dickson, John, *Ph.D.*

In a catalogue in which verbal subject and name-title entries are interfiled, integrate the name and subject "scope" references when appropriate.

b)   References applicable to several headings
    Aktiebolaget . . .
      Names of corporate bodies beginning with this word are entered under the next word in the name.

    Conference . . .
      Conference proceedings are entered under the name of the conference, etc., or the title of the publication if the conference, etc., lacks a name. *See also* **Symposium . . .** , **Workshop . . .** , etc.

    Catholic Church. *Sacra . . .*
      Sacra is omitted from the heading for an administrative body of the Catholic Church when it occurs at the beginning of the name, e.g., for the Sacra Rota Romana, *see* **Catholic Church.** *Rota Romana.*

c)   Earlier and later headings

   i)   Simple situations (usually only two headings involved).

Name change
American Material Handling Society
   see also the later heading
International Material Management Society

International Material Management Society
   see also the earlier heading
American Material Handling Society

Merger of two bodies to form a third
Screen Writers' Guild
   see also the later heading
Writers Guild of America, West

Radio Writers Guild
   see also the later heading
Writers Guild of America, West

Writers Guild of America, West
   see also the earlier headings
Radio Writers Guild
Screen Writers' Guild

   ii)   Complex situations requiring more explanation (usually more than two headings involved). Make explanatory references with the same information under each of the headings.

Complete information available
England
   This heading is used for official publications issued before 1536. For official publications issued 1536-1706, *see* **England and Wales.** For official publications issued 1707-1800, *see* **Great Britain.** For official publications issued 1801 to date, *see* **United Kingdom.**
   Make a similar reference under **England and Wales** *and* **Great Britain** *and* **United Kingdom**

Westminster Bank
   The Westminster Bank and the National Provincial Bank merged in 1969 to form the National Westminster Bank. Works of these bodies are entered under the name used at the time of publication.
   Make the same reference under **National Provincial Bank** *and* **National Westminster Bank**

United Kingdom. *Ministry of Technology*
This ministry was set up in 1965 and incorporated the Department of Scientific and Industrial Research. It was amalgamated with the Board of Trade to form the Department of Trade and Industry in 1971. In 1974 the Department of Trade and Industry was replaced by the Department of Energy, the Department of Industry, the Department of Prices and Consumer Protection, and the Department of Trade. For works of these bodies, *see* their names as subheadings of **United Kingdom.**
Make a similar reference under the heading for each of these government bodies

American-Asian Educational Exchange
The American-Asian Educational Exchange was founded in 1957. In 1962 the name was changed to American Afro-Asian Educational Exchange. In 1967 the name American-Asian Educational Exchange was resumed.
Works of this body are found under the name used at the time of publication.
Make the same reference under **American Afro-Asian Educational Exchange**

Incomplete information available
Zambia. *Ministry of Mines and Mining Development*
The Ministry of Mines and Mining Development was created about 1970.
For related bodies *see also*
Zambia. *Ministry of Lands and Mines*
Zambia. *Ministry of Mines*
Zambia. *Ministry of Mines and Co-operatives*
Make a similar reference under the heading for each of these government bodies

iii) Multiple headings for one series of meetings. Make the same explanatory reference under each of the conference headings involved.

Symposium on the Plasma Membrane (*1961 : New York, N.Y.*)
Publications of this series of meetings are found under the following headings or titles:
3rd: **Symposium on the Plasma Membrane** (*1961 : New York, N.Y.*)
4th: Connective tissue
5th: Differentiation and development
7th: **Symposium on Macromolecular Metabolism** (*1965 : New York, N.Y.*)
8th: Contractile process
9th-   : **Basic Science Symposium**
Make the same explanatory reference under the heading for the 7th and for the 9th- symposia

> **Technical Thick Film Symposium** (*1st : 1967 : Palo Alto, Calif., and Los Angeles, Calif.*)
> Publications of this series of meetings are found under the following headings:
> **Technical Thick Film Symposium** (*1st : 1967 : Palo Alto, Calif., and Los Angeles, Calif.*)
> **Symposium on Hybrid Microelectronics** (*2nd : 1967 : Boston, Mass.*)
> **Hybrid Microelectronics Symposium** (*3rd : 1968 : Rosemont, Ill.*)
> **International Hybrid Microelectronics Symposium** (*5th : 1970 : Beverly Hills, Calif.*)
> *Make the same explanatory reference under the heading for each of the symposia*

26.3C2. Acronyms. If, in the catalogue, initials with full stops are filed differently from initials without full stops, and more detailed guidance than a *see* reference is required, make an explanatory reference under each form.

> **N.A.T.O.**
> *see* **North Atlantic Treaty Organization**
> When these initials occur in a title or other heading without spaces or full stops, they are filed as a single word.
> *Make a similar explanatory reference under* **NATO**

In the context of such a catalogue, if the abbreviated form does not consist entirely of the initial letters of the name, make the references from the form with the letters represented as separate initials only if they might be so construed.

> **S.A.C.L.A.N.T.**
> *see* **Supreme Allied Commander, Atlantic**
> When these initials occur in a title or other heading without spaces or full stops, they are filed as a single word.
> *Make a similar explanatory reference under* **SACLANT**

However, make a *see* reference without explanation if only one reference is to be made.

26.4. UNIFORM TITLES

26.4A. When this rule calls for a reference to (or from) a uniform title, take it as requiring a reference to (or from) a name heading and uniform title in appropriate cases.

26.4B. *See* references

26.4B1. Different titles or variants of the title. Refer to the uniform title from the different titles and variants of the title under which the work has been published or cited in reference sources.[2]

---

2. However, make an added entry under the title proper of the work being catalogued (see 21.30J) if it differs from the uniform title.

Lied der Nibelungen
see **Nibelungenlied**

Beethoven, Ludwig van
Moonlight sonata
see **Beethoven, Ludwig van**
Sonatas, piano, no. 14, op. 27, no. 2, C♯ minor

Dickens, Charles
Personal history of David Copperfield
see **Dickens, Charles**
David Copperfield

Australia
Commonwealth of Australia Constitution act
see **Australia**
Constitution

In the case of translated titles, refer to the uniform title and the appropriate language subheading, when appropriate.

Red book of Hergest
see **Llyfr coch Hergest.** *English*

Flaubert, Gustave
Sentimental education
see **Flaubert, Gustave**
Éducation sentimentale. English

26.4B2. Titles of parts of a work catalogued independently. If separately published parts of works are catalogued independently, refer from the titles of such parts in the form of subheadings under the uniform title for the whole work. *Optionally*, make an explanatory reference as instructed in 26.4D2.

Tolkien, J.R.R.
Lord of the rings. 2, Two towers
see **Tolkien, J.R.R.**
Two towers

Proust, Marcel
À la recherche du temps perdu. 1, Du côté de chez Swann
see **Proust, Marcel**
Du côté de chez Swann

26.4B3. Titles of parts catalogued under the title of the whole work. If separately published parts of a work are catalogued under the uniform title of the whole work, refer from the titles of such parts, if they are distinctive, to the uniform title of the whole work.

Old Testament
see **Bible.** *O.T.*

Genesis (*Book of the Bible*)
see **Bible.** *O.T. Genesis*

Ruth rabbah
  see **Midrash rabbah.** *Ruth*

Verdi, Giuseppe
  Celeste Aïda
    see **Verdi, Giuseppe**
      Aïda. Celeste Aïda

Schumann, Robert
  Soldatenmarsch
    see **Schumann, Robert**
      Album für die Jugend. Nr. 2, Soldatenmarsch

26.4B4. Collective titles. When a collection of, or a selection from, a person's works is catalogued under a collective uniform title, refer from the name and title taken from the chief source of information or found in a reference source to the name and collective title, unless the title taken from the chief source of information or found in a reference source is the same as, or very similar to, the collective title.

  Dante Alighieri
    Tutte le opere
      see **Dante Alighieri**
        Works

  Andersen, H.C.
    Eventyr
      see **Andersen, H.C.**
        Fairy tales

  Balzac, Honoré de
    Due studi di donna e altri racconti
      see **Balzac, Honoré de**
        Selections. Italian

26.4C. *See also* **references**

26.4C1. When related works, other than those that are parts of other works, are entered in the catalogue under different uniform titles, make *see also* references between them unless one or both of the references are made unnecessary by added entries.

  Kerr, Orpheus C.
    Cloven foot
      see also **Dickens, Charles**
        Edwin Drood
        (*The Kerr work is an adaptation of* Edwin Drood. *Added entry under Dickens makes a see also reference from* **Dickens, Charles.** Edwin Drood *unnecessary*)

  Klage
    see also **Nibelungenlied**

Nibelungenlied
  see also **Klage**

Catholic Church
  Breviary
    see also **Catholic Church**
          Liturgy of the hours

Catholic Church
  Liturgy of the hours
    see also **Catholic Church**
          Breviary

26.4D. Explanatory references

26.4D1. General rule. Make an explanatory reference when more detailed guidance than a *see* or *see also* reference is required.

Pentateuch
  For the Pentateuch as a whole, *see* **Bible.** *O.T. Pentateuch.* For an individual book of the Pentateuch, *see* the name of the book as a subheading of **Bible.** *O.T.* (e.g., **Bible.** *O.T. Genesis*).

26.4D2. Titles of parts of a work catalogued independently. *Optionally*, if separately published parts of a work are catalogued independently, make an explanatory reference from the name heading (when appropriate) and uniform title of the main work to any such parts.

Arabian nights
  For separately published parts of this collection, *see*
Ali Baba
Sindbad the sailor
[*etc.*]

Tolkien, J.R.R.
  Lord of the rings
  For the separately published parts of this work, *see*
Tolkien, J.R.R.
  Fellowship of the ring
  Two towers
  Return of the king

Proust, Marcel
  À la recherche du temps perdu
  For the separately published parts of this work, *see*
Proust, Marcel
  Du côté de chez Swann
  À l'ombre des jeunes filles en fleurs
  Côté de Guermantes
  [*etc.*]

26.4D3. Collective titles. When the same title is used as the title proper (or the opening phrase of the title proper) of works that are assigned different uniform titles, one or more of which is a collective uniform title (see 25.8–25.10), refer to the name heading and collective uniform title with an appropriate explanation.

> **Turgenev, I.S.**
> Phantoms
> For separate publications of this work in English, *see*
> **Turgenev, I.S.**
> Prizraki. English
> For collections in English with titles beginning with
> *Phantoms*, *see*
> **Turgenev, I.S.**
> Selections. English

26.5. REFERENCES TO ADDED ENTRIES FOR SERIES AND SERIALS

26.5A. Series

26.5A1. If an added entry is made under the heading for a series to which separately catalogued parts belong, refer to the heading for the series from different forms of the heading under which it might reasonably be sought.

> **Food and Agriculture Organization of the United Nations**
> FAO soils bulletin
> *see* FAO soils bulletin

> Industries Assistance Commission report
> *see* **Australia.** *Industries Assistance Commission*
> Industries Assistance Commission report

> Study topics in physics
> *see* **Bolton, W.**
> Study topics in physics

26.5B. Serials

26.5B1. If an added entry is made under the heading for a serial, refer to that heading from different forms under which the serial might reasonably be sought.

> **ITAL**
> *see* Information technology and libraries

> **I.T.A.L.**
> *see* Information technology and libraries

26.6. REFERENCES INSTEAD OF ADDED ENTRIES COMMON TO MANY EDITIONS

26.6A. If a number of added entries under the same heading are required, *optionally* replace them by appropriate references.

Hamlet
For editions of this work, *see*
Shakespeare, William
Hamlet

Bible
Luther, Martin
For editions of the whole Bible translated by Luther, *see*
Bible. *German. Luther*

26.6B. Alternatively, in such a case, make one added entry under the common heading and include in it a reference to the main entry.

Hamlet
Shakespeare, William
Hamlet : an authoritative text, intellectual backgrounds, extracts from the sources, essays in criticism / William Shakespeare ; edited by Cyrus Hoy. — New York : Norton, [1963]
xii, 270 p. : ill. ; 21 cm. — (Norton critical editions ; N306)
For other editions, *see* **Shakespeare, William.** Hamlet

CAPITALIZATION

Contents

General Rules

English Language

Foreign Languages

General Rules

A.1. INITIALS AND ACRONYMS

A.1A. Capitalize the letters of an initialism or acronym used by a corporate body according to the predominant usage of the body.

> AFL-CIO
>
> Unesco

A.1B. Capitalize words in a personal, place, or corporate name as instructed in the rules for the language involved (see A.12–A.52). For such names used in headings, see also A.2.

A.2. HEADINGS FOR PERSONS, PLACES, AND CORPORATE BODIES

A.2A. General rule

A.2A1. In all cases, capitalize the first word of each heading and subheading.[1] Capitalize other words in personal, place, and corporate names used as headings and corporate names used as subheadings as instructed in the rules for the language involved.

> **Alexander,** *of Aphrodisias*
>
> **De la Mare, Walter**
>
> **Musset, Alfred de**
>
> **Cavour, Camillo Benso,** *conte di*
>
> **Third Order Regular of St. Francis**
>
> **Société de chimie physique**
>
> **Ontario.** *High Court of Justice*
>
> **Norske Nobelinstitutt**
>
> **El Greco Society**

A.2B. Words or phrases characterizing persons

A.2B1. Capitalize a word, or the substantive words in a phrase, characterizing a person and used as a heading (see also 22.11D and A.13H1). Capitalize proper names contained in such a phrase as instructed in the rules for the language involved. Capitalize a quoted title within a personal name heading as instructed in A.4A.

> **Physician**
>
> **Lady of Quality**
>
> **Citizen of Albany**
>
> **Author of Early impressions**

---

1. If a personal name begins with the Arabic article *al* in any of its various orthographic forms (e.g., *al*, *el*, *es*) or with the Hebrew article *ha* (*he*), do not capitalize it, whether written separately or hyphenated with the following word.

A.2C. Additions to certain headings for persons

A.2C1. Capitalize additions to headings for persons made according to the instructions in certain rules (e.g., 22.11, 22.12, 22.15A, 22.19) as instructed in the rules for the language involved. If the addition is given in parentheses (see 22.11A and 22.19A), capitalize the first word of the addition and any proper name.

Moses, *Grandma*	**John,** *Abbot of Ford*
Deidier, *abbé*	**Thomas** (*Anglo-Norman poet*)
Alfonso XIII, *King of Spain*	**Brown, George,** *Rev.*

A.2D. Additions to names of corporate bodies

A.2D1. Capitalize the first word of each addition to the name of a corporate body. Capitalize other words in the addition as instructed in the rules for the language involved.

Bounty (*Ship*)

Knights Templar (*Masonic order*)

Regional Conference on Mental Measurement of the Blind
 (*1st : 1951 : Perkins Institution*)

A.3. UNIFORM TITLES

A.3A. Individual uniform titles

A.3A1. Capitalize an individual uniform title as instructed in A.4.

[Hard times]

Bava kamma

Nicene Creed

[De bello Gallico]

A.3B. Collective uniform titles

A.3B1. Capitalize only the first word of a collective uniform title (see 25.8–25.10 and 25.34).

[Works]

[Short stories]

[Instrumental music]

[Polonaises, piano]

A.3C. Additions to uniform titles

A.3C1. Capitalize the first word of each addition to an individual uniform title or a collective uniform title. Capitalize other words in the addition as instructed in the rules for the language involved.

Seven sages of Rome (*Southern version*)

Guillaume (*Chanson de geste*)

Genesis (*Middle High German poem*)

[Sketches by Boz. German. Selections]

[Poems. Selections]

[Goyescas (Opera)]

[Iliad. Book 1. Selections]

In additions to uniform titles for music, do not capitalize words (including abbreviations) indicating medium of performance (see 25.30B), words (including abbreviations) accompanying serial numbers and opus or thematic index numbers (see 25.30C), or words accompanying statements of key (see 25.30D), unless the word is, or the abbreviation stands for, a proper name. Do not capitalize *arr.*

> [Trios, piano, strings, no. 2, op. 66, C minor]
>
> [Sonatas, piano, K. 457, C minor]

A.4. TITLE AND STATEMENT OF RESPONSIBILITY AREA

A.4A. Title elements (general rule)

A.4A1. Capitalize the first word of a title (title proper, alternative title, parallel title, quoted title, etc.).[2] Capitalize other words as instructed in the rules for the language involved. See A.20 for the capitalization of names of documents.

> The materials of architecture
>
> The 1919/1920 Breasted Expedition to the Far East
>
> Les misérables
>
> IV informe del gobierno
>
> Eileen Ford's a more beautiful you in 21 days
>
> Journal of polymer science
>
> Sechs Partiten für Flöte
>
> Still life with bottle and grapes
>
> The Edinburgh world atlas, or, Advanced atlas of modern geography
>
> Coppélia, ou, La fille aux yeux d'émail
>
> Strassenkarte der Schweiz = Carte routière de la Suisse = Carta stradale della Svizzera = Road map of Switzerland
>
> The greenwood tree : newsletter of the Somerset and Dorset Family History Society
>
> Quo vadis? : a narrative from the time of Nero
>
> King Henry the Eighth ; and, The tempest
>
> An interpretation of The ring and the book
>
> Selections from the Idylls of the king
>
> ... / by the Author of Memoirs of a fox-hunting man
>
> A dictionary of American English on historical principles
>
> Les cahiers du cinéma
>
> The anatomical record
>
> "Reprinted from The anatomical record, vol. 88, Jan.-Mar. 1944"
>
> A supplement to The journal of physics and chemistry of solids
>
> Separate from La revista de derecho, jurisprudencia y administración

---

2. If a romanized title (title proper, alternative title, parallel title, quoted title, etc.) begins with the Arabic article *al* in any of its various orthographic forms (e.g., *al*, *el*, *es*) or with the Hebrew article *ha* (*he*), do not capitalize the article, whether written separately or hyphenated with the following word.

> ha-Milon he-hadash : Ivri-Angli, Angli-Ivri
>
> (Milon *is considered the first word and is therefore capitalized*)

A.4B. Titles preceded by dashes indicating incompleteness

A.4B1. Do not capitalize the first word of a title if it is preceded by a dash indicating that the beginning of the phrase from which the title was derived has been omitted.

> —and master of none

A.4C. Certain titles of serials that have merged or been absorbed

A.4C1. When one serial absorbs or merges with another and incorporates that serial's title with its own, do not capitalize the first word of the incorporated title unless the rules for the language involved require its capitalization for another reason.

> Farm chemicals and crop life   *not*   Farm chemicals and Crop life

A.4D. Grammatically independent titles of supplements and sections of an item

A.4D1. If the title proper of an item that is supplementary to, or a section of, another item consists of two or more parts that are not grammatically linked (see 1.1B9, 12.1B4, and 12.1B5), capitalize the first word of the title of the second and subsequent parts.

> Faust. Part one
>
> Advanced calculus. Student handbook
>
> Journal of biosocial science. Supplement
>
> Acta Universitatis Carolinae. Philologica

If the title of the part is introduced by an alphabetic or a numeric designation beginning with a word, capitalize also that word.

> Progress in nuclear energy. Series 2, Reactors

A.4E. General material designation

A.4E1. Do not capitalize the word(s) in a general material designation.

> [music]
>
> [map (braille)]
>
> [computer file]

A.4F. Statement of responsibility

A.4F1. In the statement of responsibility element, capitalize as instructed in the rules for the language involved all personal and corporate names; titles of nobility; terms of address, honour, and distinction; and initials of societies, etc., accompanying personal names. In general, do not capitalize other words.

> ... / by Mrs. Charles H. Gibson
>
> ... / by Walter de la Mare
>
> ... / by Alfred, Lord Tennyson
>
> ... / by a Lady of Quality
>
> ... / International Symposium on the Cataloguing, Coding, and Statistics of Audio-Visual Materials ; organised by ISO/TC 46 Documentation in collaboration with IFLA and IFTC, 7-9 January 1976 in Strasbourg

A.5. EDITION AREA

A.5A. If an edition statement (or a statement relating to a named revision of an edition) begins with a word or an abbreviation of a word, capitalize it. Capitalize other words as instructed in the rules for the language involved.

> Household ed.
>
> Facsim. ed.
>
> 1st standard ed.
>
> Neue Aufl.
>
> Rev. et corr.
>
> Wyd. 2-gie
>
> World's classics ed., New ed. rev.

A.6. MATERIAL (OR TYPE OF PUBLICATION) SPECIFIC DETAILS AREA

A.6A. If the material (or type of publication) specific details area begins with a word or an abbreviation of a word, capitalize it. Capitalize other elements as instructed in the rules for the language involved.

> Scale 1:500,000
> Computer program (2150 statements)
>
> Vol. 1, no. 1 (Jan./Mar. 1974)-
> No 1 (juil. 1970)-

A.7. PUBLICATION, DISTRIBUTION, ETC., AREA

A.7A. General rule

A.7A1. Capitalize the names of places, publishers, distributors, and manufacturers as instructed in the rules for the language involved. Capitalize also the shortened form of name of a publisher, distributor, etc., when used as instructed in 1.4D4.

> Montréal
>
> Coloniae Agrippinae
>
> The Hague
>
> Den Haag *but* 's-Gravenhage
>
> T. Wall and Sons
>
> The Museum (i.e., *The British Museum*)
>
> Presses universitaires de France
>
> O.L.F. (i.e., *Office de la langue française*)

A.7B. Initial words or abbreviations not part of a name

A.7B1. In general, if an element begins with a word or abbreviation not an integral part of the name of the place, publisher, distributor, manufacturer, etc., capitalize the word or abbreviation. Do not capitalize other words or abbreviations not part of a name unless the rules for the language involved require their capitalization. Capitalize only the *s* of *s.l.* Do not capitalize *s.n.*

> V Praze
>
> Londini : Apud B. Fellowes
>
> Lipsiae : Sumptibus et typis B.G. Teubneri

569

New York : Released by Beaux Arts

New York : The Association

Wiesbaden : In Kommission bei O. Harrassowitz

Toronto : Published in association with the Pulp and Paper Institute of Canada by University of Toronto Press

[S.l. : s.n.]

A.8. PHYSICAL DESCRIPTION AREA

A.8A. Capitalize proper nouns and certain technical terms appearing in this area as instructed in the rules for the language involved. Do not capitalize other words, including those appearing first in the area.

leaves 81-144

1000 p. in various pagings

310 leaves of braille

... : ill., col. maps, ports. (some col.)

on 1 side of 1 sound disc (13 min.)

1 videoreel (ca. 75 min.)

12 slides : sd., col.

205 leaves of braille and Nemeth code

A.9. SERIES AREA

A.9A. General rule

A.9A1. Capitalize the title proper, parallel titles, other title information, and statements of responsibility of a series as instructed in A.4.

Great newspapers reprinted

Master choruses for Lent and Easter

Jeux visuels = Visual games

Concertino : Werke für Schul- und Liebhaber Orchester

Golden guides. Nature

Standard radio supersound effects. Trains

Acta Universitatis Stockholmiensis. Stockholm studies in history of literature

Publicación / Universidad de Chile, Departamento de Geología

A.9B. Terms used in conjunction with series numbering

A.9B1. Do not capitalize a term such as *v.*, *no.*, *reel*, *t.*, that is part of the series numbering unless the rules for a particular language require capitalization (e.g., noun capitalization in German). Capitalize other words and alphabetic devices used as part of a numbering system according to the usage of the item.

Deutscher Planungsatlas ; Bd. 8

Exploring careers ; group 8

Music for today. Series 2 ; no. 8

Typewriting. Unit 2, Skill development ; program 1

National standard reference data series ; NSRDS-NBS 5

A.10. NOTE AREA

A.10A. Capitalize the first word in each note or an abbreviation beginning a note. If a note consists of more than one sentence, capitalize the first word of each subsequent sentence. See A.4A–A.4D for the capitalization of titles. Capitalize other words as instructed in the rules for the language involved.

Title from container

Facsim. reprint. Originally published: London : I. Walsh, ca. 1734

A.11. STANDARD NUMBER AND TERMS OF AVAILABILITY AREA

A.11A. Capitalize letters that are part of a standard number.

ISSN 0305-3741

Do not capitalize qualifiers added to a standard number or to a price.

ISBN 0-435-91660-2 (cased)

$1.00 (pbk.)

£4.40 (complete collection). — £0.55 (individual sheets)

Capitalize the first word of the statement giving the terms on which the item is available if the statement appears without a price.

ISBN 0-902573-45-4 : Subscribers only

Free to high school students

English Language

A.12. GENERAL RULE

A.12A. The rules for English-language capitalization basically follow those of the *Chicago Manual of Style*. Certain rules that differ have been modified to conform to the requirements of bibliographic records and long-standing cataloguing practice.

A.12B. Where a rule prescribes the capitalization of the name of a person, corporate body, or place, or of a title of nobility, term of honour, appellation, epithet, etc., understand this to mean that each separate word or initial is to be capitalized excepting articles, prepositions, and conjunctions. However, in a place name, capitalize an article that forms an accepted part of the name according to gazetteers.

A.12C. Capitalize a plural generic term when it precedes the distinctive nouns in two or more proper names. Do not capitalize the generic term when it follows the nouns.

Saints Constantine and Helen

Secretaries of Defense and State

Lakes Erie and Ontario

but

Industry and Trade departments

Authorized and Revised versions

A.12D. For the capitalization of roman numerals, see C.2B3.

A.13. PERSONAL NAMES

A.13A. General rule

A.13A1. Capitalize the name of a person (including initials).

D.H. Lawrence	Benjamin Franklin
H.D.	C. Day-Lewis
John the Baptist	

A.13B. Names with prefixes

A.13B1. If a name includes a prefix from a language other than English (e.g., *de*, *des*, *la*, *l'*, *della*, *von*, *von der*), follow the usage of the person with regard to capitalization of the prefix. In case of doubt, capitalize it.

Daphne du Maurier; du Maurier

Eva Le Gallienne; Le Gallienne

Mark Van Doren; Van Doren

Mazo de la Roche; de la Roche

A.13C. Titles preceding the name

A.13C1. Capitalize any title or term of honour or address that immediately precedes a personal name.

Dame Judi Dench	President Carter
Field Marshal Sir Michael Carver	Prime Minister Pierre Trudeau
Gen. Fred C. Weyand	Queen Elizabeth II
Grandma Moses	Rabbi Stephen Wise
John Henry Cardinal Newman	Senator Hubert H. Humphrey
Mrs. Humphry Ward	Sir Gordon Richards
Pope Paul VI	Sister Mary Joseph

A.13D. Ordinal numerals following names of sovereigns and popes

A.13D1. Capitalize an ordinal number expressed as a word(s) used after the name of a sovereign or pope to denote order of succession.

King George the Sixth

John the Twenty-third

A.13E. Titles following a name or used alone in place of a name

A.13E1. Royalty, nobility, baronets. Capitalize a title of royalty or nobility.

Elizabeth II, Queen of the United Kingdom; the Queen

Charles, Prince of Wales; the Prince of Wales; the Prince

Frank Pakenham, Earl of Longford; the Earl of Longford; the Earl

Do not capitalize *bart.*

Sir Thomas Beecham, bart.
    (*A baronet is not a member of the nobility*)

A.13E2. Religious titles. Capitalize a religious title.

>His Holiness Paul VI, Pope; the Pope

>Most Rev. and Rt. Hon. Frederick Donald Coggan, Archbishop of Canterbury; the Archbishop of Canterbury

>the Reverend Michael O'Sullivan, Pastor of Saint Peter's Church; the Pastor

>the Dalai Lama

A.13E3. Civil and military titles. Do not capitalize a civil or military title.[3]

>Jimmy Carter, president of the United States; the president of the United States; the president

>James Callaghan, prime minister; the prime minister

>the Hon. Walter Stewart Owen, lieutenant-governor of British Columbia; the lieutenant-governor of British Columbia; the lieutenant-governor

>Warren Earl Burger, chief justice of the United States; the chief justice of the United States; the chief justice

>Gen. Bernard A. Rogers, chief of staff, U.S. Army; the general

>James F. Calvert, rear admiral, USN

>Hubert H. Humphrey, senator from Minnesota, the senator from Minnesota; the senator

>Kingman Brewster, ambassador to the United Kingdom; the ambassador to the United Kingdom; the ambassador

A.13E4. Professional and academic titles. Capitalize the title of a named professorship. In general, do not capitalize other professional and academic titles.

>W. Carson Ryan, Kenan Professor of Education; the professor

>Robert Paul Bergman, associate professor of fine arts; the professor

>R.F. Bennett, president of the Ford Motor Company of Canada; the president

>Olga Porotnikoff, secretary, IFLA Committee on Cataloguing

A.13F. Certain other terms following names

A.13F1. Capitalize the name or abbreviation of an academic degree, honour, religious order, etc.

>C.D. Needham, Fellow of the Library Association

>R.C. Strong, Ph.D., F.S.A.

>Father Joseph Anthony Barrett, S.J.

>Ralph Damian Goggens, Order of Preachers

Capitalize *esquire*, *junior*, or *senior* (and their abbreviations) following a name.

>John Mytton, Esq.

>John D. Rockefeller, Jr.

---

3. Capitalize such words as *president, prime minister*, and *governor* as instructed in A.18B when they designate the office rather than a particular person occupying the office.

A.13G. Terms of honour and respect

A.13G1. Capitalize a term of honour or respect.

Her Majesty	Your Excellency
His Royal Highness	Your Grace
His Holiness	Your Honour

A.13H. Epithets

A.13H1. Capitalize an epithet occurring with, or used in place of, a personal name.

the Iron Chancellor

Old Hickory

Bonnie Prince Charlie

Elroy "Crazy Legs" Hirsch

Jerome H. (Dizzy) Dean

Abraham Lincoln, the Great Emancipator

A.13J. Personifications

A.13J1. Capitalize a personification.

A dialogue between Death and a beautiful lady

Let Fame sound the trumpet

A.14. NAMES OF PEOPLES, ETC.

A.14A. Capitalize the name of a people, race, tribe, or ethnic or linguistic group.

Africans	Polynesians
Celts	Scandinavians
Germans	Slavs
Hottentots	Teutons
Mongols	Yoruba

Capitalize an adjective derived from such a name.

African	Scandinavian

Capitalize the name of a language.

English	Estonian

A.15. PLACE NAMES

A.15A. Geographic features, regions, etc.

A.15A1. Capitalize the name of a geographic feature, region, etc. Do not capitalize a descriptive adjective not part of an accepted name.

Arctic Circle

Arctic Ocean

Asia; Asian continent

Atlantic; South Atlantic; southern Atlantic

Central America; central European (*but* Central Europe *when referring to the geopolitical entity*)

Cheviot Hills

the Continent (i.e., Europe); continental Europe; the European continent; Continental customs

East; the Orient; Far East(ern); Near East(ern); Middle East(ern); Eastern customs; oriental (adjective); eastern Europe (*but* Eastern Europe *when referring to the geopolitical entity*); the East (U.S.)

Great Lakes

Great Slave Lake

Isthmus of Suez

Mississippi Delta

North Temperate Zone

Sea of Marmara

South America; South American continent

Southeast Asia; southern Asia

Strait of Dover

Tropic of Capricorn; the tropics

the West, Far West, Middle West, Midwest (U.S.); western, far western, midwestern

A.15B. Political divisions

A.15B1. Capitalize the name of a political division (e.g., a country, state, province, city). Capitalize a word such as *empire*, *kingdom*, *state*, *country*, and *city* following a proper name if it is a commonly accepted part of the name. Do not capitalize such a word when used alone to indicate a political division.

Austrian Empire; the empire

Eleventh Congressional District; the congressional district

New York City; the city of New York

Simcoe County; the county

Sixth Precinct; the precinct

Washington State; the state of Washington

A.15C. Popular names

A.15C1. Capitalize a popular name of a place, or the name of a legendary place.

Atlantis	New World
Bay Area	Old World
Benelux	the Nutmeg State
the Channel (English Channel)	Old Dominion
City of Brotherly Love	Panhandle
Erin	the Potteries
Eternal City	South Seas
Latin Quarter	the Village
Middle Earth	the West End

A.16. NAMES OF STRUCTURES, STREETS, ETC.

A.16A. Capitalize the name of a building, monument, or other structure; and the name of a road or street. Do not capitalize words such as *avenue*, *bridge*, *hotel*, and *park* when they are used alone. See A.18E for the capitalization of names of buildings in which religious bodies meet.

> the Capitol
> Central Park; the park
> Cleopatra's Needle
> Drury Lane Theatre; the theatre
> Forty-second Street
> Hoover Dam; the dam
> Iroquois Lock
> Jacques Cartier Bridge; the bridge
> Oxford Circus; the circus
> Pyramid of the Sun; the pyramid
> Royal Air Force Memorial

A.17. DERIVATIVES OF PROPER NAMES

A.17A. Do not capitalize a word derived from a personal or place name when it is used with a specialized meaning.

> angstrom unit   italicize
> arabic numbers   malapropism
> bikini   melba toast
> bourbon whiskey   nile green
> burnt sienna   raglan sleeves
> cologne   roman type
> diesel engine   timothy grass
> hamburger   vernier telescope

A.18. NAMES OF CORPORATE BODIES

A.18A. International organizations and alliances

A.18A1. Capitalize the name of an international organization or alliance.

> Central Treaty Organization
> Common Market
> Hanseatic League; Hansa
> Holy Alliance
> International Monetary Fund
> Little Entente
> Organization of African Unity
> Triple Alliance, 1882
> United Nations; United Nations Security Council; the Security Council; the council
> World Health Organization

A.18B. Government bodies

A.18B1. Capitalize the full name of a legislative or judicial body; administrative department, bureau, or office; armed force (or component part of an armed force); or an accepted shortened form of its name. Do not capitalize other incomplete designations (except abbreviations) or adjectives derived from such a name.

> Agency for International Development
> Atlantic Fleet
> Canadian Armed Forces
> Canadian Citizenship Branch
> Central Office of Information
> Circuit Court of the United States; the federal Circuit Court
> Commission on Post-Secondary Education in Ontario
> Congress; the Ninety-fifth Congress; congressional
> Court of Appeals of the State of Colorado
> Department of State; State Department
> District Court for the Southern District of New York; district court
> Division of Education for the Disadvantaged
> Domestic Council Committee on Illegal Aliens
> First Army; the First
> First Infantry Division
> House of Commons
> House of Representatives; the House; the lower house of Congress
> Juvenile and Domestic Relations Court; juvenile court; domestic relations court
> Middlesex Regiment; the Diehards; the regiment
> Ministry of Agriculture, Fisheries, and Food
> Parliament; parliamentary
> Peace Corps
> President of the United States (i.e., the office)
> Prime Minister (i.e., the office)
> Queen's Bench Division of the High Court of Justice
> Royal Air Force
> Royal Gloucestershire Hussars
> Twenty-first Regiment of U.S. Infantry
> United States Court of Appeals for the Second Circuit; court of appeals
> United States Navy

A.18C. Political parties

A.18C1. Capitalize the name of a political party and of its members.

> Communist Party of Great Britain; Communist(s)
> Democratic Party; Democrat(s)
> Liberal Party; Liberal(s)
> Nazi Party; Nazi(s)

A.18D. Political and economic systems

A.18D1. Do not capitalize the name of a political or economic system or school of thought or its proponents unless derived from proper nouns. In general, do not capitalize names of political groups other than parties.

anarchism		mugwumps
capitalism		nationalism
egalitarianism		right wing
fascism		socialist bloc
farm bloc	*but*	
independent(s)		Benthamism
mercantilism		Marxism
monarchism		Thatcherism

A.18E. Other corporate bodies

A.18E1. Capitalize the name of an institution, association, conference, company, religious denomination or order, local church, etc. (see A.19D1 for the names of religions), or of a department or division. Do not capitalize an article preceding the name, even when a part of the official name. Do not capitalize a generic word (e.g., *society*, *company*, *conference*) when used alone or with an article (but see A.7A1).

Abbey of Mont Saint-Michel

American Library Association

the Board of Regents of the University of California

Boy Scouts of America; a Boy Scout; a Scout

Canadian National Railways

Church of England

Christian Brothers

Church of the Redeemer

Conference, 1980 Advances in Reactor Physics and Shielding

Congregation Anshe Mizrach

Fifty-second Annual Meeting of the American Historical Association

First Baptist Church

Garrick Club

General Council of the United Church of Canada

General Foods Corporation

Green Bay Packers; the Packers; the team

Independent Order of Odd Fellows; IOOF; an Odd Fellow

Iowa Falls High School

League of Women Voters

Midwest Baptist Conference

Mosque of Sidi Okba

National Bank of New Zealand, Ltd.

National Dance Theatre Company of Jamaica

Order of Preachers

Presbyterian Church in Canada

Printed Circuit World Expo '81 West

Reference Section of the Canadian Library Association

Second Vatican Council; Vatican II

Society of Jesus; Jesuits; a Jesuit

Special Session on Ordered Fields and Real Algebraic Geometry

Synod of Whitby

Temple Israel

Textile Workers Union of America; the union

Toronto Symphony Orchestra

Young Men's Christian Association

A.19. RELIGIOUS NAMES AND TERMS

A.19A. Deities

A.19A1. Capitalize the name of a deity and any term referring to the Christian Trinity.

Adonai	Mars
Allah	Messiah (Jesus Christ)
the Almighty	Minerva
Astarte	the Omnipotent
Brahma	Prince of Peace
Christ	Providence
the Father	Son of God
the First Cause	Son of Man
Hera	the Supreme Being
Holy Ghost	Vishnu
Holy Spirit	the Word
Jehovah	Yahweh
King of Kings	Zeus
Lamb of God	

A.19A2. Do not capitalize a pronoun referring to the name of a deity unless capitalization is necessary to avoid ambiguity.

God as I understand him

The appearance of Christ after his resurrection

but

God gives man what He wills

Trust Him who doeth all things well

A.19A3. Do not capitalize words derived from the names of deities.

God's fatherhood, kingship, omnipotence

Jesus' sonship

godlike

messianic hope

christological   *but*   Christ-like

579

A.19B. Names of Satan

A.19B1. Capitalize a word specifically denoting Satan.

> the Devil
>
> His Satanic Majesty
>
> Lord of the Flies
>
> Lucifer

but

> a devil; the devils
>
> devilled eggs
>
> the devil's advocate

A.19C. Revered persons

A.19C1. Capitalize an appellation of a revered person such as a prophet, guru, saint, or other religious leader.

the Apostle to the Gentiles	Mother of God
the Baptist	Our Lady
the Beloved Apostle	Panchen Lama
the Blessed Virgin	the Prophet (i.e., *Mohammed*)
Buddha	the Twelve
the Fathers; church fathers	the Virgin (i.e., *Mary*)
the Mahatma	

A.19D. Religions

A.19D1. Capitalize the name of a religion, sect, or specific religious movement. Capitalize also a name describing its members and any adjective derived from such a name. See A.18E for the names of denominations, orders, local churches, etc.

> Anglicanism; an Anglican; Anglican communion
>
> Arianism; Arian heresy
>
> Buddhism; a Buddhist; Buddhist ideas
>
> Catholicism; a Catholic
>
> Christian Science; a Christian Scientist
>
> Dissenter
>
> Islam; Islamic; Muslim
>
> Judaism; Orthodox Judaism; Reform Judaism; an Orthodox Jew
>
> Lutheranism; a Lutheran
>
> Protestantism; a Protestant
>
> Shinto
>
> Theosophy; Theosophist
>
> Vedanta
>
> Zen; Zen Buddhism
>
> Zoroastrianism

A.19E. Religious events and concepts

A.19E1. Capitalize the name of a major Biblical or religious event or concept.

Armageddon	the Hegira
the Assumption of the Virgin	Judgement Day
the Captivity (Babylonian)	the Last Supper
the Crucifixion	Redemption
the Enlightenment (Buddhism)	the Second Advent

A.19F. Creeds and confessions

A.19F1. Capitalize the name of a creed or confession.

Augsburg Confession

Nicene Creed

the Thirty-nine Articles

A.19G. The Eucharist

A.19G1. Capitalize a term referring to the Eucharist.

Communion	the Lord's Supper
the Divine Liturgy	the Mass
Holy Communion	

A.19H. Sacred Scriptures

A.19H1. Capitalize the title of a sacred scripture, one of its divisions, a group of books, or an individual book.

Holy Bible	Apocrypha
Holy Scriptures	Five Scrolls
Sacred Scriptures	Historical Books
New Testament	Minor Prophets
Old Testament	Pentateuch
New Covenant	History of Susanna
Gospels	Song of Songs
Acts of the Apostles	Koran
Apocalypse of John	Qu'ran
Epistles of Paul	Zend-Avesta
	Talmud Yerushalmi

A.19H2. Capitalize *book* when it refers to the entire Bible; otherwise, do not capitalize it.

the Book

but

the book of Proverbs

the book of the Prophet Isaiah

the second book of Kings

A.19J. Special selections from the Bible

A.19J1. Capitalize the first word of the name of a special selection from the Bible that is commonly referred to by a specific name.

the Beatitudes	the Nunc dimittis
the Decalogue	the Shema
the Lord's prayer	the Sermon on the mount
the Miserere	the Ten commandments

A.19K. Versions of the Bible

A.19K1. Capitalize the name of a version of the Bible (see 25.18A11).

Authorized Version	New English Bible
Confraternity Version	Septuagint
Jerusalem Bible	Vulgate
New American Standard Bible	

A.20. NAMES OF DOCUMENTS

A.20A. Capitalize the formal, or conventional, name of a document such as a charter, constitution, legislative act, pact, plan, statement of policy, or treaty.

Articles of Confederation

Atlantic Charter

Bill of Rights

British North America Act

Civil Rights Act of 1964

Constitution of Virginia; the constitution

Declaration of Independence

Fourteenth Amendment (U.S. Constitution)

Magna Charta

Marshall Plan; the plan

Reform Bill

Third Five Year Plan (India)

Treaty of Versailles; the treaty

Universal Copyright Convention; the convention

In case of doubt whether the title of a document is its formal or conventional name, capitalize the title according to other rules in this appendix.

An act to amend the constitution and to prohibit taxes on property . . .

A.21. NAMES OF HISTORICAL AND CULTURAL EVENTS AND PERIODS

A.21A. Capitalize the name of an historical or cultural event and of a major historical or cultural period.

Age of Discovery	Norman Conquest
Battle of Dunkirk	Operation Deep Freeze
Boxer Rebellion	Reformation
Dark Ages	Second Battle of the Marne
Elizabethan Age	Second World War
French Revolution	Siege of Leningrad
Grand National Steeplechase	Thirty Years' War

A.22. DECORATIONS, MEDALS, ETC.

A.22A. Capitalize the name of a particular decoration, medal, or award.

Bronze Star Medal

Congressional Medal of Honor

Iron Cross

Victoria Cross

A.23. NAMES OF CALENDAR DIVISIONS

A.23A. Capitalize the name of a month of the year or day of the week.

January

Monday

Do not capitalize the name of a season.

winter

A.24. NAMES OF HOLIDAYS

A.24A. Capitalize the name of a secular or religious holiday and of a religious season.

Advent	Fourth of July
Boxing Day	Lent
Christmas Day	Ramadan
Epiphany	Saint Patrick's Day
Feast of the Annunciation	Thanksgiving

A.25. SCIENTIFIC NAMES OF PLANTS AND ANIMALS

A.25A. Capitalize the Latin name of a phylum, class, order, family, or genus, and names of intermediate groupings (e.g., subclasses). Do not capitalize the name of a species or subspecies even if it is derived from a proper name. Do not capitalize English derivatives of scientific names.

Arthropoda (*phylum*)

Insecta (*class*)

but arthropod (*from* Arthropoda)

A.26. GEOLOGIC TERMS

A.26A. Capitalize the distinctive word(s) in the name of a geologic era, period, etc. Do not capitalize words such as *era* and *period* and modifiers such as *early*, *middle*, or *late* when used only descriptively.

Eocene epoch

Jurassic period

Lower Triassic period

Mesozoic period

but

the early Miocene

the late Eocene

A.27. ASTRONOMICAL TERMS

A.27A. Capitalize the name of a planet, satellite, star, constellation, asteroid, etc. Do not capitalize the words *sun*, *moon*, and *earth* except, in the case of *earth*, when the word is used in conjunction with the names of other planets (e.g., *The planet Mars lies between the Earth and Jupiter*).

Alpha Centauri	Mercury
Canis Major	the Milky Way
Little Dipper	North Star

A.28. SOIL NAMES

A.28A. Capitalize the name of a soil classification.

Alpine Meadow	Half Bog
Chernozem	Prairie

A.29. TRADE NAMES

A.29A. Capitalize a trade name, variety name, or market grade. Do not capitalize a common noun following such a name.

Choice lamb (*market grade*)

Formica (*trade name*)

Orlon (*trade name*)

Polaroid film (*trade name*)

Red Radiance rose (*variety*)

Yellow Stained cotton (*market grade*)

A.30. SINGLE LETTERS USED AS WORDS OR PARTS OF COMPOUNDS

A.30A. Capitalize the pronoun *I* and the interjection *O* (*Oh*). Capitalize a single letter used as part of a compound word whether or not hyphenated. Capitalize a letter that refers to a letter of the alphabet as such.

A major	vitamin B
H-bomb	X-ray
U-boat	Y is for yellow

A.31. HYPHENATED COMPOUNDS

A.31A. If the rules require the capitalization of a hyphenated compound, capitalize the first part, and capitalize the second, etc., part if it is a noun or a proper adjective or if it has the same force as the first part.

Twentieth-Century	Blue-Black
Basket-Maker	Secretary-Treasurer

A.31B. Do not capitalize the second part if it modifies the first part or if the two parts constitute a single word.

French-speaking

Twenty-five

Co-ordinate

A.32. HYPHENATED PREFIXES

A.32A. Do not capitalize a prefix joined by a hyphen to a capitalized word unless other rules require its capitalization.

ex-President Roosevelt	trans-Siberian
pre-Cambrian	un-American

Foreign Languages

A.33. GENERAL RULE

A.33A. Apply the rules for the capitalization of English (A.12–A.32) to the capitalization of a foreign language unless a contrary rule is provided in a section below treating that language or unless the romanization table for the language adopted by the cataloguing agency provides otherwise.

A.34. CAPITALIZATION OF ROMANIZED HEADINGS AND TITLES

A.34A. Capitalize words in romanized headings and titles as instructed in A.33. If the language has no system of capitalization, capitalize the first word of a title or a sentence and the first word of the name of a corporate body or a subdivision of a corporate body. Capitalize proper names according to English usage.

A.35. BULGARIAN

A.35A. Proper names and their derivatives

A.35A1. Do not capitalize names of peoples, races, and residents of specific localities: българин; софиянец; семит.

A.35A2. Do not capitalize names of religions and their adherents: будизъм; християнство; лютеранец.

A.35A3. Do not capitalize proper adjectives: софийски улици.

A.35B. Names of regions, localities, and geographic features, including streets, parks, etc.

A.35B1. Capitalize the first word unless it is a common noun. Capitalize other words only if they are proper nouns: Орлово гнездо; Бряг на слоновата кост; Стара Загора; Охридско езеро; село Белица; Червеният площад; ул. Шипка.

A.35C. Names of countries and administrative divisions

A.35C1. Capitalize the first word and proper nouns in names of countries and administrative subdivisions: Обединена арабска република; Народна република България; Софийска област; Министерство на селскостопанското производство.

A.35D. Names of corporate bodies

A.35D1. Capitalize only the first word and proper nouns in the names of corporate bodies: Българска комунистическа партия; Организация на обединените народи; Държавна библиотека "Васил Коларов"; Български червен кръст.

A.35E. Titles of persons

A.35E1. Capitalize свети and titles of royalty, high government officials, and high ecclesiastical officials if they are followed by a name: Министър Даскалов; Свети Климент.

A.35E2. Capitalize any title occurring in conjunction with the name of a well-known personage: Отец Паисий; Хаджи Димитър; Бачо Киро.

A.35E3. In general, do not capitalize other titles: министър; крал; отец; професор; отец Борис.

A.35F. Personal pronouns

A.35F1. Do not capitalize аз.

A.35F2. Capitalize Вие (Вий), Ви, Вас, and Вам when used in formal address.

A.35G. Names of calendar divisions

A.35G1. Do not capitalize the names of days of the week and of months.

A.35H. Names of historic events, etc.

A.35H1. Capitalize the first word and proper nouns in the names of historic events, etc.: Първата световна война; Великата октомврийска социалистическа революция; Възраждането; Битката при Косово поле.

A.36. CZECH (BOHEMIAN)

A.36A. Proper names and their derivatives

A.36A1. Capitalize only the distinctive word in geographic names consisting of a distinctive word and a generic word: *Tichý oceán*.

586

A.36A2. Capitalize the first word and any other word that is a derivative of a proper name in names of streets: *U invalidovny*; *Na růžku*; *Na Smetance*.

A.36B. Names of corporate bodies

A.36B1. In general, capitalize only the first word in names of corporate bodies: *Československá republika*; *Česká akademie věd a umění*; *Bratří čeští*; *Milosrdní bratří*.

A.36B2. Do not capitalize names of branches of schools, conservatories, universities, ministries, and departments of government: *ministerstvo školství*; *závodní rada*.

A.36C. Titles of persons

A.36C1. Do not capitalize titles of persons: *doktor*; *král*; *ministr*; *svatý*.

A.36D. Personal pronouns

A.36D1. Do not capitalize *já*.

A.36D2. Capitalize the pronouns of formal address: *Ty, Tvůj, Tobě*; *Vy, Vám*; *Vás, Váš*.

A.36E. Names of calendar divisions

A.36E1. Do not capitalize the names of days of the week and of months.

DANISH. *See* Scandinavian languages.

A.37. DUTCH

A.37A. Single letter as the first word

A.37A1. Capitalize the first word of a sentence if it is the interjection *O*, the pronoun *U*, or a letter referring to a letter of the alphabet as such (e.g., *A is een aapje*).

A.37A2. Do not capitalize any other single letter that is the first word of a sentence or the first word of a proper name. Capitalize the next word: *'s Avonds is het koud*; *'k Weet niet wat hij zegt*; *'s Gravenhage*.

A.37B. Prefixes in personal names

A.37B1. Capitalize the prefixes *de, ten, van*, if not preceded by the Christian name.

A.37C. Personal pronouns

A.37C1. Do not capitalize *ik*.

A.37C2. In general, capitalize *U, Uw*, and *Gij* in personal correspondence.

A.37D. Names of calendar divisions

A.37D1. Do not capitalize the names of days of the week and of months.

A.38. FINNISH

A.38A. Names of corporate bodies

A.38A1. Capitalize only the first word and proper nouns in names of state and local government agencies, courts, and church bodies: *Erillinen komppania Kontula*; *Helsingin kaupunginkirjasto*; *Kauppa- ja teollisuusministeriö*; *Kirkon ulkomaanasiain toimikunta*; *Korkein oikeus*; *Suomen Unesco-toimikunta*.

A.38A2. In general, capitalize only the first word and proper nouns in names of scientific and economic institutions of the state: *Kansallismuseon esihistoriallinen osasto*; *Geodeettinen laitos*; *Helsingin yliopisto*. Exceptions: *Suomen Akatemia*; *Suomen Pankki*.

A.38A3. In the names of other institutions, societies, and firms, follow the usage of the body. If the usage is not known, capitalize all words.

A.38B. Names of buildings

A.38B1. Capitalize proper nouns in the names of buildings: *kaupungintalo*; *Helsingin kulttuuritalo*.

A.39. FRENCH

A.39A. Proper names and their derivatives

A.39A1. Do not capitalize names of members of religious groups, sects, religious orders, political and other organizations, names of religions, and names of languages: *les jésuites*; *les démocrates*; *le bouddhisme*; *l'anglais* (the English language).

A.39A2. Do not capitalize adjectives derived from names of members of religious groups, sects, religious orders, political and other organizations, names of religions, names of languages, geographic names, and adjectives denoting nationality: *la religion catholique*; *la région alpine*; *le peuple français*.

A.39A3. Capitalize nouns denoting nationality: *les Français*.

A.39A4. Do not capitalize a common noun used as a generic word in a geographic name: *la mer du Nord*; *l'île aux Oiseaux*.

A.39B. Names of corporate bodies

A.39B1. In general, capitalize the first word, any adjectives preceding the first noun, the first noun, and all proper nouns in the names of corporate bodies: *Société de chimie physique*; *Grand Orchestre symphonique de la R.T.B*; *Église réformée de France*. Notable exceptions: *Société des Nations*; *Nations Unies*.

A.39B2. Capitalize the nouns and adjectives in hyphenated corporate names: *le Théâtre-Français*.

A.39C. Prefixes in names of persons

A.39C1. Capitalize prefixes consisting of an article or a contraction of an article and a preposition: *La Fontaine*; *Du Cange*.

A.39D. Titles of persons

A.39D1. Do not capitalize titles designating rank or office: *le roi*; *le ministre*; *le pape Léon X*.

A.39D2. Capitalize titles of address and titles of respectful address or reference: *Monsieur*; *Mme de Lafayette*; *Son Éminence*; *Sa Majesté le roi de France*.

A.39D3. Do not capitalize *saint* (*sainte*, etc.) when it refers exclusively to a person; otherwise capitalize it: *saint Thomas More*; but *la cathédrale Saint-Lambert*; *l'été de la Saint-Martin*.

A.39E. Personal pronouns

A.39E1. Do not capitalize a personal pronoun.

A.39F. Names of calendar divisions

A.39F1. Do not capitalize the names of days of the week and of months.

A.39G. Miscellaneous

A.39G1. Do not capitalize *rue* and its synonyms: *rue de la Nation*; *avenue de l'Opéra*.

A.39G2. Do not capitalize *église* when it indicates a building: *l'église Notre-Dame*. Capitalize it when it refers to the Church as an institution.

A.39G3. Capitalize *état* when denoting the nation: *le Conseil d'État*.

A.40. GERMAN

A.40A. Nouns

A.40A1. Capitalize all nouns and words used as nouns: *das Buch*; *das Geben*; *die Armen*; *das intime Du* (reference to the word *du*).

A.40B. Proper names and their derivatives

A.40B1. In general, do not capitalize proper adjectives: *die deutsche Sprache*.

A.40B2. Capitalize adjectives derived from personal names when used in their original meaning: *die Lutherische Übersetzung*; *die Platonischen Dialoge*. Do not capitalize them when they are used descriptively: *die lutherische Kirche*; *die platonische Liebe*.

A.40B3. Capitalize indeclinable adjectives derived from geographic names: *Schweizer Ware*; *die Zürcher Bürger*.

A.40B4. Capitalize adjectives, pronouns, and numerals used as parts of a name or title: *Alexander der Grosse*; *das Schweizerische Konsulat*; *Seine Excellenz*; *Friedrich der Zweite*; *Bund der Technischen Angestellten und Beamten*; *der Erste der Klasse* (expressing rank). See also A.40D1b.

589

A.40C. Pronouns

A.40C1. Do not capitalize *ich*.

A.40C2. Capitalize *Du*, *Ihr*, *Dein*, and *Euer* and their inflected forms when used in correspondence.

A.40C3. Capitalize *Sie* and *Ihr* and their inflected forms when used in formal address.

A.40D. Miscellaneous

A.40D1. Do not capitalize the following:
  a) pronouns (see also A.40C): *jemand, ein jeder, der eine . . . der andere, etwas anderes, die übrigen*
  b) numerals (see also A.40B4): *die beiden, alle drei, der vierte* (indicating numerical order)
  c) adverbs: *mittags, anfangs, morgen, montags, aufs neue, fürs erste, im voraus*
  d) verbal phrases: *not tun, schuld sein, haushalten, preisgeben, teilhaben, wundernehmen, ausser acht lassen, zuteil werden, zumute sein*
  e) adjectives modifying nouns that are implied if the noun has been expressed elsewhere in the same sentence: *Hier ist die beste Arbeit, dort die schlechteste.*

A.41. HUNGARIAN

A.41A. Proper names and their derivatives

A.41A1. Do not capitalize nouns denoting nationality: *az oroszok*.

A.41A2. Do not capitalize adjectives derived from proper names: *budapesti*.

A.41B. Titles of persons

A.41B1. Capitalize titles used in direct address: *Felséges Uram*.

A.41B2. Do not capitalize titles of nobility, including those consisting of an adjectival term derived from place of origin, etc.: *gróf Teleki Pál*; *körmendi Frim Jakab*.

A.41C. Personal pronouns

A.41C1. Do not capitalize *én*.

A.41C2. Capitalize pronouns used in formal address: *Maga*.

A.41D. Names of calendar divisions

A.41D1. Do not capitalize the names of days of the week and of months.

A.42. ITALIAN

A.42A. Proper names and their derivatives

A.42A1. Do not capitalize names of members of religious groups, sects, religious orders, political and other organizations, names of religions, and names of languages: *i protestanti*; *i benedettini*; *un democratico*; *il buddhismo*; *il francese* (the French language).

A.42A2. Do not capitalize adjectives derived from names of members of religious groups, sects, religious orders, political and other organizations, names of religions, names of languages, geographic and personal names, and adjectives denoting nationality: *la religione cattolica*; *la flora alpina*; *il popolo italiano*; *iconografia dantesca*.

A.42A3. Capitalize nouns denoting nationality: *gl'Italiani*.

A.42B. Names of corporate bodies

A.42B1. In general, capitalize only the first word, proper nouns, religious terms, and the word following an adjective denoting royal or pontifical privilege in the names of corporate bodies: *Istituto nazionale di fisica nucleare*; *Accademia nazionale de Santa Cecilia*; *Università cattolica del Sacro Cuore*; *Pontificio Seminario francese*; *Chiesa evangelica italiana*. Notable exceptions: *Società delle Nazioni*; *Nazioni Unite*; *Croce Rossa*.

A.42C. Titles of persons

A.42C1. Do not capitalize titles of persons except for ceremonial titles consisting of a possessive pronoun and a noun expressing an abstract quality: *signora*; *il signor Donati*; *il duca d'Aosta*; *Umberto I, re d'Italia*; but *Sua Santità*; *Sua Altezza Reale il principe Umberto*; *le LL. MM. il re e la regina*.

A.42C2. Do not capitalize *san* (*santo*, etc.) when referring exclusively to a person; capitalize it when it is abbreviated and when it is an integral part of the name of a place, a building, etc.: *san Francesco d'Assisi*; but *S. Girolamo*; *Castel Sant'Angelo*.

A.42D. Personal pronouns

A.42D1. Do not capitalize *io*.

A.42D2. Capitalize the pronouns of formal address: *Ella*; *Lei*; *Loro*.

A.42E. Names of calendar divisions

A.42E1. Do not capitalize the names of days of the week and of months.

A.42F. Names of centuries

A.42F1. Capitalize the proper names of centuries: *il Cinquecento*; *il Seicento*; but *il sedicesimo secolo*.

A.42G. Miscellaneous

A.42G1. Do not capitalize *via* and its synonyms: *via Vittorio Veneto*; *corso Umberto I*.

A.42G2. Do not capitalize *chiesa* when it indicates a building: *la chiesa di S. Maria degli Angeli*. Capitalize it when it refers to the Church as an institution.

A.42G3. Capitalize *stato* when denoting the nation: *Consiglio di Stato*.

A.43. LATIN

A.43A. Follow the instructions in A.12–A.32.

NORWEGIAN. *See* Scandinavian languages.

A.44. POLISH

A.44A. Proper names and their derivatives

A.44A1. Do not capitalize names of residents of cities and towns: *warszawianin*.

A.44A2. Do not capitalize adjectives derived from proper names: *mickiewiczowski*.

A.44A3. Do not capitalize names of religions and their adherents and names of members of religious orders: *katolicyzm*; *katolik*; *mahometanin*; *jezuici*.

A.44A4. Capitalize each part of a compound geographic name unless the distinctive word is in nominative case and can stand alone; in that case, capitalize only the distinctive word: *Morze Bałtyckie*; but *jezioro Narocz*.

A.44A5. Do not capitalize geographic names applied to wines, dances, etc.: *tokaj*; *krakowiak*.

A.44A6. Do not capitalize names of administrative districts and geographic adjectives: *województwo poznańskie*; *diecezja łomżyńska*.

A.44B. Names of corporate bodies

A.44B1. Capitalize all words except conjunctions and prepositions in the names of corporate bodies: *Towarzystwo Naukowe w Toruniu*; *Ewangelicko-Augsburski Kościół*.

A.44C. Titles of persons

A.44C1. Do not capitalize titles of persons except in direct address: *papież*; *król*; *święty*.

A.44D. Personal pronouns

A.44D1. Do not capitalize *ja*.

A.44D2. Capitalize the pronouns of formal address: *Ty, Tobie, Twój*; *On, Ona, Jego, Jej, Jemu*; *Wy, Wam, Was*.

A.44E. Names of calendar divisions

A.44E1. Do not capitalize the names of days of the week and of months.

A.44F. Names of historic events, etc.

A.44F1. Do not capitalize names of historic events and wars: *pokój wersalski*; *wojna siedmioletnia*.

A.45. PORTUGUESE

A.45A. Derivatives of proper names

A.45A1. Do not capitalize derivatives of proper names: *os homens alemães*; *os franceses*.

A.45B. Titles of persons

A.45B1. Capitalize names of positions or posts of dignitaries and words that designate titles: *o Arcebispo de Braga*; *o Duque de Caxias*; *o Presidente da República*; *Senhor Professor*.

A.45C. Personal pronouns

A.45C1. Do not capitalize *eu*.

A.45D. Religious terms

A.45D1. Capitalize *igreja* when referring to the Church as an institution.

A.45E. Names of calendar divisions

A.45E1. Do not capitalize the names of days of the week and of months.

A.46. RUSSIAN

A.46A. Proper names and their derivatives

A.46A1. Do not capitalize prefixes, prepositions, and conjunctions forming part of a proper name, except when they are connected to the following part of the name by a hyphen: фон Клаузевиц; ван Бетховен; Ван-Гог.

A.46A2. Do not capitalize names of peoples, races, and residents of specific localities: араб; таджик; москвичи.

A.46A3. Do not capitalize the names of religions and their adherents: католицизм; католик.

A.46A4. Do not capitalize proper nouns that are parts of adverbs: по-пушкински.

A.46B. Names of regions, localities, and geographic features, including streets, parks, etc.

A.46B1. Do not capitalize a common noun forming part of a geographic name: мыс Горн; остров Рудольфа; канал Москва-Волга.

A.46B2. Capitalize a common noun forming an integral part of a name: Кривой Рог; Белая Церковь; Богемский Лес.

A.46B3. Capitalize the common noun if it is a foreign word that has not become a part of the Russian language: Рю-де-ла-Пе (Рю—meaning street, Пе—meaning peace); Сыр-Дарья (Дарья—meaning river).

A.46B4. Do not capitalize the title or rank of the person in whose honour a place is named: остров королевы Виктории; мыс капитана Джеральда.

A.46B5. Do not capitalize adjectives derived from geographic names: московские улицы.

A.46B6. Do not capitalize geographic names applied to wines, species of animals, birds, etc.: мадера; херес; сенбернар.

A.46C. Names of countries and administrative divisions

A.46C1. Capitalize the first word in the commonly accepted names of groups of countries: Балканские страны.

A.46C2. Capitalize unofficial but commonly accepted names of countries, cities, and territorial divisions: Советский Союз; Страна Советов; Приуралье; Белокаменная (for Moscow).

A.46C3. Capitalize administrative divisions of the USSR as follows:

a) Capitalize every word in the names of republics and autonomous republics: Башкирская Автономная Советская Социалистическая Республика.

b) Capitalize only the first word in the names of provinces, autonomous provinces, territories, regions, and village soviets: Алма-Атинская область; Приморский край; Коми-Пермяцкий национальный округ; Егоршинский район; Краснинский сельсозет.

c) Capitalize every word in the names of the highest Soviet and non-Russian governmental units and Communist Party organizations except those in parentheses and партия : Верховный Совет СССР (also of the Union republics and autonomous republics); Совет Союза, Совет Национальностей; Всесоюзная Коммунистическая партия (большевиков); Рейхстаг; Конгресс США; Правительствующий Сенат.

d) Capitalize only the first word and proper nouns in the names of other governmental units: Государственная плановая комиссия СССР; Народный комиссариат иностранных дел; Военный совет Закавказского военного округа.

e) Do not capitalize the names of bureaus when used in the plural and when used in a general sense: советы народных комиссаров; народный комиссариат.

f) Capitalize Совет in Совет депутатов трудящихся : Загорский районный Совет депутатов трудящихся.

A.46D. Names of corporate bodies

A.46D1. Capitalize only the first word and proper nouns in names of corporate bodies: Академия наук СССР; Книжная палата; Профессиональный союз работников высшей школы и научных учреждений; Дом книги.

A.46D2. If part of the name of a corporate body is in quotation marks, capitalize only the first word and proper nouns within the quotation marks: завод "Фрезер"; совхоз "Путь к социализму".

A.46D3. If a corporate body is also known by a part of its name, capitalize the first word of the part when it appears in conjunction with the full name: Государственный ордена Ленина академический Большой театр (Большой театр).

A.46D4. Do not capitalize the following words in the names of congresses, conferences, etc.: съезд; конференция; сессия; пленум.

A.46D5. Do not capitalize совет when used to refer to the council of a society or institution.

A.46E. Titles of persons

A.46E1. Capitalize the titles of the highest government officials: Председатель Совета Народных Комиссаров; Маршал Советского Союза.

A.46F. Pronouns

A.46F1. Do not capitalize я.

A.46F2. Capitalize pronouns of formal address: Вы; Вам; Вас.

A.46G. Names of calendar divisions

A.46G1. Do not capitalize the names of days of the week and of months.

A.46H. Names of historic events, etc.

A.46H1. Capitalize the first word, the distinctive word, and proper nouns in the names of historic periods and events: Великая Октябрьская социалистическая революция; Возрож-дение; Третья республика; Парижская коммуна; Кровавое воскресенье; Ленский расстрел; Бородинский бой.

A.46H2. Do not capitalize the names of the five-year plans: третья сталинская пятилетка; *but* соревнование имени Третьей Сталинской Пятилетки.

A.46H3. Do not capitalize война in the names of wars: Франко-Прусская война; Русско-Японская война; Великая Отечественная война; Отечественная война.

A.47. SCANDINAVIAN LANGUAGES

A.47A. Derivatives of proper names

A.47A1. Do not capitalize adjectives derived from proper names: *europeisk*; *køben-havnsk*; *luthersk*; *svensk*.

A.47B. Names of corporate bodies

A.47B1. In general, capitalize the first word and the word following an adjective denoting royal privilege in the names of corporate bodies. Capitalize other words, such as proper nouns, according to the appropriate rule: *Kungl. Biblioteket*; *Ministeriet for kulturelle anliggender*; *Selskabet for dansk skolehistorie*.

A.47C. Compound names

A.47C1. In general, capitalize only the first word of a compound name, other than a compound personal name: *Förenta staterna*; *Kronborg slot*; *Norske kirke*.

A.47D. Titles of persons

A.47D1. In general, do not capitalize titles of persons: *fru Larsen*; *kong Haakon VII*; *Gustav, prins av Vasa*.

A.47E. Personal pronouns

A.47E1. Danish. Do not capitalize *jeg*. Capitalize *De*; *Dem*; *Deres*. Capitalize the familiar form *I* (you) to distinguish it from *i* (in).

A.47E2. Norwegian. Do not capitalize *jeg*. Capitalize *De*; *Dem*; *Deres*; *Dykk*; *Dykkar*.

A.47E3. Swedish. Do not capitalize *jag*. Capitalize *Ni*, *Eder*, and *Er* in correspondence.

A.47F. Names of calendar divisions

A.47F1. Do not capitalize the names of days of the week, of months, and of holidays: *jul*; *nyår*.

A.48. SERBO-CROATIAN (ROMAN AND CYRILLIC ALPHABETS)

A.48A. Proper names and their derivatives

A.48A1. Do not capitalize names of peoples and races: *bijelac*; *crnac*; *semit*.

A.48A2. Do not capitalize proper adjectives: *srpskohrvatski jezik*.

A.48A3. Do not capitalize names of religions and their adherents: *katoličanstvo*; *katolik*.

A.48B. Names of regions, localities, and geographic features, including streets, parks, etc.

A.48B1. Capitalize only the first word and proper nouns: *Tetovska kotlina*; *Velika Morava*; *Bliski istok*; *Ulica bosanska*; *Ulica Branka Radičevića*; *Trg žrtava fašizma*; *Park bratstva i jedinstva*.

A.48C. Names of administrative divisions of countries

A.48C1. Do not capitalize names of administrative divisions of countries: *primorsko-krajiška oblast*; *zagrebački kotar*.

A.48D. Names of corporate bodies

A.48D1. Capitalize only the first word and proper nouns in the names of corporate bodies: *Jugoslovenska akademija znanosti i umjetnosti*; *Udruženje književnika Srbije*; *Hrvatsko narodno kazalište u Zagrebu*; *Savez komunista Jugoslavije*; *Centralni komitet Saveza komunista Jugoslavije*.

A.48E. Titles of persons

A.48E1. Do not capitalize titles of persons: *predsednik Tito*; *kralj Georg*; *ministar*, *sveti Petar*. However, capitalize *sveti* when it appears in the name of a holiday (see A.48H2).

A.48F. Personal pronouns

A.48F1. Do not capitalize *ja*.

A.48F2. Capitalize the pronouns of formal address: *Ti, Tvoj, Ti*; *Vi, Vam, Vas, Vaš*.

A.48G. Names of calendar divisions

A.48G1. Do not capitalize names of days of the week and of months.

A.48H. Names of historic events, holidays, etc.

A.48H1. Capitalize proper nouns in the names of historic periods and events: *kameno doba*; *srednji vijek*; *oktobarska revolucija*; *boj na Mišaru*; *prvi srpski ustanak*.

A.48H2. Capitalize the first word and proper nouns in the names of holidays: *Božić*; *Veliki četvrtak*; *Nova godina*; *Sveti Petar*.

A.49. SLOVAK

A.49A. Follow the instructions in A.36.

A.50. SLOVENIAN

A.50A. Proper names and their derivatives

A.50A1. Do not capitalize names of peoples and races: *arijec*; *semit*; *črnec*.

A.50A2. Capitalize only the distinctive words in the names of nationalities that consist of more than one word: *severni Korejec*; *zahodni Nemec*.

A.50A3. Do not capitalize proper adjectives: *slovenski jezik*.

A.50A4. Do not capitalize the names of religions and their adherents: *katolicizem*; *katoličan*.

597

A.50B. Names of regions, localities, and geographic features, including streets, parks, etc.

A.50B1. Capitalize only the first word and proper nouns: *Ziljska dolina*; *Novo mesto*; *Škofja Loka*; *Daljni vzhod*; *Otok kraljice Viktorije*; *Rtič dobrega upanja*; *Ulica stare pravde*.

A.50C. Names of countries and administrative divisions

A.50C1. Capitalize the first word and proper nouns in the names of countries and administrative subdivisions: *Federativna socialistična republika Jugoslavija*; *Združene države Amerike*.

A.50D. Names of corporate bodies

A.50D1. Capitalize the first word and proper nouns in the names of corporate bodies: *Društvo slovenskih književnikov*; *Državna založba Slovenije*.

A.50E. Titles of persons

A.50E1. Do not capitalize titles of persons: *predsednik*; *sekretar*; *doktor*; *maršal Tito*; *kralj Matjaž*; *sveti Peter*. However, capitalize *sveti* when it appears in the name of a holiday (see A.50H).

A.50F. Personal pronouns

A.50F1. Do not capitalize *jaz*.

A.50F2. Capitalize the pronouns of formal address: *Ti, Tebe, Tebi, s Teboj*; *Vidva, Vidve, Vaju, Vama*; *Vi, Vas, Vam, z Vami*.

A.50G. Names of calendar divisions

A.50G1. Do not capitalize the names of days of the week and of months.

A.50H. Names of historic events, holidays, etc.

A.50H1. Capitalize proper nouns in the names of historic events, holidays, etc.: *ledena doba*; *renesansa*; *francoska revolucija*; *boj na Mišaru*; *prva srbska vstaja*; *božič*; *velika noč*; *Sveti Peter*.

A.51. SPANISH

A.51A. Derivatives of proper names

A.51A1. Do not capitalize derivatives of proper names: *las mujeres colombianas*.

A.51A2. Do not capitalize adjectives used substantively: *los franceses*.

A.51B. Titles of persons

A.51B1. Capitalize titles of honour and address only when they are abbreviated: *señor*, *Sr.*; *doctor*, *Dr.*; *general*, *Gral.*

A.51B2. Capitalize *Su Excelencia*, *Su Majestad*, etc., when used alone, whether written out or abbreviated. Do not capitalize these words when they are used with a name or another title: *su majestad Juan Carlos*; *su majestad el Rey*.

A.51C. Personal pronouns

A.51C1. Do not capitalize *yo*.

A.51C2. Capitalize the pronouns of formal address: *Vd.*, *Vds.* (*Ud.*, *Uds.*)

A.51D. Religious terms

A.51D1. Capitalize *iglesia* when it refers to the Church as an institution.

A.51E. Names of calendar divisions

A.51E1. Do not capitalize the names of days of the week and of months.

A.51F. Questions within a sentence

A.51F1. In general, do not capitalize the first word of a question occurring within a sentence: *Cuando viene la noche ¿cómo se puede ver?*

SWEDISH. *See* Scandinavian languages.

A.52. UKRAINIAN

A.52A. Follow the instructions in A.46.

ABBREVIATIONS

Contents

B.1. GENERAL RULE

B.1A. Use abbreviations in catalogue entries as instructed in B.2–B.8. Use the abbreviations prescribed in B.9–B.15.

B.2. HEADINGS

B.2A. Use only the following categories of abbreviations in headings:

1) those that are integral parts of the heading (e.g., *St.* (Saint)), if the person or corporate body uses the abbreviation
2) designations of function (e.g., *comp.*) (see 21.0D)
3) certain names of larger places added to the name of another place (see 23.4) or to the name of a corporate body (see 24.4C2)
4) certain terms used with dates (e.g., *b.*, *fl.*) (see 22.17)
5) distinguishing terms added to names of persons, if they are abbreviated in the source from which they are taken (see 22.15B, 22.19B).

B.3. UNIFORM TITLES

B.3A. Use only the following categories of abbreviations in uniform titles:

1) those that are integral parts of the title
2) designations of parts of a work as instructed in a particular rule (e.g., *N.T.* (New Testament)) (see 25.18A2)
3) the ampersand (&) in listing languages.

B.4. TITLES AND STATEMENTS OF RESPONSIBILITY

B.4A. Use only the following categories of abbreviations in the title and statement of responsibility area, any statement of responsibility in the edition area, and titles and statements of responsibility in the series area and contents notes:

1) those found in the prescribed sources of information for the particular area
2) *i.e.*, *et al.*, and their equivalents in nonroman scripts (see 1.0F, 1.1F5).

B.5. OTHER PARTS OF THE CATALOGUE ENTRY

B.5A. Abbreviate words elsewhere in the catalogue entry, subject to the limitations specified in footnotes to B.9. However, do not do so if the brevity of the statement makes abbreviations unnecessary or if the resulting statement might not be clear. Do not use a single-letter abbreviation to begin a note. Do not abbreviate words in quoted notes.

B.6. CORRESPONDING WORDS IN ANOTHER LANGUAGE

B.6A. Use an abbreviation for the corresponding word in another language if the abbreviation commonly used in that language has the same spelling. In case of doubt, do not use the abbreviation.

B.7. COMPOUND WORDS

B.7A. Use a prescribed abbreviation for the last part of a compound word (e.g., *Textausg.* for *Textausgabe*).

B.8. INFLECTED LANGUAGES

B.8A. In inflected languages, use the abbreviation of a word listed in B.9–B.15 in the nominative case for an inflected form of that word. If, however, the abbreviation includes the final letter(s) of the word, modify the abbreviation to show the final letter(s) of the inflected form (e.g., литература, лит-ра; литературы, лит-ры).

B.9. ROMAN ALPHABET ABBREVIATIONS

(Footnotes for this listing appear on pages 604 and 605.)

TERM	ABBREVIATION	TERM	ABBREVIATION
aastakäik	aastak	centimetre, -s	cm.
Abdruck	Abdr.	century	cent.[5]
abgedruckt	abgedr.	cetakan	cet.
Abteilung, Abtheilung	Abt.	chapter	ch.
accompaniment	acc.	circa	ca.
afdeling	afd.	číslo	čís.
aflevering	afl.	colored, coloured	col.
altitude	alt.[1]	Compagnia	Cia.
alto	A[2]	Compagnie	Cie
and	&[3]	Compañía	Cía.
and others	et al.	Company	Co.
Anno Domini	A.D.	compare	cf.
approximately	approx.	compiler	comp.[6]
årgang	årg.	confer	cf.
argraffiad	arg.	copyright	c
arranged	arr.	Corporation	Corp.
arranger	arr.	corrected	corr.
átdolgozott	átdolg.	corregido	corr.
Auflage	Aufl.	corretto, -a	corr.
augmenté, -e	augm.	corrigé, -e	corr.
augmented	augm.	część	cz.
aumentada	aum.	declination	decl.[1]
aumentato	aum.	deel	d.
Ausgabe	Ausg.	del (Danish, Norwegian, Swedish)	d.
avdeling	avd.	département	dép.
Band	Bd.	Department	Dept.
band	bd.	diameter	diam.
Bändchen	Bdchn.	died	d.
Bände	Bde.	diena	d.
baritone	Bar[2]	djilid	djil.
bass	B[2]	document	doc.
Before Christ	B.C.	dopunjeno	dop.
bilangan	bil.	drukarnia	druk.
binary coded decimal	BCD	edición	ed.
bind	bd.	edition, -s	ed., eds.
black and white	b&w	édition	éd.
bogtrykkeri	bogtr.	editor	ed.[6]
boktrykkeri	boktr.	edizione	ed.
book	bk.	enlarged	enl.
born	b.	equinox	eq.[1]
bővített	bőv.	ergänzt	erg.
broj	br.	erweitert	erw.
Brother, -s	Bro., Bros.[4]	establecimiento tipográfico	estab. tip.
Buchdrucker, -ei	Buchdr.	et alii	et al.
Buchhandlung	Buchh.	et cetera	etc.
bulletin	bull.	évfolyam	évf.
bytes per inch	bpi	facsimile, -s	facsim., facsims.
capitolo	cap.		
část	č.		

TERM	ABBREVIATION	TERM	ABBREVIATION
fascicle	fasc.	manuscript, -s	ms., mss.
fascicule	fasc.	mėnuo	mėn.
flourished	fl.	metai	m.
folio	fol.	metre, -s	m.
following	ff.	mezzo-soprano	Mz[2]
foot, feet	ft.	miesięcznik	mies.
frame, -s	fr.	millimetre, -s	mm.
frames per second	fps	minute, -s	min.
fratelli	f.lli[4]	miscellaneous	misc.
Gebrüder	Gebr.[4]	monophonic	mono.
gedruckt	gedr.	Nachfolger	Nachf.[4]
genealogical	geneal.	nakład	nakł.
godina	g.	nakladatelství	nakl.
government	govt.	naukowy	nauk.
Government Printing Office	G.P.O.	neue Folge	n.F.
		new series	new ser.
Handschrift, -en	Hs., Hss.	New Testament	N.T.
Her (His) Majesty's Stationery Office	H.M.S.O.	no name (of publisher)	s.n.
		no place (of publication)	s.l.
Hermanos	Hnos.[4]	nombor	no.
hour, -s	hr.	nomor	no.
id est	i.e.	Nonae	Non.
Idus	Id.	nouveau, nouvelle	nouv.
illustration, -s	ill.	number, -s	no.
illustrator	ill.[6]	numbered	numb.
imienia	im.	numer	nr.
imprenta	impr.	numero (Finnish)	n:o
imprimerie	impr.	numéro (French)	no
inch, -es	in.	numero (Italian)	n.
inches per second	ips	número (Spanish)	no.
including	incl.	Nummer	Nr.
Incorporated	Inc.[4]	nummer	nr.
introduction	introd.	nuovamente	nuov.
izdája	izd.	odbitka	odb.
izmenjeno	izm.	oddział	oddz.
jaargang	jaarg.	Old Testament	O.T.
Jahrgang	Jahrg.	omarbeidet	omarb.
javított	jav.	oplag	opl.
jilid	jil.	opplag	oppl.
Kalendae	Kal.	opracowane	oprac.
kiadás	kiad.	opus	op.
kilometre, -s	km.	otisk	ot.
kniha	kn.	page, -s	p.
knjiga	knj.	paperback	pbk.
kötet	köt.	part, -s	pt., pts.[7]
księgarnia	księg.	parte	pt.
leto	l.	partie, -s	ptie, pties[7]
librairie	libr.	phonogram (copyright)	p
Lieferung	Lfg.	photograph, -s	photo., photos.[8]
Limited	Ltd.[4]	plate number, -s	pl. no.
livraison	livr.	poprawione	popr.
maatschappij	mij.	portrait, -s	port., ports.

TERM	ABBREVIATION	TERM	ABBREVIATION
posthumous	posth.	supplement	suppl.
predelan	pred.	svazek	sv.
preface	pref.	szám	sz.
preliminary	prelim.	tahun	th.
printing	print.[9]	talleres gráficos	tall. gráf.
privately printed	priv. print.	Teil, Theil	T.
projection	proj.[1]	tenor	T^2
proširen	proš.	tipografía, tipográfica	tip.
przekład	przekł.	tiskárna	tisk.
przerobione	przerob.	title page	t.p.
pseudonym	pseud.	tjetakan	tjet.
publishing	pub.	tome	t.
quadraphonic	quad.	tomo	t.
redakcja	red.	towarzystwo	tow.
refondu, -e	ref.	translator	tr.[6]
réimpression	réimpr.	typographical	typog.
report	rept.	typographie, typographique	typ.
reprinted	repr.	udarbejdet	udarb.
reproduced	reprod.	udgave	udg.
reviderade	revid.	udgivet	udg.
revisé, -e	rev.	uitgaaf	uitg.
revised	rev.	uitgegeven	uitg.
revolutions per minute	rpm	uitgevers	uitg.
revu, -e	rev.	umgearbeitet	umgearb.
right ascension	RA^1	unaccompanied	unacc.
riveduto	riv.	Universitäts-Buchdrucker, -ei	
ročník	roč.		Univ.-Buchdr.
rocznik	rocz.	upplaga	uppl.
rok	r.	utarbeidet	utarb.
rozszerzone	rozsz.	utgave	utg.
second, -s	sec.	utgiven	utg.
série	sér.	uzupełnione	uzup.
series	ser.	verbesserte	verb.
sešit	seš.	vermehrte	verm.
signature	sig.	volume, -s	v.
silent	si.	volume, -s	vol., vols.[10]
sine loco	s.l.	vuosikerta	vuosik.
sine nomine	s.n.	vydání	vyd.
skład główny	skł. gł.	wydanie	wyd.
soprano	S^2	wydawnictwo	wydawn.
sound	sd.[8]	wydział	wydz.
stabilimento tipográfico	stab. tip.	założba	zal.
stereophonic	stereo.	zeszyt	zesz.
številka	št.	zväzok	zv.
stronica	str.	zvezek	zv.
superintendent	supt.		
Superintendent of Documents	Supt. of Docs.		

---

1. Use only in recording mathematical data in entries for cartographic materials.
2. Use only in notes to indicate voice range of vocal works.
3. Use only in uniform titles in listing languages.

B.10. CYRILLIC ALPHABET ABBREVIATIONS

TERM	ABBREVIATION	TERM	ABBREVIATION
без имена	б.и.	издание	изд.
без имени	б.и.	издательство	изд-во
без імені	б.і.	имени	им.
без места	б.м.	Императорский	Имп.
без месца	б.м.	институт	ин-т
без міста	б.м.	исправленный	испр.
без място	б.м.	исследовательский	иссл.
видання	вид.	інститут	ін-т
видавництво	вид-во	књига	књ.
відповідальний	відп.	книгоиздательство	кн-во
военный	воен.	книга	кн.
всероссийский	всерос.	комитет	ком-т
всесоюзный	всес.	литература	лит-ра
вступление,		література	літ-ра
вступительный	вступ.	медицинский	мед.
выдавецтва	выд-ва	музыкальный	муз.
выпуск	вып.	народный	нар.
географический	геогр.	науковий	наук.
геологичецкий	геол.	научный	науч.
главный	глав.	областной	обл.
год	г.	оборонный	обор.
головний	гол.	обработанный	обраб.
городской	гор.	общество	об-во
государственный	гос.	ответственный	отв.
губернский	губ.	отделение	отд-ние
державний	держ.	палітычны	паліт.
дзяржаўны	дзярж.	педагогический	педагог.
диссертация	дисс.	переработанный	перер.
дополненный	доп.	пересмотренный	пересм.
державен	држ.	полиграфический	полигр.
държавен	държ.	политический	полит.
друкарня	друк.	політичний	політ.
електричний	електр.	предисловие	предисл.
енергетичний	енерг.	преработен	прер.
железнодорожный	жел-дор.	промышленность	промышл.
заглавие	загл.	радянський	рад.
и другие	и др.	редакция	ред.
и так далее	и т. д.	рік	р.
и тому подобное	и т. п.	рэдакцыя	рэд.

4. Use only in names of firms and other corporate bodies.

5. Use in headings and in indicating the period when a manuscript was probably written.

6. Use only in a heading as a designation of function (see 21.0D).

7. Do not use in recording the extent of the item in the case of music.

8. Do not use in general or specific material designations.

9. Do not use in recording the date of printing in the publication, distribution, etc., area (see 1.4F6, 1.4G4, and 2.4G2).

10. Use at the beginning of a statement and before a roman numeral.

TERM	ABBREVIATION	TERM	ABBREVIATION
селскостопански	сел.-стоп.	товариство	т-во
сельскохозяйствен-ный	с.-х.	товарищество	т-во
сільськогоспо-дарський	с.-г.	том	т.
		транспортный	трансп.
скорочений	скор.	украинский	укр.
советский	сов.	университетский	унив.
сокращенный	сокр.	управление	упр.
социалистический	социалист.	учебный	учеб.
социальный	соц.	финансовый	фин.
статистический	стат.	химический	хим.
страница	стр.	хімічний	хім.
строительный	строит.	художественный	худож.
текстильный	текстил.	центральный	центр.
теоретический	теорет.	часть	ч.
технический	техн.	экономический	экон.
типография	тип.	электрический	электр.
типо-литография	типо-лит.	энергетический	энерг.
		юридический	юрид.

B.11. GREEK ALPHABET ABBREVIATIONS

TERM	ABBREVIATION	TERM	ABBREVIATION
Ἀδελφοί	Ἀφοί	ἐπηυξημένη	ἐπηυξ.
ἀναθεωρημένη	ἀναθ.	καὶ ἄλλοι	κ.ἄ.
ἄνευ ὀνόματος	ἄ.ὀ.	μέρος	μέρ.
ἄνευ τόπου	ἄ.τ.	Πανεπιστήμιον	Παν.
ἀριθμός	ἀρ.	Σύλλογος	Σύλλ.
βελτιωμένη	βελτ.	τεῦχος	τεῦχ.
δελτίον	δελτ.	τμῆμα	τμ.
δηλαδή	δηλ.	τόμος	τ.
ἔκδοσις	ἔκδ.	Τυπογραφεῖον	Τυπογρ.
Ἐκδοτικός Οἶκος	Ἐκδοτ. Οἶκος		

B.12. HEBREW ALPHABET ABBREVIATIONS

TERM	ABBREVIATION	TERM	ABBREVIATION
אויסנאבע	אויסג.	חסר מוציא לאור	חמו"ל
אויפלאנע	אויפל.	חסר מקום	ח"מ
און אנדערע	א"א	טייל	טל.
אן ארט	א"א	טעות דפוס	ט"ד
אן פארלאג	אפ"ג	יארנאנג	יארג.
באנד	בד.	מהדורה	מהד'
גליון	גל'.	מספר	מס'
דאס הייסט	ד"ה	נומער	נומ.
זאת אומרת	ז"א	פארבעסערטע	פארב.
חוברת	חוב'	פארמערטע	פארמ.

B.13. ABBREVIATIONS USED IN CITING BIBLIOGRAPHIC SOURCES

B.13A. Use common, self-explanatory abbreviations of the type listed below in citing the source of data used in the catalogue entry, provided the use of abbreviations does not obscure the language of the source cited.

TERM	ABBREVIATION	TERM	ABBREVIATION
American	Amer.	directory	direct.
annuaire	ann.	encyclopedia	encycl.
annuario	ann.	English	Engl.
anuario	an.	history	hist.
bibliography	bibl.	Katalog	Kat.
biography	biog.	literature	lit.
British	Brit.	littérature	litt.
catalog(ue)	cat.	museum	mus.
cyclopedia	cycl.	national	nat.
diccionario	dicc.	report	rept.
dictionary	dict.		

B.14. NAMES OF CERTAIN COUNTRIES, STATES, PROVINCES, TERRITORIES, ETC.

B.14A. Use the following abbreviations of the names of certain countries and of states, provinces, territories, etc., of Australia, Canada, and the United States when used:

1) as additions to certain other place names (see 23.4)
2) as additions to names of certain corporate bodies (see 24.4C and 24.9)
3) as additions to the name of the place of publication or distribution in the publication, distribution, etc., area (see 1.4C3)
4) in notes.

Do not abbreviate the name of a city or town even if it has the same name as a state, etc., listed below (e.g., *Washington, D.C.* not *Wash., D.C.*). Do not abbreviate any place name that is not in the list.

NAME	ABBREVIATION	NAME	ABBREVIATION
Alabama	Ala.	Illinois	Ill.
Alberta	Alta.	Indiana	Ind.
Arizona	Ariz.	Kansas	Kan.
Arkansas	Ark.	Kentucky	Ky.
Australian Capital		Louisiana	La.
Territory	A.C.T.	Maine	Me.
British Columbia	B.C.	Manitoba	Man.
California	Calif.	Maryland	Md.
Colorado	Colo.	Massachusetts	Mass.
Connecticut	Conn.	Michigan	Mich.
Delaware	Del.	Minnesota	Minn.
District of Columbia	D.C.	Mississippi	Miss.
Distrito Federal	D.F.	Missouri	Mo.
Florida	Fla.	Montana	Mont.
Georgia	Ga.	Nebraska	Neb.

NAME	ABBREVIATION	NAME	ABBREVIATION
Nevada	Nev.	Saskatchewan	Sask.
New Brunswick	N.B.	South Australia	S. Aust.
New Hampshire	N.H.	South Carolina	S.C.
New Jersey	N.J.	South Dakota	S.D.
New Mexico	N.M.	Tasmania	Tas.
New South Wales	N.S.W.	Tennessee	Tenn.
New York	N.Y.	Territory of Hawaii	T.H.
New Zealand	N.Z.	Texas	Tex.
Newfoundland	Nfld.	Union of Soviet Socialist	
North Carolina	N.C.	Republics	U.S.S.R.
North Dakota	N.D.	United Kingdom	U.K.
Northern Territory	N.T.	United States	U.S.
Northwest Territories	N.W.T.	Vermont	Vt.
Nova Scotia	N.S.	Victoria	Vic.
Oklahoma	Okla.	Virgin Islands	V.I.
Ontario	Ont.	Virginia	Va.
Oregon	Or.	Washington	Wash.
Pennsylvania	Pa.	West Virginia	W. Va.
Prince Edward Island	P.E.I.	Western Australia	W.A.
Puerto Rico	P.R.	Wisconsin	Wis.
Queensland	Qld.	Wyoming	Wyo.
Rhode Island	R.I.	Yukon Territory	Yukon
Russian Soviet Federated			
Socialist Republic	R.S.F.S.R.		

B.15. NAMES OF THE MONTHS

Use abbreviations of the names of the months in languages not listed below if they appear in style manuals for the language concerned.

BELORUSSIAN	BULGARIAN	CZECH	DANISH
студз.	ян.	led.	jan.
лют.	февр.	ún.	febr.
сак.	март	břez.	marts
крас.	април	dub.	april
май	май	květ.	maj
чэрв.	юни	červ.	juni
ліп.	юли	červen.	juli
жнівень	авг.	srp.	aug.
верас.	септ.	září	sept.
кастр.	окт.	říj.	okt.
ліст.	ноем.	list.	nov.
снеж.	дек.	pros.	dec.

DUTCH	ENGLISH	ESTONIAN	FRENCH
jan.	Jan.	jaan.	janv.
feb.	Feb.	veebr.	févr.
maart	Mar.	märts	mars
apr.	Apr.	apr.	avril
mei	May	mai	mai
juni	June	juuni	juin
juli	July	juuli	juil.
aug.	Aug.	aug.	août
sept.	Sept.	sept.	sept.
oct.	Oct.	okt.	oct.
nov.	Nov.	nov.	nov.
dec.	Dec.	dets.	déc.

GERMAN	GREEK, MODERN	HUNGARIAN	INDONESIAN
Jan. (Jän.)	'Ιαν.	jan.	Jan. (Djan.)
Feb.	Φεβρ.	feb.	Peb.
März	Μάρτ.	márc.	Mrt.
Apr.	'Απρ.	ápr.	Apr.
Mai	Μάϊos	máj.	Mei (Mai)
Juni	'Ιούν.	jún.	Juni (Djuni)
Juli	'Ιούλ.	júl.	Juli (Djuli)
Aug.	Αΰγ.	aug.	Ag.
Sept.	Σεπτ.	szept.	Sept.
Okt.	'Οκτ.	okt.	Okt.
Nov.	Νοέμ.	nov.	Nop.
Dez.	Δεκ.	dec.	Des.

ITALIAN	LATIN	LATVIAN	LITHUANIAN
genn.	Ian.	jan.	saus.
febbr.	Febr.	feb.	vas.
mar.	Mart.	marts	kovas
apr.	Apr.	apr.	bal.
magg.	Mai	maijs	geg.
giugno	Iun.	junijs	birž.
luglio	Iul.	julijs	liepa
ag.	Aug.	aug.	rugp.
sett.	Sept.	sept.	rugs.
ott.	Oct.	okt.	spalis
nov.	Nov.	nov.	lapkr.
dic.	Dec.	dec.	gr.

MALAYSIAN	NORWEGIAN	POLISH	PORTUGUESE
Jan.	jan.	stycz.	jan.
Feb.	febr.	luty	fev.
Mac	mars	mar.	março
Apr.	april	kwiec.	abril
Mei	mai	maj	maio
Jun	juni	czerw.	junho
Julai	juli	lip.	julho
Og.	aug.	sierp.	agosto
Sept.	sept.	wrzes.	set.
Okt.	okt.	paźdz.	out.
Nov.	nov.	listop.	nov.
Dis.	des.	grudz.	dez.

ROMANIAN	RUSSIAN	SERBO-CROATIAN		SLOVAK	
Ian.	янв.	јан.	siječ.	l'ad.	jan.
Feb.	февр.	фебр.	velj.	ún.	feb.
Mar.	март (мартъ)	март	ožuj.	brez.	mar.
Apr.	апр.	април	trav.	dub.	apr.
Mai	май	мај	svib.	kvet.	máj
Iunie	июнь (іюнь)	јуни	lip.	červ.	jún
Iulie	июль (іюль)	јули	srp.	červen.	júl
Aug.	авг.	ауг.	kol.	srp.	aug.
Sept.	сент.	септ.	ruj.	zári.	sept.
Oct.	окт.	окт.	list.	ruj.	okt.
Noem.	ноябрь	нов.	stud.	list.	nov.
Dec.	дек.	дэц.	pros.	pros.	dec.

SLOVENIAN	SPANISH	SWEDISH	UKRAINIAN	WELSH
jan.	enero	jan.	січ.	Ion.
feb.	feb.	febr.	лют.	Chwef.
mar.	marzo	mars	бер.	Maw.
apr.	abr.	april	квіт.	Ebr.
maj	mayo	maj	трав.	Mai
jun.	jun.	juni	чер.	Meh.
iul.	jul.	juli	лип.	Gorff.
avg.	agosto	aug.	серп.	Awst
sept.	sept. (set.)	sept.	вер.	Medi
okt.	oct.	okt.	жовт.	Hyd.
nov.	nov.	nov.	лист.	Tach.
dec.	dic.	dec.	груд.	Rhag.

NUMERALS

Contents

C.1. GENERAL RULE

C.1A. Apply the following rules to all items published in the nineteenth century or later. Apply them also to items published before the nineteenth century unless rules 2.12–2.18 instruct otherwise.

C.2. ARABIC VS. ROMAN

C.2A. Headings

C.2A1. Use roman numerals in headings for persons (e.g., rulers, popes) and for corporate bodies identified by names including roman numerals unless, in the case of a corporate body, a particular rule instructs otherwise (see 24.7B2).

> **John XXIII,** *Pope*
>
> **XXth Century Heating & Ventilating Co.**

C.2A2. In uniform titles, use roman numerals that are integral parts of the name of the work.

> **Sancho II y el cerco de Zamora**

In the case of numerals used to identify particular parts of a work, follow the instructions in the appropriate rule (see 25.6A2 and 25.18A3).

C.2B. Description

C.2B1. Substitute arabic numerals for roman in the following areas and elements of the bibliographic description:

a) in an edition statement
b) in the material (or type of publication) specific details area unless a particular rule directs otherwise (see 3.3B2) or unless C.2B2 applies
c) in the date of publication, distribution, etc., element
d) in the other physical details element of the physical description area
e) in the series numbering in the series area unless C.2B2 applies.

C.2B2. Use roman numerals in the areas and elements listed in C.2B1 if the substitution of arabic numerals makes the statement less clear (e.g., when roman and arabic numerals are used in conjunction to distinguish the volume, section, series, or other group from the number, part, or other division of that group).

> (The Washington papers ; vol. IV, 36)

C.2B3. When using roman numerals, give them in capitals except those used in paging or page references and those appearing in lowercase in the chief source of information or in quoted notes. Use lowercase roman numerals in paging or page references even when capitals appear in the item.

> xliii, 289 p.

C.3. ARABIC NUMERALS VS. NUMBERS EXPRESSED AS WORDS

C.3A. Headings

C.3A1. Retain numbers expressed as words in the names of corporate bodies unless a particular rule instructs otherwise (see 24.7B2).

> **Four Corners Geological Society**

C.3A2. Retain numbers expressed as words in uniform titles if they are an integral part of the name of the work. In the case of numbers used to identify particular parts of a work, follow the instructions in the appropriate rule (see 25.6A2 and 25.18A3).

> **Quinze joies de mariage**

C.3B. Description

C.3B1. Substitute arabic numerals for numbers expressed as words in the following areas and elements of the bibliographic description:

a) in an edition statement
b) in the material (or type of publication) specific details area unless a particular rule directs otherwise (see 3.3B2)

c) in the date of publication, distribution, etc., element
d) in the physical description area
e) in the series numbering.

C.4. NUMERALS BEGINNING NOTES

C.4A. Express a numeral that is the first word of a note in words unless the note is a quotation. In the latter case, give the numeral as it appears in the source.

> First ed. published in 1954
>
> "5th anniversary printing"—T.p. verso
>
> Four no. a year, 1931; 5 no. a year, 1932-1934

C.5. ORIENTAL NUMERALS

C.5A. In cataloguing Arabic alphabet, Far Eastern, Greek, Hebrew, Indic, etc., materials, substitute roman numerals or Western-style arabic numerals for numerals in the vernacular as instructed in the following rules.

C.5B. Use roman numerals in romanized headings for persons identified by numerals (e.g., rulers).

C.5C. Use Western-style arabic numerals in romanized headings for corporate bodies and in uniform titles.

> **Thawrat 25 Māyū, 1969**
>
> **Lajnah al- 'Ulyā li-Iḥtifālāt 14 Tammūz**

C.5D. Use Western-style arabic numerals in the following areas and elements of the bibliographic description:

1) in an edition statement
2) in the material (or type of publication) specific details area unless a particular rule directs otherwise (see 3.3B2)
3) in the date of publication, distribution, etc., element
4) in the physical description area
5) in the series numbering.

C.5E. Consider inclusive dates and other numbers to be a single unit in languages that are read from right to left.

> 1960-1965   *not*   1965-1960

Add punctuation to the left of the inclusive dates or numbers.

> .1973-1976

C.6. INCLUSIVE NUMBERS

C.6A. Give inclusive dates and other inclusive numbers in full.

> 1967-1972
>
> p. 117-128

C.7. ALTERNATIVE DATES

C.7A. When alternative dates of birth or death are given in headings for persons (see 22.17), give the second of the alternatives as it is spoken.

> *d.* 1506 *or* 7
> *d.* 1819 *or* 20
> *b.* 1899 *or* 1900

In all other cases, give the numbers in full.

C.8. ORDINAL NUMERALS

C.8A. In the case of English-language items, record ordinal numerals in the form 1st, 2nd, 3rd, 4th, etc.

C.8B. In the case of other languages, follow the usage of the language if ascertainable.[1]

> 1er, 1re, 2^e, 3^e, *etc.*
> (*French*)
> 1., 2., 3., *etc.*
> (*German*)
> 1°, 1^a, 2°, 2^a, 3°, 3^a, *etc.*
> (*Italian*)

C.8C. For Chinese, Japanese, and Korean items, accompany the arabic numeral by the character indicating that the numeral is ordinal.

C.8D. If the usage of a language cannot be ascertained, use the form 1., 2., 3., etc.

---

1. A useful source for the form of ordinal numerals in European languages is: Allen, C.G. *A Manual of European Languages for Librarians.* — London ; New York : Bowker, 1975.

GLOSSARY

This glossary contains definitions of most of the technical bibliographic and cataloguing terms (for both print and nonprint materials) used in these rules. The terms have been defined only within the context of the rules. For definitions of other terms, consult the standard glossaries of bibliographic and library terms or technical dictionaries.

Access point. A name, term, code, etc., under which a bibliographic record may be searched and identified. *See also* Heading.

Accompanying material. Material issued with, and intended to be used with, the item being catalogued.

Activity card. A card printed with words, numerals, and/or pictures to be used by an individual or a group as a basis for performing a specific activity. Usually issued in sets. *See also* Game, Kit.

Adaptation (Music). A musical work that represents a distinct alteration of another work (e.g., a free transcription); a work that paraphrases parts of various works or the general style of another composer; a work that is merely based on other music (e.g., variations on a theme). *See also* Arrangement (Music).

Added entry. An entry, additional to the main entry, by which an item is represented in a catalogue; a secondary entry. *See also* Main entry.

Added title page. A title page preceding or following the title page chosen as the basis for the description of the item. It may be more general (e.g., a series title page), or equally general (e.g., a title page in another language). *See also* Series title page.

Alternative title. The second part of a title proper that consists of two parts, each of which is a title; the parts are joined by *or* or its equivalent in another language (e.g., *The tempest, or, The enchanted island*).

Analytical entry. An entry for a part of an item for which a comprehensive entry is also made.

Analytical note. The statement in an analytical entry relating the part being analyzed to the item of which it is a part.

Anonymous. Of unknown authorship.

Architectural rendering. A pictorial representation of a building intended to show, before it has been built, how the building will look when completed.

Area. A major section of the bibliographic description, comprising data of a particular category or set of categories. *See also* Element.

Arrangement (Music). A musical work, or a portion thereof, rewritten for a medium of performance different from that for which the work was originally intended; a simplified version of a work for the same medium of performance. *See also* Adaptation (Music).

Art original. An original two- or three-dimensional work of art (other than an art print (q.v.) or a photograph) created by the artist (e.g., a painting, drawing, or sculpture, as contrasted to a reproduction of a painting, drawing, or sculpture).

Art print. An engraving, etching, lithograph, woodcut, etc., printed from the plate prepared by the artist.

Art reproduction. A mechanically reproduced copy of a work of art, generally as one of a commercial edition.

Artefact. Any object made or modified by one or more persons.

Atlas. A volume of maps, plates, engravings, tables, etc., with or without descriptive text. It may be an independent publication or it may have been issued as accompanying material (q.v.).

Audiorecording. *See* Sound recording.

Author. *See* Personal author.

Author-title added entry. *See* Name-title added entry.

Author-title reference. *See* Name-title reference.

Binder's title. A title lettered on the cover of an item by a binder, as distinguished from a title on the publisher's original cover. *See also* Cover title, Spine title.

Braille. Material intended for the visually impaired and using embossed characters formed by raised dots in six-dot cells. Nemeth code is a form of braille used in mathematics.

Broadsheet. *See* Broadside.

Broadside. A separately published item consisting of a piece of paper, printed on one side only and intended to be read unfolded; usually intended to be posted or publicly distributed. Examples of broadsides are proclamations, handbills, ballad-sheets, news-sheets. *See also* Sheet.

Caption title. A title given at the beginning of the first page of the text or, in the case of a musical score, immediately above the opening bars of the music.

Carrier. *See* Physical carrier.

Cartographic material. Any material representing the whole or part of the earth or any celestial body at any scale. Cartographic materials include two- and three-dimensional maps and plans (including maps of imaginary places); aeronautical, navigational, and celestial charts; atlases; globes; block diagrams; sections; aerial photographs with a cartographic purpose; bird's-eye views (map views), etc.

Case binding. A method of binding in which a hard cover is made separately from the book and later attached to it.

Cased. *See* Case binding.

Catalogue. 1. A list of library materials contained in a collection, a library, or a group of libraries, arranged according to some definite plan. 2. In a wider sense, a list of materials prepared for a particular purpose (e.g., an exhibition catalogue, a sales catalogue).

Chart. An opaque sheet that exhibits data in graphic or tabular form (e.g., a wall chart).

Chart (Cartography). *See* Map.

Chief source of information. The source of bibliographic data to be given preference as the source from which a bibliographic description (or portion thereof) is prepared.

Chinese style. *See* Traditional format (Oriental books).

Chorus score. A score of a vocal work showing only the chorus parts, with accompaniment, if any, arranged for keyboard instrument. *See also* Vocal score.

Cinefilm. *See* Motion picture.

Close score. A musical score giving all the parts on a minimum number of staves, normally two, as with hymns.

Collaborator. One who works with one or more associates to produce a work: all may make the same kind of contribution, as in the case of shared responsibility (see 21.6), or they may make different kinds of contributions, as in the case of collaboration between an artist and a writer (see 21.24). *See also* Joint author, Mixed responsibility, Shared responsibility.

Collection. 1. Three or more independent works or parts of works by one author published together. 2. Two or more independent works or parts of works by more than one author published together and not written for the same occasion or for the publication in hand.

Collective title. A title proper that is an inclusive title for an item containing several works. *See also* Uniform title 3.

Colophon. A statement at the end of an item giving information about one or more of the following: the title, author(s), publisher, printer, date of publication or printing. It may include other information.

Coloured illustration. An illustration in two or more colours. (Neither black nor white is a colour.)

Compiler. 1. One who produces a collection by selecting and putting together matter from the works of various persons or bodies. 2. One who selects and puts together in one publication matter from the works of one person or body. *See also* Editor.

Compound surname. A surname consisting of two or more proper names, sometimes connected by a hyphen, or conjunction, and/or preposition.

Computer file. A file (data and/or programs) encoded for manipulation by computer.

Condensed score. A musical score giving only the principal musical parts on a minimum number of staves, and generally organized by instrumental sections.

Conference. 1. A meeting of individuals or representatives of various bodies for the purpose of discussing and/or acting on topics of common interest. 2. A meeting of representatives of a corporate body that constitutes its legislative or governing body.

Container. Any housing for an item, a group of items, or part of an item that is physically separable from the material being housed. *See also* Physical carrier.

Continuation. 1. A supplement (q.v.). 2. A part issued in continuance of a monograph, a serial, or a series.

Conventional name. A name, other than the real or official name, by which a corporate body, place, or thing has come to be known.

Conventional title. *See* Uniform title.

Corporate body. An organization or group of persons that is identified by a particular name and that acts, or may act, as an entity. Typical examples of corporate bodies are associations, institutions, business firms, nonprofit enterprises, governments, government agencies, religious bodies, local churches, and conferences.

Cover title. A title printed on the cover of an item as issued. *See also* Binder's title, Spine title.

Cross-reference. *See* Reference.

Data set name. *See* File name (Computer files).

Diorama. A three-dimensional representation of a scene created by placing objects, figures, etc., in front of a two-dimensional painted background.

Direct access (Computer files). The use of computer files via carriers (e.g., disks, cassettes, cartridges) designed to be inserted into a computer or its auxiliary equipment by the user. *See also* Remote access (Computer files).

Distributor. An agent or agency that has exclusive or shared marketing rights for an item.

Double leaf. A leaf of double size with a fold at the fore edge or at the top edge of the item. *See also* Traditional format (Oriental books).

Edition: Books, pamphlets, fascicles, single sheets, etc. All copies produced from essentially the same type image (whether by direct contact or by photographic or other methods) and issued by the same entity. *See also* Facsimile reproduction, Impression, Issue, Reprint.

Edition: Computer files. All copies embodying essentially the same content and issued by the same entity.

Edition: Other materials. All copies produced from essentially the same master copy and issued by the same entity. A change in the identity of the distributor does not mean a change of edition. *See also* Facsimile reproduction, Issue.

Edition: Unpublished items. All copies made from essentially the same original production (e.g., the original and carbon copies of a typescript).

Editor. One who prepares for publication an item not his or her own. The editorial work may be limited to the preparation of the item for the manufacturer, or it may include supervision of the manufacturing, revision (restitution), or elucidation of the content of the item, and the addition of an introduction, notes, and other critical matter. In some cases, it may involve the technical direction of a staff of persons engaged in creating or compiling the content of the item. *See also* Compiler.

Element. A word, phrase, or group of characters representing a distinct unit of bibliographic information and forming part of an area (q.v.) of the description.

Engineering drawing. *See* Technical drawing.

Entry. A record of an item in a catalogue. *See also* Heading.

Entry word. The word by which an entry is arranged in the catalogue, usually the first word (other than an article) of the heading. *See also* Heading.

Explanatory reference. An elaborated *see* or *see also* reference that explains the circumstances under which the headings involved should be consulted.

Explicit. A statement at the end of the text of a manuscript or early printed book, or at the end of one of its divisions, indicating its conclusion and sometimes giving the author's name and the title of the work.

Extent of item. The first element of the physical description area. It gives the number and the specific material designation of the units of the item being described and, in some cases, other indications of the extent (e.g., duration). *See also* Specific material designation.

Facsimile reproduction. A reproduction simulating the physical appearance of the original in addition to reproducing its content exactly. *See also* Reprint.

Fascicle. One of the temporary divisions of a printed item that, for convenience in printing or publication, is issued in small installments, usually incomplete in themselves; they do not necessarily coincide with any formal division of the work into parts, etc. Usually the fascicle is protected by temporary paper wrappers. It may or may not be numbered. A fascicle is distinguished from a part (q.v.) by being a temporary division of a work rather than a formal component unit.

File, Computer. *See* Computer file.

File name (Computer files). A designation used in a computer system to identify a file. Sometimes, a file name is called a "data set name." For external designations of a computer file, *see* Title proper.

Filing title. *See* Uniform title.

Filmstrip. A length of film containing a succession of images intended for projection one at a time, with or without recorded sound.

Flash card. A card or other opaque material printed with words, numerals, or pictures and designed for rapid display.

Format. In its widest sense, a particular physical presentation of an item.

Format (Texts). The number of times the printed sheet has been folded to make the leaves of a book (e.g., folio (one fold giving two leaves), quarto (two folds giving four leaves)).

Full score. *See* Score.

Game. An item or set of materials designed for play according to prescribed or implicit rules and intended for recreation or instruction. *See also* Activity card, Kit, Toy.

General material designation. A term indicating the broad class of material to which an item belongs (e.g., *sound recording*). *See also* Specific material designation.

Globe. A model of the earth or other celestial body, depicted on the surface of a sphere.

Graphic. A two-dimensional representation whether opaque (e.g., art originals and reproductions, flash cards, photographs, technical drawings) or intended to be viewed, or projected without motion, by means of an optical device (e.g., filmstrips, stereographs, slides).

Half title. A title of a publication appearing on a leaf preceding the title page.

Harmony (Bible). 1. An arrangement of passages of the Bible on the same topic into parallel columns so that similarities and differences may be compared readily. 2. An interweaving of such passages into a continuous text.

Heading. A name, word, or phrase placed at the head of a catalogue entry to provide an access point. *See also* Access point.

Impression. All copies of an edition of a book, pamphlet, etc., printed at one time. *See also* Issue, Reprint.

Incipit. The opening words of a manuscript or early printed book, or of one of its divisions. It frequently includes the word "incipit" or its equivalent in another language. An incipit at the beginning of a work often contains the name of the author and the title of the work.

Initial title element. The word or words selected from the title of a musical work and placed first in the uniform title for that work. If no additions to the initial title element are required by the rules, it becomes the uniform title for the work.

International intergovernmental body. An international body created by intergovernmental action.

International Standard Book Number (ISBN). *See* Standard number.

International Standard Serial Number (ISSN). *See* Standard number.

Issue. Copies of an edition forming a distinct group that are distinguished from other copies of that edition by minor but well-defined variations (e.g., a new impression of a book for which minor revisions have been incorporated into the original type image). *See also* Impression, Reprint.

Item. A document or set of documents in any physical form, published, issued, or treated as an entity, and as such forming the basis for a single bibliographic description.

Jacket (Sound disc). *See* Sleeve.

Japanese style. *See* Traditional format (Oriental books).

Joint author. A person who collaborates with one or more other persons to produce a work in relation to which the collaborators perform the same function. *See also* Shared responsibility.

Key-title. The unique name assigned to a serial by the International Serials Data System (ISDS).

Kit. 1. An item containing two or more categories of material, no one of which is identifiable as the predominant constituent of the item; also designated "multimedia item" (q.v.). 2. A single-medium package of textual material (e.g., a "press kit," a set of printed test materials, an assemblage of printed materials published under the name "Jackdaw"). *See also* Activity card, Game.

Leaf. One of the units into which the original sheet or half sheet of paper, parchment, etc., is folded to form part of a book, pamphlet, journal, etc.; each leaf consists of two pages, one on each side, either or both of which may be blank.

Machine-readable data file. *See* Computer file.

Macroform. A generic term for any medium, transparent or opaque, bearing images large enough to be read easily by the naked eye. *See also* Microform.

Main entry. The complete catalogue record of an item, presented in the form by which the entity is to be uniformly identified and cited. The main entry may include the tracing(s) (q.v.). *See also* Added entry.

Main heading. The first part of a heading that includes a subheading (q.v.).

Manuscript. Writings (including musical scores, maps, etc.) made by hand, typescripts, and inscriptions on clay tablets, stone, etc.

Map. A representation, normally to scale and on a flat medium, of a selection of material or abstract features on, or in relation to, the surface of the earth or of another celestial body.

Map section. *See* Section (Cartography).

Masthead. A statement of title, ownership, editors, etc., of a newspaper or periodical. In the case of newspapers it is commonly found on the editorial page or at the top of page one, and, in the case of periodicals, on the contents page.

Mechanical drawing. *See* Technical drawing.

Microfiche. A sheet of film bearing a number of microimages in a two-dimensional array.

Microfilm. A length of film bearing a number of microimages in linear array.

Microform. A generic term for any medium, transparent or opaque, bearing microimages. *See also* Macroform.

Microopaque. A sheet of opaque material bearing a number of microimages in a two-dimensional array.

Microscope slide. A slide designed for holding a minute object to be viewed through a microscope or by a microprojector.

Miniature score. A musical score not primarily intended for performance use, with the notation and/or text reduced in size.

Mixed authorship. *See* Mixed responsibility.

Mixed responsibility. A work of mixed responsibility is one in which different persons or bodies contribute to its intellectual or artistic content by performing different kinds of activities (e.g., adapting or illustrating a work written by another person). *See also* Joint author, Shared responsibility.

Mock-up. A representation of a device or process that may be modified for training or analysis to emphasize a particular part or function; it usually has movable parts that can be manipulated.

Model. A three-dimensional representation of a real thing. *See also* Toy.

Monograph. A nonserial item (i.e., an item either complete in one part or complete, or intended to be completed, in a finite number of separate parts).

Monographic series. *See* Series 1.

Motion picture. A length of film, with or without recorded sound, bearing a sequence of images that create the illusion of movement when projected in rapid succession.

Multimedia item. An item containing two or more categories of material, no one of which is identifiable as the predominant constituent of the item; also designated "kit" (q.v.).

Multipart file. A bibliographic entity that consists of more than one computer file (q.v.).

Multipart item. A monograph complete, or intended to be completed, in a finite number of separate parts.

Multivolume monograph. *See* Multipart item.

Music (large print). A term used as a general material designation for printed music intended for use by the visually impaired.

Musical presentation statement. A term or phrase found in the chief source of information of a publication of printed music or a music manuscript that indicates the physical presentation of the music (e.g., score, miniature score, score and parts). This type of statement should be distinguished from one that indicates an arrangement or edition of a musical work (e.g., vocal score, 2-piano edition, version with orchestra accompaniment, chorus score).

Musical work. 1. A musical composition that is a single unit intended for performance as a whole. 2. A set of musical compositions with a group title (not necessarily intended for performance as a whole). 3. A group of musical compositions with a single opus number.

Name-title added entry. An added entry consisting of the name of a person or corporate body and the title of an item.

Name-title reference. A reference made from the name of a person or a corporate body and the title of an item.

Object. A three-dimensional artefact (or replica of an artefact) or a naturally occurring entity. *See also* Realia.

Other title information. A title borne by an item other than the title proper or parallel or series title(s); also any phrase appearing in conjunction with the title proper, etc., indicative of the character, contents, etc., of the item or the motives for, or occasion of, its production or publication. The term includes subtitles, avant-titres, etc., but does not include variations on the title proper (e.g., spine titles, sleeve titles).

Overhead projectual. *See* Transparency.

Overlay. A transparent sheet containing matter that, when superimposed on another sheet, modifies the data on the latter.

Parallel title. The title proper in another language and/or script.

Part. 1. One of the subordinate units into which an item has been divided by the author, publisher, or manufacturer. In the case of printed monographs, generally synonymous with volume (q.v.); it is distinguished from a fascicle (q.v.) by being a component unit rather than a temporary division of a work. 2. As used in the physical description area, "part" designates bibliographic units intended to be bound several to a volume. *See also* Part (Music).

Part (Music). 1. The music for one of the participating voices or instruments in a musical work. 2. The written or printed copy of one or more (but not all) such parts for the use of one or more performers, designated in the physical description area as *part*.

Patronymic. A name derived from the given name of a father.

Personal author. The person chiefly responsible for the creation of the intellectual or artistic content of a work.

Phonorecord. *See* Sound recording.

Photocopy. A macroform photoreproduction produced directly on opaque material by radiant energy through contact or projection.

Physical carrier. A physical medium in which data, sound, images, etc., are stored. For certain categories of material, the physical carrier consists of a storage medium (e.g., tape, film) sometimes encased in a plastic, metal, etc., housing (e.g., cassette, cartridge) that is an integral part of the item. *See also* Container.

Piano [violin, etc.] conductor part. A performance part for a particular instrument of an ensemble work to which cues have been added for the other instruments to permit the performer of the part also to conduct the performance.

Piano score. A reduction of an orchestral score to a version for piano, on two staves.

Picture. A two-dimensional visual representation accessible to the naked eye and generally on an opaque backing. Used when a more specific term (e.g., art original, photograph, study print) is not appropriate.

Plan. A drawing showing relative positions on a horizontal plane (e.g., relative positions of parts of a building; a landscape design; the arrangement of furniture in a room or building; a graphic presentation of a military or naval plan).

Plan (Cartography). *See* Map.

Plate. A leaf containing illustrative matter, with or without explanatory text, that does not form part of either the preliminary or the main sequence of pages or leaves.

Plate number (Music). A numbering designation assigned to an item by a music publisher, usually printed at the bottom of each page, and sometimes appearing also on the title page. It may include initials, abbreviations, or words identifying a publisher and is sometimes followed by a number corresponding to the number of pages or plates. *See also* Publisher's number (Music).

Portfolio. A container for holding loose materials (e.g., paintings, drawings, papers, unbound sections of a book, and similar materials) consisting of two covers joined together at the back.

Praeses. A faculty moderator of an academic disputation, normally proposing a thesis and participating in the ensuing disputation.

Predominant name. The name or form of name of a person or corporate body that appears most frequently (1) in the person's works or works issued by the corporate body, or (2) in reference sources, in that order of preference.

Preliminaries. The title page(s) of an item, the verso of the title page(s), any pages preceding the title page(s), and the cover.

Printing. *See* Facsimile reproduction, Impression, Issue, Reprint.

Producer. 1. A person or corporate body that has artistic and/or intellectual responsibility for the form and content of an item. 2. An individual or organization that has responsibility for the technical aspect(s) (e.g., mixing of sound), manufacture or production of an item.

Profile (Cartography). A scale representation of the intersection of a vertical surface (which may or may not be a plane) with the surface of the ground, or of the intersection of such a vertical surface with that of a conceptual three-dimensional model representing phenomena having a continuous distribution (e.g., rainfall).

Pseudonym. A name assumed by an author to conceal or obscure his or her identity.

Publisher's number (Music). A numbering designation assigned to an item by a music publisher, appearing normally only on the title page, the cover, and/or the first page of music. It may include initials, abbreviations, or words identifying the publisher. *See also* Plate number (Music).

Radiograph. A photograph produced by the passage of radiation, such as X rays, gamma rays, or neutrons, through an opaque object.

Realia. An artefact or naturally occurring entity, as opposed to a replica. *See also* Object, Toy.

Recto. 1. The right-hand page of a book, usually bearing an odd page number. 2. The side of a printed sheet intended to be read first.

Reference. A direction from one heading or entry to another.

Reference source. Any publication from which authoritative information may be obtained. Not limited to reference works.

Reissue. *See* Issue, Reprint.

Related body. A corporate body that has a relation to another body other than a hierarchical relation (e.g., one that is founded but not controlled by another body; one that only receives financial support from another body; one that provides financial and/or other types of assistance to another body, such as "friends" groups; one whose members have also membership in or an association with another body, such as employees' associations and alumni associations).

Related music. *See* Adaptation (Music).

Releasing agent. An agent or agency responsible for the initial distribution of a motion picture.

Remote access (Computer files). The use of computer files via input/output devices connected electronically to a computer. *See also* Direct access (Computer files).

Reprint. 1. A new printing of an item made from the original type image, commonly by photographic methods. The reprint may reproduce the original exactly (an impression (q.v.)) or it may contain minor but well-defined variations (an issue (q.v.)). 2. A new edition with substantially unchanged text. *See also* Facsimile reproduction.

Respondent (Academic disputations). A candidate for a degree who, in an academic disputation, defends or opposes a thesis proposed by the praeses (q.v.); also called the "defendant."

Romanization. Conversion of names or text not written in the roman alphabet to roman-alphabet form.

Running title. A title, or abbreviated title, that is repeated at the head or foot of each page or leaf.

Score. A series of staves on which all the different instrumental and/or vocal parts of a musical work are written, one under the other in vertical alignment, so that the parts may be read simultaneously. *See also* Chorus score, Close score, Condensed score, Miniature score, Part (Music), Piano [violin, etc.] conductor part, Piano score, Short score, Vocal score.

Secondary entry. *See* Added entry.

Section (Cartography). A scale representation of a vertical surface (commonly a plane) displaying both the profile where it intersects the surface of the ground, or some conceptual model, and the underlying structures along the plane of intersection (e.g., a geological section).

Section (Serials). A separately published part of a serial, usually representing a particular subject category within the larger serial and identified by a designation that may be a topic, or an alphabetic or numeric designation, or a combination of these. *See also* Subseries.

Sequel. A literary or other imaginative work that is complete in itself but continues an earlier work.

Serial. A publication in any medium issued in successive parts bearing numeric or chronological designations and intended to be continued indefinitely. Serials include periodicals; newspapers; annuals (reports, yearbooks, etc.); the journals, memoirs, proceedings, transactions, etc., of societies; and numbered monographic series. *See also* Series 1.

Series. 1. A group of separate items related to one another by the fact that each item bears, in addition to its own title proper, a collective title applying to the group as a whole. The individual items may or may not be numbered. 2. Each of two or more volumes of essays, lectures, articles, or other writings, similar in character and issued in sequence (e.g., Lowell's *Among my books*, second series). 3. A separately numbered sequence of volumes within a series or serial (e.g., *Notes and queries*, 1st series, 2nd series, etc.).

Series title page. An added title page bearing the series title proper and usually, though not necessarily, other information about the series (e.g., statement of responsibility, numeric designation, data relating to publication, title of the item within the series).

Shared authorship. *See* Shared responsibility.

Shared responsibility. Collaboration between two or more persons or bodies performing the same kind of activity in the creation of the content of an item. The contribution of each may form a separate and distinct part of the item, or the contribution of each may not be separable from that of the other(s). *See also* Joint author, Mixed responsibility.

Sheet. As used in the physical description area, a single piece of paper other than a broadside (q.v.) with manuscript or printed matter on one or both sides.

Short score. A sketch made by a composer for an ensemble work, with the main features of the composition set out on a few staves. *See also* Close score, Condensed score.

Sine loco (s.l.). Without place (i.e., the name of the place of publication, distribution, etc., is unknown).

Sine nomine (s.n.). Without name (i.e., the name of the publisher, distributor, etc., is unknown).

Sleeve. A protective envelope for a sound disc, made of cardboard or paper.

Slide. Transparent material on which there is a two-dimensional image, usually held in a mount, and designed for use in a projector or viewer.

Sound recording. A recording on which sound vibrations have been registered by mechanical or electrical means so that the sound may be reproduced.

Specific material designation. A term indicating the special class of material (usually the class of physical object) to which an item belongs (e.g., *sound disc*). *See also* General material designation.

Spine title. A title appearing on the spine of an item. *See also* Binder's title, Cover title.

Standard number. The International Standard Number (ISN), (e.g., International Standard Book Number (ISBN), International Standard Serial Number (ISSN)) or any other internationally agreed upon standard number that identifies an item uniquely.

Standard title. *See* Uniform title.

Statement of responsibility. A statement, transcribed from the item being described, relating to persons responsible for the intellectual or artistic content of the item, to corporate bodies from which the content emanates, or to persons or corporate bodies responsible for the performance of the content of the item.

Subheading. Part of a corporate heading other than the main heading (q.v.).

Subordinate body. A corporate body that forms an integral part of a larger body in relation to which it holds an inferior hierarchical rank.

Subseries. A series within a series (i.e., a series that always appears in conjunction with another, usually more comprehensive, series of which it forms a section). Its title may or may not be dependent on the title of the main series. *See also* Section (Serials).

Supplement. An item, usually issued separately, that complements one already published by bringing up-to-date or otherwise continuing the original or by containing a special feature not included in the original. The supplement has a formal relationship with the original as expressed by common authorship, a common title or subtitle, and/or a stated intention to continue or supplement the original. *See also* Sequel.

Supplied title. A title provided by the cataloguer for an item that has no title proper on the chief source of information or its substitute. It may be taken from elsewhere in the item itself or from a reference source, or it may be composed by the cataloguer.

Surname. Any name used as a family name (other than those used as family names by Romans of classical times).

Tactile materials. Materials with raised symbols and/or differently textured surfaces that are intended for use by the visually impaired.

Technical drawing. A cross section, detail, diagram, elevation, perspective, plan, working plan, etc., made for use in an engineering or other technical context. *See also* Architectural rendering.

Text. 1. A term used as a general material designation to designate printed material accessible to the naked eye (e.g., a book, a pamphlet, a broadside). 2. The words of a song, song cycle, or, in the plural, a collection of songs.

Text (large print). A term used as a general material designation for a printed text intended for use by the visually impaired.

Text (tactile). A term used as a general material designation for material intended for the visually impaired and presented as embossed textual information composed by use of any system of touch reading and writing, excluding braille systems. Examples include Moon type and New York point.

Thematic index. A list of a composer's works, usually arranged in chronological order or by categories, with the theme given for each composition or for each section of large compositions.

Title. A word, phrase, character, or group of characters, normally appearing in an item, that names the item or the work contained in it. *See also* Alternative title, Binder's title, Caption title, Cover title, Half title, Parallel title, Running title, Spine title, Supplied title, Title proper, Uniform title.

Title frame. A frame containing written or printed material not part of the subject content of the item.

Title page. A page at the beginning of an item bearing the title proper and usually, though not necessarily, the statement of responsibility and the data relating to publication. The leaf bearing the title page is commonly called the "title page" although properly called the "title leaf." *See also* Added title page.

Title proper. The chief name of an item, including any alternative title but excluding parallel titles and other title information.

Title screen (Computer files). In the case of a computer file, a display of data that includes the title proper and usually, though not necessarily, the statement of responsibility and the data relating to publication.

Toy. An object designed for imaginative play or one from which to derive amusement. *See also* Game, Model, Realia.

Tracing. 1. A record of the headings under which an item is represented in the catalogue. 2. A record of the references that have been made to a name or to the title of an item that is represented in the catalogue.

Traditional format (Oriental books). A format consisting of double leaves with folds at the fore edge and with free edges sewn together to make a fascicle. Usually several fascicles are contained in a cloth-covered case.

Trailer. A short motion picture film consisting of selected scenes from a film to be shown at a future date, used to advertise that film.

Transcription (Music). *See* Adaptation (Music), Arrangement (Music).

Translator. One who renders from one language into another, or from an older form of a language into the modern form, more or less closely following the original.

Transliteration. *See* Romanization.

Transparency. A sheet of transparent material bearing an image and designed for use with an overhead projector or a light box. It may be mounted in a frame.

Uniform title. 1. The particular title by which a work is to be identified for cataloguing purposes. 2. The particular title used to distinguish the heading for a work from the heading for a different work. 3. A conventional collective title used to collocate publications of an author, composer, or corporate body containing several works or extracts, etc., from several works (e.g., complete works, several works in a particular literary or musical form).

Version (Bible). A particular translation of the Bible or any of its parts. For the broader use of *version* for other works, to designate a type of adaptation, see 21.10.

Verso. 1. The left-hand page of a book, usually bearing an even page number. 2. The side of a printed sheet intended to be read second.

Videorecording. A recording on which visual images, usually in motion and accompanied by sound, have been registered; designed for playback by means of a television set.

View (Cartography). A perspective representation of the landscape in which detail is shown as if projected on an oblique plane (e.g., a bird's-eye view, panorama, panoramic drawing, worm's-eye view).

Vocal score. A score showing all vocal parts, with accompaniment, if any, arranged for keyboard instrument. *See also* Chorus score.

Volume. 1. In the bibliographic sense, a major division of a work, regardless of its designation by the publisher, distinguished from other major divisions of the same work by having its own inclusive title page,[1] half title, cover title, or portfolio title, and usually independent pagination, foliation, or signatures. This major bibliographic unit may include various title pages and/or paginations. 2. In the material sense, all that is contained in one binding, portfolio, etc., whether as originally issued or as bound after issue.[2] The volume as a material unit may not coincide with the volume as a bibliographic unit.

Work (Music). *See* Musical work.

---

1. The most general title page, half title, or cover title is the determining factor in deciding what constitutes a bibliographic volume (e.g., a reissue in one binding, with a general title page, of a work previously issued in two or more bibliographic volumes is considered to be one bibliographic volume even though the reissue includes the title pages of the original volumes).

2. Such a composite volume may contain either two or more bibliographic volumes of the same work or two or more works published independently.

INDEX

Compiled by K. G. B. BAKEWELL; updated by JEAN WEIHS

The index covers the rules (including introductions to the rules) and appendices, but not examples or works cited in any of the rules or appendices. *App. D* indicates that a term is defined in Appendix D (Glossary).

As the rules are based upon bibliographic conditions rather than specific cases, kinds of work have been indexed only when actually named in a rule (e.g., concordances and other kinds of related works named in Rule 21.28). There is no entry under *Encyclopedias, Directories,* etc., because they could represent several bibliographic conditions.

Rules for description have been indexed only to the general chapter (chapter 1) unless there is an amplification or amendment in a later chapter dealing with the description of a specific kind of material.

The index is arranged according to *ALA Filing Rules* / Filing Committee, Resources and Technical Services Division, American Library Association. – Chicago : American Library Association, 1980.

Abbreviations used in the index

App.	Appendix
n	Footnote

Appellations involving names of known persons (*see also* Given names, etc.; Words or phrases)
"*see also*" references, 26.2C2
Appendices, explanation, 0.10
Approximate date of publication, distribution, etc., 1.4F7
Arabic alphabet, names in, 22.22
Arabic article *al, see al* (Arabic article)
Arabic numerals
books of the Bible, 25.18A3
corporate names and places, "see" references, 26.3A5
date of edition, 1.4F1
date of publication or printing, early printed monographs, 2.16F
edition statement, early printed monographs, 2.15A
medium of performance, music, 25.30B1
series numbers, 1.6G1
substitution for roman numerals, App. C.2B1
substitution for spelled-out numerals, App. C.3B1
substitution of Western-style arabic numerals for oriental numerals, App. C.5A, C.5C–C.5D
uniform titles, 25.6A
Arabic script, personal names in, romanization, 22.3C2
Aranyakas
references, 25.18L
uniform titles, 25.18H
Archbishops, *see* Bishops, etc.
Archdioceses, 24.27C2–24.27C3
autocephalous, 24.3C3
Architectural renderings, definition, App. D
Archival cataloguing, designations in heading, 21.0D1
Areas of description (*see also* Edition area; Material (or type of publication) specific details area; Note area; Physical description area; Publication, distribution, etc., area; Series area; Standard number and terms of availability area; Title and statement of responsibility area)
definition, App. D
organization of description, 1.0B
Arguments presented by lawyers, 21.36C8
Arias, 21.19B1
Armed services, 24.18A (type 8), 24.24
capitalization, App. A.18
Arrangements (musical works) (*see also* Adaptations)
definition, App. D
entry, 21.18B
uniform titles, 25.35C
Arrangers, designation in heading, 21.18B
Art galleries, *see* Corporate bodies
Art originals (*for other rules see* Graphic materials; Three-dimensional artefacts and realia)
date, 8.4F2
definition, App. D
dimensions, 8.5D4

general material designation, 1.1C1
medium and base, 8.5C1(a)
no colour given, 8.5C2
specific material designation
graphic materials, 8.5B1
three-dimensional artefacts and realia, 10.5B1
Art prints (*for other rules see* Graphic materials)
definition, App. D
dimensions, 8.5D4
process, 8.5C1(b)
specific material designation, 8.5B1
Art reproductions (*for other rules see* Graphic materials; Three-dimensional artefacts and realia)
definition, App. D
dimensions, 8.5D4
entry
one work, 21.16B
two or more works, 21.17
general material designation, 1.1C1
notes on originals, 8.7B22
reproduction method, 8.5C1(c)
specific material designation
graphic materials, 8.5B1
three-dimensional artefacts and realia, 10.5B1
Art works, adaptations, 21.16; *see also* Art reproductions
Artefacts (*for other rules see* Three-dimensional artefacts and realia)
definition, App. D
not intended primarily for communication
date of manufacture, 10.4F2
no place of publication recorded, 10.4C2
no publisher, distributor, etc., recorded, 10.4D2
Articles, *see* Initial articles
Artistic form of item, *see* Nature, scope or artistic form of item
Artists
collaborations with writers, 21.24
graphic materials, 8.1F1
ASCII characters, file characteristics, computer files, 9.7B8
Aspect ratio, motion pictures, 7.5C1–7.5C2
Associations, *see* Corporate bodies; Societies
Astarte, capitalization, App. A.19A1
Asteroids, capitalization, App. A.27A
Astronomical terms, capitalization, App. A.27
Atharvaveda, 25.18G
Athletic contests, as corporate bodies, 21.1B1
Atlases (*for other rules see* Cartographic materials)
declinations, 3.3D2
definition, App. D
dimensions, 3.5D2
number of maps in, 3.5C1–3.5C2
pagination, 3.5B3
specific material designation, 3.5B1
Auctors, academic disputations 21.27A n6
Audience of item, notes on, 1.7B14
cartographic materials, 3.7B14
computer files, 9.7B14

Cartridges, microfilm, specific material designation, 11.5B1; *for other rules see* Microforms

Cartridges, sound, *see* Sound cartridges

Case binding, definition, App. D

Cases (cartographic materials), as sources of information, 3.0B2

Cases, court, 21.36

Cases (printed monographs), description, 2.5B1, 2.5B18

Cassettes, computer files
  dimensions, 9.5D1(c)
  specific material designation, 9.5B1

Cassettes, film, *see* Film cassettes

Cassettes, microform, specific material designation, 11.5B1; *for other rules see* Microforms

Cassettes, sound, *see* Sound cassettes

Cast (motion pictures and videorecordings, sound recordings) *see* Performers

Catalogue, definition, App. D

Cathedrals, 24.3G; *see also* Churches

Catholic Church (*see also* Holy See; Liturgical works; Mass; Popes; Religious orders)
  apostolic designations, 24.27D
  central administrative organs, 24.27C4
  concordats, 21.35C
  councils, 24.27A
  dioceses, etc., 24.27C3
  liturgical works, uniform titles, 25.20, 25.23

CDs, *see* Compact discs; Computer optical discs

Celestial charts (*for other rules see* Cartographic materials)
  coordinates, 3.3D2
  magnitude, 3.7B8

Central administrative organs of the Catholic Church, 24.27C4

Centre track, sound recordings, 6.5C5

Centuries, capitalization, Italian language, App. A.42F

Ceramic designs, *see* Art works

Chamber music combinations, uniform titles, 25.30B3

Change of literary form, 21.10

Change of name (*see also* Variant names)
  corporate bodies, 24.1C
    explanatory references, 26.3C1
  localities of corporate bodies, 24.4C4
  personal names, 22.2C
    "see" references, 26.2A1
  place names, 23.3

Change of persons or corporate bodies responsible for a work, 21.3

Change of title proper, 21.2
  without change in sequence of numbering, serials, 12.3B3

Changes in frequency, serials, 12.7B1

Changes in pagination, printed monographs, 2.5B5

Channel Islands, additions to place names, 23.4D2

Channels, sound, number of, sound recordings, 6.5C1, 6.5C7

Čhaofā (Thai names), 22.28B2

Chapters of corporate bodies, additions to, 24.9; *see also* Branches

Characterizing words or phrases (*see also* Words or phrases)
  capitalization, App. A.2B
  headings for, 22.11D

Charges to juries, 21.36C5

Charters, 21.33
  capitalization, App. A.20A

Charts (*for other rules see* Cartographic materials; Graphic materials)
  aerial, *see* Cartographic materials
  aeronautical, *see* Cartographic materials
  celestial, *see* Cartographic materials; Celestial charts
  declinations, 3.3D2
  definition, App. D
  double sided (graphic materials), 8.5C1(d)
  general material designation, 1.1C1
  navigational, *see* Cartographic materials
  specific material designation (graphic materials), 8.5B1

Chief executives, decrees of, 21.31B1

Chief source of information (*see also* Sources of information)
  definition, App. D
  lack of, 1.0A2, 1.1B7
  several, 1.0H

Chiefs of state, *see* Heads of state, etc.

Children
  adaptations for, 21.10
  of royal persons, additions to names, 22.16A4

Chinese language, ordinal numerals, App. C.8C

Chinese names
  containing a non-Chinese given name, 22.24
  Indonesian names derived from, 22.26F

"Chinese style" printing, *see* Traditional format (Oriental books)

Chip cartridge, computer files
  dimensions, 9.5D1(b)
  specific material designation, 9.5B1

Choice of personal names, *see* Personal names, choice

Choir book, specific material designation, 5.5B1

Choral music, uniform titles, 25.30B9, 25.34C1 n13

Choreographers, added entries, 21.20

Choreographies, 21.28; *see also* Related works

Chorepiscopus added to names, 22.16C

Chorus scores (*for other rules see* Music; *see also* Vocal scores)
  definition, App. D
  specific material designation, 5.5B1
  uniform titles, 25.35D

Christ, capitalization, App. A.19A1

Christian liturgical works, uniform titles, 25.19–25.20, 25.22–25.23

Christian names, *see* Forenames; Given names, etc.

Christian religious orders, *see* Religious orders

Christian Trinity, capitalization, App. A.19A1

sound recordings
  edition statement, 6.2B5
  entry, 21.23D
  extent, 6.5B3
  notes on, 6.7B10
  title and statement of responsibility
    area, 6.1G
  three-dimensional artefacts and realia,
    10.1G
    edition statement, 10.2B5
  music, 25.24–25.35
  "see" references, 26.4B4
  uniform titles, 25.8–25.12
Collectors of field material, sound recordings,
  6.1F1
Colleges of universities, 24.13A (type 5)
Collotypes, *see* Art reproductions
Colon, use of, *see* Punctuation of description
Colonies, governors of, 24.20D
Colophon
  as source of information
    early printed monographs, 2.13A
    music, 5.0B
    printed monographs, 2.0B
    serials, 12.0B
  definition, App. D
Colour
  cartographic materials, 3.5C1, 3.5C3
  computer files, 9.5C1
  graphic materials, 8.5C2
  microforms, 11.5C3
  motion pictures and videorecordings, 7.5C1,
    7.5C4, 7.7B10(c)
  three-dimensional artefacts and realia,
    10.5C2
Colour printing, early printed monographs,
  2.18E1
Colour process or recording system, motion
  pictures and videorecordings, 7.7B10(c)
Colour separation films, 7.7B10(d)
Coloured illustrations, printed monographs,
  2.5C3
  definition, App. D
Colouring, hand (early printed monographs),
  2.18F1
Columns, number of (*see also* Pagination)
  ancient, medieval, and Renaissance
    manuscripts, 4.5B1
  early printed monographs, 2.17A1, 2.18E1
Combined notes, 1.7B22
Comma, use of, *see* Music, uniform titles;
  Personal names, entry element;
  Punctuation of description
Command districts (armed forces), 24.24
Commentaries, 21.13
Commercial films without title proper, 7.1B2;
  for other rules see Motion pictures and
  videorecordings
Commissions, manuscript, without title, 4.1B2
Commissions to international and
  intergovernmental bodies, 24.18A (type
  11), 24.26
Committees (*see also* Corporate bodies)
  government agencies, 24.18A (type 2)
  joint, 24.15

of legislative bodies, 24.21B
subordinate and related corporate bodies,
  24.13A (type 2)
Communion, Holy, capitalization, App.
  A.19G1
Compact disc (computers), *see* Computer
  optical discs
Compact discs, notes, 6.7B10
Companies (*see also* Corporate bodies)
  capitalization, App. A.18E1
  members of (sound recordings), 6.1F2
  military services, *see* Armed services
Compilations, *see* Collections
Compilations, film, *see* Motion pictures and
  videorecordings
Compilers (*see also* Editors)
  added entries, 21.30D
  collections of treaties, 21.35F
  definition, App. D
  designation in heading, 21.0D1
  law reports, 21.36A
  laws, etc., 21.31B1, 21.31C
Complainants (trials), designation in heading,
  21.36C2
Complete works (collective titles), 25.8
  music, 25.34
Completed serials
  dates, 12.4F2
  numeric and/or alphabetical, chronological,
    or other designation, 12.3F
  specific material designation, 12.5B2
Complex numbering of serials, 12.7B8
Complicated pagination, printed monographs,
  2.5B8
Component branches of armed forces, 24.24
Components, number of, extent, 1.5B3
Composers, statement of responsibility, sound
  recordings, 6.1F
Composition
  date (music)
    in description, 5.1B1
    uniform titles, 25.30E
  form (music, notes), 5.7B1
  place (music, uniform titles), 25.30E
  type (music, uniform titles), 25.30, 25.34C
Compound names, capitalization, Scandinavian
  languages, App. A.47C
Compound surnames, 22.5C
  definition, App. D
  hyphenated, 22.5C3
  married women using maiden name and
    husband's surname, 22.5C5
  nature uncertain, 22.5C6
  place names following surnames, 22.5C7
  preferred or established form known, 22.5C2
  "see" references, 26.2A3
  words indicating relationship following
    surnames, 22.5C8
Compound words
  abbreviations, App. B.7
  capitalization
    hyphenated prefixes, App. A.32
    hyphenated words, App. A.31
    initial letters, App. A.30
Compressed files, 9.0B1

Film loops, specific material designation, 7.5B1; *for other rules see* Motion pictures and videorecordings

Film reels, specific material designation, 7.5B1; *for other rules see* Motion pictures and videorecordings

Film trailers, *see* Trailers, film

Films (*see also* Microforms; Motion pictures and videorecordings)
  base, motion pictures and videorecordings, 7.7B10(e)
  gauge, sound track films, 6.5D3
  nature, microform, 11.7B10
  sound recordings on, chief source of information, 6.0B1

Films, sound track, *see* Sound track films

Filmslips (*for other rules see* Graphic materials)
  frames, 8.5B2
  gauge, 8.5D2
  multipart, 8.5B5
  sound, 8.5C1(e)
  specific material designation, 8.5B1

Filmstrips (*for other rules see* Graphic materials)
  definition, App. D
  frames, 8.5B2
  gauge, 8.5D2
  general material designation, 1.1C1
  multipart, 8.5B5
  sound, 8.5C1(e)
  specific material designation, 8.5B1

Fine grain duplicating films, 7.7B10(d)

Finnish language, capitalization, App. A.38

Firms (*for other rules see* Corporate bodies)
  capitalization, App. A.18E1
    Finnish language, App. A.38A3

First level of description, 1.0D1
  cartographic materials, 3.0D
  title proper, 1.1B5

Five year plans, capitalization, Russian language, App. A.46H2

Flash cards (*for other rules see* Graphic materials)
  colour, 8.5C2
  definition, App. D
  general material designation, 1.1C1
  sound, 8.5C1(e)
  specific material designation, 8.5B1

Fleets, *see* Armed services

Flemish, *see* Dutch language

Flip charts (*for other rules see* Graphic materials)
  double-sided, 8.5C1(d)
  extent, 8.5B3
  multipart, 8.5B5
  specific material designation, 8.5B1

Folded leaves, printed monographs, 2.5B11

Folded manuscripts, dimensions, 4.5D1

Folded sheets
  cartographic materials, 3.5D1
  printed monographs, dimensions, 2.5D4

Folders, description, 2.5B1

Foliation of manuscripts, 4.5B1
  added to uniform titles, 25.13B

ancient, medieval, and Renaissance manuscripts, 4.7B23

Foreign languages, capitalization, App. A.33–A.52

Forenames as part of phrases, 22.11B; *see also* Given names, etc.

Form (artistic) of item, *see* Nature, scope or artistic form of item

Form, literary, change of, 21.10

Form of composition, music, 5.7B1

Form of print, films, 7.7B10(d)

Formal notes, 1.7A3

Format
  definitions, App. D
  early printed monographs, 2.17C

Formats, alternative, 1.5A3, 1.7B16
  cartographic materials, 3.7B16
  computer files, 9.7B16
  graphic materials, 8.7B16
  microforms, 11.7B16
  motion pictures and videorecordings, 7.7B16
  music, 5.7B16
  printed monographs, 2.7B16
  serials, 12.7B16
  sound recordings, 6.7B16

Forms
  illustrative matter, printed monographs, 2.5C2
  manuscript, *see* Manuscripts

Forms of name, *see* Variant forms of name

Founding date added to names of corporate bodies, 24.4C6

fps, use of
  motion pictures, 7.5C5
  sound recordings, 6.5C3

Fragments, collective titles, 25.10

Frames (graphic materials)
  as sources of information, 8.0B1
  multipart filmslips, etc., 8.5B5
  number of, 8.5B2, 8.7B18

Frames (microfiches), number of, 11.5B2

Frames per second
  motion pictures, 7.5C5
  sound track films, 6.5C3

Frames (videodiscs)
  number of, 7.7B10(j)
  of still images, duration, 7.5B2

Fraternal orders, 24.3C2

Free transcriptions, music, 21.18C; *see also* Adaptations; Arrangements

Free translations, *see* Adaptations

French language
  capitalization, App. A.39
  ordinal numerals, App. C.8B
  surnames with prefixes, 22.5D1

Frequency of serials, 12.7B1
  accompanying material, 12.5E1, 12.7B11

Friends, Society of, yearly meetings, 24.27A1 n14

Full scores, *see* Scores

Full stop, use of, *see* Punctuation of description

Fullness of names
  corporate and place names, "see" references, 26.3A3

uniform titles, omission, 25.2C
Initial title elements, definition, App. D
Initial words not part of a name, publication, distribution, etc., area, capitalization, App. A.7B
Initialisms, *see* Acronyms
Initials
as last element of Indonesian names, 22.26C1(c)
as pseudonyms, name-title references, 26.2B4
as surnames, entry under, 22.5A
denoting academic degrees or membership in organizations, added to identical names entered under surname, 22.19B
entry under, 22.5A, 22.10
name-title references, 26.2B2
"see" references, 26.2A2–26.2A3
in compound words, capitalization, App. A.30A
in title proper, 1.1B6
of Christian religious orders, added to personal names, 22.16D
of corporate names
capitalization, App. A.1A, App. A.4F
explanatory references, 26.3C2
omission from statement of responsibility, 1.1F7
preferred form, 24.2D
presentation, 24.1A
"see" references, 26.3A3–26.3A4
of personal authors entered under surname
additions to, 22.18
references from, 26.2A2
of place names, "see" references, 26.3A3–26.3A4
of ships' names, omission, 24.5C4
Inserts, serials, 12.7B18
Insets, cartographic materials, 3.7B18
Institutes (subordinate corporate bodies), 24.13A (type 5)
Institutions (*see also* Corporate bodies)
added to chapters, branches, etc., of corporate bodies, 24.9
added to corporate names, 24.4C5
added to uniform titles for liturgical works, 25.22A(2)
capitalization, App. A.18E1
Finnish language, App. A.38A3
Instrumental ensembles, uniform titles, 25.30B5
Instruments, musical, *see* Medium of performance (music)
Integral sound systems
filmstrips and filmslips, 8.5C1(e)
slides, 8.5C1(g)
Integration of explanatory references, 26.3C1
Intellectual level of item, *see* Audience of item
Intended audience of item, *see* Audience of item
Intergovernmental agreements, *see* Treaties, intergovernmental agreements, etc.
Intergovernmental bodies, *see* International and intergovernmental bodies
Interjection *Oh*, capitalization, App. A.30

Internal user labels, *see* Labels (computer files)
International and intergovernmental bodies
agreements contracted by, *see* Treaties
ancient bodies, 24.3C2
definition, 21.33A n9, App. D
delegations to, 24.18A (type 11), 24.26
heads of, 24.20C2
language, 24.3B
International organizations and alliances, capitalization, App. A.18A
International Standard Bibliographic Description (General), 0.22, 0.25–0.26
International Standard Book Numbers, *see* Standard numbers
International Standard Serial Numbers, *see* Standard numbers
International treaties, etc.
capitalization, App. A.20A
entry, 21.35
uniform titles, 25.16
Internegative films, 7.7B10(d)
Internunciature, Apostolic, 24.27D
Interpolations in entry, 1.0C
language and script, 1.0E
Interpositive films, 7.7B10(d)
Interpretations, 21.13
Interviews, reports of, 21.25
Introductory phrases omitted from uniform titles, 25.3B
ips, use of, sound recordings, 6.5C3
Ireland, additions to place names, 23.4D2
Irregular numbering of serials, 12.7B8
Irregular pagination of printed monographs, 2.5B8
ISBD(G), 0.22, 0.25–0.26
ISBN, *see* Standard numbers
Islamic names in Arabic alphabet, 22.22
Isle of Man, additions to place names, 23.4D2
Ism (names in Arabic alphabet), 22.22C–22.22D
Israel, persons living in, romanization of names, 22.3C2
ISSN, *see* Standard numbers
Issue (*see also* Impressions; Reprints)
as edition statement, 1.2B3
definition, App. D
Issue statements, Arabic numerals used, App. C.2B1(a), C.3B1(a), C.5D(1)
"Issued with" notes, serials, 12.7B21; *see also* "With" notes
Italian language
capitalization, App. A.42
surnames with prefixes, 22.5D1
Item, definition, App. D
manuscripts, 4.5B2 n2
Item numbers, *see* Numbers, borne by item
Items made up of several types of material, *see* Kits; Mixed material items; Multimedia items
Items, number of, manuscripts, 4.5B2

Jackets (sound recordings), *see* Sleeves
Jain canon, *see* Jaina Āgama
Jain names, 22.25

Localities, *see* Local place names; Place names
Locally assigned file or data set name, computer files, 9.7B20
Location of accompanying material, *see* Accompanying material, notes on
Locations, *see* Local place names; Place names
Long other title information, 1.1E3
Long title proper, 1.1B4
   music, uniform titles, 25.27C
Longitude, cartographic materials, 3.3D1
Loops, film (specific material designation), 7.5B1
Loose-leaf publications, 2.5B9
Lord, added to personal names, 22.12B
Lord's Supper, capitalization, App. A.19G1
Low reduction, microforms, 11.7B10
Lower-case roman numerals, use of, App. C.2B3
Ltd., omission from corporate names, 24.5C1

m. per sec., use of, sound recordings, 6.5C3
Machine-readable data files, *see* Computer files
Machines, *see* Three-dimensional artefacts and realia
Macroform, definition, App. D; *see also* Microform
Magnitude, celestial charts, 3.7B8
Main entries
   definition, 21.0A, App. D
   reasons for, 0.5
   selection, 21
Main heading, definition, App. D
Main menus, sources of information, computer files, 9.0B1
Major or *minor*, added to uniform titles, music, 25.30D1
Malay names, 22.27
Malayalam names, 22.25B2
Malaysian place names, additions to, 23.4C
Mangku (*Mangkoe*) (Indonesian names), 22.26C1(b)
Manuals
   accompanying graphic materials, as sources of information, 8.0B1
   computer files, *see* Documentation
   of religious observance, *see* Liturgical works
Manufacture, date and place of, 1.4G
Manufacturer, 1.4G
   capitalization, App. A.7A1
   computer files, 9.4G
   graphic materials, 8.4G
   motion pictures and videorecordings, 7.4G
   serials, 12.4G
   sound recordings, 6.4G
   three-dimensional artefacts and realia, 10.4G
Manuscript additions to early printed monographs, 2.18F1
Manuscript cartographic items (*for other rules see* Cartographic materials)
   description, 3.5B1
   dimensions, 3.5D1
Manuscript volumes without title, 4.1B2
Manuscripts, 4
   date area, 4.4
   definition, 4.0A, App. D

general material designation, 1.1C1, 4.1C
music, 5.5B1
note area, 4.7
physical description area, 4.5
reproductions, 1.11
sources of information, 4.0B
title and statement of responsibility area, 4.1
uniform titles, 25.13
   Bible, 25.18A12
   liturgical works, 25.22B
Map sections, specific material designation, 3.5B1; *for other rules see* Cartographic materials
Map views, scale, 3.3B7; *for other rules see* Cartographic materials; *for definitions see* Sections (cartography)
Maps (*for other rules see* Cartographic materials)
   collections, physical description, 2.5B18
   definition, App. D
   dimensions, 3.5D1
   general material designation, 1.1C1
   illustrative matter, printed monographs, 2.5C2
   number, in an atlas, 3.5C1–3.5C2
   of imaginary places, scale, 3.3B7
   reproductions, 1.11
   scale, *see* Scale
   specific material designation, 3.5B1
   with nonlinear scales, scale, 3.3B7
Marchionesses, *see* Titles of honour, nobility, address, etc.
Marines, *see* Armed services
Market grades, capitalization, App. A.29A
Marks of omission, *see* Omission, marks of
Marquesses, *see* Titles of honour, nobility, address, etc.
Married women
   addition of terms of address to names, 22.15B
   Thai names, 22.28C2
   using maiden name and husband's surname, 22.5C5
Mass (liturgical works)
   capitalization, App. A.19G1
   uniform titles, 25.23B–25.23C
Masthead
   as source of information, serials, 12.0B1
   definition, App. D
Material
   cartographic materials, 3.5C1, 3.5C4
   manuscripts, 4.5C1
   three-dimensional artefacts and realia, 10.5C1
Material designations, *see* Extent, statement of; General material designation; Specific material designation
Material (or type of publication) specific details area, 1.3
   arabic numerals used, App. C.2B1(b), C.3B1(b), C.5D(2)
   capitalization, App. A.6
   explanation, 0.25
   notes on, 1.7B8

(Mixed responsibility, works of *cont.*)
    texts, 21.10–21.15
  new works, 21.24–21.27
  sound recordings, 21.23
Mnemonic structure of rule numbering, 0.23
Mock-ups (*for other rules see* Three-dimensional artefacts and realia)
  definition, App. D
  specific material designation, 10.5B1
Mode of access, computer files, 9.7B1(c)
Models (*for other rules see* Three-dimensional artefacts and realia)
  definition, App. D
  general material designation, 1.1C1
  specific material designation, 10.5B1
Moderators, *see* Religious officials
Modern Indic names, 22.25B
Modern laws, uniform titles, 25.15A
Modi vivendi between Holy See and national governments, 21.35C1
Modifications of works, 21.9
  art works, 21.16–21.17; *see also* Art reproductions
  musical works, 21.18–21.22
  texts, 21.10–21.15
Modified letters, *see* Diacritical marks
Modulation frequency, videotapes, 7.7B10(f)
Mohammedan names in Arabic alphabet, 22.22
Mǫm Čhao, *Mǫm Lūang*, and *Mǫm Rātchawong* (Thai names), 22.28B2
Monarchs, *see* Royalty
Monasteries (*see also* Churches)
  added to uniform titles, liturgical works, 25.22A(2)
  headings, 24.3G
Monastic orders, *see* Religious orders
Monastics, Buddhist, 22.28D1
Monographic series, *see* Series
Monographs (*see also* Early printed monographs; Printed monographs)
  changes in responsibility for, 21.3A
  changes in title proper, 21.2B
  definition, App. D
  multipart, analysis, 13.2
Monophonic sound recordings, 6.5C7
Months of the year
  abbreviations, App. B.15
  capitalization, *see* Calendar divisions, capitalization
Monuments, capitalization, App. A.16
Moon, capitalization, App. A.27A
Moon-type works, *see* Braille works
Mortgages, manuscript, without title, 4.1B2
Mosques, 24.3G; *see also* Churches
Motion pictures and videorecordings, 7
  definition, 7.0A, App. D
  edition area, 7.2
  entry under corporate body, 21.1B2(e)
  general material designation, 1.1C1, 7.1C
  note area, 7.7
  physical description area, 7.5
  publication, distribution, etc., area, 7.4
  series area, 7.6
  sources of information, 7.0B

specific material designations, 7.5B1
standard number and terms of availability area, 7.8
title and statement of responsibility area, 7.1
with subtitles, uniform titles, 25.5C
Mottoes, early printed monographs, 2.14C
Mounting, cartographic materials, 3.5C1, 3.5C5
Movements, musical works, 21.18C
Moving images, videodiscs consisting of
  duration, 7.5B2
  notes, 7.7B10(j)
Ms, use of
  manuscripts, 4.7B1
  music, 5.5B1
  uniform titles, 25.22B
Mss, use of, 4.7B1
Mullahs, *see* Religious officials
Multilevel description
  analysis, 13.6
  cartographic materials, 3.0J
  items made up of several types of material, 1.10D
  supplementary items, 1.9B
Multilingual . . . , *see also* Multiscript . . .
Multilingual chronological designations, serials, 12.3C3
Multilingual edition statements, 1.2B5
  cartographic materials, 3.2B4
  computer files, 9.2B6
  microforms, 11.2B4
  motion pictures and videorecordings, 7.2B4
  music, 5.2B4
  printed monographs, 2.2B4
  revisions, 1.2D2
  serials, 12.2B3
  sound recordings, 6.2B4
  three-dimensional artefacts and realia, 10.2B4
Multilingual musical presentation statements, 5.3B1
Multilingual numeric and/or alphabetic designations, serials, 12.3B2
Multilingual places of publication, 1.4C1
Multilingual publishers, distributors, etc., 1.4D2
Multilingual serials, notes on language, 12.7B2
Multilingual sources of information, 1.0H1(d)
Multilingual statements of responsibility, 1.1F11
  named revisions of editions, 1.2E3
Multilingual texts, pagination in opposite directions, 2.5B15
Multilingual titles proper, 1.1B8; *see also* Parallel titles
Multimedia items, 1.10; *see also* Kits
  definition, App. D
  general material designation, 1.1C1, 1.1C4, 1.10C1, 2.1C2
Multipart files (computers)
  definition, App. D
  number of records, etc., 9.3B2(c)
Multipart items
  cartographic materials, scales, 3.3B4–3.3B6
  change of publisher, etc., during course of publication, 1.4D5

(Parentheses, use of *cont.*)
    fuller forms of personal names, 22.18
    governments, 24.6B–24.6D
    heads of state, etc., 24.20B
    local churches, 24.10
    names entered under given name, etc., 22.19A
    place names, 23.4A
    radio and television stations, 24.11
    religious officials, 24.27B
    spirits, 22.14
    Thai nobility, 22.28C1
   in uniform titles:
    additions (general), 25.5B–25.5D
    liturgical works, 25.22
    music, 25.30B1, 25.30B7, 25.30C3, 25.30E, 25.31B–25.31C, 25.32A2, 25.35B
    treaties, 25.16A, 25.16B2
Parks, capitalization, App. A.16A
   Bulgarian language, App. A.35B
   Russian language, App. A.46B
   Serbo-Croatian language, App. A.48B
   Slovenian language, App. A.50B
Part (music), definition, App. D
Partial contents, *see* Contents notes
Particles, names with, *see* Prefixes, surnames with
Parts of works
   definition, App. D
   description
    computer files, specific material designation, 9.5B1
    music, specific material designation, 5.5B1–5.5B3
    printed monographs, 2.5B18
   uniform titles, 25.6
    explanatory references, 26.4D2
    liturgical works, 25.23
    musical works, 25.32
    sacred scriptures, 25.18
    "see" references, 26.4B2–26.4B3
Pasticcios, 21.19B
Pastoral letters of popes, patriarchs, bishops, etc., 21.4D1
Patriarchates
   autocephalous, 24.3C3
   Catholic Church, 24.27C3
Patriarchs (*see also* Bishops, etc.)
   Buddhist, 22.28D3
   official communications of
    entry, 21.4D1
    headings, 24.27B1
Patronymics
   definition, App. D
   in names in Arabic languages, 22.22C–22.22D
   Romanian, 22.7
   with given names, 22.28B
Peace treaties, *see* Treaties
Peculiarities in numbering of serials, 12.7B8
Peculiarities of items, *see* Library's holdings
Peerage, United Kingdom, explanation of, 22.6A1 n10, 22.12A1 n13
Peers and peeresses, *see* Titles of honour, nobility, address, etc.

Peoples, *see* Races
Percussion, groups of instruments, uniform titles, 25.30B5
Performance, duration of, *see* Duration
Performance, medium of, *see* Medium of performance
Performers
   groups of, as corporate bodies, 21.1B2(e)
   motion pictures and videorecordings, 7.7B6
   sound recordings
    added entries, 21.23
    notes on, 6.7B6
    statements of responsibility, 6.1F1
Period, use of, *see* Punctuation of description
Periodicals, *see* Serials
Periods, historic and cultural, *see* Historic events, etc.
Peripherals, computer files, 9.7B1(b)
Persian language, personal names in, romanization, 22.3C2
Personal authors (*see also* Personal names; Statements of responsibility)
   changes in, 21.3
   definition, 21.1A1, App. D
   entry, general rule, 21.1A2
   works erroneously or fictitiously attributed to, 21.4C
   works of single authorship, 21.4A
Personal names
   additions to
    Buddhist monastics, ecclesiastics, and patriarchs, 22.28D
    Burmese and Karen names, 22.23
    capitalization, App. A.2C
    distinguishing identical names, 22.17–22.20
    Indic names, 22.25B3
    Indonesian names, 22.26G
    Malay names, 22.27D
    names consisting of or containing initials, 22.18
    names entered under given name, etc., 22.16
    names entered under surname, 22.15
    saints, 22.13
    spirits, 22.14
    Thai names, 22.28B–22.28C
    titles of nobility and honour, 22.12
   as title proper, 1.1B3
   capitalization, App. A.13
    in headings, App. A.2A
    in statements of responsibility, App. A.4F
   change of name, 22.2B
   choice, 22.1
    among different forms of the same name, 22.3
    among different names, 22.2
   entry element, 22.4
    Arabic alphabet, names in, 22.22
    Buddhist monastics, ecclesiastics, and patriarchs, 22.28D
    Burmese and Karen names, 22.3
    Chinese names containing a non-Chinese given name, 22.24
    given name, etc., 22.8
    Icelandic names, 22.9B

(Place names *cont.*)
    chapters, etc., of corporate bodies, 24.9
    civil and criminal courts, 24.23A
    conferences, etc., 24.7B4
    corporate names, 24.4C2–24.4C4
    embassies, consulates, etc., 24.25
    exhibitions, fairs, festivals, etc., 24.8B
    local church names, 24.10B
    papal diplomatic missions, etc., 24.27D
    radio and television stations, 24.11
  added to uniform titles, liturgical works, 25.22A(2)
  additions to, 23.4
  as headings for corporate bodies, 24.3E
  capitalization, App. A.15
    Bulgarian language, App. A.35B–A.35C
    Czech language, App. A.36A1
    French language, App. A.39A2, A.39A4
    Polish language, App. A.44A4–A.44A6
    Russian language, App. A.46B
    Serbo-Croatian language, App. A.48B
    Slovenian language, App. A.50B
  changes of name, 23.3
  following surnames, 22.5C7
  in entry under given name, 22.8A
  in Indonesian names, 22.26E
  including a term indicating a type of jurisdiction, 23.5
  language, 23.2
  references, 26.3
  use, 20.2, 23.1
Place of composition, added to uniform titles, music, 25.30E
Place of manufacture, 1.4G
  computer files, 9.4G
  graphic materials, 8.4G
  motion pictures and videorecordings, 7.4G
  serials, 12.4G
  three-dimensional artefacts and realia, 10.4G
Place of printing, etc.
  cartographic materials, 3.4G
  music, 5.4G
  printed monographs, 2.4G
Place of publication, distribution, etc., 1.4C
  abbreviations, 1.4C3–1.4C4, App. B.14
  capitalization, App. A.7A1
  computer files, 9.4C
  early printed monographs, 2.16B–2.16C
  graphic materials, 8.4C
  three-dimensional artefacts and realia, 10.4C
Place of writing (manuscripts)
  as part of title proper, 4.1B2
  notes on, 4.7B8
Plainsong settings of Ordinary of Mass, 25.23C
Plaintiff (trials), optional designation in heading, 21.36C2
Planets, capitalization, App. A.27A
Plans (cartographic materials), dimensions, 3.5D1; *see also* Maps; Cartographic materials
Plans (illustrative matter, printed monographs), 2.5C2
  definition, App. D

Plans (political, etc., documents), capitalization, App. A.20A
  Russian language, App. A.46H2
Plants, scientific names of, capitalization, App. A.25
Plate numbers, music (*see also* Publisher's numbers), 5.7B19
  definition, App. D
Plates (printed monographs), 2.5B10
  definition, App. D
Players (actors, etc.), *see* Performers
Playing cards, specific material designation, 3.5B1; *for other rules see* Cartographic materials
Playing speed
  sound recordings, 6.5C1, 6.5C3
Playing time, *see* Duration
Plays (collective titles), 25.10
Pleas (court cases), 21.36C8
Plucked instruments, uniform titles, music, 25.30B5
Plural generic terms, capitalization, App. A.12C
Plus sign, use of, celestial charts, 3.3D2; *see also* Punctuation of description
Pockets (printed monographs)
  containing accompanying material, 2.5E2
  containing illustrative matter, 2.5C6
Poems (collective titles), 25.10
Poems, early, 25.12A
Poera (Indonesian names), 22.26C1(b)
Points of the compass, capitalization, App. A.15A1
Policy, statements of, capitalization, App. A.20A
Polish language, capitalization, App. A.44
Political divisions, capitalization, App. A.15B
Political jurisdictions, *see* Governments; Jurisdiction . . .
Political parties (*for other rules see* Corporate bodies)
  American state and local elements, 24.16
  capitalization, App. A.18C
    French language, App. A.39A1–A.39A2
    Italian language, App. A.42A
Political systems, capitalization, App. A.18D
Polyester film base, 7.7B10(e)
Polyglot (uniform titles), 25.5C
  Bible, 25.18A10
Popes (*see also* Catholic Church; Holy See)
  additions to names, 22.16B
  capitalization of numerals following names, App. A.13D
  capitalization of titles, App. A.13E2
    French language, App. A.39D
  entry of works by, 21.4D
  headings for, 24.27B2
  official communications of
    entry, 21.4D1
    headings, 24.27B
    uniform titles, 25.24
"Popular" music, arrangements, uniform titles, 25.35C2
Popular names of places, capitalization, App. A.15C

(Reel *cont.*)
>no dimensions given, 9.5D1(d)
>specific material designation, 9.5B1

film, specific material designation, 7.5B1

microfilm, specific material designation, 11.5B1

sound recordings, as sources of information, 6.0B

sound tape, *see* Sound tape reels

Reel-to-reel tapes (*for other rules see* Sound recordings)
>chief sources of information, 6.0B1
>number of tracks, 6.5C6

Reference sources
>definition, 22.1B n1, App. D
>for corporate bodies, definition, 24.1A n2
>for liturgical works, 25.19A n8
>for manuscripts, as sources of information, 4.0B1
>for names written in Arabic alphabet, 22.22 n19
>for personal names, definition, 22.1B n1
>for thematic index numbers, 25.30C4 n11–25.30C4 n12
>for titles of nobility, honour, etc., 22.6A1 n9, 22.12A1 n14, 22.12B1 n15

References, *see also* Explanatory references; Name-title references; "See also" references; "See" references
>Bible, 25.18A6
>bibliographic, etc., *see* Bibliographic citations
>Buddhist scriptures, 25.18F3
>corporate names, 26.3
>definition, App. D
>form of, 26.1F
>general rule, 26.1
>personal names, 26.2
>place names, 26.3
>replacing added entries, 21.29G, 26.6
>Talmud, Mishnah, and Tosefta, 25.18D
>to added entries for series and serials, 26.5
>to published descriptions, manuscripts, 4.7B15
>uniform titles, 25.2E, 26.4
>Vedas, Aranyakas, Brahmanas, Upanishads, Jaina Āgama, and Avesta, 25.18L

Regiments, *see* Armed services

Regions, capitalization, App. A.15A
>Bulgarian language, App. A.35B
>Russian language, App. A.46B
>Serbo-Croatian language, App. A.48B
>Slovenian language, App. A.50B

Reign, years of, *see* Date(s) of reign

Reissues (*see also* Issue; Reprints)
>dates, 1.4F3
>edition statements, 1.2D3
>statements of, serials, 12.2B1(e)

Related corporate bodies, definition, App. D; *for rules see* Subordinate and related corporate bodies

Related music, *see* Adaptations

Related works, 21.28; *see also* Adaptations
>added entries, 21.30G
>described as supplementary items, 1.9

"see also" references, 26.4C1

Relationship, words indicating, following surnames, 22.5C8

Release, country of, motion pictures and videorecordings, 7.7B9

Release date, motion pictures and videorecordings, 7.4F1

Releasing agents, motion pictures and videorecordings, 7.4D1, 7.4E1
>definition, App. D

Relief models (*for other rules see* Cartographic materials)
>dimensions, 3.5D3
>scale, 3.3B8
>specific material designation, 3.5B1

Religion, name in, "see" references, 26.2A1

Religions, names of, capitalization, App. A.19D
>Bulgarian language, App. A.35A2
>French language, App. A.39A1–A.39A2
>Italian language, App. A.42A
>Polish language, App. A.44A3
>Russian language, App. A.46A3
>Serbo-Croatian language, App. A.48A3
>Slovenian language, App. A.50A4

Religious bodies, 24.27; *see also* Religions; Religious denominations; Religious orders
>as corporate bodies, 21.1B1
>capitalization
>>Finnish language, App. A.38A1
>>French language, App. A.39A1–A.39A2
>>Italian language, App. A.42A1
>international, conventional names, 24.3C2

Religious constitutions, 21.4D1

Religious denominations, capitalization, App. A.18E1

Religious events and concepts (*see also* Historic events, etc.)
>capitalization, App. A.19E

Religious holidays, *see* Holidays

Religious laws, 21.1B2(b)

Religious leaders (*see also* Bishops, etc.; Popes; Religious officials)
>capitalization, App. A.19C1

Religious movements, capitalization, App. A.19D1

Religious names and terms (*see also* Bishops, etc.; Popes)
>additions to names, 22.16D
>capitalization, App. A.19
>>Portuguese language, App. A.45D
>>Spanish language, App. A.51D
>Indic names, 22.25B4

Religious observances, manuals of, *see* Liturgical works

Religious officials (*see also* Bishops, etc.; Popes)
>capitalization of titles, App. A.13E2
>headings for, 24.27B

Religious orders
>added to personal names, 22.16D
>added to uniform titles, liturgical works, 25.22A(3)
>capitalization, App. A.18E
>>following personal names, App. A.13F1

early printed monographs, 2.14F
graphic materials, 8.1F
items lacking collective title, 1.1G3
lack of, 1.1F2
manuscripts, 4.1F
microforms, 11.1F
motion pictures and videorecordings, 7.1F
music, 5.1F
notes on, 1.7B6
  cartographic materials, 3.7B6
  computer files, 9.7B6
  graphic materials, 8.7B6
  manuscripts, 4.7B6
  microforms, 11.7B6
  motion pictures and videorecordings, 7.7B6
  music, 5.7B6, 5.7B18
  printed monographs, 2.7B6
  serials, 12.7B6
  sound recordings, 6.7B6, 6.7B18
  three-dimensional artefacts and realia, 10.7B6
printed monographs, 2.1F
relating to edition, 1.2C
  computer files, 9.2C
relating to named revisions of an edition, 1.2E
relating to series, 1.6E
relating to subseries, 1.6H3
serials, 12.1F
sound recordings, 6.1F
uniform titles, omission from, 25.3B
with other title information, 1.1E4
States
abbreviations, App. B.14
added to corporate names, 24.4C2
added to names of royalty, 22.16A1
added to place names, 23.4C
added to place of publication, 1.4C3
capitalization, App. A.15B1
  French language, App. A.39G3
  Italian language, App. A.42G3
Statistical tables, notes on, *see* Contents notes
Statutes, *see* Laws, etc.
Stereographs (*for other rules see* Graphic materials)
dimensions not given, 8.5D3
frames, 8.5B2
multipart, 8.5B5
Stereophonic sound recordings, 6.5C7
Still images, videodiscs consisting of frames of, duration, 7.5B2, 7.7B10(j)
Stock shots (*for other rules see* Motion pictures and videorecordings)
lack of title proper, 7.1B2
notes, 7.7B18
Streets, capitalization, App. A.16
Bulgarian language, App. A.35B
Czech language, App. A.36A2
French language, App. A.39G1
Italian language, App. A.42G1
Russian language, App. A.46B
Serbo-Croatian language, App. A.48B
Slovenian language, App. A.50B
String quartets, uniform titles, 25.30B3

String trios, uniform titles, 25.30B3
Structure of AACR2, 0.3–0.4, 0.6, 0.23, 20.1
Structure of entries, 0.6, 20.1
Structures, *see* Buildings
Study prints, specific material designation, 8.5B1; *for other rules see* Graphic materials
Style of AACR2, 0.2
Style of entries, 0.11
Style of writing (ancient, medieval, and Renaissance manuscripts), 4.7B23
Subcommittees, *see* Corporate bodies
Subdivisions of publishers, sound recordings, 6.4D2
Subheading, definition, App. D
Subjects, manuscripts relating to, without title, 4.1B2
Subordinate and related corporate bodies
definition, App. D
headings, 24.12–24.16
"see" references, 26.3A7
Subordinate entry of government agencies, 24.18–24.19
Subordinate religious bodies, 24.27C
Subordinate units
of corporate bodies, *see* Subordinate and related corporate bodies
of legislative bodies, 24.21B
Subseries (*see also* Sections of serials)
definition, App. D
entry, *see* Related works
statement of, 1.6H
Subtitles, *see* Other title information
Successive designations of serials, 12.3G
Suites (musical works), uniform titles, 25.32B2
Summary of content of item, in notes, 1.7B17; *see also* Contents notes
computer files, 9.7B17
graphic materials, 8.7B17
manuscripts, 4.7B17
microforms, 11.7B17
motion pictures and videorecordings, 7.7B17
printed monographs, 2.7B17
sound recordings, 6.7B17
three-dimensional artefacts and realia, 10.7B17
Sun, capitalization, App. A.27A
Supplements
capitalization of titles, App. A.4D
definition, App. D
description, 1.9
entry, 21.28; *see also* Related works
notes on, 1.7B11
title proper, 1.1B9
to serials
  notes, 12.7B7(j)
  statements of responsibility, 12.1F4
  title proper, 12.1B3–12.1B6
Supplied title, definition, App. D; *for rules see* Title proper, lack of
Supreme patriarchs, Buddhist, 22.28D3
Suria and *Surja* (Indonesian names), 22.26C1(b)
Surnames
definition, App. D

(Surnames *cont.*)
  entry under, 22.4B2–22.4B3, 22.5
    additions to, 22.15, 22.19B
    Chinese names containing a non-Chinese
      given name, 22.24
    compound, *see* Compound surnames
    Indonesian names of Chinese origin,
      22.26F
    Malay names, 22.27B
    modern Indic names, 22.25B
  in entry under title of nobility, 22.6A
  manuscripts relating to, without title, 4.1B2
  references from
    Buddhist supreme patriarchs, 22.28D3
    Thai names, 22.28A, 22.28C1
  romanization, 22.3C2
  with prefixes, *see* Prefixes, surnames with
Surya (Indonesian names), 22.26C1(b)
Suspension of publication, serials, 12.7B8
Sutan (Indonesian names), 22.26D
Swami (early Indic names), 22.25A
Swedish, *see* Scandinavian languages
Symbols
  at the beginning of titles, capitalization of
    words following, App. A.4B
  in edition statement, 1.2B2
  in statements of responsibility, 1.1F9
  in title proper, 1.1B1
  replacement, 1.0E
Symposia, *see* Conferences; Corporate bodies
Synagogues, 24.3G; *see also* Churches
Synods
  headings, 24.27C2
  official messages to, entry, 21.4D1
System requirements, computer files, 9.7B1(b)

t., capitalization, App. A.9B1
Table book, specific materials designation,
  music, 5.5B1
Table-talk, 21.25
Tables
  not illustrations, 2.5C1
  notes on, *see* Contents notes
Tables, genealogical (illustrative matter,
  printed monographs), 2.5C2
Tactile
  added to general material designation, 1.1C1
  added to specific material designation,
    graphic materials, 8.5B6
Tactile data, cartographic materials, 3.5B5
Tactile materials (*see also* Braille works; Text
  (tactile))
  definition, App. D
  general material designation, 1.1C1
  manuscripts, statement of extent, 4.5B3
  music, 5.5B3
  serials, 12.5B3
  specific material designation, graphic
    materials, 8.5B1
Takhallus (names in Arabic alphabet), 22.22D
Talmud
  references, 25.18D
  uniform titles, 25.18B
Tamil names, 22.25B2

Tape cartridges, computer
  dimensions, 9.5D1(b)
  specific material designation, 9.5B1
Tape cartridges, sound, number of tracks,
  6.5C6; *for other rules see* Sound
  recordings
Tape reels, computer
  dimensions, 9.5D1(d)
  specific material designation, 9.5B1
Tape reels, sound, *see* Sound tape reels
Tapes, length, motion pictures and
  videorecordings, 7.7B10(b)
Tapes, sound, *see* Sound tapes
Tapestries, *see* Art works
Technical drawings (*for other rules see* Graphic
  materials; *see also* Architectural
  rendering)
  colour not given, 8.5C2
  definition, App. D
  dimensions, 8.5D6
  general material designation, 1.1C1
  reproduction method, 8.5C1(j)
  specific material designation, 8.5B1
Telegrams without title, 4.1B2
Television stations, additions to, 24.11
Telugu names, 22.25B2
Temples, 24.3G; *see also* Churches
Tenor
  abbreviation for, 5.7B1
  omitted from uniform titles when
    distinguishing musical instruments,
    25.30B4
Terminology of AACR2, 0.2
Terms indicating incorporation (corporate
  names)
  omission, 24.5C
  transposition, 24.5C2
Terms of address (*see also* Titles of honour,
  nobility, address, etc.)
  added to identical names entered under
    surname, 22.19B
  as part of phrases, 22.11B
  Burmese and Karen names, 22.23B
  capitalization, App. A.13C1
  early Indic names, 22.25A
  married women, 22.15B
  "see" references, 26.2A3
  Thai names, 22.28A
Terms of availability, 1.8D
  additions to, 1.8E
  capitalization, App. A.11
  facsimiles, etc., 1.11E
Terms of honour and respect, capitalization,
  App. A.13G
Territorial designations (*see also* Countries;
  Place names)
  added to place names, 23.4
  in titles of nobility, 22.6B1
Territories, occupied, governors of, 24.20D
Territories (USSR), capitalization, Russian
  language, App. A.46C3(b)
Testaments (Bible), uniform titles, 25.18A2
Text (large print), definition, App. D
Text (tactile), definition, App. D

Texts
   adaptations, 21.10
   as sources of information
      accompanying graphic materials, 8.0B1–8.0B2
      accompanying motion pictures and videorecordings, 7.0B1–7.0B2
      accompanying sound recordings, 6.0B1–6.0B2
      accompanying three-dimensional artefacts and realia, 10.0B1
   definition, App. D
   general material designation, 1.1C1
   illustrated, 21.11
   in two languages with pages numbered in opposite direction, 2.5B15
   modifications of, 21.10–21.15
   of religious observances, *see* Liturgical works
   opening words of (early printed monographs), as title proper, 2.14A
   revisions, *see* Revisions
   translations, 21.14
   with biographical/critical material, 21.15
   with commentary, 21.13
   with music, notes on language, 5.7B2
Thai names, 22.28
Thematic index numbers
   added to uniform titles, music, 25.30C1, 25.30C4
      capitalization of accompanying words, App. A.3C1
   definition, App. D
Theological creeds, *see* Creeds, theological
Thermoform
   cartographic materials, 3.5B5
   graphic materials, 8.5B6
   music, 5.5B3
   printed monographs, 2.5B23
Theses, *see* Dissertations
Third level of description, 1.0D3
   parallel titles, 1.1D2
Thorough bass, uniform titles, music, 25.30B4
Three-dimensional artefacts and realia, 10
   colour, 10.5C2
   definition, 10.0A
   edition area, 10.2
   general material designation, 10.1C
   material, 10.5C1
   note area, 10.7
   physical description area, 10.5
   publication, distribution, etc., area, 10.4
   series area, 10.6
   sources of information, 10.0B
   specific material designations, 10.5B
   standard number and terms of availability area, 10.8
   title and statement of responsibility area, 10.1
Three-dimensional cartographic materials, scale, 3.3B8; *for other rules see* Cartographic materials
Tipitaka (Buddhist scriptures), 25.18F1

Title (*see also* Alternative titles; Binder's title; Caption title; Collective titles; Cover title; Half title; Other title information; Running titles; Spine title; Supplied title; Title proper; Uniform titles)
   added entries under, 21.30J
   changes in, *see* Title proper, changes in
   definition, App. D
   entry under, *see* Title entry
   facsimiles, etc., 1.11B
   lack of, *see* Title proper, lack of
   preceded by dashes, capitalization, App. A.4B
   references, 26.4
      initial articles omitted, 26.1A
   variations in, *see* Variations in title
Title and statement of responsibility area, 1.1
   abbreviations, App. B.4
   capitalization, App. A.4
   cartographic materials, 3.1
      sources of information, 3.0B3
   computer files, 9.1
      sources of information, 9.0B2
   early printed monographs, 2.14
   facsimiles, etc., 1.11B
   graphic materials, 8.1
      sources of information, 8.0B2
   manuscripts, 4.1
      sources of information, 4.0B2
   microforms, 11.1
      sources of information, 11.0B2
   motion pictures and videorecordings, 7.1
      sources of information, 7.0B2
   music, 5.1
      sources of information, 5.0B
   printed monographs, 2.1
      sources of information, 2.0B2
   serials, 12.1
      sources of information, 12.0B1
   sound recordings, 6.1
      sources of information, 6.0B2
   three-dimensional artefacts and realia, 10.1
      sources of information, 10.0B2
Title cards (aperture cards), chief source of information, microforms, 11.0B1
Title entry, 0.6, 21.1C
   adaptations of music, 21.18C
   adaptations of texts, 21.10
   capitalization, App. A.4A
   citations, digests, etc., of court reports, 21.36B
   reports of interviews or exchanges, 21.25
   sacred scriptures, 21.37
   sound recordings, 21.23C
   theological creeds, etc., 21.38
   treaties, intergovernmental agreements, etc., 21.35A2
   works of shared responsibility, 21.6C2
   works of unknown or uncertain authorship, 21.5
Title frames
   definition, 11.0B1, App. D
   graphic materials, 8.5B2
   microforms, chief source of information, 11.0B1

added to uniform title, 25.18A11
alternatives to version, 25.18A12
capitalization, App. A.19K
definition, App. D
manuscripts, 4.7B9
stories, uniform titles, 25.12B
texts in different literary forms, entry, 21.10
Verso, definition, App. D
Vertical exaggeration, cartographic materials, 3.3B8
Vertically cut discs, notes, sound recordings, 6.7B10
Very high reduction, microforms, 11.7B10
Vessels, as corporate bodies, 21.1B1; *see also* Ships
Videocartridges, specific material designation, 7.5B1; *for other rules see* Motion pictures and videorecordings
Videocassettes, specific material designation, 7.5B1; *for other rules see* Motion pictures and videorecordings
Videodiscs (*for other rules see* Motion pictures and videorecordings)
  diameter, 7.5D4
  duration, 7.5B2, 7.7B10(j)
  number of frames, 7.7B10(j)
  specific material designation, 7.5B1
Videorecordings (*for other rules see* Motion pictures and videorecordings)
  definition, App. D
  general material designation, 1.1C1
  videorecording system, 7.7B10(f)
Videoreels, specific material designation, 7.5B1; *for other rules see* Motion pictures and videorecordings
Videotapes (*for other rules see* Motion pictures and videorecordings)
  gauge, 7.5D3
  generation of copy, 7.7B10(g)
  length, 7.7B10(b)
  number of lines and fields, 7.7B10(f)
Views (cartography) (*for other rules see* Cartographic materials)
  definition, App. D
  scale, 3.3B7
  specific material designation, 3.5B1
Violin conductor part, specific material designation, 5.5B1; *for other rules see* Music; *for definition see* Piano conductor part
Virgin Mary, capitalization, App. A.19C1
Viscounts and viscountesses, *see* Titles of honour, nobility, address, etc.
Vishnu, capitalization, App. A.19A1
Visual data, cartographic materials, 3.5B5
Visually impaired, cartographic materials for, 3.5B1; *for other works for the visually impaired see* Braille . . . ; Tactile . . .
Vocal music (*for other rules see* Music)
  abbreviations, 5.7B1
  medium of performance, *see* Medium of performance (music)
  terms, 25.30B9–25.30B10, 25.34C1 n14

Vocal scores (*for other rules see* Music; *see also* Chorus scores)
  additions to uniform titles, 25.35D
  definition, App. D
  specific material designation, 5.5B1
Vocal works (*for other rules see* Music)
  notes on texts, 5.7B2
  translations, uniform titles, 25.35F1
Voices (music) *see* Medium of performance (music)
Volumes
  definitions, App. D
  number of
    atlases, 3.5B3
    early printed monographs, 2.17A1
    manuscript collections, 4.5B2
    music, 5.5B1–5.5B2
    printed monographs, 2.5B17–2.5B24

Wales (*see also* United Kingdom)
  additions to place names, 23.4D
Wall charts (Cartographic materials) (*for other rules see* Cartographic materials)
  specific material designation, 3.5B1
Wall charts (Graphic materials) (*for other rules see* Graphic materials)
  dimensions, 8.5D6
  specific material designation, 8.5B1
Warrants without title, 4.1B2
Wars, capitalization
  Polish language, App. A.44F
  Russian language, App. A.46H3
West, capitalization, App. A.15A
Width (*see also* Dimensions; Gauge)
  cartographic materials, 3.5D1
  manuscripts, 4.5D
  printed monographs, 2.5D2
  single sheets, 2.5D4
  sound cassettes, 6.5D5
  sound tape reels, 6.5D6
  sound track films, 6.5D3
Wills without title, 4.1B2
Wind quintets, uniform titles, 25.30B3; *for other rules see* Music
Winds, groups of instruments, uniform titles, 25.30B5
"With" notes, 1.7B21
  cartographic materials, 3.7B21
  computer files, 9.7B21
  graphic materials, 8.7B21
  microforms, 11.7B21
  motion pictures and videorecordings, 7.7B21
  music, 5.7B21
  printed monographs, 2.7B21
  serials, 12.7B21
  sound recordings, 6.7B21
  three-dimensional artefacts and realia, 10.7B21
Wives, *see* Married women
Woodcuts, early printed monographs, 2.17B1
Woodwind quartets, uniform titles, 25.30B3
Woodwinds, groups of instruments, uniform titles, 25.30B5
Word processor, notes, computer files, 9.7B1(a)

675

Set in Times Roman by Impressions Book and Journal Services, Inc.

Printed on Glatfelter and bound by Data Reproductions

The paper used in this publication meets the minimum requirements of American
National Standard for Information Sciences—Permanence of Paper for Printed
Library Materials, ANSI Z39.48-1992. ♾